THE
SECRET CODE
OF THE
STEP PYRAMID
OF DJOSER AT SAKKARA
ANCIENT WISDOM REVEALED

Steve Kallman

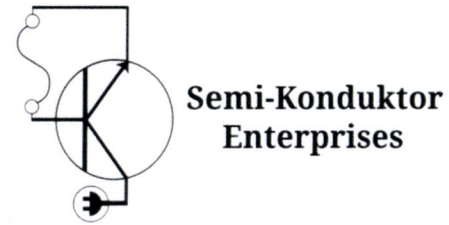

Semi-Konduktor
Enterprises

Copyright © 1993-2021 by Stephen R. Kallman
Copyright © 2022 by Semi-Konduktor Enterprises, LLC

All rights reserved. No part of this publication may be reproduced, distributed, or transmitted in any form or by any means, including photocopying, recording, or other electronic or mechanical methods, without the prior written permission of the publisher, except in the case of brief quotations embodied in critical reviews and certain other noncommercial uses permitted by copyright law.

For permission requests, write to the author, addressed "Attention: Permissions" at stevekallman@gmail.com.

Ordering Information:
For details, contact: stevekallman@gmail.com or stevekallman.com.

ISBN: 978-1-66786-498-3

Printed in the United States of America on SFI Certified paper.

First Edition

Dedication

In deepest gratitude, this book is dedicated to Jean-Philippe Lauer,
Abd'el Hakim Awyan ("Hakim") and Grandfather

All of whom, in their own way, contributed much to the realization of this book.

Meeting Jean-Philippe Lauer (center left) in April, 1990 with Abd'el Hakim Awyan, (far right), and some of our tour group members.

Table of Contents

Preface 1

1. Unexpected Discoveries – A Personal Journey..3

2. Imhotep – The First Renaissance Man in History 15

3. Imhotep the Physician – The South Entrance Hall and Human Anatomy....................................21

   The South Entrance Hall and Ḥeb-Sed Court Medical Center..24

   The South Entrance Hall and the Human Genome..46

   The East Chapels, Temple 'T' and Per-Nefer ("House of Beauty") 50

   The East Chapels 54

   Temple 'T' 59

   The Per-Nefer ("House of Beauty") 61

4. Imhotep the Priest – The South Entrance Hall and the Weighing of the Heart Ceremony............73

   The Weighing of the Heart Ceremony...75

   The 'Magic Number 2' 79

5. Imhotep the Grand Vizier – The South Entrance Hall and the Civil Government of Egypt.........83

6. Imhotep the Architect, Astronomer and Sculptor – Building Egypt's First *Mega Mortuary Temple* 89

   Before There Was a Step Pyramid...90

   The Great South Court..97

   Mastaba M₃ and the Eleven Pit Tombs Mystery 98

   The Central Burial Chamber and Vertical Shaft 100

   The South Tomb 106

   The South Tomb Chapel 110

   The North and South Pavilions 110

   The Enclosure Walls 116

   The Ḥeb-Sed Court 123

   The Serdab 130

   The North Mortuary Temple 132

   The North Court 134

   The Three Western Massifs (Storage Magazines or Tombs) 138

   Building Egypt's First Mega Mortuary Temple..139

Repurposing and Rebuilding the Pre-Existing Structures 140

Finishing the South Tomb and the Three Mastabas 142

The First Enclosure Wall and the Old Serdab 143

The Construction of the Four-Tier Pyramid and the Initial Design Phase of the North Court 145

The Six-Tier Step Pyramid and the Second North Mortuary Temple 147

Recent Unexpected Discoveries 148

7. Imhotep the Scribe and Mathematician – The Tradition of Sacred Geometry and the Design of the Step Pyramid Enclosure 151

A Brief Introduction to Sacred Geometry and Its Use in Architectural Design 151

The Use of Architecture as a Repository of Hidden Esoteric Wisdom 155

The Use of Sacred Geometry in the Design of the Step Pyramid 158

The Second Enclosure Wall That Was Never Constructed 167

The Six-Tier Step Pyramid Enclosure 168

Sacred Geometry and the South Entrance Hall / Ḥeb-Sed Court Quadrant 172

The Sacred Geometry of the Entrance Vestibule and the Enclosure Wall 190

The Tradition of Using Sacred Geometry by Ancient Egyptian Architects Before and After Imhotep 192

The Funerary Enclosure of Khasekhemwui at Abydos 193

The Funerary Enclosure of Peribsen at Abydos 200

The Step Pyramid of Sekhemkhet 201

Sacred Geometry and the Secret Symbol in the King's Chamber of the Great Pyramid of Giza 208

The Mystery of the Sakkara Ostracon 210

Final Thoughts 219

8. Imhotep the Sage and Scribe – Another Gate and Departure from the World of Spirit 221

9. Imhotep the Immortal – The End of One Journey and the Beginning of Another 239

Illustration and Photo Credits 243

Bibliography 244

Notes 246

Index 251

Preface

This book will never be finished.

I know what you're thinking: No self-respecting author should ever admit this at the beginning of their book. Not to mention the fact that you're holding a completed manuscript in your hands. But the things I have discovered – and uncovered – about ancient Egyptian culture, customs, religion and their beliefs leads me to suspect that, while we know a great deal about ancient Egypt, it is but the tip of the iceberg. Quite possibly, this will always be so. This book will never be the last word on this subject; nor should it be. Peeling back the layers of hidden esoteric knowledge is an ongoing quest and sometimes when we bring to light some previously concealed knowledge, the possibility also exists that we may accidentally tap into something lying deep within ourselves that we had never known existed before.

Though it may be entirely impossible to gain a complete, thorough understanding of the world of ancient Egypt, we need to try to see their world as the Egyptians did. As challenging as that is, we will be the richer for it as this wonderful ancient culture has much to teach us – if we have courage enough to learn – and provided we rid ourselves of any preconceived notions we may have.

My fascination with ancient Egypt began decades ago when I was in grade school, and later in high school. I was fortunate to have a wonderful teacher in grade school, Mr. Ed Kochmann, who taught history with such a passion and joy that one couldn't help but share in the excitement his retelling the stories of history gave to his students. In high school, I was fortunate to have teachers who allowed us to explore ancient civilizations without forcing on us any preconceived ideas about those civilizations.

In the early 1970s, I purchased I. E. S. Edwards' classic book, *The Pyramids of Egypt*. I spent hours staring at the photos and illustrations, especially those of Pharaoh Djoser's Step Pyramid and the pyramids at Giza. My thirst to know more about ancient Egypt increased many times over after the good fortune of finding employment in the "Trade Books" department of my college bookstore. My boss, who was a member of the Theosophical Society, introduced me to a number of esoteric topics as well as encouraged my continued interest in ancient Egypt. It did not take long for me to amass a sizable library of books related to ancient Egypt. Over time, the desire to encounter firsthand the land of the Nile resulted in two trips I took in 1988 and 1990.

When approaching the Step Pyramid Enclosure as I did so many years ago, the first thing you see is the magnificent South Entrance Gate that leads to the equally stunning South Entrance Hall. It is a testament to its design by Imhotep – Djoser's vizier, architect, physician and the all-round genius – as well as the man who excavated and reconstructed it, Jean-Philippe Lauer. Through the efforts of Mr. Lauer and others, the world has been given back a monument of consummate grace and beauty.

During my 1990 trip to Egypt, I stumbled upon a relatively overlooked piece of stonework lying near the surface in an obscure part of the Step Pyramid Enclosure at Sakkara. Few people are aware of this artifact's existence, and by itself, it hardly merits any mention when there is any discussion of Djoser's mortuary temple. However, this rather extraordinarily carved block of limestone appears to be part of a much greater puzzle that I've become obsessed with since I first laid eyes on it over 30 years ago. More than that, it has become a catalyst to learn more about Djoser's incredible monument and the man who designed it – Imhotep.

During this incredible journey, I discovered things that contradict the common narratives about the Step Pyramid Enclosure. Visitors are often told the Enclosure Wall surrounding the Step Pyramid has only one entrance, but such may not necessarily be the case. From such small discoveries, like a relatively unknown object few people ever get to see, there sometimes comes great inspiration to explore new ideas and new perspectives. It is my fervent wish that what I uncovered so many years ago will also inspire you to see the ancient world with a fresh pair of eyes as it did for me.

This book started as speculative article for the magazine, *KMT, A Modern Journal of Ancient Egypt*. Though the article was a very raw attempt at displaying my enthusiasm for what I had found at Sakkara, I submitted it in mid-1993, just four years after the founding of the magazine. The editor, Dennis Forbes, was probably busy with his new venture, and did not have time to get the article into publishing shape. It is a tribute to Dennis' patience with my greenhorn writing skills, but in the end, I withdrew the article, and the document spent the better part of 25 years locked away in my closet.

A few years prior to retiring after spending 40 years in the computer industry, I dusted off the article, and was amazed at just how *awful* it was. Bad grammar, poor and incomplete illustrations, incoherent and outright wrong conclusions about what I had discovered was only just the beginning. I thank my lucky stars that Mr. Forbes never published the article. I don't think I would have lived down the embarrassment.

So, what has changed in the intervening 32 years? Newer computer software and technology have also helped shape my discoveries into what I believe is a better attempt at writing. In addition, the Internet has provided access to even greater sources of research that the local library never could. (Maybe it's because I once worked in a bookstore, but I still love to hang out in libraries. There's no better place to exercise the mind than the quiet ambiance of the John G. White Collection at the Main Branch of the Cleveland Public Library.) I have been able to tap into the most recent articles concerning new research and excavations in Egypt. From these many new sources, I corrected my initial twisted logic, but also found a wealth of new information that stimulated me to learn even more, giving me a better foundation with which to present my ideas and theories with greater accuracy and clarity. (I uncovered so much new information as I was doing research for this book, in both written and intuitively derived material, that the first line in this preface almost became a self-fulfilling prophecy.) Knowing more has yet to still be uncovered, I believe many future discoveries about the Step Pyramid will continually shed new light on this wonderful monument, allowing us to realize what a fantastic work of genius it truly is.

I do not claim to be an Egyptologist, though I do share their passion for the subject. A better term for my unfettered enthusiasm for this topic would be "armchair archeologist". As for why I have this continued fascination with ancient Egypt, its monuments, its spiritual heritage and its people – both ancient and modern – I must defer to one of my favorite authors, Barbara Mertz, an Egyptologist in her own right who wrote many wonderful Egyptology-centered mysteries under the pen name, Elizabeth Peters:

The question is not, why am I interested in ancient Egypt, but why isn't *everyone* interested in ancient Egypt?

Barbara Mertz, Author and Egyptologist

It is my fervent wish to inspire all who read this book to take a fresh look at the wonders of this ancient culture with a *new set of eyes*, and feel the excitement of diving into such a complex and profound subject as I have. In so doing, perhaps the reader will 'remember' what our ancestors were trying teach us from so long ago.

Steve Kallman, 2022

The ancients knew something, which we seem to have forgotten.

Albert Einstein, German Physicist

Unexpected Discoveries – A Personal Journey

The South Entrance Gate and the Step Pyramid

A new idea that challenges an old paradigm rarely appears as a sudden flash of inspiration in the mind. One inspired idea often leads to another, and another and yet another. This can be as exhilarating as it is frustrating. Not knowing where a new idea will lead has a tendency to move you in a different direction than intended. Sometimes this requires leaving a pet theory behind as some newly discovered information, of which you were not previously aware, pops out of nowhere and your cleverly crafted hypothesis no longer holds water. More often than not, it is the slow, methodical, and sometimes accidental, connecting of many seemingly unrelated dots that lead to the revelation of a much grander design. Inevitably, any new idea must first be plausible, and then ascertained to be even possibly true before it can eventually be proven probable. When the last piece of a puzzle falls into place, a much greater whole than the sum of the individual parts will be finally revealed.

When we visit the monuments of King Djoser, we enter the enclosure by the only ancient entrance, which is placed in the east side of the enclosure wall, 27 meters from the south-east corner. [1]

The only gate, at the southern end of the eastern portion of the perimeter wall, leads into the great hall. [2]

The only actual doorway, which has now been rebuilt, was situated near the southern corner of the east side, where two towers flanked a narrow passage leading to the entrance colonnade. [3]

The temenos or girdle wall of the Step Pyramid is composed of numerous bastions making an articulated facade. Although there are fourteen gateways in it, only one is an actual entry. [4]

It is clear from the above quotations that most Egyptologists believe the Funerary Enclosure of Djoser at Sakkara has only one entrance, which is located in the southeastern corner. Known today as the South Entrance Gate or Entrance Hall, this is the main entrance that everyone uses to enter and exit this great monument. While it is true the South Entrance Gate is the only entrance in the perimeter wall, it is far from the only *gate* or *opening*, as I will show with the evidence that I (literally) uncovered while walking around the Step Pyramid Enclosure.

The author at the Step Pyramid of Sakkara in 1990
(And, yes, that's 25 pounds of camera equipment I was hauling around Egypt for more than two weeks!!)

While it seems the Great Pyramid of Giza and the two pyramids nearby get the most attention from people travelling to Egypt, or learning about its past, the Step Pyramid of Djoser, only nine miles away, is often relegated to just a half-day side trip on most tour itineraries. Covering thirty-seven acres, there is a great deal to take in at the Step Pyramid, so it is little wonder that much of what there is to see often goes unnoticed by the average tourist.

I had been to Egypt once before in 1988, but did not have the opportunity to explore and spend much time at the Step Pyramid at Sakkara as I had wanted. On my second trip to Egypt in April 1990, I was fortunate to have a second free day at the Step Pyramid site to investigate areas that I did not get a chance to see previously. Without the usual clamor of other tourists, I was virtually alone in the ruins of this once magnificent temple, and soon found myself in the area northeast of the North Pavilion, sometimes known as the "House of the North". (*Fig.1-1*, red arrow).

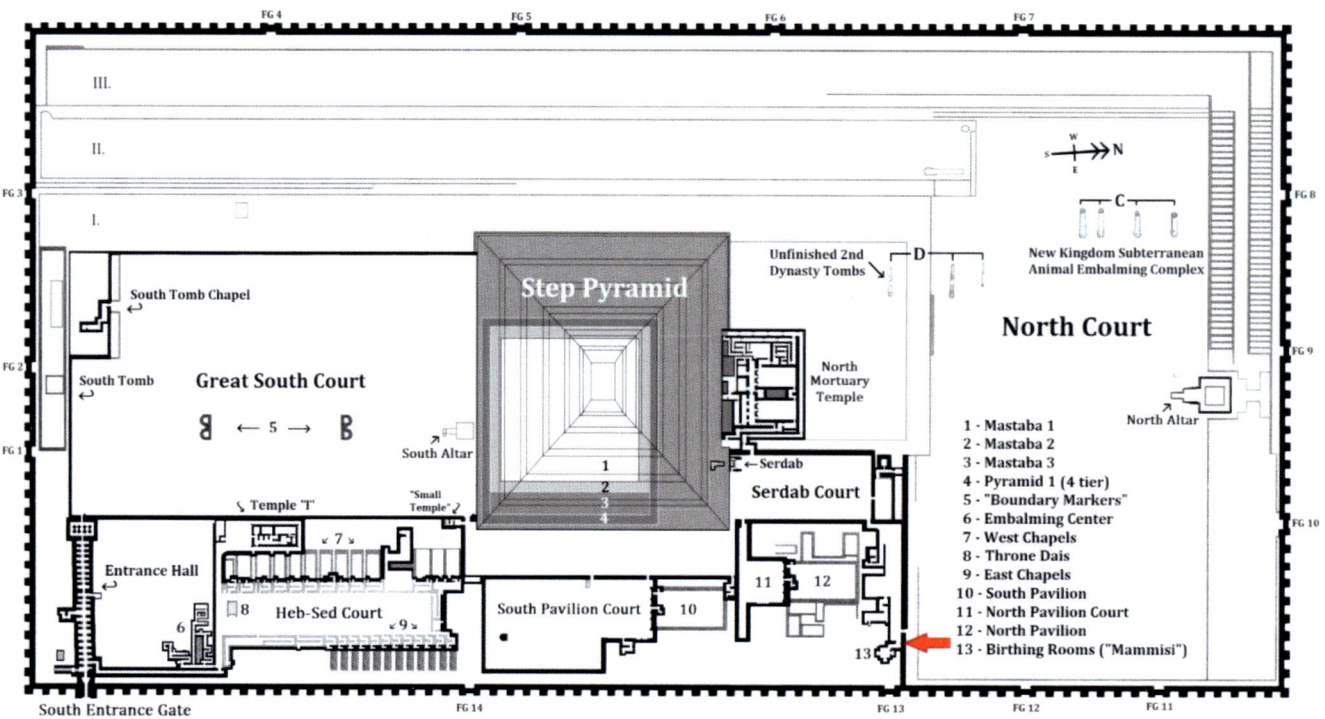

Fig. 1-1 – The Step Pyramid Enclosure of Djoser (the prefix "FG" denotes False Gates 1 through 14)

As I wandered around the area, I tried to envision how this temple must have looked in its prime. I spotted a group of stone blocks behind the North Pavilion that appeared to be arranged for eventual reconstruction (*Fig. 1-2*). The late Mr. Jean-Philippe Lauer and his team must have been greatly challenged to make sense of the immense pile of stones around the site in order to excavate and rebuild the Step Pyramid Enclosure when excavations began in the late 1920s. It must have been like trying to assemble a jigsaw puzzle – one with most of the pieces missing and without a reference photo to go by.

Fig. 1-2 – Step Pyramid Enclosure, northeast of the North Pavilion looking southwest

In this corridor of jumbled stones, I came upon a somewhat oval-shaped stone, half-buried under a lot of sand, food wrappers and empty film boxes (!). Curiosity got the best of me, and I removed the dirt and debris from the stone's hollow cavity to reveal a very delicately rendered piece of artwork. I initially thought it was the ear of a large, toppled, mostly hidden statue. (*Go figure!*) It was then that I realized this ear-shaped stone was not part of a statue, but rather a complete, freestanding work of art in and of itself. Impressed with how gracefully sculpted it was, I photographed the stone and the surrounding area (*Fig. 1-3*). After covering up the stone with sand to prevent any further damage, I continued my outing at Sakkara without giving it another thought.

Until later, that is.

Fig. 1-3 – Northeast of the North Pavilion looking west into the interior of the Step Pyramid Enclosure

Besides being an *armchair archeologist*, I am also somewhat of an architectural detective. I enjoy figuring out how and why an architect chose to design buildings the way they did. When I returned home, I poured over the photos from my trip and took a closer look at this unique object. I couldn't put my finger on it. Something seemed very strange about it, yet familiar at the same time. After staring at it for a while, it suddenly dawned on me: **This was a doorpost socket!** The conclusion was inescapable; it could be nothing else!

As can be seen in both *Figs. 1-3* and *1-4*, the interior of the socket is smaller at the bottom than at the top as it slopes inward at an angle from the outer lip to the bottom of the semi-oval stone. It is asymmetrical in shape, unlike a regular semi-circular door socket where the interior sides are normally perpendicular to the socket's base. The streaks of discoloration on the interior of the socket indicate there was once a working doorpost installed in it. A doorpost, probably made of wood, could have only made these streaks as it rotated within the socket when the door attached to the doorpost opened and closed. More than that, the shape of the interior of the socket itself gives silent proof that the door installed there long ago was a ***self-closing*** one.

It is barely discernable, but the very faint topmost streak, which does not run parallel to the ground as it would in a typical semi-circular doorpost socket, is proof positive of this. Rather, it slopes sharply upward, from right to left, to a barely perceptible peak within an inch or so of the top of the socket before gently dropping down to the left side of the socket's interior. The reason that I knew the socket was for a self-closing door was because I repaired a set of bi-directional swinging doors in the bookstore where I worked more than a decade and a half before! Those doors had hinges with the same sloping shape as the doorpost socket that I had found many years and thousands of miles later (see *Fig. 1-7*).

Fig. 1-4 – Close-up of the doorpost socket for a self-closing door

This particular door socket's half-oval shape indicates it must have contained an equally unusually shaped doorpost as well. The bottom of the doorpost of the now-missing *self-closing* door must have been beveled to conform to the more rounded and steeply sloped right side of the socket instead of having a squared-off bottom as with a typical doorpost (see *Fig. 1-3*).

The self-closing door would move up and down ever so slightly in the socket as it swung open and shut. When the door opened, the steeply curved bottom of the doorpost would squeeze against the less curved, more perpendicular left side of the socket as seen in *Fig. 1-4*, forcing the door to move ***up*** in the socket well. Since temple doors were fairly large and heavy, and sometimes even clad in copper or gold, the very weight of the door would tend to push the doorpost ***down*** from the narrowed left part of the socket's interior towards the doorpost *well* (i.e. the right side) forcing the door to swing shut. Given the gentle slope of the socket's interior, a heavy door would only have to rise up a half-inch or less to force the door to close on its own.

The doorpost socket I stumbled upon is unlike the sockets for other false doors that are scattered throughout the Step Pyramid complex (*Figs. 1-5* and *1-6*, red arrows). It certainly was not the usual type of doorpost socket found in many other Egyptian temples. Most of those other temple doorpost sockets had interior sides that were perpendicular to their base, and the thickness at the top of the socket was the same as at the bottom. This is also true of the upper doorpost sockets installed in the lintel of a temple's entrance gate. Examples of these are the false doors of the West Chapels of the Ḥeb-Sed Court, and in the South Entrance Hall's stone doors (see *Fig. 1-11*, red arrows). Fashioned from stone, these false doors were immovable and permanently fixed in place, but their design imitated functioning doors most commonly found in temples and domestic architecture of the period. More importantly, there did not appear to be any remains of a corresponding false stone door near this unique doorpost socket similar to the other false doors in the Step Pyramid Enclosure (see *Figs. 1-3* and *1-4*).

Fig. 1-5 – False Door of West Chapel 4.

Note the false door made of stone and its upper and lower doorpost sockets (red arrows). (Manna Nader).

Fig. 1-6 – Close-up of the false door socket of West Chapel 4.

Note the straight, perpendicular sides of the interior of the doorpost socket.

Similar designs for self-closing doors are still very much in use today. Sometimes called gravity hinges, these hinges are used on free-swinging saloon or cafe doors, or on the bidirectional doors installed in many commercial kitchens. Look closely and you will see a similar design to the ones used in those doors and their ancient equivalent located in the Step Pyramid Enclosure (*Fig. 1-7*).

Further evidence of an exit-only door installed at this location is the clear depiction of the sloping interior of this socket in the architectural drawings of J.-P. Lauer (*Fig. 1-8*).

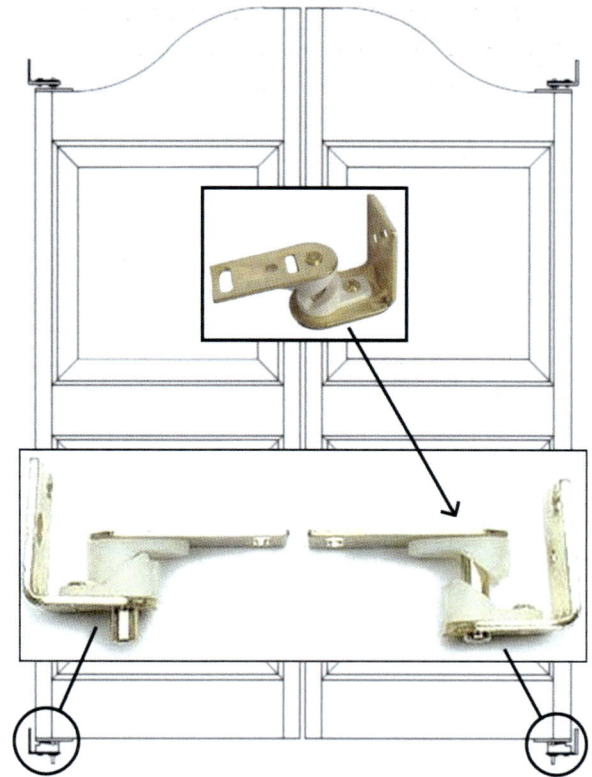

Fig. 1-7 – A typical saloon door with gravity hinges (inset)
Note the sloping sides of the plastic ramp-like parts on the right hinge analogous to the sloping interior of the doorpost socket in *Fig. 1-4*.

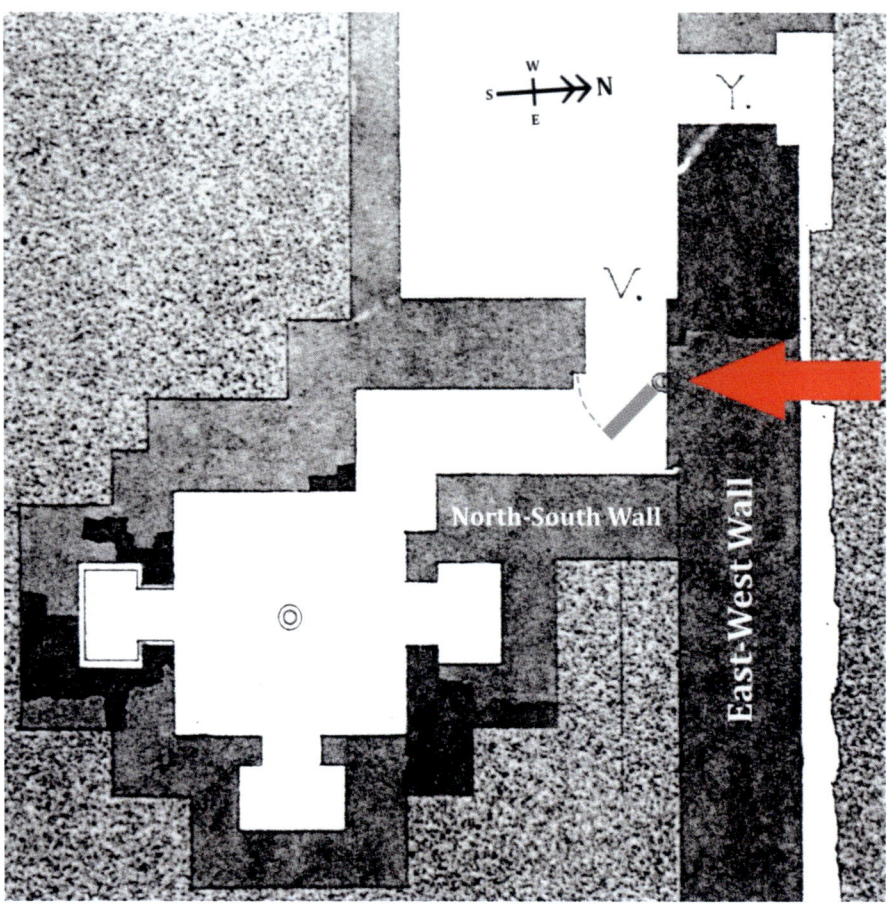

Fig. 1-8 – The area west of the North Exit Gate (False Gate 13)
The red arrow points to the doorpost socket for a self-closing door (hypothetical door added by author)

Jean-Philippe Lauer was the lead architect of a team headed by the English Egyptologists Cecil M. Firth and James Quibell who began the first excavations and rebuilding of the Step Pyramid and its environs in 1926. Their seminal work, *Excavations at Saqqara: The Step Pyramid*, published in 1935, has been the major source material for this book. (Wherever I mention these three throughout this work, it is in reference to their book. Though other books and papers about the Step Pyramid exist, I have found that first impressions from the initial excavations often still hold after all the intervening years.) The red arrow in *Fig. 1-8* shows the location of the door socket I uncovered (quite literally) in 1990. If you look closely, the hemispheric circle depicting this socket shows it as having one circle inside the other, exactly as it looks in situ. This speaks to Jean-Philippe Lauer's dedication to represent the massive scale and complexity of the Step Pyramid Enclosure accurately despite its ruinous state. For that, we should be eternally grateful to the man who spent more than 70 years working at Sakkara. I just hope my meager efforts to convey a deeper meaning to this ancient wonder are up to the standards of Mr. Lauer's work that has inspired this book.

While there is no evidence for an exit passageway leading out of the enclosure at this location, one may well have existed here at one time. In *Fig. 1-9*, the view looks east towards the cleft between the two walls near where the doorpost socket is located. The socket itself lies just behind the short wall seen in the left foreground; the same short wall also referenced by the letter '**Y**' in *Figs. 1-3* and *1-9*.

Fig. 1-9 – Area near the North Exit Gate looking east

If the oval-shaped stone were really a doorpost socket that was part of a working door assembly, then construction of a passageway exiting the Enclosure to the east must have existed at one time. It would then have jutted to the south a short distance behind the far wall (in the background with the wire fence on top of it) to finally exit through what is known these days as False Gate 13 (at the bottom of *Fig. 1-10*). The area between the missing north-south wall just to the east of the doorpost socket and False Gate 13 shown in *Fig. 1-10* was filled in with stone rubble and sand. It is possible the sand and rubble material visible in *Fig. 1-9* to the left of the wall in the background is part of the rubble infill used to reinforce the finished walls of the exit corridor, or perhaps, is just windblown debris that accumulated over the centuries, or both.

It also appears that part of a north-south wall that formed the doorway for the self-closing door is missing (marked at 'V') as *Fig. 1-10* seems to indicate. Since another short north-south wall that lays perpendicular to the east-west wall of the North Court no longer exists, perhaps it was constructed using different less stable and easily removed material than the surrounding enclosure walls. If so, this may be proof that at one time there was a passageway leading out of the Step Pyramid Enclosure.

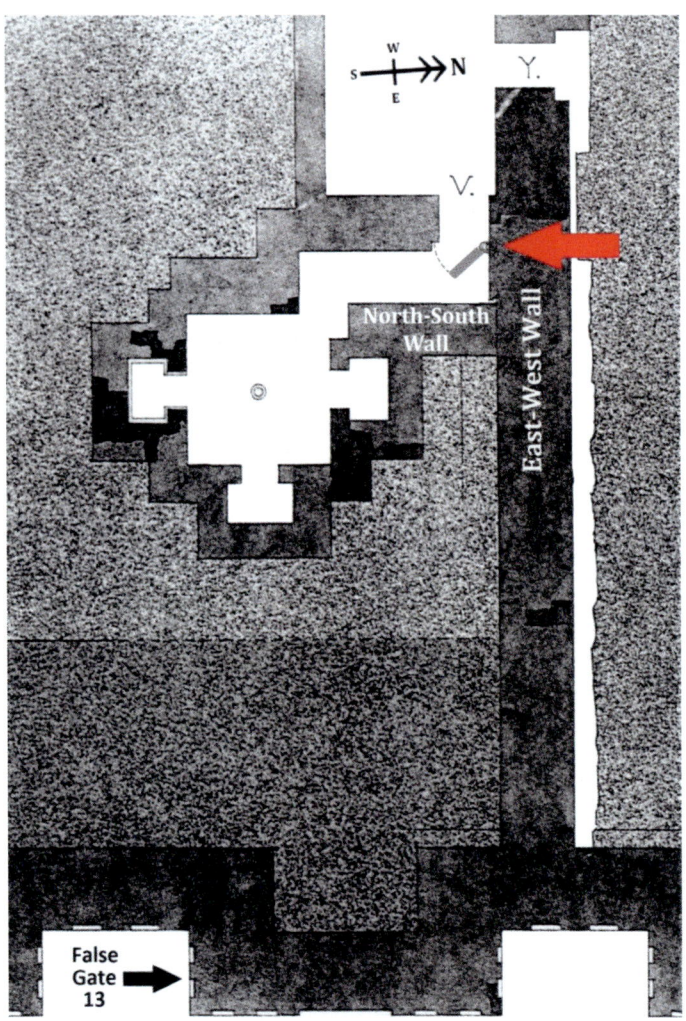

Fig. 1-10 – The area near False Gate 13 and the doorpost socket

No doubt, the existence of a doorpost socket for a self-closing door implies changes were made to the Step Pyramid Enclosure at one point for some reason, and the corridor leading out of what is now False Gate 13 was filled in. It was common to renovate and repurpose Egyptian temples during their long history, so an exit passageway leading out of a true gate as part of the original design of the Step Pyramid Enclosure is certainly possible.

The highly unusual design of the doorpost socket indicates that it was only a one-way exit, and if so, there would not have been a handle affixed to the outside of the door. Having a one-way door leading out to the exterior of this temple would prove to be a unique feature when compared to all the other great temple of ancient Egypt.

How can it be determined if any of this is true? Sometimes the answer to a question comes from asking another question.

Consider this: A passageway with a self-closing door implies that it was to be restricted and one-way only, unlike the South Entrance Gate where there are only decorative non-functioning stone doors. If so, then logically there would not have been a handle installed on the outside of a functional self-closing door that was located here, or this doorpost socket's design would have been made much simpler. In addition, if there was no exit corridor leading out of the enclosure and the passageway only led to a small, multisided room, and if a self-closing door without an exterior handle was installed here, no one could leave that small room (as seen in *Figs. 1-8* and *1-10*). *Not a great design choice if that's the case!* The other choice is that the original door was removed altogether once the North Exit Gate was transformed into False Gate 13.

That the design of this socket near the North Exit Gate (*as I refer to it*) was unique in that several other flat-bottomed sockets of false, open doors exist in the Entrance Hall and Ḥeb-Sed Court. Carved in stone to mimic the standard design for doors typically found in ancient Egyptian temples and domestic architecture, these non-functional false doors look as if they were capable of motion, one part inside the other (see *Figs. 1-5* and *1-6*).

Inside the entrance to the South Entrance Hall, the *always-open* stone doors feature a beveled fake doorpost at the base of the doors, along with the imitation upper sockets at the top of the doors (*Fig. 1-11*). The symbolism of these *always-open doors* will be explained in a later chapter. Having speculated that there was indeed a North Exit Gate, there are two ways of interpreting the North Exit Gate's importance as it fits into the overall scheme of the Step Pyramid Enclosure-one more traditional, the other symbolic.

Fig. 1-11 – South Entrance Hall stone door with imitation doorpost sockets (arrows)

If there were, in fact, two gates in the Step Pyramid Enclosure Wall, it would be quite typical for any temple of this, or for that matter, *any* period of ancient Egyptian history. American Egyptologist, James H. Breasted, wrote of an inscription attributed to the reign of King Sneferu describing the construction of two cedar wood doors for the king's palace. The names given for these doors were *Exalted Is the White Crown of Sneferu upon the South Gate*, and *Exalted Is the Red Crown of Sneferu upon the North Gate*. In a footnote to this inscription, Breasted relates the following:

These are the names of two gates or parts of the palace of Sneferu: one for the South and one for the North. We have thus the double name of a double palace, which, like the organs of the government, was double, to correspond with the old kingdoms of South and North. These two gates are still preserved in the palace of the Empire as seen in the Amarna tombs. The palace front was always referred to as the "double façade" or "double gate" (Rwty);... The state temples also were double; each had a "double façade," and the hypostyle was divided into north and south by the central aisle. The division of the palace audience hall will have been the same. [5]

Sneferu was the first king of the Fourth Dynasty, and began his reign approximately 40 to 50 years after the death of Netjerikhet Djoser. Breasted implies that it was already customary to place two gates in palace and temple walls by the time Sneferu ascended to the throne. If so, then it is probable that building two gates in a palace or temple structure would not have become a long-standing tradition in the short number of years between Djoser's death and the beginning of Sneferu's reign if doing so had only started after Djoser's death. Having two gates in the Step Pyramid Enclosure must mean it was standard practice long before Djoser's time.

To show the care and attention to detail inherent in Imhotep's design, the stone doors in the Entrance Vestibule depict a remarkable feature which, had these been wooden doors, were imitated perfectly in stone. The pin at the top of the north door (left diagonal arrow, *Fig. 1-12*) sits a little farther out from the wall than the south stone door (see *Fig. 1-11*) as indicated by the vertical line (bottom arrow, *Fig. 1-12*), which is called *piano hinge* today. Had these replicas been working wooden doors, the south door would have been closed first, followed by the north door, which would then overlap the south door (*Fig. 1-13*). This virtually substantiates that the carefully crafted design of the doorpost socket near False Gate 13 is no aberration. Since Imhotep was capable of incorporating such meticulous details into this easily overlooked part of the Entrance Vestibule, then it is entirely likely the self-closing door and its socket, being an equally unique feature in the Step Pyramid Enclosure, was a deliberate design choice on Imhotep's part.

Fig. 1-12 – North Stone Door in the Entrance Vestibule

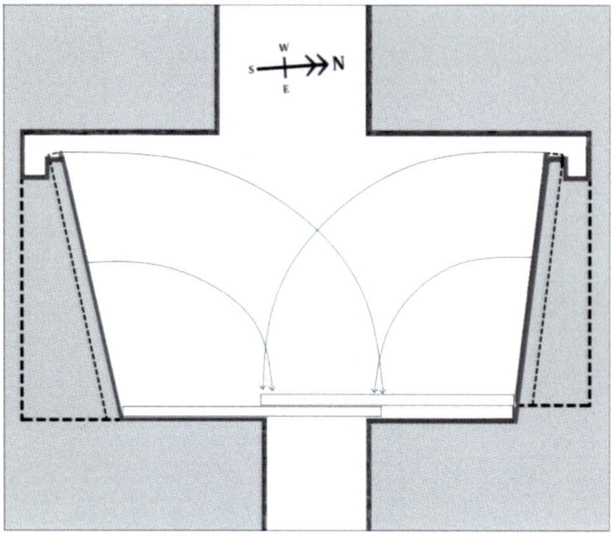

Fig. 1-13 – How the stone doors of the Entrance Vestibule would have operated had they been made of wood

In all my years of studying ancient Egyptian architecture, one thing is inescapably certain: When it comes to the design of these ancient monuments, there are no accidents or coincidences. Further, the Egyptians always incorporated two important architectural elements into their temples, never only just one. Constructing two pylons, two rows of sphinxes, two obelisks in front of the pylons, and so on, was the standard architectural practice of the day. By this reasoning alone, a North Exit Gate had to exist at some time as a spiritual and architectural counterbalance for the South Entrance Gate. This echoes the one concept that pervades all of ancient Egyptian thought and religion, that is, *duality*. It is because of the Egyptians' seeming obsession with duality that Imhotep's design of the Step Pyramid Enclosure had a dual purpose in mind-one for the living and one for the dead. It may not be apparent at first given the obvious reasons for constructing any of ancient Egypt's mortuary temples, but I believe a heretofore hidden function was also part of the day-to-day activity of Djoser's Step Pyramid Enclosure. *More on this later.*

Because the tradition of double gates may have predated Djoser's reign by a few centuries, Imhotep, the great architect of Djoser's funerary monument, would therefore have naturally included two gates in his design, which most scholars also believe to be a faithful reproduction of the Djoser's palace in Memphis. It is interesting to note the persistent use of *double gates* continued throughout the long history of ancient Egypt, often embodied in the quintessentially ancient Egyptian architectural element: The ubiquitous double-entrance pylons seen in practically every temple along the Nile (*Fig. 1-14*).

Fig. 1-14 – The Temple of Isis at Philae

If a North Exit Gate with a self-closing door really did exist, then the next logical question is: What purpose would this gate have served in the overall design of the Step Pyramid Enclosure? Naturally, there is a great deal of symbolism inherent in a North Exit Gate even existing in the first place. This is based on a philosophy subscribing that ancient Egyptian temples were more than a continued rehashing of stylistic formulae, and contained a sincere outpouring of unique religious and spiritual expression in their architectural elements.

From this point of view, constructing two gates in the Enclosure Wall may well have had some sort of ritual significance. *Consider this possibility*: After a procession of nobility, priests and courtiers entered the South Entrance Gate from the east, they would complete a ritual or ceremony in the Great South Court or perhaps at the North Funerary Temple at the base of the Step Pyramid. Then the retinue would then exit through the North Exit Gate, making a complete circuit through the Step Pyramid Enclosure. Thus, they imitated the daily movement of the sun, which held a great significance in ancient Egyptian society from even before the predynastic era. They would do so with deep reverence as the solar cycle was reminiscent of the cycle of birth and death. However, this was only one of several possibilities that I uncovered during my subsequent investigation of this temple.

After making the grand intuitive leap that there was more to this unusual stone doorpost socket than met the eye, I was motivated to do more research about Djoser's Step Pyramid, and spent the last few years becoming reacquainted with the Step Pyramid Enclosure, learning a great many new things including about its chief architect, Imhotep, along the way. One cannot look at this unique doorpost socket without marveling at the kind of intellect and persistence it must have taken to create something so exceptional. Its graceful curves and elegant design speaks of a man that must have possessed a great sense of aestheticism that was well beyond his contemporaries, and that was highly praised for his intellectual acumen, not only in ancient times, but also for hundreds of years after his death.

The Step Pyramid is the most unique pyramid in Egypt, as well as being the first. It is as if they broke mold once its construction was complete. The more I researched, the more amazed I became by the level of skill and originality inherent in the Step Pyramid Enclosure's design. Like peeling back the layers of an onion, more things started to be revealed once I began researching in earnest. One jaw-dropping revelation after another kept surfacing to the point that I kept asking: Why is the existence of a long-forgotten piece of sculpted stonework so important to the overall scheme of the Step Pyramid Enclosure? What other secrets are hiding within the old temple that no one seems to know about?

It only took 30 years to find out.

It is by logic that we prove, but by intuition that we discover.

Henri Poincaré, French Mathematician

Imhotep – The First Renaissance Man in History

The first Figure of a Physician to stand out clearly from the Mists of Antiquity.

Sir William Osler, Canadian Physician

Before there can be any study of the Step Pyramid Enclosure of Djoser, proper due must be given to the man who designed it.

Imhotep was a Vizier, (i.e., Prime Minister) of Egypt and Chief Royal Architect during Djoser's reign, as well as allegedly being a physician. His name means *One Who Comes in Peace*, and his unique stature in ancient Egyptian history can be judged simply by examining his many titles, [6] some of which were ascribed to him in later dynasties:

1) Grand Vizier of Egypt, (i.e., "Chancellor of the King of Lower Egypt", "The first one under the King" or "One who is near the head of the King" (similar to the title "Fan Bearer on the Right" in later dynasties)
2) Imhotep, the Carpenter and the Sculptor (chief sculptor or overseer of sculptors and chief carpenter)
3) Chief Royal Architect
4) Chief of All Works of the King
5) Chief Royal Physician (or, Magician-Physician)
6) Chief Lector Priest or *Kheri-heb* (High Priest or *Wab-priest*) of Ra at Heliopolis (Onu)
7) Chief Judge
8) Bearer of the Royal Seal ("Seal Bearer of the King of Egypt")
9) Director (Administrator) of the Great Mansion (either the King's palace or the temple of Ra Atum)
10) Overseer of the King's Records
11) Supervisor of 'that which Heaven brings, the Earth creates and the Nile brings'
12) Supervisor of everything in this entire land
13) Sage and Scribe
14) Astronomer
15) Royal Representative
16) The Hereditary Noble

Except for the manner in which the pharaohs depicted their conquests, their triumphs and other deeds, the ancient Egyptians were not prone to excessive hyperbole about the events of a non-royal person's life. Granted, a member of the upper-class elite could record the greatest moments of their life on the walls of their tomb if they had in some way served the royal family. However, these often over-bloated, self-aggrandizing accomplishments were usually confined to the dark and dusty interior of the family tomb, and were not meant for public consumption. With Imhotep, this was clearly the exception. Even though he was not believed to be of royal blood, he was lauded with praise and honors long after his death by not only Egyptians, but also by the Greek and Roman conquerors of Egypt who lived millennia after him.

Such was the intellectual brilliance and depth of his abilities, that Imhotep became deified as a god thousands of years after his death. He was associated with the god Thoth, and as such, became the patron of scribes, physicians, architects and mathematicians. Statues of Imhotep were erected in many temples where priests prayed to him for guidance before tending to the needs of the sick or wounded (*Fig. 2-1*). Ordinary people also possessed small statues of him in their homes (*Fig. 2-2*), and would invoke his name to intercede with the gods on their behalf to effect a rapid cure for their injuries or illnesses.

Fig. 2-1 – An Invocation to I-em-hetep, the Egyptian Deity of Medicine

While doing research for this book, I noted many authors use the term *polymath* to describe Imhotep. I had not heard the term before, but the definition fits Imhotep like a glove:

Polymath "pŏl'ē-măth"

1. An individual whose knowledge spans a significant number of subjects, known to draw on complex bodies of knowledge to solve specific problems. [7]
2. A person of great or varied learning. [8]
3. A person with extraordinarily broad and comprehensive knowledge. [9]
4. A person of encyclopedic learning. [10]

Based on historical records of how Imhotep was held in such high regard by so many for so long a period of time, it is not much of a stretch of the imagination to say he was, perhaps, the first *Renaissance Man* in history. What he accomplished in his lifetime compares easily to the likes of Leonardo da Vinci, Benjamin Franklin, Thomas Jefferson, Galileo Galilei, Michelangelo Buonarroti, Alexander Borodin, Blaise Pascal, Sir Isaac Newton and Abū Rayhān al-Bīrūnī; all brilliant in their own way in their own fields. Yet, if there is any validity to the legends surrounding Imhotep, it appears he was well versed in many disciplines, and excelled in each.

Fig. 2-2 – A typical votive statuette of Imhotep as a scribe

There are many excellent biographies of Imhotep, so I will not try to rehash their content. Chief among his modern biographers is Jameson B. Hurry, whose 1926 book, *Imhotep, The Egyptian God of Medicine* sums up the more important aspects of his life and career. Though he is one of ancient Egypt's most famous personages, there is actually very little proof that can corroborate the details of his life. For as famous and revered as Imhotep was during the long history of ancient Egypt, it is indeed ironic there was very little written about the man during his lifetime.

Based on carbon-14 dating of samples of wood taken from the interior of the Step Pyramid, general agreement is that Imhotep designed and built the Step Pyramid Enclosure at Saqqara for Pharaoh Netjerikhet Djoser circa 2663 BCE,[11] including the pioneering use of stone columns for structural support. [12] Yet, some have argued that the ancient Egyptians never credited Imhotep as the architect of the Step Pyramid, or that he was the first person to use dressed stone extensively in his architectural designs,[13] though the Greek historian, Manetho, later credited him with these innovations.

As we continue our examination of the Step Pyramid Enclosure, it will become evident that what we can readily see in its design could only have been a product of someone with Imhotep's acumen and genius, but because of his position in ancient Egyptian society, he was the only one that could have realized its construction.

At one time, Imhotep was thought to be an almost mythological figure, but some factual evidence of Imhotep's existence and fame comes from a large stele carved on a rock on Sehel Island near Aswan in southern Egypt (*Fig. 2-3*).

First discovered in the late 19th century by the eminent Egyptologist Charles Wilbour; it was inscribed considerably later than the Third Dynasty during the rule of the Greek Ptolemies, about 200 BCE. Commonly known as the Famine Stele, it describes a seven-year drought due to lower than normal flooding of the life-giving Nile during the reign of King Djoser.

Fig. 2-3 – Famine Stele of Netjerikhet Djoser on Sehel Island, Aswan, Egypt

In the tale carved on this boulder, Djoser's trusted advisor, Imhotep, tells him to give lands and gifts to the Temple of Khnum, the god believed to be the creator of the human race (though, ironically, in Imhotep's time, the father of all creation including humans was considered to be the Memphite god, Ptah). According to the stele, Djoser followed Imhotep's advice, which greatly pleased Khnum. Soon, the annual Nile floods returned to normal levels, as did the plentiful harvests.

The story on the Famine Stele resembles that of Joseph, son of Jacob of the Bible, a Hebrew whose jealous brothers sold him into slavery. Through his gift for interpreting several disturbing dreams for the pharaoh, he became overseer of the grain harvests during seven years of plenty in preparation for seven years of drought. Some contend that Joseph and Imhotep was the same person, but this is not likely, as Joseph probably lived between 800 to 1400 years after Imhotep, possibly during the Second Intermediate Period. It is more likely the author of Joseph's story, who allegedly lived in Egypt among royalty and may have had access to key ancient records, adopted part of Imhotep's story and integrated it into his historical narrative of the Hebrew people. Conversely, it is highly improbable that Egyptian priests appropriated the story of a Hebrew slave turned royal advisor that originated from a tribe that had not lived in Egypt for over a thousand years.

Within the enclosure of Djoser's mortuary complex, there is an area called the North Court. In the North Court, there is a double row of about 80 storage granaries (*Fig. 2-4*). Several Egyptologists believe these granaries were constructed for symbolic reasons only, but evidence of wheat, barley and fruits was found in underground storage chambers below the granaries. If the story written on the Famine Stele is remotely true then the storage of large quantities of food in these granaries makes sense.

Fig. 2-4 – The Double Row of Granaries in the Step Pyramid's North Court

Some think Imhotep was born a commoner and rose to his exalted status because Pharaoh Djoser saw in him a great intellect and chose him to be his Vizier, Chief Physician and Chief Architect. In reality, Imhotep was born into an elite family that was ensconced in the government of Egypt. One of Imhotep's titles, *The Hereditary Noble*, clearly indicates a birth in the upper echelon of Egyptian society. His father, Kanofer, also held the title of Royal Architect, which lends credence to this idea. In families that were part of the Egyptian bureaucracy, the eldest son would often inherit their father's job and title.

Though it is likely the priests of Khnum were indulging in a campaign of blatant political posturing to bolster their claim to some land, it is clear that later generations still had great respect for Imhotep's wisdom and intelligence. By invoking Imhotep's name, the priests of Khnum may have wanted to add credibility to their land claim.

This is supported by a graffito found in a quarry in the Wadi Hammamat,[14] a valley that was used as a trade route and stone quarry located between the Red Sea and the ancient city of Koptos (the ruins of which are within the modern-day city of Qift, north of Luxor). The inscription dates from the first period of occupation by the Persians (the Twenty-seventh Dynasty, 525-404 BCE), and shows the architect Khnumibre who was *Superintendent of Works in Upper and Lower Egypt* (i.e., Vizier) during the reign of the pharaoh Darius I. The graffito purportedly honors every architect going all the way back to the Third Dynasty beginning with Kanofer, followed by his son, Imhotep. It then skips forward in time to Rahotep, a Vizier and Architect of the Nineteenth Dynasty, and ends with the architect Khnumibre. This list was meant to legitimize Khnumibre's status as Royal Architect, and corroborates how the hereditary bureaucracy operated in Egypt throughout most of its history. Indirectly, it virtually proves Imhotep's family was associated with the royal family as well as Imhotep's probable birth in Memphis, the royal capital. Khnumibre would not have even needed to mention Imhotep and his father, Kanofer, if they were not connected with the royal family in some way, thus reinforcing Khnumibre's lineage as rightful holder of the Office of Vizier.

The erroneous presumption of a common birth is most likely due to Imhotep being confused with another great man of ancient Egypt, Amenhotep, Son of Hapu. Though he was actually a commoner at birth, Amenhotep, Son of Hapu held a number of high offices during the reign of Amenhotep III. Among his many titles were Architect, Priest, Scribe, Manager of the Estates of the King's daughter and *Fan Bearer on the Right*, a title often given to the Pharaoh's most trusted counselor. Amenhotep, Son of Hapu was even allowed to build his own mortuary temple next to the king's, a rare honor for anyone let alone one of such a humble birth.[15]

During the era of the Old Kingdom when Imhotep lived, the building of such large temple complexes may have only just begun. At its height, the Great Temple of Ptah at Memphis was as large as the Temples of Amun and the temples of several other gods constructed at Karnak during the New Kingdom, but the eventual enlargement of the Memphite temples would happen in a much later time. The Temple of Ra at Onu (Heliopolis) was a different story. Imhotep, as well as being Vizier, Physician and Architect was also a Priest of Ra. Even in the Old Kingdom, the Heliopolitan temples were large. Perhaps the Temple of Ra-Atum along with the funerary enclosures at Abydos of the previous pharaohs of the First and Second Dynasties is what inspired Imhotep to use stone to build on such a large scale at Sakkara.

In his own lifetime, Imhotep was widely known as the Vizier of Egypt, and perhaps, acknowledged as the Royal Architect due to his supervision of the construction of the Step Pyramid complex of Djoser as well as being the architect of the unfinished funerary monument of Djoser's successor, Sekhemkhet. However, his reputation as a healer came much later. A healing sanctuary within the mortuary temple at Deir el-Bahari of the Eighteenth Dynasty ruler, Hatshepsut, was dedicated in Imhotep's honor. [16] In the later Ptolemaic period, votive chapels and small temples were also constructed in his honor.

On the island of Philae is the Temple of Isis, built by Ptolemy II Philadelphus (285–246 BCE) starting 380 BCE and his successor, Ptolemy III Euergetes (who reigned 246–221 BCE) with later additions by the Roman emperors Augustus, Tiberius and Hadrian. Tucked away behind the colonnade near the First Pylon is the Temple of Imhotep (*Fig. 2-5*), also called the Temple of Asclepius, who was the father of Greek medicine.

Fig. 2-5 – The Temple of Imhotep in the Temple of Isis, Philae

On the west bank of the Nile River nestled in a little valley beneath towering cliffs is a small settlement called Deir el-Medina though in its day, it was known as Set-Maat, or *The Place of Truth*. This was the village of the artisans and craftsmen that excavated and decorated the tombs of the kings and queens in the Valley of the Kings, the Western Valley and the Valley of the Queens. One of several temples in the northern part of the village, the Temple of Hathor and Maat (*Fig. 2-6*) was built by Ptolemy IV Philopator (222–205 BCE) even though the village itself was no longer occupied by that time. Inscriptions in the temple indicate it was dedicated to two architects from centuries gone by, Imhotep and Amenhotep, Son of Hapu.

Fig. 2-6 – Temple of Hathor and Maat, Deir el-Medina

"Hail to you, kind-[hearted] god,
Imhotep son of Ptah!
Come to your house, your temple in Thebes,
May its people see you with joy!
Receive what is presented there,
Inhale the incense,
Refresh your body with libation!"

"One and all exalt your kindness!
For you heal them,
You revive them,
You renew your father's (Ptah) creation.
They bring you their donations,
Bear to you their gifts,
Proffer you their goods;
That you eat the offering loaves,
That you swallow the beer,
With your brothers, the elder gods,
And feed the worthy spirits with your surpluses."

(From the *Hymn to Imhotep*, Temple of Hathor and Maat, Deir el-Medina) [17]

Arguably, Imhotep probably was only incidentally known as a Royal Physician during his lifetime, so what explains people praying to him as a demigod for several millennia after his death to receive a cure for their illnesses (see *Fig. 2-1*).

The Edwin Smith Surgical Papyrus is one of the few medical papyri we have from ancient times, and was attributed to Imhotep by the scribe who wrote it, even if such authorship cannot easily be verified (*Fig. 2-7*). Of the entirety of known ancient works concerning medicine and surgical procedures, the Edwin Smith Papyrus is the oldest.

It contains the first known descriptions of cranial sutures, the external surface of the brain, and cerebral spinal fluid. It also contains the diagnosis, treatment, the prognosis of 48 medical issues, and is the earliest writing explaining trepanation, a standard method of relieving pressure on the brain.[18]

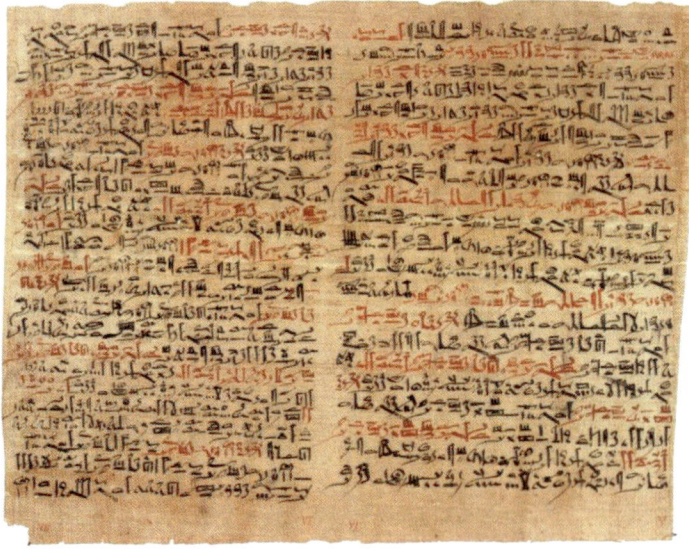

Fig. 2-7 – A fragment of the Edwin Smith Surgical Papyrus, attributed to Imhotep (circa 1600 BCE)

If Imhotep actually wrote some or all of the text in the Edwin Smith Papyrus, then there can be no doubt of his genius for mastering several widely divergent disciplines.

Grand Vizier, Chief Architect and Chief Lector Priest were among Imhotep's many titles and would have been sufficient to assure his renown when he was alive, and possibly for several generations afterward. Nevertheless, Imhotep's reputation as a physician is how we even know about him today. Yet, when writing about Imhotep, the Egyptologist, James Peter Allen, states:

The Greeks equated him with their own god of medicine, Asclepius, although ironically there is no evidence that Imhotep himself was a physician. [19]

It is unquestioned that Imhotep was more highly regarded as a physician in ancient times than any of his other titles would have guaranteed, but no one seems to have asked the obvious question:

Why?

Why pay tribute to a man who was no more than a distant memory, and was given the greatest honor a mere mortal could attain; that of being treated as equal to the gods, and could perform feats of medical magic as if he was still alive? Was it because of his alleged skills as a doctor, or was it something else?

A simple enough question, yet I could never find a reasonable answer. It would not be enough to ascribe to him a prodigious healing ability as evidenced by the existence of medical papyri attributed to him by many ancient peoples if he was simply a very good doctor. There had to be more to this riddle.

This single nagging question that would not let go for over 30 years motivated me to look even deeper into the life of Imhotep and his design of the Step Pyramid complex after stumbling onto a relatively obscure piece of stonework in a rarely visited part of the Djoser mortuary temple.

What follows is the culmination of that journey.

The journey of a thousand miles begins with a single step.

Lao Tsu, Chinese Philosopher

Imhotep the Physician – The South Entrance Hall and Human Anatomy

The ancient Egyptians were great observers of the natural world around them. In many ways, they were the world's first natural scientists. Their worldview, and consequently their religion, was an outgrowth of what they could easily witness in relation to nature in their daily lives. There is a universal inclination in all humans to speculate about a person's true nature, why they are alive and what happens after death. Over the millennia, it is probable that many Egyptians had profound moments of deep spiritual introspection while reflecting upon the meaning of life. Living alongside the tranquility of a gently flowing Nile River has a tendency to do that. Such observations of their natural world grew into a system of beliefs that incorporated the metaphors of *gods* and *goddesses* to explain their observations of nature and its rhythm. This spiritual imagery explained life in general to the ancient Egyptians, and more importantly, what awaited them in the Afterlife.

The Nile River was the slow, inexorable force that regularly gave and sustained life and constant renewal despite the vast expanse of deadly, unforgiving desert on either side of it. The Nile was the center of all life in ancient Egypt, and in many ways, the evolution of ancient Egyptian religion mimicked the natural cycles of the Nile River itself because its riverbed would meander within its flood plain on a regular basis to the extent that its position after the annual inundation was rarely the same. This necessitated the development of proficient surveying skills to determine property boundary lines after the inundation receded. Metaphorically, ancient Egyptians navigated the changes in their world in terms of both religion as well as politics, with a skill unlike most contemporaneous cultures, in that Egyptian society maintained a guiding moral and ethical framework that was as constant as it was flexible. Despite these changes, the ancient Egyptians always remained focused in their quest to *Live-in-Truth*, (i.e. *maat*) and tried their best to live within those self-revealed truths.

Ancient Egyptian religion did not resemble the more modern notion of what constitutes a religious creed. Rather, it grew out of an organic relationship with nature, and did not have any strict canon attached to it. In one sense, ancient Egyptian religion was many religious traditions that developed and changed over the millennia. Having no fundamental doctrine, the stories or myths were allowed grow and evolve in an organic fashion. Ancient Egyptian religion did not change in a *revolutionary* sense where a new messiah or teacher would come along espousing some radical new idea, which then replaced or totally modified the *old* religious concepts (Akhenaten being the only exception, and even then, it's debatable that his new Aten-based religion was all that revolutionary).

Instead, it was more *evolutionary* which allowed for the addition of new gods and stories to the prevailing religious mythology. Adding of new ideas and gods into previously accepted fundamental spiritual truth may seem foreign to us today, but it was a natural outgrowth of a profound, mysterious belief system that readily accepted other new ideas without adhering to a rigid dogma. It was one which saw in nature a lack of separation among its many manifestations, which in turn is how new gods could be added to the Egyptian pantheon over the thousands of years of their history without having to replace the old ones. In truth, they were like spiritual *hoarders* because they never *threw away* any of the old gods.

Religion, like the Nile River, was the single-most unifying force in ancient Egypt, more than even the state. Mighty temples of stone lined the banks of the Nile for a thousand miles providing a sense of permanence that is the hallmark of living life focused on spiritual ideals and beliefs. This is in direct contrast to the Egyptians' impermanent mud brick dwellings that are symbolic of their everyday life on Earth. One could not help but be cognizant of the powerful, underlying social and legal structure within those equally commanding stone structures that was fundamental to all of Egyptian culture.

While some of these new gods, and their priesthoods, eventually usurped power and prominence in Egyptian society to the point of resembling a political power grab, it was only because of the average Egyptian's insulated way of life that allowed the major temples at Karnak, Memphis, Heliopolis and other places to become the supreme authority in ancient Egyptian culture. Such dominance even displaced the role of the pharaoh at times, but this only occurred when there was a power vacuum at the top of a weak central government, and only manifested because of the mostly subtle control that the temples had over everyone, including the monarchy. However, this was not the norm during the time of Pharaoh Djoser's reign known as the Old Kingdom. That would have to wait until at least the end of the Middle Kingdom and later during the New Kingdom.

The belief in dozens of supernatural beings to explain the inner workings of nature may seem superstitious and primitive to someone who treats science and religion as two distinctly separate schools of thought. Nevertheless, we in the modern world must refrain from looking at the ancient Egyptian world through the lenses of our own reality, and put aside those filters if we can. We need to see how ancient Egyptians viewed themselves and their place in this grand cosmos and seek to understand how they saw life and nature. A multi-layered viewpoint of the world in ancient Egyptian society was the norm; a perspective that understood a human being is a soul composed of nine distinctly different bodies that simultaneously coexist between the physical world, the world of spirit, and everything in between. While the physical body (the **khat**) was the only one of the nine left behind after death, they it believed to be as important as the others, for it was the link to the person's past life that enabled them to become immortal in their future life in the spiritual realms. Coincidentally, the nine bodies are the same number as the Ennead, the nine primeval gods of ancient Egypt. Perhaps there is a paradoxical correlation between these two concepts which ably expresses the maxim attributed to Hermes Trismegistus, (who is often associated with the ancient Egyptian god, Thoth) of *as above, so below*. They are:

Khat	The Physical Body	Considered as a part of the soul, it is the vessel that contains the other parts of the soul while alive, and is the link between the soul in the Afterlife and one's earthly life. If the physical body was destroyed, the *Ka* could also be destroyed.
Ib	The Heart	The Key to the Afterlife; records every life experience
Ren	The True Name	The soul would live for as long as that name was spoken.
Bâ	The Personality (ego)	That which makes that makes a person unique. Capable of traveling between the spiritual and physical worlds before and after death.
Ka	The Vital Spark or energy body	A vital concept in the soul as it distinguishes the difference between a living and a dead person
Akh	The Immortal Self; the *Ba* and *Ka* united	The transformed immortal self that offered a magical union of the *Ba* and *Ka*.
Sahu	The Judge	An aspect of the *Akh* which would come to a person as a ghost or while asleep in dreams
Sechem	The Master of the Material World	This was another aspect of the *Akh* which allowed it have the power to control one's surroundings.
Shuyet	The Shadow	The shadow contained another part of what made each person unique.

The Nine Bodies of a Human Being

The material sciences of our modern era are limited to studying physical or material phenomena. It is impossible to use them to study the world of spirit since they are different from physical reality. If the ancient peoples of the Nile were like us today, and were inclined to compartmentalize logic and reason from belief and spirituality, they still would see no difference between science and religion. To them, the natural world they saw around them was an outgrowth of a greater spiritual reality; an expression of a Divine Spirit or energy, sometimes referred to as Atum, or Ra-Atum, the *Complete One*, or *The One-Who-Created-Himself-Out-Of-Nothing*. To the average ancient Egyptian, *nature* and *supernature* were the same and separating the two would invite chaos. To live an orderly and meaningful life would be *Living-in-Truth*, or *ankes-em-maat*. To *Live-in-Truth* is to live one's life in accordance with Divine Order (*maat)*, and be in harmony with the immutable laws of nature, or as we would put it today, respecting the laws of physics. If they did not, they would be in conflict with nature, and be in danger of losing their soul for all of eternity. It would be the same if we attempted to repeal the Law of Gravity by jumping out of an airplane in flight without a parachute!

In a more esoteric and deeper sense, the gods and goddesses of ancient Egypt were not actual *beings* in the traditional sense of the word (though some have speculated they may have been at one time). Instead, the *gods* of ancient Egypt should be thought of as *nature principles*; archetypes of a greater system that encompasses all of nature, a kind of metaphor that describes the way the universe works. As further proof of this, the ancient Egyptian word for god is *ntr* (pronounced 'neter'), which we have inherited from ancient Egypt as it is the root origin of our word for *nature*.

Gardiner Sign List No. – R8   '*ntr'*, "god" or "goddess"

The creation and development of ancient Egyptian religious views and systems of belief may seem unconnected to any reasonably scientific-like observations of nature, but unlike our current Western European-centric philosophical belief systems, the ancient Egyptians did not see themselves as separate from the world in which they lived. Simply put, the ancient Egyptians saw no difference between their lives in the physical world and the spiritual realm they would return to after death; their beliefs about the world of the Afterlife greatly resembled their lives in this world.

Into this world where people embraced the differences between life and death, medical science and spirituality, politics and philosophy without taking notice of the apparent contradictions was born Imhotep. Being able to draw on two or more dissimilar ways of perceiving the world in his work would have come easily to him. As F. Scott Fitzgerald once wrote, "The test of a first-rate intelligence is the ability to hold two opposed ideas in the mind at the same time, and still retain the ability to function." [20] Being capable of multilayered thinking is the best description of the genius that is Imhotep.

What sets Imhotep apart in the ancient world was his ability to juggle two or more complex and disparate concepts when tasked with designing and building the Step Pyramid Enclosure. It is entirely possible that Imhotep the Physician influenced and inspired Imhotep the Architect when he was designing his greatest architectural achievement. If we were to apply the age-old architectural design principle of *form follows function* to the work of Imhotep, then it might be possible to determine the function of the various architectural elements contained within the form of the architecture of the Step Pyramid complex.

However, the symbolism inherent in these design elements may be based on a hidden, unknown tradition of spiritual knowledge and wisdom that we may have difficulty comprehending having no analogous tradition or custom in the modern world. The secret code contained in the architectural language of the Step Pyramid and its enclosure is as distant to us as the real spiritual meaning that led to its construction.

It has always been my desire to know and understand the spiritual wisdom of ancient Egypt. In this respect, I was most fortunate to encounter an Egyptian *indigenous wisdom keeper*, that is, one who keeps alive the great spiritual teachings of his people as well as being an archeologist, Abd'el Hakim Awyan, or *Hakim*, as he was more widely known. I did not know it at the time, but what I learned from my tour guide, Hakim, on those two trips to Egypt eventually gave me the opportunity to reveal what has long been *hidden in plain sight* and show the brilliance of Imhotep the Architect.

Hakim was born in 1926 in the village of Nazlet el-Samman that lies at the edge of the Giza Plateau in the shadow of the Sphinx and the Great Pyramid, and lived there until his death in 2008. He learned many oral traditions of Egypt from his maternal uncle, Zaki Mahmoud Awyan, who was also an antiquities dealer. Zaki taught Hakim much about Egyptian history and its antiquities, and later adopted him as his son. At age six, Hakim's uncle sent him to study with a Sufi master, Ismail, who taught him the wisdom innate within Sufism, which is the mystical teachings of Islam. However, as Hakim would later say, the greatest gift Ismail gave him was to learn to meditate. Utilizing this skill, he would meditate in the *holy places* at all the archeological sites in Egypt, deriving profoundly powerful insights and to *walk with the Neters*, that is, to be *one with the gods*, or more accurately, be in harmony with the natural world in all its manifestations.

Abd'el Hakim Awyan, "Hakim" (1926-2008)

In this respect, I believe Hakim was listening to the *intelligence of the heart* much like his ancestors. As such, he gave freely from his heart as he frequently spoke of the ancient spiritual wisdom of Egypt to the thousands of people that were fortunate to have met him during the fifty-six years he served as a tour guide in Egypt.

Hakim also worked at Giza with Dr. George Reisner of Harvard University and the Boston Museum of Fine Arts. As a result, he fell in love with archeology, and graduated from Fouad University in 1952 with dual degrees in Egyptology and archeology. He later did graduate work at Leiden University in Holland in the 1960s. Having one foot in the world of science and archeology and another in the world of metaphysics and mysticism gave him a unique viewpoint when teaching ancient Egyptian history and culture.[21]

It was during our tour group's visit to Sakkara that I first heard Hakim speak of an ancient tradition about the Ḥeb-Sed Court (Hakim called it *the House of the Spirit* or *House of the Ka*, as it would have been known in ancient times). Besides being the site for the *sed*-festival, Hakim said it was also used as a center for healing.

The South Entrance Hall and Ḥeb-Sed Court Medical Center

Fig. 3-1 – Ḥeb-Sed Court – West Chapels '0', 1, 2, 3 and 4

In *Fig. 3-1* and the artistic reconstruction of the Ḥeb-Sed Court by J.-P. Lauer (*Fig. 3-5*), there are two alcoves with a set of stairs in front of West Chapels 1 and 2. Most Egyptologists believe the construction of these two alcoves was to hold stone statues of Pharaoh Netjerikhet Djoser, one statue wearing the White Crown of Upper Egypt and the other statue wearing the Red Crown of Lower Egypt. While this is certainly plausible, there are some difficulties with this theory. Hoisting a pair of stone statues into the two alcoves would have proven daunting at best given our current knowledge of Third Dynasty building techniques. However, many reliefs depicting *sed*-festival rituals show just such a type of raised platform for the king to sit on (*Fig. 3-2*), and for which the dais with two sets of stairs (foreground, *Fig. 3-1*) was no doubt used for these ceremonies.

Fig. 3-2 – Pharaoh seated on his throne during the Ḥeb-Sed

Fig. 3-3 – West Chapel 1 Stairs

Because of the unfinished state of seven statues found near the Ḥeb-Sed Court (*Fig. 3-4*), it is unlikely that the alcoves held any permanent statues based on the incomplete state of the Step Pyramid Enclosure as a whole. It is doubtful that there was any intention to install the stone statues in the alcoves as *Fig. 3-2* depicts the king seated on just such a raised platform. Therefore a critical and dispassionate look at the Ḥeb-Sed Court as rebuilt by J.-P. Lauer forces us to reexamine this presumption.

Fig. 3-4 – Three of the seven unfinished statues found near the South Pavilion Court

When viewing the West Chapels of the Ḥeb-Sed Court , one must ask how heavy stone statues weighing more than a ton were supposedly lifted more than 3 meters (10 feet) above ground level into the two alcoves (*Fig. 3-5*). It is certain the steps, which are not flat and slope **downward** in front of the alcoves; were not used to lift such heavy statues into place (*Fig. 3-3*). No self-respecting architect would design such an oddly shaped staircase for such a difficult task. First, it would prove nearly impossible to muscle a pair of statues that high using a sloped staircase, thus making it more difficult than necessary. In addition, the stairs would more than likely been damaged in the process.

If there were stone statues installed in these two chapel alcoves, then the construction of the current staircases probably occurred **after** the installation of any statues into the alcoves (if statues were even installed in them at all). However, given the transient nature of celebrating the *Ḥeb-Sed*, it is more probable that the placement in the alcoves of temporary lighter-weight wooden effigies of the king that were later removed at the end of the *sed*-festival allowed the Ḥeb-Sed Court to function as a medical center once again. More likely still, Djoser may have sat in the alcoves during the *sed*-festival ceremonies. It may seem like a small matter whether stone statues were installed in these alcoves or not, but as we will see, it changes the nature of what the true function of the Ḥeb-Sed Court would become after Djoser passed away.

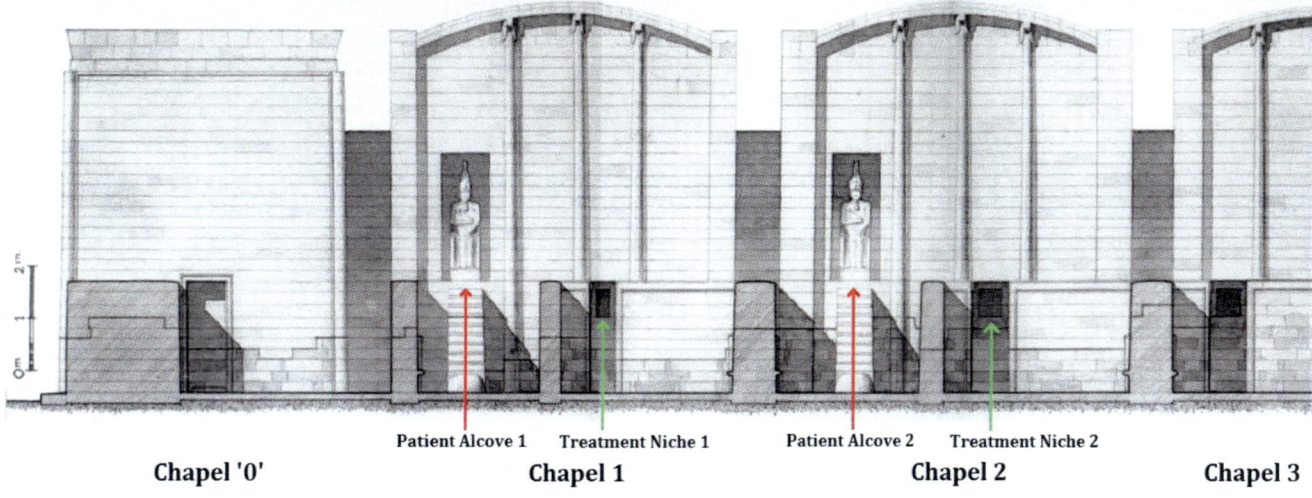

Fig. 3-5 – Ḥeb-Sed Court – West Chapels

According to Hakim, a patient coming to the Ḥeb-Sed Court for medical treatment would use their intuition, or *intelligence of the heart*, to guide them to sit in one of the two elevated alcoves accessible by the stairs in front of West Chapels 1 and 2. The physician/priest would be in the lower level of the chapel and sing or chant specific tones or frequencies into the head-high treatment niche that acted as a type of resonator to affect a healing for the patient sitting in the alcove above. After this healing session, the priest would also prescribe any additional cures. We do not know why patients chose one of the chapels over the other. Maybe one chapel was for men and the other for women. Who knows? Some secrets remain hidden today.

In another scenario, the patient would be lying on a bed-like table inside one of the other West Chapels, and using the niche of the chapel, the priest would intuitively focus his attention on the person on the table. Using sound once again, he would determine the best course of corrective treatment, and affect the proper healing for his patient – *or so the story goes*.

Is Hakim's story too fantastic to be true? While it is true there is no archeologically based evidence of its veracity, it is also true that archeologists cannot *dig up* oral traditions concerning history, spiritual wisdom and beliefs. There is more to ancient Egyptian culture and history than can be revealed with a spade and trowel as archeologists can only uncover tangible artifacts from the dust of time. Oral traditions, such as those related by wisdom keepers as Hakim, are an integral part of many cultures in Africa. What is often amazing to Western scientists when they examine these ancient and traditional stories more carefully is how precise they are, both in their historical accuracy and in scientific validity.

Curiously, Hakim also said there were water channels beneath the Ḥeb-Sed Court connected to the chapels that amplified the sound of the priests' chanting and aided the acceleration of the healing process. There is no direct proof such water channels existed, but if they did, it is a fact that sound moves about 4.3 times faster through water than through the air, thus amplifying the frequency of any sound going through the water. No doubt it would be difficult to locate any such underground channels today (supposedly there were 22 of them) because the Nile River has migrated several kilometers to the east since the Step Pyramid Enclosure was built along with any evidence of where the ancient water table was at that time.

However, between 2005 and 2007, a team from the Latvian Scientific Mission used ground-penetrating radar (GPR) to investigate the underlying strata beneath the Step Pyramid Enclosure up to 50 meters (164 feet) deep (see Chapter 6, *Figs. 6-83, 6-84* and *6-85*). Thus far, there have been the identification of several underground cavities and galleries, along with three previously unknown corridors extending from the eastern Dry Moat to the third, fourth and fifth pit tombs, and a tunnel connecting the South Tomb to one of the underground chambers beneath the Step Pyramid. [22] Maybe the 22 water channels Hakim alluded to will eventually be found some day.

While using sound to heal the sick may seem strange, recent experiments have used extremely high frequencies to kill cancer cells[23] showing that it is possible to cure diseases with these resonant sounds. The universe in which we all live is nothing more than energy manifested as frequency and resonance. To use sound frequencies to alter the biology of a diseased body back to a state of proper equilibrium is not outside the realm of distinct possibilities.

Is this what Hakim alluded to when speaking about the healing techniques of the ancient Egyptian priests who worked at the Step Pyramid healing center? It is difficult to say without knowing the methods employed by those priests, but there is a need for much more research on both of these ancient and the modern healing modalities.

This may seem superstitious and primitive compared to our modern allopathic medical practices. However, along with prescribing various *medications* (primitive though they were) that were in common use at that time, the priests were, perhaps, the world's first psychologists by using what we nowadays call the *placebo effect*, whether they knew it or not. Often hotly debated among more materialist-thinking physicians, the reality of the placebo effect and its place in treating patients is highly controversial. However, the fact of the matter is that it is real as evidenced by virtually every responsible and reliable drug trial includes using a placebo as a control with a certain number of subject patients to see if the new drug is both safe and effective. These are called triple-blind, placebo-controlled studies. If a drug is no more or even less effective than using a placebo, then the drug is considered unsuccessful for its intended use.

In this vein, I spoke with a doctor many years ago about drug trials in general, and the use of placebos in the trials. He told me a story of one of his patients who took part in a trial for a drug intended for use in treating rheumatoid arthritis. As part of the drug trial, this particular patient was unknowingly in the placebo control group instead of the group given the drug. When the patient went for a post-trial consult with the doctor, he mentioned his happiness with how the drug helped relieve the pain in his knees from which he had suffered for many years. When the doctor told him he was one of the control subjects that was given only the placebo, the fellow just laughed, and said he didn't care, because he was now pain free even though it was obvious his own mind/body healing mechanism was what *cured* him.

The documented use of the Ḥeb-Sed Court as a festival site and as a copy of the royal palace that Djoser could take with him into the hereafter is not in question here. Rather, the real question is what purpose did the Ḥeb-Sed Court serve **after** the festivities were over and all the revelers had gone home. In general, *Ḥeb-Sed* buildings were meant to be temporary structures made of perishable materials such as wood and reed matting to be used during the thirtieth anniversary celebration of a pharaoh's ascension to the throne (though most Pharaohs didn't live that long, so many celebrated their *sed*-festival jubilees much earlier in their reigns). Thereafter, *sed*-festivals were held every four years or so. (The Pharaoh Amenhotep III of the Eighteenth Dynasty had three *Ḥeb-Sed* jubilees during his 37-year reign.) Having a *sed*-festival center made of permanent material like stone made no sense given the irregularly of celebrating the festival. The use of stone in the construction of a *Ḥeb-Sed* venue would not return until the New Kingdom some 1300 years later, mostly in the Eighteenth and Nineteenth Dynasties.

Initially, when Hakim spoke about the Ḥeb-Sed Court being a *hospital*, I didn't make the connection to the discovery of a doorpost socket for a self-closing door. A few years later, though, I remembered what Hakim said, and I knew there was more to this doorpost socket – and the Step Pyramid Enclosure as a whole – than met the eye! It was then I started to delve more deeply into its architecture to see if what Hakim said might possibly be true.

Is there any evidence that confirms the Ḥeb-Sed Court was also a medical center? For the longest time, I sensed a symbolic representation of the human spine was integral to the design of the Entrance Hall. (*It was in there, somewhere!*) Certainly, many things did not add up.

First, there are 24 vertebrae in the spine, but only 42 columns. Even if two columns represented one vertebra, there were not enough columns to go around! Second, even though I intuitively knew that perhaps the *spaces between the columns* represented the spine, there were only 22 spaces between the Entrance Hall columns. After examining the plan of the Entrance Hall for what seemed to be an eternity, I suddenly realized the trapezoid-shaped room located just after the narrow entrance corridor looked very familiar! After consulting an anatomical chart of the spine, I had a *light bulb moment* and everything started to fall into place.

It may seem strange at first, but looking at the plan of the South Entrance Gate and colonnaded Entrance Hall with a little bit of imagination, a stylized rendering of the human spine can be seen outlined by the **spaces** defined by the colonnade. The representation of the human spine is easier to spot when inverting the black-and-white details of the Entrance Hall (*Fig. 3-6*).

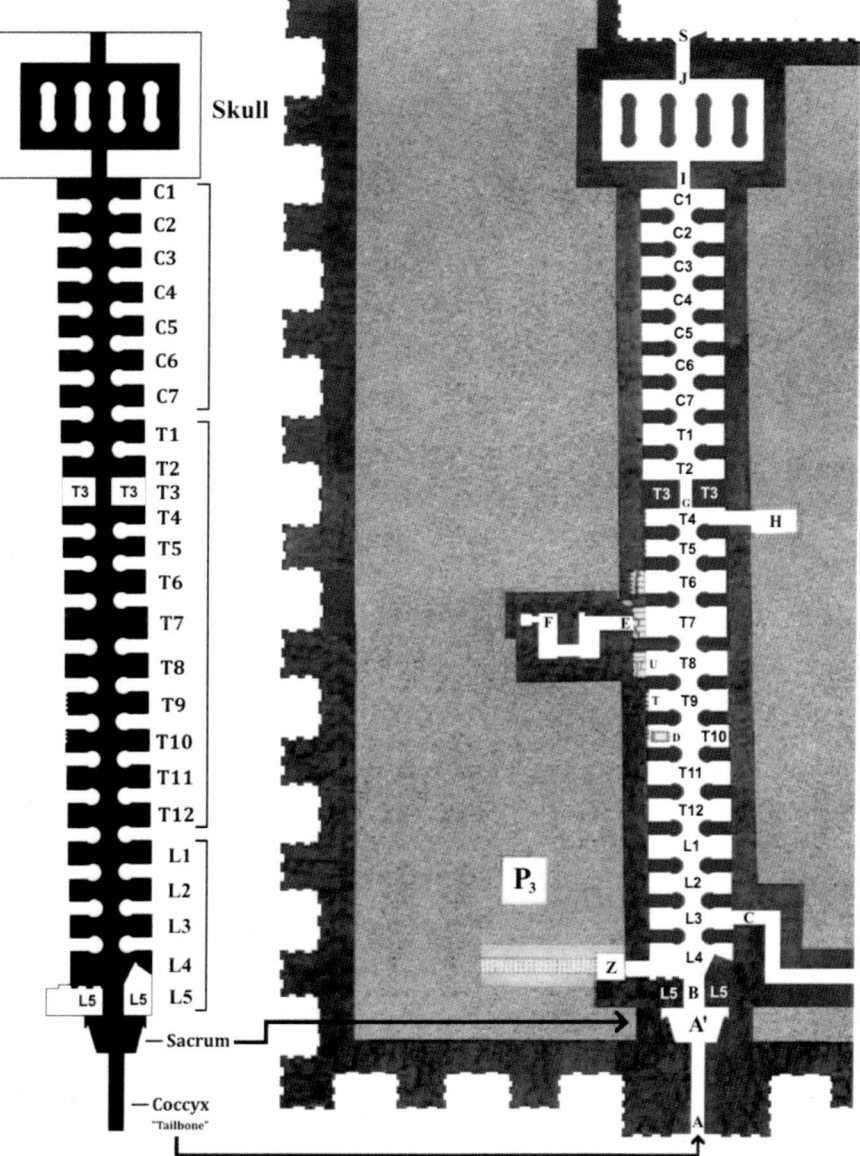

Fig. 3-6 – The South Entrance Hall and its reverse image as the Human Spine and Skull

Rather than using the semi-round and square columns to create a symbolic metaphor in stone for the human spine, Imhotep opted to create a new *rule* for viewing the human spine within his design: *the space between walls and columns is the equivalent of bone*; or to put it simply, *space-equals-bone*. This inconspicuously and subtly incorporates the human spine within the design of the South Entrance Hall inspiring *those who have eyes to see*.

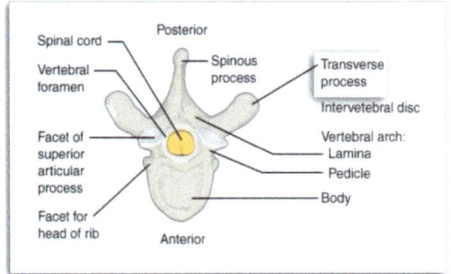

One can see the round central core of the spinal column with the two outward jutting side bones of each vertebra called 'transverse processes' (*Fig. 3-7*). These transverse processes are represented by the horizontal spaces between the columns of the long Entrance Hall as seen in *Fig. 3-8*.

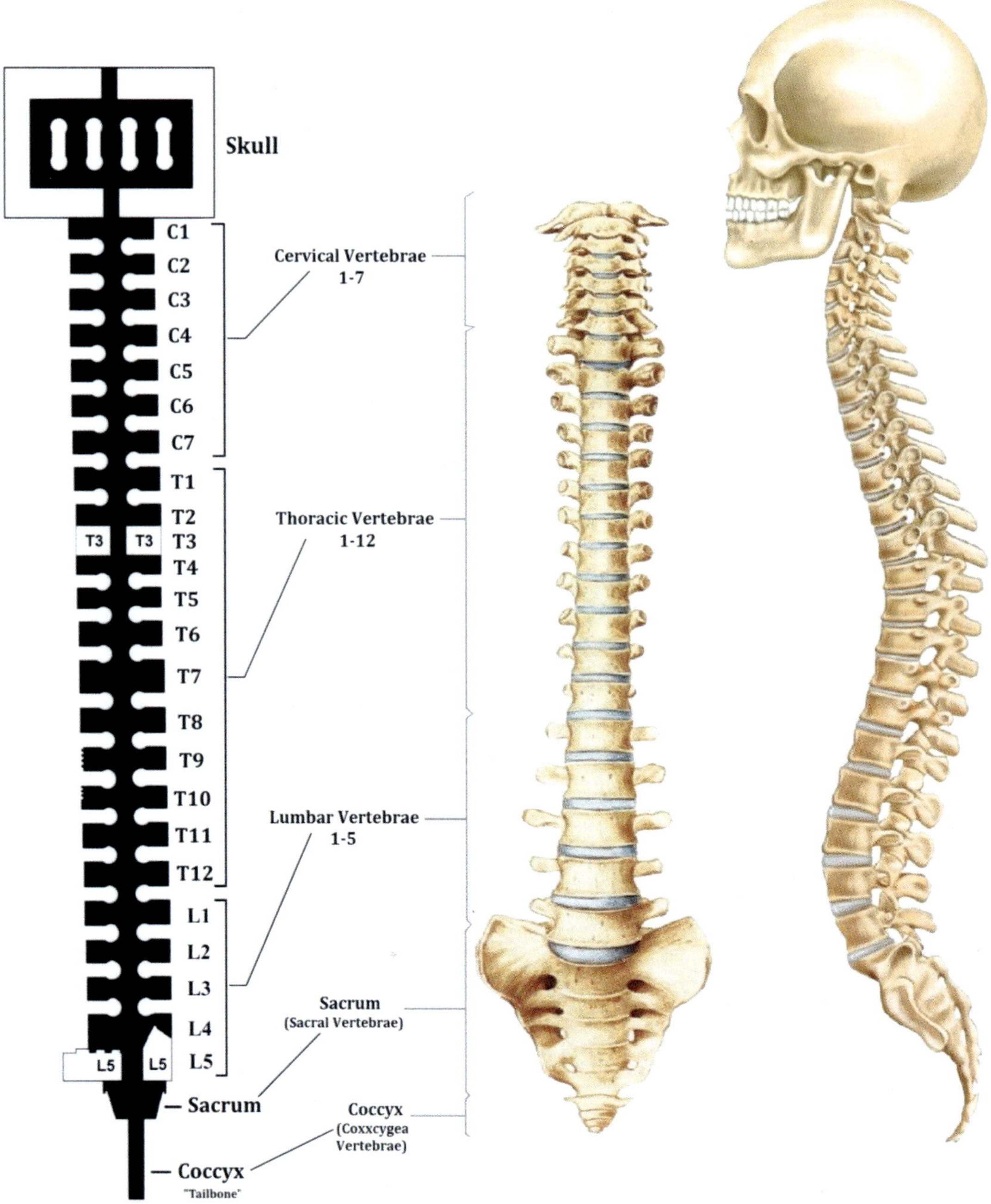

Fig. 3-7 – Top view of a vertebra showing the Transverse Processes

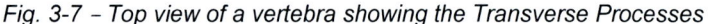

Fig. 3-8 – The inverse image of the South Entrance Hall and Anterior (Frontal) View of the Human Spine and Side View with Skull

Entering the South Entrance Gate, the first anatomical feature defined is within the entrance corridor itself. This very long, narrow corridor leading into the Entrance Hall is analogous to the five fused bones of the *coccyx*, more commonly known as the tailbone. After exiting this corridor, one enters a trapezoid-shaped room (marked as **A′**) that has two simulated permanently open doors made of stone (see Chapter 1, *Figs. 1-11, 1-12* and *1-13*). This unusually shaped room leading into the inner recesses of sacred space clearly imitates the triangular shape of the sacrum, or the mass of knitted bones sitting just above the coccyx.

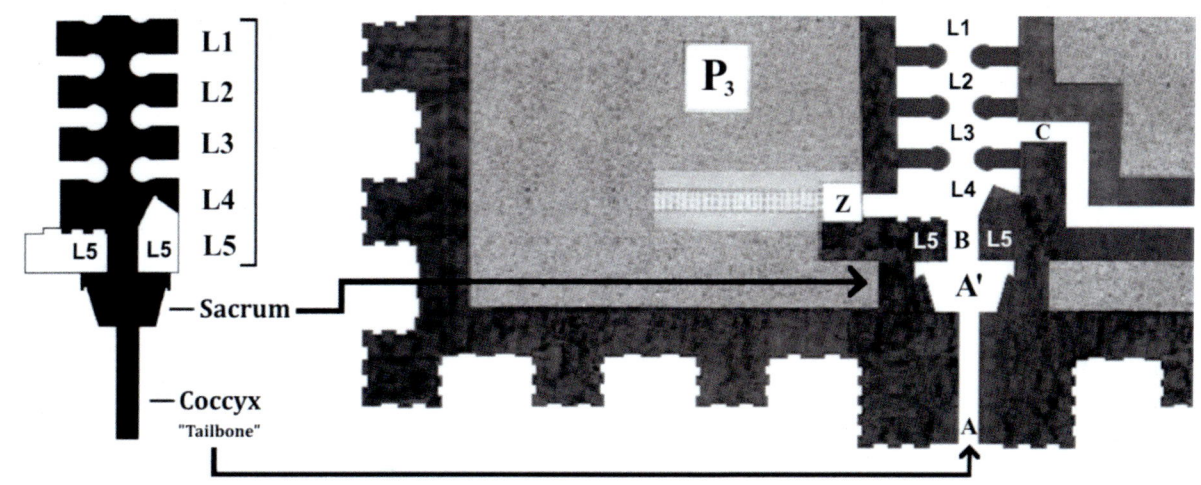

Fig. 3-9 – The South Entrance Gate – Coccyx to L1 of the Spine

Leaving this small Entrance Vestibule, one enters another short, narrow passageway (marked as '**B**' in *Figs. 3-9* and *3-10*). If you have any familiarity with human anatomy, you would not be wrong in thinking this '**B**' corridor should represent the fifth lumbar vertebra (**L5**) assuming Imhotep was still using his '*space-equals-bone*' rule. Instead, the two very large square, boxy doorframes are stand-ins for the **L5** vertebra. The reason for this exception to the *rule* will be explained later in this chapter.

Fig. 3-10 – The north 'L5' Stone Door next to the 'L4' space in the foreground

Exiting the small '**B**' corridor situated between the **L5** columns, one enters another small open area with one more *always-open* door made of stone attached to the north (right) doorframe (*Figs. 3-10* and *3-11*). This space corresponds to the fourth lumbar vertebra (**L4**).

Just before the first columns of the Entrance Hall proper is a doorway to the left exiting out of the Entrance Hall to the south (marked as '**Z**'). This doorway purportedly led to a set of stairs that permitted access to the top of the Enclosure Wall, much like the walls of a military outpost or city walls. The undulating bastions that are on the exterior of the Enclosure Wall are an imitation of this sort of military architecture.

Fig. 3-11 – From behind the 'L5' Stone Door.

Beyond the stone door is the L4 space that leads out to the doorway marked on J.-P. Lauer's plans as 'Z' where a stairway that went to the top of the Enclosure Wall was once located (see Fig. 3-9)

The pit designated as **P₃** in J.-P. Lauer's plan (*Fig. 3-12*) as it presently exists was an entrance to a small set of unfinished underground chambers that would have connected to the South Tomb had it been completed. At one time, it also may have been a well for use by the temple staff and visitors during the time when the Step Pyramid Enclosure was a functioning temple. Egypt during the Third Dynasty was far more verdant and green, unlike the desert environment we see today. The Nile River at that time was much closer to the plateau where the Step Pyramid Enclosure is located than it is now. The Nile probably started to migrate eastward in its river channel many centuries later during the great drought that occurred at the end of the Old Kingdom (Sixth and Seventh Dynasties), at which time the well would have also dried up enabling it to be filled part-way up and used as an entrance for a tomb.

However, if it was never a water well, and it pre-existed the construction of the South Entrance Gate and Entrance Hall, one must wonder why Imhotep chose to include it within the confines of the Enclosure Wall. If it was not an entrance to an unfinished tomb, and it had no other significance when Imhotep started construction of the southeast quadrant of the Step Pyramid Enclosure, he could have just filled it in, and no one would know it ever existed to this day. Such small things as this pit seem to have their own mysteries associated with them.

Fig. 3-12 – The P₃ Pit Tomb (originally a water well?)

Continuing west down the Entrance Hall, on the north (right) side, situated between the first and second set of columns, is a doorway (*Fig. 3-13*) to a long corridor (marked as '**C**' in *Fig. 3-9*) that leads to the Ḥeb-Sed Court. The location of this doorway corresponds to the third lumbar vertebra in the spine (**L3**). It is at the **L3** vertebra that the last neural path of the spinal cord exits and joins up with the rest of the sympathetic nervous system.

The **L3** vertebra also aligns with the area of the abdomen where the small and large intestines are located. If this *L3 hallway* was meant to call our attention to this point, then perhaps the Ḥeb-Sed Court and the group of corridors and rooms preceding it are a large-scale model of the central nervous system and the intestinal tract, upon which we'll elaborate further as we continue our investigation.

*Fig. 3-13 – The **L3** Doorway to the Ḥeb-Sed Court*

In addition to the **L3** vertebra, the **L4** vertebra is where the organs of the lower abdomen also reside, including the bladder, the internal reproductive organs and the small and large intestines. This might be a bit of a stretch, but perhaps a small room was located just west (to the right) of the south doorway leading from the **L4** space (marked as '**Z**', *Fig.3-11*). This doorway led to stairs that gave access to the top of the Enclosure wall. The location of just such a room next to this stairway would allow a person to shake off the dust of the desert, or even for more personal hygiene needs, such as having chamber pots or latrine chairs available to weary travelers. As strange as this idea may sound, it makes perfect sense to place such a room at this spot given its anatomically symbolic position along the length of the Entrance Hall. In many temples, small rooms such as this would have been located just inside the temple near the entrance, perhaps for use to perform a cleansing or purification ritual prior to entering the main sanctuary. This hypothesis depends on whether there was a room just after the **L4** doorway between the stairway (marked as '**Z**') and Pit **P**$_3$ that was filled in at the time the Entrance Hall was constructed or later (see *Fig. 3-9*).

Fig. 3-14 – The South Entrance Hall – Vertebrae T12 to T6 of the Spine

Between the sixth and seventh columns on the south side of the Entrance Hall analogous to the tenth thoracic vertebrae (**T10**) is a rectangular object that is depicted on J.-P. Lauer's plans of the Entrance Hall (marked as '**D**' in *Fig. 3-14*). Firth called this object the *Lion Base*. Some speculate that it may have been the base of a statue, an offering table or something altogether quite different. More about the Lion Base later in this chapter.

Between the ninth and tenth set of columns is an entrance to a U-shaped room whose function is unknown at this time, though Firth seemed to think it was a chapel of some sort. It is equally possible that it was a restroom referred to above. If so, the small room marked as '**F**' would have had a latrine chair installed in it, and a washbasin located near the entrance to the chamber (marked as '**E**').

It was here that the base of a statue was found with the two feet of Djoser standing on the Nine Bows, the traditional enemies of Egypt. This statue base was made famous because Imhotep's name and titles were inscribed upon it, (red rectangle in *Fig. 3-15*) a most unusual occurrence in ancient Egypt because there was never an instance before or after Imhotep's time where the king permitted the architect of his funerary monument to sign his work, so to speak.

The name of Imhotep

Imhotep's titles read "Chancellor of the king of Lower Egypt, First after the king of Upper Egypt, Administrator of the Grand Palace, Hereditary Lord, High Priest of Heliopolis, Imhotep the architect, the sculptor, the maker of stone vases ..."

Fig. 3-15 – The base of a statue of Djoser with Imhotep's name (in red rectangle)

If the **T7** chamber was a latrine or privy at one time, in all likelihood someone moved this statue base here in antiquity from another location, possibly the space between the columns marked as '**U**', or more likely, from elsewhere in the Enclosure because the top part of the statue depicting Djoser's body was never found here or anyplace else.

In this location along the spine (**T7**), the lungs, diaphragm and their associated organs are located. The U-shape of this alleged chapel is suggestive of the two lungs on either side of the trachea, bronchus and, of course, the heart. Though the lungs run the length of the spine between **T1** and just above **T8**, it is just below **T3** where the trachea (windpipe) branches out into the two bronchia. Each bronchus of the windpipe attaches to the lungs, and it is at **T7** where the last of the bronchia attaches to the lungs.

In many esoteric teachings, the spiritual discipline of learning to control the breath (or *prana* as it is called in the Hindu tradition) is a method of focusing one's attention in order to cross the gateway or intersection between the spiritual and the physical worlds. This obviously would be important to the priests that lived and worked in this temple in that the practice of disciplined breathing and chanting would be an integral part of their daily rituals.

The fourth thoracic vertebra (**T4**) is located between the twelfth and thirteenth set of columns of the Entrance Hall (*Fig. 3-16*). Located just outside the north wall of the Entrance Hall is situated a small chamber. Attached to the **T4** vertebra, a rib is connected which goes diagonally down and around to the front of the sternum (breastbone). Located within the abdominal cavity behind where the **T4** rib connects to the sternum (*Fig. 3-14*) is the pericardium, and within it, the heart. Ancient Egyptian writings often spoke of *the intelligence of the heart*, for they regarded the heart as the seat of wisdom – or more accurately – the center where the higher intuitive functions reside. It would therefore be natural that Imhotep honored the sacred heart center by designing a room to be located at this position along the Entrance Hall corridor.

Fig. 3-16 – The South Entrance Hall – Vertebrae T5 to T1 of the Spine

If Imhotep meant for the Entrance Hall to be an anatomically correct representation of the human body, it is obvious the location of the **T4** *heart chamber* is not quite right since the heart's position is in the chest cavity along the spine between the **T4** and **T6** vertebrae. However, if we view the human body from the front (anterior), the *heart chamber* is in the anatomically correct position on the left (north) side of the body. To clarify, when looking at a plan of the Entrance Hall (*Fig. 3-6*), north is on the right and equals the left side of the body. South is on the left side of the plan and equals the right side of the body. This is yet another example of Imhotep *hiding something in plain sight*, inspiring the observer to go beyond using only intellectual and logical reasoning to perceive what lies hidden in this *anatomy textbook* made of stone. (And yes, it really is a coincidence that J.-P. Lauer designated this room on his plans with the letter '**H**'.) Since this *heart chamber* also figures prominently in another of the multiple layers of hidden wisdom contained in the Step Pyramid Enclosure's design, Imhotep needed to make some accommodations in order to incorporate in the same space all of the secret wisdom he wished to convey. Its size and position at this particular spot will make sense as we proceed further in our investigation.

After the **T4** *heart chamber*, there are two square columns (marked as '**G**' in *Fig. 3-16*). These columns are a curious anomaly within the context of the Entrance Hall, and are analogous to the third thoracic vertebra (**T3**). Once again, Imhotep suspends his use of the *space-equals-bone* rule, this time for a very good reason. As discussed before, symbolic representations of most of the vertebrae are visible in the outline of the spaces between the columns along the length of the Entrance Hall (once you know they are there).

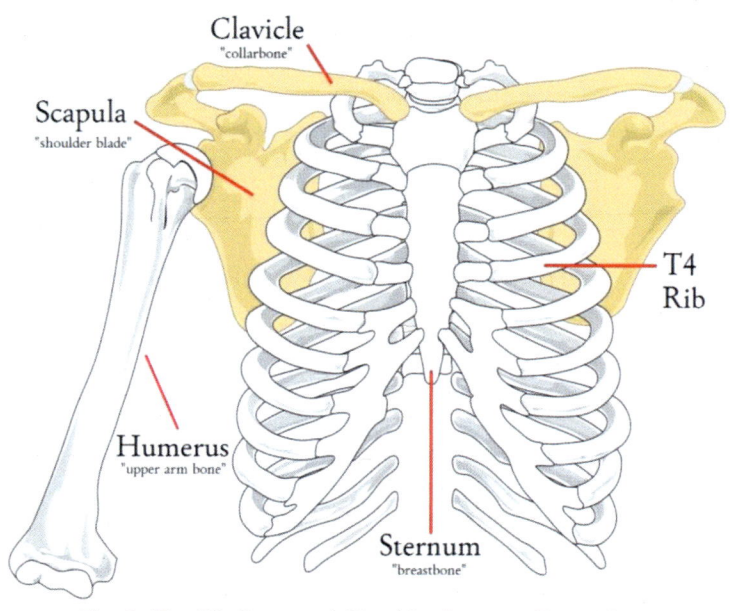

Fig. 3-17 – Rib Cage and Shoulder Bones – Front View

Why Imhotep reversed the symbolism for the third thoracic (**T3**) and fifth lumbar vertebrae (**L5**) is not readily apparent. These two vertebrae are unique inasmuch as they are the attachment points for the bones of the extremities (the arms and legs) at or near these locations in the spinal column. The collarbones (*clavicle*) connect to the breastbone (*sternum*) near where the **T1** and **T2** vertebrae are located (*Fig. 3-17*). Connected to the other end of the collarbones are the shoulder blades (*scapula*), which attach to the rib cage and shoulders by three muscle groups. The upper arm bones (*humerus*) then connects to the end of shoulder blades. Actually, the *clavicle* and *scapula* straddle the part of the ribcage where vertebrae **T2**, **T3** and **T4** are located, with the shoulder and arm structures aligning perpendicularly with the **T3** vertebra and its rib.

Just below the **L5** vertebra, is the **sacrum** (*Fig. 3-18*). Attached to the **sacrum** is the pelvic girdle (with its two ear-shaped bones called *coxa*), to which the ball-and-sockets of the hip joints and the leg bones (*femurs*) are connected.

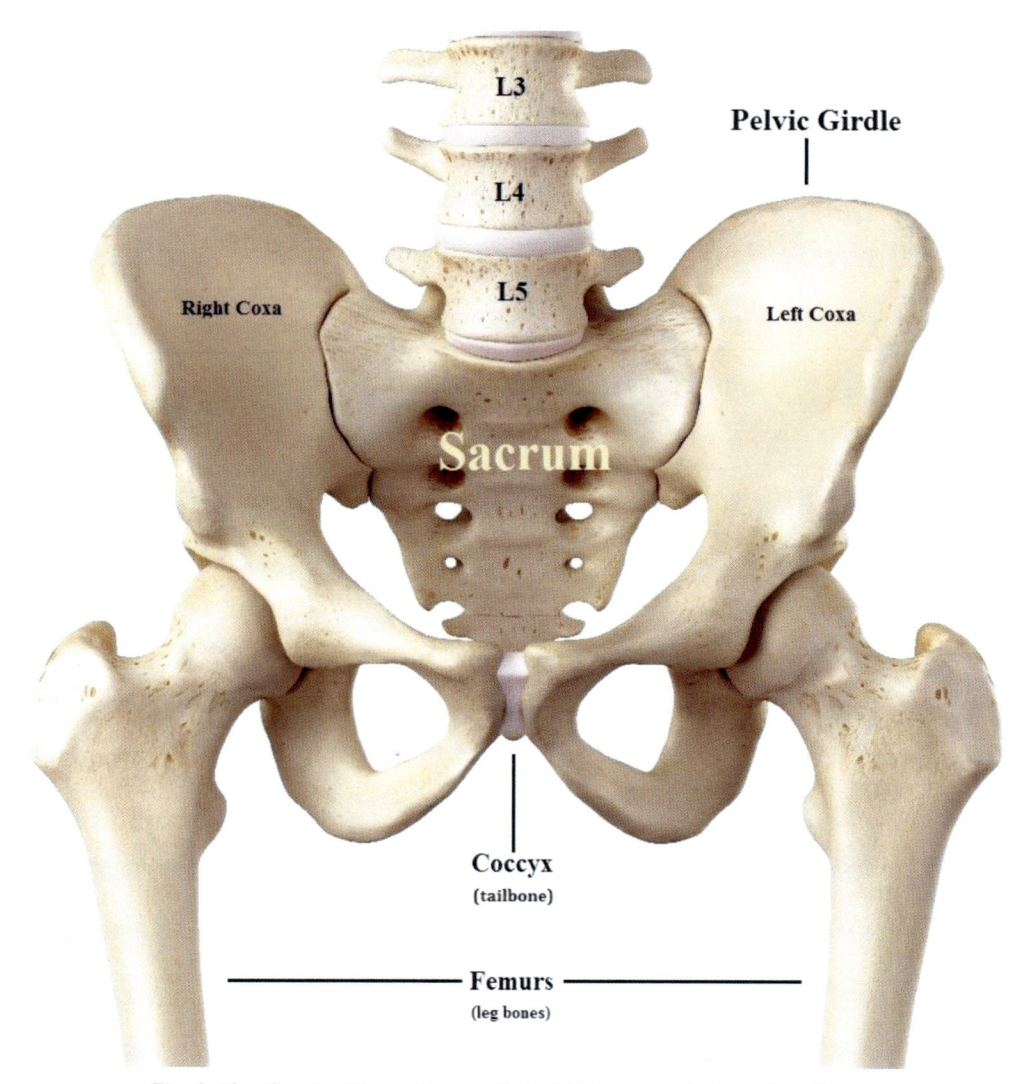

Fig. 3-18 – Frontal View of Lower Spinal Column and Upper Leg Bones

With the representations in stone of the **L5** and **T3** vertebrae being the reverse of the implicit representations of the other vertebrae by the empty spaces between the semi-round Entrance Hall columns, it appears Imhotep is deliberately breaking his *space-equals-bone* rule. These two exceptions were ultimately consistent with the structure of the human body. In so doing, Imhotep compels the observer to *think outside the box*, requiring them to recognize some of the finer details of human anatomy by intuition alone. In this respect, the healthcare facility located in the Ḥeb-Sed Court may well have been like a modern-day teaching hospital where healer-priests learned the medical arts. The Entrance Hall would have been an excellent teaching aid for this purpose, a rather impressive and imposing one at that even if not readily apparent at first.

Here at last is the definitive proof that Hakim was right all along!

Clearly, the *always-open* stone doors in the *Sacrum Room* Entrance Vestibule and the *L5 Columns* located just inside the South Entrance Gate offer mute testimony that the Step Pyramid Enclosure was a medical center in addition to being a mortuary temple. Every hospital in the world never closes its doors, because hospitals are a 24 hours a day, 7 days a week operation that offer emergency and inpatient care, and need to remain open all the time. Perhaps the tradition of hospitals never shutting their doors began here in ancient Egypt.

Continuing along to the end of the Entrance Hall and arriving at the twenty-fourth space (which is the first cervical vertebra (**C1**, or *atlas*), we come upon a small enclosure containing four transverse double columns (*Fig. 3-19*). Despite it sometimes being referred to as the *transverse vestibule*, J.-P. Lauer called this room the Exit Vestibule as it leads out to the Great South Court. [24]

Fig. 3-19 – The Exit Vestibule at the end of the South Entrance Hall and Vertebrae C1 of the Spine and Skull

As there are no more vertebrae after the atlas (**C1**), then, logically, the walls of the Exit Vestibule represent the skull as it sits atop the spinal column. The four double columns within this small enclosure may well symbolize the four lobes of the human brain (frontal, parietal, occipital and temporal lobes) divided into its two cerebral hemispheres on either side of the central longitudinal fissure (i.e., the split between the two hemispheres of the brain, marked as '**I**' and '**J**' in *Fig. 3-19*).

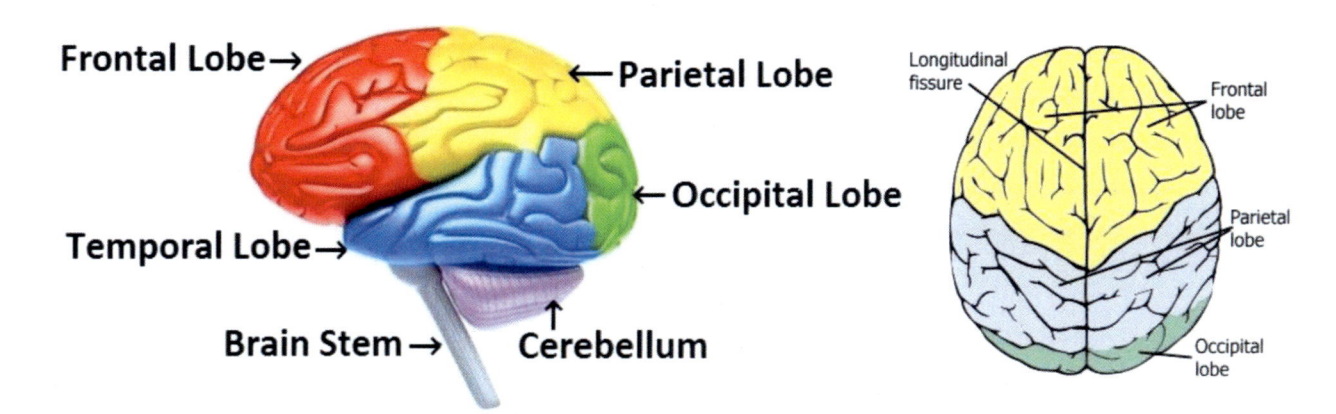

Fig. 3-20 – The Brain and Its Major Constituent Parts

Using the formula, *space-equals-bone* once again, we can see that Imhotep has accounted for the nine major bones of the human skull in the design of the Exit Vestibule as well (*Figs. 3-21* and *3-22*).

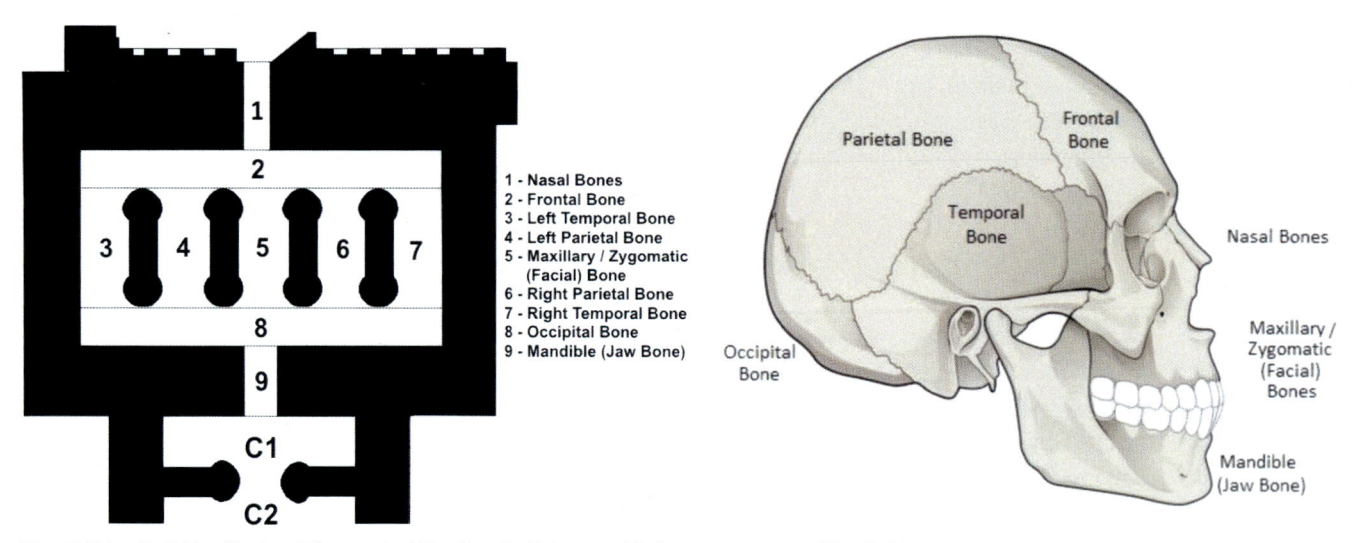

1 - Nasal Bones
2 - Frontal Bone
3 - Left Temporal Bone
4 - Left Parietal Bone
5 - Maxillary / Zygomatic (Facial) Bone
6 - Right Parietal Bone
7 - Right Temporal Bone
8 - Occipital Bone
9 - Mandible (Jaw Bone)

Fig. 3-21 – Exit Vestibule at the end of the South Entrance Hall

Fig. 3-22 – The Skull and its Major Bones

It is a peculiarity of ancient Egyptian architectural drawings that, instead of creating a three view plan (top view plus two or more elevation views) as we do today, Egyptian architects showed all three dimensions in a single two-dimensional plane. Rather than being a frontal view as was used for depicting the spine, the Exit Vestibule is a flattened bottom view of the skull with the nasal bones at the top and the mandible (jaw) bones at the bottom. It is also the frontal view of a person who has raised their head to the heavens in a manner of prayer or supplication to the gods.

Imhotep seems to have had a fondness for hiding parts of the human anatomy *in plain sight* within the design of Djoser's funerary temple. To that end, the *always-open* door (*Fig. 3-23*) of the Exit Vestibule (marked by the letter '**S**' in *Fig. 3-24*) leading out to the Great South Court resembles the nasal bones when viewed in profile. Since the passageway marked with the letter '**S**' represents the nasal bones, this adds further proof that Imhotep disguised the human spine and skull in the Entrance Hall and Exit Vestibule design.

Fig. 3-23 – The Exit Vestibule and the 'Always-Open' Stone Door

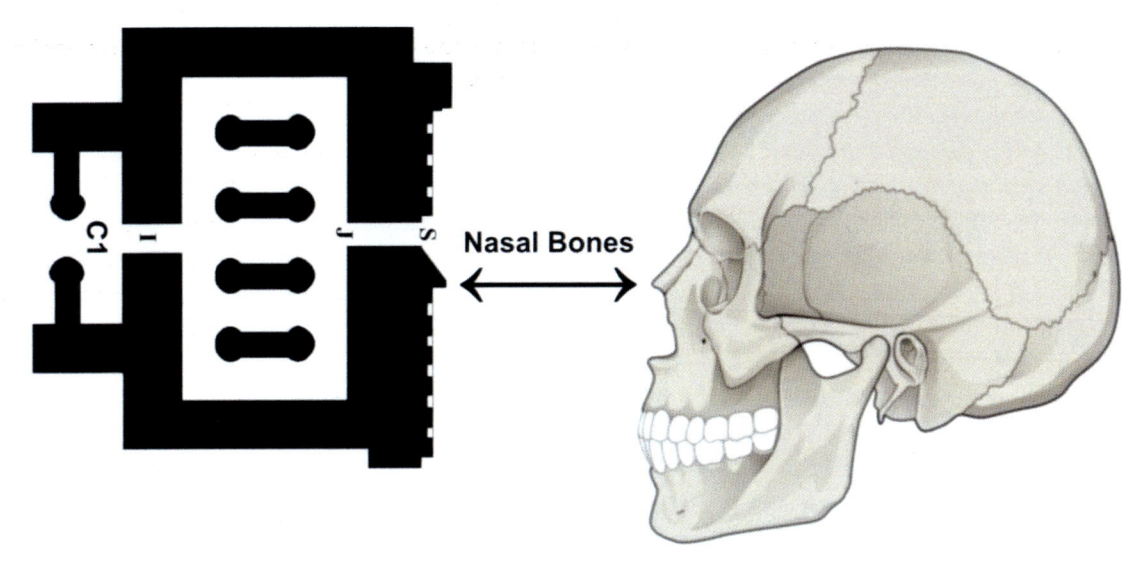

Fig. 3-24 – Additional proof of hidden knowledge in the design of the Step Pyramid Enclosure

In the description of the five major architectural elements discussed above, four groups of internal body organs are associated with spaces between the sixth and eleventh columns of the Entrance Hall's south side. The organs and the vertebrae they align with are the stomach (**T6**), lungs (**T7**), and liver (**T8/T9**). The large and small intestines span many vertebra, but generally, they stretch between **T10** and **L4**. These internal organs are the same ones the ancient Egyptians preserved in separate canopic jars for inclusion with the other burial goods (*Fig. 3-25*). The special treatment these organs received is reflected in the unique fluted stonework decorating the five walls between the sixth and eleventh columns (*Fig. 3-6*), and line up with the South Tomb. There is some mystery as to what the South Tomb may have been used for and what its symbolic meaning may have been, but some Egyptologists have speculated that this tomb may have been the repository for the four canopic jars containing Djoser's internal organs, and maybe even his placenta (though this idea has never gained much traction).

Fig. 3-25 – Canopic jars with stopper lids representing the heads of the Four Sons of Horus (left to right)

Qebehsenuef, the falcon-headed god, guarded the intestines.
Hapy, the baboon-headed god, guarded the lungs.
Duamutef, the jackal-headed god, guarded the stomach.
Imsety, the human-headed god, guarded the liver.

The fifth element, the **T4** *heart chamber*, was given special placement on the north side of the Entrance Hall, distinctly separate from the rooms or chambers associated with the four other major internal organs located on the Entrance Hall's south side. This affirms the special nature of the heart in ancient Egyptian culture and religion by separately embalming and placing the heart back into the abdominal cavity of the mummy, treating it with great reverence.

We should not be too surprised that Imhotep would have also included representations of these organs within the design of this funerary temple/medical center. If the priests and priestesses serving in this temple knew of the hidden meanings behind the various architectural elements of Djoser's temple, it is unlikely the average ancient Egyptian was aware of them. Whatever esoteric and exoteric wisdom these architectural features may have represented, they certainly do not seem random in their choice of position along the Entrance Hall.

Obviously, the representation of the human spine isn't rendered to scale. It wasn't meant to be. The human spine was only one of many hidden secrets designed into the Entrance Hall. If Imhotep intended the plan of the Entrance Hall to have the same proportions as the human spine, it would have been too obvious, not to mention structurally unsound with inherent design flaws causing many engineering problems.

As we investigate the Step Pyramid Enclosure further, it will become apparent that Imhotep's design for the Entrance Hall exists on many levels. The prevailing theory is that Imhotep did not use freestanding columns in the Entrance Hall, and chose to attach them to the outer walls for the sake of engineering safety. Perhaps, he had some concerns about the structural loads on the columns since this was the first time anyone had attempted to use stone in such a grandiose and unique manner. This may be true, but a much bigger picture has emerged that questions this idea.

In essence, the columns of the Entrance Hall serve not only a structural purpose, but Imhotep also subtly imbued secret, esoteric wisdom within his design as well. As an architect, Imhotep was well aware of sound engineering principles even when using less permanent materials such as timber and reed bundles used in domestic and civil architecture to support roofs and interior structures. (Reed bundles are actually deceptively strong as the aggregate load spreads out over the sum total of the reeds contained in the column just as ropes made of individually fragile hemp fibers are extremely strong and durable.) It is plain to see that Imhotep was not afraid to design and build freestanding columns, or he would not have built the four transverse double columns in the Exit Vestibule in the manner he did.

If the Entrance Hall was a cleverly disguised model of the human spine, it is tempting to ask why the depiction of the spinal column was not in stone. To answer this, we must again view the structure of the Step Pyramid Enclosure, not from the physical world that we can readily see, but from a spiritual or non-physical dimension. From the perspective of physical reality, we are unable to perceive non-physical reality using the five physical senses because of their inherent limitations. It would be like trying to use a pair of binoculars to view the surface of Mars. Though this is highly speculative, the same might be true when one attempts to perceive the physical world from higher dimensions. Symbolically then, everything outside the Enclosure Wall relates to the physical world we live in. By *travelling west* through the South Entrance Gate, a person leaves the world of the flesh and enters the world of the spirit, and what lies within the walls of the Step Pyramid Enclosure is a metaphor for the Afterlife.

When viewed from the perspective of the spiritual realms, what is solid matter (i.e., the physical world including the human body) is now invisible, and what was once invisible to the physical world (i.e., the higher-dimensional space that permeates and surrounds all matter) now becomes visible. In this same way, the symbolic representation of the spine in the space between the columns and walls of the Entrance Hall mirrors this reversal of perspective. As the ancient Egyptians believed the totality of a human being comprised a physical body and up to eight other distinctly separate quasi-physical and non-physical *bodies* or aspects, it is no wonder that Imhotep incorporated these same notions of a physical/non-physical reality in his creation of the Step Pyramid and its environs.

This explanation may seem more of a modern interpretation of Imhotep's design of the Step Pyramid Enclosure than what his original intentions would indicate. The notion of creating something more transcendent and intangible in the way of *experiencing* a building that is dedicated to expressing spiritual ideals has always been a part of religious architecture from even before Imhotep's time. It was, and still is, a primary focus of later architects, such as the men who built the great cathedrals of Europe.

Architects do not *design buildings*, as such; they *define interior spaces* by using architectural elements, such as walls, pillars, windows, doors, and so on. Every architect working today must concern themselves, not only with what materials to use and how to use those materials to best the effect a good design, but also with the space that will be defined by the walls, floors and ceilings of the final plan. In essence, the space inside the building is equally important as the materials used to create it.

To architects and engineers, *form must follow function*. The design of every building must adequately provide for the needs of the people using that building in order to embody its stated purpose. An architect should not indulge in whimsy or *artsy-ness*, unless the building will be a temporary one, or will deliberately manifest the extremes of popular taste necessitating the inclusion of elements of garishness or *kitsch*, as in an amusement park, or the speculative designs for a *city of the future*. If they deviate too much from their client's wishes, they run the risk of not adhering to any sort of guiding principles that were part of the original design criteria for the building and will ultimately fail to provide for the needs of the client.

Granted, there are examples of architects pushing the boundaries of design and form to create a new architectural *language* which then becomes the new standard by which all other new buildings are judged. Such architects as Frank Lloyd Wright, Ludwig Mies van der Rohe, Walter Gropius, Le Corbusier and Philip Johnson have created milestones of architectural design which were highly controversial and almost reviled when they were first revealed, but as time has gone by, their designs have become more readily accepted and commonplace, and their architectural language has become the norm.

The best way of looking at any building is to recognize its impact is due, not from the materials that make up its structure, but rather how those walls, windows, doors, ceilings, and so on, define the interior space. Architects working today concern themselves a great deal with how all the various architectural elements work together to make a specific impression on a person as they first enter into the architect's creation. This speaks to how a rather mundane experience of just walking into, say an office building or a shopping mall, can be transformed into an *event*, or be made something very special, not unlike the feelings of awe one experiences when entering a Gothic cathedral. It is all a calculated effect. Frank Lloyd Wright, the most famous American architect of the 20th century, was fond of saying that "Architecture is nothing more than music cast in stone". Great architecture transcends the materials that makes up its constituent parts, and goes beyond just providing shelter. As great music will inspire and uplift the hearer, so too does great architecture move the soul and kindle a greater expansion of the self when encountering such monumental buildings.

The defining of the interior space is as much a part of any building design as are the bricks and mortar of its walls and the openings for doors and windows that are part of its structure. This explains why the spinal column and skull is implied by the space between the stonework of the Entrance Hall. Imhotep went beyond creating just an impressive and inspiring work of architecture with its unique use of stone when he designed the spaces between the columns to represent the human spine.

Additionally, the Entrance Hall as a symbolic representation of the spinal column raises the possibility that ancient Egyptian priests and priestesses were aware of a fire-like energy associated with the divine feminine known as *kundalini*. This bioelectrical energy ascends the spinal column from the base of the spine to the top of the skull resulting from the practice of intense spiritual disciplines. When the *kundalini* energy surges up the spinal column, episodes of extremely lucid spiritual states can occur. A person walking through the South Entrance Hall out of the Exit Vestibule to the interior of the Enclosure not only becomes a proxy for the soul leaving the body at the point of death, but can also represent the *kundalini* energy as it ascends the spinal column. Both events are similar in that when a person experiences either one, an increased awareness of higher, non-physical dimensions is possible. Imhotep's design of the Entrance Hall, with its emphasis on the human spine and the implied association with becoming aware of greater states of reality, may have had a profound influence on subsequent generations of Egyptian priests and priestesses that worked at the Step Pyramid Enclosure.

The spine as a spiritual metaphor had its genesis in the Memphis/Sakkara area with the Cult of Ptah (*Fig. 3-26*). In the ancient Egyptian pantheon, Ptah was venerated as the Architect/Creator of the Universe. One of the many symbols associated with him is the *djed* pillar. The *djed* pillar has four rings and two plumes, and can represent either the number 42 or the number 24. It is a stylized rendering of Ptah's spinal column, and represents the great stabilizing force that kept the Universe in Divine Order, or *maat* (*Fig. 3-27*). In the same way, the spine is the single-most stabilizing element in the human body just as a column or pillar is the most important structural element in a building.

Fig. 3-26 – The god Ptah   *Fig. 3-27 – Pharaoh Seti I raising and venerating the Djed Pillar – Temple of Abydos*

The number 42 had a great cultural and religious significance in ancient Egypt. It was highly integrated into their society on both the sacred and profane levels, and was primarily associated with esoteric spiritual beliefs, but not exclusively. The human spine has 24 major bones. This led me to an amazing realization: **The (profane) number 24 is the *mirror image* of the (sacred, divine) number 42. Metaphorically then, it can be said that human beings, who have 24 major vertebrae in their spine, are the mirror image of their Creator as symbolized by the number 42 (the djed pillar, or spine of Ptah). Therefore, it is no coincidence the South Entrance Hall contains both the Sacred Number 42 (the total number of columns), and the profane number 24 (the spaces between the columns).** In a book of ancient spiritual wisdom, it states, "God created man in his own image". Perhaps another *book* made of stone that echoes this truth already existed in the form of the South Entrance Hall of the Step Pyramid Enclosure long before the writing of that other book.

This shows that Imhotep's knowledge of sacred wisdom was quite profound in that the ancient Hermetic maxim of *as above, so below* was not just an intellectual exercise known only to a few select priests. It was put into a grand architectural form for all to behold, provided they had *eyes to see* beyond the visage of amazingly beautiful precision stonework. If Djoser's Funerary Enclosure was also a working hospital, then there would be no better inspiration for its design than the human body. Knowing all this, it does not take too long to see that ancient Egyptians incorporated anatomical symbolism into everyday objects and images as well as their spiritual lives.

Two universally recognizable icons from ancient Egypt are the Red and White Crowns of Egypt's kings and the unified version of both crowns symbolizing a unified Egypt (*Fig. 3-28*). The Red and White Crowns were also symbolic representations of certain body parts.

White Crown of Upper Egypt

"Hedjet"

Red Crown of Lower Egypt

"Deshret"

Double Crown of the Unified Egypt

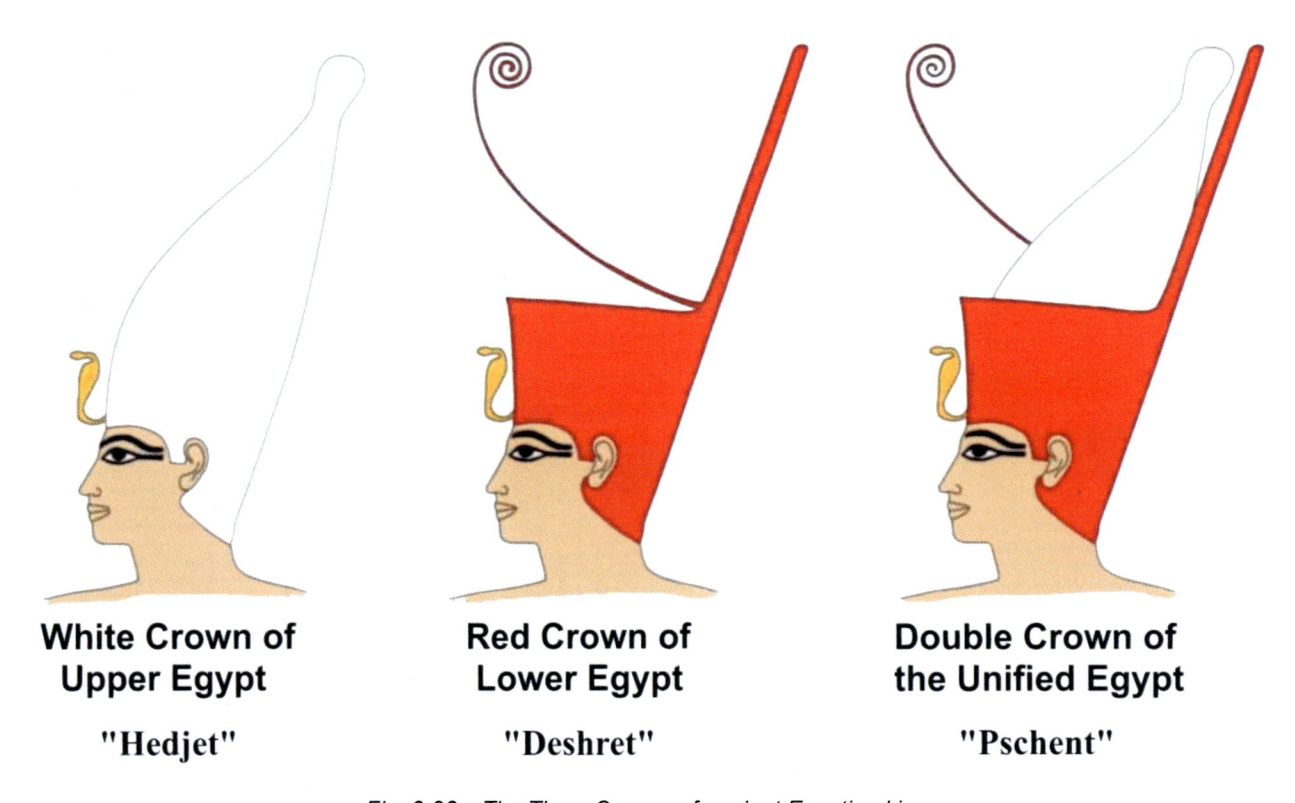

"Pschent"

Fig. 3-28 – The Three Crowns of ancient Egyptian kings

The White Crown of Upper Egypt resembles the shape of the pericardium [25] (and has *nothing* to do with bigheaded extraterrestrials!). The pericardial sac surrounds and protects the heart. To ancient Egyptians, the heart was the most important organ in the body because they believed it to be the seat of wisdom and the place where the soul resided. Physically, the heart is inherently vulnerable, but the pericardium surrounds it and is its second line of defense after the rib cage. Metaphorically, the pericardium is the angel with sword in hand standing guard at the gates to the heart. The little bulb at the top of the White Crown represents the pulmonary trunk that contains a major vessel of the human heart originating from the right ventricle (*Fig. 3-29*). It branches into the right and left pulmonary arteries, leading to their respective lungs, from which comes the *breath of life* (*prana*).

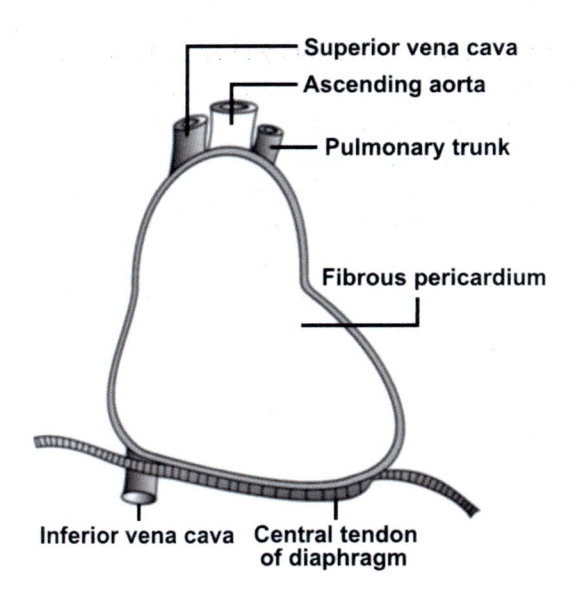

Fig. 3-29 – Pericardium and Pulmonary Trunk

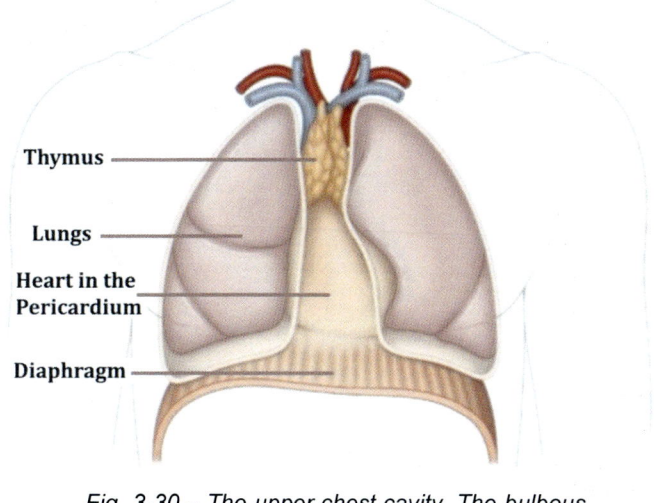

Fig. 3-30 – The upper chest cavity. The bulbous top of the pericardium is behind the thymus gland

A variation of the White Crown is the *Atef* crown worn by Osiris (*Fig. 3-31*), the God of the Underworld or Afterlife. The *Atef* crown is a White Crown with two ostrich feathers on either side of it. These feathers represent the two lobes of the thymus gland, which sit atop the pericardium behind the sternum (*Fig. 3-30*). The thymus gland is the primary manager of the body's immune system – the chief of defense. It produces T–cells that play a critical role in the immune system response and protects the body from foreign invaders, not unlike the duty of a pharaoh to protect his people from the *Nine Bows*, the traditional hostile enemies of Egypt.

Fig. 3-31 – Osiris wearing the Atef crown

The Red Crown represents the rib cage that surrounds and protects the pericardium and the heart. The raised part at the back of the Red Crown is the cervical section in the upper spinal column that sits between the rib cage and the skull. As noted above, the spinal column is associated with the djed pillar of Ptah that symbolizes the singular unifying and stabilizing force of the Universe, and with it, the implication of the necessity for pharaoh to maintain stability and avoiding chaos when ruling the country. (Hakim thought the Red Crown may have represented the female uterus and womb, but this may not be correct in this context.)

The spiral part attached to the Red Crown may symbolize several different things. The easiest explanation is that it mimics the curly streak beneath the eye of Horus, the falcon god, who was always associated with the divine nature of the pharaoh.

Gardiner Sign List No. – D10   'w3ḏt', "wedjat eye"

It may even represent the hieroglyph for the number 100, perhaps expressing the desire that the pharaoh should live a hundred years.

Gardiner Sign List No. – V1   'št, nwh', "hundred"

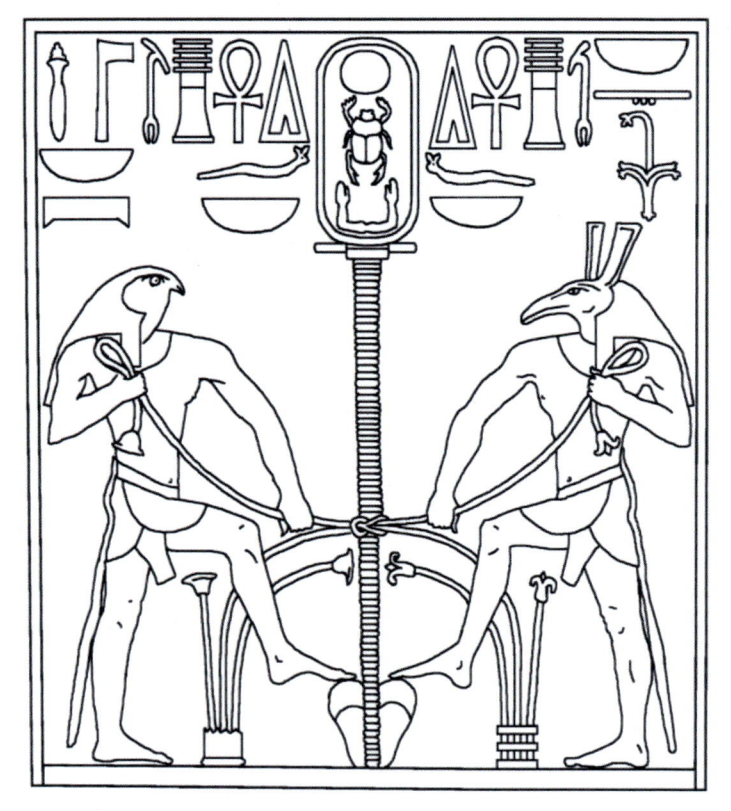

Fig. 3-32 – Horus and Seth binding the Two Lands

Additionally, the *rope* translation symbolizes the unification of Egypt as exemplified in depictions of the gods Horus and Seth binding the Two Lands together using ropes made from lotus and the papyrus plants, the symbols for Upper and Lower Egypt (*Fig. 3-32*). The *sema* hieroglyph is the symbol for the Two Lands.

Gardiner Sign List No. – F36 'sm3', "unite" and "lung"

Inherent in the meaning of *to unite* is the source of pharaoh's right to rule a united Egypt, but it also represents his responsibility to maintain *maat* and keep Egypt's political structure stable. As the *sema* hieroglyph also symbolizes the lungs and the trachea, this shows another use of body parts to illustrate esoteric concepts. It is also significant that the name of pharaoh (i.e., *he who unifies the Two Lands*) is encircled by a rope – the *cartouche* (see text at *Fig. 6-3*).

Physical matter in the Universe frequently organizes into the shape of spirals on the macro and micro levels, which are common patterns observable in nature (*fig. 3-33*). The spiral attached to the Red Crown may well be a reflection of what ancient Egyptians observed in the natural world around them.

Fig. 3-33 – Spirals found in nature

The design and shape of crowns from any age or civilization have always had underlying symbolic meanings of some kind. In the case of ancient Egyptian crowns, the symbology of the Red and White Crowns may also have had multiple layers of meanings. Just like the spiral shape shown above, other shapes tend to repeat in nature, even in widely different forms. Besides being a representation of the pericardium found in the human body, the White Crown may have embodied some other element found in nature.

In a book by Jonathan Meader and Barbara Demeter,[26] the authors speculate the White Crown of Upper Egypt was a representation of the white water lily bud in its closed up pre-dawn appearance before the rising sun causes it to open its blossoms (*Fig. 3-34*). The bulb at the top of the White Crown symbolizes the sun.

Fig. 3-34 – The White Crown of Upper Egypt as inspired by the White Waterlily

The white water lily, or lotus, is itself a symbol of Upper Egypt, just as the papyrus was the symbol for Lower Egypt. This is consistent with the ancient Egyptians' incorporation of symbols derived from nature into their esoteric philosophy as well as exoteric expression in the form of capitals used on columns in their temples (*Fig. 3-35*).

Fig. 3-35 – Lotus and Papyrus Column Capitals and their inspirations from nature

While the theory put forth by Mr. Meader and Ms. Demeter has a certain charm to it, we cannot discount the possibility the shape of the White Crown resembles that of the pericardium, either. Ancient Egypt's *heart-centered* spiritual philosophy and symbology can attest to that. Though it is a natural human inclination to believe only one of these two concepts must be the correct one, we should be open to the possibility that *both* are correct since multi-layered meanings for just about anything seem to have been the norm in ancient times.

Representations of other body parts also found their way into ordinary everyday objects. Every architect in ancient Egypt possessed one particular ubiquitous tool that was the standard unit of measure used during Egypt's long history: the cubit (*Fig. 3-36*). In theory, the length of these cubits was based on the measurement of the Pharaoh's arm from the elbow to the tip of the middle finger. It was then subdivided into seven palms with each palm further subdivided into four fingers. There were several different cubits in use during the long history of ancient Egypt, the most common one being the Royal Cubit (20.682 inches/52.50 centimeters long), and occasionally the Sacred Cubit (25.025 inches/63.520 centimeters long).

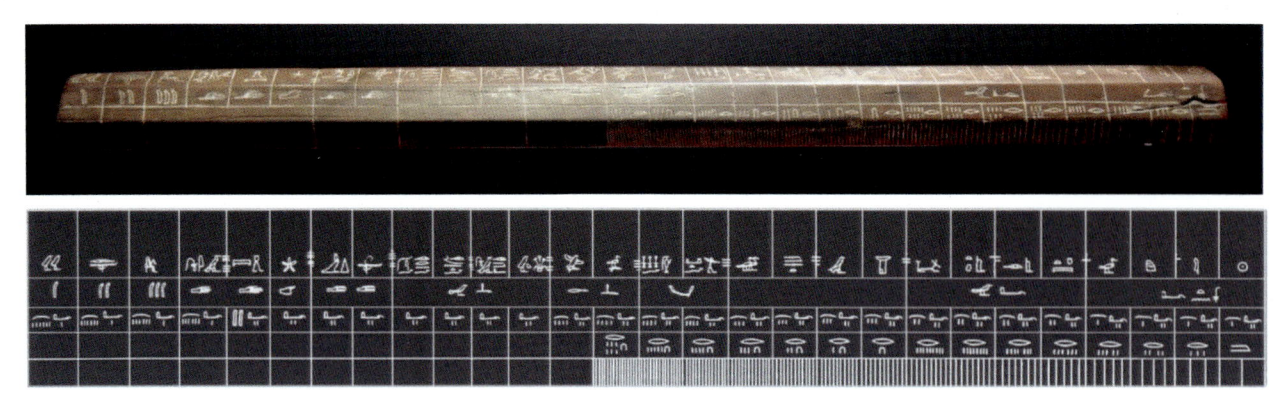

Fig. 3-36 – The Cubit Rod of Maya – Eighteenth Dynasty

Additionally, over 60 hieroglyphs in the Egyptian lexicon depict various parts of the human body. From the design of their temples, to the crowns of their kings and even in mundane, everyday things like hieroglyphs, it should not surprise us that ancient Egyptians could have easily used the human body as a template to express their deeply esoteric spiritual concepts.

However, one important question remains: Why was the human body incorporated into so many facets of ancient Egyptian culture, sometimes in a symbolic, hidden manner?

The answer is very significant if not readily apparent: **Because everybody has one**.

At the risk of being too obvious (and possibly a little flippant), it is the single-most common point of reference we all share in the course of our human experience. It is the one thing we can all relate to when it comes to our lives both physical and spiritual. In essence, the physical body is a metaphysical metaphor of every one of the nine levels of existence in which the ancient Egyptians believed a human simultaneously lives. The human body, with all its limitations, is the temporary habitation of the soul, and is also a creation of Divine Energy (Ra-Atum) as is everything in the Universe. It is little wonder the ancient Egyptians were, perhaps, the first people to embrace the notion that our bodies are a holy temple, and should be revered as such, but also that every temple was (a representation of) a body, and should be viewed in that context.

The ancient Egyptians believed it was an absolute necessity to preserve the physical body as much as possible through mummification to ensure their survival in the Afterlife. The physical body (the **khat**) was a type of anchor that enabled the spirit, or **ka**, to live in the *Field of Reeds*; also known as *Sekhet-Aaru*, the Egyptian heaven. As has been shown before, a complete human being consisted of nine separate *bodies*. Mummification allowed the whole human being, including the former residence of soul (the physical body) to live in the Afterlife for eternity.

In ancient Egypt, life and death were considered to be but two different stages of the spirit's cosmic journey. In our modern vernacular, we would say they are *two sides of the same coin*. Their Afterlife resembled their life on Earth to the point that they saw no difference between the two. Their focus on everyday concerns of life in this world did not cause them to ignore their spiritual lives, which is often a misinterpretation as ancient Egyptians being preoccupied with death. In essence, they did not consider themselves as human beings who had spiritual experiences; they saw themselves as spiritual beings having a human experience. The only reason many are of the opinion that ancient Egyptians were *obsessed* with death is that virtually the only source of knowledge we have about them comes from their tombs and sacred religious texts like the *Book of the Dead*; a rather distorted view of the real human beings they truly were.

Regardless of whether or not we believe the ancient Egyptians thought the human body was important enough to symbolically represent and embody it (*pun intended*) in the design of their temples, they thought it was important, and imperative enough to do so. We should not be so cavalier as to readily dismiss this notion out of hand.

The Step Pyramid Enclosure was not unique in that various architectural elements incorporated the human body in its design. As detailed in his monumental book *The Temple of Man*, the Swiss-born Egyptologist, R. A. Schwaller de Lubicz spent more than fifteen years doing research at the Temple of Amun at Luxor. He concluded that the architects of the Luxor temple designed it to be a giant model of the human body, concealing it in a highly mystical, esoteric language within the temple structure itself (*Fig. 3-37*).

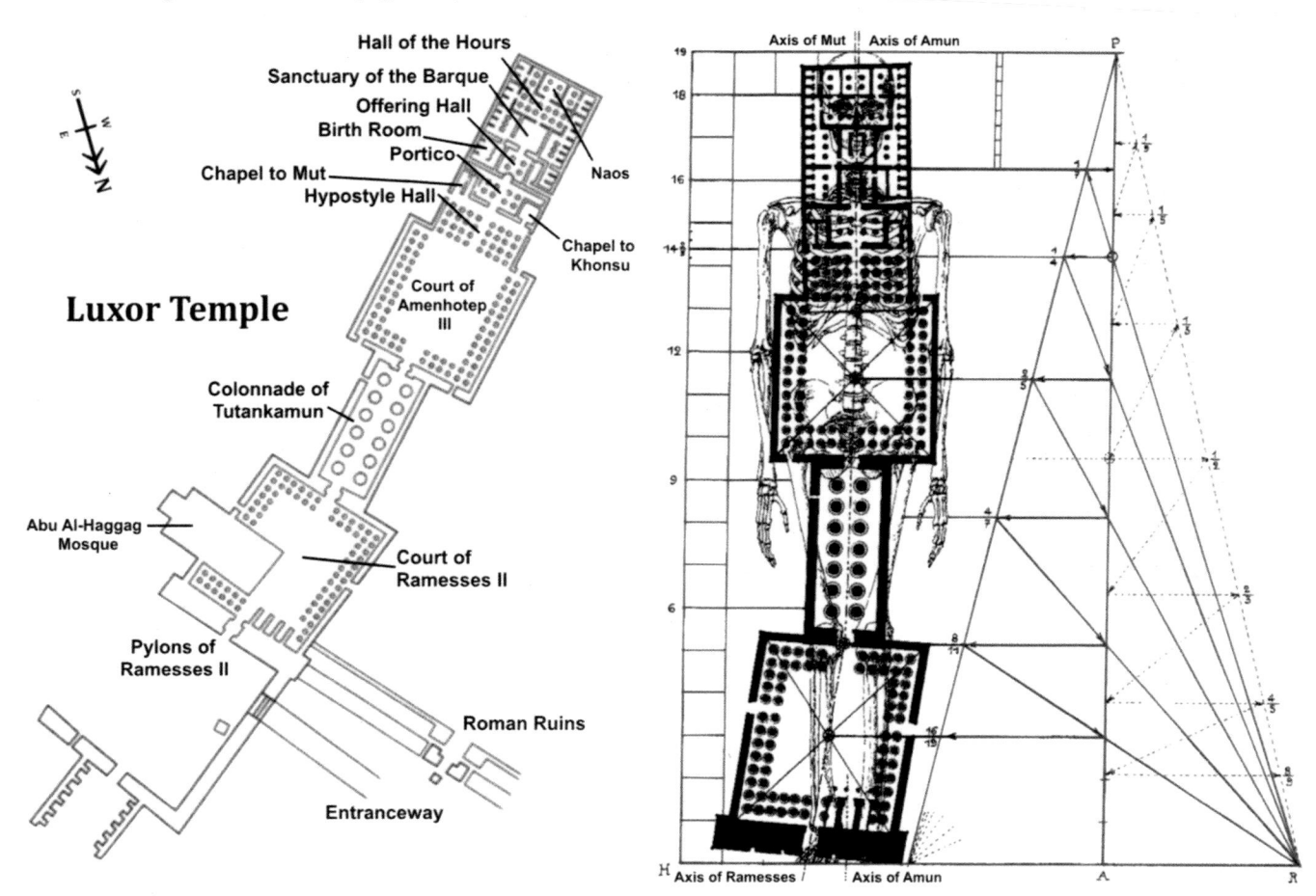

Fig. 3-37 – Luxor Temple and its relationship to the human body

The metaphor of the *body as a temple* was widely used in the ancient world, due in part to such temples at Sakkara and Luxor, which incorporated elements of the human anatomy in their designs. There are several references in the Bible (John 2:18-21 and I Corinthians 6:19), and quite possibly other ancient texts that used this same allegory. The ancient Greeks certainly equated the body with a temple. The original Olympic Games, for example, were part athletic contest and part religious festival celebrating the ideal of the human body at the Temple of Apollo in Olympia, Greece. If not actually having been responsible for inspiring the *body as temple* metaphor, then perhaps the ancient Egyptians created these *temples as bodies* to be visible representations of that principle.

The temples scattered throughout Egypt served many functions besides the deification of the god or pharaoh honored by its construction. Our modern notion of a somber, cloistered atmosphere pervading temple environs was not always the case in ancient Egypt. Certainly, there was a formal and reverential mood in the inner most sanctums of the temple, but temples were also the social centers of the communities, not unlike the local town square of our own modern era. Rather than the forced solemnity of a modern church or cathedral, ancient Egyptian temples were, in many instances, the scene of gaiety and revelry because of the many religious and secular festivals celebrated throughout the year. Many tomb paintings plainly show that ancient Egyptians loved to have a good time. (After all, they invented beer!) They were definitely not obsessed with death, as is commonly believed. Rather, the opposite was true: they enjoyed life to the fullest! These festivities and moments of merriment were also a part of temple life.

The South Entrance Hall and the Human Genome

Having discovered that Imhotep embedded the anatomy of the human spine into the design of the South Entrance Hall, I looked for additional symbolic expressions of human anatomy secretly hidden in stone. At the same time, I hesitate to reveal more of what I have discovered regarding additional elements of the human anatomy implied in the design of the South Entrance Hall. The reason is that it is so fantastic that it stretches the boundaries of credulity, and yet, it cannot be readily ignored!

Knowing there are 40 semi-round and 4 square columns (the **L5** and **T3** pairs of columns, *Figs. 3-9* and *3-16*), I looked for any anatomical features with the number 44 as part of their makeup. As I was perusing an anatomy textbook, I vaguely remembered the number 44 had something to do with chromosomes. I wondered: Was Imhotep clever enough to include the structure of human DNA in his design? I felt incredulous at first, but then I decided to do some further research.

Apparently, my memory hadn't failed me: Human cells contain 23 pairs of chromosomes, for a total of 46 chromosomes. Twenty-two of these pairs, called autosomes, are identical in both males and females, so there was only a need to construct one set of 22 pairs of columns. The 23rd pair, the sex chromosomes, differs between males and females: two Y-chromosomes for the female gender, and one X- and one Y-chromosome for the male (*Fig. 3-38*).

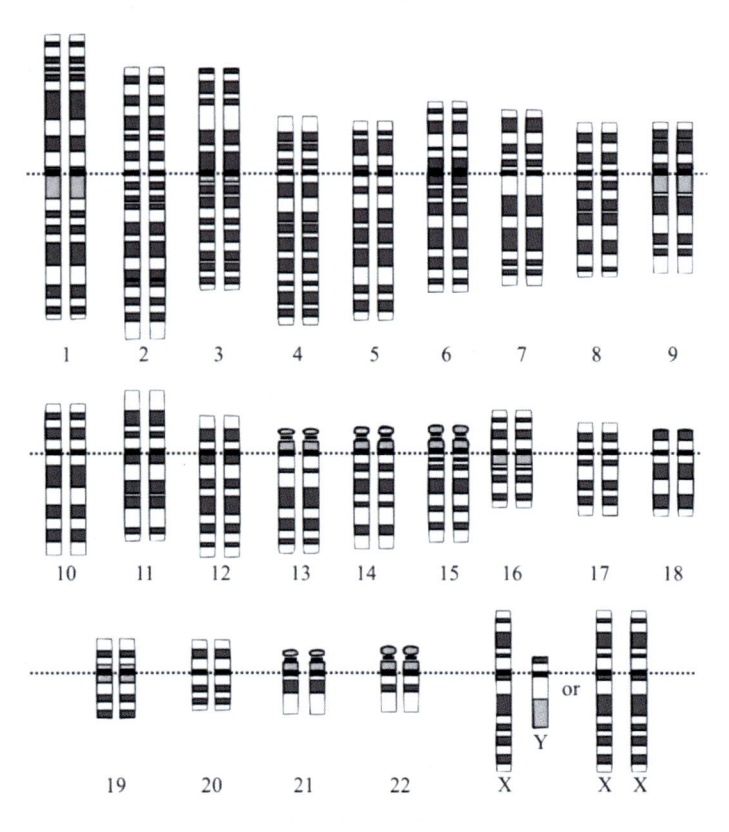

Fig. 3-38 – Graphical representation of pairs of chromosomes (diploid karyotypes), showing the organization of the human genome. This shows both the male (XY) and female (XX) versions of the 23rd chromosome pair (lower right). Chromosomes are shown aligned at their centromeres.

However, something did not add up. Certainly, the 20 pairs of semi-round columns plus the 2 pairs of square columns could be related to the 22 base pairs of chromosomes, but there did not seem to be a single pair of columns representing the twenty-third and last pair of sex chromosomes. While it is true that at the end of the Entrance Hall there are two square features that resemble the square **T3** columns, these structures that lead into the small Exit Vestibule containing the 4 semi-round double columns weren't columns as such. Instead, they were part of the wall structure of the Exit Vestibule and not freestanding columns. I looked at the South Entrance Hall repeatedly, and I began to think this idea was nothing more than a flight of fantasy with no hope of a resolution in sight. Try as I might, I could not find a link between the architectural elements of the Entrance Hall and the basic structure of human DNA.

Then, as I continued exploring, another thought came to me: Was Imhotep *hiding something in plain sight* once again? As I was about to give up, I remembered: The last pair of sex chromosomes was so different that Imhotep *broke the rules* again to show their inherent differences! It was now all so very clear: The 4 columns in the Exit Vestibule at the end of the Entrance Hall reproduced in stone the 4 differentiated chromosomes for each of the male and female genders' 23rd sex chromosome!

This intuitive insight led to an even bigger question: How could the ancient Egyptians have known about the existence of human DNA millennia before its discovery (or re-discovery) in the late 19th and early 20st centuries? Ancient Egypt was not a technologically advanced civilization like ours, so they obviously could not have known – *or could they*?

Moreover, if they did not have any way of discovering or understanding the basic principles of human genetic structure and development, how did the ancient Egyptians, and specifically, Imhotep, gain this knowledge? Where did it come from if not Egypt? This was definitely *going down a (different) rabbit hole* than I expected.

Implicit in these questions and observations is the possibility that the human genome was known by a hitherto undocumented and unidentified culture; a much earlier civilization that passed this knowledge down to later generations including the Egyptian priesthood that would have wanted to keep it secret. In order to do this, they would have altered its *appearance*, so to speak, to hide its inherent importance. As Imhotep was Chief Priest at the Temple of Ra at Heliopolis, it is almost certain he would have had access to such deeply esoteric and secret teachings if they existed at all.

If the existence of human DNA was known, and passed down to successive generations of Egyptian priests, it is entirely likely they did not realize its true import. Rendering such profound knowledge about the genetic structure of humans into a more symbolic, quasi-mythological framework would be necessary to disguise its importance to the human anatomy. The average priest would not have understood the *treasure* in their possession, and after a time, the wisdom contained in this knowledge would have become less and less evident, until a time came when such information was lost altogether due to political or social upheaval (*Fig. 3-39*).

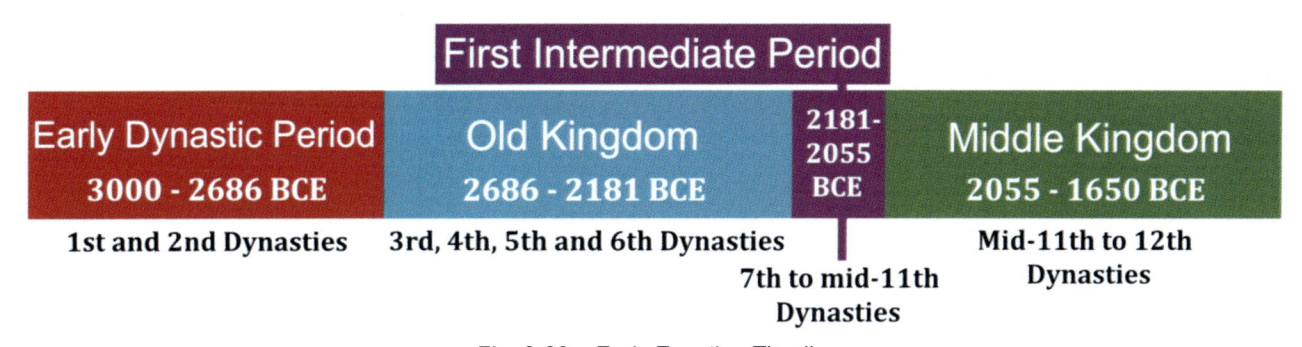

Fig. 3-39 – Early Egyptian Timeline

A logical candidate for such a dark, chaotic period would come at the end of the Old Kingdom during the First Intermediate Period, which comprised most of the Seventh Dynasty through the early part of the Eleventh Dynasty. During this period, political factions of the north (centered at Hierakonpolis), and the south (located at Thebes) were in a nearly constant state of war.

> **The temples were not merely pillaged and violated, but their finest works of art were subjected to systematic and determined vandalism, which shattered the splendid granite and diorite statues of kings into bits, or hurled them into the well in the monumental gate of the pyramid-causeway. Thus, the foes of the old regime wreaked vengeance upon those who represented and upheld it. The nation was totally disorganized.** [27]

If this were the case, then much in the way of sacred knowledge and wisdom, secret or otherwise, could have been lost, never to be preserved by later generations of priests after the internal conflicts of the First Intermediate Period had ended.

Though some might feel that ancient Egypt was technologically inferior as compared to our modern society, I long abandoned any feelings of technological superiority when standing before such wonders as the Great Pyramid and the Step Pyramid. To design, engineer and organize the construction of such awe-inspiring monuments speaks of a people graced with tremendous insight, foresight and tenacity. To belittle or underestimate their technological achievements is to do our own selves a great disservice as it prevents us from seeing the magic of larger possibilities than what we can readily perceive.

The ancient Egyptians were a highly advanced civilization possessing a technology we have yet to duplicate let alone understand. When we say *technology*, the first thing that comes to most people's minds is a piece of machinery with lots of moving parts. Egyptian technology, such as it was, may not have had any moving parts, yet the Egyptians could move mountains of stone to create monuments that have stood the test of time. The possession of a high degree of technical sophistication extends to ancient Egyptian medical knowledge as well.

In that light, I need to mention one more curious thing about the South Entrance Hall. The top view of the 4 semi-round double columns in the Exit Vestibule (*Fig. 3-40*) resemble the telophase part of mitosis, which is the process of a single cell subdividing into two cells (*Fig. 3-41*). Telophase occurs just before the two parts of the single cell become two separate cells.

Fig. 3-40 – The Four Double Columns of the Exit Vestibule at the end of the South Entrance Hall

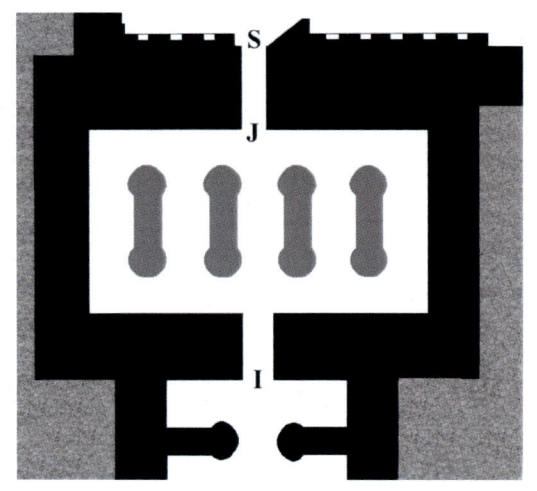

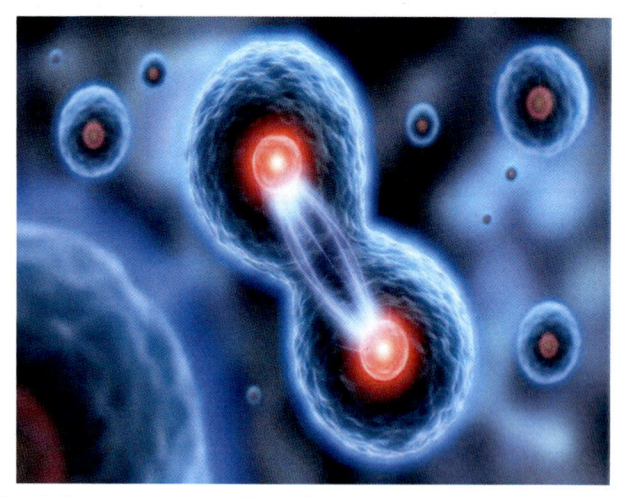

Fig. 3-41 – Telophase of the mitosis process (i.e., cell division)

If the ancient Egyptians were aware of the structure of DNA, the mechanics of cell biology would not have been beyond their reach. It is only speculation that at that time they may have possessed some knowledge of the complexities of human anatomy down to the cellular level. If this knowledge came from an earlier, technologically advanced civilization, they may not have even known or understood what was contained in the sacred scrolls that were passed down to them. Any attempts to gain a deeper understanding of this knowledge, and to use it in their medical practice would become mere mimicry without knowing what they had inherited from the remote past.

There is some scant knowledge of just such a civilization that may have existed tens of thousands of years before the earliest dynasties of Egypt. References to a very ancient civilization existing before pre-dynastic Egypt come from a stele known as the Palermo Stone, the Royal Canon of Turin Papyrus and several other ancient sources. The Palermo Stone (*Fig. 3-42*) is one of seven fragments known as the Royal Annals of the Old Kingdom (ca. 3150–2283 BCE) which records the kings of the First Dynasty to the early part of the Fifth Dynasty. The Royal Canon of Turin dates from the reign of Ramesses II (1279–1213 BCE), and details previous monarchs of ancient Egypt. Though information is scarce, a civilization called the *Shemsu-Hor* (or *Shesu-Hor*) apparently predated the first king of Egypt, Menes, by several thousands of years.

Fig. 3-42 – The Palermo Stone

R. A. Schwaller de Lubicz translated the name of these people as *Followers of Horus*. The British Egyptologist, E. A. E. Reymond, believes the translation of *Shesu-Hor* should be the *People of Horus*. However, the late Egyptian *wisdom keeper*, Hakim, who kept alive the indigenous oral traditions of his people, believed a more accurate translation should be *People of the Realized Man*. According to some oral traditions as retold by Hakim and others,[28] the term, or title of *Hor* (or *Horus*) in pre-dynastic times meant *realized man*, meaning a person who had become "enlightened" after successfully integrating the heart and the mind into a unified whole expressed as having an *intuitive intellect*.

The pharaoh is the symbolic representation of just such a *self-realized* person when he wears the Double Crown (symbolizing the heart, or center of higher intuitive function) on his head (symbolizing the mind and intellect, or the center of logic and reason). In essence, a *self-realized person* raises their consciousness when the intuitive self (the heart) unites with the intellectual self (the brain), and achieves the balanced state of *maat*, or *Living-in-Truth*, thus emulating or becoming one with the gods. It was only in later dynastic times when the term *Horus* became associated with a hawk-headed divine personage, and later, with royalty.

Oddly enough, the heart-brain connection has only recently been (re-)discovered. Research conducted by Dr. Paul Pearsall, Dr. Gary Schwartz of the University of Arizona and Dr. John Andrew Armour from the University of Montreal, Canada and the HeartMath Institute on the effects experienced by heart transplant recipients has begun to question whether thinking – and especially memory – exists solely in the brain. From this and other research, the discovery that the heart is not just a perpetually beating muscle is being reported. The heart has over 40,000 brain-like neurons that are in constant communication with the brain, and is the largest generator of electromagnetic signals in the body. In a sense, the heart *thinks*. Its magnetic energy is 5000 times more powerful than the brain, and detectable up to 6 feet away from the body. Even more fantastic, the EKG (electrocardiogram) is 10 to 100 times larger than an EEG (electroencephalogram) of the brain. As Dr. Pearsall once said,

The heart is a connective organ; a gentle organ. It's a different type of intelligence. Until the recent past, science has glorified the brain. The questions we need to ask as scientists is "Is that the only place these things happen? Is there another source of intelligence?' The heart may be, based on current science, a sentient, thinking, feeling, remembering organ. And if we just glorify the brain, we'll never be open to the possibility that another organ 'thinks'.[29]

Did Imhotep – and ancient Egyptians in general – *know* there was *some sort* of undefined, yet tangible connection between the heart and the brain? If they *intuitively sensed* this connection by way of the *intelligence of the heart*, did they retrieve this knowledge from records left by a vaguely remembered, historically distant civilization? Is there a source for this knowledge that has yet to be discovered? Answers to these questions will be revealed as we continue our search for hidden codes and secrets.

If anything, Old Kingdom *wisdom keepers* would have possessed more knowledge about the *Shemsu-Hor* than later generations after the turmoil of the First Intermediate Period. If the Royal Canon of Turin and the Palermo Stone are historically accurate, and the *Shemsu-Hor* existed upwards of 30,000 years before the first dynasties of Egypt, then it could be they were a very highly developed civilization. They may well have passed down its knowledge of medical science and the human genome, as well as the connection between the brain and the heart to later generations of Egyptians. Even so, any documents from this technologically advanced culture would probably have been incomprehensible to the Egyptian priesthood that possessed them. Over the millennia, this lack of understanding the sophisticated technical basis of this inherited wisdom led to its transformation into the language of myth, legend and symbolic archetypes designed for easier consumption by a less sophisticated population. Despite this, a smaller, inner circle of dedicated priests would have kept the real meaning of this ancient medical knowledge secret. If there came a time when these profound secrets were lost, then we, the heirs of ancient Egypt's cultural and spiritual heritage, would have no idea about the extent of the wisdom they once possessed.

The possibility that ancient Egyptians were once keepers of advanced knowledge of human biology among other technologies without knowing its true meaning is reminiscent of a phenomenon called *cargo cults*. During World War II, Japanese and American military personnel occupied the Melanesia group of islands in the South Pacific. These occupying armed forces brought with them hitherto unknown material goods along with their weapons of war. Although the term *cargo cult* is considered pejorative and condescending in its presumption that Melanesian society was simple and backward, it nevertheless expresses the idea that these native populations associated prosperity with the arrival of white foreigners that brought with them unimagined wealth in the form of material goods brought by planes to their islands.[30]

Fig. 3-43 – "Cargo Cult" effigies and artifacts

After World War II, religions sprang up on the islands of Vanuatu, Pentecost, and Papua New Guinea whose adherents worshiped effigies of airplanes. The islanders made masks resembling airman's helmets and goggles, carved out *runways* in the jungle replete with torch-lit *landing lights*, and wore *headphones* made of coconut shells while manning *control towers* as a form of ritual magic (*Fig. 3-43*). To this day, they perform ceremonies where the men paint 'USA' on their chests and march around carrying bamboo replicas of rifles with fixed bayonets. In doing so, they hope the men who flew cargo and fighter aircraft that once visited their island will return and *deliver the goods*, bringing with them the prosperity described by their tribal elders who were alive at the time.

While not an exact correlation to the modern phenomena of *cargo cults*, the *Shemsu-Hor* could have left behind knowledge of specific advanced technologies preserved by the pre- and early dynastic Egyptians in the form of myths and legends. Though there are no traces of *Shemsu-Hor*, a civilization as presumably advanced as they were could have fallen into disarray and chaos and subsequently disintegrated for any number of reasons, whether due to war, climactic change or an enormous geological upheaval.

Whatever the circumstances of their demise, knowledge about the civilization of the *Shemsu-Hor* would not have taken long to vanish; so it's remarkable that any record of them exists today. Studies have shown that it would only take about a thousand years for evidence of any civilization, even one as technologically advanced as our own, to completely disappear and be swallowed up by the forces of nature.[31] It is, therefore, not surprising that we have virtually no information or evidence of the *Shemsu-Hor* left to examine. We can only guess who the *Shemsu-Hor* really were, and what the ancient Egyptians knew about them, if anything at all.

On the other hand, is this all just another coincidence? Only time will tell.

The East Chapels, Temple 'T' and *Per-Nefer* ("House of Beauty")

For many years, I struggled with the traditional explanation of why the Ḥeb-Sed Court was included in the design of Djoser's funerary temple with the most elegant and beautiful example of craftsmanship by ancient Egyptian architects and stonemasons from the Old Kingdom. Yet, the prevailing opinion is that its construction was for a single purpose, for a single day of festivities to celebrate the ascension to the throne of a single man, Netjerikhet Djoser.

Something about that interpretation just didn't ring true for me.

Why, I thought, would someone go through the trouble of building such a beautifully elaborate architectural masterpiece to use it only once, and never use it again? Whenever I thought about the Step Pyramid Enclosure and the Ḥeb-Sed Court in particular, this interpretation felt wrong on so many levels. Though earlier kings may have celebrated *sed*-festivals within their funerary enclosures at Abydos, there is no evidence of *Ḥeb-Sed* buildings ever being built within those enclosures. However, I could not shake this feeling until I discovered the symbolic relationship between the South Entrance Hall and the human spine.

We have been so conditioned to hearing that every ancient Egyptian mortuary monument such as the Step Pyramid Enclosure was built solely as a testament to the oversized egos of ancient Egyptian pharaohs that built them, and the priests that staffed these funerary temples were only concerned with perpetuating the dead king's memory. From what we now know to be the hidden secret of the Step Pyramid Enclosure's true purpose once its function as Djoser's burial site was complete – now this can be put to rest (*at least a little*).

What was the s*ed*-festival? What significance did it have in ancient Egyptian cultural life and what was its role in maintaining political stability?

The s*ed*-festival, also known as the *Ḥeb-Sed*, or *Feast of the Tail* (for the tail of a bull that was attached to the back of the pharaoh's garment), was a celebration with two purposes. Already observed as early as the First Dynasty, the s*ed*-festival was generally held to commemorate the king's thirtieth year on the throne, though sometimes it was held earlier as the kings in the ancient world, like their subjects, didn't always have long life spans. If a king lived long enough, the festivals occurred every three to four years after his first *Ḥeb-Sed*. For example, Amenhotep III celebrated three s*ed*-festivals during his reign.

These celebrations, often referred to as the *King's Jubilee*, signified the rejuvenation of the king so he could continue to rule. The king performed a ceremony during the s*ed*-festival called *encompassing the field* or *running the boundary markers*. Running around two sets of boundary markers that symbolized Upper and Lower Egypt showed the king was physically capable of continuing to rule. This simple, yet highly important ritual, blessed by the gods and witnessed by his people, bound the king and his subjects together into a cohesive, unified culture that lasted well over 3000 years.

We know that during the Old Kingdom (ca. 3100 BCE–2181 BCE), s*ed*-festival buildings were often temporary at best. This was because the *Ḥeb-Sed* was not only celebrated once in a king's reign, but also because the festival itself was held in several places along the Nile since the pharaoh needed to be seen by as many of his subjects to cement his rule throughout all of Egypt. This required an easily dismantled set of structures for ease of transport. However, in the New Kingdom (ca. 1570 BCE–1069 BCE), they were mostly constructed using more permanent materials such as stone or mudbrick.

We in the modern era have difficulty comprehending the reasons why such structures like the Ḥeb-Sed Court were used only once or twice, never to be used again. We have no cultural reference point to relate to it. Going through the effort of designing and building such an elegant collection of *chapels*, false or otherwise, to be used only once during the life of Pharaoh Netjerikhet Djoser, then discarded like a used tissue, goes against everything for which architects generally strive. Today's architects want to ensure that their designs are built for long-term use, and go to extreme lengths to ensure they are compliant with their clients' needs and wishes. They also strive to engineer buildings with safety and durability in mind so the structure will last for an extremely long time. No doubt, this was equally true of ancient architects as well.

While such *one-off* construction projects literally littered the landscape of ancient Egypt in the form of tombs, pyramids and mastabas, the presence of a *sed*-festival venue constructed of stone within Djoser's funerary monument was extremely unusual, and speaks to a use that lasted long after Djoser was laid to rest in his tomb. It is indisputable that Imhotep was the Chief Royal Physician as well as being Pharaoh Netjerikhet Djoser's Grand Vizier (Prime Minister) and Chief Royal Architect, and quite possibly during the reigns of several other kings as well. Honored and deified by generations of ancient Egyptians for thousands of years after his death attests to this. Knowing that the South Entrance Hall contains a symbolic representation of the human spine, it should come as no surprise that Imhotep, as a practicing physician, would also want to improve the standard of health-care in his country.

Because he was also the Grand Vizier of Egypt, Imhotep quite probably had enough influence with Djoser to allow him to design the Ḥeb-Sed Court with a more permanent secondary use after Djoser had *flown to the West*. Having an 'eternal' *Ḥeb-Sed* structure may have appealed to Djoser's ego and vanity, but nonetheless, he gave his Vizier permission to acquire the necessary materials and resources to turn the Ḥeb-Sed Court into a permanent health care facility once the need for holding the *Ḥeb-Sed* ceremonies were over. As the Grand Vizier of Egypt, Imhotep would also have the power to requisition the essential materials and skilled labor to build his vision for a new type of medical center.

If anything, Netjerikhet Djoser – by way of his Vizier, Chief Royal Architect and Chief Royal Physician, Imhotep – displayed compassion and kindness towards his people by building a hospital within the confines of his mortuary temple to care for the medical needs of his people long after he departed to the *Field of Reeds*. It may seem preposterous to suggest a funerary complex built to serve the needs of King Djoser and his family in the Afterlife should also serve the needs of the living as a health care facility for the city of Memphis, and by extension, all of Egypt. The ancient Egyptians believed the main purpose of such funerary monuments as the Step Pyramid was to have one's name spoken aloud for eternity, guaranteeing immortality in the Afterlife by maintaining the connection to your previous life on Earth by the simple act of people speaking your name. However, from what I discovered about the symbolism inherent in the Entrance Hall and the Ḥeb-Sed Court, the real reason for the construction of the Step Pyramid Enclosure is, I feel, less narrowly focused.

Prior to investigating the architecture of the Step Pyramid Enclosure, I had no answer as to Imhotep's veneration for more than 2000 years after his death as the Patron of Physicians and the recipient of prayers for healing. It is clear from the graffiti written by ancient visitors to the Step Pyramid Enclosure that Imhotep's design of this mortuary temple was highly regarded by later generations of Egyptians who came to see and marvel at its beauty, even if they did not know who actually designed it. However, it is far more likely Imhotep's stature as a physician grew from the medical facility he established within the Enclosure than for any other factor. The subsequent fame the Step Pyramid hospital garnered in providing excellent medical care (for the period) ensured the name of Netjerikhet Djoser – and his Vizier, Imhotep – be spoken forever. Based on some of the graffiti found throughout the Step Pyramid complex, it appears Djoser got his wish as his name was spoken with deepest reverence for hundreds of years after his death (see Chapter 6).

The Ḥeb-Sed Court medical center should rightly be considered the first genuine hospital in history; and though I have no proof of this, it may have even served to train many generations of physician–priests during its existence. Medical treatment in the early dynastic period was perhaps haphazard at best, with the training of physicians coming by way of apprenticeships of sons learning their physician-fathers' craft similar to apprenticeships of sons devoted to learning the skills of a carpenter or stonemason from their fathers. As the practice of medicine was a family affair, most physicians' practiced in their own homes or the homes of their patients (*Fig. 3-44*).

Due to their well-deserved reputation, Egyptian doctors were considered the best in the ancient world. It is possible that following the construction of the Ḥeb-Sed Court hospital, many physician–priests practiced medicine together in the same location instead of in their individual homes. This would have led to a more standardized level of medical care than had been previously known. It could even have inspired the treatment of the sick by priests and priestesses staffing many of the other temples built during the ensuing centuries.

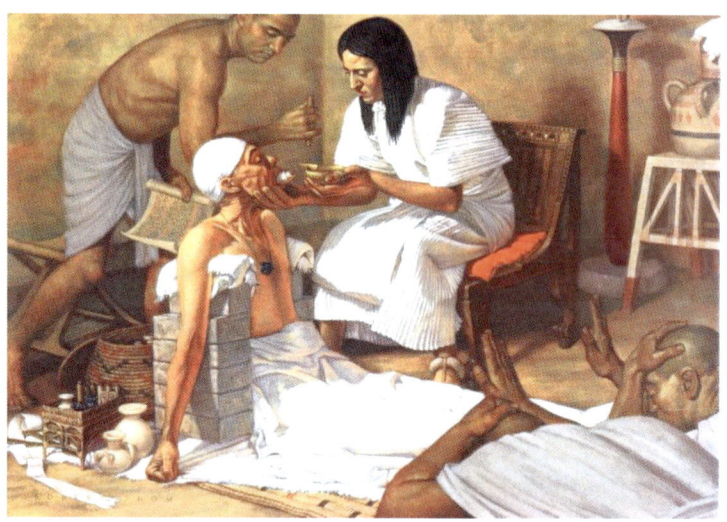

Fig. 3-44 – An Egyptian Doctor practicing in his home

If the Ḥeb-Sed Court doubled as a hospital, why has there no mention of it being used as such been unearthed during the course of any archeological investigation to date?

One simple answer is that an archeologist that is not looking for such a connection–or doesn't believe it even exists–probably won't find one. More to the point, no one in ancient Egypt needed to mention the Ḥeb-Sed Court was a medical facility. Up until the end of the Old Kingdom, knowledge of the Step Pyramid Enclosure as a working hospital would have been so common that it was unnecessary to record such a thing. It is much like writing on a milk carton "This milk is treated with the method of bacterial decontamination developed by Louis Pasteur", instead of just printing, "pasteurized", on its front. There's no need to memorialize Louis Pasteur as the one who developed the process for killing harmful bacteria in milk. Another example is that when you go to buy a car, nowhere in the sales literature does it read, "This fine automobile utilizes the internal combustion engine as invented by Jean Joseph Etienne Lenoir and further improved by Nikolaus Otto". It is unnecessary to state the obvious, and in the end, it's not even relevant.

Another factor is that during the long history of Egypt and long after the Ḥeb-Sed hospital ceased operations, the founding of a medical center in the Step Pyramid might not have been popular knowledge outside the small circle of healer–priests who staffed most Egyptian temples. They would not have written down the history of their medical profession, as it was mostly an oral tradition passed from one generation of priests to the next. Moreover, as time went on, every temple in Egypt was also the local hospital, though not necessarily in the modern sense (*Figs. 3-45* and *3-46*). In addition to serving in the temple as officiants for religious rites and ceremonies, priests were also physicians who treated the local populace for various ailments or injuries if the few extant medical papyri are any indication. Such is the legacy of Imhotep and the medical center he created at Sakkara that inspired the codification of medical knowledge and produced the likes of the Edwin Smith Surgical Papyrus.

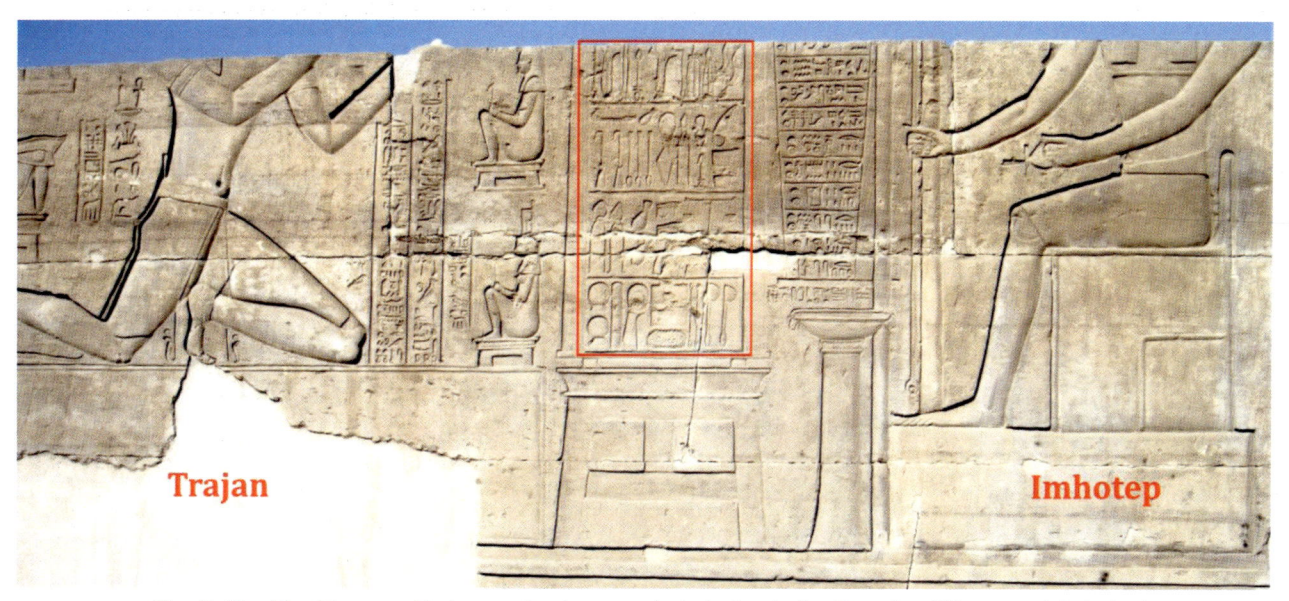

Fig. 3-45 – The Emperor Trajan paying homage to Imhotep in the Temple of Horus and Sobek at Kom Ombo, Egypt. Between them, surgical instruments are inscribed on the wall (red rectangle).

On a wall in the Temple of Horus and Sobek, the emperor Trajan is depicted giving tribute to the god, Imhotep. In this relief, surgical instruments that are quite similar to modern ones are inscribed along with two figures of the goddess Isis sitting on birthing chairs. (See *Fig. 8-19* in chapter 8.) This implies this temple also served as a maternity hospital. It was probably a medical school as well since the prominent displaying of surgical instruments would serve as a kind of teaching tool.

Fig. 3-46 – The Sanatorium (or Infirmary) at the Temple of Hathor, Dendera, which later became a monastery for the nearby Coptic Church

The East Chapels

As stated before, the Ḥeb-Sed Court may have incorporated a representation of the central nervous system in its design. There are twelve structures sometimes referred to as chapels or shrines lined up along the eastern side of the Ḥeb-Sed Court. Each of these small buildings has what appear to be two small rooms in front of them, which lead to a small niche in the back. If you look at the plan of these *chapels* (*Fig. 3-47*), the maze-like structure of the walls defining the two rooms of each of the twelve chapels is reminiscent of the undulating folds of the surface of the human brain (*Fig. 3-48*). **Symbolically, therefore, the twelve East Chapels are analogous to the twelve pairs of cranial nerves.**

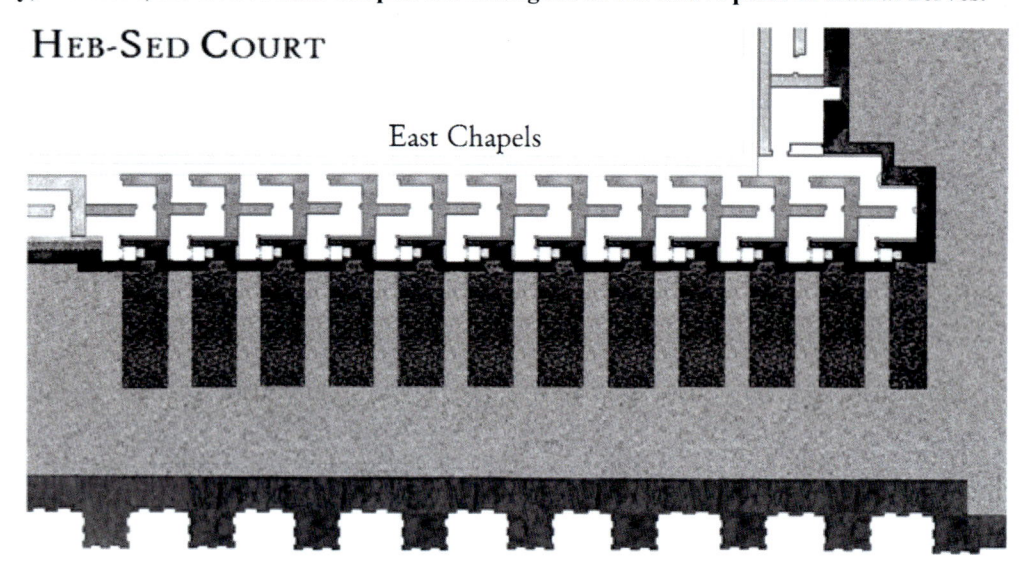

Fig. 3-47 – The East Chapels of the Ḥeb-Sed Court, northeast section

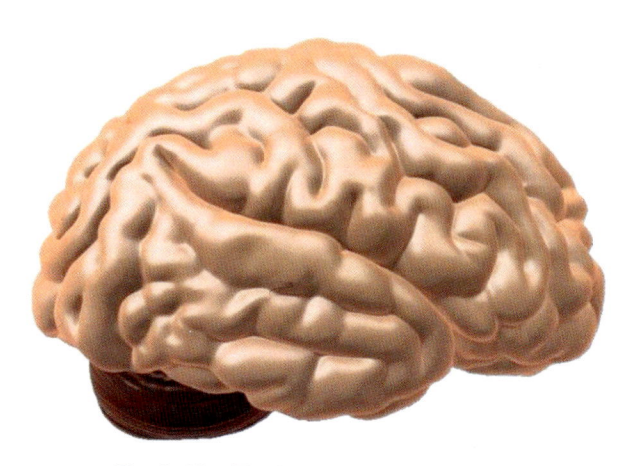

Fig. 3-48 – The Human Brain – Side View.

The winding serpentine walls in front of the twelve East Chapels (*Fig. 3-47*) imitate the undulating surface of the brain

Many Egyptologists believe the ancient Egyptians had little or no regard for the importance of the human brain; as it was not preserved with the internal organs that were stored in the four canopic jars included in a person's grave goods (*Fig. 3-25*). Most often, the brain was rarely removed during mummification, but when it was removed, the brain was scraped out of the skull through the nose and just thrown away. However, an ancient Egyptian physician probably knew the brain had a vital function as there are numerous examples of surgical procedures being performed on people's skulls based on the evidence of trepanning (i.e., the removal of a section of the skull to gain access to the brain) from several mummies and medical papyri found in Egypt. The fact that only the internal organs and not the brain were mummified is probably more due to the fact of the difficulty of removing the brain without damaging the skull than anything else.

While modern science realizes the brain's true value, the ancient Egyptians did not seem to value it as much. A modern analogy is the removing of the engine from an automobile. The make and model of the car would still be apparent even with the motor missing. According to Egyptian religious beliefs, the mummified body (the *khat*) would still be recognizable by the *ka*, or spirit. The Egyptians believed that when they would visit the tomb of a departed family member to celebrate their loved one's life, the *ka* of the deceased would still recognize its former *residence* when it returned to symbolically share a meal with their relatives. The brain is unnecessary at that point. In this context, it was only necessary to preserve the internal organs in order for the spirit of the deceased person to partake symbolically of the spiritual essence of the food left with the mummy's grave goods. Food left behind in a person's tomb symbolized the connection of the soul with its past life on Earth. To have a good time in the Afterlife, one needed to have that connection with the social aspect of communal eating they had when they were alive.

Inevitably, one must ask: Why build in stone what was in earlier times intended to be only a temporary building made of wood or reeds (*Fig. 3-49*)? The answer is that the Ḥeb-Sed Court's conversion into a hospital occurred before or shortly after Djoser had *flown to the West*. Being a hospital most of the time does not exclude the use of the Ḥeb-Sed Court as a *sed*-festival venue every four years or so, or vice versa.

When looking at the Step Pyramid Enclosure solely as a funerary monument, it would be very easy to believe the twelve structures on the east side of the Ḥeb-Sed Court functioned as chapels meant for the worship of some kind to a god or gods, though which gods has never been made clear. More than that, during the Old Kingdom, Egyptians worshipped a group of nine primary gods called the Ennead of Heliopolis: Ra-Atum, Shu, Tefnut, Geb, Nut, Osiris, Isis, Seth and Nephthys–sometimes adding Horus, the son of Osiris and Isis, to this primary group, leaving two chapels available for a pair of unknown gods. Several other gods could be suitable candidates, but these ten gods were the principle ones worshipped at Memphis at the time.

Fig. 3-49 – Two of the twelve East Chapels as reconstructed by J.P. Lauer. These are stone replicas of the typical temporary tent-like accommodations used during the Ḥeb-Sed

However, assuming the Ḥeb-Sed Court was also a center for medical treatment for most of its existence, it is likely the East and West Chapels had many other functions as well and not restricted to only one possible use. Philosophically speaking, it has become apparent there are many layers with multiple hidden meanings existing in the design of the Step Pyramid, all at the same time.

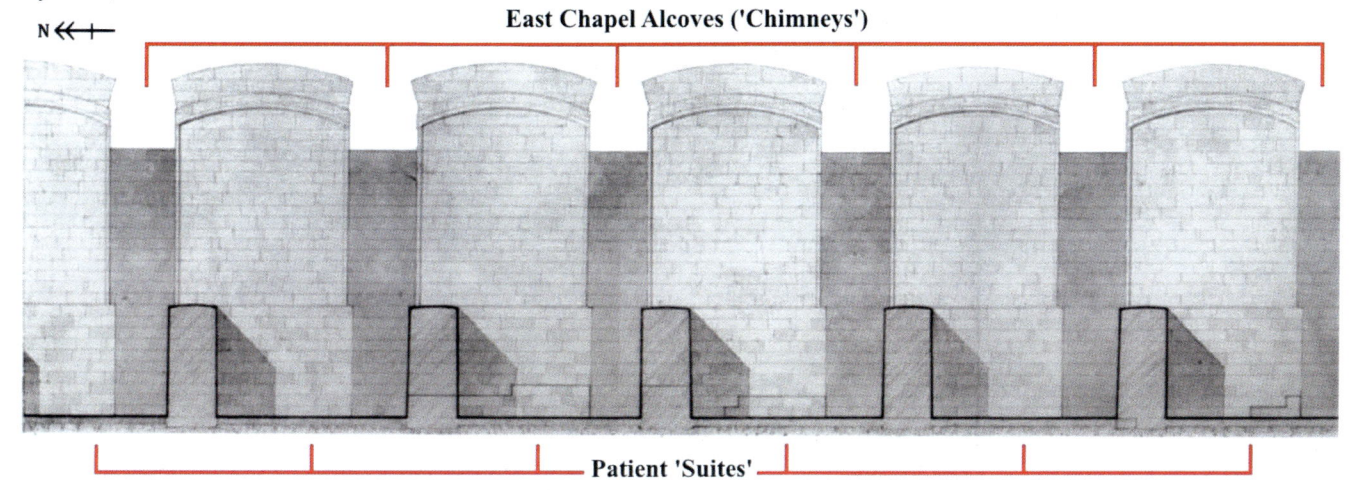

Fig. 3-50 – Ḥeb-Sed Court – East Chapels Patient Suites

During the *sed*-festival, these *chapels* were most likely used as guest accommodations for the royal retinue attending the jubilee. After the Ḥeb-Sed, patients visiting the Step Pyramid medical facility might have had to stay longer after receiving initial health–care. To that end, these twelve, two–room *suites* in the East Chapels of the Ḥeb-Sed Court were used for overnight stays by individual patients for a variety of reasons:

- Recovery after a surgical procedure.
- Continuing medical care for an illness.
- To commune with a god during dreamtime. (The famous ancient Greek physician, Asclepius, used this technique later in his clinic.)

The suites had two rooms, an antechamber just inside the door, and an inner bedroom for the patient (*Figs. 3-51* and *3-52*). Each of these rooms was approximately 1.5 meters (5 feet) wide. Though they may not look like it, these rooms were large enough to accommodate a small cot-like bed in the second of the two rooms that made up a *chapel*. The outer room could also accommodate a family member who was helping care for the patient. The walls of the patient suite were approximately 9 meters (10 feet) tall, affording some privacy. These two front rooms most likely had a detachable roof made of rectangular wooden frames covered with cloth, reeds or even papyrus stalks that lay on top of the walls allowing sunlight to both heat the inner rooms during cooler weather as well as the benefit of sunlight being a natural disinfectant.

Fig. 3-51 – Several partially reconstructed East Chapels
The antechamber is to the right and
the sleeping quarters is to the left

Fig. 3-52 – An East Chapel patient suite
The patient sleeping area is between the wall in
the foreground and the latrine alcove in the rear

The rear alcove was open to the sky as they are today (*Figs. 3-49* and *3-50*). These alcoves would have had a chamber pot, or latrine chair for the patient's use (*Fig. 3-53*). [32] There was also enough space for a clay or metal brazier filled with igneous rocks like granite that would have wood or other organic matter burning within it to keep the sleeping quarters warm during the winter months.

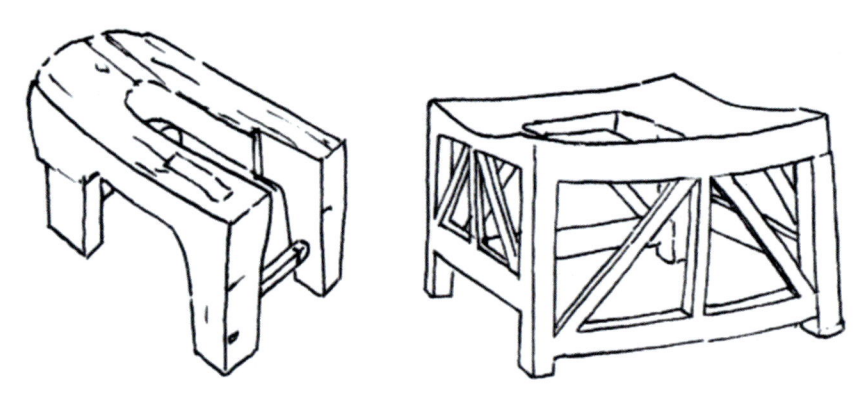

Fig. 3-53 – Two typical latrine chairs from Thebes

Above the latrine chair and set into the north wall of the alcove was a niche similar to those in the West Chapels. An oil lamp for lighting and/or an incense burner to neutralize the odors of the latrine chair was placed inside these niches. On a side note, most latrines in ancient Egypt would preferably have had a window facing north to allow the prevailing northerly breezes to flush out the bad odors (*pun intended*).

Here is a conclusive validation of Imhotep's inherent genius. Because of the Ḥeb-Sed Court's north-south orientation, a slight breeze passing over the arched roofs of these *chapels* produced a Venturi effect inducing a lower pressure above the alcove much like the wings of a modern aircraft. This caused a more efficient updraft to draw up and out of the patient suite any odors from the latrine chair or smoke from the oil lamps, incense burners or brazier, thus functioning in the same way a chimney does in a modern house.

In the colder winter months, natural sunlight would heat these rooms with the removal of the wood–framed, cloth–covered roof during the day. At night, with the roof placed back onto the top of the walls, the stones walls would retain their heat and radiate it back into the rooms supplementing the heat produced by the clay pots or braziers that were installed in the alcove. Organic material like wood or reeds piled on top the rocks inside the braziers and set alight, would heat the patient's room. Even when the fire died down, the still-hot rocks provided ample heat on their own. In the hotter summer months, they reversed the process with the roof in place covering the patient suites during the day. Since heat rises, the roof would be removed at night to cool the room. While it seems unusual for patients to stay overnight in what is essentially an outdoor room, having a removable roof in the Ḥeb-Sed Court patient suites provided patients with the natural healing effects of fresh air, which can kill viruses, along with sunlight's natural germicidal effects that also provides an ample source of vitamin D.

Fig. 3-54 – A West Chapel alcove similar to ones in the East Chapels

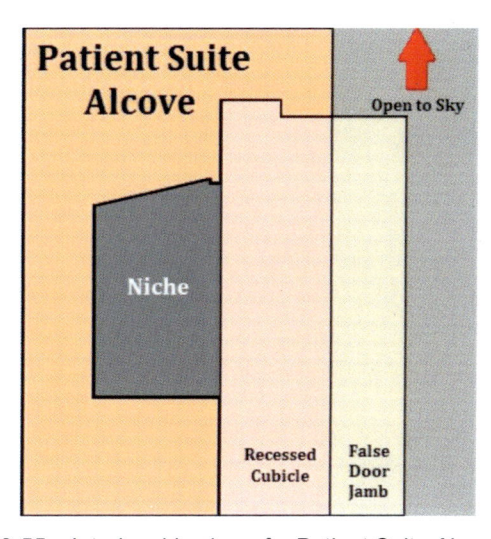

Fig. 3-55 – Interior side view of a Patient Suite Alcove

Looking at *Figs. 3-54* and *3-55* you can see a niche in the rear of a West Chapel alcove. Assuming this niche is identical to the ones in the East Chapels, it is about head high. The roof of the niche itself sloped upwards to easily allow smoke generated by an incense burner or lamp to billow up out of the niche and up the alcove's *chimney*. The existence of these niches virtually confirms these twelve *chapels* were, in fact, patient suites because their design prevented any smoke to build up and be trapped. This speaks to these rooms' use for a long-term stay of the medical center's patients, not for the temporary ritualistic worship of a god.

On the southeast side of the Ḥeb-Sed Court were two larger versions of the twelve smaller patient suites (*Fig. 3-56*).

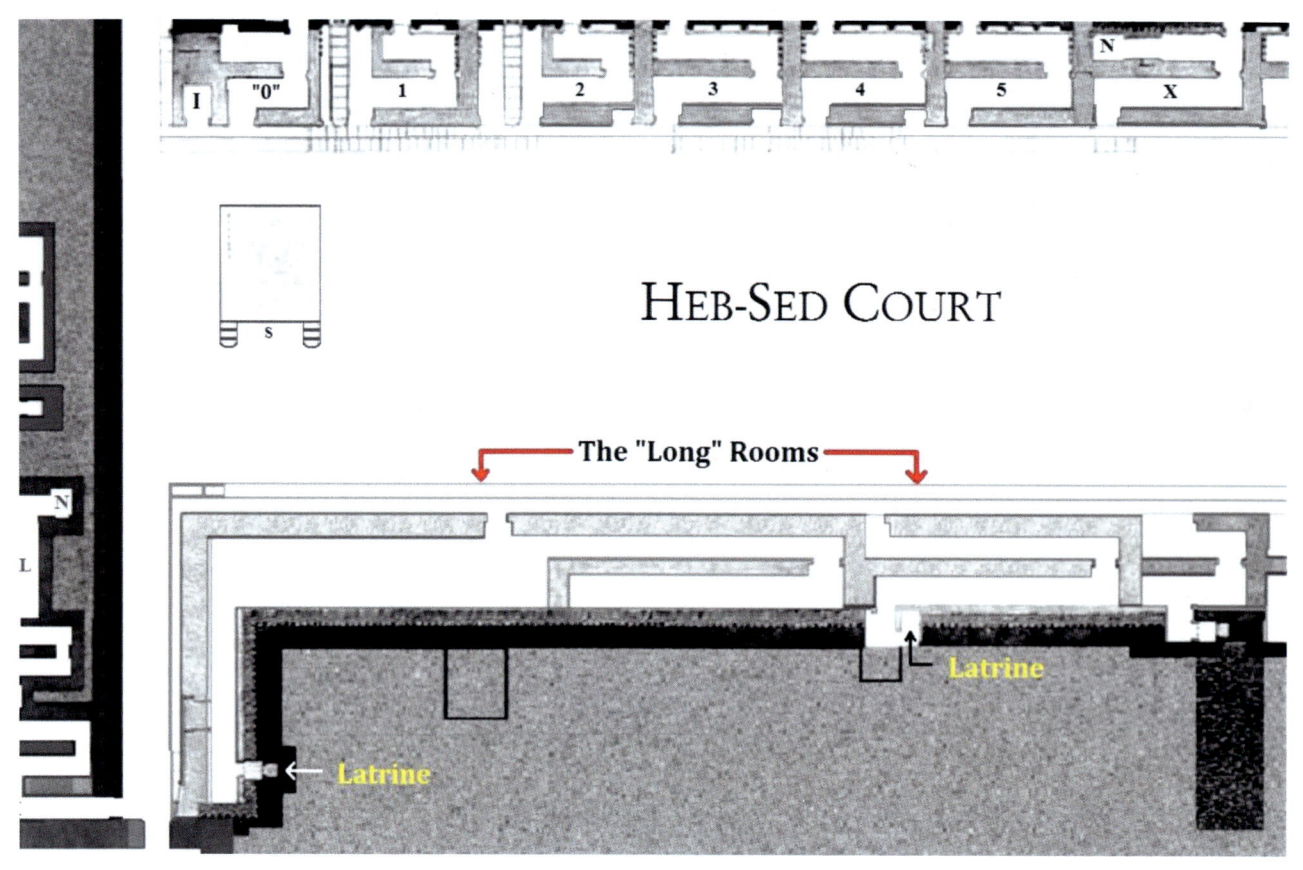

Fig. 3-56 – Ḥeb-Sed Court – The "Long" Rooms

These larger rooms have the appearance of dormitory–style accommodations. They may have been used for patients with less critical care needs: possibly one room was used for male patients and the other for female patients. Another possibility is that relatives of patients who were assisting with caring for a family member, and could not be accommodated in the antechamber of the patient's suite, may have used these rooms as well.

There is modern evidence these types of outdoor quarters are highly effective in helping a patient recover from illness. During the Spanish Flu Pandemic of 1918, doctors had no choice but to house the overflow of patients outdoors in tents because of the overwhelming demand for indoor bed space (*Fig. 3-57*). They subsequently discovered that patients in these outdoor accommodations recovered much faster due to their exposure to sunlight. The combination of fresh air and sunshine reduced patient deaths, along with reducing infections among the medical staff. Herein lies the additional evidence that supports the East Chapels' use as open-air suites for patients was certainly possible.

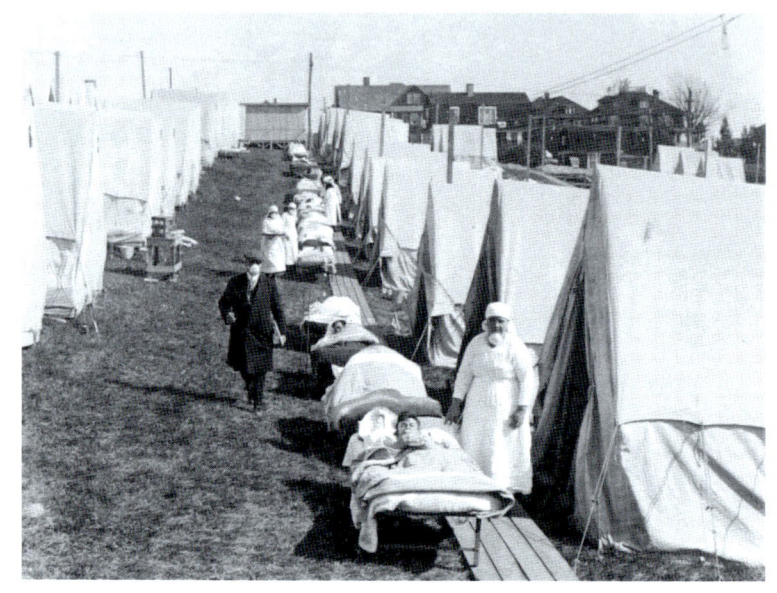

Fig. 3-57 – Influenza patients getting sunlight in an emergency open-air hospital in Boston, 1918

Temple 'T'

Fig. 3-58 – Temple 'T' (looking NE from the Great South Court)

Temple 'T' sits just to the west of the Ḥeb-Sed Court behind the West Chapels (*Fig. 3-58*). Even in its semi-demolished state, it is still an impressive structure, and must have been even more elegant and beautiful in antiquity. While the true function of the temple has never been ascertained, Firth believed it was a *robing room* or a place the king used to rest during the *Ḥeb-Sed* ceremonies. However, I believe another room within the Ḥeb-Sed Court quadrant may have fulfilled that function [see *The Per-Nefer* ("House of Beauty") section below].

Fig. 3-59 – Temple 'T' looking NW from the 'Mystery Building'

Fig. 3-60 – Interior of Temple 'T' as reconstructed by J.-P. Lauer

In keeping with the idea that the conversion of Ḥeb-Sed Court into a medical center took place after the completion of the *sed*-festival ceremonies, it is possible that Temple 'T' had a new function related to its use in a medical facility (*Fig. 3-61*). To that end, Temple 'T' became the Ḥeb-Sed Court hospital's surgical suite as well as being used to triage (i.e., consult and treat) incoming patients after its function for the *sed*-festival was complete. (Here again is yet another wonderful coincidence as J.-P. Lauer labeled the building used for *triage* as Temple 'T'.)

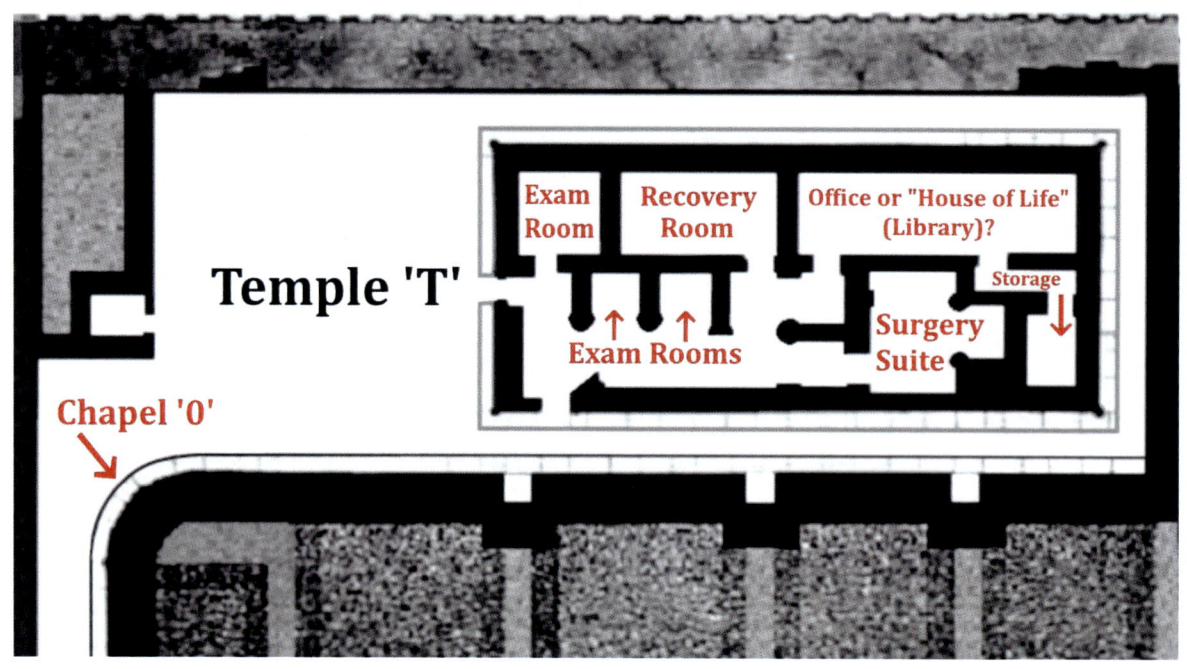

Fig. 3-61 – Temple 'T' as repurposed for a surgery and triage center

On top of the walls surrounding the room designated as the Surgery Suite there are several *djed* pillar friezes (*Fig. 3-62*). *Djed* pillars were associated with the god Ptah, the chief god of Egypt's capital, Memphis. Ptah is the ancient creator god who existed before everything, and by the force of his mind, created the Universe. Ptah was also the patron god of craftsmen and architects.

Fig. 3-62 – Temple 'T' Surgury Suite (?) with djed pillars adorning the lintels above the doors

Ptah's wife was the lion-headed warrior goddess, Sekhmet. When in a bad mood, she was associated with both war and blood, but in her calmer moments, she became docile like her alter ego, Bastet, the cat goddess. In this guise, she was the patron goddess of physicians and healing. By including the *djed* pillar above the walls of the surgery suite and elsewhere, no doubt Imhotep wished to honor his two patron gods, and at the same time giving us another clue as to what purpose these rooms may have served.

The rounded corner at the rear of West Chapel '0' (*Fig. 3-63*) permitted easier transportation of patients being carried on stretchers from a recovery room in the Temple 'T' to a *patient suite* in the Ḥeb-Sed Court East Chapels.

On a side note: J.-P. Lauer labeled the small forecourts in front of most of the West Chapels with a number or letter. He never labeled the southernmost West Chapel (the one with the curved rear wall) though he did label two small rooms on its façade and within its interior. For ease of identification, I have chosen to call it West Chapel '0'.

Fig. 3-63 – The rear of Chapel '0' near Temple 'T'

The *Per-Nefer* ("House of Beauty")

Fig. 3-64 – The rooms at the end of the passageway leading from the South Entrance Hall to the Ḥeb-Sed Court [33]

Near the end of the corridor leading from the Entrance Hall to the Ḥeb-Sed Court (*Fig. 3-64*) are some rather oddly shaped *rooms*, if they can be called that. Resembling more of a collection of hallways than functionally usable rooms, one must wonder what purpose these spaces may have served. As stated before, architects often work on the premise that "form follows function", and while some sort of function may dictate the final form, sometimes the resultant structure does not have the appearance of being terribly functional. That seems to be case here.

Firth, Quibell, or Lauer never speculated on the purpose these long rooms and corridors served after they excavated and reconstructed the Step Pyramid Enclosure in the 1920s and 1930s. Some have suggested they were *robing rooms* for guests' use during the *Ḥeb-Sed* ceremonies, or perhaps storage rooms, or may have even been the temple library (called the *Per Ankh* or *House of Life*). All these explanations are certainly plausible, and they might all have been true at one time or another, but I felt there was something was incomplete about these theories when I studied the plans of this part of the Enclosure.

To discover a possible function for these strangely shaped rooms, we have to return to the Entrance Hall to a space between two of the columns near the **T7** Lung *chapel* representing the **T10** vertebra. During the initial excavations of the Entrance Hall, a rectangular stone object in the space between these two columns was discovered (marked by the letter '**D**' in *Fig. 3-65*), and was christened the *Lion Base* because of the lion heads that were once attached to it (*Fig. 3-67*). Firth thought the Lion Base was found in its original location, not having been moved in over 50 centuries (*Fig. 3-66*). If that is true, why were most of the lion heads no longer attached to its perimeter? Most likely because the lion heads were dislodged when the Lion Base was moved to the location in the Entrance Hall where it was discovered.

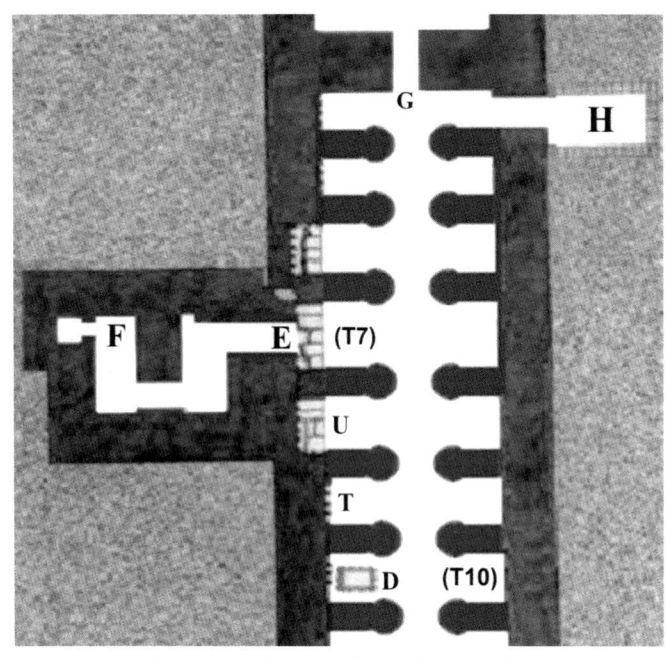

Fig. 3-65 – Section of the Entrance Hall near the south U-shaped 'chapel'

Fig. 3-66 – The Lion Base in situ after its discovery
Note the missing lion heads from its perimeter that were probably broken off in antiquity

Fig. 3-67 – The Lion Base with nine of the 14 lion heads reattached

At this point, you may well ask, is there a connection between the Lion Base and the elongated passages and rooms just south of the Ḥeb-Sed Court? What clues did Imhotep leave behind that can tell us their intended function? Having no other examples from ancient Egypt with which we can compare, we can only guess as to their purpose, because buildings with similarly designed rooms and passageways do not appear to have been constructed after the Third Dynasty.

Apparently, the Lion Base was not unique because there was a similar lion-headed throne platform depicted in the *Ḥeb-Sed* scenes from the sun temple of the Pharaoh Niuserre at Abu Ghurob (*Fig. 3-68*). [34]

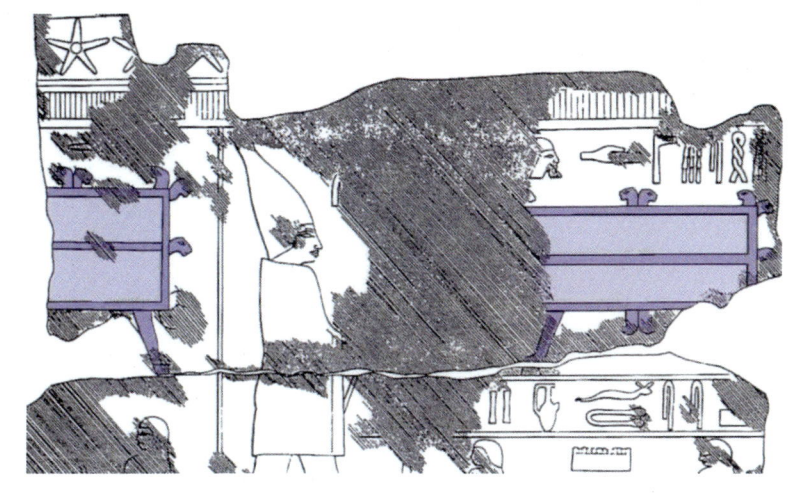

Fig. 3-68 – A Lion Platform (left) from the Fifth Dynasty Pharaoh Niuserre's sun temple (above)

What purpose did the Lion Base serve, and why was it discovered in the middle of the Entrance Hall? Firth described the Lion Base as an "altar-like object of limestone decorated with lions' heads" that was, perhaps, a bedstead. [35] J. E. Quibell thought it might be a throne-base. [36] The Lion Base in its original condition had three lion heads attached to each of its short sides, and four heads on its longer sides (*Fig. 3-67*). This arrangement mimics the Step Pyramid Enclosure Wall that has three false gates on the shorter north and south walls, and four false gates on the longer east and west walls. In ancient Egyptian mythology, the number 14 was associated with death and resurrection because of its association with the god, Osiris, who was killed by his brother, Seth, cut up Osiris' body into 14 parts and scattered the remains along the length of the Nile River. Osiris' wife, Isis, retrieved her husband's body parts, reassembled them and resurrected Osiris, who then became the god of the Underworld. This may give a clue as to its intended purpose.

One thing is certain: Besides having a practical use, the Lion Base also probably had a symbolic reason for lion heads adorning its perimeter. While today, we consider the lion to be the *king of beasts*, it may well be that in ancient Egypt the lion became associated with royalty as the *Beast of Kings*. Observing the behavior of lions in the wild may have influenced how the succession of kings in ancient Egypt developed over many centuries. What follows is just another example of how the ancient Egyptians perceived the natural world around them, and incorporated their observations into various aspects of their culture and society.

Royal succession in ancient Egypt bears no resemblance to how later monarchies chose their next king. Rather than the heir apparent succeeding his father because he was the king's son (as in Western monarchies), a crown prince of Egypt became pharaoh at his father's passing because he was the son of the Pharaoh's Chief Royal Wife, or one of his others wives if the Chief Royal Wife did not have a son. This mimics the behavior of lions in their natural habitat where a single male lion sires children with a group (*pride*) of related female lions. Once a younger male member of the pride matures and comes of age, his father drives him off, and the son goes off to find his own pride of females with which to mate. When a younger male evicts from the pride the older lion that is no longer able to fend off the new *king* who then asserts his dominance, the lion pride's DNA is continually refreshed with new blood. The DNA of the related female lions is the one constant factor in the lion family relationships, with a new male *heir* ruling the pride for about thirty to 40 years until they die or replaced by a new interloper.

In emulating the family dynamics of the lion kingdom, the ancient Egyptian female royal family members possessed the power behind the throne (reminiscent of female lions possessing a consistent line of inherited DNA), while the male king wielded that political power. Anyone who married a royal princess (or *solar princess*, as they were sometimes called) could legitimately claim the throne of Egypt. This is why pharaohs would often marry their own daughters to keep this matrilineal succession within the royal family. Except in the time of the Late Period (712–322 BCE), pharaohs never gave their daughters in marriage to a foreign king. This prevented anyone other than a native Egyptian royal family member to sit on the throne of Egypt.

A simple examination of the Lion Base shows what it is not: because of the raised lip that surrounds its top, we can safely assume the Lion Base was not a platform for a statue. Every statue excavated at the Step Pyramid was carved from a single block of stone with a base integrated into it, negating a need for a separate platform (see *Fig. 3-4*). Lifting a multi-ton statue onto the top of the Lion Base might have led to damaging the raised lip, and what little damage there is can be attributed to the usual wear and tear that is often seen on 4700-year-old artifacts.

Fig. 3-69 – Room 'V' near the Ḥeb-Sed Court

Returning to the rooms and corridors in question, we can see a curious feature in Room '**V**' (far left side of *Fig. 3-64*) of a large, platform-like structure in the middle. When I first saw this old excavation photo, I was quite puzzled. While its dilapidated state is probably due to the deconstruction that took place millennia ago, the rectangular inset in the middle of the raised platform (arrow, *Fig. 3-69*) makes no sense from either a design or stone harvesting point of view.

Why would someone that is taking stone for reuse elsewhere remove the stones from the middle of the platform and not from the perimeter first? For that matter, why leave a hollowed out space in what is obviously meant to be a platform?

The thought then occurred to me that if the Lion Base was really a *wooden bedstead* or *seat* executed in stone, then the Lion Base might have originally been installed in this hole on the platform in Room '**V**'. This implies that room '**V**' would have been sleeping quarters for the king to rest during *sed*-festival ceremonies instead of Temple '**T**', and the serpentine nature of these long corridors would provide ample privacy. If the Lion Base is slightly smaller than the empty inset, the plan of Room '**V**' might well be a reproduction of the royal apartments in the king's palace at Memphis.

Another possible use for the Lion Base was as an offering table. The raised lip would keep the offering, possibly an animal sacrifice, and any blood from spilling off the sides of the table. The two grooves at the back of the Lion Base suggest one of two things: given their jagged appearance, the grooves could be just the typical damage often seen on an artifact that is over 4700 years old. Conversely, the grooves could be part of the original design of the offering table when first sculpted, or their uneven appearance could have been the result of damage done in the past. Better photographs or an up-close inspection will be able to tell what these grooves really are.

If used as an offering table for blood sacrifices, the two grooves at its rear (see *Figs. 3-66* and *3-67*) would allow any blood that pooled on the surface of the Lion Base to drain away into vessels set at its rear. If true, this is similar to the function of a pair of lion-headed embalming tables (*Fig. 3-70*) found in a subterranean gallery in the North Court by August Mariette in 1889 (marked as '**C**' in *Fig. 1*-2, Chapter 1). (One way to prove this is to spray the Lion Base with Luminol to see if any blood residue becomes evident.) Originally thought to be from the First or Second Dynasties, the Lion Tables and construction of gallery '**C**' probably originated in the Eighteenth Dynasty or later.

Fig. 3-70 – One of two Lion-Headed Embalming Tables found in the Subterranean Gallery 'C' in the North Court of the Step Pyramid Enclosure

Even though the two Lion Tables were used for embalming animals as part of the animal burials at the Serapeum, [37] their resemblance to the Lion Base suggest a similar usage. Because no apparent scorch marks are visible on the Lion Base's surface, burnt offerings were probably never made on it.

If it was indeed an offering table, or even a throne-base used by Djoser during his *sed*-festival, its original location may have been on top of the South Altar located at the south side of the Step Pyramid in the Great South Court. If so, then the South Altar should be re-designated as a throne dais. In either case, it probably ended up in the Entrance Hall because centuries after it was no longer an active mortuary temple, the Step Pyramid Enclosure was gradually stripped of its precious limestone casing and walls for reuse elsewhere. Given the location where it was discovered, it is easy to speculate the Lion Base was probably being hauled out of the Enclosure, and whoever was removing it gave up trying to do so for any number of reasons; most likely because it was too heavy and cumbersome to continue dragging it out of the Enclosure.

Fig. 3-71 – Apis Bull Embalming (natron) Table – Sakkara
Note the lion bed carved on the outside of the table

Moreover, the Lion Base may have been repurposed for a completely different use after it had served as an offering table, bed platform or throne base. It may seem strange to suggest this because the Step Pyramid Enclosure has never been thought of as a medical center (until now), but the Lion Base's secondary function may have been that of a natron table. Natron tables were used during the mummification process to dry out the body as well as the internal organs which were placed into canopic jars for inclusion with the mummy in it tomb. *Fig. 3-71* shows a large natron table used for embalming Apis bulls at Sakkara. Embossed on its side is a replica of a lion bed that is evocative of the lion heads on the Lion Base and the two lion-headed embalming tables (*Fig. 3-70*). The existence of subterranean gallery 'C' in *Fig. 1-2* also proves that mummification was performed within the Step Pyramid Enclosure, so having an embalming center near the Heb-Sed Court hospital may have been a long-standing tradition and certainly plausible.

When I first studied this part of the Step Pyramid Enclosure, the shapes of these rooms are not what you would normally associate with any particular purpose. After studying them for a long time, I concluded they must be symbolic in the same way the South Entrance Hall had a symbolic meaning relating to human anatomy. When looking at a top view of these strangely shaped rooms, they bear a striking resemblance to human entrails spread out on a natron table for preservation during the mummification process. Oddly enough, verification of this came from seeing hieroglyphs in the shape of these rooms. I do not know how I made the intuitive leap to arrive at such a conclusion, but when I started to compare their shapes to hieroglyphs, it became apparent I was on the right track.

The first room that resembles a hieroglyph (marked as 'O' in *Fig. 3-64*) is at the end of hallway 'II'.

Turning the plan 180°, the 'O' room looks like the hieroglyph for '**intestine**' (*Fig. 3-72*).

Gardiner Sign List No.	Hieroglyph	Represents
F46	⊂⊃	Intestine

This became a vital clue as I investigated further.

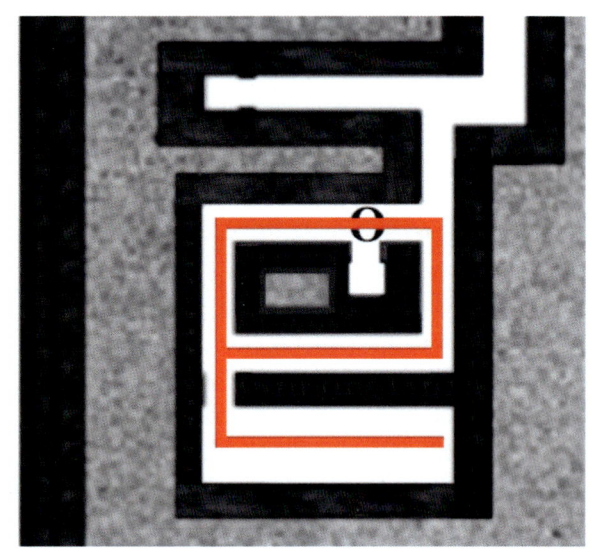

Fig. 3-72 – Room 'O' – "Intestine Room"

Turning the plan 90° to the right, and looking at the serpentine corridor between the Roman numeral 'I' and the letter 'L', we see something that resembles another hieroglyph (*Fig. 3-73*).

Gardiner Sign List No.	Hieroglyph	Represents
N25	⋯	Mountain range; sandy hill-country over green cultivation

Most often translated as 'foreign land, hill country' or 'desert', in certain contexts it can also mean '**necropolis**' or '**upland tomb**' which is certainly within keeping of the function of this funerary temple.

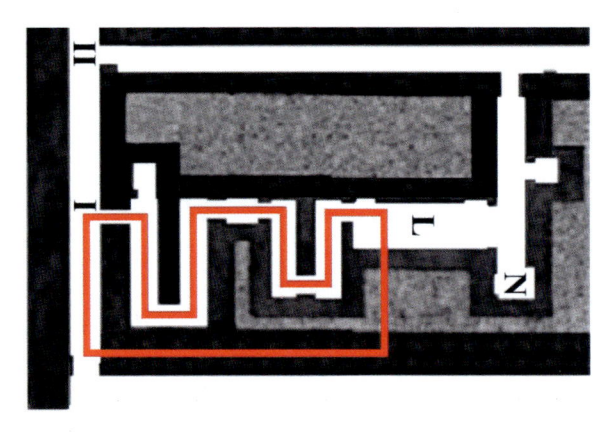

Fig. 3-73 – Room L – "Necropolis Room"

As noted above, there is what appears to be a very oddly shaped structure in the middle of Room '**V**' (as seen in *Fig. 3-68*). It may have been a platform for the Lion Base if its original location was here (*Fig. 3-74*).

Gardiner
Sign List No.   Hieroglyph   Represents

R8   ⎡   Flag, "god" or goddess"

The shape is like the hieroglyph *ntr*, meaning '**god**'. In the context of its location, it could mean, *the king is now one with the gods, or is now a god himself*. This room may have also served as Djoser's bedroom during the *sed*-festival. If it is a platform for the Lion Base as a bedstead, its shape is in keeping with the notion that the king himself was a god.

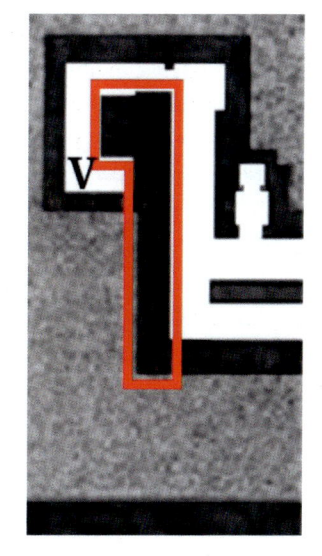

Fig. 3-74 – Room V – The "Neter Room"

In the corridors marked by the letter 'R' (above of the Roman numeral **III**) is a hieroglyph that can be interpreted two ways. First, it can be viewed as a variation of the hieroglyph for '**intestine**' (*Fig. 3-75*).

Gardiner
Sign List No.   Hieroglyph   Represents

F49   ⌇   Intestine
                              (Variant of F46)

Obviously another confirmation of the intended use for this collection of rooms and corridors.

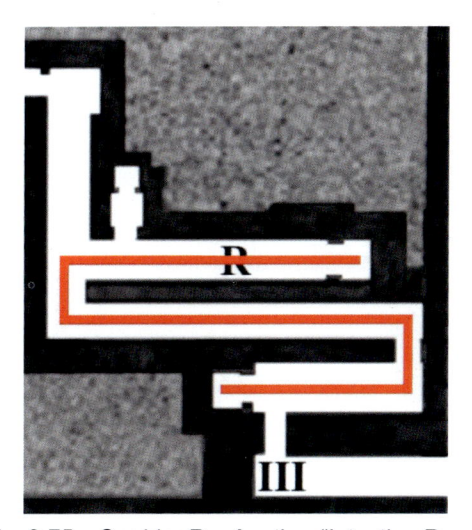

Fig. 3-75 – Corridor R – Another "Intestine Room"

Secondly, when rotated 90° to the right, this same corridor takes on a different meaning (*Fig. 3-76*).

Gardiner
Sign List No.   Hieroglyph   Represents

O5   ⊔   Winding Wall

This hieroglyph can be interpreted as "a street", "lowing" (as in the sound made by cattle) or '**traverse**'. Though it seems a bit of a stretch, keep in mind that Imhotep to would often ascribe more than one secret meaning to an architectural feature.

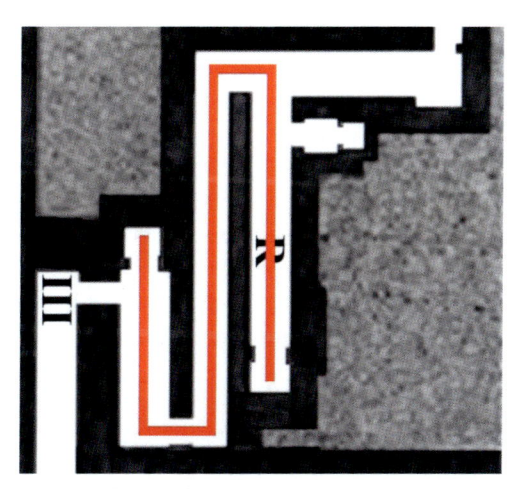

Fig. 3-76 – Corridor R – "Winding Wall"

Taken as a whole, it is unknown what symbolic meaning (if any) Imhotep was attempting to convey with the shapes of hieroglyphs embedded in the design of these rooms. Going out on a limb, though, one possible interpretation when taking all these disguised hieroglyphs together may be, **"The King has *traversed* the *western hill country* over the *far mountains of the gods* to join them in the *Field of Reeds* (the Afterlife)."**

Or something to that effect.

Perhaps the term *far mountain* may even refer to the Step Pyramid, which is itself a man-made mountain. Whatever the hidden message may be, the choice of hieroglyphs was not accidental or capricious. The hieroglyphs Imhotep chose to use were always in the context of where they appear in the Step Pyramid Enclosure, and never just random.

Finally, the last hieroglyph depicted here is implied by the space between the walls of Room '**V**' instead of the walls themselves (*Fig. 3-77*). Using empty *space* to convey a hidden meaning is in keeping with what Imhotep did in the South Entrance Hall.

Gardiner
Sign List No.   Hieroglyph   Represents

U19   Adze

The adze was a tool used by stonemasons and woodcarvers alike to refine their work after a stone or piece of wood had been rough-cut.

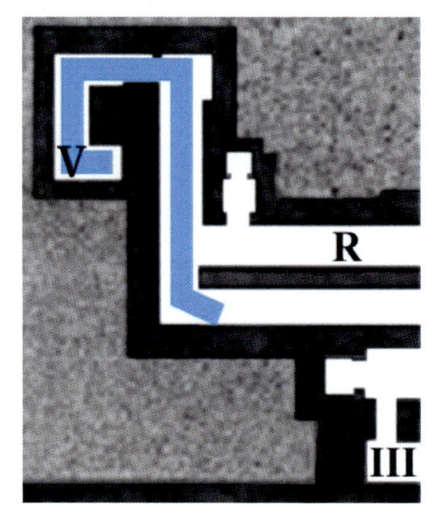

Fig. 3-77 – Corridor R and Room V – The "Adze Room"

In addition, the adze was used in the *Opening of the Mouth* ceremony performed during burial rituals prior to putting the body in the tomb (*Fig. 3-78*). Symbolically, performing this ceremony ensured the newly deceased person could speak upon entering the Afterlife, enabling them to properly defend themselves during the *Weighing of the Heart* ritual trial (see Chapter 4).

Fig. 3-78 – Opening of the Mouth Ceremony
(From the tomb of Tutankhamun)

As seen in the Entrance Hall where Imhotep created a symbolic metaphor by using *space* to denote the human spine in his design, it is well within reason that a hidden hieroglyph can be located here in Room '**V**' (*Fig. 3-76*). As he was a High Priest of Ra-Atum (the *Complete One*), perhaps Imhotep would not see the empty vastness of *space* as being truly devoid of life, but saw in it the Progenitor of the Potential. In addition, defining a space to impart an esoteric truth is in keeping with Imhotep's use of the spaces between the columns of the Entrance Hall to depict the human spine and skull.

Putting all these clues together, only one conclusion made sense to me: after the completion of the *sed*-festival, Room '**V**' as well as the other nearby rooms were converted into a mummification or embalming center, often referred to as *Per Nefer*, or the *House of Beauty*, though it seems odd to associate *death* with the notion of *beauty*. (Never let it be said the ancient Egyptians did not possess a sense of irony!) In this context, the hieroglyph for 'beauty' can also mean 'good' or 'happy'. This certainly is in keeping with their beliefs of what lies beyond the veil of life in heaven. The hieroglyph itself represents the heart and windpipe, so associating the sign for 'beauty' with embalming a body is not so farfetched.

Gardiner Sign List Nos. – O1 and F35   '*pr nfr*', "House of Beauty"

Finally, the dimensions of the Lion Base are 1.05 meters wide by 0.62 meters deep by 0.35 meters high (3.44 feet x 2.03 feet x 1.15 feet).[38] As you can tell from its relatively small size, the Lion Base might not be able to accommodate the typical bed used by ancient Egyptians, which have legs at their extreme corners. For a person standing 5 feet tall or less (the average height of an ancient Egyptian male) would necessitate a radical design change from the norm. Nothing is impossible, but given its relatively small size, the Lion Base was probably not a bedstead at all like the ones we know. (Sorry Mr. Firth, Mr. Quibell seems to have gotten this one right.) Still, Room 'V' may have served as a place of rest for the king with the placement of a bed on its platform during the Ḥeb-Sed. The shape of the room in the form of the hieroglyph for 'god' (*ntr*) lends credence to this inasmuch the belief was that on Earth the pharaoh was a god.

If we take stock of every available artifact from ancient Egypt, I would wager that there has not been a discovery of a bedstead made of limestone. If the initial installation of the Lion Base was in Room 'V', and was to be a temporary fixture for use only during Djoser's *sed*-festival, then from a practical standpoint, it does not make sense to create such a heavy piece of furniture for what is essentially a domestic setting. For example, when we look at the beds found in the tomb of Tutankhamun (*Fig. 3-79*), all are made of gilt-covered wood and are light in weight. A limestone bedstead in a room south of the Ḥeb-Sed Court only makes sense if you are going to repurpose it later, in this case, reusing the Lion Base as a natron table.

Fig. 3-79 – Tutankhamun's lion headed bed

My guess is the first use of the Lion Base was as a throne-base or offering table situated on the South Altar, which should be thought of more as a throne dais and not an altar. This is where Djoser would have sat prior to running around the B-shaped *boundary markers* as part of the Ḥeb-Sed. After completion of the *sed*-festival, the Lion Base was possibly repurposed as a natron table when the Ḥeb-Sed Court became a medical center. This means Room 'V' underwent a conversion from being the king's bedchamber. First, the lightweight bed was removed from the stone platform. Then, with the extraction of several stones from the center of the platform, the Lion Base was inserted into the vacated space.

Further indirect proof that these rooms south of the Ḥeb-Sed Court were an embalming center is that every modern hospital has a morgue where the bodies of deceased patients are kept prior to sending the remains to the local coroner, a mortuary or funeral home. This ancient Egyptian medical center was no different in that respect. The inclusion within a hospital of a facility that prepared the body for burial (in this case, by way of embalming) in the event of a patient's death would be appropriate then as it is today.

The only mystery to uncover now is how the Lion Base wound up in the Entrance Hall where it clearly wasn't meant to be. Given several possibilities of its intended purpose, it is highly unlikely that the original installation of the Lion Base was in the place of its discovery in the Entrance Hall. The Entrance Hall functioned as a ceremonial processional space leading to the Great South Court and the interior of the Step Pyramid Enclosure as a whole. If the Lion Base were truly a "bedstead" or "throne-base", then it definitely would not have been its original location. (Taking a nap on a stone bedstead in the middle of a ceremonial corridor is highly unlikely, and not very comfortable, either.) With its darkened interior, making offerings would also be impractical if not impossible, especially if it were a burnt offering. Moreover, kings generally do not like sitting on a throne hidden halfway down a dark corridor out of the spotlight.

We have already mentioned how hard it must have been to remove the Lion Base had it originally been located on top of the South Altar. If the excavation photos from the 1920's are any indication, much of the Step Pyramid Enclosure was littered with massive piles of stone and dirt that had piled up over the centuries, so moving a heavy object like the Lion Base would make it that much more difficult. Proof of this comes from the fact that most of the lion heads had broken off during the move (see *Fig. 3-66*). However, if Room 'V' was its original home, how did the Lion Base get to the **T10** space in the Entrance Hall? One possibility is that as the Lion Base was being moved, it had to be hoisted up and over the top of the infill material just north of the Entrance Hall as this was the easiest way to get it out rather than maneuvering it through the Embalming Center's winding corridors. Apparently, mudbricks filled in the **L3** doorway on the Entrance Hall's north side, [39] so that path was blocked.

By that time, much destruction and deconstruction had taken place, and the walls and infill were reduced from their original height with much of the stone carted away. Taking this route over the infill seems to have been their only choice. This opens up another mystery: Since the **L3** doorway was the only way in or out of the Ḥeb-Sed Court after the completion of the *sed*-festival, why and when was the doorway to the Ḥeb-Sed Court hospital bricked up? My suspicion is that during the removal of the stones from the Step Pyramid Enclosure to build the Monastery of St. Jerome or other projects, whoever was doing the harvesting wanted a nice big chunk of limestone to use. However, they didn't realize how difficult it was to move such a heavy block from Room '**V**' over the accumulated massive piles of dirt and rubble that accumulated over the centuries, and just dumped the Lion Base in the space between two pillars in the Entrance Hall that I have designated as **T10** (see Fig. 3-65).

Having come this far in our investigation of the Step Pyramid Enclosure, one thing becomes evident the more we examine the architecture of this incredible monument:

The person who designed the Step Pyramid Enclosure must surely have had a working knowledge of human anatomy.

If we were to search for definitive proof of Imhotep's skill as a physician, we need only look at his monumental work as an architect, for in that sense, the proof of his being a physician is *hiding in plain sight*, and cannot be considered a coincidence. Instead of referring to the festival courtyard with its elaborate and elegant *chapels* strictly as the *Ḥeb-Sed Court*, perhaps we should call it the "Imhotep Memorial Hospital and *Per-Nefer* ("House of Beauty") Embalming Center".

Is all this the product of wild ideas imprinting a modern interpretation of an ancient monument? Maybe, but it might be the design of a modern hospital's patient care center is a product of this temple's design that is *baked into* our genes. For example, the inclusion of an embalming center/mortuary into the design of a hospital may be a tradition unconsciously remembered from ancient Egypt whose civilization lasted over 4000 years. Genetic imprinting of many facets derived from ancient Egypt would take that long to become part of all human DNA that has since been passed down to us. Over time, the notion of a hospital functioning with a separate mortuary might be part of our genetic *inheritance* from ancient Egypt unconsciously organizing our modern ideas along similar lines as those of the ancient Egyptians.

Our personal beliefs are more than the ideas and philosophies inherited from our parents, siblings, authority figures of all kinds and society in general. Embedded in our DNA is what we believe to be the *order of the Universe*, passed down by countless ancestors from millennia ago. It is easily demonstrable that the repetitive pattern of behavior of any species be it man or animal, will alter its DNA, and become inbred with succeeding generations.

Domesticated cats' behavior is good example of this observation. In ancient times, cats were just another wild animal living on the periphery of the communities of humans. As humans became more settled and developed farming as a source of food and less dependent on hunting and gathering, cats noticed mice and other rodents – their primary food source – in the cereal grains the *two-legged creatures* harvested and stored near their homes. Soon, a kind of *rapprochement* ensued where farmers allowed the cats roam freely in their storage bins to catch and kill the vermin found there.

No one knows when it happened, but one day, a cat came bearing a *gift* of a dead mouse to a farmer. Though he was surprised at the cat's boldness, the farmer gave the cat some sort of reward for its efforts – perhaps a small fish the farmer had caught in the nearby river – which the cat gratefully accepted, and scampered off with it new prize. (This may seem farfetched, but I personally observed this behavior when visiting the Greek island of Fourni. A cat came onto the dock where a fisherman had just returned with his fresh catch of the day. The fisherman obviously knew the cat, and gave it a little fish, which the cat eagerly grabbed and ran off with its *reward*.) This inbred behavior is typical in today's housebound cats who will bring a *dead* toy to a *staff member* of its human entourage for some much needed affection or food. (Yes, I really meant *staff member*. It is a well-known fact among pet parents that dogs have masters, but cats have staff!) Perhaps this peculiar behavior of cats is another example of genetic imprinting after being worshipped as gods for centuries in ancient Egypt.

It isn't necessary to view ancient Egyptian temples through the lens of only one philosophical viewpoint. By readjusting our personal *filters*, we can begin to see these ancient wonders much as the ancient Egyptians did. It would be easy to say that what I have postulated in this book is the product of a fevered, overactive imagination filtered through a 21st century mind-set. It is true we create our personal beliefs from our own experiences in the modern world, but maybe – just maybe – these experiences are not so different from those of our ancestors. Though the world of ancient Egypt and our own are light years apart, we share the one thing that transcends time and space – our humanity. The ancient Egyptians are not the static images found on monuments and in burial chambers. They were flesh and blood human beings much like us in many ways; with the same hope, wishes and dreams we all have in common. Certainly, the external details of our lives today versus those in ancient Egypt are radically different, but maybes the way we view our world and how we create what we think are new ideas are really part our genetic makeup inherited from the ancient Egyptians – at least partly – and we don't really know or recognize it.

To expand our vision beyond the limitations of our present-day personal paradigms, we need to realize that life is a voyage of self-discovery. It just takes a little bit of courage to weigh anchor, and sail on to our next great adventure.

When you change the way you look at things, the things you look at change.

Max Planck, German Physicist

Imhotep the Priest – The South Entrance Hall and the Weighing of the Heart Ceremony

Virtually every recent photograph of the interior of the South Entrance Hall shows a somewhat brightly lit and sunny environment. Back in ancient times; however, it was more than likely to have had a dark and closed-in feeling to it. The effect of small clerestory windows situated high up in the walls near the roof of the Entrance Hall kept it quite dimly lit at all times. Further enhancing this mysterious atmosphere, the half-columns were painted red, and the small alcoves between the columns painted black. This was intentional, as the Entrance Hall was an allegory for the dark tunnel that a person goes through after leaving the world of the flesh. Moving towards a bright light at the end of this passageway, the newly freed soul enters the bright and luminous world of spirit.

Fig. 4-1 – The South Entrance Hall as it may have appeared in ancient times

As seen in *Fig. 4-1*, Imhotep has recreated what has been reported by thousands of people who have died and come back to tell the tale. The most prevalent story told by persons that have had near death experiences is that when they left their body, they felt compelled to move towards a bright light at the end of a long, dark tunnel.

One can only wonder if Imhotep knew about this phenomenon, but in modern times, many patients declared clinically dead and subsequently resuscitated tell their doctors what they experienced when they *died*. While doctors were often skeptical at first, after so many patients repeatedly telling the same story, they eventually had to accept the possibility of life after death. In Imhotep's day, the certainty of life after death was never in doubt. As a physician, Imhotep would no doubt have attended the passing of many of his patients. It is entirely feasible Imhotep would have had patients who told similar stories if they returned from the dead.

Another possibility is that as a lector priest trained in the Temple of Ra-Atum at Heliopolis, Imhotep may have had a similar out-of-body experience resulting from a deep meditation, or even as part of an initiation ritual. In either case, the effect of entering a darkened Entrance Hall before exiting into the brilliant, intense light of the Egyptian sun would have been quite impressive and inspiring; much like the feeling of intense awe upon entering the soaring, lofty heights of a Gothic cathedral.

In addition to doctors observing the near death experience, relatives and hospice workers have also observed something curious when sitting at the bedside of a person during the final stage of life. Many have reported seeing a glowing orb of white light rising from the top of the person's head when they take their last breath. In fact, in a couple of different studies where palliative caregivers (those who take care of terminally ill patients) were interviewed, between one-third to one-half reported seeing a radiant light enveloping the entire room in the moments after the death of the patient, which was also witnessed by family members.[40]

To an ancient Egyptian, '*going to the West*' symbolized a person's soul moving from the world of the living to the underworld of the Afterlife, known as the *Am Duat*. This journey, mirrored in the natural world with the daily journey of the sun being *reborn* every day in the east, and *dying* every evening at sunset as it sets below the western horizon. Pharaohs of ancient Egypt were always associated with the falcon-headed god, Horus. At his passing, the announcement of the pharaoh's death was declared with "The Falcon has flown to heaven, and (his successor) has arisen in his place", or more simply put, "The Falcon has flown to the West". In Western tradition, the expression most often used is "The King is dead; long live the (next) king".

It has become clear to this point that Imhotep was capable of embedding multiple layers of esoteric wisdom into his design of the Step Pyramid Enclosure. To that end, a person entering the Step Pyramid Enclosure from the east, and walking down the Entrance Hall, is quite literally *going to the west*. Because the Exit Vestibule symbolically represents the human head, leaving the Entrance Hall out through the Exit Vestibule into the Great South Court, imitates a person's soul leaving the body from the top of the head to continue their journey to the next world. In essence, they have moved from the world of the living to the world of the dead (or immortal ones, according ancient Egyptian religious thought). By extension, the area within the Step Pyramid's Enclosure Walls is a symbolic representation of the *Am Duat* under the reign of Osiris, the God of the Underworld. Everything outside the Enclosure Walls represents the world that the soul has left behind. Though this is highly speculative, if ancient Egyptians (and especially Imhotep when working as a physician) had observed a wispy, shining ball of light leaving from a person's head at the moment of their death, then this would be absolute proof that Imhotep embodied the human spine and skull into the design of the Entrance Hall.

An indirect proof that ancient Egyptians may have known about this phenomena are statues of various pharaohs with the protective effigy of a falcon wrapping its wings around the king's neck which some think is the god Horus. However, depictions of Horus portray him with a falcon head on a human body. For this reason, the falcon on the neck of a pharaoh may actually represent the **ba**, or personality of the king, unified after death with the **ka**, the spiritual essence or life force of the soul, together becoming the **akh**, or the transfigured self. In other illustrations, the portrayal of the **ba** is a human-headed falcon representing the person's spirit flying above their body after mummification. If the falcon sitting behind the head of a pharaoh represents the king's spirit in the moments after death, then it is reasonable that the ancient Egyptians believed the soul exited the body from the area of the head. In the thousands of years of ancient Egyptian history, it is quite likely this observation took place many, many times.

Fig. 4-2 - Statue of Khafre with Horus Falcon

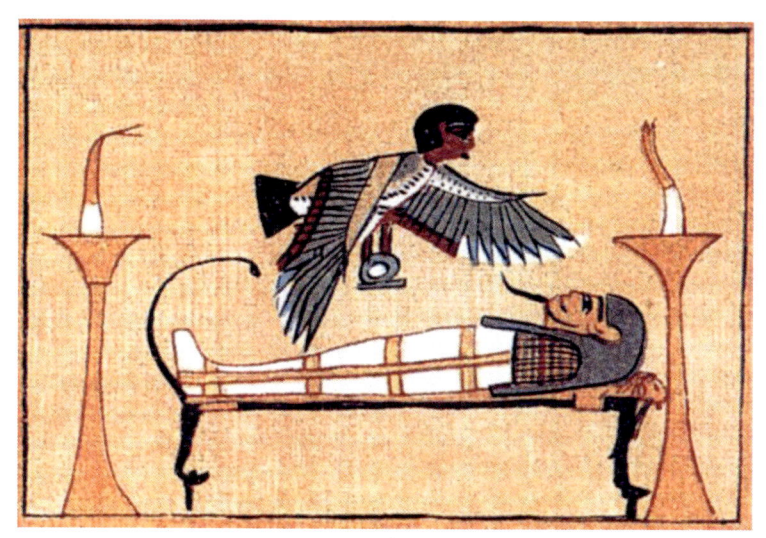

Fig. 4-3 - The Ba of the deceased Ani hovering over his mummy holding the hieroglyphic sign 'shenu', which means 'circuit (of the sun)', implying the completion of the life cycle

The Weighing of the Heart Ceremony

Since everything within the Step Pyramid Enclosure symbolically relates to the Afterlife, the interior of the enclosure duplicates characteristics of the *Field of Reeds* (*Sekhet-Aaru*). Because the Entrance Hall is inside the Enclosure, it also has a function directly involving a certain stage in the experience of the Afterlife, namely the *Weighing of the Heart Ceremony*.

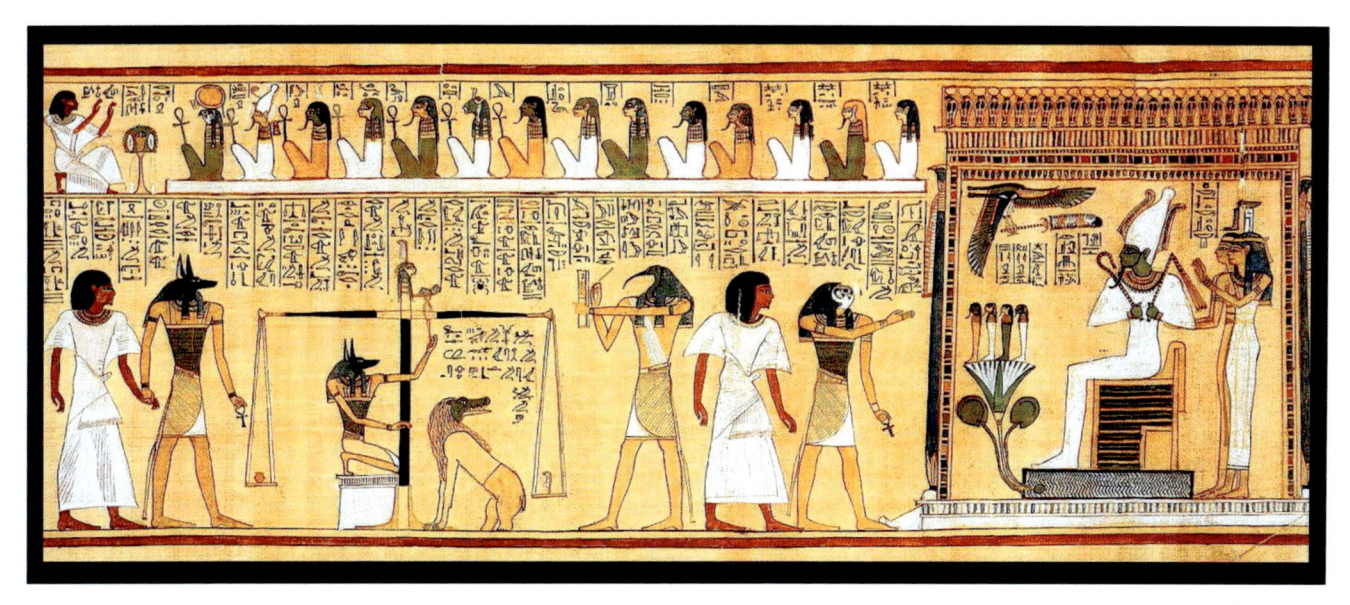

Fig. 4-4 – The Weighing of the Heart Ceremony -The Papyrus of Hunefer

On the left, Anubis weighs the deceased Hunefer's heart on the Scales of Maat, with Thoth recording the outcome. Ammit, the Devourer, waits behind Thoth to see if she gets a free meal today! On the right, Horus leads the newly 'justified' Hunefer into the presence of Osiris, the God of the Underworld, his wife, Isis, and her sister Nephthys before continuing on to the Afterlife.

The most important and elaborate funerary rituals practiced in ancient Egypt were reserved for royalty and the elite. The average person would have felt fortunate even to have a coffin, let alone one with scenes and spells from the *Book of the Dead* painted on it. Priests or a tomb artisans working as a kind of side job often produced such coffins. If you were *really* lucky, or at the least very wealthy, important funerary rituals like purification, mummification and the Opening of the Mouth Ceremony would be performed after your death.

Fig. 4-5 – Another version of The Book of Going Forth into the Light from Deir el-Medina showing all 42 Assessor-gods in the top two registers

Ancient Egyptians believed that after they were buried, their journey in the Afterlife began by going through the gates of the *Am Duat*, and correctly reciting the name of each gate's guardian permits them to continue on to the next phase known as the Weighing of the Heart Ceremony. As part of this ceremony, the jackal-headed god, Anubis, led the newly arrived person into the Hall of Judgment to recite the so-called 42 negative confessions before a tribunal of 42 Assessors or Judges. The negative confessions were declarations of their innocence from having committed sinful deeds beginning with the words "I have not..." such as "I have not *stolen*" or "I have not *uttered lies*". If they passed these tests, Anubis guided them to the next test in the Hall of Maat. This resembles the *life review*, often related by those who have had a near death experience.

The 42 Principles of Maat (The Negative Confessions)

1. I have not committed sin.
2. I have not committed robbery with violence.
3. I have not stolen.
4. I have not slain men or women.
5. I have not stolen food.
6. I have not swindled offerings.
7. I have not stolen from God/Goddess.
8. I have not uttered lies.
9. I have not carried away food.
10. I have not cursed.
11. I have not closed my ears to truth.
12. I have not committed adultery.
13. I have not made anyone cry.
14. I have not felt sorrow without reason.
15. I have not assaulted anyone.
16. I am not deceitful.
17. I have not stolen anyone's land.
18. I have not been an eavesdropper.
19. I have not falsely accused anyone.
20. I have not been angry without reason.
21. I have not seduced anyone's wife.
22. I have not polluted myself.
23. I have not terrorized anyone.
24. I have not disobeyed the Law.
25. I have not been exclusively angry.
26. I have not cursed God/Goddess.
27. I have not behaved with violence.
28. I have not caused disruption of peace.
29. I have not acted hastily or without thought.
30. I have not overstepped my boundaries of concern.
31. I have not exaggerated my words when speaking.
32. I have not worked evil.
33. I have not used evil thoughts, words or deeds.
34. I have not polluted the water.
35. I have not spoken angrily or arrogantly.
36. I have not cursed anyone in thought, word or deeds.
37. I have not placed myself on a pedestal.
38. I have not stolen what belongs to God/Goddess.
39. I have not stolen from or disrespected the deceased.
40. I have not taken food from a child.
41. I have not acted with insolence.
42. I have not destroyed property belonging to the God/Goddess

During the ceremony, Anubis placed their heart, or ***ib***, on a scale weighing it against the Feather of Truth, the symbol of the goddess of truth, order and justice, Maat. The ibis-headed god, Thoth, the scribe of the gods and the god of wisdom, would record these proceedings. If their heart was deemed to be as light or lighter than the Feather of Truth, implying it was devoid of evil, the deceased person would be declared *true of voice* and ushered into the presence of Osiris, the god of the Underworld by his son, Horus. If their heart weighed too much, this meant it was heavy from all of the misdeeds and transgressions they committed during their lifetime, a ferocious goddess called Ammit would eat their heart. Ammit, also known as the Devourer or Destroyer, was the most unique of the gods. She possessed the head of a crocodile, the forepaws of a lion and the hindquarters of a hippopotamus, embodying the three most vicious, predatory animals in all of ancient Egypt. To have one's heart eaten by Ammit meant the destruction of your soul, and you would cease to exist forever. (*Not a good thing!*)

If they passed this final test, Horus, the falcon-headed god, led the person into the presence of his father Osiris, the God of the Underworld, who sits on the Throne of Maat. Isis, his wife and her sister Nephthys, stand behind Osiris. Upon learning of the deceased person's honor and truthfulness from Horus, Osiris admits them into the Afterlife to reside in the *Field of Reeds* (*Sekhet-Aaru*) where they live for eternity in much the same manner as they had lived their life on Earth.

As discussed before, the ancient Egyptians considered the heart to be the seat of wisdom, or the source of higher intuitive faculties. It was not only the primary organ of the body; it functioned as the gateway to that *other realm* which lies beyond the five senses. To listen to, and be in harmony with the Wisdom of the Heart would forever connect a person to the Divine Source that created them and the Universe they lived in. If they did so, they would be *Living-In-Truth*, or *maat*, that is, Divine Order, harmony and balance. Thus, they would attain the highest level of intelligence and knowledge possible and live the fullest life for any human to guarantee immortality in heaven.

Secondly, the heart was believed to be the repository of a person's emotions, intellect, will and morality, and within it was recorded the sum total of a person's behavior and actions during their lifetime. The heart was the only ritually mummified abdominal organ by wrapping in special bandages, and for the wealthy, a heart scarab placed upon it for protection. The reinsertion of the heart into to the chest cavity occurred prior to wrapping the body in linen to complete the mummification process.

Based on the finding of statues parts in the Entrance Hall during the initial excavations in the 1920s and 1930s, Egyptologists Wolfgang Helck and Hans Goedicke thought the Entrance Hall was a "statue palace" with the placement of statues in between the columns. Helck was of the opinion that one or more statues of the pharaoh stood in as a proxy during the resurrection rituals performed in the Entrance Hall after Djoser's death by his successor. Goedicke, on the other hand, thought statues of the gods stationed between the columns were a symbolic part of a judgment ritual involving the pharaoh, perhaps similar to the Weighing of the Heart Ceremony.[41]

The one problem with either theory is that there is no evidence of the installation of statues in the Entrance Hall, and the statues parts that were uncovered in the 1920s and 1930s may not have been in their original location. It is certain that the installation of 42 statues of the gods of judgment between the columns did not occur since there are only 39 spaces between the columns for at the most, 40 statues because of several passageways and rooms that exit from the sides of the Entrance Hall along its length. Besides, the very dark interior as it originally existed would have made it very difficult to see the statues even if they *were* there, negating whatever intention for placing them there in the first place.

Just as the human spine was concealed within the architecture of the Entrance Hall, so too was the Weighing of the Heart Ceremony. As it is readily apparent, there are 42 pillars lining the length of the Entrance Hall – 40 semi-round and the two square **T3** columns. These columns symbolically represent the 42 Judges or Assessors who examined the behavior of deceased Egyptians during their recent life in the Weighing of the Heart Ceremony. These columns actually symbolize this ancient after-death ritual, not the spaces between the columns as some have asserted. The reason most have missed the connection of these 42 columns to the Weighing of the Heart Ceremony is that the two square columns were not considered to be columns like the 40 other semi-round columns. This is another of the hidden secrets created by Imhotep.

The four double columns of the Exit Vestibule also played a symbolic role in the Weighing of the Heart Ceremony, though the symbolism is not quite as apparent as with the other 42 columns in the Entrance Hall. In virtually every written depiction of the Weighing of the Heart Ceremony, there are eight gods who are almost always depicted in one form or another depending on how detailed the scribe who wrote the papyrus wanted to make it.

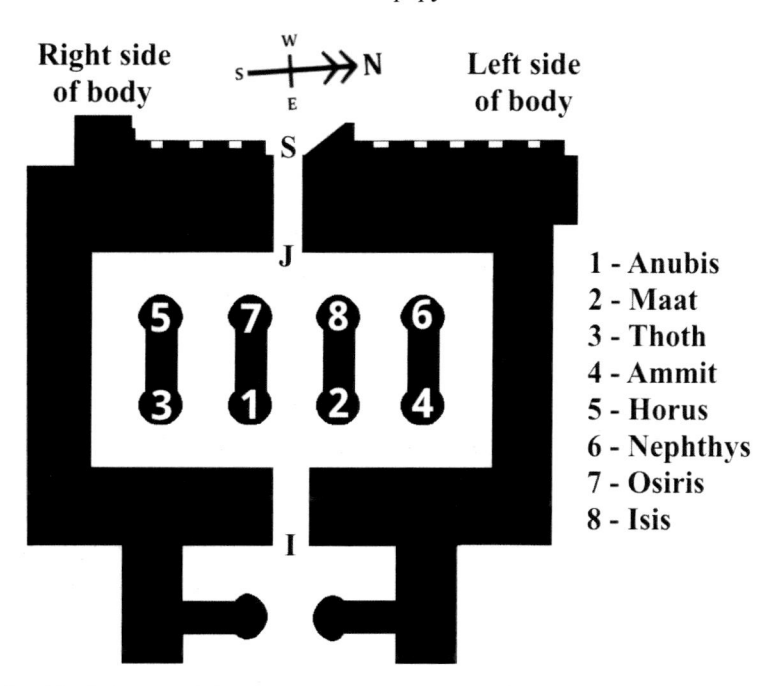

Fig. 4-6 – The 4 Double Columns of the Exit Vestibule and the 8 Gods and Goddesses associated with them

1 - Anubis
2 - Maat
3 - Thoth
4 - Ammit
5 - Horus
6 - Nephthys
7 - Osiris
8 - Isis

When looking at a top-view plan of the Entrance Hall and Exit Vestibule, we are viewing the human body as if from the front (anterior). In *Fig. 4-6*, the four female goddesses who are most often shown in various copies of the Weighing of the Heart Ceremony are associated with the two double pillars located on the north side of the Exit Vestibule (i.e., left side of the body). The two double pillars on the south side (i.e., right side of the body) are associated with the male gods.

This aligns with several esoteric traditions where the left side of the body is the feminine or introverted, receptive side, and the right side is the masculine or extroverted, active side. Despite the appearance of being arbitrary as to which half-column represents which god, it is generally consistent with the order in which the deceased person encounters each god in the Weighing of the Heart Ceremony depending on which copy of the *Book of the Dead* you are studying. Since there is no official canon of this text, every copy of it discovered thus far was custom made for its owner.

It is unclear if the average Egyptian knew the South Entrance Hall was an allegorical representation of the experience of transitioning to the Afterlife. If they did, they knew that when they entered the South Entrance Gate, they were symbolically leaving the world of the living, and were literally *going to the west* through the Entrance Hall with its 42 pillars representing the 42 Assessors (*Fig. 4-7*). In so doing, they were taking part in a proxy trial from the Weighing of the Heart Ceremony. Leaving the Exit Vestibule and its representations of the eight gods one meets before entering the Afterlife, they entered the Great South Court, symbolically arriving at the *Field of Reeds*, the Egyptian heaven. They may have even taken part in a ceremony of some sort at the South Altar near the base of the Step Pyramid. To complete the circuit of this sacred ritual, they would walk past the South Pavilion, the North Mortuary Temple and pass behind the North Pavilion to leave through the North Exit Gate.

By leaving the Step Pyramid Enclosure through the North Exit Gate, a person has symbolically left the realm of spirit to be reborn into flesh. Having a one-way door installed in this gate reinforces the notion that one cannot return to the world of the spirit in the same way one has left it. The only way a person can re-enter the spiritual dimension is to go through the death process or some other method of spiritual transformation or physical transfiguration when one symbolically *goes to the west* by walking through the South Entrance Hall. This is alluded to in many spiritual texts including the *Book of the Dead*, (which should more rightly be translated as *The Book of Going Forth by Day*, or even perhaps, given the current research on near death experiences, it could even be called *The Book of Going Forth into the Light*).

If Imhotep truly embedded portions of the *Book of Going Forth into Light* into the design of the South Entrance Hall, then it is safe to say he has given us one of Egypt's oldest and most revered religious texts, albeit one written in stone and not papyrus.

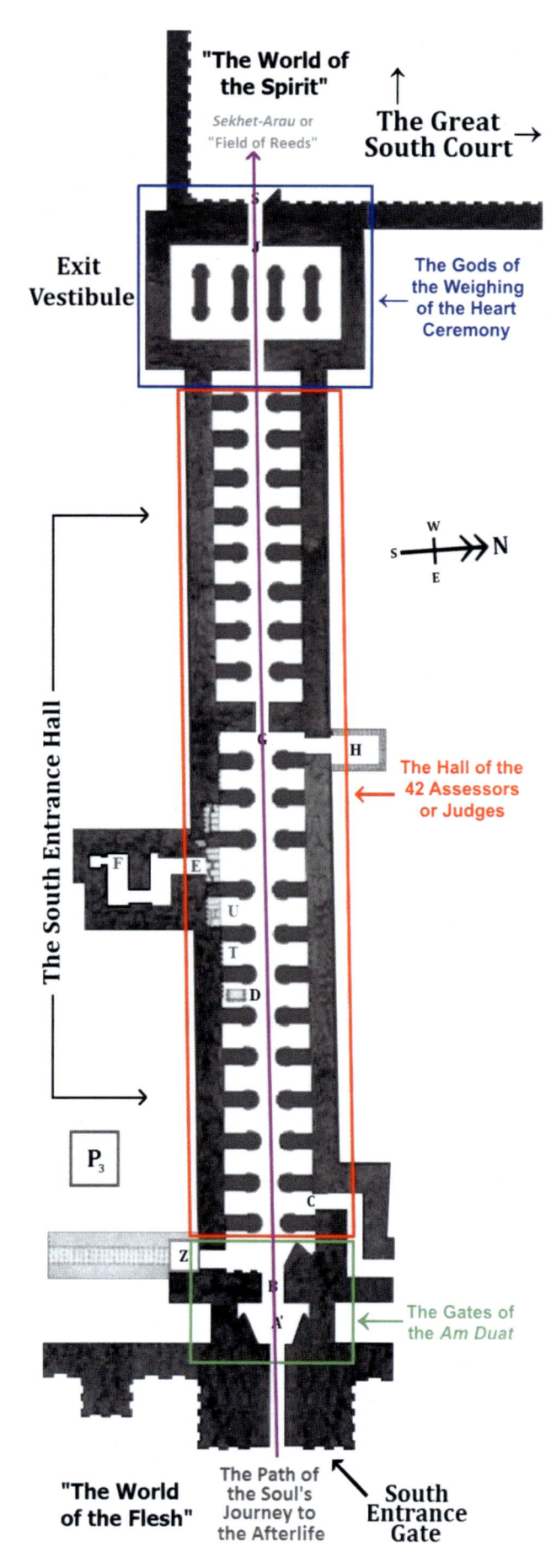

Fig. 4-7 – The South Entrance Hall as a metaphor for the Weighing of the Heart Ceremony

The 'Magic Number 2'

In Chapter 1, there was brief discussion on the concept of duality in relationship to the number of gates (2) typically found in Egyptian temples of the Third Dynasty and later. Having two of anything in sacred architecture was the norm as well as almost everything in ancient Egyptian life. Because the principle of duality was so universal in ancient Egyptian culture and society, it was inevitable it found its expression in their sacred architecture as well. The most obvious is the set of double pylons found on virtually every ancient Egyptian temple as previously shown in Chapter 1. Even a temple built by the Ptolemaic Greeks dedicated to two different gods near the town of Kom Ombo is a perfect illustration of this pervasive concept of duality (*Fig. 4-8*).

Fig. 4-8 – The Double Temple of Horus the Elder and Sobek at Kom Ombo

One possible esoteric reason why Imhotep extensively used the number 2 is the relationship between squared numbers. In the Squared Number Table below, we see that the *difference* between the differences of two squared numbers is always the same, that is, 2. From there, the number 2 reduces to zero (0).

A Whole Number	The Whole Number Squared	The *Difference* Between the Squares of the Two Numbers	The *Resulting Difference* Between the Differences	The *Difference* Between the Resulting Differences
10	$10^2 = 100$	------	------	------
9	$9^2 = 81$	100 - 81 = 19	------	------
8	$8^2 = 64$	81 - 64 = 17	19 - 17 = 2	------
7	$7^2 = 49$	64 - 49 = 15	17 - 15 = 2	2 - 2 = 0
6	$6^2 = 36$	49 - 36 = 13	15 - 13 = 2	2 - 2 = 0
5	$5^2 = 25$	36 - 25 = 11	13 - 11 = 2	2 - 2 = 0
4	$4^2 = 16$	25 - 16 = 9	11 - 9 = 2	2 - 2 = 0
3	$3^2 = 9$	16 - 9 = 7	9 - 7 = 2	2 - 2 = 0
2	$2^2 = 4$	9 - 4 = 5	7 - 5 = 2	2 - 2 = 0
1	$1^2 = 1$	4 - 1 = 3	5 - 3 = 2	2 - 2 = 0

The Squared Number Table

Although it was never explicitly articulated or documented in any of their religious texts, the number 2 is directly related to the concept of duality that permeated virtually every aspect of ancient Egyptian life. Duality was the one constant that tacitly articulated their beliefs concerning the underlying mechanism of the natural world around them, (i.e., *maat*, or Divine Order). Sunrise/sunset, good/evil, Seth/Horus, birth/death, inundation/rejuvenation are but some of the facets of this overarching belief system.

Though seemingly the most logical reduction from 2 (i.e., seeing nature and the universe through the lens of duality) in the Squared Number Table would be to further reduce it to 1 (symbolically viewing everything in nature as being interconnected and never separate from one another), an ancient Egyptian priest of the Old Kingdom might have understood something more profound. Zero (0) symbolically represents the Infinite Void or the place from where the god Ra-Atum created himself. In the more ancient creation myths, Atum is the Primal Creator, and created the first gods Shu, the god of peace, lions, air and wind, and Tefnut, the goddess of rain and moisture. Their children were Geb and Nut, the gods of the earth and sky, respectively. Geb and Nut's children were Osiris, Isis, Nephthys and Seth. This is the ennead of the nine ancient Egyptian gods honored and worshipped throughout its history.

The principle cult center in the Old Kingdom for Ra-Atum was Heliopolis where Imhotep was a high priest. Ra-Atum was often referred to as "he who created himself out of nothing". It is difficult for many in the modern world to wrap their heads around this concept, so most of us will categorize this idea as a fanciful myth or allegorical fiction and let it go at that. However, I believe it is probable that Imhotep knew there was something more to the notion of 'creating something out of nothing'. If he did, it is likely he embedded the *Magic Number 2* into his design of the Step Pyramid and its structures to inspire those who seek greater knowledge and wisdom to look past the concept of duality. Though not readily apparent, Imhotep used architectural design and the language of Sacred Geometry to give expression to these deeply esoteric teachings, albeit in a form that is not so easily discernible, not unlike the mysteries of the Universe itself.

In the book of Genesis 1:2, it says, "In the beginning was the Void. And the earth was without Form and Void; and darkness was upon the face of the deep. And the Spirit of God moved upon the face of the waters". It was allegedly written by a man who grew up in Egypt before leading his people to a new life in the land of their ancestors. Is it possible this man, who lived in the royal court, could have had access to this esoteric wisdom from the deepest, sacred teachings taught only in the inner sanctums of Egypt's temples?

As the consciousness of the human race continues to expand, the belief that duality is the inherent substructure of all of nature will slowly evolve towards seeing the singularity of nature/supernature. In order to progress to that level of awareness, one cannot eventually come to realize the Oneness of all of Creation without first realizing the Void is where the Universe itself was created (i.e. *Everything was created from Nothing*).

The *Magic Number 2* (i.e., duality) stands at the threshold of the Void and the heart of all creation. The act of creating anything in the physical world is a two-fold process: first, we create it in our minds, and second, then it manifests in physical form. It can be no other way. Did Imhotep secretly embed this great wisdom about duality and the *Magic Number 2* in the Step Pyramid Enclosure in order to teach us this? Is he showing us we can only approach spiritual Oneness with all of Creation by seeing the inherent limitations of duality, even while embracing it, and in the end, leaving it behind to recognize that everything is a single expression of an Infinite Universe? Is Imhotep acknowledging the innate natural creative energy of the Universe through the *Magic Number 2*? Perhaps when he repurposed the North and South Pavilions from the derelict, incomplete and unused mastabas they had become into a grand teaching tool, Imhotep was reaching out to us over the centuries to look beyond the obvious, and see things as they truly are.

There are many examples of the *Magic Number 2* throughout the Step Pyramid Enclosure. Although not readily or easily discernible, the *Magic Number 2* is rooted in the architecture of the Exit Vestibule at the end of the Entrance Hall. As shown earlier in this chapter, the Exit Vestibule has a greater meaning on so many levels other than serving as the entrance to the Great South Court. In one context, the Exit Vestibule serves as a gateway for the soul as it stands at the threshold of beginning another journey into the Afterlife. The Entrance Hall also uses architectural elements to embody duality in that one moves from a *compressed* space (the Entrance Hall) into an *expansive* space (the Great South Court).

In another context, the shape of the Exit Vestibule's double columns resembles that of the telophase of the mitosis process at the beginning of life where single cells repeatedly subdivide in two as discussed in Chapter 3, (see *Figs. 3-40* and *3-41*). This is inherently mathematical in that **multiplication can only occur through division**. Since the number of cells always doubles at every stage, this process continuously expresses the *Magic Number 2*. In this context, the Exit Vestibule symbolically becomes a different doorway for the continuity of life: the creation of a new physical human body wherein the soul resides during its next earthly journey. Consequently, the design of the double columns of the Exit Vestibule adds another layer of meaning related to birth, and is the perfect symbol for this Universal Creative Force.

Part of this *meaning of life* story also relates the Sacred Number 42 to the *Magic Number 2* in the gestation cycle of a human body from the moment of conception. The 2 cells at the beginning of the reproductive cycle divide into 4 cells, which then divides into 8, 16, 32, 64 cells, and so on, **until after *42* cell division iterations, a baby is born with a body consisting of about 10 trillion cells!** (By comparison, an adult human body is comprised of about 37.2 trillion cells.) It is difficult know if the ancient Egyptians knew of the relationship of the Sacred Number 42 to the cell division process and its importance to the creation of life. I can't help but think this advanced knowledge was passed down to the ancient Egyptians, who, it seems, did not grasp its significance because the underlying details seem to have degenerated over the millennia into myth and legend. Nevertheless, perhaps a certain ancient Egyptian architect/physician/priest knew of *something* stemming from a very secret oral tradition of esoteric wisdom that he subsequently incorporated into the design of the Step Pyramid Enclosure.

Life and death are one thread, the same line viewed from different sides.

Lao Tzu, Chinese Philosopher

Imhotep the Grand Vizier – The South Entrance Hall and the Civil Government of Egypt

In ancient Egypt, the central government revolved around the persona of the king. The king left the day-to-day operation of the civil government to his Viziers, or Prime Ministers. In later dynasties when a united Egyptian empire became too large for one vizier to handle the job, there were two viziers, one for the North and one for the South. Though there were probably two viziers during Djoser's reign, we know the most about only one – Imhotep.

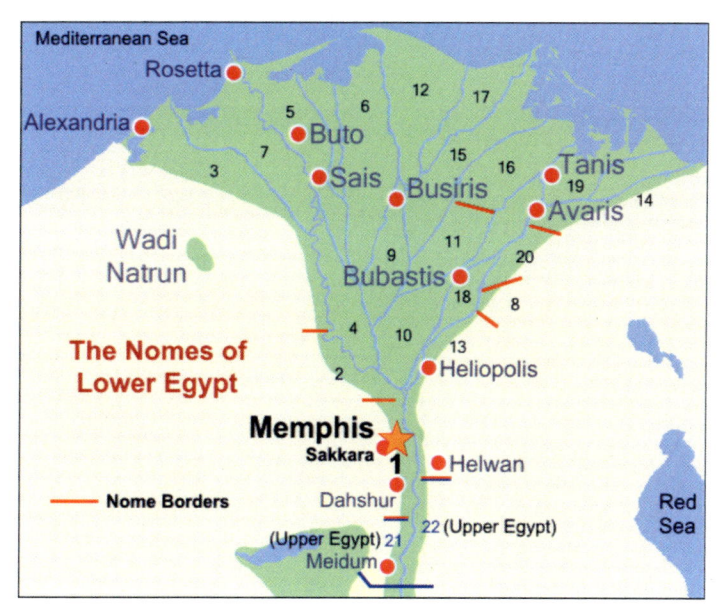

Fig. 5-1 – The 20 Nomes of Lower Egypt

While the central government ruled by pharaohs such as Netjerikhet Djoser and administered by viziers like Imhotep, 42 nomes or states run by nomarchs or governors, made up the substructure of Egyptian civil government. Nomarchs were similar to the titled nobility of medieval Europe, and the system in ancient Egypt was very much like the European feudal system of lords, dukes and earls that owed their position to the king. Though the nomarchs sometimes passed their title and office to their sons, the pharaoh could replace them if he felt they were incompetent or corrupt.

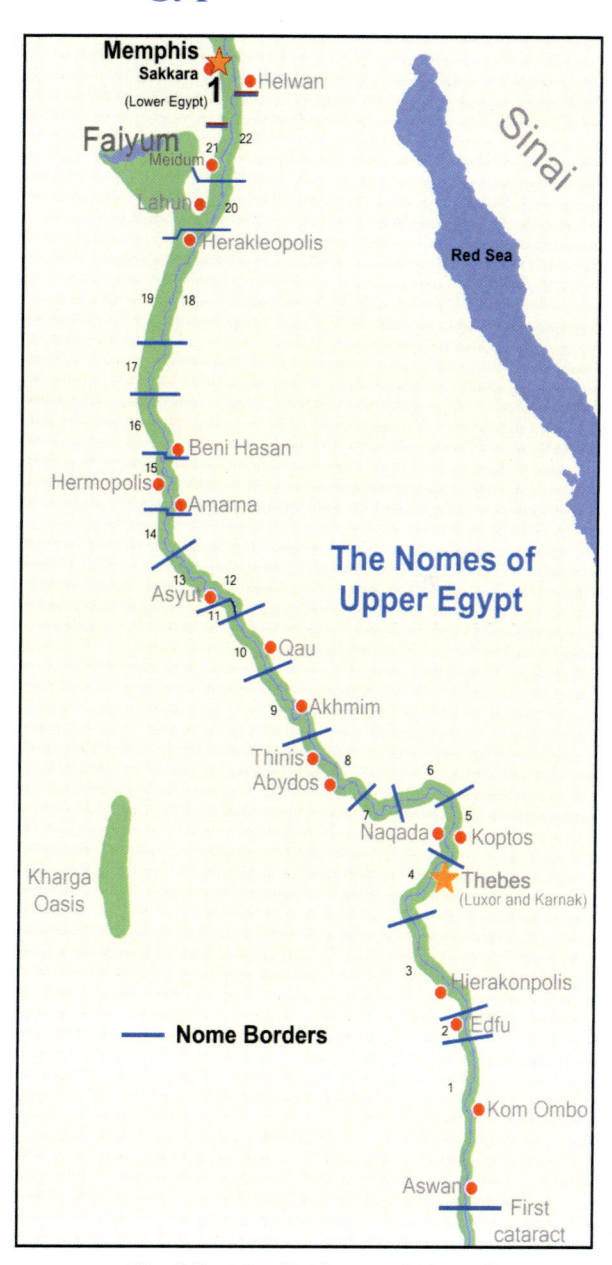

Fig. 5-2 – The 22 Nomes of Upper Egypt

In time of war, in addition to the major temples sending their temple guards to aid in the fighting, the nomarchs sent men from their villages to fight alongside the pharaoh's troops. Being farmers and local villagers, these men were not professional soldiers, but were trained by the troops of the king's standing army prior to battle. Some of these village soldiers acquitted themselves in battle so well that they received the same honors as the professional soldiers of the pharaoh's retinue.

Here is another manifestation of the Sacred Number 42 (nomes), divided by (the *Magic Number*) 2 regional groups – the North, or Lower Egypt, comprising 20 nomes; and the South, or Upper Egypt, consisting of 22 nomes. (The Egyptian *wisdom keeper*, Hakim, taught that 42 different tribes settled in the Nile valley that later became the unified nation of Egypt with its 42 nomes.) That Imhotep embedded the governmental structure of Egypt into the design of the South Entrance Hall is plain to see: there are 42 columns and 42 nomes. Many have said that 42 statues representing the gods of the 42 nomes were installed between the columns of the Entrance Hall. Basically, this is impossible. As shown in Chapter 4, when looking at a plan of the Entrance Hall, there are at most 39, or possibly 40 spaces to place statues between the 42 columns and doorways occupy the rest of the spaces. In addition, there is no direct evidence on the installation of statues at any point within the Entrance Hall. Further, the columns were painted red, and the alcoves between the columns painted black. Along with the inherent dark atmosphere of the Entrance Hall, it is unlikely any of these alleged statues could have been easily seen if at all. Once again, the only logical architectural elements that symbolize the 42 nomes would be the 42 columns of the Entrance Hall, and not the spaces between them.

While doing some research on the internet, I came across a number of videos made by people who visited the Step Pyramid. Despite their good intentions, many tour guides in Egypt get some of the finer details wrong when explaining the importance of the archeological sites they visit. (*That's okay – they mean well. There's an awful lot to learn about ancient Egyptian history after all.*) Some tour guides will tell you the South Entrance Hall has 42 columns; others may say it has only 40 columns. While it is apparently true there are only 40 columns, what often prevents anyone from associating the 42 nomes with the columns of the Entrance Hall is that, in their present incomplete stage of restoration, there are 40 semi-round columns and what looks like two square columns (the **T3** columns).

I say *looks like*, because in his book, *The Pyramids of Sakkarah*, Jean-Philippe Lauer illustrated what he thought the Entrance Hall may have looked like in the past (*Fig. 5-3*).[42]

However, there is more to this than meets the eye.

Looking down the corridor in this illustration, one can see a doorway. This is where the two **T3** columns are located. Part of the anomalous nature of the square **T3** columns is that Lauer's artistic reconstruction of the South Entrance Hall shows the two square columns as being part of a doorway with a lintel between them stretching up to the ceiling.[43] Looking closer at Lauer's drawing, it does not depict a door installed in the doorway. This can be confirmed, as there are no remnants of doorpost sockets in the floor adjacent to these two square columns.

Still, something is wrong with this picture. To my way of thinking, this just didn't feel right.

Fig. 5-3 – J.-P. Lauer's reconstruction of the South Entrance Hall

The anatomically symbolic nature of the two **T3** square columns as well as the **L5** columns has already been discussed in Chapter 3. While it is plausible the two square columns formed part of a doorway, why did Imhotep put a doorway (without a door, no less) in the middle of an Entrance Hall meant to be used for ritual processional purposes?

What purpose would this oddly placed doorway have served? Are the two square columns meant to stand alone, or are they a structural element that is part of a doorway? Did the doorway's incorporation in this part of the Entrance Hall serve some ritual purpose? Is the purpose, perhaps, symbolic? If so, what is it?

To clarify this further, we must define what is a column or pillar. Simply put, a column or pillar is an architectural element or upright structure that performs a load-bearing function, and supports an arch or superstructure such as a roof or ceiling. Being an architect himself, Jean-Philippe Lauer must have believed the existence of two square columns meant a doorway with a lintel above it was located here at one time. If putting a doorway at this location makes no sense, either architecturally or symbolically, then chances are the two square **T3** columns are just columns, and nothing else. If the two square columns were really part of a doorway as Lauer thought, they are still columns since they perform a structural load-bearing function. In short, if it holds up a roof, it's a column, regardless of anything else attached to it.

By now, it has become readily apparent Imhotep hid a great many things *in plain sight* within his design for the Step Pyramid Enclosure. A symbolic representation of the civil government of Egypt is just one of those not-so-hidden secrets.

Leaving the Entrance Hall to go out to the Great South Court, we pass through the Exit Vestibule with its four rectangular freestanding columns. In the middle of the Great South Court are two capital B-shaped objects (*Fig. 5-4*).

Fig. 5-4 – The north "boundary marker" in the Great South Court

While their purpose is not readily apparent, these B-shaped structures are thought to be symbolic *boundary markers* representing the borders of Upper and Lower Egypt around which the king would run as part of the *sed*-festival held on the thirtieth anniversary of his reign. As mentioned before, by running around these *boundary markers*, the Pharaoh symbolically encircles his kingdom and renews his right to rule the whole of Egypt. We don't know why their shape looks like the capital letter '**B**', but they do resemble similar semi-circular glyphs found on representations of Djoser and other kings running the *sed*-festival course like the ones found in the blue-faience rooms under the Step Pyramid and the South Tomb.

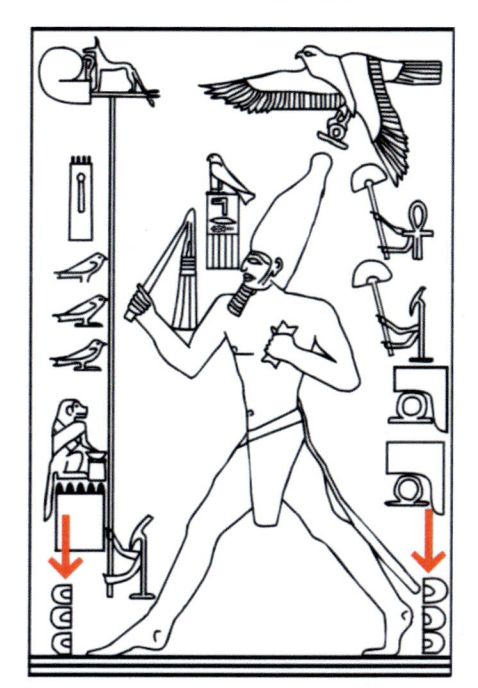

Fig. 5-5 – Pharaoh Djoser running in the sed-festival
Note the semi-circular symbols (red arrows) that are similar to the two 'capital B'-shaped boundary markers in the Great South Court.

Fig. 5-6 – Pharaoh Hatshepsut running the Ḥeb-Sed course with the Apis bull. The red arrow indicates the "boundary markers" (Manna Nader, Gabana Studios, Cairo)

Since the 42 columns of the South Entrance Hall correspond to the 42 nomes of Egypt's civil government, the First and Second Nomes of Lower Egypt are represented by the two pillars situated just before the two square **T3** columns bounded by the **T4** and **T5** spaces (just above the double red lines in *Fig. 5-7*). To the right (north) of the **T4** space is the chamber marked by the letter '**H**'. As shown in Chapter 3, this chamber symbolizes the heart and its position inside the rib cage. Once again, the ancient Egyptians regarded the heart as the most important organ in the body.

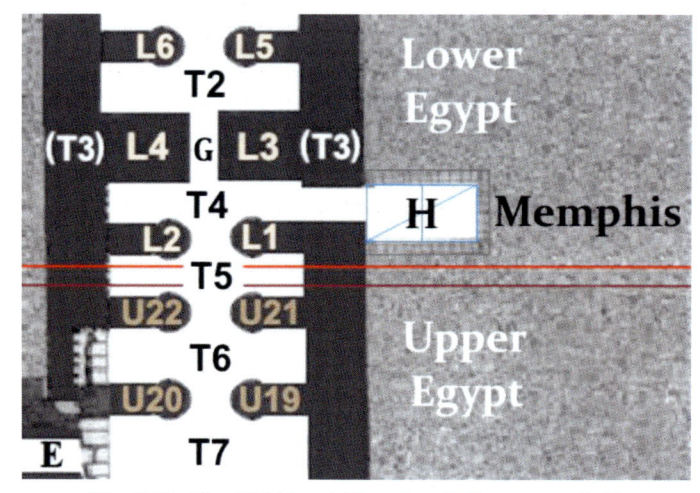

Fig. 5-7 – The 'T4' Heart Chamber ('H') as a symbolic representation for the capital of Egypt, Memphis

While it is possible the two square columns in the middle of the Entrance Hall were not part of a wall structure with a lintel spanning the space above the corridor, there may be a symbolic reason for having a doorway in the middle of a ceremonial passageway.

The capital of Egypt, Memphis was located in the First Nome of Lower (Northern) Egypt. If the Entrance Hall was also a symbolic representation of the civil government structure of Egypt's 42 nomes, the semi-round column that represents the First Nome of Lower Egypt is next to the small room (marked as '**H**' in *Fig. 5-7*). It is no accident the '**H**' room, or *Heart Chamber*, is adjacent to that column. Here is yet another layer of hidden meaning to the Entrance Hall.

In essence, Imhotep is symbolically telling us the 'H' (Heart) Chamber represents Memphis – the capital city of Egypt for many millennia – and the *heart of Egypt*.

Fig. 5-8 – Artist's conception of the ancient city of Memphis and the Temple of Ptah (J. C. Golvin)

Moreover, if Imhotep immortalized his hometown, Memphis, in this part of the Entrance Hall, then the two square **T3** columns adjacent to the *Heart Chamber*, besides doing double duty as representing the Third and Fourth Nomes, may well symbolize part of a certain architectural feature long associated with the ancient city of Memphis.

The original name for Memphis was *Hut-Ka-Ptah* ('Temple of the *Ka* of Ptah') or *Hiku-Ptah*. (The Greeks altered this to *Aegyptus*, which eventually became *Egypt*, the name for the entire country.) Later, the city of *Hut-Ka-Ptah* was called *Inebu-hedj*, which translates as *white walls* because of the famous white, plaster covered walls that encircled the city. The name of the city during the Middle Kingdom (ca. 2055-1650 BCE) was *Ankh-Tawy* meaning *Life of the Two Lands*, and during the New Kingdom its name was *Mennefer*, (which the Greeks pronounced as "Memphis"), and means *enduring and beautiful*. The white walls of Memphis provided protection for the city against any invading forces, and may have even have kept the city dry during the months of the inundation.

Lauer thought the Enclosure Wall itself was a giant metaphor for the famous "white walls" of Memphis, and the 14 false gates represented the city gates in that wall. [44] Even though the capital city of Egypt was probably known as *Hut-Ka-Ptah* during the Third Dynasty, colloquially it might have been called "white walls" before any formal name change to the later *Inebu-hedj*. If this is so, the two square **T3** columns could indeed have been part of a wall structure with a doorway that symbolized the *white walls* of Memphis, as seen in Lauer's illustration. The symbolic placement of a wall and doorway at this location along the Entrance Hall confirms this possibility; otherwise, a clumsily placed wall with a doorway in the middle of the processional passageway serves no practical or ceremonial purpose. Personally, I think the two square **T3** columns may have only been standalone columns, but Imhotep could once again be layering multiple meanings onto the same architectural elements forcing us to look beyond just one explanation for its symbology.

O, Memphis, my city, beauty forever! You are a bowl of love's own berries, (a) dish set for Ptah your god, (the) god of the handsome face.

From the ancient Egyptian love poem, "Oh, I'm Bound Downstream on the Memphis Ferry" [45]

Imhotep the Architect, Astronomer and Sculptor – Building Egypt's First *Mega Mortuary Temple*

That the Nile River was the greatest gift any ancient culture could have possessed cannot be said often enough. It was life giving for certain, but the Nile's long, navigable corridor for transporting people and materials of all kinds permitted ancient Egypt to have such a remote central government that could still unite and run such a far-flung country was fairly unique in the ancient world. You could travel the 700-mile length of Egypt in a matter of days, where in other places and countries, such a journey over land would take weeks or even months.

Yet, despite an ever-changing outlook influenced by world events and a constantly evolving political landscape, Egyptian's lives were mainly focused around their local villages and towns. Even when they did venture down the Nile to one of the larger cities like Memphis or Thebes, ancient Egyptian tourists were as awestruck with the size and scale of the monuments their ancestors had built as we are today. We have expressions of admiration about the Step Pyramid from more than 1400 years later left by Egyptians in the form of graffiti, some of which is found written on the walls of the South Pavilion (*Fig. 6-1*). Keeping in mind the three (or four) great pyramids at Giza were also in near pristine condition, these lavish testimonials are all the more remarkable for their emotional accolades to the beauty and splendor of the Step Pyramid Enclosure.

The scribe, Ahmose, son of Iptah, came to see the Temple of Djoser. He found it as though heaven were inside it, Re rising within. Let loaves and oxen and fowl and all good and pure things fall to the *Ka* of the justified Djoser; may heaven rain fresh myrrh, may it drip incense! [46]

Fig. 6-1 – Some of the graffiti found in the Step Pyramid Enclosure

The ancient Egyptians were a passionate people. One need only read their love poetry to get a sense that they showed their emotions without holding anything back. To read the effusive language displayed in these graffiti inscribed in the South Pavilion of the Step Pyramid Enclosure and elsewhere, one can only conclude the scribe who penned these words was overwhelmed at the sight of the Step Pyramid and its environs. In order to elicit these flowery, poetic words, it is safe to conclude Djoser's mortuary temple and its buildings must have been in reasonably good condition. For us in the modern world, we are at a disadvantage when trying to envision what it must have been like to see these ancient temples and monuments that, in their prime, evoked a sense of wonder – and respect – for the people that built them.

The general consensus is that when Imhotep was commissioned by Netjerikhet Djoser to construct his tomb, very little existed on the Sakkara plateau where the tomb was to be built, with the exception of one of the Western Massifs, and two mortuary mastabas just below and to the south of the plateau. These mastabas covered the entrances to the tombs of Hotepsekhemwy and Ninetjer, the first and third kings of the Second Dynasty (see *Fig. 8-7*). Based on my observations, something else entirely may be closer to the truth concerning what Imhotep found before designing his king's final resting place.

What follows is a suggested sequence of the construction of the Step Pyramid and it ancillary buildings within the Enclosure Walls. It is based on findings and field reports from the initial excavations and the subsequent rebuilding of the Step Pyramid and its surrounding buildings in the 1920s and 1930s, right up to recent 21st century excavations, preservation work and discoveries above and below ground. To be certain, what is propose here is sometimes the result of grand leaps of intuition by the author and others. However, it is speculation based on previous excavation work and documentation done on the monument beginning with the initial excavations and preservation work by Firth, Quibell, Lauer and others, as well as simple observations, which at the outset appears to contradict long-established archeological evidence, but in fact, does utilize the very same evidence to arrive at several different conclusions.

Before There Was a Step Pyramid

Prior to explaining the design and construction of the Step Pyramid and its surrounding structures, we must first review what was happening in Egypt at that time. We cannot separate the building of this mighty temple from the political climate of the period before Djoser and Imhotep began any construction. There is a reason history is often called *viewing the past though the mists of time*. Not only are certain historical events shrouded in mystery, but also, events of the past are often seen through the distortions induced by a lack of credible historical data. With little reliable evidence, archeologists often find it necessary to raise *reading between the lines* to the level of a high art form.

Our view of the ancient past gets a little muddy the farther back in time we go. Such is the case with the political landscape of the latter half of the Second Dynasty leading to the beginning of the Third Dynasty and the reign of Netjerikhet Djoser. The Second Dynasty, it seems, is one of those 'black holes' of history where hundreds of questions go in and few answers come out. Even though we have a an almost complete understanding of the history of the First Dynasty, there is a dearth of reliable information that has been unearthed concerning the Second Dynasty and what we do have is sketchy at best. Even the names and number of kings who ruled is subject to a great deal of debate. This indicates an unstable, turbulent political situation at best and outright conflict at worst. Consequently, if you asked ten Egyptologists their thoughts concerning the Second Dynasty, you'd probably get twenty different opinions!

We do not know the circumstances surrounding the fall of the First Dynasty and the rise of the Second Dynasty. While proof of this rather tenuous, it is alleged that the subsidiary tombs surrounding the sepulcher of First Dynasty pharaohs were for the bodies of their courtiers and servants, who were supposedly murdered upon the pharaoh's death and sent with him into the Afterlife. This may have been the underlying reason that led to the Second Dynasty kings overthrowing the kings of the First Dynasty. It is easy to see that if the kings of the First Dynasty took several of the elite bureaucracy with them to the grave, they would have sown the seeds of their own destruction. Wiping out in one fell swoop a portion of the state's administrative class would lead to political chaos, at least temporarily, following the death of these First Dynasty kings until new bureaucrats could rise up in their predecessor's place. Ostensibly, the stopping of this practice occurred when the Second Dynasty took over the reins of power, and the subsidiary tombs that surrounded the king's mastaba tombs waited for their owners to die a natural death.

Yet, could it be the tombs of a pharaoh's family and courtiers surrounding his mastaba eventually became purely symbolic? Courtiers throughout ancient Egypt's history always wished to have their tomb near the tomb of their king, much like the extensive eastern and western mastaba cemeteries at Giza. Once the First Dynasty practice of sending the pharaoh off to the Afterlife with his retinue of servants had ended, perhaps the reason behind the necessity for subsidiary tombs inspired the creation of the *ushabti* figures. Little *ushabti* statuettes that populated the grave goods of later Egyptian kings to accompany them into the Afterlife would do the bidding of the king much like his servants had done during his life without actually having to kill them. *Fig. 6-2* shows what a Second Dynasty king's mastaba with its subsidiary tombs may have looked like after completion.

Fig. 6-2 – A typical Second Dynasty royal mastaba with surrounding subsidiary tombs for courtiers (J. C. Golvin)

Several kings of the Second Dynasty are well established: the first three, Hotepsekhemwy, Raneb (or Nebra) and Ninetjer; and the last king, Khasekhemwui. The kings from the middle of the dynasty are less well known, and the history of this part of the dynasty is very muddy. The names that have come down from this period are Weneg, Senedj, Neferkara, Neferkasokar, Hudjefa, Seth-Peribsen, Sekhemib-Perenmaat and Nubnefer. Several of the above names may refer to the same king, but we don't know for sure. Part of the confusion lies in the fact that kings in ancient Egypt had up to five different names associated with them. These are the *Nebty* (or *Two Ladies*) name, the throne name, the Horus name, a possible Golden Horus name, and the king's personal name. (For example, the pharaoh "Djoser" may have been his personal name, and Netjerikhet was his Horus name.)

The name Hudjefa appears in several lists of kings, but 'hudjefa' literally means "unknown" in ancient Egyptian. "Hudjefa" may even refer to the fifth (or sixth) king of the Second Dynasty, Seth-Peribsen, since it appears that this king became a "non-person" to later generations. (As you can see in *Fig. 6-3*, we don't even have any statues of him.) Nevertheless, it seems somewhat certain that the ephemeral king Sekhemib-Perenmaat was an earlier Horus name for Seth-Peribsen, who may have changed his name to represent a move away from portraying the king as the *son of Horus* to one associated with Horus' mortal enemy, Seth. Shifting such traditional allegiances may have tainted Peribsen's reputation where his name was not included in several New Kingdom kings lists. Whatever the reason for such an exclusion, it appears Seth-Peribsen only ruled in the south of Egypt having no power in the north, and as a result left little in the way of official records.

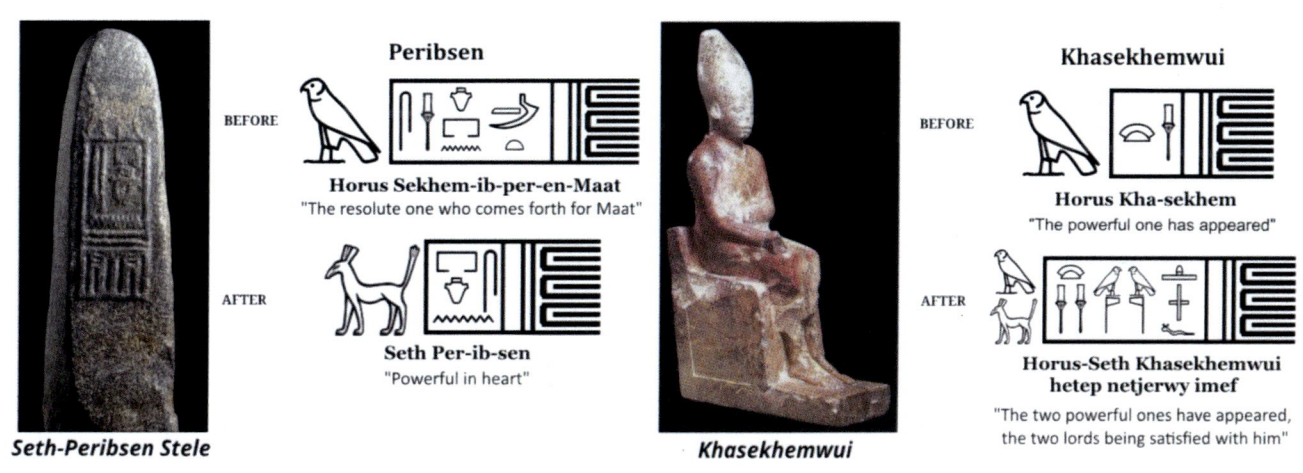

Fig. 6-3 – Names changes of key figures of the Second Dynasty

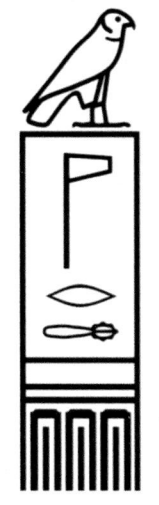

On a side note: Most people know that the pharaoh's name was enclosed in an oval-shaped hieroglyph called a *cartouche*. Up until the early Fourth Dynasty, the king's name was enclosed in a rectangle atop a square resembling an architectural façade called a *serekh*. This is akin to referring to the Executive Branch of the United States government as the "White House". The transition from *serekh* to *cartouche* implies that the description of a king went from an architecturally based meme relating to the king's palace to one based on the immortal god-like nature of the king. The hieroglyph the *cartouche* is based on is the coiled rope-shaped *shen* hieroglyph, which represents the completion or the circuit of the eternal sun. As the sun is the eternal presence in the sky, the *shen* can also mean immortal or eternal. Therefore, whoever's name is in a *cartouche* is thought to be immortal like the gods.

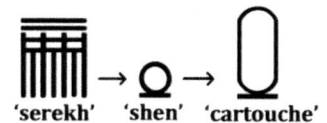

The serekh of Netjerikhet Djoser

'serekh'   'shen'   'cartouche'

A text found at the Ptolemaic Temple of Horus at Edfu describes a supposedly mythical war that took place between Horus and Seth and their followers. [47] However, there is some debate among Egyptologists as to whether this civil war was an actual conflict between two different factions aiming to seize power during the Second Dynasty.[48] [49] Aiden Dodson, however, takes a middle view:

While some attempts have made to link the civil war (if real) to the reign of the Horus Ninetjer (*third king of the Second Dynasty)***... any echoes are more likely to refer to the latter part of the period. It is with Seth-Peribsen's reign and later that we see possible signs of a breakdown in national cohesion, only ending in the final reign of the dynasty** (*i.e., Khasekhemwui*). [50]

The reign of a late Second Dynasty king named Khasekhem seems to have been marked by armed conflict as evidenced by inscriptions found at an unused mortuary enclosure of his at Hierakonpolis in southern Egypt, about 114 kilometers north of Aswan. Several stone vases were unearthed whose inscriptions read as being from "The Year of Fighting the Northern Enemy". Also found at Hierakonpolis were two statue bases that record the deaths of 47,209 northern enemies. From this, it is safe to say the end of the Second Dynasty was a return to stability from a time of great upheaval and internal conflict. It may also have led 'Khasekhem' to change his name to '*Khasekhemwui*', which may have signaled the coming of peace after a terrible civil war. [51]

History, they say, is the story told by the victors, and the first casualty of any war is the truth. It is hard to dismiss the possibility of a period of internal strife during the last years of the Second Dynasty. A certain degree of caution needs to be exercised when viewing the events surrounding the last kings of the Second Dynasty as a battle between *light* and *dark* factions, mainly because there is scant evidence for any real assessment to be made of the historical record. Accounts we do have from ancient Egypt too often resemble politicized bombast and over-bloated rhetoric. We need to set aside the filters of our present civilization, and not interpret the reign of purported *bad boy* Peribsen as a decent into pure evil necessitating the intervention of the *good king* Khasekhemwui. The fact is Khasekhemwui had both Horus and Seth on his *serekh*, the cartouche-like box surrounding his royal name (see *Fig. 6-3*). The translation of his complete name is "The powerful ones have appeared, the two lords being satisfied with him", indicating some sort of *rapprochement* between the two factions during his reign. We do know Khasekhemwui's wife and Djoser's mother, Nimaathap, was a princess from the North, implying a ceasing of hostilities between the South and North. It's too easy for us to say that Peribsen *embraced the dark side* of the cult of Seth with Khasekhemwui riding in on his white horse and saving Egypt by returning it to the *light*. Good drama, but bad history.

Early excavations at the Step Pyramid uncovered over 40,000 stone vessels (*Fig. 6-4*). These vessels mostly had the names of First and Second Dynasty kings engraved on them, but only one vessel had Djoser's name on it. There is some thought that Djoser was reusing these stone vessels for his own grave goods, but this seems unlikely as it would be easier to make new stoneware than to dig up vessels from dozens of older tombs to plunder their pottery for reuse. Whenever a pharaoh recycled anything from a previous king's reign, it was usually to obtain larger building materials or statues that were later incorporated into new buildings with the new king's cartouche carved over the old king's name.

Fig. 6-4 – A few of the 40,000 stone vessels found in the Step Pyramid

One possible scenario would be that Djoser found the tombs of earlier kings had been desecrated and looted. To better preserve what was left of his ancestors' remains and/or grave goods, he relocated them to his own mortuary complex. What circumstances occurred which led to those king's tombs to be plundered remains to be discovered, but internal political strife would be at the top of the list as the cause for Djoser to preserve the contents of his predecessors' tombs. On the other hand, it may be that Djoser merely built over the tombs of earlier kings that were present on the Sakkara plateau, or just incorporated them within his mortuary enclosure, leaving what remained of those kings' and their families' possessions where he found them. Or maybe the true answer is a combination of these two proposals.

Perhaps the South Tomb within the Enclosure was to be Djoser's personal tomb to be close to the tombs of his ancestors that lay underground nearby beneath Western Massif II and elsewhere. The Central Burial Chamber beneath Mastaba M_1/M_2, the pit tombs beneath Mastaba M_3 and the unfinished or unused mastaba tombs that became the North and South Pavilions may not have been part of any plan to reuse them because the extent of the despoilment of the other king's graves wasn't known in the beginning. Consequently, the decision to move as much of the grave goods to Djoser's funerary enclosure was made only after carefully accessing the damage to the earlier tombs. Another possibility is they left the grave goods where they found them, and Djoser constructed his mortuary buildings over these older tombs.

The events surrounding the last years of the Second Dynasty should not be given such a shallow interpretation in which our modern culture has a habit of indulging by presenting only two extremes with no middle ground of interpretation. Things were probably not so clear-cut back in the days of the Second Dynasty. Given all the changing of Pharaonic names to align with either Horus or Seth or both, it is safe to say something happened at the end of the Second Dynasty, which bears a resemblance to some kind of conflict between two camps espousing divided and shifting loyalties. At the very least, we have no clue as to what Khasekhemwui, or his contemporaries, may have felt about the events of his reign, and maybe we should just leave it at that.

That being said, however, it is likely that Djoser reigned over a relatively recently reunited Egypt after a period of internal strife – if not outright civil war – between the North and South. This may explain his desire to allocate space to earlier kings in his own burial complex at Sakkara. Maybe there were intrusions and looting of burial sites during the conflict that prompted Djoser to secure the remains and grave goods of his predecessors and their relatives. This would explain the large number of chambers built beneath the storage magazine Western Massif II that contained the remnants of Second Dynasty grave goods. Even the large number of pottery with seals of many of the kings of the First and Second Dynasties found in the Step Pyramid itself gives silent testimony to Djoser's desire to preserve the remains of his ancestors.

If the use of these massifs was not to store Djoser's personal grave goods, or to even stockpile food in the event of drought, but rather for burials – or more accurately – reburials, then any supposition that at least Western Massif II was built in the Second Dynasty would be correct. Until a thorough excavation of the subterranean chambers beneath these massifs and cataloguing of any items found in them is undertaken, we will never know for sure.

The first stage of constructing the eventual Step Pyramid was a series of simple mastabas, an Arabic word meaning *stone bench*. The first was Mastaba M₁. The addition of Mastaba M₂ occurred almost immediately afterward, and is only just a shell that surrounds Mastaba M₁. Soon after, there was an extension (designated as Mastaba M₃) added to the east side of Mastabas M₁/M₂, which covered the eleven pit tombs that had previously been excavated. Then there was the construction of the penultimate four-tier Step Pyramid P₁ on top of Mastabas M₁/M₂/M₃, extended later to become the six-tier Step Pyramid P₂ we see today (*Fig. 6-5*). It is probable that along with these six stages of construction, there were designs or the building of several Enclosure Walls of various sizes as well. (52)

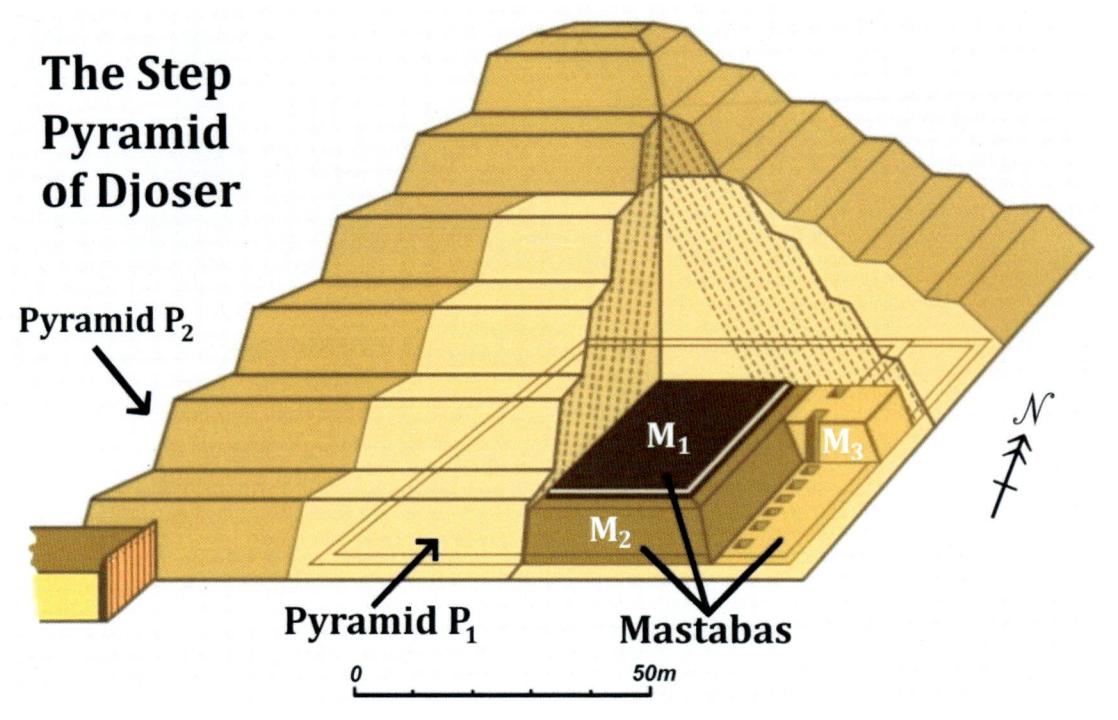

Fig. 6-5 – The Step Pyramid's successive stages of construction

How and when the construction of these first mastabas happened leads to an interesting mystery if not some confusion.

The first impression made on anyone looking on the South face of the pyramid, and seeing the embedded mastaba with its course of small stones laid horizontally and separated by thick layers of clay, [*Fig. 6-6*] contrasting so sharply with the much larger stones of the pyramid laid in plunging [inward sloping] courses, must be that *the mastaba dates from an earlier period; that it was the tomb of an ancestor, or of the founder of the dynasty, preserved from pious or economic motives*. So great a change in the character of the masonry, it would seem, is most unlikely to have been adopted suddenly in the middle of the building of the pyramid.

The argument still appears weighty, but one fact alone is fatal to it. *The original mastaba was not oblong as a mastaba should be, but square, just like the internal building of the Meidum pyramid.*

The successive stages - two or three in number - of the mastaba, and three of the pyramid, show that great changes in design took place in both: changes of method are also possible. The seal with Djoser's name on the masonry of one of the tombs below the mastaba shows that the burial in it took place during the King's reign.

Further, the great pit in which Djoser was interred could not have been dug if the mastaba was already there. We seem then to be safe in assuming that the mastaba was built by Djoser. (53) (Emphasis and clarification added.)

This is an interesting conundrum. Firth first proposed that the building of Mastabas M₁/M₂ was much earlier, long before Djoser allowed Imhotep to build a unique four-tier Step Pyramid. Firth later changed his mind, and concluded that Mastabas M₁/M₂ were part of the original design of the Step Pyramid for the sole reason that they are square, and not rectangular like other mastaba tombs in the area. This presumption seems flimsy to me. If having a square mastaba is Firth's only argument against predating the Step Pyramid mastabas to "an earlier period" before construction of the four-tier Step Pyramid P₁ began, then his observation concerning the difference in stonework between the mastabas and the subsequent pyramids confirms that Imhotep did not start his construction project with a blank sheet of papyrus. Rather he was continuing a building project that had started much earlier than Djoser's reign, and just utilized parts of buildings that already existed. Stranger still is that J.-P. Lauer's original plans of the Step Pyramid Enclosure depicted Mastabas M₁/M₂ as being rectangular. In a later revision of those plans, Mastabas M₁/M₂ became square, and along with Mastaba M₃, making the three mastaba tomb complex more rectangular. When and why Lauer made the change remains unclear. Invariably, it is all guesswork inasmuch as the Step Pyramid covers up most of the three mastabas, and their true size and shape are not readily discernible.

Fig. 6-6 – The south face of the Step Pyramid in 1990 showing the original mastabas on the lowest course before the completion of renovations covered them up in the 21st century (see cover)

Firth's argument seems sound at first. Most mastabas of the First and Second Dynasties were rectangular. However, square mastabas do exist such as the Mastaba of Kagemni near the Pyramid of Teti (*Fig. 6-7*). In addition, the square mastabas of Sesheshet Idut, Kainer, Isi, Ni-ankh-Ptah, Herimeru, and the square-*ish* mastabas of Khenut and Nebt, all of which are near the Pyramid of Unas just to the south of the Step Pyramid (*Fig. 6-8*).

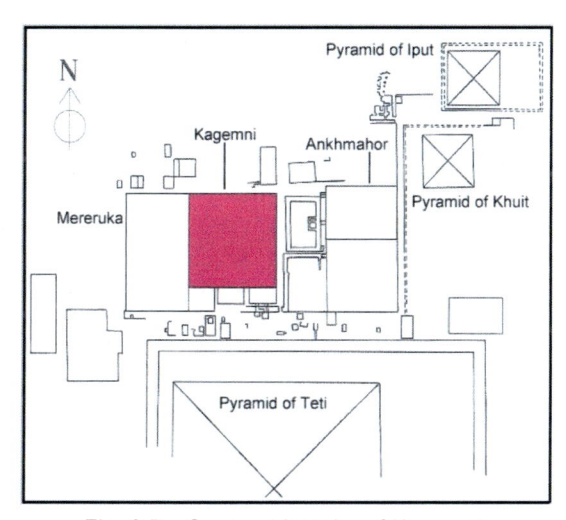

Fig. 6-7 – Square Mastaba of Kagemni 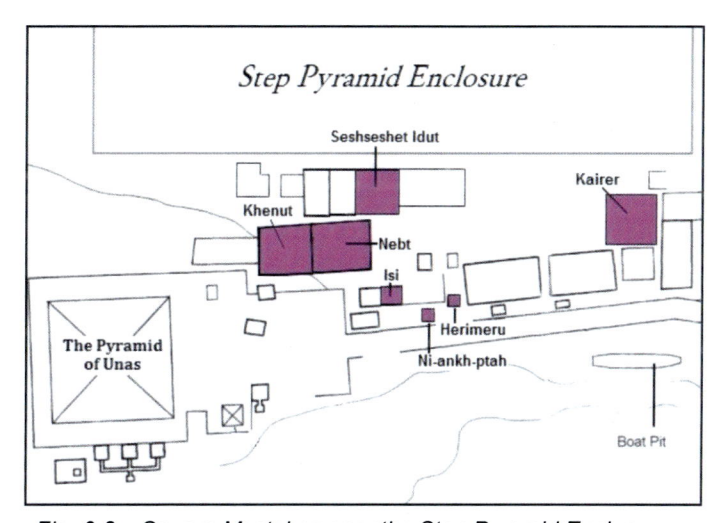   *Fig. 6-8 – Square Mastabas near the Step Pyramid Enclosure*

Furthermore, the placement of seals in the Subterranean Chambers bearing Djoser's name could have occurred after the original (M₁) and subsequent mastabas (M₂ and M₃) were built, perhaps closer to the time of Djoser's burial. Instead of Imhotep constructing Mastaba M₁, perhaps he rebuilt or renovated it, resulting in Mastaba M₂, and possibly M₃ before conceiving the four-tier Step Pyramid P₁. We must also remember Imhotep was breaking new ground architecturally speaking, and starting with an already existing square mastaba would not have mattered to him.

Sometimes small and seemingly unrelated details are used to *connect the dots* in order to create a path to a working theory when more exacting and unambiguous road signs derived from verifiable facts are not available. Though these mastabas are from the later Fifth Dynasty, relying on the existence – or non-existence – of a *square mastaba* to date the construction of the Step Pyramid seems tenuous. Basing a dating hypothesis solely on the shape of Mastabas M₁/M₂ from the initial construction phase of Djoser's mortuary complex has some serious difficulties associated with it. Ultimately, it is missing the whole point. While I believe that Firth should have gone with his first impression, I believe he would have been amenable to seeing other possibilities as to who built Mastabas M₁/M₂ and the later Mastaba M₃. Firth was writing at the beginning stages of excavating the Step Pyramid and its environs, but sadly, he passed away five years before publication of the seminal work outlining what his associates, James E. Quibell and Jean-Philippe Lauer uncovered later. This should not deter us from seeking other possible explanations for "who built what when" as we look to flesh out the details with what we may subsequently discover in our quest to understand the past, in general, and this monument specifically.

Firth was right, though: the excavation of the Central Burial Chamber came first, and the installation of the large granite sarcophagus thereafter. Only then could the construction of the first mastaba (M₁) occur. Quite possibly, it was meant for a First or Second Dynasty king. After the entombment of this unknown king, the plan was to have hundreds of stone boulders form a type of plug to insert into the top of the pit shaft. (Part of this *plug* and its remnants fell onto the top of the granite sarcophagus due to an earthquake in 1992. Shoring up and repairing the Central Burial Chamber roof began in 2008 and finished five years later. See the National Geographic film *Saving Egypt's Oldest Pyramid*).

In any event, whoever commissioned the construction of the pit tomb below what would eventually become Mastaba M₁ did not live long enough for burial within it. A vacant, partially constructed tomb presented to Imhotep for repurposing could have had the beginnings of a mastaba above a burial shaft, and possibly the eleven pits tombs, being excavated. Then, there were further improvements made including the addition of Mastaba M₂. Because Mastaba M₃ is technically not a mastaba, it is more of a *lean-to* on the east side of Mastaba M₂, and doesn't surround Mastabas M₁/M₂. Covering the eleven pit tombs with M₃ probably occurred much later, closer to the time when the construction of the four-tier Step Pyramid took place. Excavation of the North Descending Passage occurred about this time, but from the inside of the Central Burial Chamber out to the surface. The exterior entrance of the North Descending Passage was subsequently covered over when the four-tier pyramid was upgraded to the present six-tier Step Pyramid. Imhotep was likely involved in these renovations as well.

Building a pyramid isn't easy, especially if no one had built one before to use as a prototype. This was the daunting task facing Imhotep as he attempted to create something without a reference model for inspiration, and on a scale not previously imagined or attempted.

Though it continues to evoke the same degree of appreciation today as it did in the past, the Step Pyramid Enclosure is a flawed masterpiece. Despite its beauty of form and grace in the execution of its design, Djoser's mortuary temple was incomplete at his death according to C. M. Firth, who began the restoration work on the Step Pyramid in the 1920s.

> **The great monument was never finished. Under the pyramid the long chamber, decorated with tile work on one side only, was on the other still in the masons' hands. In the Ḥeb-Sed court lay large statues only roughed out; by the E. side of the pyramid, stones pierced from both sides and useless for building were not cleared away: the whole of the northern quarter [North Court] was still apparently an empty space used to store materials.**
>
> **Yet the pyramid itself had received its casing; the temples were roofed; the great tomb at the south end was complete; so was the enclosure wall. In this [wall], no entrance wide enough to admit materials, or indeed large numbers of men, had been left, and as much [of the] work [remained] to be done, men and materials must have come over the wall; perhaps by the big ramp we found in the [North] court, east of the altar.** [54] [Emphasis added for clarity]

The difficulty in ascertaining the exact sequence of events that occurred during construction – and eventual dismantling – lies in the fact the whole of the complex was in an almost constant state of redesign, upgrading and reconstruction from its beginning, coupled with its near destruction over the many centuries after it ceased to be a working temple. Lauer believed there were at least six phases of construction during the life of the Step Pyramid Enclosure (*Fig. 6-8*). There is no reason to doubt this claim looking at the different architectural styles of the various buildings within the complex and construction methods needed to build them.

The Great South Court

Upon exiting the South Entrance Hall, we enter a vast open space to the south of the Step Pyramid known as the Great South Court (*Fig. 6-9*). An expansive courtyard, the Great South Court was used for *Ḥeb-Sed* rituals and possibly other ceremonies and public gatherings. Toward the south are the South Tomb and its attached South Tomb Chapel. In the center are two so-called capital B-shaped *boundary markers* symbolizing the northern and southern borders of Egypt used during the *sed*-festivals. The Step Pyramid is to the north with the South Altar at its base, and an entrance next to it excavated more than 2000 years later by the Persian kings of the Twenty-sixth Dynasty whose capital was in Sais. Nearby are three niche-like rooms close to a passageway that leads to the North and South Pavilions.

This courtyard originally contained only a few buildings. In its northeast corner stood *a small temple with three niches* and a low limestone altar, which was attached to the south side of the Step Pyramid. This altar was accessed by a small ramp, in front of which a bull's head was found in a cavity lined with limestone. [55] [Emphasis added.]

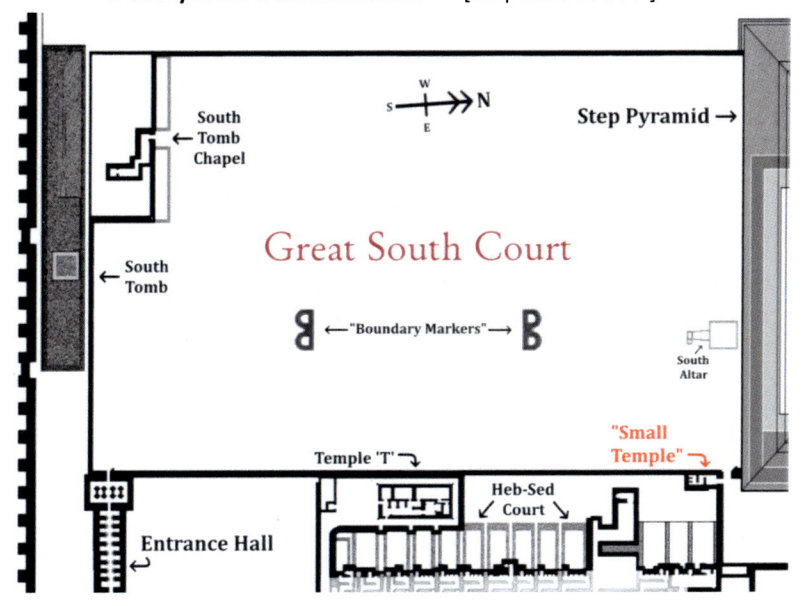

The *small temple* (*Figs. 6-10* and *6-11*) referred to here could have been a chapel dedicated to the Memphite Triad of the gods Ptah, his consort Sekhmet, and their son Nefertum. If so, the view towards the three small chambers and their statues would have been obscured because they are behind a pair of large walls, neither one of which is a "low, limestone altar". With its proximity to the Great South Court, which is a large open venue for public gatherings, it becomes apparent this *chapel's* design does not lend itself to being a quiet place of devotion for these three gods, or any other deities. Closer examination of this alleged chapel leads to a far different conclusion.

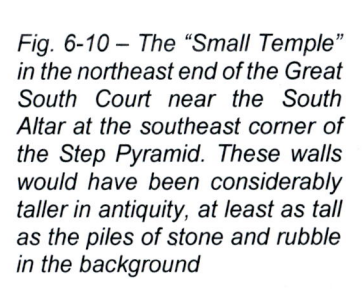

Fig. 6-9 – The Great South Court

Fig. 6-10 – The "Small Temple" in the northeast end of the Great South Court near the South Altar at the southeast corner of the Step Pyramid. These walls would have been considerably taller in antiquity, at least as tall as the piles of stone and rubble in the background

First, it is located in an otherwise nondescript and out-of-the-way location of the Great South Court next to the southeast corner of the Step Pyramid. Since crowds of people gathering for *sed*-festivals and other celebrations in the nearby Great South Court tended to be quite noisy, this would break the ambiance of an ideal setting for reverent worship. Therefore, it would not be in keeping with the quiet confines of a typical Old Kingdom Egyptian temple.

Second, the design of this *small temple* is a bit awkward. When one enters, you are facing a blank wall (*Fig. 6-10*). On the right side of the first wall is an opening leading to another smaller room with a doorway on the left side of a second wall. Passing through this second doorway, you encounter with three small niches where, in theory, very small statues of gods or goddesses were housed. The space between the second wall and the three chambers is quite cramped (*Fig. 6-11*), and doesn't fit the solemn character of what we believe a votive chapel such as this would normally have been. Worshipping any god in the confines of this small space would be extremely difficult, and hiding the statues of gods from a direct line of sight, or requiring a circuitous, serpentine route in order to view them would not have been the norm in a typical ancient Egyptian Old Kingdom temple.

Fig. 6-11 – The three small chambers at the rear of the "Small Temple" (upper right)

Even if none of the above is true, it is my belief the three tiny rooms in this *temple* at the end of the long east wall of the Great South Court are not really chapels at all. Instead, Imhotep made provisions for one of life's most basic necessities, and certainly the most common human experience after childbirth: that of urinary and bowel elimination. It is my belief these three small niches, and several other similar small chambers scattered throughout the Step Pyramid Enclosure, are simply lavatories, toilets, restrooms, or any other euphemism you care to use. Obviously, what occurred inside these small chambers would not be the worship of a god. The placement of chamber pots or latrine chairs (see *Fig. 3-53*) in these niches was for the temple staff or guests attending the Ḥeb-Sed to use, not to mention the many patients of the hospital or their families. Therefore, the function of the two intrusive modesty half-walls was not to force a reverential distance between worshipers and their gods, but to provide a degree of privacy for patrons of these restrooms.

We in the modern world tend to think of the ancient Egyptians in terms of the faded, time-ravaged artwork from tombs and temples, not the human beings they were. It may seem strange to offer such an unusual alternative interpretation for the function of these and other small niche-like rooms within the complex, but we must remember that ordinary humans lived and worked in this temple on a daily basis. The purpose of this and other mortuary temples was not solely limited to taking care of the dead. They also had to provide for the needs of the living as well.

Mastaba M₃ and the Eleven Pit Tombs Mystery

The north side of the Great South Court is where the Step Pyramid is located. Prior to the completion of renovations finished in 2020, the mastaba tombs that preceded the construction of the Step Pyramids could be easily seen (*Fig. 6-5*). Sometimes, the eleven pit tombs under Mastaba M₃ are referred to as the Tombs of the Royal Family despite the lack of evidence that any of Djoser's family members were entombed there. In fact, it is highly unlikely these tombs were for Djoser's family at all. If the eleven pit tombs were to eventually be used for Djoser's family, it would have necessitated that *every one of them predecease him by several years* because these pit tombs were covered over by the construction of

Mastaba M₃. This was followed shortly thereafter by the construction of the four-tier Step Pyramid, thus preventing any further burials. Exactly whom the tombs were supposed to hold remains a mystery, but it seems unlikely to have been members of Djoser's family. More than likely, they were meant for the burial of families associated with earlier kings because of the large number of First and Second Dynasty pottery found in the Subterranean Chambers beneath the Step Pyramid and Western Massif II.

Indications of this come from accounts of the original excavation done in the early twentieth century.

> **The centerpiece of the Saqqara tableau is the Step Pyramid of Djoser (the Horus Netjerykhet). When the king's builders began this unprecedented creation in stone, the site may have already been a royal reserve. Immediately south, there are two large sets of underground galleries, over 130 m (427 ft.) long and entered by passages from the north. On the basis of seal impressions found within them, they are considered to be the tombs of the first and third kings of the Second Dynasty – Hotepsekhemwy and Ninetjer, both of whom, unlike Peribsen and Khasekhemwui later in the dynasty, did not have tombs at Abydos. The tombstone of the second king of the Second Dynasty, Raneb, was found in the area, suggesting that another royal tomb remains to be found.**

> **(Rainer) Stadelmann believes that the galleries were once topped by mastabas, similar to Djoser's South Tomb.** (56)

Also, during the initial stages of excavation, there were found numerous…

> **Fragments of archaic stelae bearing the names of the "royal daughters Intkaes and Ḥetepḥernebti" also appeared; the first found were naturally considered as funeral stelae and led to hopes of the family cemetery, hopes [which were] not fulfilled. In the next season these stelae had become too numerous and too uniform in the text they bore for this explanation to hold.**

> **Moreover, during Zoser's [reign] they had been taken down and reused in the interior of walls, even given to apprentices to practice on with their boring tools. It was concluded that they must have been boundary marks needed in laying out the site and during the ceremonies of foundation; afterwards [they were used]… as building material.**

> **Near the entrance of the pyramid on the north a great heap of fragments of stone vases, alabaster and diorite for the most part, was found, evidently carried out from the underground passages: among them were some bearing inscriptions of no less than eight kings of the first three dynasties - Udimu, Azib, Semerkhet, Ka'a, Ḥotepsekhemui, Reneb, Netherymu, Sekhemib.** (57) [Clarification added]

These small clues point to burials of kings and royal family members from earlier dynasties near where the Step Pyramid Enclosure was eventually constructed. Indirect evidence for this comes from 40,000 stone urns and other pottery with the name of First and Second Dynasty kings. Ironically, only one of these urns had Djoser's name on it. Further proof of Djoser preserving the remains and tomb goods of his ancestors is that only one intact mummy has been recovered: **a female body found in one of the eleven shaft tombs under Mastaba M₃ dates to several generations before Djoser, possibly the early Second Dynasty**. If this older woman wasn't one of Djoser's contemporary relatives, then we need to ask a relevant question: Did ancient Egyptians move mummies to another tomb if the original tomb had been compromised in some way?

There is clear evidence of royal reburials occurring during the Twenty-first or Twenty-second Dynasties (1069 to 720 BCE). Dozens of royal mummies were found in several caches in the late 19th century in the Valley of the Kings west of Luxor. These mummies were reinterred from plundered tombs by priests of the period attempting to preserve their kings and queens from further despoilment. However, there is no evidence that this custom occurred during the Old Kingdom. Logically then, the presence of the mummy of this older female beneath Djoser's Step Pyramid suggests that she was probably interred in this pit tomb shortly after her demise where she was found millennia later in the 20th century. This implies that she was already in her original – and only – tomb when Imhotep began to build Djoser's mortuary complex, and goes along with the discovery of thousands of pottery from earlier dynasties found in side chambers beneath the Step Pyramid.

It is probable that Djoser did not move thousands of pieces of First and Second Dynasty pottery, along with the remains of persons from earlier dynasties to his mortuary complex, but rather constructed Mastabas M₁/M₂/M₃ for his burial and left the mummies and pottery in place to be found in the 20th Century. It then becomes apparent that Djoser was preserving the memory as well as the bodies of his ancestors. Either that or he was repurposing tombs on the Sakkara plateau belonging to those older kings or their families that were left unused for some reason, and did not have to move any grave goods like pottery in order to preserve them.

It is, therefore, entirely possible that Imhotep, or even his father, the Royal Architect Kanofer, used extant buildings in the initial design of Djoser's mortuary complex, or perhaps, used them to preserve the remains of the kings who preceded Djoser. This may seem unusual, but ancient Egyptian pharaohs did not portray their predecessors from an earlier dynasty as being from separate families. Dynasties are more of a concept of kingship advocated by the Greeks, like the Greek historian Manetho, who was among the first to group the kings of ancient Egypt into distinctly different dynasties. Quite possibly, Djoser demonstrated respect for his predecessors by preserving their remains in order to legitimize his ascension to the throne (as did successive pharaohs), and in so doing, he showed that he was but one of a long line of legitimate rulers. If Djoser was indeed the son of Khasekhemwui, supposedly the last king of the Second Dynasty, and the brother of Sanakht, (possibly the first king of the Third Dynasty), then for Djoser to honor their burials and include them in his own mortuary temple at Sakkara would not be so unusual.

Other recovered body parts, including a foot initially thought to be from Djoser's mummy, were probably from intrusion burials of a much later time, e.g., the Twenty-sixth Persian Dynasty. This suggests that none of Djoser's family were entombed here prior to the construction of Mastaba M_3 that entirely covered the eleven pit tombs, nor were these pit tombs intended for his relatives.

Based on casual observations of the tunnels beneath the Step Pyramid, the rock strata seems to be mostly uniform with few fissures or fragmented seams that can send a tunnel off in a different unintended direction if the other subterranean tunnels just a few meters above the eleven pit tombs are any indication. There appears to be no reason for excavating the eleven pit tombs in such a haphazard and meandering fashion other than those that did so were not very careful (see *Figs. 6-83* and *6-85*). When you look at how precise and clean the details of the stonework prevalent throughout the Step Pyramid Enclosure, it becomes apparent this is a reflection of Imhotep's personality and the subsequent work he did by insisting on straight lines and near-perfect symmetry when excavating the underground chambers. Witness the straightness of the North Descending Passage, and most of the underground passages associated with the Central Burial Chamber. For that reason, it does not take much to believe that Imhotep and his work crews had nothing to do with the excavation of the eleven pit tombs. For the most part, we can conclude that any underground passage that isn't perfectly straight (within reason) indicates a hurried or rushed excavation of these tombs by one of Djoser's predecessors, which by itself implies a time of a possibly turbulent political climate and social upheaval.

In conclusion, the Mastaba M_3 pit tombs probably pre-existed the building of Step Pyramid's First Enclosure. Given the meticulousness and care with which Imhotep used in the design and construction of the Step Pyramid and the buildings within the Enclosure Walls, it is unlikely he would have dug out the M_3 tombs in such an irregular and uneven fashion. The excavation of these pit tombs was somebody else's handiwork. The straightness of the North Descending Passage from the Central Burial Shaft out to the surface is proof of this.

The Central Burial Chamber and Vertical Shaft

The Central Burial Chamber of the Step Pyramid beneath Mastabas M_1/M_2 is one of the largest in Egypt, made all the more remarkable since it was part of the first pyramid to be constructed. It is 7.3 meters (23.95 feet) square at the top, 10.6 meters (34.78 feet) square at the bottom and 29.5 meters (96.78 feet) deep. The sarcophagus at the bottom of the Central Burial Chamber is of a most peculiar design. In ancient Egypt, the sculpting of most sarcophagi included hollowing out a single block of granite or limestone to accept a wooden coffin with a stone lid placed on top. Instead, the Step Pyramid sarcophagus is constructed of 32 slabs of granite fitted together to create a stone box with several of the stone slabs resting on top to form its lid. It sits atop 24 pillars, each made of six stacked stone bricks (*Figs. 6-12* and *6-13*). A granite plug is fitted into a hole at the north end of the sarcophagus through which the body of the king allegedly would have been inserted.

Fig. 6-12 – The underside of Djoser's sarcophagus showing the precarious nature of its 24 support pillars

Upon entering the Central Burial Chamber for the first time, Firth and company faced some interesting challenges.

> **The beam** [stone slab] **furthest to the South** [on top of the sarcophagus] **has been overturned and it was its edge, projecting from the debris,...** [See *Figs. 6-13* and *6-16*]
>
> **On the** (North) **face** [of the burial chamber]**... above the pile of stones we see the mouth of the great constructional incline** [i.e., North Descending Passage] **and the doorway in the middle of it***; its threshold seemed to us mysteriously high so long as we supposed it to have opened on to the floor of the chamber* [i.e. the top of the sarcophagus] *in which the granite plug once hung suspended.*
>
> **In the south wall of the pit are sockets cut to receive the ends of the great beams of wood from which the stopper** [granite plug on top of the sarcophagus] **was hung and lowered; there are other holes to correspond on the North. Higher up is the tall recess already mentioned.** [58]
>
> **At the north end** [of the sarcophagus] **is the great plug which closed it; it must once have been sunk flush with the floor** [i.e. the top of the sarcophagus] **but someone has raised it a little... Perring** [an English Egyptologist who entered the burial chamber in 1837]**... gave reasons for thinking that Zoser was never buried here, pointing out that no fragment of a mummy or skeleton could be found after a careful search, that a body could not be withdrawn by the present opening unless it were first broken up, and that if it were broken up some fragment would surely be left.**
>
> **The argument is not conclusive and the fact that the plug was lowered is against it. But it is at any rate evident that the body was not brought in a coffin.** [59] (Clarification and emphasis added)

If we take into consideration the views of Firth and others, then it is safe to conclude that Djoser was buried somewhere else other than the South Tomb or the Central Burial Chamber of the Step Pyramid. Based on the fact that only a few bone fragments were found in the burial chambers, then it likely Djoser was buried in an as yet undiscovered chamber beneath the Step Pyramid itself, somewhere nearby within the Enclosure, or the traditional site for pharaonic burials at Abydos. This is not so farfetched inasmuch as the Latvian Scientific Mission under the directorship of Dr. Bruno Deslandes has recently discovered what looks to be several previously unknown tunnels beneath the plateau on which the Step Pyramid sits (see *Figs. 6-83* through *6-86*). These chambers and/or tunnels along with the multitude of chambers and tunnels beneath Western Massif II still require more detailed exploration. If Djoser was buried elsewhere, was the Central Burial Chamber finished in a manner to foster the belief that Djoser was buried in the Step Pyramid to thwart future tomb raiders? (Or, maybe, archeologists?)

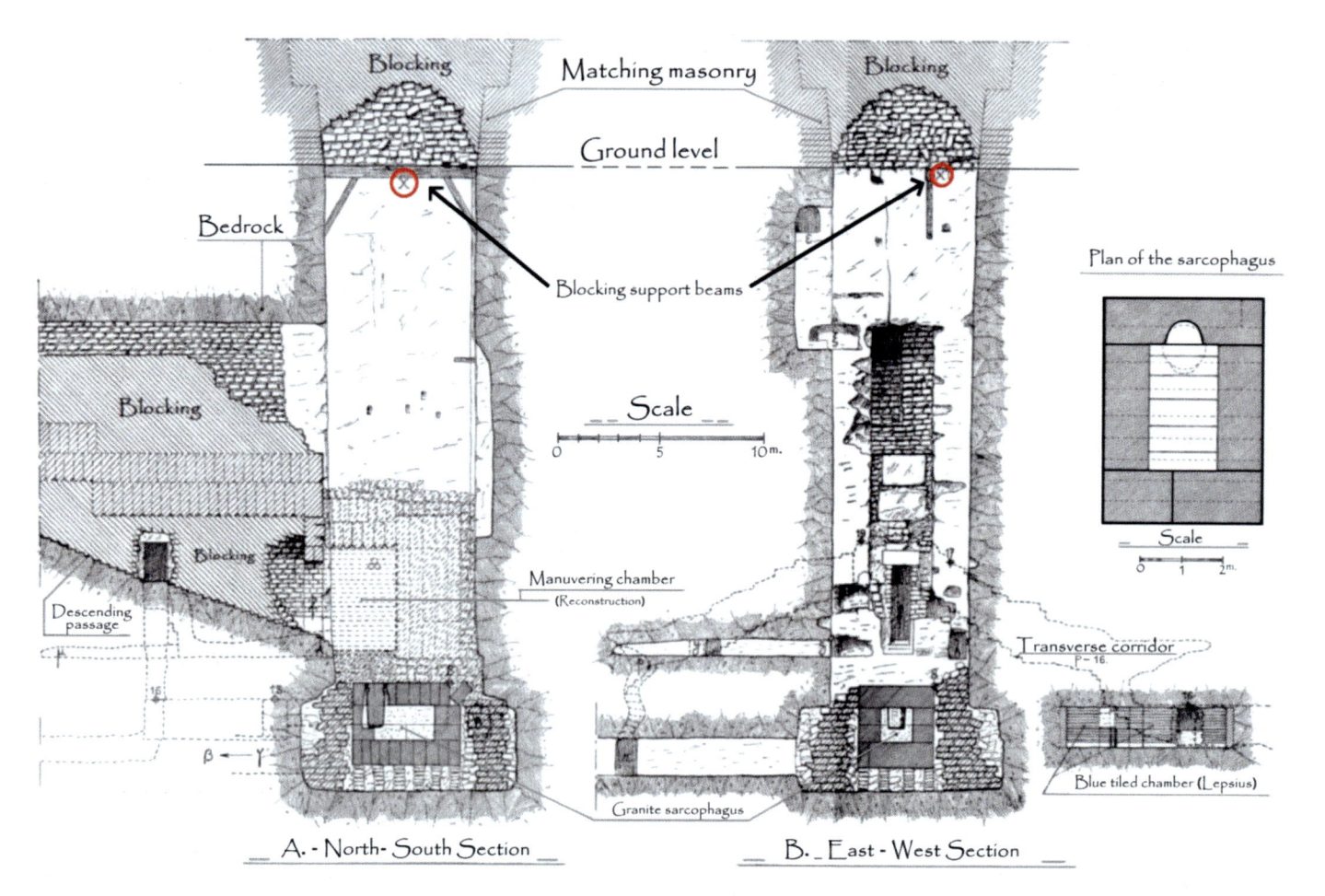

Fig. 6-13 – Sectional views of the Central Burial Chamber beneath the Step Pyramid

During the excavation of the burial vault in the early 20th century, rocky debris was found surrounding the sarcophagus on all sides level with its top (*Fig. 6-14*). Instead of being freestanding, the excavators believed the sarcophagus was, instead, a granite-lined cavity set into the floor of the burial shaft with ten granite slabs and a giant plug that, when it was uncovered, was not sitting flush with the top of it. They further concluded this debris originally fell from the blockage at the top of the Central Burial Chamber's roof, similar to the stones that had fallen from the earthquake in 1992.

Fig. 6-14 – The sarcophagus in the Central Burial Chamber
Note the debris surrounding the sarcophagus that is level with its top

Eventually, careful removal of the enormous quantity of stone rubble on the floor of the shaft revealed the true size and nature of this immense sarcophagus. [60] It quickly became obvious the sheer quantity of this debris could not have come solely from the roof of the central burial shaft. Indeed, Imhotep himself may have also found this very same rubble in situ when he started to repurpose this unused mastaba for the king's entombment.

Additionally, more of the rubble may have come from part of the excavation of the North Descending Passage. If so, Imhotep deliberately left this new material in the Burial Chamber to save time and labor, and to make it easier and less dangerous when bringing Djoser's body into the chamber during his funeral. Leaving this rocky debris where it was also has the advantage of stabilizing the sarcophagus (which sits precariously on only 24 pillars made of loose rocks) in the event of an earthquake (see *Fig. 6-12*).

The unique design for this sarcophagus implies it was lowered, one granite slab at a time (32 in all) down the vertical shaft above the burial vault, because the North Descending Passage did not exist at that time. This can be proven by the existence of a beam – one of two that originally existed – still in place, high up in the burial shaft (at 'X' circled in red in *Fig. 6-13*) near ground level. It is possible these two beams were used to lower the sarcophagus sections into the burial shaft when it was still open to the sky. If the excavation of the North Descending Passage and Central Burial Shaft had occurred at the same time, it would have been easy to move a typical, much smaller one-piece sarcophagus down the descending passage. After lowering the large, multi-segment sarcophagus piecemeal down the North Descending Passage once it was fully excavated, placement of a wooden beam needed for the sole purpose of raising and lowering the granite plug would have to be installed above the sarcophagus a little higher than the last step of the descending passage. Yet, there is no evidence of such beams installed at an ideal height of about 5 meters above the sarcophagus as there was in the South Tomb Main Burial Chamber. If so, they would have been left in place much as the support beams that still exist higher up in the shaft.

Fig. 6-15 – The Central Burial Chamber
The red line indicates the last step of the North Descending Passage (in the background) that is 7 meters above floor level

Supporting this hypothesis are several sets of hieroglyphs along the sides and top of the granite slabs that comprise the sarcophagus. These are an architect's markings instructing the work crew on how to assemble the sarcophagus once the granite slabs were brought down into the burial chamber. (These are not unlike the assembly instructions one gets with furniture kits.) The curious thing is that the person supervising the assembly of the sarcophagus did so in reverse of how it should have been as indicated by these markings! [61] In other words, the blocks and the granite plug marked for the south side were installed on the north side; blocks for the east side were installed on the west, and so on. From this, I concluded that Imhotep had nothing to do with the construction of this tomb shaft and its sarcophagus because he would not allow such sloppy work from his work crews.

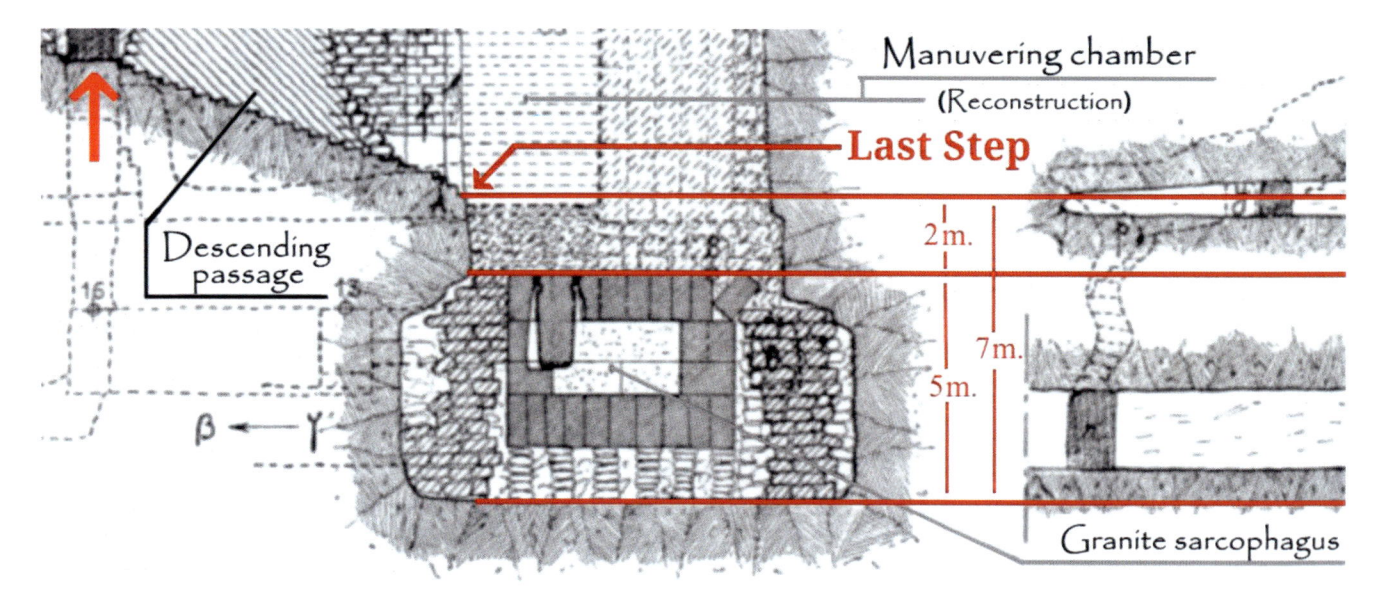

Fig. 6-16 – The Central Burial Shaft's Last Step (see also Fig. 6-15)

When entering the burial chambers of most, if not all, Old Kingdom pyramids or mastabas, *the descending passages are either level with the floor of the burial chamber, or an easy single step down*. If entering the chamber from an ascending passageway, whose exterior entrance is below the level of the burial chamber floor, *the passage ends at floor level, or just slightly below* and is easily accessed by a few steps like at the end of the Grand Gallery of the Great Pyramid at Giza.

This led me to conclude that Imhotep found the Central Burial Chamber in pretty much the same condition as it was found in the late 19th and early 20th centuries. Additionally, the last step of the North Descending Passage is over 7 meters (23 feet) above floor level and 2 meters (6.56 feet) above the sarcophagus (the red line in *Figs. 6-15* and *6-16*) at the point where it enters the Central Burial Chamber. Even Firth noticed this oddity as shown by the quotation above. This implies that Imhotep ordered the excavation of at least part of this passage from the inside out to the surface, leaving some of the excavation rubble to surround the sarcophagus. This happened long after the original excavation of the tall central vertical shaft and installation of the sarcophagus for one of Djoser's predecessor. It is possible that two crews excavated the descending passage working from both the inside and outside. Try as they might to meet in the middle, they slightly miscalculated and had to make adjustments at the end. The short landing (red arrow, *Fig. 6-16*) hints at this.

Even though some have suggested the purpose of the North Descending Passage was to remove construction debris from the Burial Chamber [62] this does not seem reasonable. The Central Burial Shaft is 29.5 meters (96.78 feet) deep with the descending passage opening 7 meters (23 feet) above floor level. This means excavation up to that point required that all of the construction waste from the first 22.5 meters (73.82 feet) went up and out the top of the shaft, with only the last 7 meters (23 feet) of excavation work using the new descending passage for waste removal. *Not very efficient!*

If construction of the Central Burial Chamber and the North Descending Passage occurred at the same time, then logically, the last step of the descending passage would be level with the Burial Chamber floor as in other pyramids, and the North Descending Passage would be much longer than as it presently exists. This would also make installing a *regular* sarcophagus much easier once the burial chamber was completed. This may seem like a small, insignificant detail, but as we continue our investigation, it will become more apparent that some of the buildings that now exist in the Step Pyramid Enclosure were not the handiwork of Imhotep. Maybe he wished to preserve the work of one of his predecessors, perhaps his father, Kanofer, who was also a Royal Architect.

The huge size of the Step Pyramid sarcophagus is reminiscent of the immense Apis bull sarcophagi – considered the largest in all of Egypt – located in the Serapeum nearby in north Sakkara. In contrast, the Step Pyramid sarcophagus is about 60% larger than any sarcophagi in the Serapeum (!). This would make it one of the largest, if not **the** largest, sarcophagus in Egypt, so using 32 granite slabs to construct it makes a great deal of sense. Though it is difficult to assess its relative size from photographs (see *Fig. 6-17*), its approximate dimensions are as follows.

Step Pyramid Sarcophagus Dimensions

	EXTERIOR	INTERIOR
Height	4.7 m. (15.42 ft.)	1.7 m. (5.58 ft.)
Width	3.9 m. (12.80 ft.)	1.6 m. (5.25 ft.)
Length	5.4 m. (17.72 ft.)	3 m. (9.84 ft.)

This could easily accommodate a mummy up to 9 feet tall (!!), though I doubt there were any such tall persons living at that time in ancient Egypt. However, *rumor has it* that the last king of the Second Dynasty and Djoser's father was over 2.44 meters (8 feet) tall. The latest translations of the Greek historian, Manetho, gives Khasekhemwui's height as "5 cubits, 3 palms". Depending on which cubit is used, be it a *remen* cubit, the short cubit, the royal cubit or some other cubit, Khasekhemwui could have been at least 7 feet tall to over 14 feet tall (!!!). Without a body to examine, it is difficult to prove, but if true, it might indicate Khasekhemwui suffered from a form of gigantism. This might also point to a completely different person originally intended for the sarcophagus. It could also go long way in explaining why Khasekhemwui may have ordered the construction of the nearby *Gisr el-Mudir* (the *Great Enclosure*) along with this burial chamber/mastaba, which duplicates the design of his tomb at Umm el-Qa'ab and his funerary enclosure, commonly known as *"Shunet el-Zebib"* (literally, "Storehouse of the Raisins"), or *Shuneh* for short, both in Abydos. The reason for going through the time, labor and expense to have two burial sites is still unclear. The Great Enclosure may have even belonged to the ephemeral king, Sanakht, who was possibly Khasekhemwui's immediate successor (see *The South Tomb* section below). It may even postdate the reign of Djoser altogether.

However, Khasekhemwui's statue in the Ashmolean Museum (*Fig. 6-3*) indicates he was of average height for an ancient Egyptian. If so, it is highly unlikely he would have commissioned a statue showing he was shorter than in real life. Another possibility is that Khasekhemwui passed along the same genetic trait for gigantism to Djoser, and the sarcophagus was for Djoser all along. However, by alleging either or both of these kings were giants may be an exaggeration, because any person over 6 feet tall in ancient Egypt would appear to be gigantic, and we have mummies from Egypt that are at least that tall and taller.

Still, there was no discovery of a complete or parts of a body or coffin in the sarcophagus when Firth and Lauer excavated it in the 1930s, adding another to list of mysteries surrounding this and many other pyramids. As the sarcophagus did not contain anyone – 9 feet tall or otherwise – knowing where Djoser was buried will remain a mystery for now. Djoser may have even intended the South Tomb to be his final resting place, though there is no evidence for this.

There is also one slight problem with the design of this sarcophagus. The granite plug inserted into the one end of sarcophagus suggests that any mummy entombed within might not have been in a sealed coffin as Firth suggested. The hole in the top of the sarcophagus into which the granite plug was installed is about 0.9 meters (3 feet) wide, certainly wide enough to insert a coffin case. However, the hole is only about 2.1 meters (6.89 feet) deep to the lip where the granite plug rests (see *Fig. 6-16*). The stone slabs forming the top lid of the sarcophagus are about 1 meter (3.28 feet) thick. This offers very little swing room to insert a coffin safely into the sarcophagus without damaging it. Eliminating the coffin would make it easier to place a mummy in this sarcophagus, but considering the difficulty in doing so, it may be the reason for not entombing the rigor mortis-stiff mummy of Djoser within it. If it was not for the fact that the sarcophagus is located in the Central Burial Chamber, its unusual design might prevent considering it as a sarcophagus at all.

As shown in *Figs. 6-14* and *6-15*, the plug does not sit flush with the top of the sarcophagus. Tomb robbers may have attempted to raise the plug to rob the contents of the sarcophagus, but then gave up because at 3 tons, it was much too heavy to lift. When excavation began in the 1920s, the slab at the south end of the sarcophagus opposite the granite plug was tilted outward (see *North-South Section A* of *Figs. 6-13* and *6-16*). If this was the work of tomb robbers, they soon gave up, as there obviously was no coffin or body in the sarcophagus, just as it was when discovered during excavations in the early 20th century.

Fig. 6-17 – Looking down into the Central Burial Chamber
Note the person in the upper right corner of the Burial Chamber for scale

The Step Pyramid underwent a 14-year renovation with the Burial Chamber and tunnels reopened in March 2020. The exposure of the 24 pillars supporting the sarcophagus occurred during the renovation (see *Fig. 6-12*), which may have been part of an earlier construction project, not something Imhotep designed. Their use suggests the architect knew of the prevalence of earthquakes in this area of Egypt, and the possible reason for the pillars' unusual design was to absorb shocks from earthquakes with the packing of the rock debris around this unusually designed sarcophagus providing extra cushioning from earth tremors. The reason why the sarcophagus was not installed directly onto the floor is unclear. Renovation of the Step Pyramid that began in 2011 included repairing and stabilizing the Central Burial Shaft's roof and removing most of the rock debris surrounding the sarcophagus. It is now possible to walk around the sarcophagus on a raised wooden platform that is even with the bottom of the sarcophagus, situated about 1.25 meters (4 feet) above the floor. This is something that was not possible up until now, and possibly not even in Imhotep's time. Presumably, most of the original rubble still lies beneath this wooden platform, which, oddly enough, helps to maintain the stability of the sarcophagus above it in the event of another earthquake. Taken together everything we have learned so far, *the sarcophagus may not have been intended to be freestanding at all!* If so, Firth's belief that the sarcophagus was set into the floor of the burial chamber surrounded by excavation rubble was the original design from the beginning.

Though Djoser could have reigned longer than the 19 years generally ascribed to him in order for the excavation of the Step Pyramid's interior tunnels and chambers to be finished, it would have been unlikely that he started and completed the entirely of all the above and below ground construction projects before his death. The enormity of the sarcophagus and the Central Burial Chamber alone meant he could have lived longer than previously thought.

However, if Djoser reigned for only 19 years, the more likely scenario is the full excavation of the vertical shaft and the installation of the sarcophagus within the Burial Chamber occurred before Imhotep was commissioned to build Djoser's funerary complex. Once construction began, the descending passage was dug out from the Central Burial Chamber northward and upward with most of the excavation debris carried up and out through the vertical shaft. Because the granite sarcophagus sits very close to the Burial Chamber's north wall, Imhotep couldn't begin excavating the North Descending Passage at floor level. He had to commence excavating the descending passage higher up in the north wall, far enough above the top of the sarcophagus to ensure adequate clearance and to prevent any damage to it. Above the Central Burial Chamber, Mastaba M₁ was completed; and the construction of Mastaba M₂ as a shell surrounding Mastaba M₁ followed shortly by the addition of Mastaba M₃ to cover the eleven pit tombs.

Many mastaba tombs of the period had vertical shafts descending into the burial chambers (*Fig. 6-18*). They generally did not have a sloping entry passage leading from outside the walls of the mastaba into the burial chamber because this would have provided easy access for tomb robbers, assuming the older mastaba tombs were designed in in a similar fashion to the Step Pyramid and South Tomb burial shafts. By extension, this design for a burial shaft and chamber, typical of Old Kingdom mastabas, should have influenced Imhotep assuming he designed all the underground tunnels and chambers of the Step Pyramid and South Tomb.

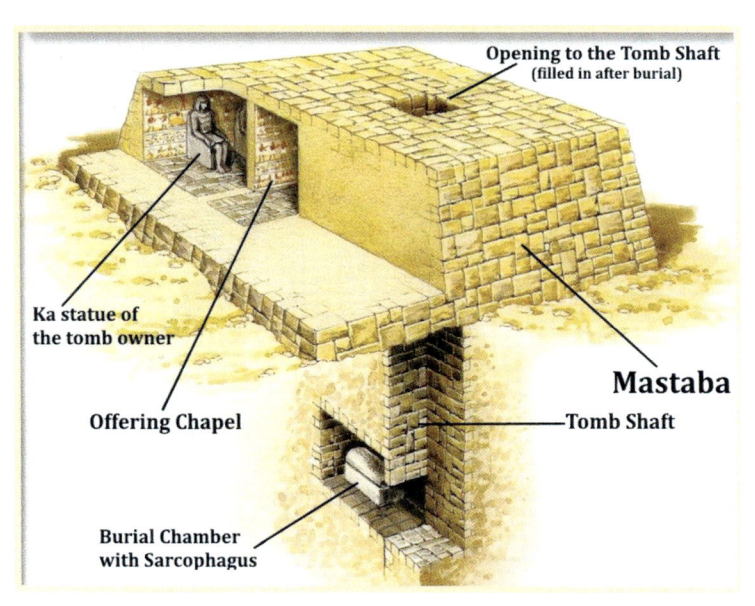

Fig. 6-18 – A typical mastaba tomb with its burial shafts

The South Tomb

The South Tomb (*Figs. 6-19* and *6-20*) is "a riddle, wrapped in a mystery, inside an enigma". It has caused much consternation and confusion among Egyptologists ever since its excavation in the 1920s. There are many theories about the purpose for the South Tomb as there Egyptologists. One theory is it housed the placenta from Djoser's birth, or even the canopic jars containing his internal organs removed during the mummification process. This is not as crazy as it first sounds. During part of the *sed*-festival ceremonies, the king wore a tight-fitting garment meant to symbolize the placenta that surrounded and protected his body prior to birth. In effect, the *Ḥeb-Sed* is a celebration of the king's rejuvenation, or rebirth, to continue to rule, much like his birth symbolizes the beginning of his life.

Another theory posits the South Tomb was a substitute memorial for one that would have been traditionally located at Abydos in southern Egypt. Several royal tombs of First and Second Dynasty kings at Abydos consisted of two elements: a funerary enclosure constructed in north Abydos, with a separate tomb located about 2 kilometers to the southeast at Umm el-Qa'ab. This theory may explain the existence of the South Tomb more than any other. Djoser may have wanted to replicate the two-part structure of earlier royal tombs in Abydos when he chose Sakkara as the location for his tomb, and wanted the South Tomb to be his final resting place. The shape of the South Tomb with its arched roofline is similar to the elongated, rectangular profile of Western Massif II, suggesting a common link to other Second Dynasty tombs.

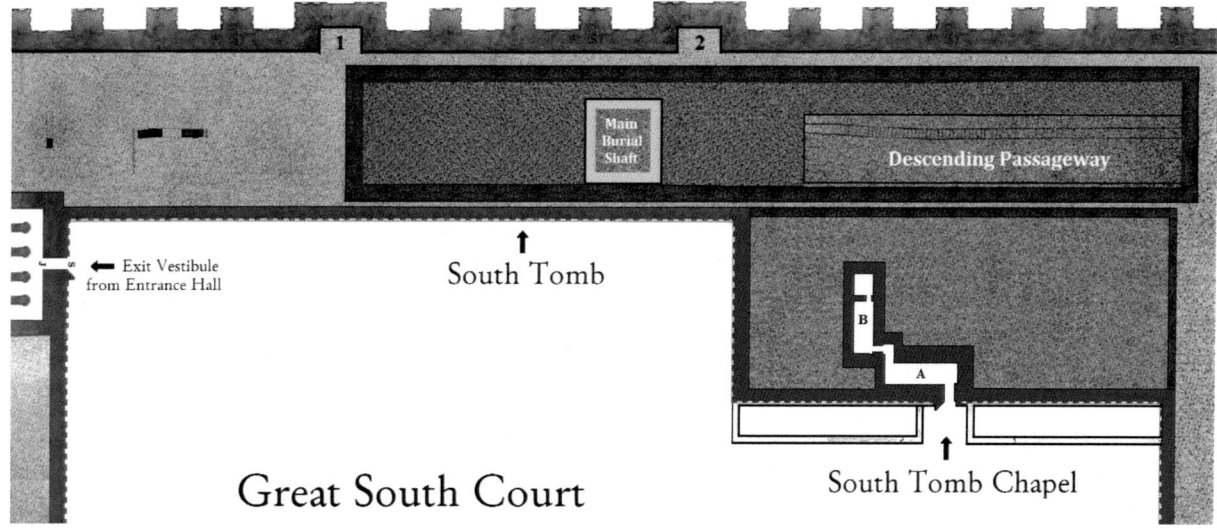

Fig. 6-19 – The South Tomb and South Tomb Chapel, top view looking south

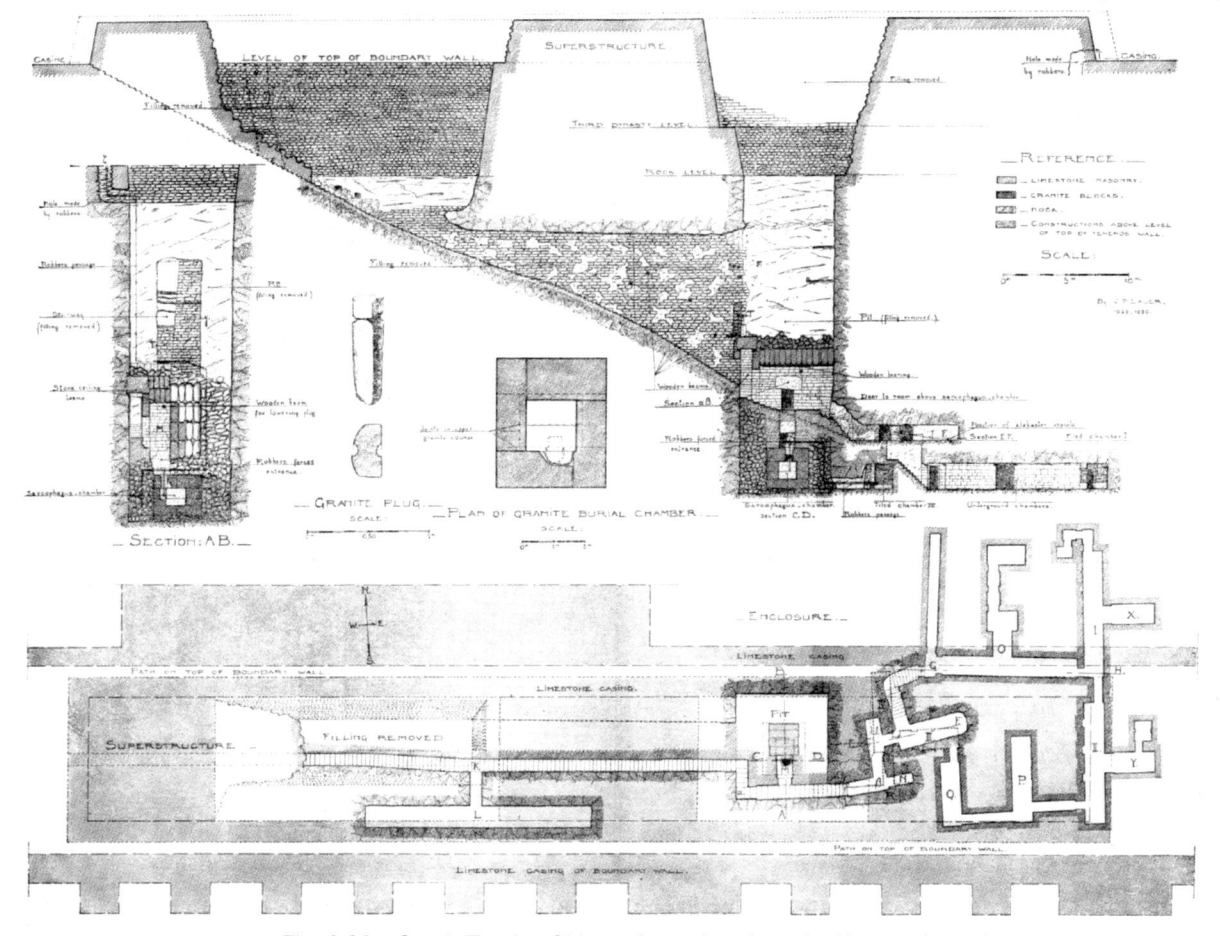

Fig. 6-20 – South Tomb – Side and top elevations, looking north

Whatever its purpose, there was no indication within this tomb to point to the reason for its construction. It does house a smaller sarcophagus in its own tomb shaft, similar in style to the one in the Step Pyramid, along with a more complete set of blue-faience tiled scenes of Djoser performing the rituals associated with the *sed*-festival (*Fig. 6-21*). This is important to remember because installation of six similar, duplicate panels related to the Ḥeb-Sed had begun in several chambers beneath the Step Pyramid, but never finished. This can only mean that Djoser must have passed away prior to their completion, and work on the Step Pyramid and its enclosure was ongoing right up until his death.

Fig. 6-21 – South Tomb Faience Chamber (reconstructed)

One or more of the above hypotheses is the most likely reason for the construction of the South Tomb. However, Imhotep may have also used it as a type of *trial piece* to experiment with using different building materials and techniques. Evidence for this comes from the aforementioned six completed panels of blue faience showing Djoser participating in the Ḥeb-Sed ceremonies. Not to mention, his work crews, sculptors and other artisans needed to hone their newly acquired skills before launching into the grand construction project that awaited them.

Although stone had been used in temple and tomb construction before, Imhotep was using stone in an entirely new way, and needed to make sure what he envisioned could be accomplished at the building site by his work crews. Imhotep had to train and teach his artisans and sculptors in the new techniques he was developing in order to build, first, the four-tier Step Pyramid and Enclosure Wall, and later, the six-tier Step Pyramid. As this was Imhotep's first time building a monument of this size using an enormous quantity of stone whereas other funerary mastabas and monuments were usually made of mudbrick, then it makes sense that Imhotep wanted to get it right the first time.

Though it may have started out as Netjerikhet Djoser's tomb prior to the building of the Step Pyramid(s), I initially thought of the South Tomb for a child inasmuch as its sarcophagus is about half the size of the one in the Step Pyramid. There was an ephemeral king between Khasekhemwui and Netjerikhet Djoser. As mentioned before, his name was Sanakht, or Horus Sa Werskhunum, or even Nebka depending on the source. He may also have even been the presumed successor to Sekhemkhet. Take your pick.

According to the Egyptologist, Nabil Swelim, Sanakht's reign only lasted for 2 months, 23 days,[63] leading me to suspect he was a child, or at least a very young man. When he became pharaoh, he did not live long enough to complete the burial rituals (which traditionally lasted between 42 and 70 days) for his supposed father, Khasekhemwui. Netjerikhet Djoser eventually completed these rituals based on clay seals bearing his name found in Khasekhemwui's tomb at Abydos, and is believed to be the true first king of the Third Dynasty. If Swelim is right, then the South Tomb may have been intended for this ephemeral Sanakht/Horus Sa Werskhunum/Nebka, and Mastabas M_1/M_2 already existed, although in an incomplete state, making it easy for Djoser to take it over for his funerary monument.

The sarcophagus at the bottom of the South Tomb's Main Burial Chamber was crafted in a similar fashion to the larger one located in the Step Pyramid's Central Burial Chamber. Though smaller, the construction of the South Tomb's sarcophagus used multiple slabs of granite to form a stone box as if it was for an actual burial. There is no evidence that the South Tomb ever contained human remains, but some think it housed the king's mummified organs stored in canopic jars, or the aforementioned king's placenta, though canopic jars are usually found in close proximity to the tomb occupant. Neither theory has gained much credence due to a lack of hard evidence to support them. As determined from J.-P. Lauer's plans, the dimensions of the South Tomb sarcophagus are as follows.

South Tomb Sarcophagus Dimensions

	EXTERIOR	INTERIOR
Height	3.1 m. (10.17 ft.)	1.3 m. (4.27 ft.)
Width	3.5 m. (11.48 ft.)	1.6 m. (5.25 ft.)
Length	4.0 m. (13.12 ft.)	1.6 m. (5.25 ft.)

Based on the above dimensions, the mummy of a 5-foot tall person – either stretched out flat or in a fetal position – can easily fit into the South Tomb sarcophagus. This means it is possible Sanakht was an adult when he passed. Because the design of the South Tomb sarcophagus is different from virtually every sarcophagus in ancient Egypt means a mummy would have to be entombed without a coffin; a most unusual burial practice given what we know of ancient Egyptian funerary customs. In order to place a body wrapped only in typical mummy linens into this peculiar design of a sarcophagus would require inserting it feet first through the hole at the top; and then reinstalling the granite plug after the funeral. However, as is the case with the body of Djoser, there has been no discovery of Sanakht's mummy.

If Djoser was meant to be buried in the South Tomb, thus duplicating the two-part concept of royal tombs at Abydos, then the South Tomb sarcophagus would be the right size for an Old Kingdom pharaoh. Since ancient Egyptians were of smaller stature than people are today, the sarcophagus in the Central Burial Chamber of the Step Pyramid would have been overly large for the body of the king. This idea led to a rather startling question: If the South Tomb's original purpose was for Djoser's burial, was the Step Pyramid sarcophagus meant to be strictly symbolic? If not, was Central Burial Chamber meant to be the tomb of an earlier king – and who was this king? Since there have not been any mummies found in either sarcophagus, where is Djoser's actual tomb?

While there's no shortage of theories concerning the reason for building the South Tomb, little attention has been paid as to ***when*** it was constructed. Was it erected before, during or after the four-tier Step Pyramid was designed and built? Was the excavation of the South Tomb Main Burial Chamber done separately and left unused for a time, and an entrance corridor and stairs added on much later to finish it? Or, was the South Tomb and its chapel constructed from beginning to end without interruption? We really don't know for certain, but whoever designed the Central Burial Chamber of the Step Pyramid must have also designed the South Tomb Main Burial Chamber because their design and construction are virtually identical. Whether Imhotep excavated it has yet to be determined. As we have already shown, both burial vaults in the Step Pyramid and the South Tomb share the same unique design in that they have a steep drop down from the last step of the descending passage to the top of the sarcophagus, about 3 meters (9.84 feet) in the case of the South Tomb Main Burial Chamber.

This led me to speculate that each of the two burial shafts and descending passages were two different building projects separated by a wide span of time because of one simple question: **Why did Imhotep design and build both the Step Pyramid and South Tomb burial chambers with two entrances?**

The simple answer is: **He didn't**. No other tomb in all of Egypt has two entrances into their burial chambers. The reasons are simple: (1) it would necessitate twice the labor and/or materials to build two entrances, and (2) having two means of entry into a tomb would give tomb robbers twice the chance of successfully robbing the tombs. *Not very practical*. (The Bent Pyramid at Dashur doesn't count. It has two burial chambers with two corresponding entry passages; one for each chamber.) In addition, Imhotep's completely different design for the burial chamber and sarcophagus in the Pyramid of Sekhemkhet, Djoser's successor, suggests he didn't design either one of these two burial chambers or sarcophagi (see Chapter 7).

Because there are two entrances for the South Tomb and the Step Pyramid burial chambers, these chambers had to pre-exist Imhotep's work to transform them into royal sepulchers. The two descending passages was Imhotep's work alone enabling him to cover over the two vertical tomb shafts, cutting off at least one of the entrances to each of the two burial chambers from thieves. In the final analysis, Imhotep found many unfinished building projects on this plateau in north Sakkara, so he incorporated what he had available into the design of an amazing mortuary complex for his king, and ultimately, for the people of Egypt. Another possibility is that these two burial chambers and their sarcophagi are symbolic only, negating the need to worry about securing them from tomb robbers.

The South Tomb Chapel

As chapels go, the South Tomb Chapel is a bit of an *odd duck*. Initially, it was thought to have housed the crowns of Netjerikhet Djoser, but this doesn't seem reasonable. Why would Djoser store his crowns so far away from his palace when he would have needed them on a regular basis while conducting the affairs of state in public when he was in residence in Memphis? Perhaps the South Tomb Chapel was a memorial chapel to perpetuate the memory of Djoser, or maybe it served as a kind of ceremonial gatehouse guarding the South Tomb's entrance directly behind the Chapel.

Inasmuch as it lies adjacent to the Great South Court, we can safely conclude its function had to do with the *sed*-festival ceremonies. The cobra frieze surrounding the top of the Chapel indicates an association with royalty. In this case, Djoser may have used it as his robing room prior to performing the *Heb-Sed* rituals. The little room in the back of room 'B' in *Fig. 6-19* may have even been the royal latrine as these types of accommodations were prevalent throughout the temple complex (*Figs. 3-45* and *3-46, 6-10* and *6-11*).

Just as with the mystery surrounding the South Tomb's role, we do not know what purpose the South Tomb Chapel may have served. Not enough of the original structure exists to determine its true function. Archeologists, professional and amateur alike, often grasp at straws, whether they make sense or not, when confronted with scant evidence surrounding ancient monuments and artifacts. This sort of intellectual exercise can be as much fun as it is frustrating.

While the funerary or *sed*-festival function of the South Tomb Chapel is unknown, it did serve a purpose related to the design of the Step Pyramid Enclosure. *More details concerning this are covered in the next chapter.*

The North and South Pavilions

The North and South Pavilions are, perhaps, two of the most unique structures among the many funerary monuments in Egypt, and in many ways, the most enigmatic. Originally, Firth thought them to be the tombs of two of Djoser's daughters or queens, Inetkaes and Hetephernebti due to fragments of boundary stelae with their names found on the site.[64] Two pit tombs, P_1 and P_2, are located nearby, but there has only been the discovery of pottery fragments from the Third Dynasty in them with no sign of the true owners of these tombs. Lauer and the German Egyptologist Herbert Ricke later speculated the North and South Pavilions were symbolic representations of royal administrative residences for the king in Upper and Lower Egypt. Then, there's a different idea altogether postulated by Egyptologist Mark Lehner.

> **Evidence suggests that the builders partially buried the dummy structure of Djoser's enclosure – the Pavilions of the North and South, the South Tomb and the *Sed* Chapels – almost immediately after they built them in the first stage. Likewise, they encased the king's mastaba in fine limestone in the first stage and then only a few years later entirely covered it with the Step Pyramid – an act which, if Stadelmann is right, they may have planned from the beginning. The half-submerging of the dummy buildings must have signified the chthonic, underworld aspect of existence after death. *And the full envelopment of the mastaba conforms to the pattern of early Egyptian monuments that successive stages conceal earlier stages.* Tomb building appears to have been part of a larger ceremonial cycle, an act of consolidation and renewal that necessitated burying finely crafted structures.**[65] (Emphasis added).

I do not have any archeological evidence to confirm the *burial theory* of the German Egyptologist, Rainer Stadelmann and others. However, it is possible to nullify Stadelmann's conclusion by asking one circuitous question. Since there are two entrances (a burial shaft and a descending passage) into both the Step Pyramid and the South Tomb, then it seems that both of the descending passages were the only ones Imhotep excavated, and the excavation of the burial shafts were completed by someone else for a different king. If Imhotep incorporated Mastaba M_1 that may have already existed on the plateau into Djoser's funerary monument as Lehner suggests, couldn't the unfinished mastabas now known as the North and South Pavilions be repurposed in the same way?

In addition, it does not seem reasonable that Imhotep went through the effort of designing and building the North and South Pavilions from the ground up as well as the other *dummy* structures only to have them covered over with dirt and rubble to resurrect a rather obscure funerary ritual. Besides feeling wrong on so many levels, this explanation seems highly improbable for one simple reason:

Imhotep had a tremendous ego!

With Chief Royal Architect and Royal Physician among his many titles, Imhotep was the second most powerful man in Egypt after the Pharaoh Netjerikhet Djoser. In that respect, he was probably no different from any man in his position, ancient or modern. With the possession of great power, coupled with a great vision, comes a great ego. It can be no other way. Otherwise, he would not have been an effective leader and organizer of such monumental projects like the Step Pyramid Enclosure along with running a kingdom the size of Egypt.

I usually don't advocate psychoanalyzing a person that has been dead for over 4700 years. However, it seems safe to say that if Imhotep had constructed the North and South Pavilions in their entirety, he would not have had them covered over in order to "send these buildings into the Netherworld where the king would reside after his death". [66] I cannot recall ever seeing this same theory promulgated elsewhere about the burial of a monument or mortuary structure as part of a ritual entombment to imitate the subterranean world of the Afterlife. That doesn't mean such examples do not exist, but they do not appear to have existed much before Imhotep's time, and in sufficient quantities to become a widespread tradition. In my estimation, the conjecture of *ritually burying* buildings seems to stretch the boundaries of believability. Large amounts of the ever-present windblown sand accumulating over the centuries, along with smaller rubble produced naturally as this temple's stonework was reused for other projects would be a better explanation for the *burial* of the North and South Pavilions.

Archeology is a guessing game. Unearth something today, make a reasonable conclusion based on your findings and all available research, and you have a good chance of arriving at a consensus consistent with sound archeological practices. However, if new information from subsequent investigations comes to light that changes or invalidates the conclusions about an earlier excavation, then it sometimes becomes more difficult to arrive at a genuine consensus that includes all the available relevant data. Archeologists are human after all, and no one likes to have their pet theory touched or violated in any way (*me included!*) despite any new subsequent data or information.

Many archeologists get caught up in the minutia of *the dig*; excavating, cataloging, preservation of the finds, documenting everything in sight, and finally, writing the final scholarly papers at the end of it all. That's okay, there's nothing wrong it. This is the inherent nature of archeology. However, trying to get a *30,000-foot view* of an ancient site is extremely difficult when your nose is only inches away from what you're excavating. This is not an indictment of the methodology of archeological fieldwork. (*Somebody has to do the dirty work, and who knows, it might also be a lot of fun!*). What is sometimes lost while unearthing the past is the simple truth that human beings built these monuments; people not unlike ourselves, with the same hopes, wishes and desires that are common to all humans, along with the same error-prone, very human personality faults and frailties.

As we have already mentioned, Firth concluded after working on the site for several years that the structures within the Step Pyramid Enclosure were never completed. He based this partly on the appearance of the mountains of dirt and rubble covering the area around the Step Pyramid site when excavation commenced in the 1920s. This might explain the belief that the North and South Pavilions were deliberately buried. Perhaps a better explanation for their half-buried condition is that when Imhotep received the commission to build Djoser's tomb at Sakkara, other structures were already present on the Sakkara plateau prior to Djoser choosing this place for his mortuary complex. Firth seems to have indirectly hinted at this possibility:

> **So fine and on so large a scale had the masonry** [of the rediscovered South Tomb] **now been proved to be, that Firth** (reasonably) **concluded... that Imhotep could not have been the first "to build a house of stone." Indeed, it seemed probable that there were large stone buildings existing in...** (Imhotep's) ***day which he felt free to use as quarries.*** [67] (Clarification and emphasis added.)

We do know the middle of three storage magazines, Western Massif II, existed prior to Djoser's reign since it is attributed to one or more unknown Second Dynasty kings. From this evidence, it is reasonable to conclude the Sakkara plateau was not devoid of any older construction projects, and those that did exist were left unfinished. At the very least, and even before the initial construction phase commenced, Mastaba M₁ and the eleven pit tombs that would eventually be covered over by Mastaba M₃ may have already stood on the Sakkara plateau (see *Fig. 6-5*), allowing Imhotep to reuse or integrate them into the Djoser mortuary temple project. Evidence for the original intended use of the North and South Pavilions is that their design is quite similar to many other mastabas for the elite of Memphis that were built in the area of north Sakkara before and after Djoser's reign. The principles that dictated the design and purpose they served, indicate when they were constructed. First and Second Dynasty mastabas were pretty much the same despite some differences.

The state in which Imhotep found these two unfinished mastabas differed greatly from the normal design features of Pharaonic mastabas of the period. Had they been further along in their construction process, it is possible the design of the Step Pyramid Enclosure would have looked very different than it does now. Subsidiary tombs of many of the mastabas at Abydos, Sakkara and elsewhere are reminiscent in concept to the eleven pit tombs beneath Mastaba M₃. Note also the curved roof of the mastaba in *Figs. 6-22* and *6-23* indicating the stylistic connection between older mastabas and the North Pavilion being an imitation of the Primeval Mound of Creation, virtually proving it was an unfinished mastaba before being repurposed by Imhotep.

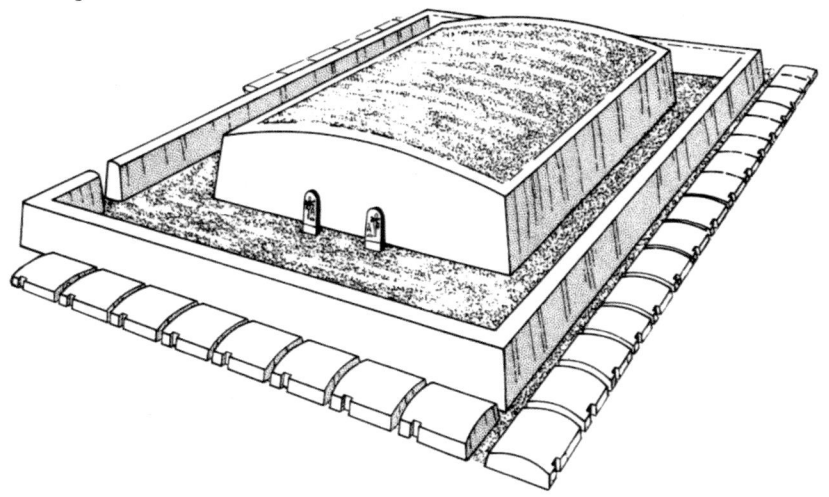

Fig. 6-22 – Reconstruction of the mastaba attributed to the First Dynasty Queen (or King) Merneith at Umm el-Qa'ab, Abydos with multiple subsidiary burial mounds surrounding it

Fig. 6-23 - The North Pavilion. Note the curved roof similar to that of Queen Merneith's mastaba

As discussed thus far, it is now possible to see the North and South Pavilions were once two partially constructed and abandoned mastabas, and their alleged ritual burial were not part of Imhotep's original design plans for Djoser's mortuary complex. This is not only based on observing the typically human character traits of men in Imhotep's position of power, but a simple scrutiny of the stratigraphy of the internal stonework of the two pavilions can tell us a great deal more. In looking at various old excavations and current photos of the North Pavilion in particular, I noticed a difference between various layers of stone *(Figs. 6-24* and *6-25)*. If Imhotep had these two mastabas covered over for any reason, it was probably for the simple fact that they already existed on the plateau where Djoser wanted to build his tomb.

Fig. 6-24 – The North Pavilion showing dissimilar sizes of stone and infill material in three different layers, implying two, or possibly three, widely separated periods of construction

Fig. 6-25 – The South Pavilion showing the same three dissimilar levels of stonework

Rather than tearing them down, Imhotep simply added one, possibly two, additional layers to both pavilions, each layer having smaller stones than the layer below it. He then designed a set of limestone façades to simulate the temporary pavilions that were often used during *sed*-festivals, and grafted these onto the two unfinished mastaba-like structures. The fact that *Layer 1* consists of larger, partially dressed stacked stones confirms that one of Imhotep's predecessors was already using cut stone to build funerary buildings like a mastaba. (Kanofer, Imhotep's father and also a Royal Architect, may have had a hand in constructing these mastabas.) If the North and South Pavilions were solely Imhotep's handiwork, he would have used a layer of consistently sized, unrefined infill material within the Pavilion's interiors similar to that found in the large area north of the Entrance Hall (see *Figs. 6-47* and *6-48*). Furthermore, he would not have had the lower *Layer 1* interior stones dressed and semi-finished when they would eventually have been covered by a second façade.

Though presently not known, there must have been a reason for not tearing down these two forlorn, unfinished mastabas. Repurposing them clearly shows Imhotep's genius, as he was able to cobble together other kings' *leftovers* like a Cobb salad [68] to fashion usable structures from what was essentially a pile of useless rubble. As we say today, Imhotep "turned a sow's ear into a silk purse". By all appearances, Imhotep merely incorporated what he found on the plateau into the design of the grand mortuary monument we see today. The most probable explanation is that before building the Step Pyramid Enclosure, Djoser and Imhotep searched the Sakkara plateau for a suitable location for Djoser's tomb. Djoser may have wanted to preserve his ancestors' tombs, even though many of them, such as Mastaba M_1 and the mastabas that later became the North and South Pavilions, were unfinished or barely started.

While there is no proof that other tombs, mastabas or other structures like the North and South Pavilions existed above or below ground on the plateau where the Step Pyramid Enclosure was eventually built (with the possible exception of Western Massif II), it doesn't disprove it either. We are only left with the evidence of the final structures as they exist today; not what the area looked like prior to the construction of the pyramid(s) and other buildings. That is one of our greatest challenges with this monument.

If these structures existed before Imhotep began to construct the first four-tier Step Pyramid, then it is unknown what symbolism they were intended to represent (if any), and what they eventually symbolized in the overall design of the Step Pyramid Enclosure as a whole. We only presume they were representations of similar pavilions used during the *Ḥeb-Sed*.

If these pavilions were deliberately covered up as part of an archaic burial ritual (as opposed to the possibility of windblown sand as the source of their concealment), Imhotep would have permitted their *burial* because he did not design them, so covering them would not have bruised his ego in the least. More than likely, though, the real reason Imhotep had the mastabas covered over with more readily available sand and rubble was to solve the problem of requiring extra labor to remove them, and instead chose to upgrade and include them into his final design as opposed to the less likely explanation of a "ceremonial burial" (*Fig. 6-26*).

Fig. 6-26 – The North Pavilion as reconstructed by J.-P. Lauer

Two more pieces of indirect evidence point to the probability that Imhotep did not design and build the underlying mastabas that became the North and South Pavilions. The presence of two pits (marked 'Pit P_1' and 'Pit P_2' in *Fig. 6-27*) just east of both pavilions accounts for Imhotep's design of the two pavilion courts, which deftly avoids surrounding or incorporating these pits into the interiors of both courts. According to Firth, these two pits contained many pieces of broken pottery and stone vases, and confirms the two pavilions were meant to be tombs and not part of a model of the treasuries of Upper and Lower Egypt. [69]

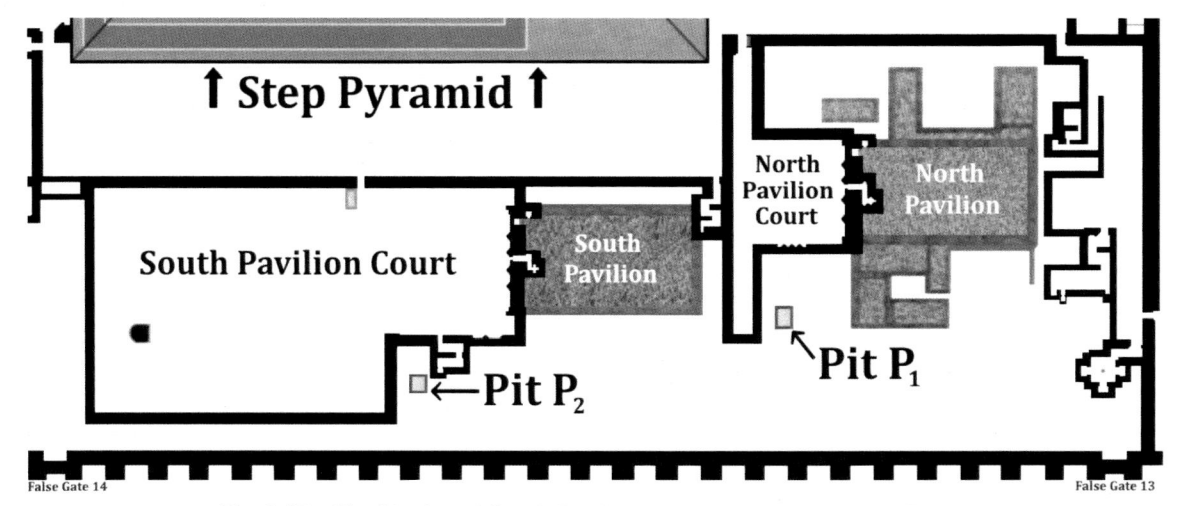

Fig. 6-27 – The North and South Pavilions and their associated Pit Tombs

The location of these two pit tombs are quite telling. If Imhotep had designed and built the North and South Pavilions, the T-shaped North Pavilion Court and the L-shaped South Pavilion Court in front of them would have looked entirely different. The two pit tombs would have been located elsewhere, with the two forecourts having more rectangular shapes instead of the odd designs they are (*Fig. 6-28*).

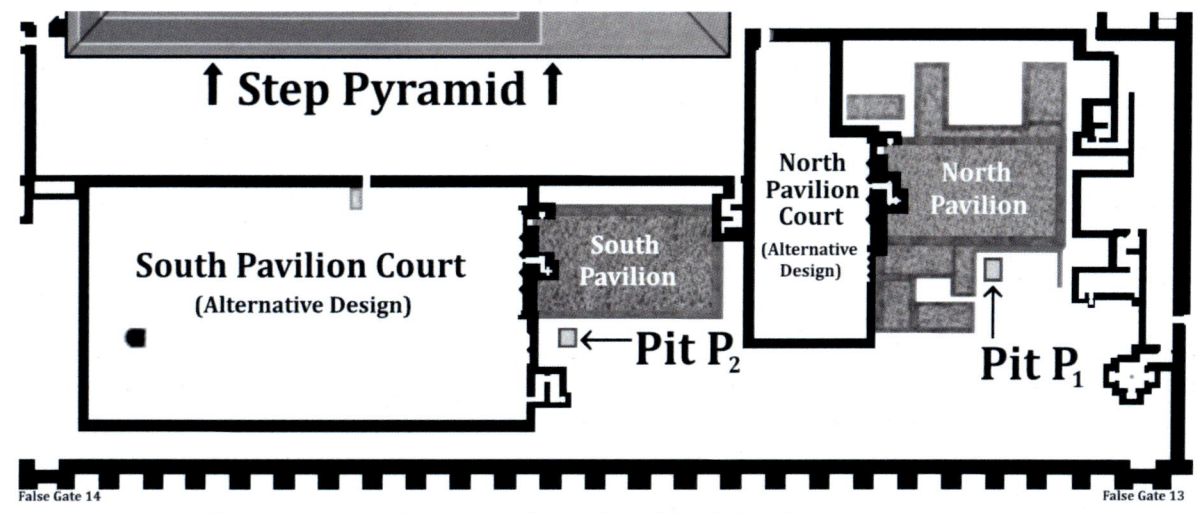

Fig. 6-28 – Alternative designs for North and South Pavilion Courts if pit tombs P1 and P2 did not pre-exist the construction of the North and South Pavilions

Because the two mastabas/pavilions and their neighboring pit tombs already existed on the Sakkara plateau when Imhotep began work on Djoser's monument, he designed the two forecourts in such a way as to avoid *bumping into* the two pit tombs. It is easy to understand why archeologists believe Imhotep built the North and South Pavilions because everything in the Step Pyramid Enclosure is mostly his work. However convoluted though this explanation may be, the existence of the pit tombs P₁ and P₂ exposes Imhotep's *secret* design solution, and the argument for Imhotep *burying* the two pavilions falls by the wayside as a result.

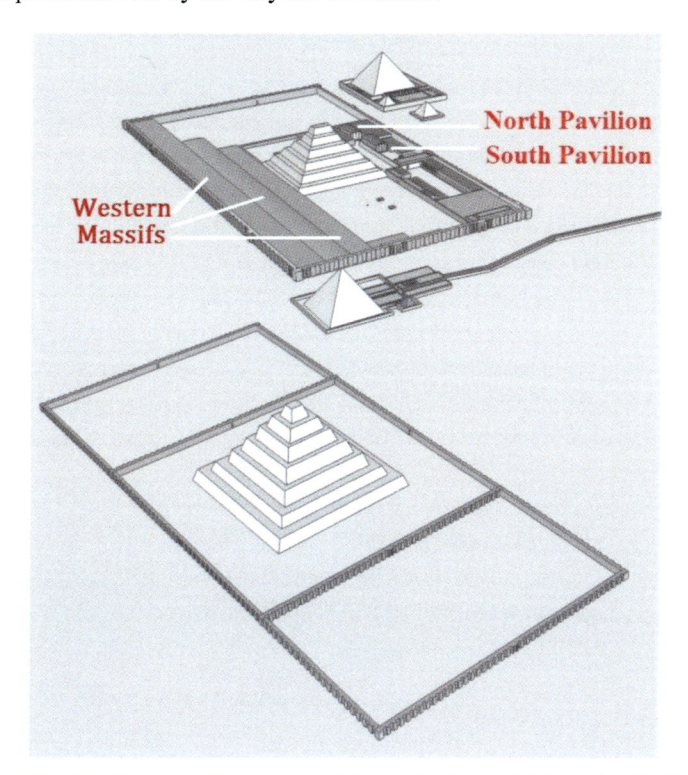

It may seem terribly obvious, but architects like everyone else are creatures of habit. If Imhotep was consistent in his activities as an architect, we should see similar design concepts manifesting in any subsequent building projects he initiated. To that end, Imhotep is believed to be the architect of the funerary complex of Djoser's successor, Sekhemkhet (*Fig. 6-29*). In this new venture for his new king, Imhotep did not include a pair of comparable pavilions or storage magazines (Western Massifs) within Sekhemkhet's mortuary complex, nor is there a 7-meter (23-foot) drop from the descending passage to the Burial Chamber's floor as in the Step Pyramid.

Fig. 6-29 – The Funerary Enclosures of Djoser (top) and Sekhemkhet (bottom) with the Fifth Dynasty Pyramids of Unas (middle) and Userkhaf (top)

The absence of similar structures to the North and South Pavilions or Central Burial Chamber design may not be the definitive proof needed for this hypothesis to be correct, but it is only because the Sekhemkhet pyramid and its enclosure were never completed. Nevertheless, the lack of a similar design for this new pyramid project points toward the possibility that two incomplete and unused mastabas and the two burial shafts in the Step Pyramid and South Tomb must have preexisted the building of Mastaba M₁, or at minimum, the four-tier Step Pyramid. In addition, the lack of at least the foundations of buildings comparable to the North and South Pavilions, erected as part of any other mortuary monument either during or after the Old Kingdom, confirms this.

As we already noted, C. M. Firth, the archeologist who supervised the first excavations of the Step Pyramid, was of the opinion that the Step Pyramid Enclosure as a whole was never finished, so the completion of all the extant structures during Djoser's lifetime would have been highly unlikely (*Fig. 6-30*).

Indirect proof of this comes by way of the U.S. television series, *Unearthed*.[70] In the episode, *The Hunt for the First Pyramid*, Egyptian archeologist, Adel Kaleny, discussed the length of time it must have taken to carve out the tunnels in the substructure of the Step Pyramid. As a demonstration, Mr. Kaleny supervised a crew of stonecutters using reproductions of the kind of copper tools Imhotep's work crew would have used. They chiseled out a large square on an empty rock face that approximates the size of one the subterranean tunnels. After Mr. Kaleny's masons cut into the rock about an inch, he literally did a rough, *back-of-the-envelope* calculation. Given the slow pace of sculpting the rock at approximately an inch per hour, and assuming a work crew or crews worked twenty-four hours a day, he estimated it would have taken 20 years to carve out all the tunnels under the Step Pyramid.

Fig. 6-30 – Netjerikhet Djoser and Imhotep
An impossibly idealized portrait of a completed Step Pyramid Enclosure that never happened

While this is only a best guess estimate of the work necessary to excavate the several miles of tunnels under the Step Pyramid, it is likely that such labor-intensive work would have taken more than the time of Djoser's reign of 19 years given by multiple sources. Assuming Djoser commissioned Imhotep to build his mortuary complex soon after taking the throne, he would have had to complete the entirety of the Step Pyramid Enclosure through the thoroughly documented six different construction phases. In the short time span of 19 years, Imhotep would have had to build Mastabas M₁/M₂, the Central Burial Chamber, then excavate eleven pit tombs and their subterranean tunnels adjacent to the mastaba's east side, and cover them over with Mastaba M₃. Then, after he finished the North and South Pavilions and the South Tomb, he could start construction on the four-tier Step Pyramid, the Ḥeb-Sed Court quadrant with the South Entrance Hall, the North Court and eventually the six-tier Step Pyramid. In addition, two, or possibly three, different Enclosure Walls would also need to be constructed, demolished and then reconstructed. Given the relatively short length of Djoser's reign, it would have been impossible to complete all of the monuments we see today because work on a pharaoh's tomb or mortuary complex would normally have stopped when he died.

For Imhotep to complete all the work outlined above during Djoser's relatively short reign, the only logical explanation is that the North and South Pavilions, Mastabas M₁/M₂ and the 11 pit tombs beneath Mastaba M₃ must have pre-existed any of the later construction projects. Another clue making this a real possibility is the slight offset (about 1.5 degrees) to the south of the South Entrance Hall, which becomes readily apparent when standing in front of the narrow South Entrance Gate doorway (see text below and *Fig. 6-33*).

The Enclosure Walls

When you approach the Step Pyramid Enclosure, the first thing you see is the temenos wall, or rather, what's left of it (*Fig. 6-31*). The Enclosure Wall, as strikingly beautiful and graceful even in its currently ruinous state, defines what Imhotep was attempting to achieve within the entirety of the complex itself. The grandeur and beauty of the South Entrance Gate and the Enclosure Wall as it may have appeared in ancient times can be surmised from its reconstruction supervised by Jean-Philippe Lauer.

The wall's most obvious feature when first encountering the very impressive South Entrance Gate is the narrow entrance corridor leading into the interior of the Step Pyramid Enclosure. Along the Enclosure Wall's entire length are small bastions erected at regular intervals said to mimic the exterior walls of many of the mastabas located in the Sakkara area (see *Fig. 6-2*). These bastions are also imitations of the walls found in military architecture of many ancient fortresses or fortified towns. Twenty-eight of these bastions are different in that their construction is in pairs to represent false gates of which there are 14: four false gates on the east and west walls, and three on each of the north and south walls.

Fig. 6-31 – The South Entrance Gate

Each gate consists of two bastions and a simulated double-door gate carved in stone between them. (Two false gates are visible on either side of several bastions in *Fig. 6-32*.) Firth felt the 14 false gates were the same as those allegedly found in the famous "white walls" surrounding the ancient capital of Memphis.[71] This may be true, but we really don't know what the ancient city of Memphis looked like, let alone the number of gates in its surrounding wall. The number of false gates (14) in Djoser's mortuary complex probably has more to do with the concept of death and resurrection than city planning.

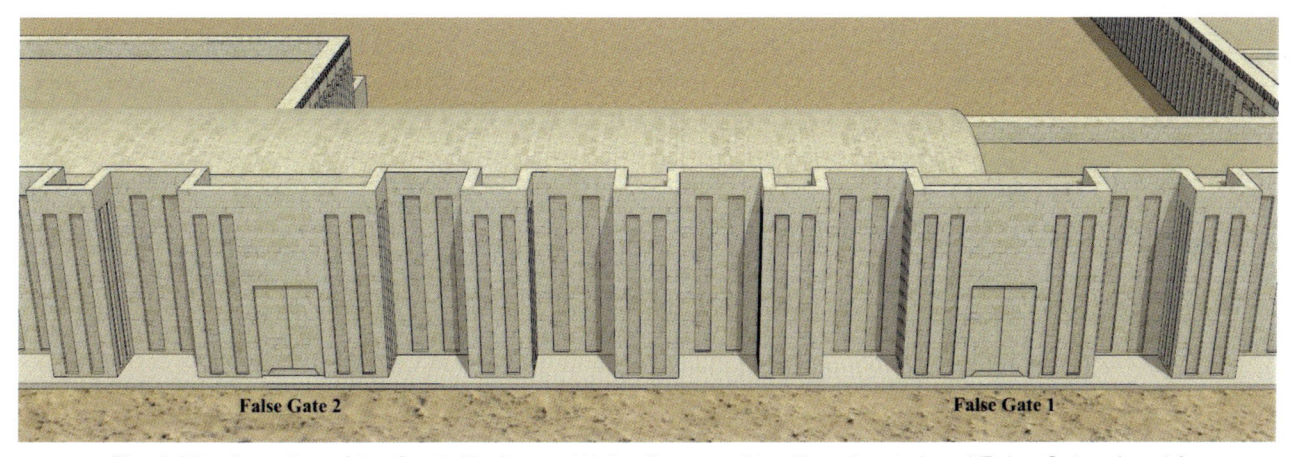

Fig. 6-32 – A section of the South Enclosure Wall with several bastions (center) and False Gates 1 and 2

As already discussed above, the number 14 is a highly significant number in ancient Egyptian mythology. According to the Egyptian legend, Osiris, the God of the Afterlife, and his brother, Seth, the God of Chaos, got into a terrible, bloody fight. Seth won, and dismembered the body of Osiris into fourteen pieces and scattered them long the length of the Nile. Isis, Osiris's wife searched for the pieces of her husband's body, but found only thirteen. The fourteenth part (the penis) was never found; said to have been eaten by fishes (!). Isis, who is acknowledged to have been a great healer and magician in her own right, reassembled Osiris' body parts, and briefly brought him back to life long enough to become pregnant by him. After burying Osiris, Isis gave birth to Horus the Younger, who later exacted revenge by killing his uncle, Seth.

Osiris eventually became God of the Underworld, and presided over the Weighing of the Heart Ceremony, judging each newly arrived deceased person to determine their worthiness to enter into the Afterlife. If not, Ammit, the dreaded goddess would devour their heart. As the God of the Underworld, Osiris – and the number 14 – became forever associated with death and resurrection, and by extension, the Afterlife. Being the natural scientists they were, maybe the ancient Egyptians derived this special meaning for the number 14 from their observations of the natural world around them. They no doubt observed the duality of 14 waxing days and 14 waning days in the 28-day cycle of the moon (*birth* followed by *death*). This 28-day cycle coincides with the natural menstrual cycle of women (*fertility* followed by *dormancy*), another manifestation of the *Magic Number 2*.

The association of the number 14 with death and resurrection seems not to have been exclusive to ancient Egypt. Perhaps this relation became a tradition passed down to later cultures. In many Christian churches, the events surrounding Easter are memorialized with vignettes or plaques installed around the interior walls of the sanctuary depicting the Stations of the Cross. In most cases, there are 14 stations (*there's that number 14 again!*) with these plaques or panels, showing the trial and crucifixion of Jesus. During Good Friday services, the congregants march around the interior, pausing at each of the 14 stations to pray or reflect on the suffering and death of Jesus.

A hidden feature of the South Entrance Gate of which most visitors are not aware is a slight 1.5° offset towards the south (left) of the main part of the Entrance Hall (*Fig. 6-33*). Lauer believed this offset was accidental possibly because the construction of the South Entrance Hall occurred before the Enclosure Wall was complete. [72] This does not seem reasonable to me inasmuch as the ancient Egyptians were highly capable surveyors as attested by the precision with which they built their pyramids and other monuments in relation to true north and the circumpolar stars. They would not have *accidentally* misaligned the Entrance Hall for this reason alone and probably constructed it at the same time the perimeter wall was being constructed. More than likely, the 1.5° offset was a deliberately constructed design feature from the very start. Although I can't prove it, I believe the South Entrance Hall aligns with the rising sun on the solstices, as it would have appeared during the time when the Step Pyramid Enclosure was built (circa 2663 to 2650 BCE).

If Imhotep had designed and built the entire group of tombs, mastabas, pavilions and other structures within the Enclosure from its inception, no doubt he would have aligned the entire Step Pyramid Enclosure in such a way as to eliminate the need to orient the Entrance Hall 1.5° towards the south. Instead, he squared up the Enclosure Wall to run parallel to the south wall of the South Tomb, and the North and South Pavilions and Mastabas $M_1/M_2/M_3$ along the east wall. Only after orienting the south and east walls with the circumpolar stars, did he design the South Entrance Hall to line up perfectly east to west so it would frame the rising sun on the summer solstice on July 19 when the star Sirius appeared on the eastern Horizon. This heralded the beginning of the season of *Akhet*, or the Inundation, which was the most important time of year as the Nile would begin overflowing its banks, depositing a new layer of silt, and ensuring a productive season of planting and harvesting a new bounty of crops.

The impression one gets when studying the Step Pyramid and its associated buildings for any length of time is that Imhotep left nothing to chance and everything within the enclosure is there for a specific reason. While we may quibble with this apparent flaw in the execution of an otherwise perfect design, the fact that the Entrance Hall isn't straight (and parallel to the Enclosure Wall) points to the fact that neither is the human spine; it's curved (see *Fig. 3-8*).

Fig. 6-33 - Looking west through the South Entrance Gate showing the 1.5° southward offset (arrow bending to the left) of the hall of pillars

Each stage of construction probably led to de-construction of various sections of the enclosure in order to accommodate the new additions. This alone can cause confusion even to the best of archeologists, excavators and restorers. The nature of a continuous renovation process by Imhotep can often lead to believing his deconstruction/reconstruction projects occurred much later. Adding to this confusion is that for many centuries afterwards, the Step Pyramid Enclosure became a quarry for local farmers, as well as a resource of easily available construction materials for the nearby villages and the Monastery of St. Jeremiah located approximately 500 meters south of the Step Pyramid.

The construction of the Enclosure Wall has beguiled tourists and archeologists alike since reconstruction began in the 1920s. The ancient Egyptians used smaller stone blocks to construct the walls because they were easier to manage and put into place, and because this supposedly was the first time stone had been so widely used to construct a mortuary temple. This may not be the case, however. The *Great Enclosure* (also known by its Arab name '*Gisr el-Mudir*'), is located to the southwest of the Step Pyramid Enclosure. It may even predate the Step Pyramid by at least a generation to the Second Dynasty with some of its walls partially constructed with stone.

It's easy to think these stone blocks were all carved with these cuts and insets chiseled into them before being assembled on-site into the Enclosure Wall because modern architects would do something similar. However, the amazing fact is the inset channels, the eight rows of incised squares and other features carved into these stone blocks were all sculpted after being installed. Preplanning the shaping of each stone prior to its use in construction would be too labor intensive to accomplish in the necessary timeframe to complete the project before Djoser was interred in his tomb. An easier construction method is suggested by the following:

1. To keep things simple (since this was purportedly the first time stone was used on this massive a scale), cut the requisite facing stone blocks to a somewhat uniform size about 1 cubit wide by one-half cubit high by three-quarter cubits deep; some larger, some smaller. This is because, even though some of the stone used in the Enclosure Wall was of a fine quality (probably obtained from the Tura quarries directly across the Nile River), there would inevitably be fractures in some of the stone preventing its use in larger block sizes. Dealing with these fractures would be easy by removing the unusable stone blocks, and reshaping it into a slightly smaller block that could still be used in the wall's construction. In short, the stone blocks in the Enclosure Wall were shaped similarly if not exactly the same size.

2. Starting from the base platform, build the wall up to the 32nd course. Place roughly quarried flat stones and rubble infill material against the interior surface of the wall during construction to better support these finer exterior stones.

3. Create a wooden template outlining the requisite profile of the vertical channels when viewed from the top. Place this template on top of the unfinished wall, draw the outline of the channels on the top of the wall and snap chalk lines down the front to the wall's base; and chisel out the channels from the top down. (In Chapter 7, *Fig. 7-69* shows this initial stage of construction on the partially constructed wall for Sekhemkhet's pyramid.)

4. Add the remaining four courses of stone blocks and incise the small squares from the 35th row at the top down to the 22nd row using another template to position the squares uniformly (*Fig. 6-34*). Smooth out the face of the walls using sandstone blocks (similar to the ones used by the sculptors seen in *Fig. 6-35*). Performing this last step of refining the wall's surface also removes any trace of the chalk lines.

Fig. 6-34 – South Entrance Gate showing the eight rows of inset squares

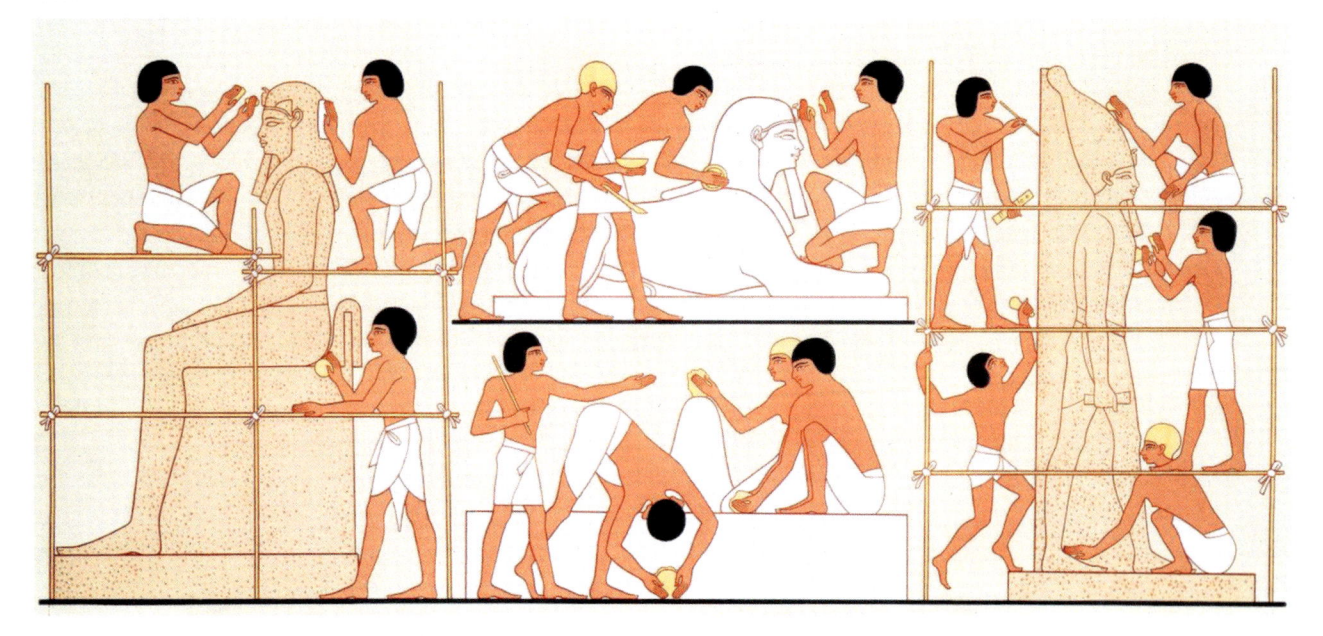

Fig. 6-35 – Sculptors using sandstone blocks and dolerite balls to polish and smooth statues in a sculptor's workshop (Eighteenth Dynasty tomb of Rekmire). These are the same tools and techniques Imhotep's artisans would have used to finish the Enclosure Wall.

This last step of sculpting the small squares on the upper fifteen courses of the Enclosure Wall has many Egyptologists puzzled. Some think these squares imitated the ends of wood beams sticking out from the wall surfaces.[73] This does not seem likely inasmuch as the Egyptians did not shape the wooden logs into squares as evidenced by the rounded imitation logs found in the Entrance Hall and North and South Pavilions (*Figs. 6-36* and *6-37*). Furthermore, why have *8 rows* of squared-off wooden beams when one row would suffice to hold up a roof? By all appearances, these incised squares bear the hallmark of dovecotes. Whether such accommodations in walls for birds were commonplace, we may never know.

Fig. 6-36 – South Entrance Hall, reconstructed roof beams

Fig. 6-37 – The South Pavilion Ceiling

Another possibility is the South Entrance Gate may be a reproduction of a gate from the palace façade in Memphis or one of its famous *white walls*. A stone plaque emulating a *serekh*, a square cartouche-like symbol, was found containing the name of Pharaoh Netjerikhet Djoser. It has the same 8 rows of incised squares and general appearance as the front of the South Entrance Gate (*Fig. 6-38*).

However, could it be Imhotep placed these 8 rows of incised squares simply for decorative purposes? It is hard for us to think of Imhotep expanding his architectural vocabulary to include a design element for the only reason of *it looked good*, but absent any other explanation, this one fits the best. If nothing else, Imhotep seemed to be perpetuating a long-held design tradition of some sort.

Fig. 6-38 – The South Entrance Gate imitates a stone plaque containing Netjerikhet Djoser's name, possibly showing a gate in the palace walls in the capital of Memphis

As the Enclosure Wall was being erected, infill material was placed behind the wall at the same time. Using a clay-based mortar as a binder between the layers of infill kept the walls stable as seen by a sizable amount of the south wall that still exists after 4700 years (*Fig. 6-39*).

Fig. 6-39 – The South Wall of the Step Pyramid Enclosure

In the following photos, the inset channels carved into the blocks of stone clearly show the method Imhotep employed in their construction. The images also show that when the Enclosure became a quarry for its rich supply of ready-made stone, many blocks from the Enclosure Wall were not very suitable for most of the building projects that occurred centuries later as they were not evenly rectangular and were highly carved and decorated. This would have required a great deal of additional shaping and sculpting prior to being reused elsewhere. As outlined above, first, there was the placement of uniform-sized stone blocks, and then the insets hewn out to create the vertical channels in the bastions that are the hallmark of the design of the Enclosure Wall (*Figs. 6-40, 6-41* and *6-42*). Of note is the lack of tool marks on the blocks attesting to the skill of Imhotep's artisans to finish the wall's exterior into a highly polished surface. This is still visible today, as a good part of the south wall still exists along with many of the more intricately never repurposed incised stones strewn about.

Fig. 6-40 – Part of a bastion from the South Enclosure Wall with a block showing an incised square carved into it that was once located at the top of the wall (Manna Nader, Gabana Studios, Cairo)

These blocks were first erected in place, and then sculpted to create the inset channels and incised squares. The quality of artisanship displayed here may be why one of Imhotep's titles was "Chief of Sculptors and Carpenters".

Fig. 6-41 – One of the bastions of the South Enclosure Wall. Note the blocks inside the inset channels seem to 'turn the corner' into the interior of the channel (Manna Nader, Gabana Studios, Cairo)

Fig. 6-42 – Inset channels showing the precision sculpting in place, and not shaped first to be set into the wall afterwards. Note the small portion of the top left stone block that appears to turn the corner (arrow) inside the channel (Manna Nader, Gabana Studios, Cairo)

The Ḥeb-Sed Court

Expanding further upon the discussion in Chapter 3, the West Chapels of the Ḥeb-Sed Court seem to be stone reproductions of buildings from the royal palace (see *Fig. 3-1*). This seems plausible even though we do not know what the royal palace actually looked like. However, these *chapels* may also be facsimiles of domestic non-royal architecture as well. Just inside the entrances of several West Chapels are curious raised reliefs along some of the interior walls of the ground floor (*Fig. 6-43*).

Fig. 6-43 – Simulated animal tethering posts inside one of the West Chapels

The first impressions of archeologists were that they looked like *pickets* or *stake fences* because they may have resembled a fence of the period. When I first saw them, they reminded me of belaying pins used on old sailing ships to tie off ropes attached to the sails (*Fig. 6-44*).

Fig. 6-44 – Belaying pins for managing the sail rigging on a sailing ship

It may seem strange to relate these architectural details to sailing ships, but Egypt was, and to some extent still is a culture centered on sailing. Though ancient Egypt was not like typical oceangoing sailing cultures like the Vikings or the Portuguese, the Nile River produced sailors who navigated it with great skill much like the American riverboat pilots of the Mississippi River during the 18th and 19th centuries. That sailing was an integral part of ancient Egyptian culture can be seen in depictions of boats in scenes painted in their tombs, but more importantly, boats were often buried alongside their funerary monuments. There are two very famous boats buried next to the Great Pyramid, 14 boat graves are located in Abydos next to the Funerary Enclosure of Khasekhemwui, Djoser's predecessor, and another boat buried next to the pyramid of Senwosret III at Dashur among others.

After pondering the *picket fence* and *belaying pin* theories for a while, it didn't seem plausible since these *chapels* were allegedly reproductions of buildings from Djoser's palace. Obviously, most houses would not have had a picket fence *inside* the entrance because such fences are normally located *outside* in front of the house.

With the above two theories falling by the wayside, I came to the realization that the Chapels numbered '1' and '2' in J.-P. Lauer's plans may have actually resembled typical homes of the time in that there were living quarters for people and domesticated animals in the same house (see *Fig. 3-3*). The ground floor would have had a stable for the animals, and the stairs in front led to the second story to the family's living quarters. I can personally attest that this type of house still exists even today because my wife lived in a similarly designed house growing up in the village of Kranochori in northern Greece in the 1950s. Her family owned a horse and a cow with its calf that were stabled in the barn located downstairs, while she and her family lived upstairs.

The intuitive insight that these carved reliefs were reproductions of something related to the use of rope such as belaying pins pointed me in the right direction. Instead of imitating a fence, these *pickets* are simulated *tethering posts*, used to tie up animals. The stone versions of these *tethering posts* show how clever the ancient Egyptians were. If you tightly tie the free end of an animal's leash to the post just above the horizontal bar, the upward flaring conical shape at the top of the post prevents the animal from pulling the leash off the pin and freeing itself. At the same time, the rope has enough slack to allow the animal to move its head up and down to keep it from choking. (*Very clever, indeed.*)

Associating the Ḥeb-Sed Court *chapels* to an average Egyptian's home should not be discounted so readily. The reasons for performing the rituals of the *Ḥeb-Sed* was to bind Pharaoh to his people – and they to him. When coming to the Ḥeb-Sed Court, the people would see these stone versions of their homes and sense an immediate connection because of their familiarity. This reinforces the idea that Djoser, through his vizier, Imhotep, was showing honor and respect to his people by recreating an image of their homes in his Ḥeb-Sed Court, which would also reinforce the people's loyalty to the king. In addition, when the Ḥeb-Sed Court was transformed into a medical center, having a familiar domestic setting goes a long way in calming a person's fear when anticipating medical treatment. It may even have allayed any ill feelings leftover from the conflicts that occurred during the latter part of the Second Dynasty.

Near the end of the row of the West Chapels is an open area designated as 'P' on J.-P. Lauer's plans (*Fig. 6-45*). It is roughly twice the width of any of the other West Chapels, but it is different in that it is open to the sky and has no façade or infill material to define it. Enclosure 'P' may well represent an animal corral or paddock from the royal palace or just about any corral for that matter. (*Yes, this is another coincidence where Lauer designated this imitation of a paddock as 'P'.*)

In the context of the Ḥeb-Sed Court as a medical center; however, Enclosure 'P' may have also served as a waiting area in the same way that hospitals today have similar rooms for patients waiting to see a doctor. The evidence for this is the small room at the back (west side) of the second room of this 'chapel' (see *Figs. 3-42* through *3-47*). It bears more than a passing resemblance to many other such small rooms found throughout the complex, such as the East Chapel Patient Suites, indicating it was meant for a patient's use while waiting to see a healer-priest (see *Figs. 6-10* and *6-11*).

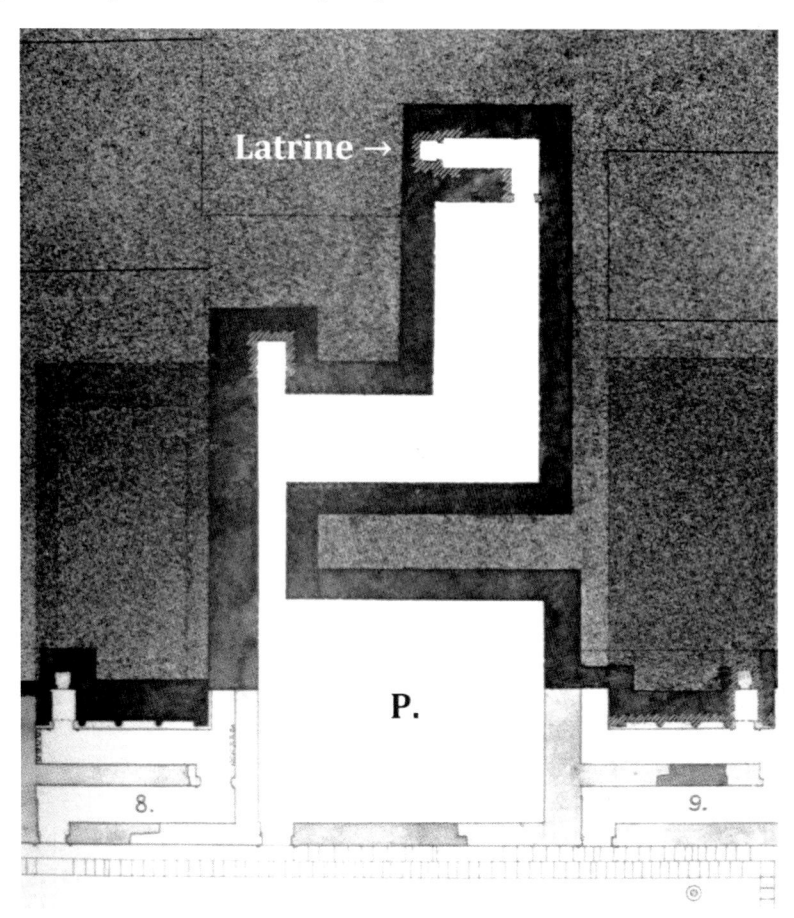

Fig. 6-45 – Ḥeb-Sed Court Enclosure 'P'

To the south of Temple 'T' in the southwest corner of the Ḥeb-Sed Court is a small building whose function is still unknown to this day, and seems to have had no obvious useful purpose (*Fig. 6-46*), hence it was given the name "Mystery Building". This structure baffled Firth and Lauer as well, and no one since has come up with a reasonable explanation for its existence. Although there is no direct evidence, this *Mystery Building* may have been the location of a temporary passageway from the Great South Court to the interior of the Ḥeb-Sed Court (*Fig. 6-47*). A small, closet-like room (marked as '**A**' in *Fig. 6-46*) was created to the south behind the doorway that once led into the interior of the Ḥeb-Sed Court, and may have been used for storage of some kind.

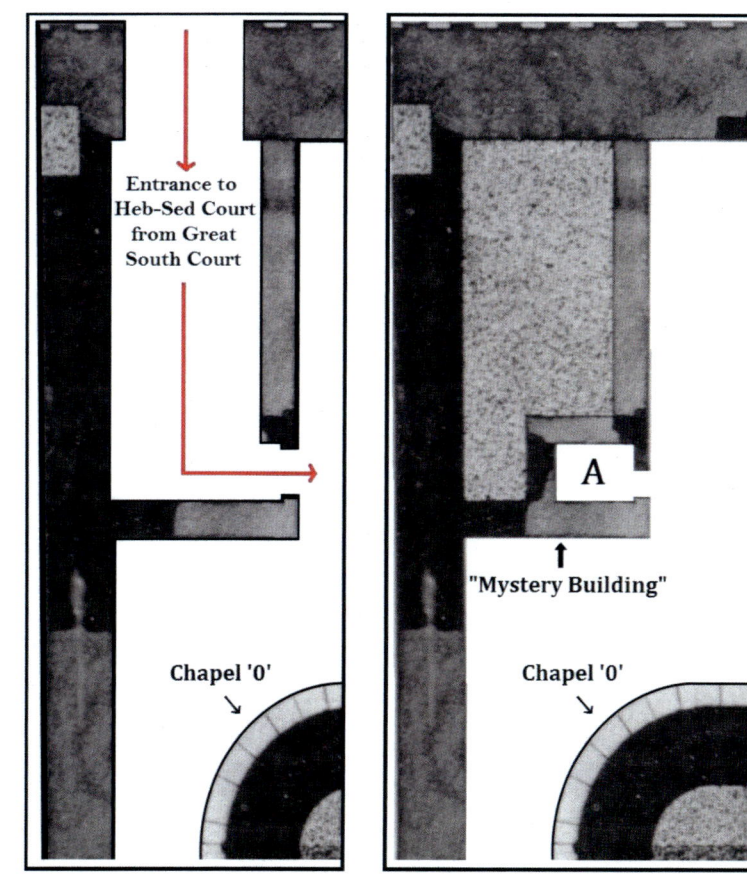

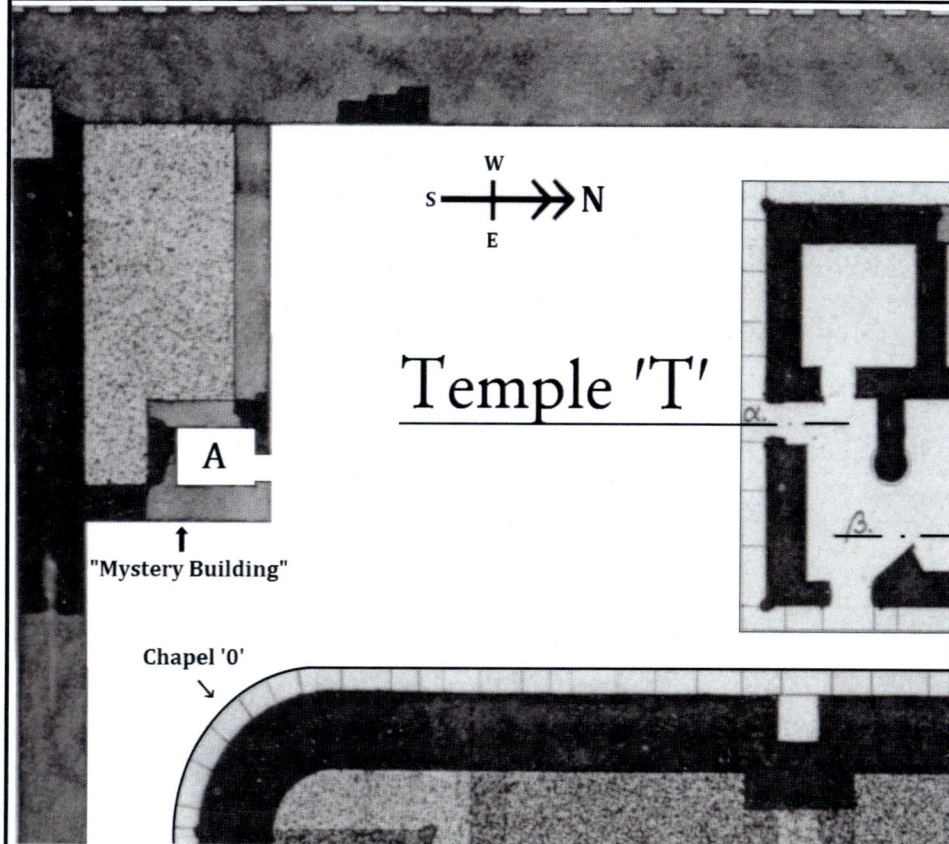

Fig. 6-46 – The "Mystery Building". Proposed Entrance to the Ḥeb-Sed Court from the Great South Court, during the sed-festival (left) and after (right)

Fig. 6-47 – View from the Great South Court near Temple 'T' showing the possible location of a temporary entrance to the Ḥeb-Sed Court

If the passage from the Great South Court through the *Mystery Building* did not exist, people would have had go back down the Entrance Hall and enter the Ḥeb-Sed Court through the '**L3** doorway' (see *Fig. 3-13*). This *Mystery Building* entrance would have only been used to allow access to the Ḥeb-Sed Court during the *sed*-festival. Then, after the conclusion of the ceremonies, stone blocks were fitted into the entrance doorway, and infill material of a slightly different size and character was placed in its interior (*Fig. 6-48*).

Different Infill Material

Fig. 6-48 – Close-up view of the two different types of infill material used where the original entrance from the Great South Court to the Ḥeb-Sed Court was located. The infill on the left uses smaller, rounder stones than the infill material on the right, which is flatter and more linear, suggesting they were constructed at two different times (Photo taken in 1990)

After the entrance from the Great South Court through the *Mystery Building* to the Ḥeb-Sed Court was sealed up, the corridor leading from the '**L3** doorway' in the Entrance Hall was the only way in or out of the Ḥeb-Sed Court. While this may be total conjecture on my part, there may have also been another temporary entrance leading from the Great South Court into the Ḥeb-Sed Court (*Fig. 6-49*).

If so, it would have been located in the northwest corner of the Ḥeb-Sed Court near the southeast corner of the Step Pyramid and near 'Chapel J' as shown in J.-P. Lauer's plans where there are four sets of feet from broken statues purported to be of Djoser and his family (*Fig. 6-50*). This northwest doorway and the one leading from the Great South Court were in all likelihood sealed off after the conclusion of the *Ḥeb-Sed* since it was unnecessary to have easier access to the other parts of Djoser's funerary temple from the Ḥeb-Sed Court. The forecourts of Chapels 9, 10, J and another small room near the East Chapel *patient suites* were repurposed as a type of *nurses station* used by healer/priests and other health care workers. This is borne out by the two latrines in Chapels 9 and 10, and the discovery of a large, heavy alabaster vase sunk into the floor in front of Chapel 9, no doubt used for ritual bathing or cleansing by the temple staff. [74]

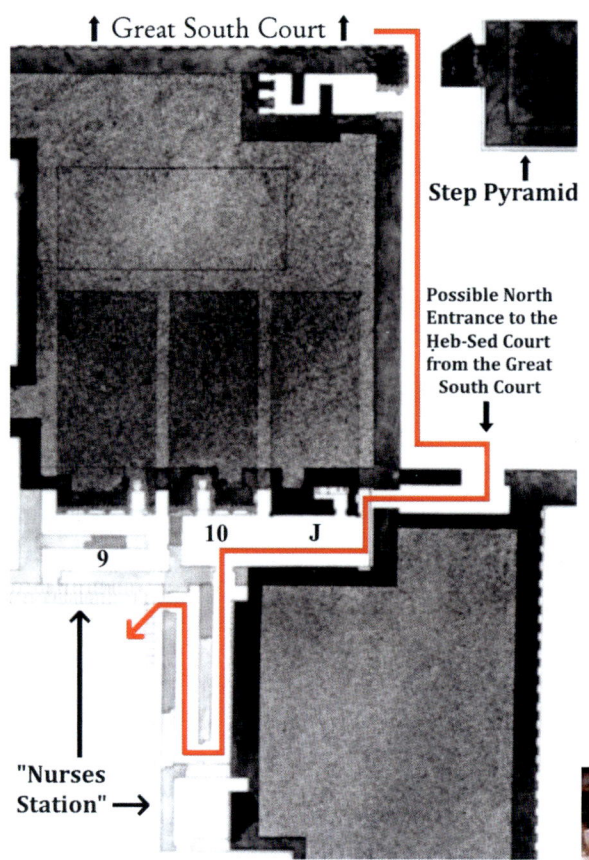

Fig. 6-49 – Another alternative entrance to the Ḥeb-Sed Court from the Great South Court

Fig. 6-50 – The feet of four statues in West Chapel 'J'

In attempting to reconcile reports from the original excavations done in the 1920s and 1930s as well as any subsequent discoveries and investigations regarding the run-down state of the Step Pyramid Enclosure, it becomes necessary to take into account various theories that try to explain the state of the temple as it exists today. Some have postulated the thousands of stones scattered about the site are the result of the simple fact that the buildings within the Step Pyramid Enclosure were incomplete at Djoser's death.

The idea that Imhotep permitted leaving unused building materials strewn about the temple complex does not seem reasonable. Leaving leftover stones from when it was under construction in the Ḥeb-Sed Court and elsewhere would not fit into the historical record of Djoser having celebrated his *sed*-festival at least once (not to mention Imhotep's ego wouldn't permit such a travesty). Instead, the appearance of an incomplete mortuary complex with many blocks of finished and unfinished stonework lying on the ground tends to resemble a structure in the process of **being dismantled** and its stonework waiting to be recycled for other uses.

Some of the stones that cluttered the Ḥeb-Sed Court when first excavated in the early 20th Century, and into the early 21st Century, may have even originally been infill material that came from behind the temple walls stonework façade. The rubble we see today was the structural support located behind the (mostly missing) finished walls. Since Imhotep was building a stone monument using new building techniques, it stands to reason his sculptors were also learning new skills, and these unfinished stones were the castoffs from just such a learning process. Photos of these stones show much damage, most likely due to poor quality stone or the inevitable mistakes made along the way during sculpting.

It is also possible these stone capitals and other blocks were for completely different construction projects, perhaps from another pyramid complex from the period of the Sixth Dynasty. During the initial excavations in the early twentieth century, an addition was uncovered attached to the north side of the *Mystery Building* (*Fig. 6-51*).

Fig. 6-51 – Storage Rooms attached to the "Mystery Building" (extreme right). Chapel 'O' is in the background

Fig. 6-52 – Papyrus Library (dark mudbricks, center) adjacent to blocks of the dismantled west wall of Temple 'T' (left)

Additionally, another a room that was clearly not part of the original construction was discovered beneath mounds of dirt and rubble. Made of mudbrick walls, it was found between the west wall of Temple 'T' and the east wall of the Great South Court (*Fig. 6-52*). A new doorway had been opened up in the west wall of Temple 'T' to allow access to this room.

In the rubble of this crude addition were a double row of bins made of mudbrick containing some papyri indicating that Temple 'T' had been converted into a construction office when pyramids of the Sixth Dynasty were being built, perhaps for the Pharaoh Teti whose pyramid is close by to the northeast of the Step Pyramid.

> **Further, the brick constructions near the 'T' temple [see *Fig. 6-53*] are dated to the end of the Old Kingdom by fragments of papyrus in a poor state of preservation, which were found there. Not far from these rooms, other fragments of papyrus in better preservation were found on the floor of small chambers [*Per-Nefer* embalming center?] to the southeast of the Ḥeb-Sed court. These papyri concern the construction of pyramids of the Sixth Dynasty ... Is it possible that the persons to whom these documents belonged were engaged in quarrying the stone of Djoser's monuments for new pyramids? It is probable that the temple of Djoser ceased to be a place of interest after about 500 B. C. owing to its partial destruction by quarrymen.** [75]

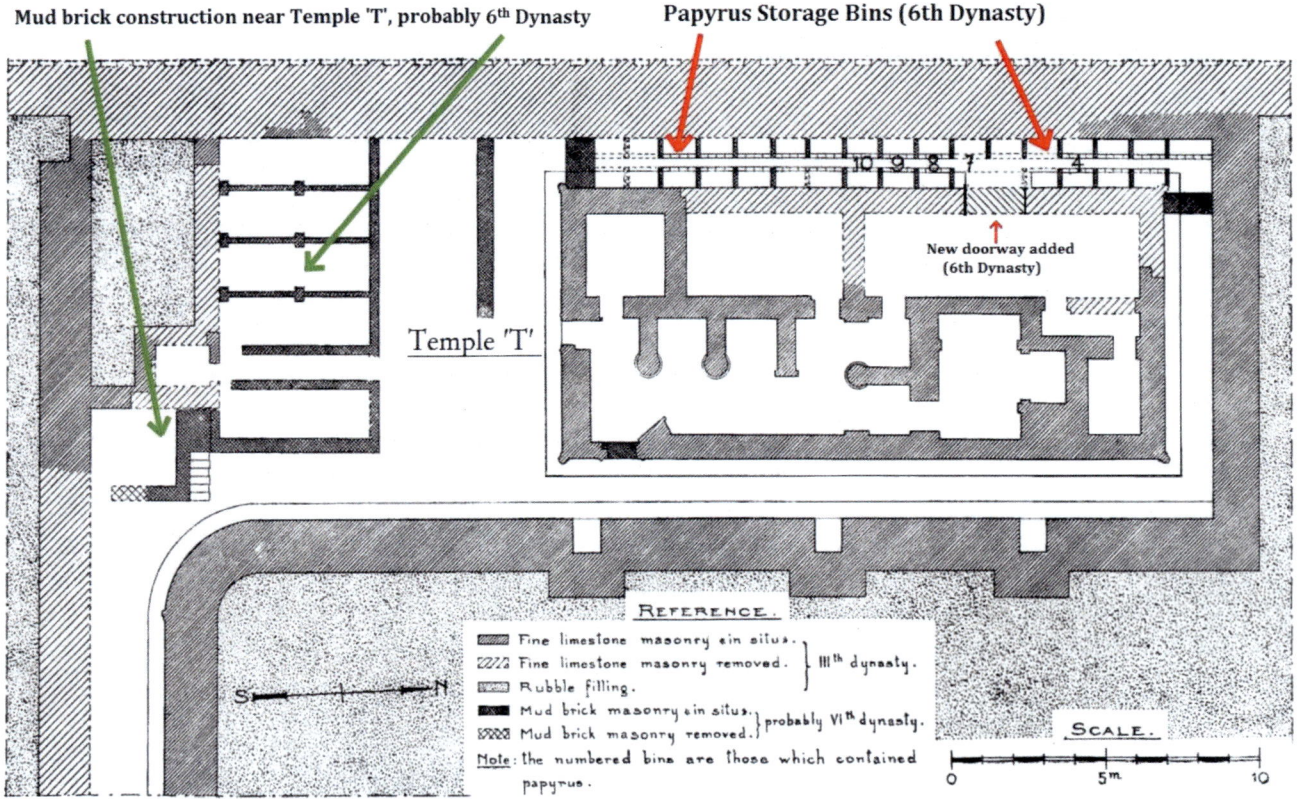

Fig. 6-53 – Late Old Kingdom renovations to Temple 'T'

For the reasons given above, it is likely activity within the Step Pyramid Enclosure related to being an active mortuary temple ceased by the end of the Old Kingdom. Storing stones for other building projects, whether it was new construction materials or stone harvested from structures within the Step Pyramid Enclosure itself, would make more sense.

However, there is an even more plausible explanation for these stone capitals lying about the Ḥeb-Sed Court than the ones put forth by Firth and others. As seen in *Figs. 6-54-A, 6-54-B* and *6-54-C* of the stone capitals from the South Enclosure Wall, raw, unfinished stones were routinely used during the entirety of the Step Pyramid building project. The fact these unfinished stones even exist should not surprise anyone. Once installed, the sculptors would begin the task of dressing these stones, carving the graceful capitals at the top of the false chapels in the Ḥeb-Sed Court, chiseling out the vertical channels in the bastions that lined the exterior of the Enclosure Wall, and so on. These same methods of sculpting temple walls in place were employed by every future generation of Egyptian stonemasons.

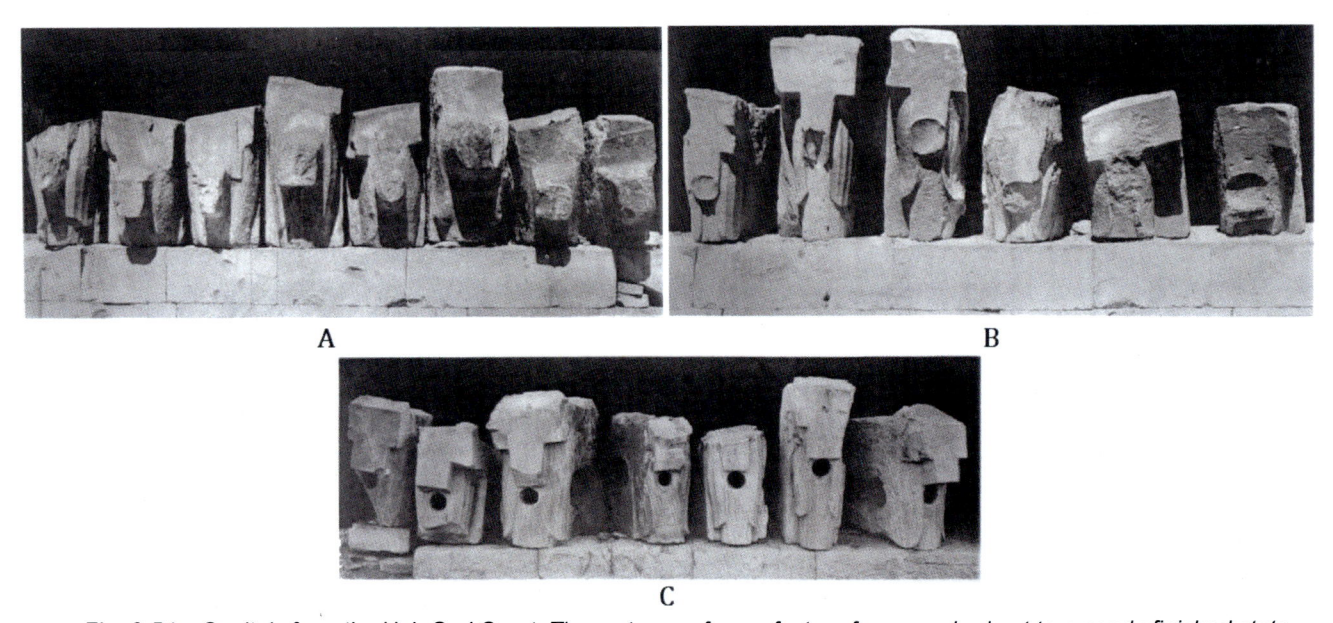

Fig. 6-54 – Capitals from the Ḥeb-Sed Court. Three stages of manufacture from roughed out to a nearly finished state

That some of these stones were left in an incomplete or unfinished state after installation in the West Chapels and elsewhere only means that the sculptors had not completed their job when Djoser died (*Fig. 6-55*). At that point, most of the construction in the Step Pyramid Enclosure would have stopped. This offers the best explanation for why these half-finished stones were found discarded millennia after being removed from their original locations while more finished stones were successfully repurposed. As the Step Pyramid was Egypt's first pyramid, the Step Pyramid Enclosure as a whole was Egypt's first "*mega mortuary temple*". For this reason, the scale and innovative nature of this project virtually guaranteed it was never going to be completed.

This fact is borne by the existence of seven unfinished statues of Djoser found near the South Pavilion (see *Fig. 3-2*). When found strewn about the Ḥeb-Sed Court during excavations done in the 20th century, these unfinished capitals gave palpable evidence that those who dismantled and harvested stones from Djoser's mortuary temple found no use for these intricately carved stones, and preferred the square or rectangular blocks for their building projects. In order to get at the more highly prized stones in these false chapels would require the removal of the capitals at the top first. They were then cast aside as unusable building material, and quarrying of the rest of the stonework could then proceed.

Fig. 6-55 – Several finished and unfinished capitals (arrow) on one of the West Chapels

Any one of these explanations, or combination of them, only points to the fact that Imhotep would not have left his king's funerary monument, and the hospital that continued to serve the people of Egypt for many generations that followed, in such an untidy state.

The Great South Court seems to have been an afterthought, but considerable design work and planning went into its construction. It was not until the four-tier Step Pyramid P₁ was in the preliminary construction phase that Imhotep convinced Djoser to create a new Great South Court with the South Entrance Hall and the Ḥeb-Sed Court between the South Tomb and the pyramid. After its use for the *sed*-festival, the newly added Ḥeb-Sed Court in the southeast quadrant would eventually become a medical facility.

Having added these features, it did not take long to convince Djoser to increase the size and number of additional tiers of the Step Pyramid to a total of six. A much smaller *sed*-festival court with a pair of requisite *boundary markers* was in the process of being built just south of the South Pavilion, but when it was decided to expand the four-tier pyramid to six-tiers, a much larger Great South Court was added to the south of the pyramid along with the new Ḥeb-Sed Court. To balance the design, Imhotep added the North Court, and may have been intended to serve as an herbal and medicinal plant garden or small farm to support the dietary and therapeutic needs of the temple staff and their patients (see *The North Court* section below).

A temple marked as **T₁** on J.-P. Lauer's plans was constructed just to the north of the four-tier Step Pyramid. We have no indication as to what the layout was of this temple or what it looked like because its footprint lies under the six-tier extension of the current Step Pyramid. Suffice to say, it may well have looked similar in some respects to the North Mortuary Temple that now abuts the north side of the six-tier Step Pyramid, as its function was to serve as the site where Djoser's funeral ceremonies took place.

In general, the area north of the Step Pyramid still contains much that is still a mystery due to the fact it has not been fully explored since the 1920s when the first archeological excavations began. The following conclusions that result from investigating this virtually unexplored part of the complex come from mostly circumstantial evidence, some archeological proof, and a lot of guesswork.

The Serdab

Just to the east of the North Mortuary Temple is a small enclosure that once housed a statue of Djoser called the Serdab, an Arabic word meaning "cellar" or "small, narrow chamber" (*Fig. 6-56*). The Serdab was positioned in such a way as to allow Djoser, in the guise of his statue, to look skyward through a pair of eyeholes towards the northern circumpolar stars(*Figs. 6-57* and *6-58*). These stars were believed to be the home of the gods and where the soul of the king would travel after death. More than that, the entire Step Pyramid Enclosure aligns with the circumpolar stars, or "indestructible ones". By evenly dividing the Enclosure east to west by thirds, the first dividing line running parallel with the east-west Enclosure wall passes through the Serdab.

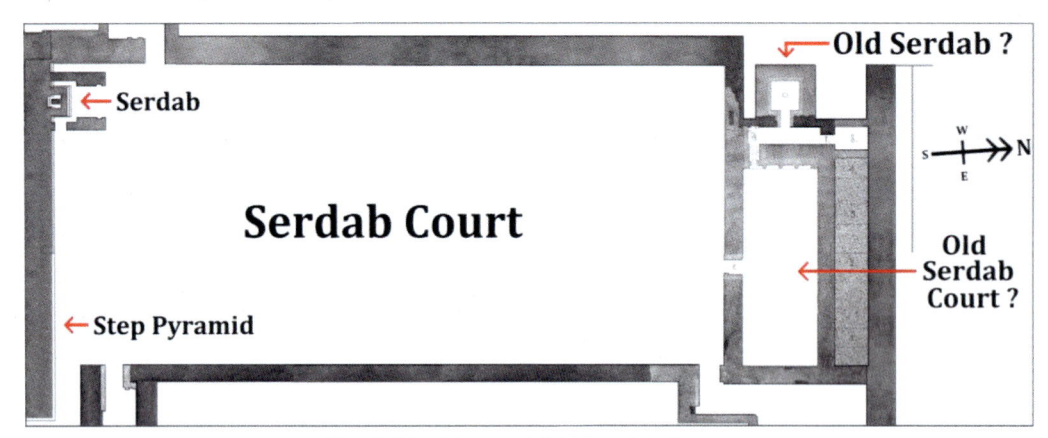

Fig. 6-56 – New and Old Serdab Courts

While examining plans of this ancient temple, it became apparent that possibly more than one Serdab was constructed during the long course of building the Step Pyramid Enclosure. One of these is what I call the *Old Serdab* (*Fig. 6-56*). While Firth or Lauer never identified it as such, it is possible it once functioned as housing for the statue of a king; either Djoser or one of his predecessors, as does the current Serdab that contained the famous statue of Djoser, now in the Cairo Museum (*Fig. 6-59*).

> **Was there any connection between "stars and pyramids"? The answer should be, "yes, there was", with certain reservations. The connection is clearly proved for the most notable of the "imperishable" stars, the circumpolar, which were used probably for their orientation,… and to which the "sighting devices" for the statue of Djoser in the Serdab of the Step Pyramid and the northern upper and lower channels of Khufu's pyramid were perhaps pointing. This theory probably also holds true for the stars of *Sah*, to which the southern upper channel of the Great Pyramid most likely pointed. A connection with Sirius, relating to a ritual in the Queen's chamber, is also probable. It is very likely that further research will disclose further, perhaps unexpected, connections between the sacred landscape of the Memphis area and the celestial realm,…** [76]

> **The *ka* statue of Djoser in the tombs at Abydos was in a serdab (a type of chamber) in the northern base of his pyramid, tilted at 17 degrees to enable it to observe the circumpolar stars through two holes.** [77]

Fig. 6-57 – The current Serdab near the North Temple

Fig. 6-58 – A copy of the statue of Djoser inside the Serdab

The shape of the "Old Serdab" (or first Serdab) looks very much like the hieroglyph for "door" or "gateway".

Gardiner Sign List No. – O32   '*sb3*', "gateway"

This is in keeping with the original intended function of a Serdab; that of a *doorway* through which the soul of the king would return to Earth from the stars to receive any offerings given to him by priests and family members tasked with keeping his memory alive. Even the *new* Serdab and its adjacent walls bear a resemblance to the *gateway* hieroglyph.

Interestingly, the "Old Serdab" faces east towards the rising sun versus the current Serdab that is oriented at a 90° difference, and faces north towards the circumpolar stars (see *Fig. 6-56*). The sun is the single-most important natural feature for all of us, and the center of spiritual life in ancient Egypt for its entire history.

The pole stars, which appear above the North Pole as the earth rotates, symbolize the idea of immortality of the soul because they appear fixed in the night sky and never rise or set.

Fig. 6-59 – The original statue of Djoser from the Serdab now in the Cairo Museum

Stranger still, there may be a possible Second Serdab, which Lauer found beneath the northernmost part of the lowest tier of the Step Pyramid. Built when the four-tier Step Pyramid was erected, and after the construction of the Old Serdab, it aligns with and is just behind (south of) the present day Serdab (*Fig. 6-60*). This now buried room is oriented east towards the rising sun, as well as to the northern pole stars. Ultimately, what the true function and meaning behind this room is anyone's guess, but the rising sun in Egyptian religion has always represented rebirth, as the sun is reborn again every day at sunrise.

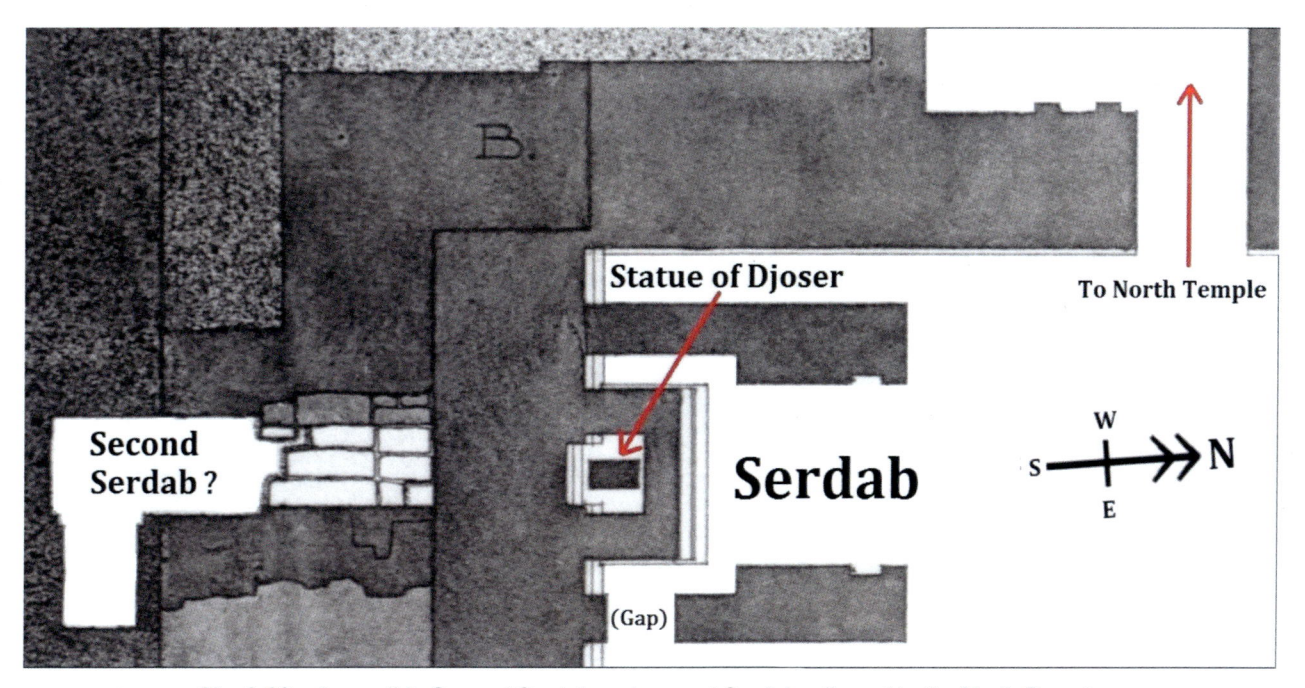

Fig. 6-60 – A possible Second Serdab and current Serdab adjacent to the North Temple

The pharaoh was regarded as a god incarnate upon the Earth. It is logical to assume that after pharaoh's death, the Egyptians believed he would rejoin the immortal gods in the stars where they resided. The reason for the double orientation of the Second Serdab may be due to a change in Egyptian religious thought during the time when the four-tier Step Pyramid and the Second Serdab were constructed. New ideas as to what pharaoh's journey into the Afterlife would look like may have been evolving at this time during the Third Dynasty, as this continually happened throughout the history of Egypt. If so, then perhaps the bi-directional alignment of this possible Second Serdab would indicate that Egyptian religion might have been becoming more cosmic-centric instead of being strictly solar-centric. It is equally possible this eastward-oriented portion of the Second Serdab is an access corridor that is similar in function to the opening in the east wall of the present Serdab that allows viewing of Djoser's statue, assuming that gap is not a modern alteration.

One last enigma to consider: Today, the replica statue of Djoser's position inside the Serdab is directly behind the two eyeholes drilled into the north-facing wall of the Serdab so that it can *see out* and view the circumpolar stars. These two eyeholes are off-center to the left (east) when viewed from the front (see *Fig. 6-57*). Yet curiously, when the Serdab was first uncovered in the 1920s, the statue was centered within the Serdab, that is, not aligned with the eyeholes (*Fig. 6-61*). This prevents the statue from *looking out* to see the stars! Obviously, those who built the Step Pyramid deliberately positioned the statue in this manner, but why is still a mystery.

Fig. 6-61 – The statue of Djoser as originally found in the Serdab. Note the statue is centered within the Serdab preventing it from directly 'seeing out' the off-center eyeholes

The North Mortuary Temple

The North Mortuary Temple (*Fig. 6-62*) has an unusual design compared to other mortuary temples of the period. Its primary purpose was apparently to serve as the venue for the funeral rituals of the dead king. Secondarily, it served to perpetuate his memory as a cultic center after internment of the pharaoh in his tomb. The final entrance into the tomb (North Descending Passage) was situated outside the north wall of the temple, meaning the pharaoh's body was never brought into the temple for any ritual purpose, but rather was interred directly into his tomb (assuming he was even buried in the Central Burial Chamber at all). This is because reaching the interior courts of the temple necessitated navigating through some narrow corridors before finally arriving at one of the two courtyards.

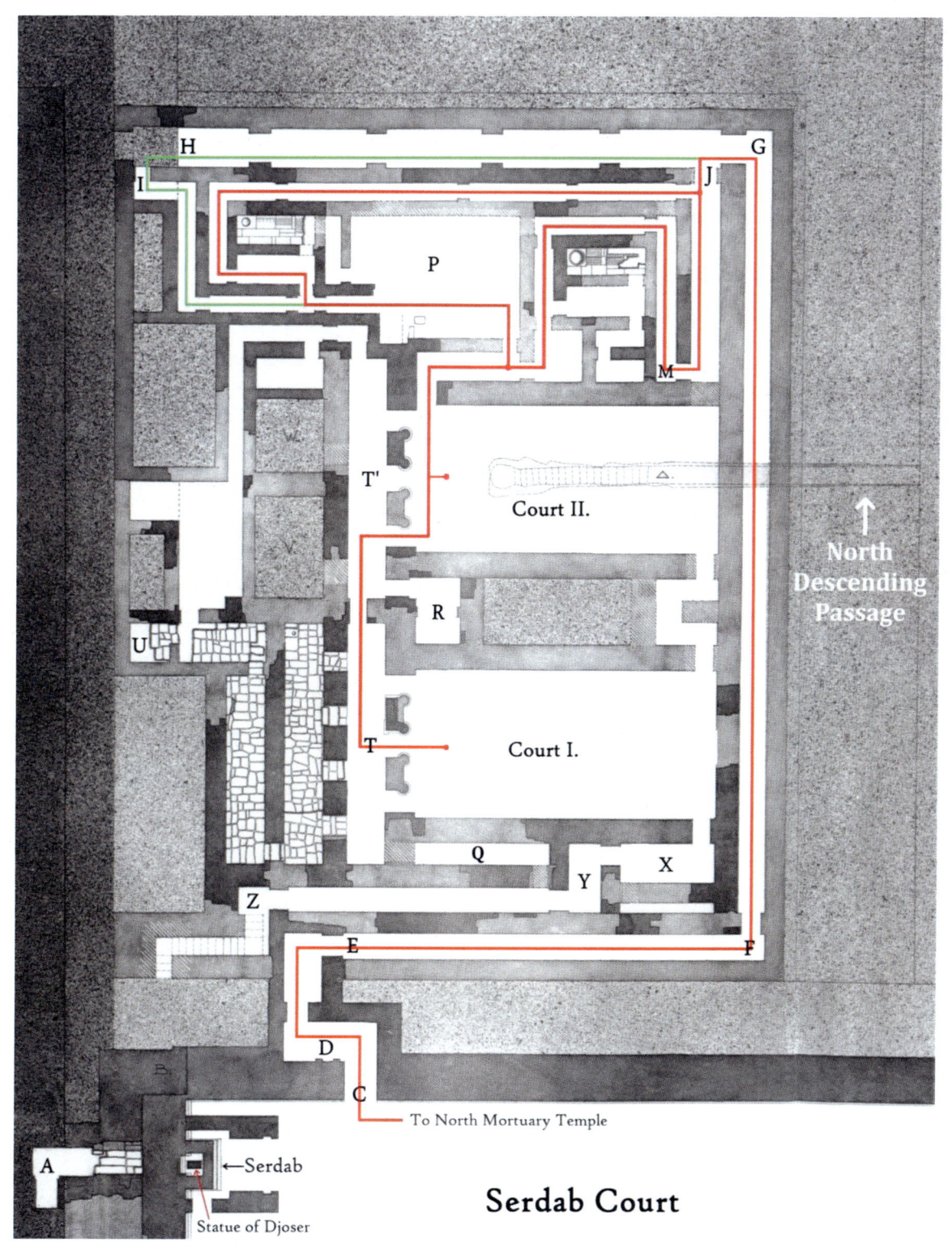

Fig. 6-62 – The North Mortuary Temple

    As can be seen by the red lines in *Fig. 6-62*, getting to the interior of the North Mortuary Temple takes a great deal of patience as its maze-like set of corridors allows for two possible ways to reach the inner courtyards. These two routes also go past two rooms that have ritual bathing bowels inset into the floor. The green line indicates another possible route to the temple interior (at letter '**H**'), but for some reason was blocked up later. Given the narrowness of the corridors, this alone would have made it virtually impossible to bring a coffin, or even a linen-wrapped mummy, into the temple, leading to the inescapable conclusion the North Temple Mortuary Temple was only for conducting pre- and post-funerary rituals, but without the king's body. It seems Imhotep had a penchant for designing indirect, circuitous routes to access a room or space, probably for some symbolic reasons, but this one exceeds all the others in the Enclosure. Like many parts of the Step Pyramid Enclosure, this temple was mostly unfinished at Djoser's death.

The North Court

In Chapter 1, we speculated on evidence for a North Exit Gate. One possible use for this North Exit Gate might have been to facilitate the moving of stone and other building materials into the Enclosure, which at this point would have been without a self-closing door. The location of this North Exit Gate was ideal during various improvements and additions, especially when Mastabas $M_1/M_2/M_3$ were in the process of being transformed into a four-tier pyramid, and later, into a six-tier pyramid. Assuming that the Enclosure Wall existed in some state of completion, it seems logical for an opening in the wall was close to where large stones were to be moved to the job site in order prevent any accidental damage to the rather narrow South Entrance Gate and colonnaded Entrance Hall. The existence of a North Gate would also serve to preserve the sense of orderliness and solemnity that the Entrance Hall imparts when entering the Step Pyramid Enclosure if any ongoing improvements were taking place after the Step Pyramid Enclosure finally *opened for business*. While there is no evidence the modifications to the area near the North Mortuary Temple occurred before the completion of the entire Enclosure Wall, there is no evidence against it, either.

The North Exit Gate could have also served a more pragmatic purpose. In the immediate vicinity of the North Exit Gate is an area neglected by most tourists and Egyptologists as well (seen at the top of *Fig. 6-63*), which on some plans of the Step Pyramid Enclosure is called the "North Court". For Egyptologists, it is not unlike the phrase *terra incognita* seen on ancient naval charts indicating uncharted and potentially dangerous territory. In addition to the Great South Court, it also seems the North Court was not part of the original design for the Step Pyramid Enclosure, but was a much later addition. Some even think the North Court along with the Great South Court represented Djoser's domain as Lower Egypt and Upper Egypt respectively. [78] However, nobody really knows what purpose the North Court served, as it was never fully completed, but I suspect that originally it was to contain a garden to grow plants and food for use by the temple staff.

Fig. 6-63 – The area behind the North Pavilion (foreground). The North Court lies just beyond the wire fence posts on top of the wall in the background

Given its rather derelict and jumbled appearance, it may be difficult to believe the North Court could have possibly contained a small garden. However, temple gardens are not unheard of. There is evidence of a temple garden at the Temple of Seti I at Abydos, and numerous trees and shrubs were planted in the Mortuary Temple of Amenhotep, Son of Hapu, Vizier to Amenhotep III. [79] In addition, at the Great Temple of Hatshepsut at Deir el Bahri there was the discovery of tree roots brought from the mysterious land of Punt that had lined the path leading up to the ramps of the temple. (Some even think Hatshepsut's temple may have been the inspiration for the famous Hanging Gardens of Babylon.)

Temple gardens may have served several purposes. An obvious one is that temple staff needs to eat on a regular basis, and fruits and vegetables could have been grown in this *north forty*. A temple garden would also have allowed the temple staff to grow the herbs and other plants necessary to create the medicines and remedies for their work as healer-priests. The proximity of such a garden would have allowed the priests to carefully supervise the growing of these highly prized plants rather than leave their cultivation to less skilled hands.

In the early part of the 20th century, the English archeologist Cecil M. Firth discovered several subterranean galleries beneath the North Court granaries (see *Fig. 2-4*). Large quantities of wheat, barley, sycamore figs, grapes and bread were found there. Some have asserted that such items were food for use by the dead in the Afterlife. While that is certainly possible, I feel this food was for the living, that is, the priests and servants who lived and worked in the temple. Depending on how far underground these subterranean chambers were, they would have provided a much cooler and drier place to store food, which makes perfect sense when you're providing for the basic necessities of a large temple staff and their patients. Certainly, it would have been far better than what was available for food storage above ground.

Strictly speaking, food buried with the dead was usually stored in close proximity to the sarcophagus, funerary equipment and other grave goods in the tomb of the deceased. This was not the case here as these foodstuffs were stored far from the known tombs located within the Step Pyramid Enclosure. Thus, a North Court garden may have been part of Imhotep's original vision to create a center for healing and agricultural trade to serve the needs of the living as well as the dead, but it is equally possible that the realization of this temple garden did not occur due to the Djoser's death.

No doubt, every temple garden would have needed an ample supply of water, and the Nile River appears to be the closest source. It may seem daunting to bring water from such a great distance, but we must remember the construction of the Step Pyramid occurred in the third millennium BCE when the Nile riverbed flowed to within at least several hundred feet of the base of the Sakkara plateau during the annual flooding. In the ensuing millennia, the Nile River migrated steadily eastward. The ever-widening strip of land between the river and the plateau on which sits the Step Pyramid complex allowed later generations to build much grander temples, such as the Great Temple of Ptah, said to be at least as large as Karnak in its heyday, and which eventually usurped the preeminence held by Djoser's funerary complex.

Having the North Exit Gate close to a garden in the North Court makes perfect sense when you realize no ready source of water is nearby. Water would have had to been carried from the Nile River, and a gate in this section of the Enclosure Wall would have made it considerably easier instead of having to bring it in through the South Entrance Gate. Even with the existence of the North Exit Gate, it would certainly be a poor second choice to require gallons of water to be carried the long distance from the Nile to irrigate the temple gardens if a better solution could be found.

Just such a solution may have appeared during excavation work in the late 1920s with the discovery of a pit near the North Altar (*Fig. 6-64*). Measuring only 1.5 meters (5 feet) deep, the pit appeared to be unfinished and unlined unlike several other pits that lead to underground chambers. If this pit was excavated as part of a planned subterranean burial chamber, its proximity to the North Altar is rather odd given the altar's ceremonial significance to make offerings of some kind.

Fig. 6-64 - North Altar and pit (arrow)

Is it possible the North Court pit was eventually to be lined with stone in order to serve as a well? We will never know as the plans for a temple garden in the North Court do not seem to have been realized, but of all the possibilities, a well in this location makes more sense than excavating more storage or burial chambers.

Digging a well to supply much needed water for a proposed garden or small located in the North Court would not be outside the realm of possibilities. There is evidence of water damage in the chambers beneath the Step Pyramid, so it appears the water table was probably much closer to the surface due to the proximity of the Nile River during the Third Dynasty. We know the ancient Egyptians were capable of excavating such wells given the simple fact the Central Burial Shaft under the Step Pyramid is 28 meters (92 feet) below grade. Excavating a well in the North Court would not be as challenging by comparison.

Evidence for a garden in or near the North Court came in 1990 when our tour guide, Hakim, showed us some seeds from the top of the North Altar that is located near the north wall of the North Court (*Fig. 6-65*). These seeds came from the blackened, charcoal-like soil just beneath the surface layer of dirt and sand covering the top of the altar. It doesn't seem likely they just blew in on the wind because there was no evidence of seeds found elsewhere, nor were there any seeds in the surface layer of dirt. In addition, the granaries, located just to the west of the North Altar along the north wall of the complex have not been used for thousands of years.

Another possible explanation for the presence of seeds on top of the North Altar may come from the altar doing double duty as a threshing floor where wheat or other seeds were separated from the chaff. If it was an altar in addition to, or separate from, being a threshing floor, the ancient ritual of sacrificing the first fruits of the harvest is what comes quickly to mind when examining these dark, carbonized seeds, and may have been a more widely held custom among ancient civilizations than we realize. I came to discover much later some evidence of the North Altar's use as an offering table (see Chapter 8). J.-P. Lauer pretty much came to the same conclusion. [80]

Fig. 6-65 – The North Altar in the North Court
Hakim (left) is showing a member of our tour group the blackened seeds found on the surface of the North Altar

Firth contradicted himself when he presumed the Enclosure Wall was finished before completion of the remainder of the complex despite his assertion that the purpose of one or more of the ramps located against the exterior of the North Court's wall was to haul construction materials to the interior of the enclosure.

While the use of a ramp to move construction materials into the interior of the Step Pyramid Enclosure is theoretically possible, a better way of accomplishing this feat would be to keep a section of the Enclosure Wall open (say, near False Gate 13 and its self-closing door) until after Djoser's funeral. Even though construction on a pharaoh's tomb would have stopped at his death, the proximity of the completed False Gate 13 (the North Exit Gate) to the North Mortuary Temple would have provided easier access to bring in stone and other materials. If this scenario is true, the ramps attached to the north Enclosure Wall were more than likely used when the harvesting of the stones from the Step Pyramid and the other parts of the Enclosure occurred in later centuries than for its construction. The stones used in the outer casing of the Step Pyramid and the limestone blocks used for floors and walls throughout the Enclosure were more desirable than the irregularly shaped stones used in the construction of the Enclosure Wall.

It has been suggested that Djoser's funeral procession entered the enclosure over one of the ramps that still partially existed as of the 1920s at the northeast corner of the North Court (*Figs. 6-66* and *6-67*). The ramps could have been used to take the royal coffin and other burial goods into the Enclosure instead of trying to negotiate through the narrow, 1 meter wide (3.28 feet) South Entrance Gate and passageways,[81] so a funeral procession through the complex by that route would be very difficult.[82]

Looking at older aerial photographs taken in the 1920s and 1930s, as well as photographs that are more recent, the ramp in question is easily visible running from outside the north wall of the Enclosure up to the base of the Step Pyramid just east of the North Mortuary Temple. In addition, there appears to be up to three more ramps in the same area of the north Enclosure Wall, plus some possible ramp-like structures in the middle of the North Court. Instead of ancient ramps, these could easily be piles of modern excavation debris, or just ordinary sand dunes.

Fig. 6-66 – The ramp (green line) that traversed the North Court, east of the North Mortuary Temple, 1928

Fig. 6-67 – Northern part of the Step Pyramid Enclosure with up to four ramps connected to the north Enclosure Wall, 1927

While it is certainly possible the northeast ramp was used for Djoser's funeral procession and possibly for other family members, it is well to ask why the ramp was left in place once the funeral rituals were complete. Even though construction of a pharaoh's mortuary complex often ceased upon his death, logically, a shorter processional ramp would have been constructed from outside the east wall and not the north wall, and would have been removed once the funeral ceremonies were completed. This would leave the pristine nature of the Enclosure completely unspoiled since the nearby Ḥeb-Sed Court was used on a daily basis as a medical center, even after the death of Djoser, not to mention priests would probably have performed cultic rituals in the North Mortuary Temple as part of keeping Djoser's memory alive.

The ramps attached to the north wall in existence even into the 20th century were likely used in the deconstruction of the Step Pyramid Enclosure. Just as it is truly difficult to date the building of a temple, it is equally difficult to know exactly when these old temples and pyramids were torn down for their precious limestone. Therefore, it is impossible to date the construction of these ramps, and their purpose. It is a given fact that most temples in ancient Egypt were renovated and reconstructed during their existence. Later, they were even dismantled to reuse the stonework for other building projects. The limestone blocks of this temple may have been more highly prized by local farmers who burned the blocks to provide a source of lime to use as fertilizer!

An alternative to constructing a ramp to allow Djoser's funeral procession to enter the Enclosure would be to use a larger opening in the wall. Leaving an opening in the wall would give easier access to the second North Descending Passage located just outside the North Mortuary Temple. The North Exit Gate is the obvious choice to do this, but it necessitated widening the passageway and without the self-closing door installed. After this, the North Exit Gate had served its purpose as the temple's design had radically changed from when the First Enclosure Wall was constructed.

Installation of exterior stones and infill material in the gap in the Enclosure Wall turned it into False Gate 13. The self-closing door may not have been reinstalled, but if it was, an exterior-facing handle would have been attached to the door allowing egress from the Mammisi birthing rooms that had just been built (see Chapter 8).

If it is certain the Enclosure Wall was completed in antiquity – as I believe it was – then Imhotep would never allow an eyesore such as a construction ramp to remain in place long after it was needed. Imhotep's pride, not to mention his work ethic, would have prevented it. The presumption that "stones pierced from both sides and useless for building were not cleared away" implies that construction ceased at some point, and these stones were left scattered about the area of the Ḥeb-Sed Court and the eastern side of the Step Pyramid. This led to the conclusion the North Court was empty and used only to store construction materials.[83] In addition, it has been suggested the pit tombs in the North Court area were meant for some unfinished Third Dynasty mastabas, and the mounds of rubbish seen today in the North Court may have been intended as infill material for these mastabas. To dedicate a fully enclosed area of the mortuary temple for the storage of building supplies contradicts Firth's discovery of foodstuffs stored in various underground bunkers that lay beneath the granaries in the northwest part of the North Court. Such large quantities of food indicates the North Court was used to store and/or grow food.

When first excavated, the presumption was that the granaries were never finished. As a result, they were considered only symbolic and later used to store building waste.[84] The granaries are clearly larger than necessary for the quantity of food often interred within the deceased person's tomb along with other burial goods, even for a king. Despite its unfinished state, the Step Pyramid complex housed a thriving priesthood that served the Memphis area community. Even though the final plan for a garden or small farm where food and other plants used in the healing arts would be grown was never realized, the North Court may have become a type of food distribution center with its many underground food storage magazines and extensive above ground granaries, say, for use in a time of drought.

The Three Western Massifs (Storage Magazines or Tombs)

When most people visit the Step Pyramid for the first time, they almost never go over to see the three Western Massifs (also known as storage magazines) on the far west side of the temple complex (*Fig. 6-68*). Odds are most Egyptologists never venture there, either. Not for any lack of archeological interest, but mostly because the importance of the Western Massifs lies underground, and it is extremely unsafe to go down into the tunnels and chambers that lie below due to highly unstable rock strata and the poorly preserved remnants of these Second Dynasty tombs.

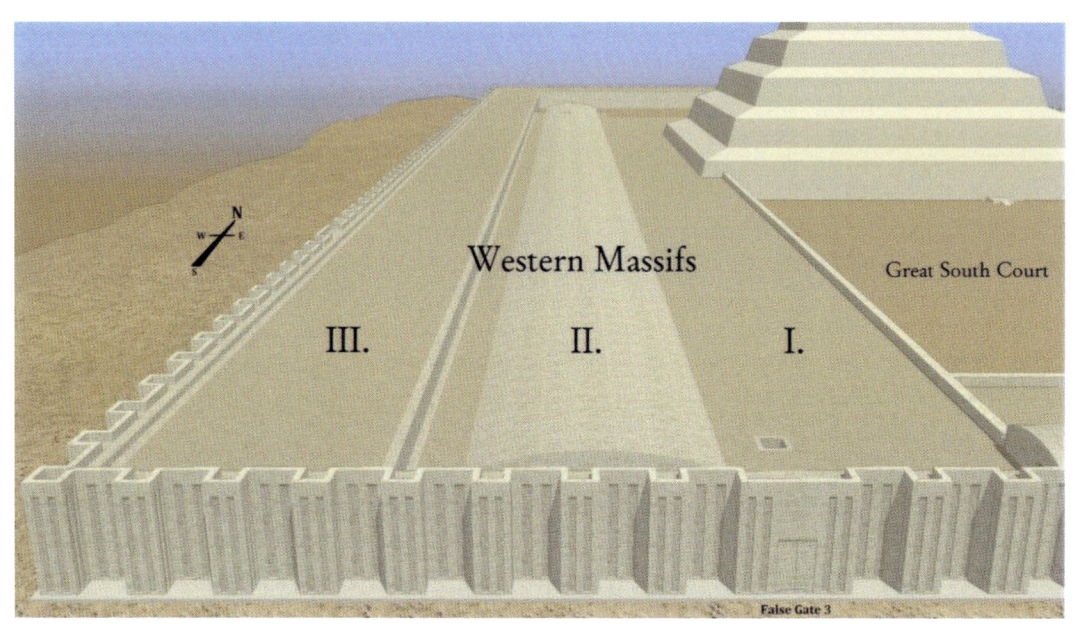

Fig. 6-68 – The Western Massifs and False Gate 3

The easternmost massif (Western Massif I) butts up against the west side of the Step Pyramid, indicating that it is either contemporaneous with the construction of the six-tier Step Pyramid, or was built shortly thereafter. Imhotep probably ordered the construction of this massif for two reasons: First, he needed to delineate the location of the western wall of the Great South Court. Next, while most of the Second Dynasty underground chambers lay beneath Western Massif II, Imhotep needed to ensure no one would build above ground in this area because doing so would compromise the structural integrity of the underground chambers that extended to the east outside the limits of the walls of Western Massif II. If nothing else, this corroborates the fact that Djoser sought to preserve and prevent any further damage to his predecessors' tombs and grave goods, as Western Massifs I and III serve no other purpose, whether it be architecturally or anything concerning religious symbolism. It is a good thing Imhotep did so, because these subterranean tunnels and chambers were structurally unsound and dangerous even back then.

Though constantly covered by the ever-present windblown sand and other rubble on the site, Lauer believed the three Western Massifs had different shapes. Because it was an earlier structure, Western Massif II had a rounded top, not unlike the South Tomb, with the other two massifs having flat tops. These two massifs – I and III – were built by Imhotep, not only to give these large structures a sense of symmetry, but also to show that Western Massif II was much older and to prevent any possible construction taking place in the future above its underground chambers.

Building Egypt's First *Mega Mortuary Temple*

No doubt, your eyes are starting to glaze over at this point, and have taken on the appearance of a *deer in the headlights* look. I freely admit to having *geeked out* [85] when doing research for this book, but please bear with me, because this will all make sense very shortly.

Reverse engineering this great monument has been the most difficult, and yet, the most rewarding part of this exploration into its past. Traditional Egyptology has given us a particular timeline of construction for the Step Pyramid complex. While most of what has been proposed concerning its various building phases is probably true, I believe what follows to be a more complete picture of the Step Pyramid's construction history.

Every work of art begins with a blank canvas. Every piece of music begins with a blank music manuscript. The construction of every building begins with a blank piece of paper. In the case of the architectural design of the Step Pyramid Enclosure, Imhotep's task didn't begin with an empty ground surface on the bluffs overlooking the Nile valley or blank piece of papyrus. Buildings and structures of various kinds already pre-existed on or around the plateau before Imhotep began work on what would eventually become the Step Pyramid(s), the ancillary buildings and Enclosure Wall. Later royal mortuary temples such as the three temples of Hatshepsut, Mentuhotep II and Thutmosis III at Deir el-Bahri, the massive Temple of Amenhotep III with the famous Colossi of Memnon standing before its front pylons and the equally majestic Ramesseum of Rameses II, owe a great deal to the Step Pyramid Enclosure of Netjerikhet Djoser. However, Imhotep needed to find inspiration from earlier temples and monuments to design Djoser's memorial structure.

An architect's work is an amalgam of the work done by their predecessors. Design ideas and principles spring from what other architects did in the past, so that any new project Imhotep undertook always built upon the work of his ancestors. (Literally, because in ancient Egypt, as previously mentioned, sons generally inherited their father's profession and position. Imhotep's father, Kanofer, was a Royal Architect, and most likely, his grandfather before that.) This is not to say that there cannot be progress in construction techniques and the use of building materials. It takes a brave architect to break long-standing and deeply ingrained traditions to make improvements, all the while maintaining alignment with the standard building practices of the time and without relying on a formulaic rehashing of past designs. What sets Imhotep apart from his contemporaries was how he used the designs of his ancestors to inspire him to take giant risks and *think outside the mastaba* to leap ahead and construct a truly unique work of architecture and art.

Imhotep was probably influenced by the designs of various mastaba tombs in Sakkara as well as several funerary enclosures located in the south at Abydos. His greatest source of inspiration may well have come from the funerary enclosure of Khasekhemwui, Djoser's predecessor (*Fig. 6-69*).

In its day, this funerary enclosure, the *"Shunet el-Zebib"*, was referred to as the *House of the Ka*. It is certainly impressive, with its inner walls measuring approximately 124 by 56 meters (407 by 184 feet) and 8 meters (26 feet) high. No doubt, the extraordinary size of this enclosure impressed Imhotep enough to attempt a design equal to this monument of Djoser's predecessor. How much this funerary enclosure inspired Imhotep will be discussed in Chapter 7.

Fig. 6-69 – The northeast gate of the Funerary Enclosure of Khasekhemwui ("Shunet el-Zebib") at Abydos

Further inspiration may well have come from the eight-tier mastaba of Nebitka in north Sakkara (*Fig. 6-70*), perhaps the first instance of the use of a stepped façade for a tomb.

Fig. 6-70 – Mastaba 3038 of Nebitka, an official during the reign of Anedjib, fifth king of the First Dynasty

Repurposing and Rebuilding the Pre-Existing Structures

When Imhotep received the commission to finish Djoser's mortuary temple, he took its design to a completely new level. Not content with using stone for the Enclosure's smaller buildings, he decided to expand the symbolic language of this mortuary temple in ways that no one had thought of before his time. A testament to Imhotep's genius is his use of a hodge-podge of cemetery refuse, which he turned into the grand monument we see today. *Fig. 6-71* portrays the best guess of what the Sakkara plateau may have looked like when Imhotep began looking for a suitable location for his king's funerary monument. The most prominent features of the plateau are the ones that no one gets to see today. These are Western Massif II, and the Subterranean Chambers accessible from Pits P_8 and P_9. Western Massif II may even be a collection of several tombs dating from the First or Second Dynasties given the number of pits (P_4, P_5, P_6, $P_{6'}$ and P_7) leading from the surface to its interior. This is only speculation since a detailed survey has never been done of this massif.

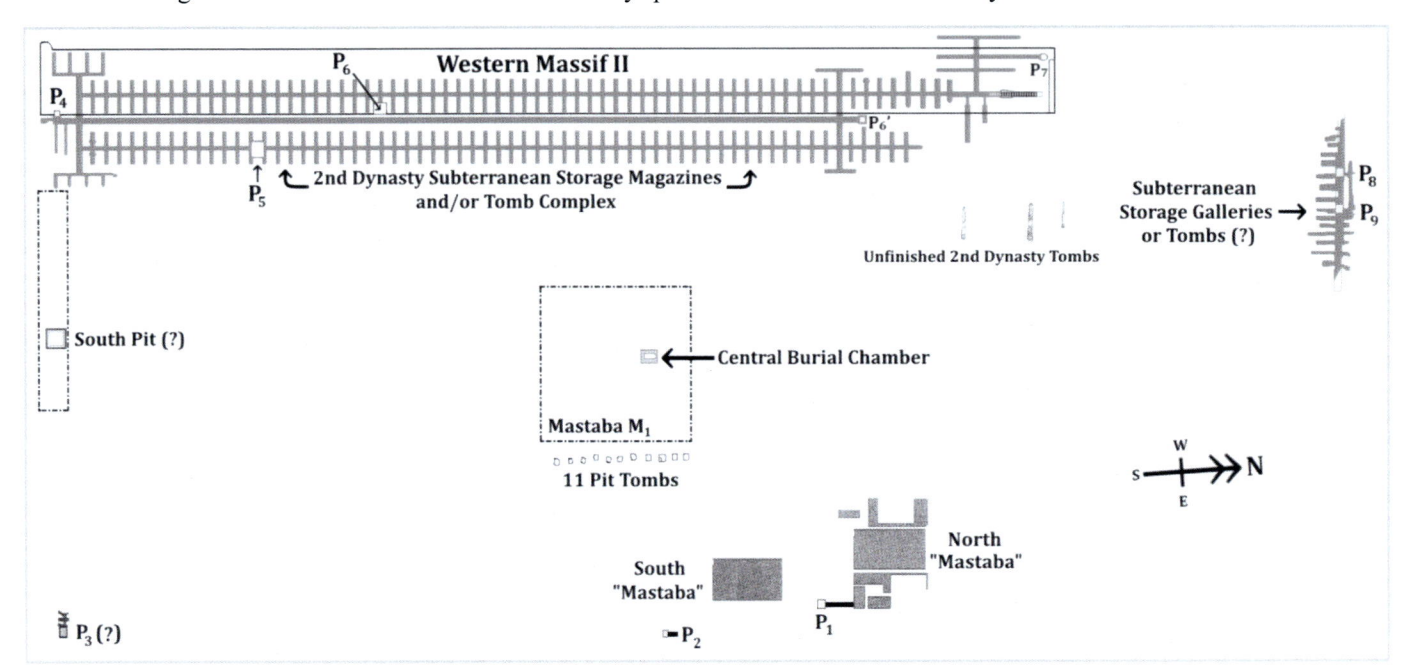

Fig. 6-71 – The Sakkara Plateau above and below ground as Imhotep may have found it prior to the construction of Djoser's funerary complex

As previously speculated in this chapter, the North and South Pavilions were already in place and were just a couple of incomplete mastabas with the pair of pit tombs (P$_1$ and P$_2$) nearby.

When Djoser and Imhotep were scouting locations for Djoser's tomb complex, Mastaba M$_1$ may have only been partially finished, as indicated by the dashed line representing the mastaba in an incomplete state in *Fig. 6-71*. The reason for doubting M$_1$ was a finished project is the existence of Mastaba M$_2$, which is more of a shell surrounding Mastaba M$_1$ than a completely integrated design. A cursory examination shows that most, if not all other mastabas from the First and Second Dynasty do not exhibit any changes after construction was complete, nor does it appear they have this kind of add-on structure. For this reason, Mastaba M$_2$ may have been built just to stabilize a half-finished Mastaba M$_1$, otherwise, why bother building Mastaba M$_2$. As noted before, the Central Burial Chamber may well have been fully excavated with its sarcophagus already installed in it when Djoser and Imhotep initially surveyed the site. The excavation of the eleven pit tombs had also occurred; and probably in the same state as we see today. It is also possible Imhotep had Mastaba M$_1$ razed to the ground if it was made of mudbrick and replaced with stone prior to constructing the four-tier Step Pyramid because the weight of a new pyramid made entirely of stone would have crushed the older mastaba.

The question marks (?) next to several features in *Fig. 6-71* relate to the uncertainty of when a particular building or structure within the Step Pyramid Enclosure was constructed. The timeline of the building of these structures is somewhat fluid and ever changing with new discoveries that inevitably answer some of these questions, but even then, more questions often arise with every newfound answer. Here are a few of the many vagaries concerning the early stages of building this monument:

1. It has always been thought that Mastaba M$_1$ was completed prior to its use (or reuse) for Djoser's tomb, but this may not necessarily be the case because of the unique shell-like characteristics of Mastaba M$_2$, as outlined above. Imhotep repeated this structural upgrade by encasing the two mastabas that later became the North and South Pavilions with new stone façades.
2. The South Pit would eventually become the South Tomb's Main Burial Chamber, although its sarcophagus may or may not have been installed when Imhotep began the task of building it. We know the Step Pyramid's sarcophagus was installed incorrectly. The South Tomb's sarcophagus was oriented with its granite plug at the south end, whereas the Step Pyramid's sarcophagus granite plug was at its north end, opposite the architect's intentions. This reinforces the theory that Imhotep was not the architect for either tomb shaft or sarcophagus. However, assuming the South Tomb Main Burial Chamber was empty and in need of a sarcophagus, Imhotep may have copied the design of the Central Burial Chamber sarcophagus, but the one made for the South Tomb is about half the size of the original.
3. The rectangular dashed lines around the South Tomb Pit in *Fig. 6-71* indicate the eventual location of the South Tomb, with the distinct possibility that its construction had already started to some extent.
4. Given its incomplete state, it is unknown what purpose Pit P$_3$ was meant to serve, but Imhotep included it within the final design for the Step Pyramid Enclosure. Was it originally a water well that had dried up, or just an unfinished pit tomb? If so, did Imhotep have a long-term plan to repurpose it?
5. The subterranean galleries (or tombs) beneath Pits P$_8$ and P$_9$ may, or may not, have existed prior to the beginning of construction of the Step Pyramid. They may have been added when the North Court was expanded during the construction phase for the six-tier Step Pyramid, and the granaries constructed above them (see *Fig. 2-4*).

The straight and orderly appearance of the plan of the tunnels and chambers beneath Western Massif II in *Fig. 6-71* is a bit deceiving. It is really just a *best guess* due to the lack of any clearing or exploration of them. Contrasting this is the random and rough look of the Subterranean Chambers beneath Pits P$_8$ and P$_9$, which were more extensively explored by Firth. As mentioned previously, fruits and grains were found in these chambers, possibly in conjunction with the two rows of granaries that would eventually be constructed above them. Whether constructed to store food or were just unused tombs that were repurposed, the true function of these chambers remains to be discovered.

The three openings to the south of these two pits and to the east of Western Massif II (marked as '**D**' on J.-P. Lauer's plan, see *Fig. 1-2*), have been dated to the Second Dynasty, and are nothing more than entrances with no finished tomb associated with them. In many respects, Imhotep needed to become an archeologist to discover what lay beneath the plateau before he could commence with designing Djoser's tomb. Not shown in *Fig. 6-71* are four entrances leading to underground rooms marked as '**C**' in *Fig. 1-2*. These openings have recently been determined to lead to an animal embalming center created during the New Kingdom, approximately 1300 years after the Step Pyramid Enclosure was built (see also Chapter 3).

Finishing the South Tomb and the Three Mastabas

After making the decision to repurpose the structures that already existed on the Sakkara plateau for Djoser's tomb, construction began in several places at roughly the same time. Though it is difficult to know precisely which structure was built first, the most logical course of action would be to begin with the South Tomb. This is simply because Imhotep was only just beginning to conceive the concept of a multi-mastaba step pyramid, and he needed to work out the construction details with the South Tomb used as a type of feasibility study before moving forward with such an enormous project.

Assuming there was no sarcophagus in the South Tomb when construction started, the first task was to lower and assemble a new half-size sarcophagus into the Main Burial Shaft that already existed, which Imhotep copied from the sarcophagus in the Central Burial Chamber of Mastaba M$_1$. Next, the excavation commenced of the South Tomb's West Descending Passage from the Main Burial Shaft to the surface. Then, the rest of the underground tunnels and chambers were excavated (*Fig. 6-72*), and completion of the famous Blue Faience Rooms could proceed (see *Fig. 6-21*).

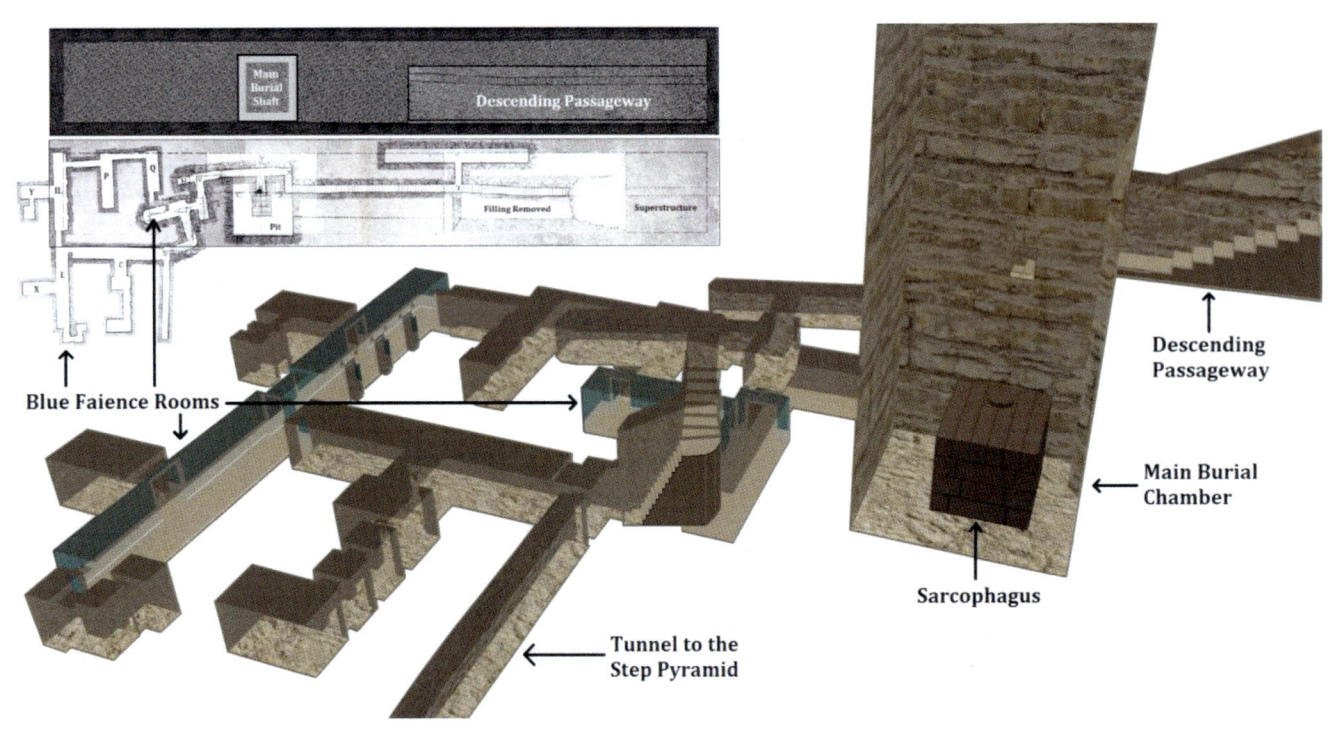

Fig. 6-72 – South Tomb Superstructure, Underground Chambers and Tunnels

While work on the underground tunnels was going on, the South Tomb's superstructure was constructed. Believing the tunnels and chambers below Western Massif II were tombs and not just storage rooms, Imhotep continued the tradition of designing a mastaba tomb with a curved roof (see *Figs. 6-22* and *6-23*, and in Chapter 7, *The Mystery of the Sakkara Ostracon*). Coincidentally, this mimics the curved roof of the nearby Western Massif II (*Fig. 6-73*, see also *Fig. 6-68*).

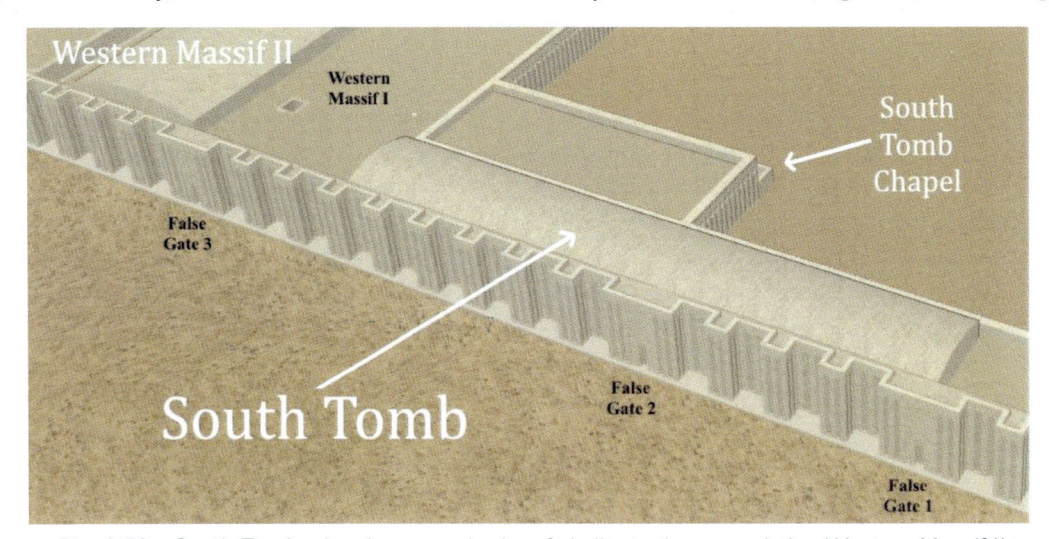

Fig. 6-73 – South Tomb, showing an arched roof similar to the pre-existing Western Massif II

Once the South Tomb was complete, Imhotep felt confident enough to begin the completion of Mastaba M₁ (*Fig. 6-74, 1*) for the next phase of construction. When that was finished, the most likely scenario to occur next was to shore up the foundation of Mastaba M₁ that may have had perpendicular walls by enveloping it with more structurally stable sloped walls of stone, turning it into Mastaba M₂ (*Fig. 6-74, 2*), otherwise, why bother encasing Mastaba M₁ if it was already structurally sound. A cursory look at other contemporary and earlier mastabas fails to show any similar wraparound walls of stone in their design indicating that Mastaba M₂ was unique in this respect.

Around the time when Mastaba M₂ was near completion, excavation of the North Descending Passage started from inside the burial shaft out to the surface (*Fig. 6-74, 3*). When the North Descending Passage and Mastaba M₂ were complete, the eleven pit tomb entrances were concealed by the added-on masonry of Mastaba M₃ (*Fig. 6-74, 4*), making Djoser's mortuary mastaba more rectangular shaped like so many other mastabas in the area, and setting the stage for the construction of the four-tier Step Pyramid.

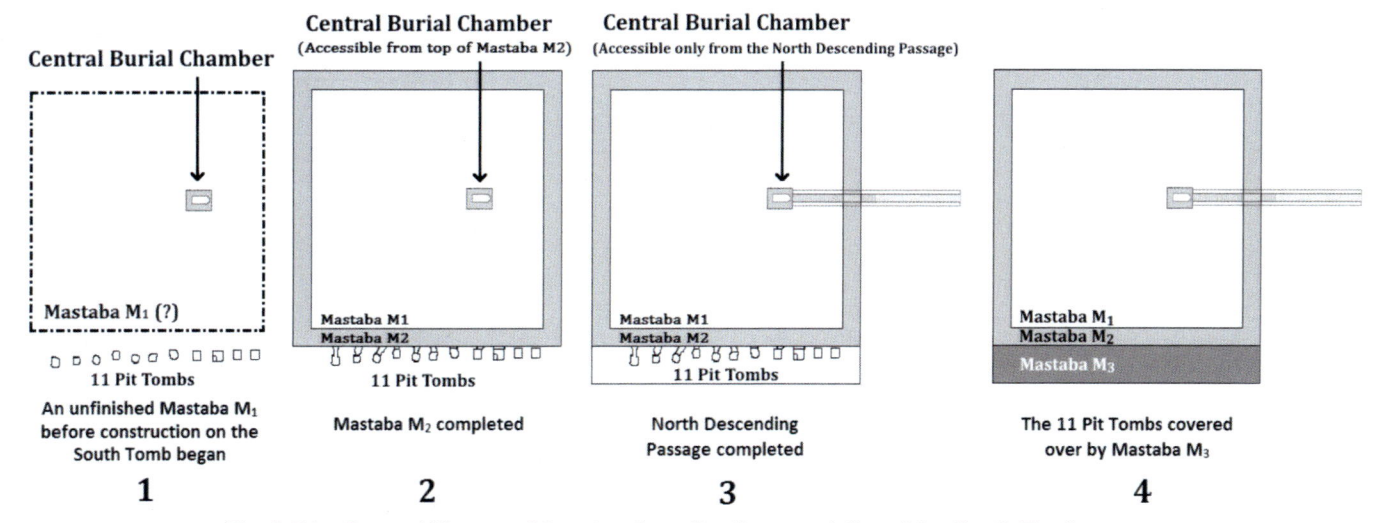

Fig. 6-74 – Second Phases of Construction after the completion of the South Tomb

The First Enclosure Wall and the Old Serdab

Near the end of the second phase of construction, adding new façades to the incomplete north and south mastabas along with additional stonework rendered them into their final forms as the North and South Pavilions. Rather than replicating the designs of his predecessors in Abydos where the kings had separate tombs and funerary enclosures, Imhotep convinced Djoser to take a grand inspirational leap and encompass his mastaba tomb and the North and South Pavilions within an enclosure wall to set it apart from all the other tombs nearby (*Fig. 6-77*).

This would duplicate the concept of a separate tomb and enclosure used at the old traditional cemetery at Abydos. As part of Imhotep's design for the North and South Pavilions, he created small courts in front of them. The South Pavilion Court became the first *sed*-festival ceremonial court, but only one D-shaped boundary marker was found in situ, unlike the later *Great South Court*, which had two B-shaped boundary markers that Djoser would encircle while running the *Ḥeb-Sed*, or *festival of the tail* (*Figs. 6-75* and *6-76*).

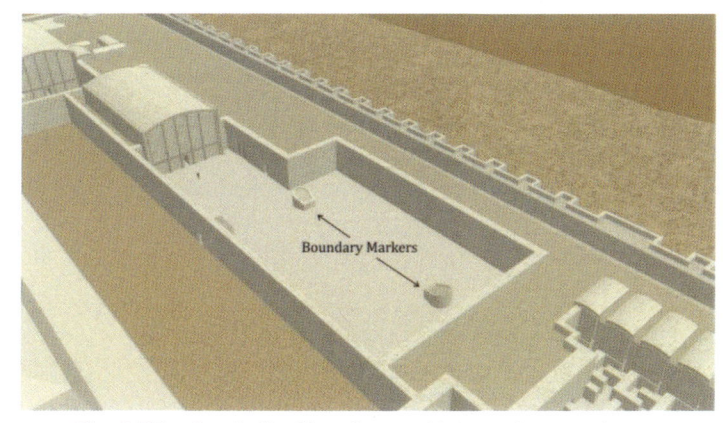

Fig. 6-75 - South Pavilion Court with boundary markers

Fig. 6-76 - The only South Pavilion Court boundary marker as excavated in the 1920s

Included within this First Enclosure Wall was what I call the *Old Serdab* and its court (see also *Fig. 6-55*). This Old Serdab may or may not have existed along with the other structures found on the Sakkara plateau before construction on Djoser's tomb began. In this plan, I have assumed Imhotep created this unique building as opposed to someone else even though other Serdabs and their statues, either within a tomb or as freestanding structures, were constructed as far back as the First Dynasty tomb of Pharaoh Qaá.[86]

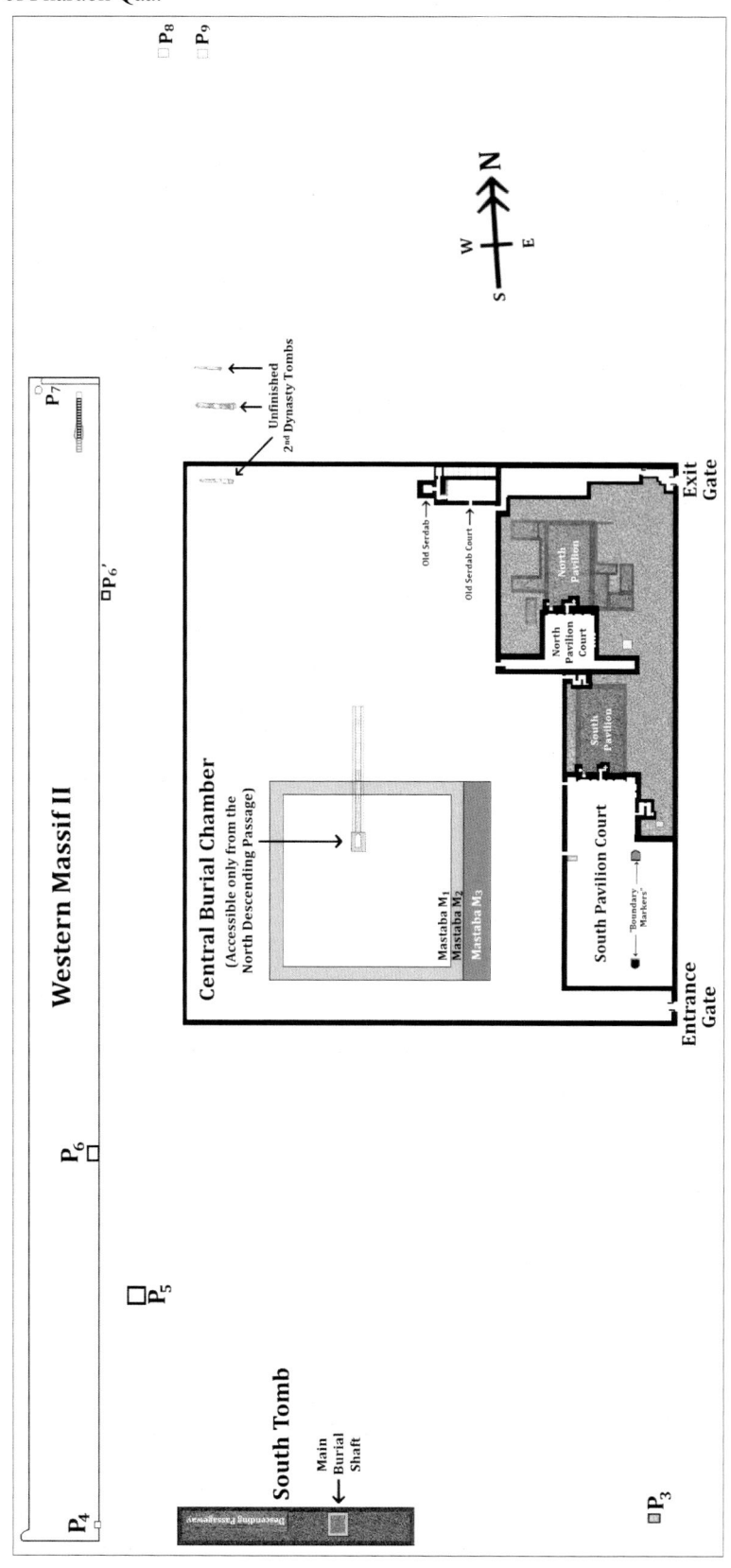

Fig. 6-77 – The First Funerary Enclosure of Netjerikhet Djoser with the above ground structures that were readily visible at the time

In keeping with the building traditions of earlier First and Second Dynasty mastabas, the smaller and shorter First Enclosure Wall may have been made of mudbrick with a smooth plaster surface. This would have appeared like the wall surfaces of the funerary enclosure of Khasekhemwui (*Fig. 6-78*). Without any evidence, it is difficult to say if the First Enclosure Wall had similar bastion-like protrusions found on the current Enclosure Wall. Remember that the Step Pyramid Enclosure underwent several revisions before Imhotep and Djoser agreed on the final design we see today.

Fig. 6-78 – Exterior Wall of the Funerary Enclosure of Khasekhemwui, North Abydos. Made of mudbrick, it had a coating of plaster, some of which is still visible at the bottom of the wall (Manna Nader, Gabana Studios, Cairo)

However, Lauer was of the opinion the First Enclosure Wall was built using fine, smooth limestone.[87] If so, this would be proof that Imhotep was already starting his innovative use of dressed stone since the walls of mastabas were generally made of plaster-covered mudbrick. Perhaps he was also inspired to use stone in the design of the Step Pyramid Enclosure from the example of the *Great Enclosure*, also known as *Gisr el-Mudir*. Though never completed, limestone was used for part of its construction. Often attributed to Khasekhemwui, it is not known for whom it was really intended since Khasekhemwui's tomb was located at Umm el-Qa'ab (*Fig. 6-79*) with his Funerary Enclosure about 2 kilometers north, both in the south of Egypt at Abydos.

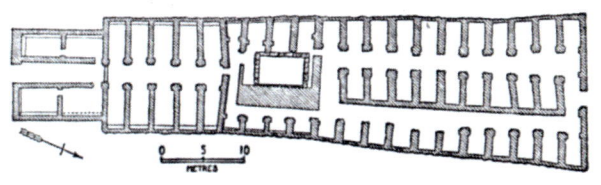

Fig. 6-79 – Khasekhemwui's tomb at Umm el-Qa'ab

At the time of completion, this first iteration of Djoser's Funerary Enclosure took on a role that perhaps was not too different from several other funerary enclosures; that being a ceremonial space, possibly to celebrate the *Ḥeb-Sed* in the South Pavilion Court among other festivities. In so doing, Imhotep copied the designs of the funerary enclosures of Djoser's predecessors by erecting a north and a south gate (see *Fig. 6-77*). This also explains why the four false gates on the east wall in the final version of the Enclosure Wall were not evenly spaced (*see Fig. 1-2*), as were the false gates on the west and north walls. Simply put, when Imhotep expanded the Enclosure northward, the two additional false gates, False Gates 11 and 12, were evenly spaced between False Gate 13 and the northeast corner of the north wall.

Virtually nothing exists of these original Entrance and Exit Gates today (False Gates 14 and 13, respectively). While it may be speculation they even existed as usable openings, the two gates would have been the main focal point of the First Enclosure Wall. Though simple in its design and construction, the First Enclosure Wall served to set the stage for what would come later when Djoser agreed to Imhotep's inspired plan to expand the enclosure to accommodate a four-tier pyramid.

The Construction of the Four-Tier Pyramid and the Initial Design Phase of the North Court

Whether it was Djoser or Imhotep who came up with the idea to create a four-tier Step Pyramid, it was necessary to enlarge the Enclosure Wall as well. When doing so, Imhotep expanded Djoser's mortuary complex to create a larger *sed-festival* venue with the Great South Court and the Ḥeb-Sed Court. As part of this expansion, Imhotep decided to include the South Tomb in this new project. The first thing Imhotep needed to do was expand the First Enclosure a little bit to the east and a considerable distance to the south in order to encompass the South Tomb within the new enclosure. The new Enclosure Wall would use the typical bastion-type wall we see today, but on a smaller scale. Lauer alluded to this possibility, [88] and speculated what the First and Second Enclosure Walls may have looked like (*Fig. 6-80*).

When I first started on this journey of rediscovering the North Exit Gate and its self-closing door, I suspected renovation and rebuilding of the Step Pyramid Enclosure took place much like other temples throughout Egypt. At some point, the North Exit Gate was closed off turning it into a false gate. Little did I know that Imhotep himself undertook and completed this renovation.

In *Fig. 6-80*, Version I shows what the northeastern corner of the complex in its first incarnation. The thick black lines indicate the original enclosure walls. For this reason, Lauer did not include a real or false gate near the doorpost socket for a self-closing door, as he believed this doorpost socket might have been part of a false door assembly similar to other false doors throughout the complex (see *Figs. 1-5* and *1-10*). However, the sloped shape of the doorpost socket and the lack of remnants of an *always-open* stone door defy this explanation. Version II shows what a new Enclosure Wall would have looked like once extended eastward and northward. Expanding on this idea a little further, *Fig. 6-81* shows what the Second Enclosure would have looked like had it been constructed with a very small North Court.

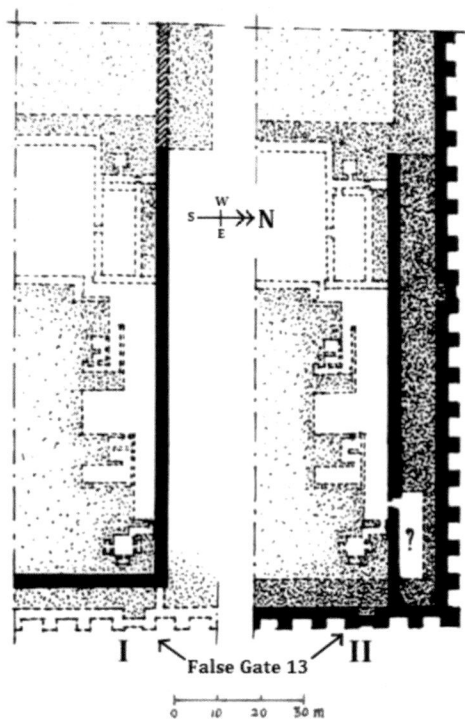

Fig. 6-80 – Two versions of what the North Exit Gate (False Gate 13) may have looked like when the First Enclosure Wall was expanded to accommodate the Four-Tier Step Pyramid

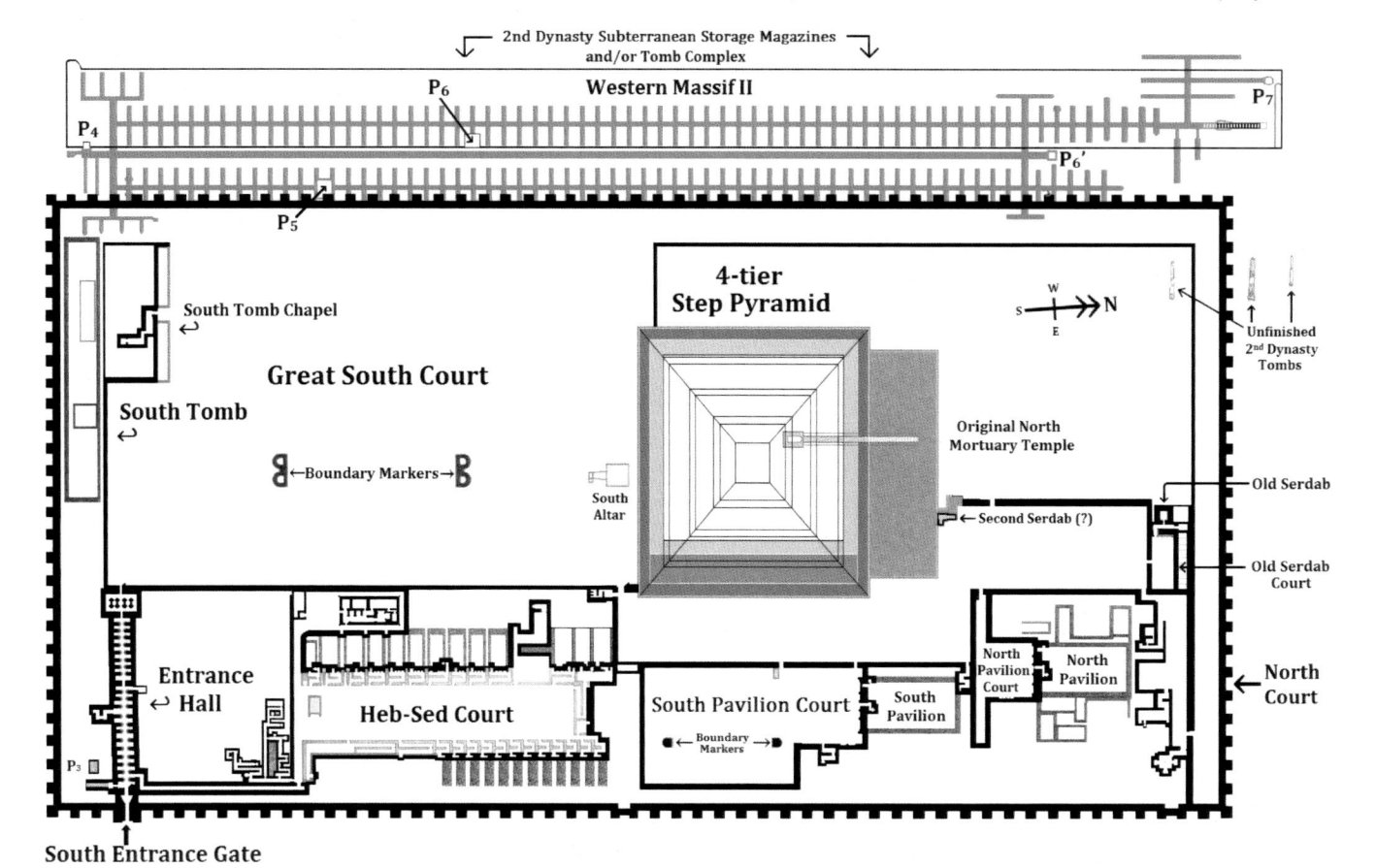

Fig. 6-81 – The Second Enclosure Wall that was never constructed

When Imhotep was planning the construction of the four-tier Step Pyramid, it became obvious the First Enclosure was not sufficiently large enough for such a grand edifice. He began designing a much larger enclosure, not only to satisfy his king's vision for the Afterlife, but also to fulfill his own vision for a health care facility that no one had dreamt of before. Though somewhat modest compared to the Step Pyramid Enclosure we know today, this second attempt at creating a grander monument became the springboard for an even greater intuitive leap with materials that beforehand were only used sparingly in other temples and monuments. Also note: This Second Enclosure Wall design uses a roughly 2:1 ratio in its dimensions, the same as the current Enclosure Wall. The reason for this will be explained further in Chapter 7.

The South Entrance Hall, Ḥeb-Sed Court and the four rooms to the north of the North Pavilion may not have been constructed at this point. No doubt, the designs for these structures were still in the planning stages in Imhotep's mind during the transition period between the completion of the three mastabas and the four-tier pyramid. When the time came to expand the complex to its present size, it would have been much easier since the basic design work had already been done. As mentioned before, what stopped Imhotep from constructing this Second Enclosure Wall was the realization that the vast system of tunnels and chambers from the Second Dynasty beneath Western Massif II would undoubtedly collapse if a wall was constructed above them creating a highly unstable situation for both the wall and the tunnels. This led to the third iteration of the Enclosure Wall we (mostly) see today. We are that much richer for this temporary setback given what Imhotep was eventually able to achieve with his final design.

The Six-Tier Step Pyramid and the Second North Mortuary Temple

Whether the design of the Second Enclosure Wall inspired the expansion of the four-tier pyramid into a six-tier pyramid, or the original plans for the Second Enclosure Wall included the final six-tier Step Pyramid is uncertain. It is unknown at what point Imhotep abandoned the construction of the Second Enclosure Wall to expand the entirety of the complex northward to encompass the Subterranean Chambers beneath Pits P_8 and P_9, and the building of a new North Altar (see *Fig. 1-2*). It is likely to have occurred when the decision to go forward with the construction of the six-tier Step Pyramid. Imhotep also placed the South Tomb inside the new enclosure wall, then stretched the new south wall due west far beyond Western Massif II to maintain the 2:1 ratio originally planned for the Second Enclosure Wall. Imhotep then constructed Western Massif III within this new Enclosure Wall (see *Fig. 6-68*) as a counterbalance to Western Massif II and the soon-to-be-built Western Massif I. This gives the western third of the complex a more aesthetically pleasing appearance, and is typical of artistic expressions as widely diverse as the Menkaure Triad statues (*Fig. 6-82*) of the Fourth Dynasty to the twin bell towers and central sanctuary of the Gothic cathedrals of Europe to the simple A-B-A sonata form in music.

Fig. 6-82 – A triad statue of Pharaoh Menkaure of the Fourth Dynasty from his valley temple at Giza, and the Gothic cathedral of Rheims, France

A new longer east wall was constructed outside the perimeter of the First Enclosure Wall to eventually meet up with a new south wall and the final north wall. This closed off the original Entrance and Exit Gates, turning them into false gates. Part of Imhotep's design for this new Enclosure Wall was the addition of twelve more false gates in keeping with the ancient Egyptian tradition of associating the number 14 with death and resurrection. From his work on the expanding the First Enclosure, Imhotep decided to build a much larger South Court to host the Ḥeb-Sed ceremonies (the much smaller South Pavilion Court just wouldn't do any more). Interestingly, the east wall of the Great South Court aligns with the west wall of the Serdab /North Pavilion that already existed. In addition, the Great South Court's east wall is exactly one-quarter the distance from the interior face of the Enclosure's east wall to its west wall's interior face. This obviously is no accident, and shows Imhotep's incredible attention to planning and detail. The plan of the Great South Court also played a part in the total design of the newly expanded area to the south of the Step Pyramid as will be further explained in Chapter 7.

A new mortuary temple was constructed at the base of the north side of the new six-tier Step Pyramid since it covered up the original mortuary temple (see *Fig. 6-62*). Because construction on this new addition began near the end of the last building phase, the new North Mortuary Temple was never fully completed.

Recent Unexpected Discoveries

Work on the reconstruction and preservation of the Step Pyramid Enclosure is ongoing to this day. The most prominent of these efforts was a study done by the Latvian Scientific Mission in 2005–2007 under the supervision of Dr. Bruno Deslandes.[89] Using ground-penetrating radar (GPR) to a depth of 50 meters, they discovered several underground cavities and galleries (*Fig. 6-83*). Chief among these are three descending corridors from the Dry Moat to the first, third and fourth pit tomb shafts beneath Mastaba M$_3$ (*Fig. 6-85*), and a fourth tunnel that ends just short of the main burial chambers (*Fig. 6-84)*. (This might go a long way in verifying Hakim's belief that there were 22 *tunnels* beneath the Ḥeb-Sed Court.)

The presence of these three tunnels coming from the eastern Dry Moat to several pit tombs beneath the Step Pyramid poses an interesting challenge. Were the tunnels excavated before or after the Mastaba M$_3$ was constructed? What was their purpose? Do they lead to other undiscovered areas beneath the Step Pyramid? More recently, there was a discovery of considerable flooding in the area circa 2700–2600 BCE. Could these descending tunnels have been used to keep the underground galleries dry by acting as a drainage system? It's interesting to speculate about these new descending corridors, and until they are excavated and entered, we won't know for certain. In the meantime, it will also be fun to think about the possibilities.

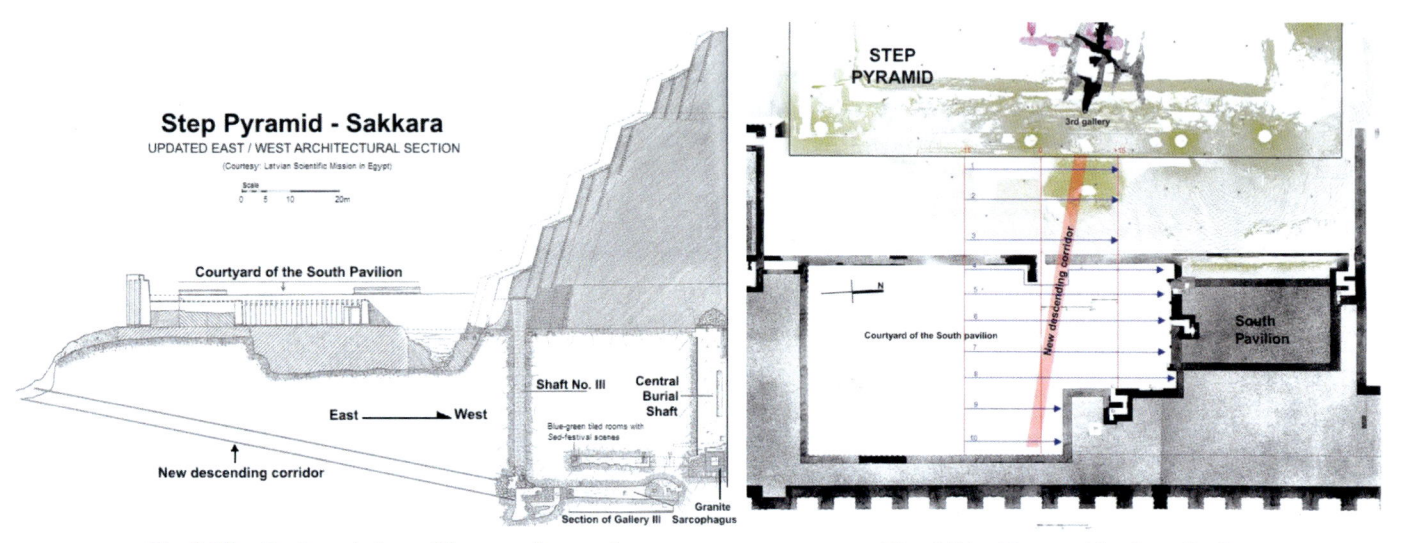

Fig. 6-83 – East-west view of the new descending corridor from the Dry Moat to the third pit tomb

Fig. 6-84 – The corridor from the Dry Moat to the third pit tomb (top view)

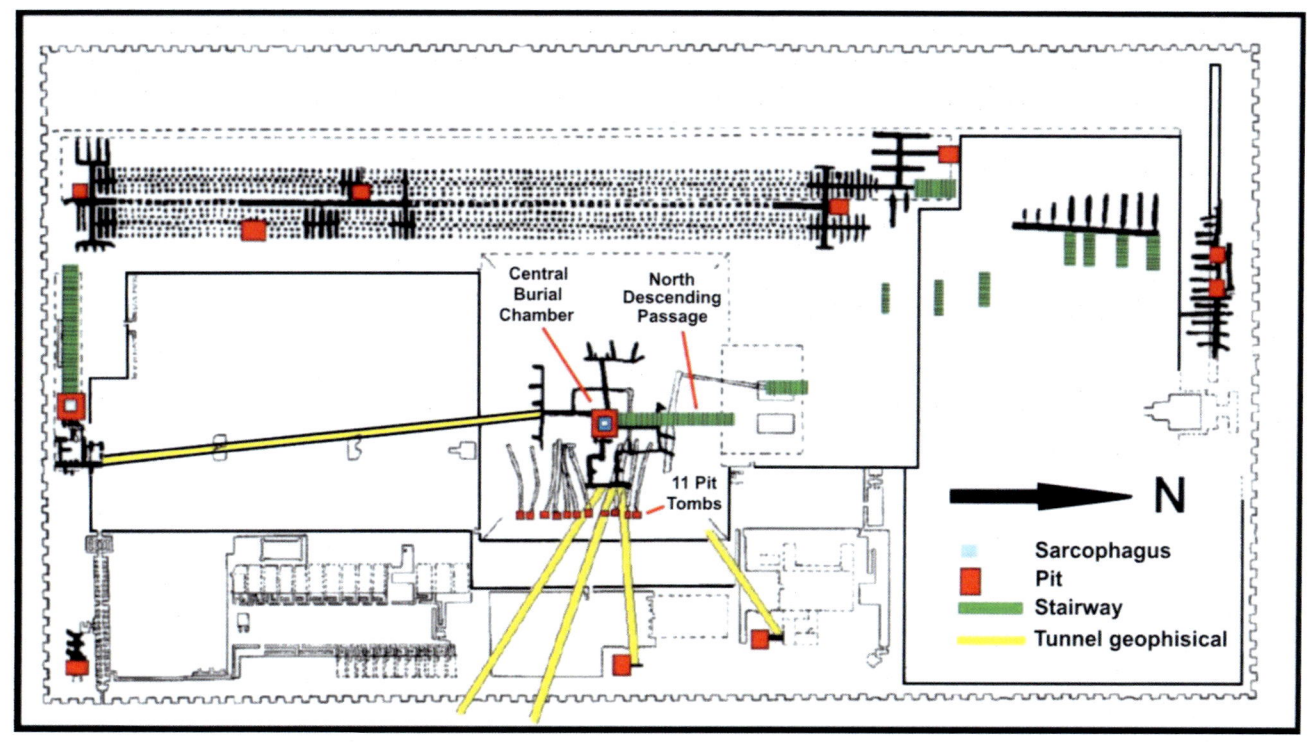

Fig. 6-85 – More tunnels and corridors discovered by the Latvian Scientific Mission

A much longer tunnel appears to join the South Tomb to the south galleries near the Central Burial Chamber beneath the Step Pyramid (*Fig. 6-86*). This poses several interesting questions regarding the integration of the South Tomb into the overall design of the Step Pyramid tomb complex.

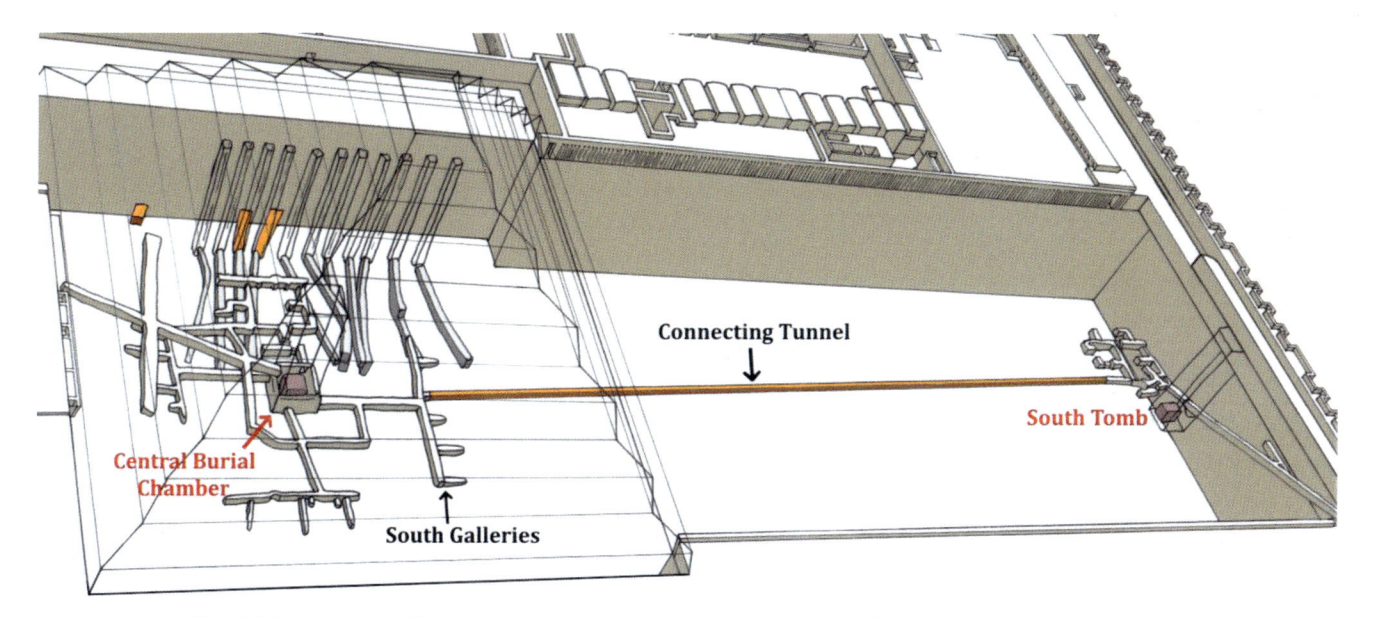

Fig. 6-86 – A newly discovered tunnel beneath the Great South Court connecting the South Tomb to the south galleries of the Central Burial Chamber beneath the Step Pyramid (Fr. Monnier)

For example, what is the symbolism of the subterranean connection between the Main Burial Chamber of the South Tomb and the Step Pyramid's south galleries? Was this tunnel a copy of similar connecting tunnels found in other cemeteries? What purpose did it serve in religious and funerary practices of the time? As much as we know about the Step Pyramid Enclosure, there will always be mysteries to unravel.

Later in 2008, the Ancient Egypt Research Associates in collaboration with the Tokyo Institute of Technology did several more surveys using the latest laser imaging technology. This survey resulted in a three-dimensional contour map of the Step Pyramid in its present condition, revealing considerably more detail than was previously obtainable using traditional archeological methods. Other projects such as the 3D Sakkara Project rendered 2D satellite data into 3D high-resolution datasets capable of producing realistic 3D visualizations of these ancient monuments. These and other such projects will go a long way in helping archeologists locate, excavate and/or preserve previously unknown and hidden archeological sites to prevent any further damage or erosion.

Finally, we must also give credit where credit is due. Imhotep may have been the guiding genius to envision the design and construction of the Step Pyramid Enclosure in a manner that was unique in ancient times, and still inspires admiration even today. He may have even possessed enough artistic skills to work and experiment with sculpting stone to develop new (for that era) and remarkable methods to do so. (One of his many titles was "Imhotep, the Carpenter and the Sculptor" or Chief Sculptor and Overseer of Sculptors and Chief Carpenter.) But it is a testament to the skill of his workforce – the artisans, sculptors and stonemasons – and their ability to render that vision with great precision into a beautiful, clean and breathtakingly elegant manner. We can only guess at what the Step Pyramid Enclosure must have looked like when it was (almost) finished.

While Imhotep was greatly revered for centuries after his passing, and even elevated to the status of a god, perhaps we should nominate for sainthood his unknown construction managers and crew for having to put up with so many change orders during the building of the Step Pyramid complex. Considering all the modifications done to Djoser's mortuary temple in a relatively short span of time, his construction supervisors must have had an infinite source of patience with all the revisions they had to implement mid-stream; tearing down just built walls and putting up new ones, adding whole new structures to an already completed project, and so on. It's too bad artists, sculptors and construction crews weren't worshiped as gods in ancient Egypt. At the very least, maybe they should have been.

A mind stretched by a new idea can never regain its original dimension.

Oliver Wendell Holmes, American jurist

Imhotep the Scribe and Mathematician - The Tradition of Sacred Geometry and the Design of the Step Pyramid Enclosure

Temples tell tales, and speak to us across the centuries in ways that mere words will always fail us. In this examination of the design of the Step Pyramid Enclosure, we will attempt explain the methods and reasons that went into its design. When we visit Djoser's mortuary temple today, one gets the impression that its creation was fully formed from the outset, and what we see now, even in its present jumbled state, was the sum of the vision of Imhotep, the genius who was its architect. This is as far from the truth as the Earth is to the sun.

Reverse engineering any building, whether it's a simple structure like a house, or one as multifaceted as the Step Pyramid Enclosure is often more difficult than designing and constructing it in the first place. Because most of the Step Pyramid's internal structure and architectural elements are hidden from view, attempting the daunting task of determining the architectural philosophy which Imhotep used to design – and redesign - the Step Pyramid Enclosure can test the patience and persistence of even the most dedicated architectural 'archeologist'.

Fortunately, Jean-Philippe Lauer's meticulously drawn plans of the complex can help us better understand the significance of Imhotep's design. Mr. Lauer's careful and disciplined work ethic reminds me of his fellow compatriot, the preeminent composer, Maurice Ravel, called "the most perfect of Swiss watchmakers" due to his perfectionist nature as a composer and the incredible precision of his orchestrations. Likewise, Mr. Lauer's painstaking attention to detail has made my work considerably easier.

Equally fortunate is that we also possess knowledge of how ancient architects used Sacred Geometry which can help us to uncover Imhotep's design philosophy, and possibly learn why he chose to include certain design elements in the manner he did. Most Egyptologists and historians in general do not ascribe the use of Sacred Geometry to the ancient Egyptians to the same degree used by other ancient civilizations. Despite that fact, I began to suspect there was, at the very least, a modicum of something resembling Sacred Geometry used in the Step Pyramid Enclosure specifically and perhaps with other Egyptian monuments as well.

The accuracy of the measurements of the Step Pyramid Enclosure as excavated and reconstructed by Jean-Philippe Lauer has some inherent flaws. This is not due to any incompetence on the part of Mr. Lauer. Rather, resources such as funding, labor, time, and so on, were unavailable to do a more exacting study and measurement of the Enclosure as a whole as well as some if its constituent parts. Not to mention that Mr. Lauer's plan shows the Step Pyramid Enclosure as it existed when it was first excavated in the late 1920s, and early 1930s. Despite the ongoing reconstruction and restoration efforts that have occurred since then, it is obvious the Step Pyramid does not look the way it did circa 2650 BCE.

In that context, the plans that I used to determine the sacred geometrical relationship between the disparate elements of the Step Pyramid Enclosure as originally drawn by Lauer should be viewed in that light. Errors inevitably have crept in for various reasons. From the work of the initial excavations, to the meticulous documenting and creation of the site plans, to publication of those plans in the 1930s, to the reproduction and digitizing of the series of books which contain those plans all have conspired to make any totally accurate assessment and measuring of the Enclosure's details that more difficult.

But, try we must.

A Brief Introduction to Sacred Geometry and Its Use in Architectural Design

Before we proceed further, it is important to understand the basics of Sacred Geometry, its use by architects to design aesthetically pleasing, yet functional architecture and its underlying symbolic meaning. Most of what we know about Sacred Geometry comes from its use in ancient cultures such as Greece and Rome. Sacred Geometry has been used to build some of the world's most iconic architecture has been proven again and again, despite the skeptical notions of many whose work denies this possibility.[90] Sacred Geometry is a means to an end. It was – and still is – used to create architecture that touches both the mind and the soul, but not slavishly adhered to, nor was it meant to be noticeable to the casual observer. If it were too obvious, it would lose its value as a tool for architects.

The use of Sacred Geometry begins with either or both, the square and/or the circle, and are used with a group of six basic shapes and their inherent mathematical ratios. These were held to be a reflection of Divine Order, and therefore, were used extensively in the design of temples and mortuary monuments. Several of the six mathematical ratios and the intrinsic irrational numbers associated with them are used most commonly in virtually all sacred, as well as non-sacred, architecture around the world (*Fig. 7-1*). They are:

The Square
The square root of two (√2 – 1.41421)

The Vesica Pisces or Double Circle
The square root of three (√3 – 1.73205)

The Progenitor of the Double Square
The square root of four (√4 – 2.0, line CI)

The Diagonal of the Double Square
The square root of five (2.23606)

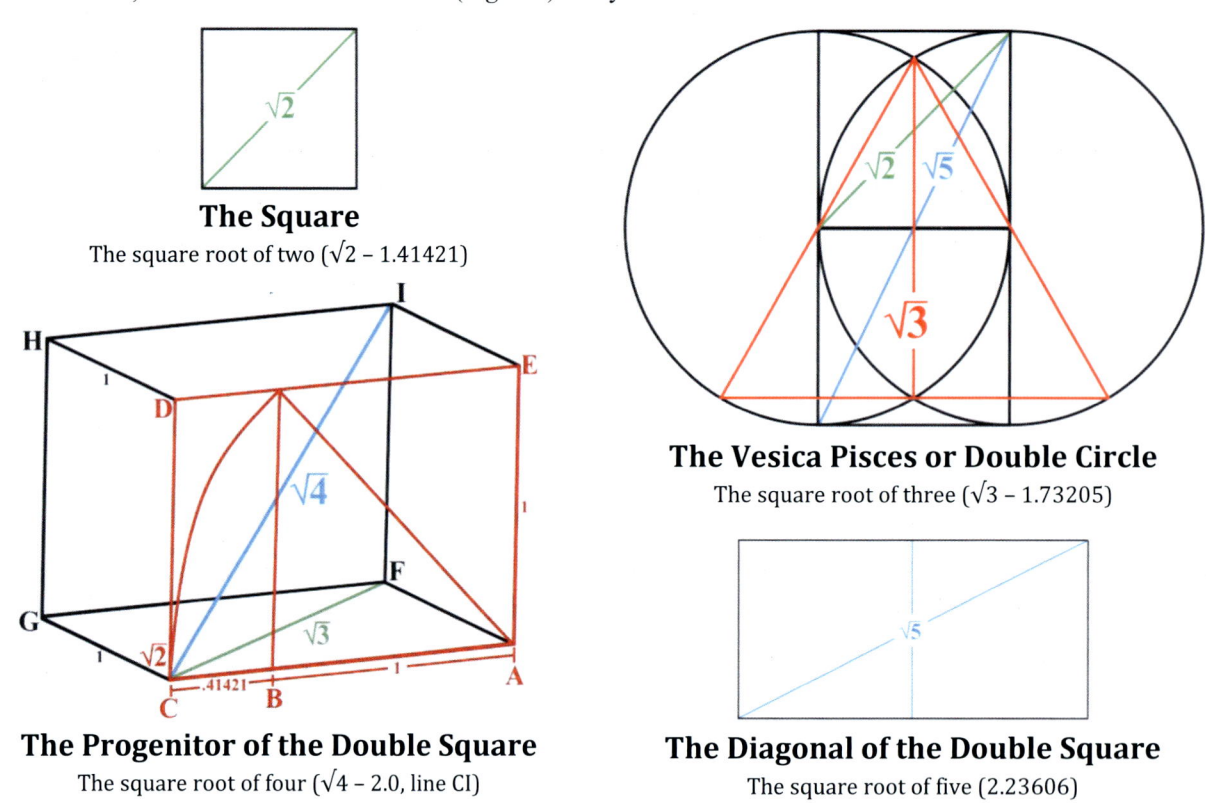

Fig. 7-1 – The Four Primary Sacred Ratios

When combining these Sacred Ratios into a single form, it would look like this:

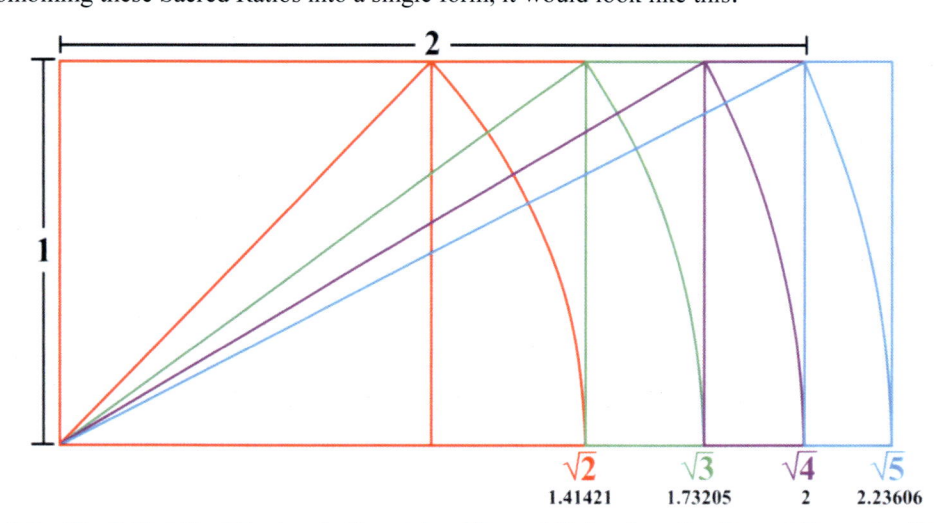

√2   √3   √4   √5
1.41421   1.73205   2   2.23606

Fig. 7-2 – The 5-Part Root Rectangle Template of Sacred Ratios from the Sacred Geometry 'Toolkit'

Though often called a *Dynamic Rectangle*, I call this the '5-Part Root Rectangle Template'. This has been used in various guises for millennia to design architecture and other works of art. In some manner, it is still used today.

An extension of the Root 5 (√5) Double Square is called the Silver Rectangle (*Fig. 7-3*). This is created by drawing an arc from the diagonal of one of the two squares making up the Double Square. Though not often used in traditional Sacred Geometry, apparently Imhotep used the Silver Rectangle extensively when designing the Step Pyramid Enclosure as will be shown further on.

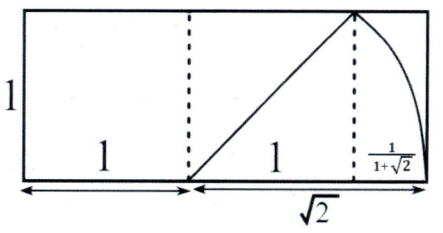

Fig. 7-3 – Silver Rectangle

Another Sacred Ratio extensively used in architectural and other design practices is the Golden Ratio. It is also known as the Golden Rectangle, Golden Mean, Golden Section or Divine Proportion because it was thought to be the most harmonious and divinely inspired of geometric designs. It is a fundamental part of this Sacred Geometry *toolkit*, and represented by the Greek letter *Phi* (Φ).

The most common representation of *Phi* is as a Rectangle (*Fig. 7-4*). It is comprised of a square plus the remainder of the rectangle equaling 0.61803 of the square, and is created in the following manner:

1. Draw a square '**ABEF**'.
2. Divide the square in two,
3. Draw a diagonal line from the midpoint '*m*' to the upper corner '**E**'.
4. Draw an arc from that corner to the extended base line of the square '**AB**'. Extend the square to create the *Phi* (Φ) Rectangle '**ACDF**'.

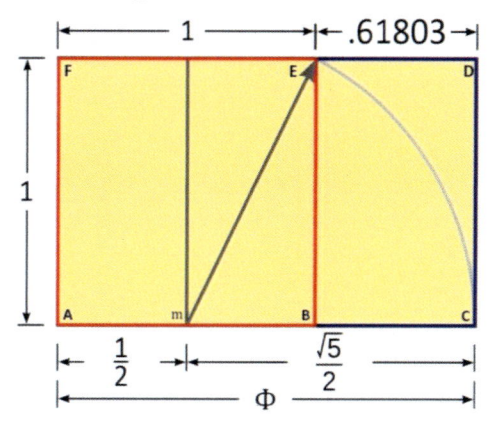

Fig. 7-4 – Construction of a Phi (Φ) Rectangle

The Golden Ratio in architectural design and other art forms has been in use for millennia. *Phi*, like *Pi* (π), is an irrational number, which are numbers that have an infinite number of non-repeating sets of consecutive digits after the decimal. For this reason, irrational numbers were believed to express the true immortal and eternal nature of the Divine, and reflected the perfect nature of the Supreme Creator. It can be expressed in the following formulas:

$$\left[\frac{BC}{AB} = \frac{AB}{AC}\right] = \frac{1+\sqrt{5}}{2} = 1.6180339887498948482\infty \text{ (often reduced to 1.61803)}$$

Translation: The ratio of the short part of the segment (BC) to the long part (AB) equals the ratio of the long part (AB) to the entire segment (AC).

Visually, this can be shown by subdividing a line in this way →

AC = 1.61803...
AB = 1
BC = .61803...

Besides using the square root of 5 (√5) to compute the value for *Phi* (Φ), it seems the number 5 also figures prominently in another formula for determining the Golden Ratio:

$$5.5 \times .5 + .5 = 1.61803 = Phi\ (\Phi)$$

Several visual representations of *Phi* use a triangle, a square or a pentagon, all within a circle, or just two lines and a triangle.

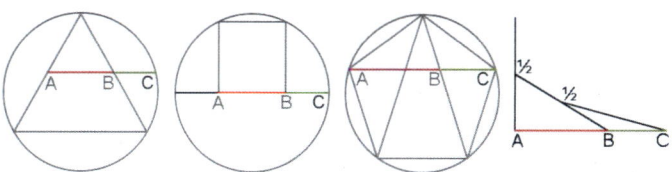

Apparently, we humans seem to be hardwired to intuitively recognize this one particular Sacred Ratio above all others. We see it unconsciously and resonate to it even if we don't know why. If the proportions of the Golden Ratio are not adhered to strictly – even just a little – we sense that something is inherently *wrong* or out of balance. This is because the universe we live in has the Golden Ratio built into it in ways we are only just beginning to understand. A recent film, *What is Reality?*, produced by Quantum Gravity Research, posited among other things, that the Golden Ratio plays a significant part of understanding the structure of our universe.[91]

The Golden Ratio equals 1.61803 and it is…
- **The Fundamental Constant of Nature**
- **Fundamental to circumscribed equilateral triangles and is weirdly ubiquitous in the universe appearing everywhere from the quantum to celestial scales.**
- **Ever so interestingly, it appears in black holes.**

The Golden Ratio is the precise point where a black hole's modified specific heat changes from positive to negative, and it is part of the equation for the lower bound on black hole entropy.

The Golden Ratio even relates the loop quantum gravity perimeter to black hole entropy.

The Golden Ratio appears deeply in both black hole physics and in quantum mechanics. The Golden Ratio appears to have startling accuracies in many other ways throughout the universe, in scales both large and small. It is so prevalent that its existence simply cannot be looked at as coincidental. A rigorous quantum gravity theory is being developed which predicts the Golden Ratio's existence is, literally, everywhere.

I'm not going to pretend to understand anything relating to the General Theory of Relativity, quantum mechanics or black hole physics, but this has led me to ask an important question: Did the ancient Egyptians consciously know about the relationship of the Golden Ratio and quantum mechanics and black hole theory? Probably not, but it is certain they intuitively understood that the Golden Ratio was integral to a balanced perspective when it came to the aesthetics used to create well-defined and properly proportioned artistic expressions from giant pyramids to the smallest works of art.

The use of the *Phi* (Φ) Rectangle (Golden Ratio) was not limited to designing temples and other monuments. Even the artists who produced some of the finest examples of stone vessels in the ancient world used the Golden Ratio to fashion their works of art. Such an example is an alabaster vase from the Tomb of Tutankhamun (*Fig. 7-5*). The grace and beauty of this piece is typical of the artifacts found in this tomb, and has few equals from the ancient world.

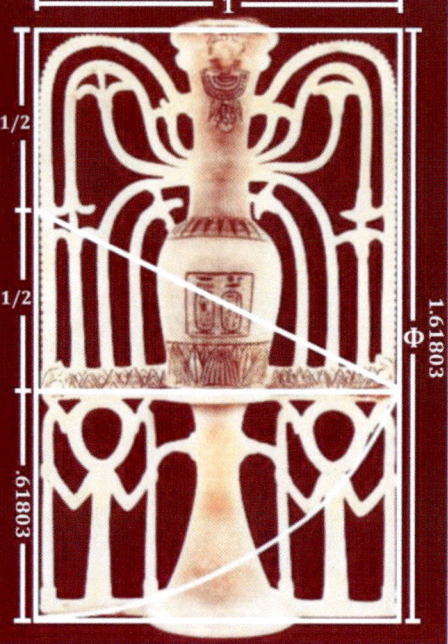

Fig. 7-5 – Alabaster Vase from the Tomb of Tutankhamun showing its design is based on the Golden Ratio Phi (Φ)

Other ancient cultures seem to have intuitively used several Sacred Ratios including *Phi* in their architecture. Two ancient Native American sites incorporate Sacred Geometry in their designs are the Sun Shrine in Mesa Verde National Park, Cortez, Colorado, and Pueblo Bonito in the Chaco Canyon Culture National Park near Nageezi, New Mexico.[92]

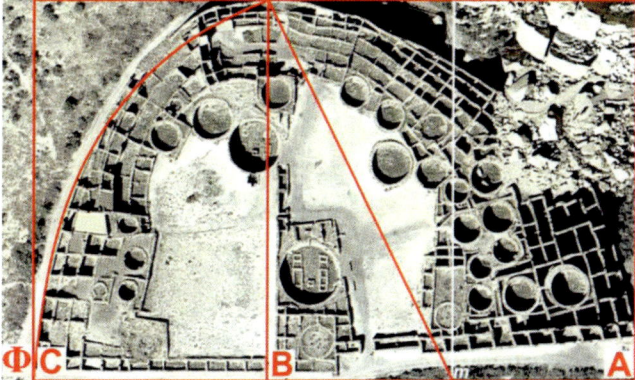

Fig. 7-6 – Sun Shrine, Mesa Verde National Park   *Fig. 7-7 – Pueblo Bonito, Chaco Canyon National Park*

Some have argued that the presence of the Golden Ratio or any other Sacred Ratio in the design of Egyptian pyramids, temples or funerary monuments is just a coincidence. The presumption is that the Greeks *imported* these design principles when the Ptolemys rebuilt several temples throughout Egypt during their reigns. This is primarily based on the fact that the ancient Egyptians produced no written evidence of their use of such ratios.[93] I would argue that there is, indeed, written evidence of the use of Sacred Geometry in their architectural designs, but they did not use papyrus to document the custom; they used stone instead. If it can be shown that the more common sacred ratios were in use in ancient Egypt beginning as early as the Second Dynasty, and continued at least to the Eighteenth Dynasty, what then? Let's find out.

If the ancient Egyptians were the originators of Sacred Geometry; then it stands to reason that they used a simpler form of the art as opposed to the more complex system that was later developed by the Greeks. Conversely, if the Egyptians were the inheritors of this Sacred Art from an earlier civilization, then any complexities may have been filtered out and reduced to the bare essentials when they designed these early monuments.

All of this is very interesting, but what does it have to do with the ancient Egyptians using Sacred Geometry to design their temples and other sacred architecture?

Sacred Geometry, when used in architectural design, is an expression of Divine Order, or at least, the laws of physics. It is a reflection of the Universe we live in and its underlying structure. Sacred Geometry imparts a sense of balance and harmony to architecture, and in the context of Egyptian culture, it aligns with the notion of *maat*.

We must always remember the ancient Egyptians generally viewed life as a multidimensional, multifaceted reality (see Chapter 3). It is not impossible that this philosophical undercurrent made its way into the designs of their religious and funerary monuments as expressing the multiple layers of meaning, some still hidden to the uninitiated and remain a mystery to this day.

The Use of Architecture as a Repository of Hidden Esoteric Wisdom

Adding the two measurements provided by Lauer and doubling it, the total length of four walls of the enclosure would be 3,136 cubits (1,643.26meters/5,391.27 feet). When divided by a thousand, the result of 3.136 is very close to that of *Pi* ($\pi \approx 3.14159\infty$). *Pi* is called an irrational number in that the numbers after the decimal have no consecutive set of repeating digits *ad infinitum*. *Phi*, the Golden Ratio (1.61803∞), is also an irrational number. Different measurements taken of the combined length of all four walls of the Enclosure are reportedly between 3,141.5 cubits (1,645.31meters/5,397.99 feet) and 3,143.40 cubits (1,647.14meters/5,404.0 feet). The differences may be attributable to the skill of the person doing the measuring, or whether measurements of the total length of the Enclosure Wall is taken along the interior surface of the wall or its exterior, as Lauer did. The difference between Lauer's value of 3,136 cubits for the perimeter of the Enclosure Wall and what we today know to be the value for *Pi* may be attributed to one of three factors:

1) As careful as the archeologists reconstructing the Step Pyramid Enclosure in the mid-20th Century tried to be, it is entirely likely that small inconsistencies introduced into their measurements were due to the simple fact that

there was near total destruction of the complex over the millennia; hampering any attempt to take accurate measurements of the site.

2) Imhotep's knowledge and understanding of the value of *Pi* (π) may be somewhat different from ours. For example, the mastaba tomb of the Second Dynasty pharaoh, Djer (*Fig. 7-8*), had a line of seven magazines in its center surrounded by 22 smaller rooms, producing a ratio of 22:7.[94] Dividing 22 by 7 produces the rounded-up result of 3.142857 that is slightly larger than the traditional value of *Pi*. It is also a rational number in that the digits after the decimal start to repeat themselves after the sixth digit, and when multiplied by a thousand is very close to the larger measurement of 3,143.40 cubits. It could be this pyramid complex was designed using an accepted mathematical practice of the time, and Imhotep used this more easily obtained number for *Pi* when you consider how difficult it was to determine fractions in ancient Egyptian mathematics. (*At least, it is for me.*) Besides, when building rather large structures like pyramids or temples, a variance of 0.00126 doesn't matter too much.

The 22:7 ratio embodied in Djer's tomb may well have been part of Imhotep's practical use of the royal cubit to determine the circumference of a circle. If you create a circle with a diameter subdivided into 7 parts called palms, the circle will have a circumference of precisely 22 palms (*Fig. 7-9*).

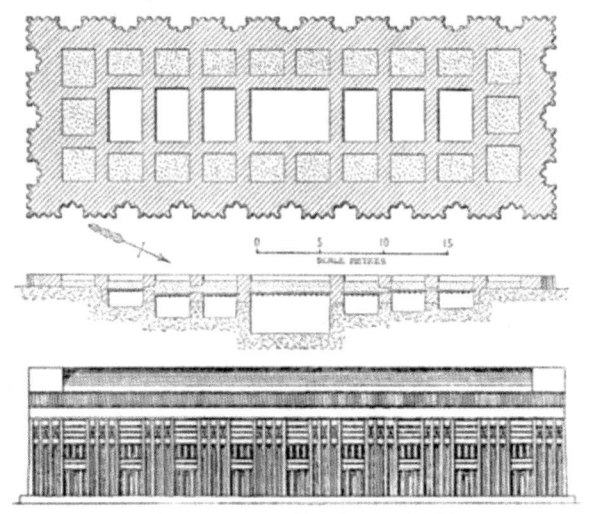

Fig. 7-8 – Mastaba Tomb No. 3471 of the Second Dynasty Pharaoh Djer

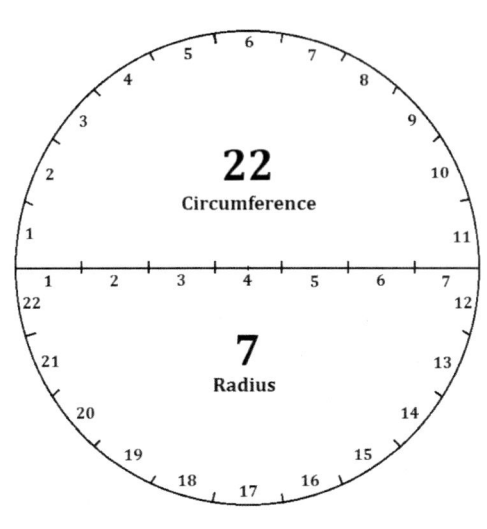

Fig. 7-9 – The 22:7 Ratio. The 'Egyptian' Value for Pi (3.14286)

3) Since we do not have any architectural plans from the period of the Third Dynasty, we have no firm idea what Imhotep's actual design of the Step Pyramid Enclosure was supposed to look like.

4) There may also be an obscure relationship with music, or more accurately, the use of sound to affect healing, which is more in keeping with the idea of the Ḥeb-Sed Court as a medical center. To the average person, when told to visualize the white notes on a piano keyboard (e.g., the C major diatonic scale C to C'), and asked how many notes are contained within an octave, most people will logically say that, since the word *octave* is the number 8 in Italian, then there must be 8 notes in an octave.

However, this is a trick question. There are only 7 diatonic notes within an octave. The eighth note (C' in our example) is the beginning of the next octave. If we were to divide 8 by 7 (8/7), the answer is 1.142857. By adding the *Magic Number 2* to this result, we get 3.14287; the same as dividing 22 by 7 (see #3 above). The use of the ratio of 8:7 could also indicate that ancient Egyptian music was more similar to modern music in that it was diatonic in nature, and did not incorporate a different type of scale, such as the pentatonic or Lydian scales, or that of later Arabic music. While this connection of ancient Egyptian architecture to music may seem tenuous, the Greek mathematician, Pythagoras, studied in the Egypt mystery schools, and in his teachings, integrated music with math and geometry together into a unified whole.

Of the four possibilities, I tend to favor the first since the measurement discrepancy amounts to less than one cubit (52.4 centimeters/20.63 inches) in the east-west walls, and 2 cubits (104.8 centimeters /41.26 inches) in the longer north-south walls. There is the possibility the discrepancy may well be deliberate on Imhotep's part as will be explained later. Nevertheless, #2 may also be true. The above examples may only be the tip of the iceberg, so to speak, as to what the ancient Egyptians regarded as the correct value of *Pi* (π). For me, explanation #2 has a certain attraction to it, but as I majored in music in college, #4 resonates with me as well (*pun intended*). Take your pick.

It appears Imhotep used the *Magic Number 2* as a common reference value in his design of the Step Pyramid Enclosure. For example, the lengths of the long north-south walls of the Step Pyramid Enclosure are 2 times the length of the east-west walls. As stated before, J.-P. Lauer also discovered several horizontal lines, which are 2 cubits long inscribed on one of the South Pavilion Court walls from which can be derived the cubit value of 52.4 centimeters/20.63 inches. (Sometimes a cubit's length is given as 52.5 centimeters, but maybe the slightly shorter value was being used at the time Imhotep designed the Step Pyramid Enclosure, through it seems it would have been hardly noticeable.) In his book, *Excavations at Saqqara, The Step Pyramid*,(95) C. M. Firth writes:

> **PLATE 1. General Plan. In Ann. Serv., vol. XXXI, pp. 59-64, Mr. Lauer has published a study of the main dimensions of the plan when converted into cubits.**
>
> *A length, evidently of 2 cubits, marked out by vertical lines in red on a wall of the South Princess'* [South Pavilion] **court gave** [52.4 centimeters] *as the cubit of the time*, **and this length divided into the main dimensions produced a long series of whole numbers with a very small margin of error. The numbers so obtained are most frequently multiples of 10 or 5. Seven times Mr. Lauer found lengths of 33 cubits and some centimeters, evidently a third of 100. This, he suggests, may have been the usual measuring cord at this period. A singular figure found no less than 5 times is 123, no doubt a lucky number. The total length of the enclosure was 1,040 cubits and its breadth 528.** (Emphasis and clarification added.)

Though located in the southwest corner on the base of the South Pavilion Court wall, Imhotep's construction crew might have utilized this 2-cubit line to provide a consistent reference tool for measuring without requiring a cubit rod to be available (see *Fig. 3-31*). Having a *key* that is a 2-cubit scale instead of only a single cubit also permits a greater level of precision when Imhotep's craftsmen made measurements during construction. As for 123 being a *lucky number*, that's just a *lucky* guess.

Imhotep was seemingly fond of using the number 2 in many places throughout the Step Pyramid complex, so perhaps the number 2 stands at the threshold to the *Void* (Chapter 4). When repurposing the burial shaft in the South Tomb, he created a second entrance by way of a descending passage. This may imply some sort of esoteric belief where two paths will always lead to the same destination, and he did it twice when he created another descending passage for the Step Pyramid's Central Burial Shaft.

If we add the *Magic Number 2* to each of the three digits in the *lucky number* 123 we get 3-4-5. Since it isn't terribly obvious, why would Imhotep do so? The 3-4-5 triangle has been a standard construction tool used by every architect and building contractor – both ancient and modern – to create perfectly squared corners when constructing a new wall. When designing the Step Pyramid Enclosure, it may be that Imhotep used the number 2 as a common reference value like that of a scale used in an architectural plan. For example, the lengths of the north-south walls of the Step Pyramid Enclosure are twice the length of the east-west walls.

To illustrate the use of the 3-4-5 triangle in the practice of building construction, let's say a building contractor drives a stake into the ground where the first corner of a new building is to be located. They then create a triangle made of rope or string whose sides are multiples of 3, 4 and 5. To gain as much accuracy as possible, most contractors will create a 3-4-5 triangle with as long a length along each side as is practical.

When laying out the foundation for a new structure, a contractor will measure out a string a little more than 24 feet in length (6 feet plus 8 feet plus 10 feet). They attach the string to the first stake and pull the string in the general direction of the opposite corner of the wall to be constructed; measures out 6 feet, attaches it to a second stake and drives the stake into the ground, keeping the string perfectly taut. From this second stake, they stretch out the string for 10 feet and attach it to a third stake, but does not yet drive it into the ground. They then measure out the remaining amount of string to 8 feet and attach it to the first stake. Stretching the two sides of the string until both lengths are perfectly taut to their limits (8 feet and 10 feet respectively), they drive this third stake into the ground.

This creates a perfect 3-4-5 triangle with a perfectly square (90°) corner at the first stake. Now the contractor can extend the lengths needed along the 6-foot and 8-foot sides of the triangle for these first two walls knowing they are perfectly square to one another. After this, he will repeat the process of measuring out another 3-4-5 triangle for the other two walls, adjusting as necessary to ensure all four walls have true 90° angles at the corners.

The construction practice outlined above is an echo from the past. Though it doesn't have the same religious connotation as its ancient counterpart, it is similar in spirit to the *Stretching of the Cord* ceremony, or *pedj-shes*, that was performed by Egyptian kings and architects when laying out the boundaries and foundations of a new temple or funerary monument (*Fig. 7-10*). Both *ceremonies* use the same 6-8-10 triangle (3-4-5 times 2) in mathematical problems and their solutions as found in the Rhind Mathematical Papyrus (RMP#53-54 and 55), as well as the Berlin Papyrus 6619.

As an architect, Imhotep was no doubt well aware of this standard method of creating perfectly squared walls. It seems the use of the 3-4-5 triangle permeated many different ancient cultures (*Fig. 7-11*).

The great Greek mathematician Pythagoras (*Fig. 7-12*) codified the use of the 3-4-5 triangle in his famous theorem ($a^2 + b^2 = c^2$), also known as Pythagorean triples. It should come as no surprise that the Greeks acquired much of their esoteric knowledge from Egypt since the ancient Greek philosopher Solon readily admitted as much.[96] The Babylonians were also aware of and used the 3-4-5 triangle as shown in the Plimpton 322 tablet housed at Columbia University, New York City.

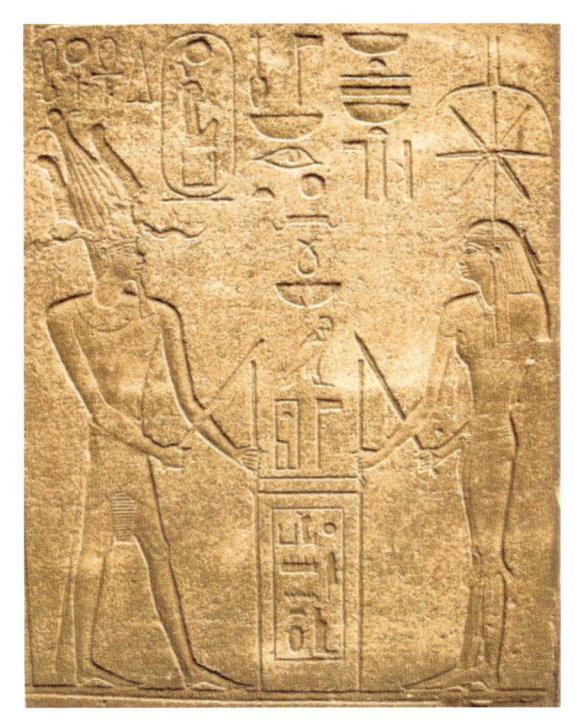

Fig. 7-10 – The "Stretching of the Cord" ceremony as depicted in the Red Chapel of Hatshepsut at Karnak

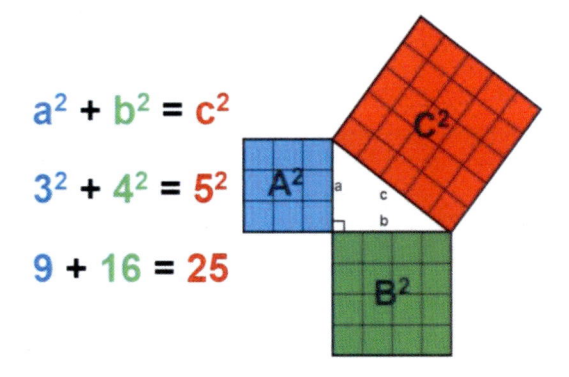

Fig. 7-11 – Pythagorean Theorem Formula

Fig. 7-12 – Pythagoras

The Use of Sacred Geometry in the Design of the Step Pyramid

When I first started to study the Step Pyramid Enclosure in depth, I took notice of the false gates in the temenos or Enclosure Wall. For the most part, the 14 false gates are evenly spaced around the perimeter of the Enclosure Wall, but the false gates in the south wall are not. I could understand the odd spacing of the four false gates in the east wall. Three of the four false gates on the east wall are evenly spaced, but the fourth gate, False Gate 14, is set apart roughly in the middle, because it was the original Entrance Gate, and the next gate in the wall as you go north, False Gate 13, was originally the Exit Gate. All Imhotep did was to evenly space False Gates 11 and 12 in the wall between False Gate 13 and the enclosure's north wall.

Every architectural plan has a key, usually located in the lower right corner, which contain symbols and their definitions that are used throughout the plan. The spacing of False Gates 1, 2 and 3, located on the south wall, seems unbalanced until you realize that Imhotep created his plans in accordance with the principles of Sacred Geometry. The three false gates are the key to understanding and confirming the use of Sacred Geometry, and three of the Sacred Ratios (*Figs. 7-1* and *7-2*) were used most often when he designed the Step Pyramid Enclosure. Imhotep expressed these ideas in stone because the three unequal spaces between the false gates embody the intertwined ratios of the Golden Ratio (*Phi*, Φ), Square (√2), and the Double Square (√5) *(Fig. 7-13)*. By all appearances, he used these three Sacred Ratios more extensively than all the other Sacred Ratios throughout the temple's design.

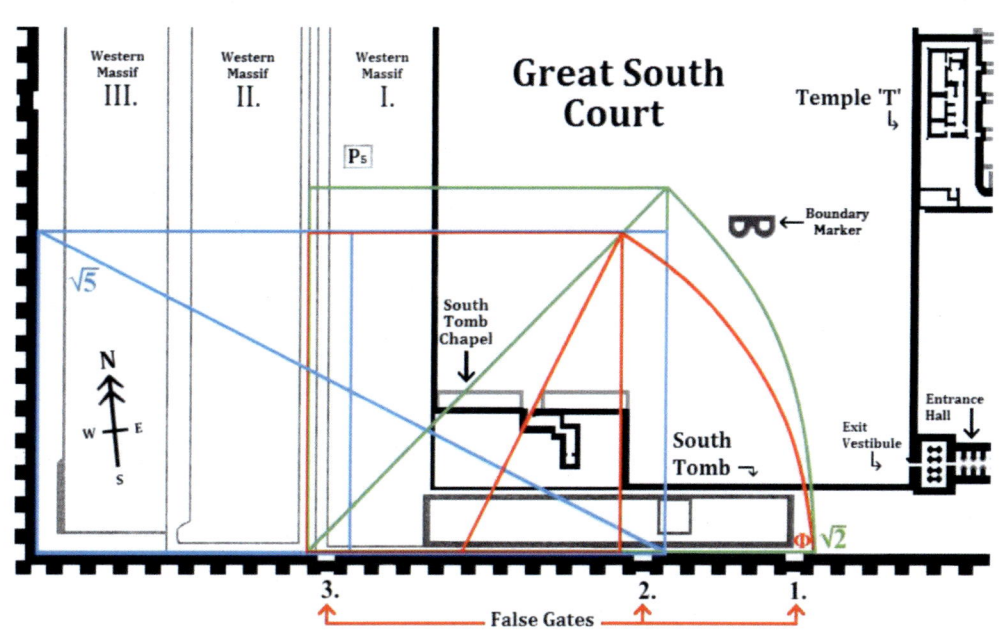

Fig. 7-13 – The Sacred Geometry Key used to design the Step Pyramid as embodied in the south False Gates

Because False Gates 1, 2 and 3 are not evenly spaced like most of the other ones, it is as if Imhotep is drawing our attention to these mute witnesses to the underlying Sacred Geometry and its use to design the Step Pyramid Enclosure as a whole. Though simple in their design and placement in the south wall of the Step Pyramid Enclosure, these three false gates silently express what may have been Imhotep's own philosophy: while not readily apparent, all things in nature are connected and interrelated, and must be kept harmoniously in balance. No doubt, this is in keeping with Imhotep's other profession as Chief Royal Physician because the human body, too, needs to be in balance, or *maat*, (*Living-in-Truth*) to maintain optimal health.

It is interesting to note that Imhotep embedded these Sacred Ratios using the three false gates in the south wall beginning at the western bastion of False Gate 3, which aligns with the trench on the east side of Western Massif II. Here is additional confirmation that Western Massif II already existed on the Sakkara plateau when Imhotep began construction on this version of the Enclosure Wall, otherwise he would have built this False Gate 3 elsewhere. During the initial design phase of this version of the Enclosure Wall, Western Massif I or Western Massif III was not yet part of his plans. That would come later. The unequal spacing of these three false gates and the embedding of the Root 2 (√2) Rectangle, Root 5 (√5) Double Square and *Phi* (Φ) Rectangles within their design shows that Imhotep was inclined to use Sacred Geometry throughout the design of the Step Pyramid Enclosure, even for the smallest and seemingly insignificant architectural element. (See the Root 5 (√5) Double Square in the '**H**' Chamber in *Fig. 5-7* and *Fig. 7-52*, which also contains a *Phi* (Φ) Rectangle in its design).

As I continued to examine Imhotep's design in greater detail, I began to suspect that he created a grid system consistent with the Sacred Geometry Ratios outlined above and *filled-in-the-blanks*, so to speak, allowing him to organize the various structures and buildings throughout the Step Pyramid Enclosure into a harmonious and balanced arrangement.

Virtually every architect uses some sort of grid system at the beginning stages of designing a new building. Most of the time, modern architects use quarter-inch graph paper for this process (*Fig. 7-14*). Geniuses like Frank Lloyd Wright might do something completely different as when he used hexagonal graph paper to design the famous Hanna

Honeycomb House with a 120° configuration (*Fig. 7-15*), not unlike Imhotep's use of the 5-Part Root Rectangle Template.

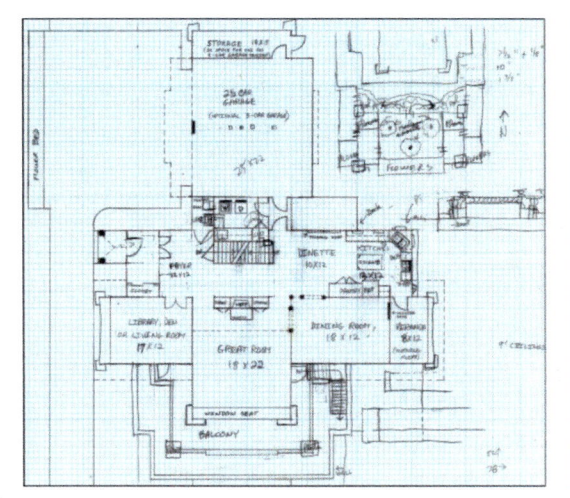

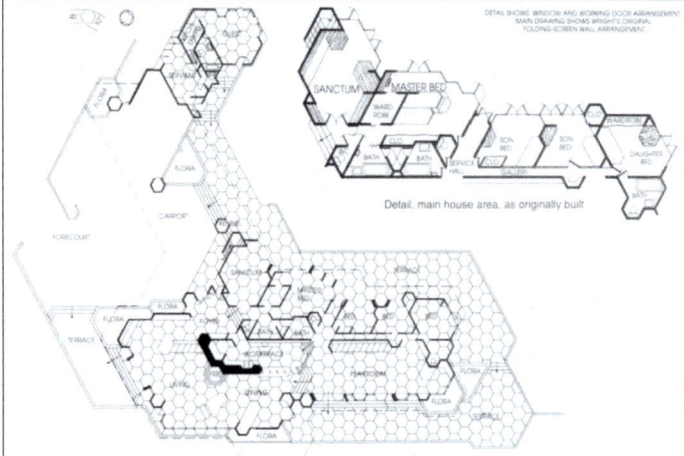

Fig. 7-14 – A rough architectural sketch by the author using ¼-inch grid paper

Fig. 7-15 – Plan of the Hanna House by Frank Lloyd Wright, located on the Stanford University campus in Palo Alto, California

Considering that architects, both ancient and modern, tend to think alike, it is probable that Imhotep used a grid system to place the various architectural elements throughout his plan for the Step Pyramid temple complex. Using the 5-Part Root Rectangle Template, he lined up various architectural elements (e.g., walls, corners, door openings, bastions, and so on) to that grid accordingly. As we proceed further in our examination of Imhotep's work, it will become obvious that the use of Sacred Geometry to define the placement of the base lines for the grid and consequently, the spacing between those lines, could not be accidental.

When working with the 5-Part Root Rectangle Template to understand how Imhotep used it in the design process for this project, I had an *oh-what-the-heck* moment, and extended the Root 5 ($\sqrt{5}$) Double Square out to the square roots of 6 ($\sqrt{6}$) and 7 ($\sqrt{7}$) (*Fig. 7-16*). As silly as this may seem, it appears Imhotep used this extended root rectangle template several times in his architectural design work. More on this later.

Nowhere in any of the literature and books about Sacred Geometry did I find any reference to the use of a root square rectangle past the Double Square ($\sqrt{5}$) because allegedly "proportions start to break down".[97] To my utter amazement, the $\sqrt{6}$ and $\sqrt{7}$ lines and arcs actually lined up with additional features within the Ḥeb-Sed Court and elsewhere in the Step Pyramid Enclosure. *Fig. 7-16* shows what this new template looks like.

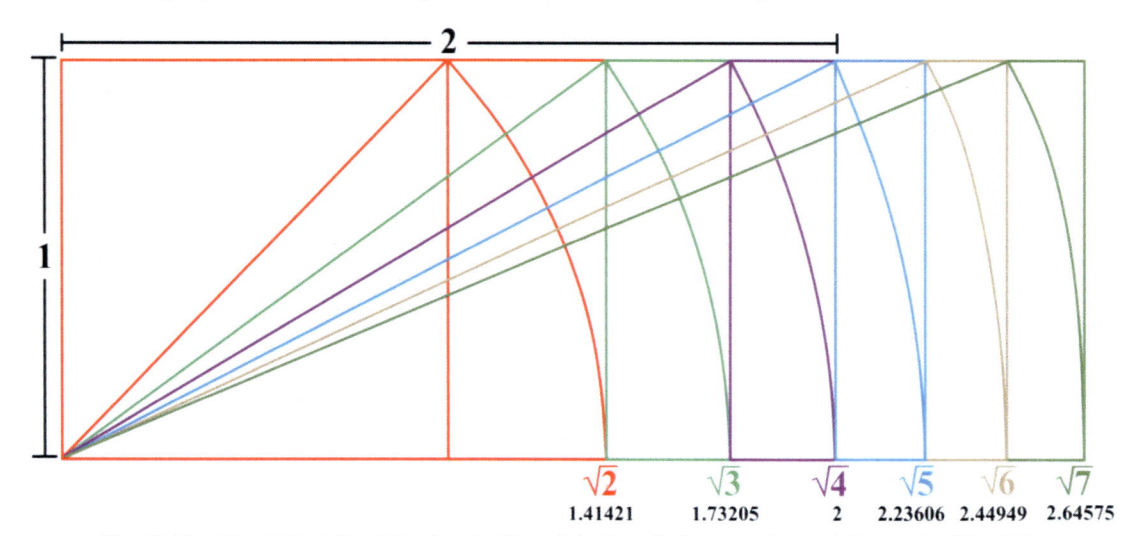

Fig. 7-16 – The 7-Part Root Rectangle Template from Imhotep's Sacred Geometry 'Toolkit'

If this was the only known instance of using a 7-Part Root Rectangle Template to design a structure in either ancient or modern times; then it's safe to say that Imhotep was far more innovative in his *out-of-the-box* thinking than just using stone to build this temple, but also when it came to designing it in the first place.

When it comes to using the 7-Part Root Rectangle Template, we are wont to ask, why seven elements? Why not use only the 5-Part Root Rectangle Template as was apparently the norm then as it is now? To answer these questions, a Fibonacci series starting with the *Magic Number 2* will result in the following sequence up to the ninth number in the series:

Sequence No. –	1	2	3	4	5	6	**7**	8	**9**
Fibonacci No. –	2	4	6	10	16	26	**42**	68	**110**

As stated previously, 42 is the most prevalent number in ancient Egypt, in both sacred and profane ways, next to the number 14. More than that, the ninth number, 110, appears to be the sound frequency in Hertz (cycles per second), that was most often used in vocalization rituals at such ancient sites as the Hypogeum at Malta, the Newgrange Passage Tomb in Ireland and Gobekli Tepe in Turkey. This specific frequency, 110 Hz, seems to facilitate altering a person's consciousness to higher states of awareness. It may also have great relevance to the Step Pyramid Enclosure because of the wisdom keeper Hakim's belief the Ḥeb-Sed Court was a medical center where using sound was part of a healer-priest's practices to affect healing. Did the priests of the Step Pyramid medical center use this tone to affect healing within their patients? We may never know, but it is certainly no coincidence. It is unknown if the ancient Egyptians used numerology in their daily lives as the number 9 represents completion, not the end of a cycle, but the beginning of a new one. It is the number of the sage, the visionary/idealist and the humanitarian. It possesses a devotion to serving humanity, providing help even during the most trying and difficult challenges. It is also loving, highly spiritual, empathetic, tolerant and intuitive through an innate connection to the Divine.

The number 7 is also a prime number (3 + 4), and along with the *Magic Number 2*, relates to another esoteric tradition. The god Amun-Re often depicted with a 2-part plumed headdress that is divided further into 7 segments (*Fig. 7-17*).

Each plume of Amun's headdress was divided into *two*, reflecting the duality of the Egyptian worldview, and each feather was divided into *seven* horizontal segments (seven being a ritually significant number). [98] (Emphasis added)

In numerology, the number 7 relates to a deeper inner wisdom. It indicates someone who is more analytical, introverted and introspective than emotional, but is still highly intuitive. It is the number of the philosopher, the seeker, the thinker and the searcher for truth for all of life's mysteries. Mysticism is the native language of the number 7, and is associated with the heart center in all its feminine aspects. In short, the number 7 is both highly intellectual and deeply spiritual at the same time.

Is this all a coincidence? Maybe, but do these numerology-based personality traits remind you of someone?

Fig. 7-17 – Amun-Re

As a prime number, the number 7 is relevant to the Vesica Pisces Double Circle, which is, perhaps, the most overlooked of the Sacred Geometric Ratios. Hidden within is the possibility that even greater esoteric wisdom can be discovered. While not readily apparent, the first five prime numbers of 2, 3, 5, 7, and 11 are represented as root squares, which can easily be determined from a slightly altered version of the Double Circle as seen in *Fig. 7-18*.

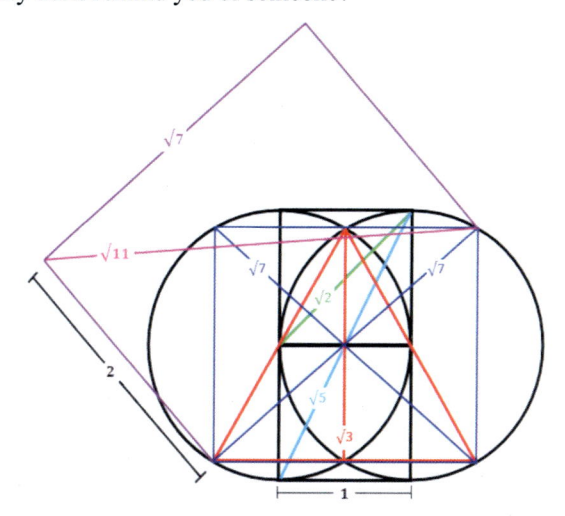

Fig. 7-18 – Expanded version of the Double Circle (Vesica Pisces)

Whether Imhotep, or any ancient architect for that matter, knew about the concept of prime numbers in this Sacred Geometric pattern is difficult to say. Until a more exacting analysis of ancient pyramids, temples and other structures is undertaken, we won't know for certain.

We have the completed Step Pyramid Enclosure as seen today with which to gauge Imhotep's work, but is it possible to know how Imhotep initially designed it using Sacred Geometry? To begin to understand Imhotep's design philosophy, we must start where he started. After completing the South Tomb, and Mastabas $M_1/M_2/M_3$ (*Fig. 7-19*), Imhotep began work on the two north and south "mastabas".

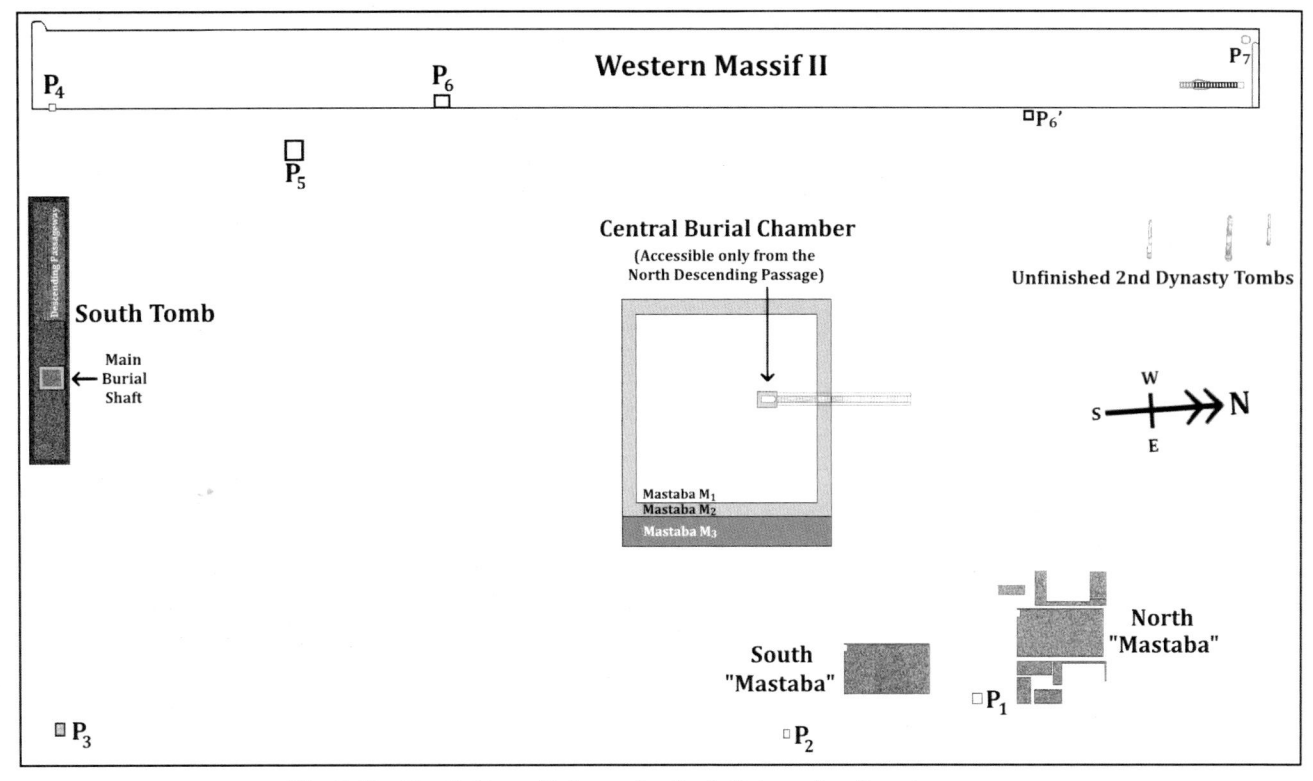

Fig. 7-19 – The Sakkara Plateau after the initial construction phase was complete. The South Tomb's completion at this phase is speculative

In the second phase of construction, the unfinished mastabas were completed with front façades, side and rear walls and arched roofs to become the North and South Pavilions (*Fig. 7-20*, see also *Fig. 6-25*).

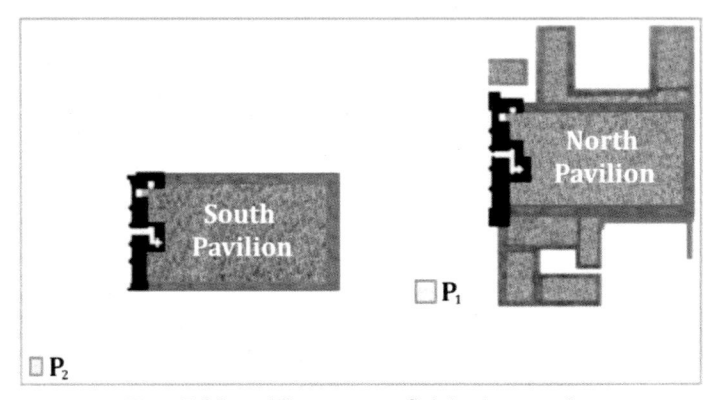

Fig. 7-20 – The two unfinished mastabas transformed into the North and South Pavilions

As part of the construction of the new façades for the two Pavilions, Imhotep took the width of the short sides of the South Pavilion, which is about 33⅓ cubits, the same dimension used many times throughout in the Enclosure. Measuring 33⅓ cubits from South Pavilion's eastern exterior face, he laid the foundations of the east section of the First Enclosure Wall, defining the east wall of the South Pavilion Court, and avoiding 'Pit P₂' in the process (*Fig. 7-21*). At this stage, he completed the design of the North Pavilion Court as well as the construction of the Old Serdab and its court.

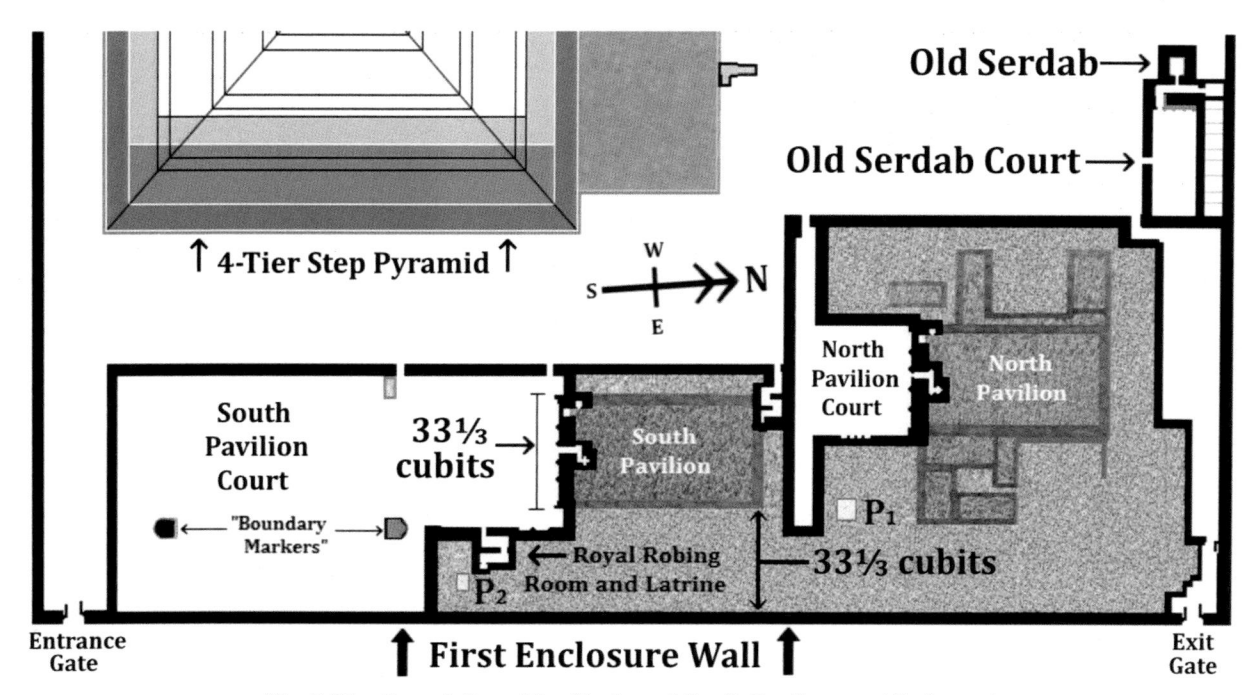

Fig. 7-21 – Completion of the North and South Pavilions and their courts

Imhotep originally planned to construct two D-shaped *boundary markers* for the South Pavilion Court, but only the south one was built (see *Fig. 6-76*). These were to be used during the *Heb-Sed* rituals when Djoser was to run around these markers as part of the ritual to seal his authority as pharaoh. In essence, the South Pavilion Court was the first *Great South Court*. This is why a royal robing room and latrine was included in its design; similar to how Room 'B' in the South Tomb Chapel may have been used when it was constructed later (see *Fig. 6-18*). Additionally, the finished Blue Faience Rooms beneath the South Tomb with their scenes of Djoser performing the *sed*-festival rituals virtually proves the use of the South Tomb Chapel as part of the *Heb-Sed* venue.

What sets Imhotep apart from every architect who came before and after him was how he took several discarded structures, and using Sacred Geometry, achieved the near impossible task of turning them into a cohesive whole. In *Figs. 7-23* and *7-24*, we can see how Imhotep used Sacred Geometry to lay out the general plan for these buildings. As I was pouring over the blueprints of the Step Pyramid, several things became apparent, revealing how Imhotep used and consistently applied Sacred Geometry to design the Step Pyramid Enclosure. This is how I became aware of certain *touch points* in Imhotep's design.

What is a "touch point" in this context? In general, when designing the Step Pyramid Enclosure, Imhotep used a grid based on the shapes of Sacred Ratios, or arcs derived from them, as an underlying foundation of what he wanted to design. Most of the time, Imhotep would lay out the interior face of virtually every wall along the lines of these Sacred Ratios. A *touch point* can be seen where grid lines or arcs from a Sacred Ratio appears to "touch" or intersect another line that runs along a wall surface, a corner or another standalone feature. If so, it can be safely assumed that it is an act of deliberate design, and not accidental or coincidence. These *touch points* will become apparent when viewing the illustrations that follow.

Whenever Imhotep designed an addition to, or modification of, any part of this funerary monument of Djoser, he always used the elements of Sacred Geometry to accomplish the task. By all appearances, Imhotep often aligned the interior surfaces of walls and the corners of two adjoining walls or other architectural elements within one of his design grids, or when using Sacred Geometric Ratios to design structures within the Enclosure, he particularly aligned interior wall surfaces against one of the Sacred Ratio's line segments. This is because the interior surface of the Enclosure Wall is always consistent. The Wall's exterior surface, with the visually undulating appearance of its bastions, is not. Other exterior wall surfaces inside the Enclosure are also too irregular, and not consistent in their shapes to allow for perfect symmetrical design. There are some exceptions of course, but this appears to be Imhotep's "rule of thumb".

What follows is an explanation of how Imhotep used Sacred Geometry to incorporate the North and South Pavilions along with Mastabas $M_1/M_2/M_3$ into a cohesive whole.

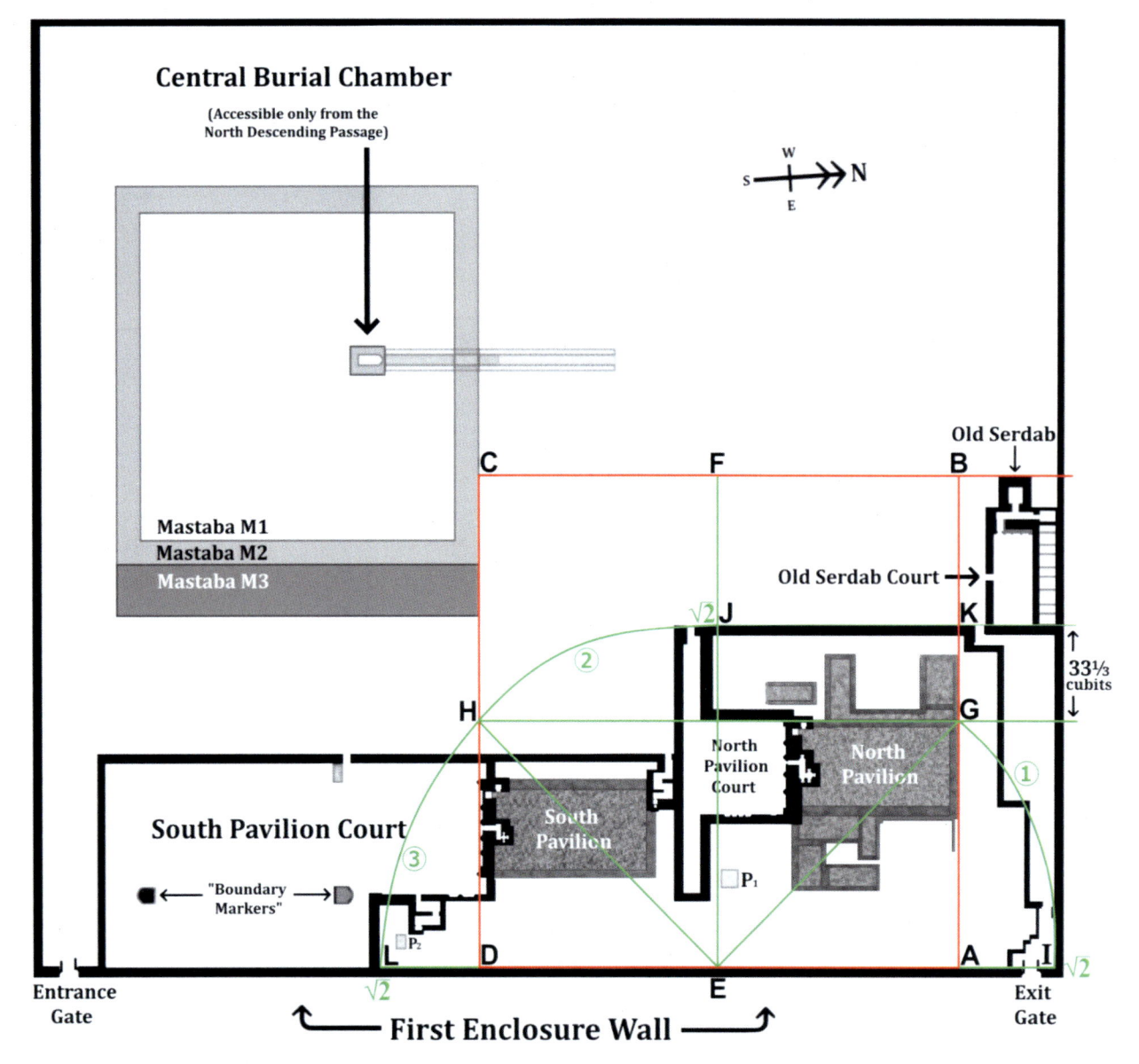

Fig. 7-22 – The use of Sacred Geometry in the design of the First Enclosure, Part 1

1) After establishing the site of the east segment of the First Enclosure Wall (see *Fig. 7-21*), the creation of three more walls in the Enclosure's interior followed. To begin, square **ABCD** encompassed the North and South Pavilions (*Fig. 7-22*). The length of the sides of the square becomes another reference dimension. When extended north, the (red) line **BC** aligns with the exterior of the narrow westernmost wall of the Old Serdab. At the beginning of the design process, Imhotep probably used line **CD** that aligns with the north face of Mastabas $M_1/M_2/M_3$ and the front of the new façade of the South Pavilion to define the thickness of the wall surrounding Mastaba M_1 that would eventually become Mastaba M_2.

2) Square **ABCD** was then subdivided further into four equal parts creating the crosshair (green) lines **EF** and **GH**.

3) The Root 2 ($\sqrt{2}$) arc ① was created from diagonal line **EG**, and delineates where the interior face of the First Enclosure's north wall was to be built.

4) The horizontal line **JK** was generated from the point where Root 2 arc ② (running between points **H** and **J**) joined line **EF**. Line **JK** was used to site the foundation of the west wall surrounding the North Pavilion mastaba cluster, as well as the interior face of the east wall of the Old Serdab Court.

5) Aligned along line **GH** is the west wall of the North Pavilion and the east face of the short west wall in the North Pavilion Court (perpendicular to the new façade of the North Pavilion).

6) Another Root 2 ($\sqrt{2}$) arc, ③, starts at point **H** and ends at point **L**. This point defined where the exterior face of the short north wall (running east-west) of the South Pavilion Court was placed in order to avoid Pit P_2 (see text at *Figs 6-27* and *6-28*). Along with arc ① and the rectangle **AGHD**, this arc creates two overlapping Silver Rectangles (see *Fig. 7-97*).

7) The distance between points **AI**, **GK** and **LD** are all **33⅓** royal cubits, the standard measurement Imhotep seems to have used throughout the design of the Step Pyramid Enclosure.

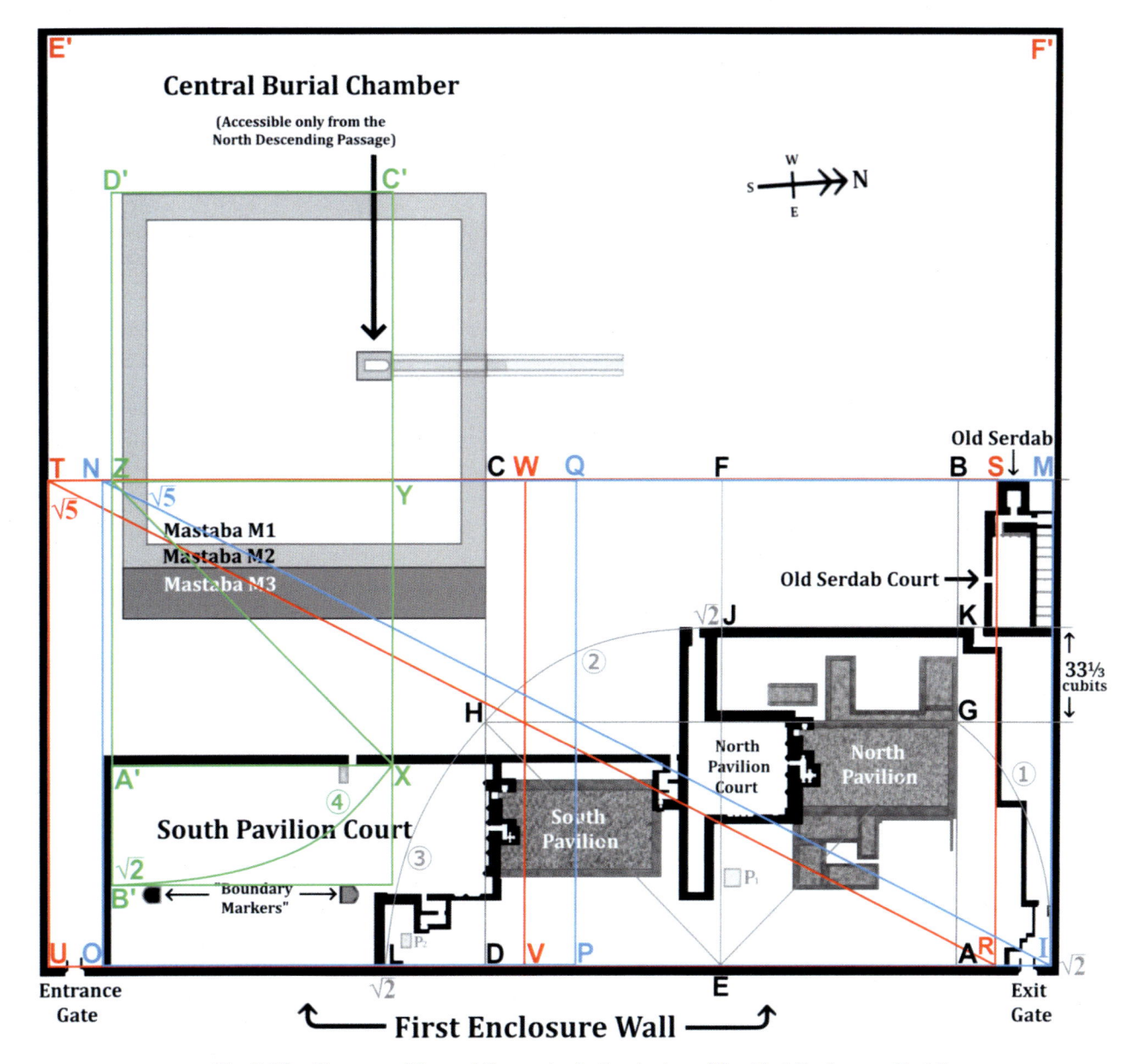

Fig. 7-23 – The use of Sacred Geometry in the design of the First Enclosure, Part 2

1) In *Fig. 7-23*, a Root 5 (√5) Double Square formed by lines **IMNO** with **PQ** as its centerline defines the south exterior face of the south wall of the South Pavilion. At one time, this wall faced onto the corridor leading from the original Entrance Gate.
2) Line **A′B′** runs along the footing of this same wall that faces the interior of the South Pavilion Court. The width between these two lines established the *standard* wall thickness for most of the temple complex. Line **A′B′** was extended westward (up) from point **A′** through point **Z** until at point **D′**, it met another line running along the west wall of Mastaba M2. Another Root 5 (√5) Double Square is formed by lines **D′C′A′X** with line **YZ** as its centerline. The eastern line **A′X** determined the location of the interior face of the western wall of the South Pavilion Court. Using the same wall thickness as the south wall, this finalized the design of the South Pavilion and its court. When viewing the completed plan of the South Pavilion Court, a Root 5 (√5) Double Square defines its overall shape and a Root 2 (√2) Rectangle is evident in the larger, southern half of the court (*Fig. 7-24*). (Oddly enough, the northern line, **C′Y**, of the topmost (western) square runs along the north wall of the Central Burial Chamber. Whether this is a coincidence, or intentional on Imhotep's part is difficult to tell.)
3) The Root 2 (√2) arc ④, created from the diagonal (line **TX**) of the lower (eastern) half of this Double Square produces a Silver Rectangle (see *Fig. 7-3*). A line then extended north (right) from the point **B′** on the south wall where arc ④ ends against which the two boundary markers were aligned (only one of which was actually constructed).
4) A third Root 5 (√5) Double Square was created along the east and south walls using points **RSTU** with line **VW** as its centerline. The north line of this Double Square (**RS**) defined the interior face of one of the north walls of the North Exit Gate passageway, the south exterior wall of the Old Serdab and part of the interior face of the Old Serdab Court wall.
5) The dimension of the south and north walls of the First Enclosure (lines **UE′** and **IF′**) was derived from the line **AU**.

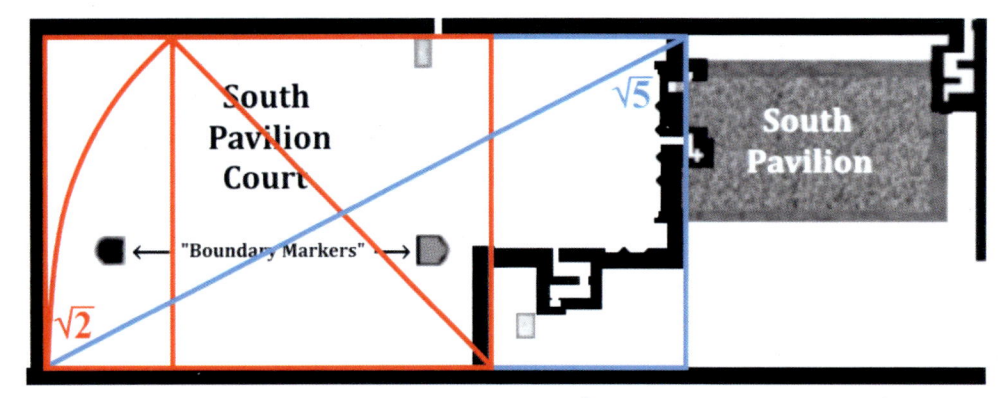

Fig. 7-24 – The South Pavilion Court conforms to both a Root 2 (√2) Rectangle and a Root 5 (√5) Double Square

When plans to upgrade the three mastabas to a four-tier Step Pyramid were formulated is unknown, but it appears to have begun shortly after the completion of the First Funerary Enclosure. The Ḥeb-Sed Court and South Entrance Hall clearly did not exist prior to the construction of the First Enclosure containing Mastabas $M_1/M_2/M_3$. Construction of the four-tier pyramid may not have occurred when the Ḥeb-Sed Court and South Entrance Hall were going up. However, it seems likely these two major structures and the four-tier pyramid were conceived together as a set piece. Part of the plans for the new additions was to build a new enclosure wall beginning a little to the east of the First Enclosure Wall to accommodate the larger structures and include the South Tomb as part of the change in the overall design philosophy.

When designing the new Enclosure Wall, Imhotep used a reference line (red line, *Fig. 7-26*) that aligns with several features of the North and South Pavilion Courts (*Fig. 7-27*), and the wall next to the passage with the self-closing door that once led out of the old North Exit Gate, which later became False Gate 13. (Lauer noticed the infill material is this new space to be of a different color and character.) In a strange ironic twist, the conception of the new Enclosure Wall and False Gate 13 gave *birth* to the *mammisi* (birthing rooms).

The green line in *Fig. 7-25* denotes the exterior face of the First Enclosure Wall (*Figs. 7-22* and *7-23*). Imhotep took half of the distance between the red and green lines (indicated by the purple line) and used this dimension to lay a foundation line for the interior face of the new Enclosure Wall (blue line). The interior face of this new wall would become one of two reference lines for the design that followed.

The newly defined space between the red and blue lines is 1½ times the distance between the red and green arrows, which is about 33⅓ cubits (17.47 meters/57.305 feet) wide; another instance of Imhotep using this reference dimension. Due to its frequent use throughout the Step Pyramid complex, Lauer thought it might have been the standard measuring cord of the period (*Fig. 7-26*).[99]

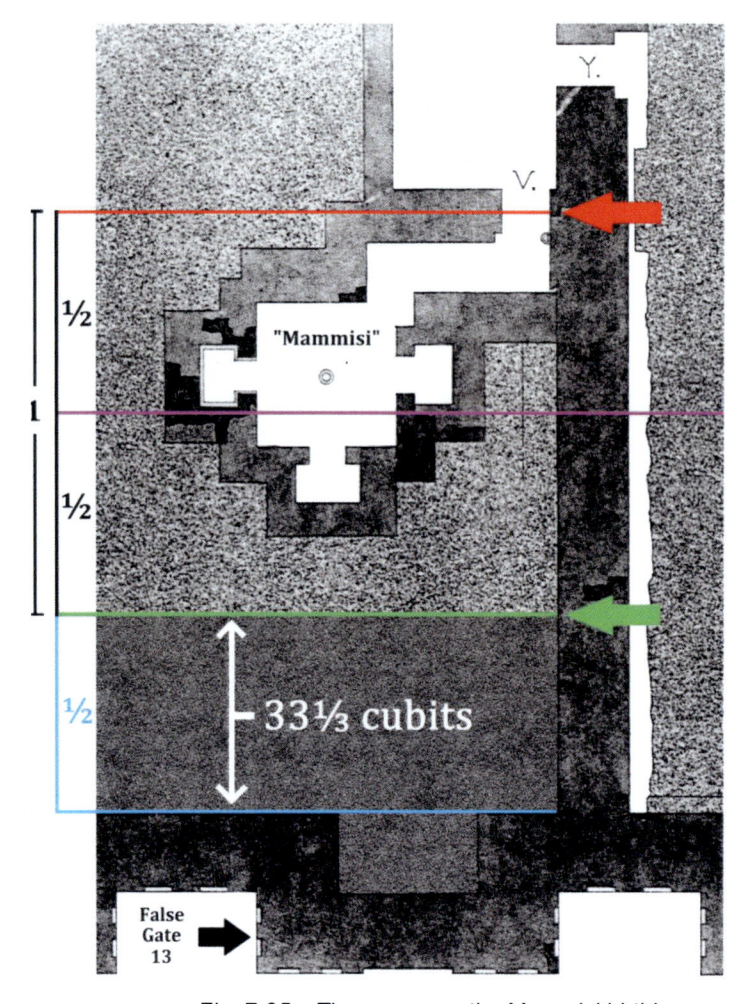

Fig. 7-25 – The area near the Mammisi birthing rooms and the new Enclosure Wall. The darker infill material was added to the space between the old wall and the new wall

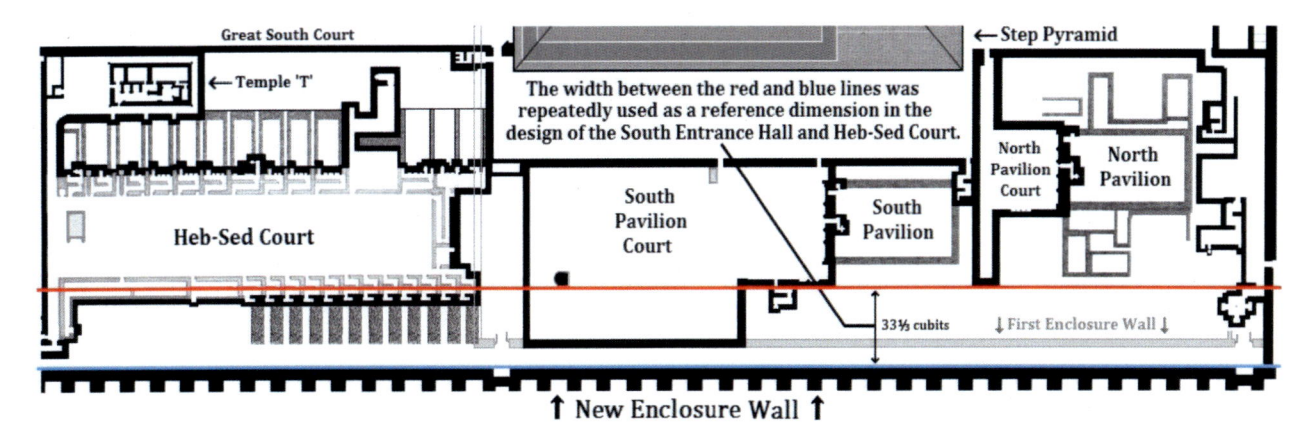

Fig. 7-26 – The reference dimension used in the design of the Entrance Hall and Ḥeb-Sed Court

The Second Enclosure Wall That Was Never Constructed

As already noted above, the Second Enclosure Wall was never constructed because the west wall of its proposed design would have been highly unstable due to the subterranean tunnels and chambers of Western Massif II over which it would have been built (see *Fig. 6-80*). My proposed design for the unbuilt enclosure is based on J.-P. Lauer and W. Kaiser's work; [100] as well as Imhotep's apparent use of Sacred Geometry in his last design of Djoser's funerary temple. This second iteration uses a Root 5 (√5) Double Square as the basis for its design (*Fig. 7-27*). Also note, the line **OD** in *Fig. 7-23* is the same line that runs along the east side of the retaining wall running north-south between the Old Serdab and the Second Serdab (red line, *Fig. 7-27*). This retaining wall became part of the design for the second, current North Mortuary Temple. The green line roughly aligns with the south side of the four-tier Step Pyramid P₁ and the interior face of the east wall in the Serdab Court that runs north-south. The centerline of the Root 5 (√5) Double Square of what would have been the Second Enclosure Wall begins at the interior corner of the north bastion of False Gate 14 (the original Entrance Gate). When extended, this line would run along the north side of the South Altar, and when complete, pass through the pointy edge of the wedge-shaped *always-open* false door near the southeast corner of the Step Pyramid.

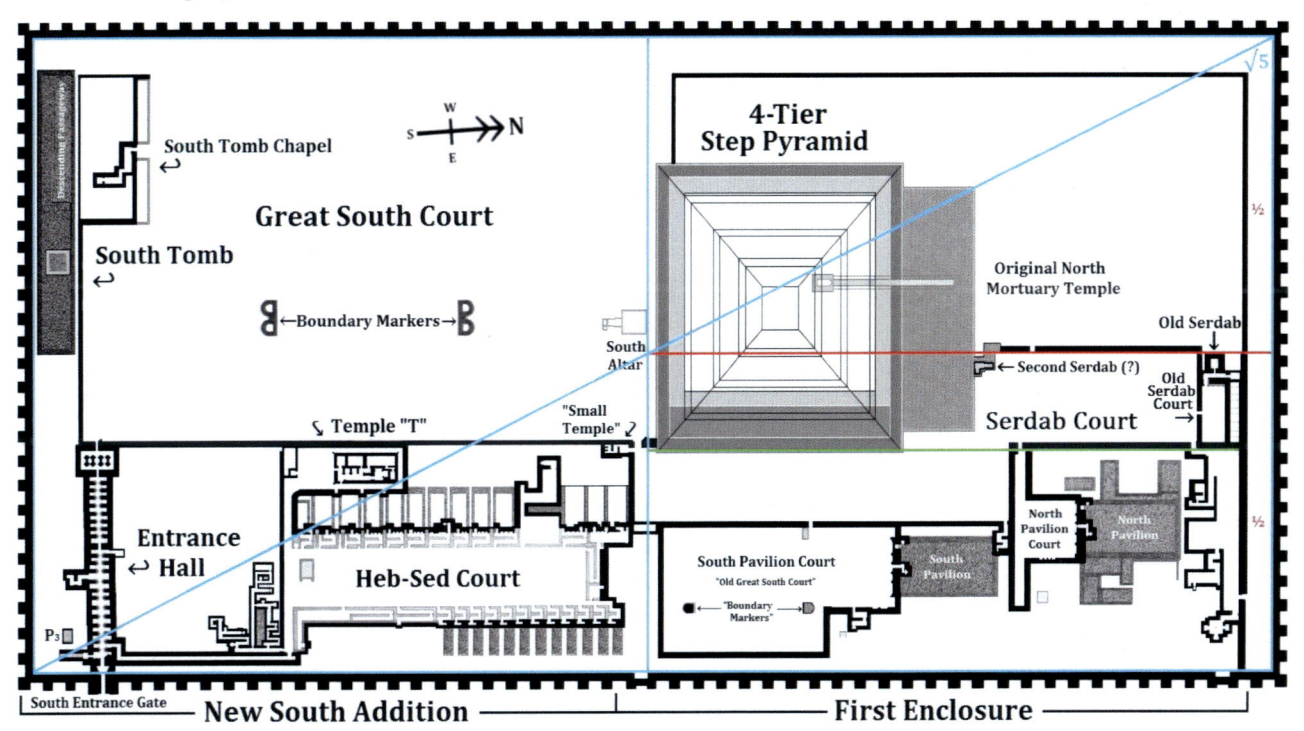

Fig. 7-27 – Within the design of the never-built Second Enclosure is a Root 5 (√5) Double Square, replicated in the Third Enclosure

Rather than abandon the plans for the South Entrance Hall and Ḥeb-Sed Court altogether when it became evident he could not build the Second Enclosure Wall, Imhotep began the expansion of the Step Pyramid Enclosure to that which we see today.

For this part of the expansion project, Imhotep planned to extend the west wall, ①, of the First Enclosure to the south in the space between the south wall of the four-tier pyramid and the South Tomb (*Fig. 7-28*). This would become part of the wall structure of the new South Tomb Chapel and the west wall of the Great South Court. Additionally, a new wall running perpendicularly west to east, ②, was built from this new wall section to the west wall of the four-tier Step Pyramid, but whose existence was probably short-lived due to the plans to expand the four-tier pyramid to six tiers (see text at *Fig. 7-33*).

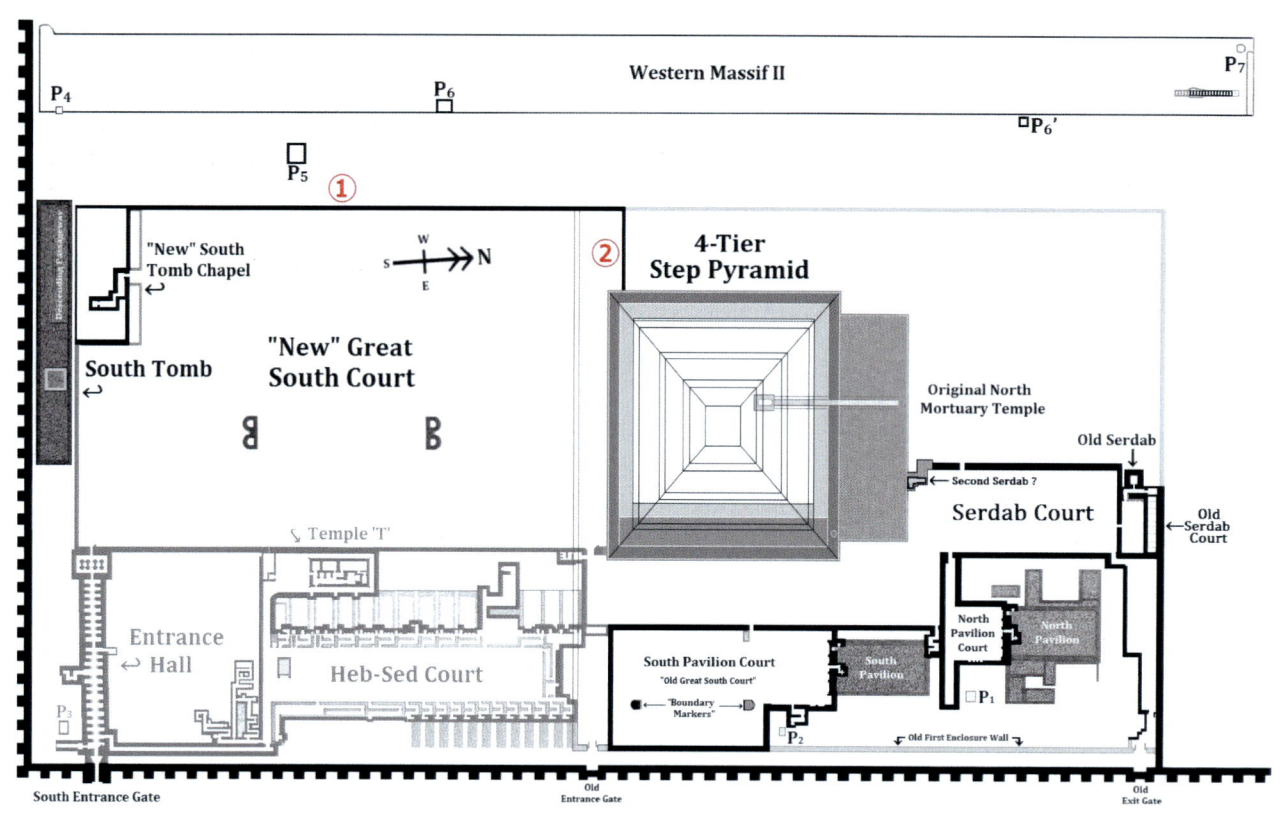

Fig. 7-28 – The intermediary design stage transitioning between the First and Third Enclosures

The Six-Tier Step Pyramid Enclosure

Completion of the design for the Third Enclosure Wall, as well as adding two additional tiers to the four-tier pyramid, was the first step in this enormous building project (*pun intended*). To understand the tradition of using Sacred Geometry during the design of this monument necessitates discovering how Imhotep used Sacred Geometry for the Step Pyramid Enclosure project. Did he lay out these grids first, and then organize what structures went where? Or, because he was given a group of unfinished structures at the outset, did he adjust and improvise as he went along in the design process? Except for the manner in which Imhotep designed Djoser's mortuary monument and his later design of Sekhemkhet's pyramid, it is likely nothing similar to the style and construction of the Step Pyramid Enclosure was ever repeated elsewhere at any time in Egypt's history. This is mostly because of the uniqueness of its design, along with the climate disaster that resulted in the First Intermediate Period occurring about 150 years later resulting in a break in cultural continuity, but also because of the rare abilities of the man who built it.

As part of the design process for the new South Entrance Hall, Ḥeb-Sed Court and virtually the entire revised plan of the Step Pyramid Enclosure, Imhotep used what we know today as the "canon of proportion". Use of this grid system was a common practice throughout the long history of ancient Egypt by artists to depict the human form as seen in virtually every sculpture and painting, as well as by architects to design temples and other buildings.

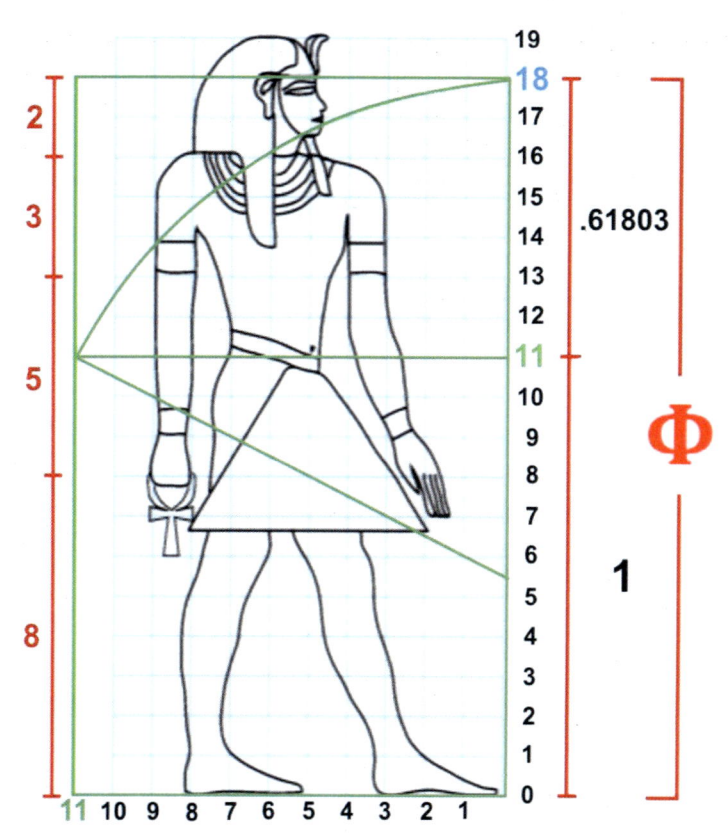

Fig. 7-29 – The canon of proportion as seen in the image of Amenhotep III from WV22 in the Valley of the Kings

A 19-by-10 grid where line ⑱ is even with the hairline was the most widely used for standing figures (*Fig. 7-29*). The canon later changed to a grid based on 20 vertical squares (a 2:1, Root 5 ($\sqrt{5}$) Double Square ratio), and later still to 22 vertical squares (with an implied 11th horizontal line, another Root 5 ($\sqrt{5}$) Double Square ratio). Even so, the concept was the same, and remained consistent for several thousand years. The canon is the hallmark of ancient Egyptian art that is easily recognizable, even to the extent that over 1200 years after the construction of the Step Pyramid Enclosure, the architects used this grid system to design the Temple of Luxor (see *Fig. 3-37*).[101]

Whether using the canon to design a building or a tomb painting, many examples still exist in various unfinished tombs today. The image of Amenhotep III [102] in *Fig. 7-29* conforms to this canon by placing line ⑪ at the naval. Symbolically, the naval represents the beginnings of life where the infant initially receives nourishment from its mother. The position of the naval is exactly at the center of the baby's body between the top of the head and the bottom of the feet. At maturity, the center of the body moves lower to where the genitalia are located, as indicated at line ⑧. This is also highly symbolic in that this is the location for the creation of human life.[103]

The relationship between lines ⑪ and ⑱ is a ratio of 11:7, from which is derived the value for the Golden Ratio *Phi* (Φ) of 1.61803 when an implied 11th vertical line is added to the 19-by-10 grid to create a *Phi* Rectangle. It doesn't take a great deal of imagination to detect an additional relationship between the ratio 11:7 and that of another irrational number. Multiplying 11 by the *Magic Number 2* gives the ratio of 22:7, which is the Egyptian value for *Pi* (π), 3.142857. Finally, the ratio of 11:7 relates to music as well. As stated in the text following *Fig. 7-9*, there are 7 diatonic notes within an musical octave, but there are also 11 semitones within the octave as well. This further implies an association with the Pythagorean notion that health and medicine, music, architecture, natural science, geometry and mathematics are all interrelated parts of a greater expression of Universal Wisdom.

Ironically, the grid also has the first four numbers (2, 3, 5 and 8) of a Fibonacci set embedded within it, which when added together, equals 18. This is another clue that the ancient Egyptians knew about and used Fibonacci ratios to design artwork and architecture.

Even though it is not readily apparent, the Egyptian canon of proportion has embedded within it a subtle reference to the seven vortexes of energy of the human body called *chakras*, which are located at certain points along the length of the spine (*Fig. 7-30*). First written about in the spiritual texts of India called the *Vedas*, it is possible that knowledge of this chakra energy system was more widespread among ancient cultures than previously thought. Though the Vedas date to around 1500 to 1000 BCE, far later than when the canon of proportion was first used in ancient Egypt, it is unknown if there was any cross-pollination of spiritual wisdom between Egypt and India in ancient times. If there was, this might explain how the canon of proportion was developed. Note that there is a separation of each chakra from the next chakra by 2 lines in the canon of proportion – another manifestation of the *Magic Number 2*.

The Relationship Between the Egyptian Canon of Proportion and the Chakra Energy System of India

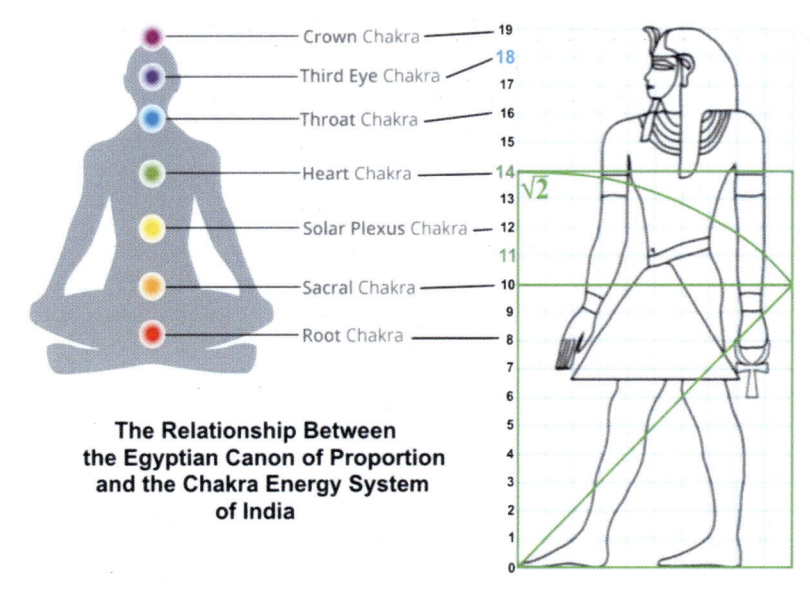

Fig. 7-30 – A comparison of Egyptian and Indian sacred wisdom

In esoteric teachings, the position of line ⑱ is located at the spot on the forehead known the *third eye*. Note that this is position of the cobra-headed *uraeus*. This is not a coincidence in that it is symbolic of the kundalini energy as mentioned in Chapter 3, which when activated, rises up from the base chakra at the bottom of the spine, causing the *third eye* to open, allowing the *realized man* to *see* and sense higher realms of existence.

The challenge to all this is to discover whether the Indian authors of the Vedas incorporated ancient Egyptian wisdom in their teachings, or vice versa.

Oddly enough, the Heart Chakra, the seat of intuitive intelligence and spiritual wisdom, aligns with line ⑭, an important Sacred Number, and the physical heart. A Root 2($\sqrt{2}$) arc derived from a 10-by-10 base square ends at line ⑭ (*Fig. 7-30*). This is the crossroads where Sacred Numbers and Sacred Geometry meet.

From a point just inside False Gate 13 on the interior of the eastern Enclosure Wall, Imhotep initially drew the base line of a 19-by-10 grid along what would have been the north wall of the Second Enclosure (green line on the far right side of *Fig. 7-31*). Once he abandoned any idea of building the Second Enclosure, Imhotep moved the base line starting at point ⓪ of this grid along the corridor wall just west of the mammisi birthing rooms. He then extended this line along the north interior wall of the Old Serdab Court (up) that runs east to west. Imhotep finished drawing out the rest of this grid using the 33⅓ cubit reference dimension by first going south (left). He aligned several important architectural features with this grid, one of which is the short wall (red arrow) just east of the Old Serdab itself that is perpendicular to the interior wall that runs along the base line of the 19-by-10 grid. Notice this short wall is exactly at the halfway point of the base line of the grid, implying the further use of Sacred Geometry in this instance.

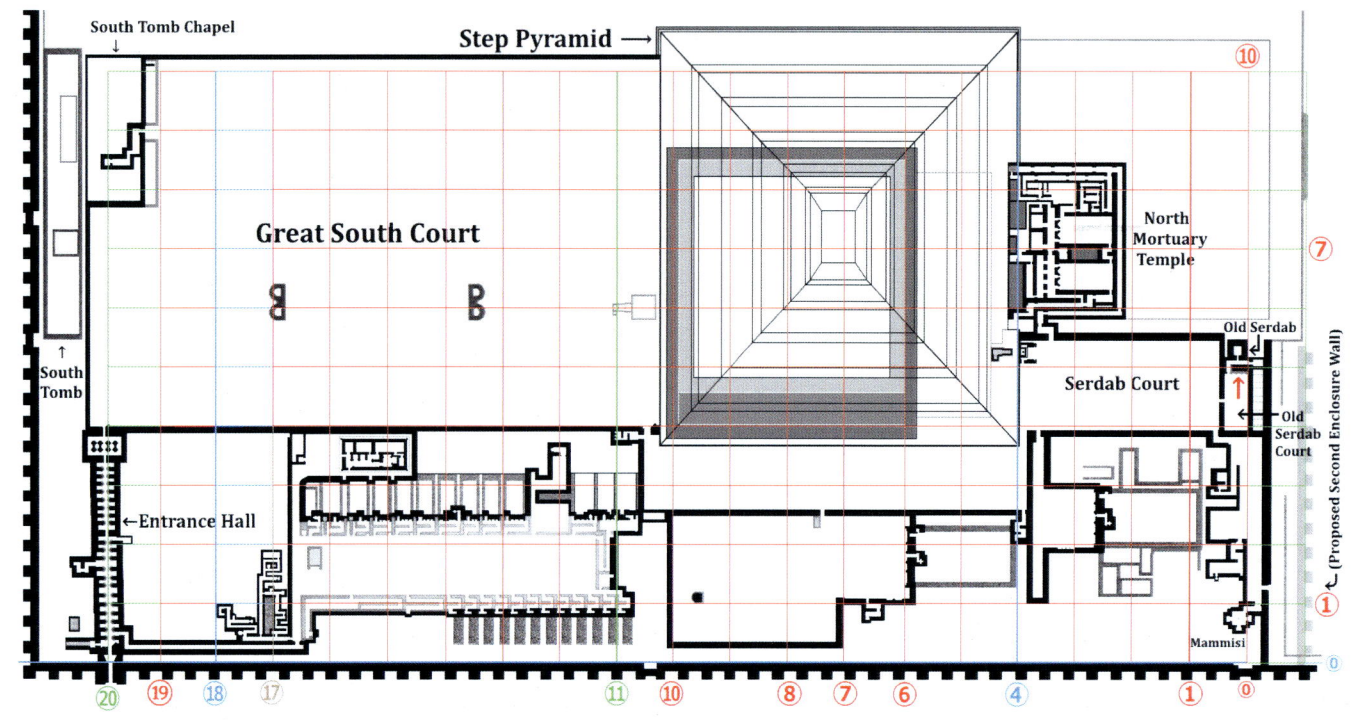

Fig. 7-31 – The Canon of Proportion as used to create the new additions to the Step Pyramid Enclosure

When looking at *Fig. 7-31*, it becomes readily apparent that Imhotep utilized the canon during the planning stages for the Step Pyramid Enclosure. Line ④ aligns with the north side of the six-tier Step Pyramid. Line ⑥ runs along the exterior façade of the South Pavilion as well as the north side of Mastabas $M_1/M_2/M_3$. Along line ⑪, Imhotep placed the north wall of the Ḥeb-Sed Court. Vertical lines ⑦, ⑩ and ⑰ align with the interior faces of several other walls. At line ⑱ is the southernmost extent of the embalming center corresponding to Room 'V'. Vertical line ⑧ is the exact midpoint of the South Pavilion Court. The horizontal line ⑦ is the midpoint between the west wall of the North Mortuary Temple and the large east wall running north to south that serves to define the Serdab Court. Various other lines align with other features within the Enclosure especially the Ḥeb-Sed Court.

At the *invisible* line, ⑳ is the South Entrance Hall. If the correlation of the 19-by-10 canon of proportion with the seven chakras is correct, perhaps the South Entrance Hall relates to a point just above the head, which ties in with the concept that the soul leaves the body from the top of the head at the time of death (see Chapter 4). It is possible the concept of an *invisible* line ⑳ as part of the canon of proportion that was used during the Old Kingdom (ca. 2700–2200 BCE) and embodied here in the Step Pyramid Enclosure may have led to the canon's modification to a 20-by-10 grid during the last years of the Eleventh Dynasty, some 600 years later.

Imhotep used a 4-by-4 section of the 19-by-10 grid to lay out the east wall of the Great South Court (*Fig. 7-32*). The area encompassing the Ḥeb-Sed Court and Embalming Center lies between lines ⑩ and ⑱. Line ⑱ is also the south line of the Root 5 ($\sqrt{5}$) Double Square (marked as 'C') that defines this space (seen in *Fig. 7-33*). With this south line extended westward to a total length of about 133⅓ cubits, the initial thickness and the base line for the western face of the Great South Court wall was determined.

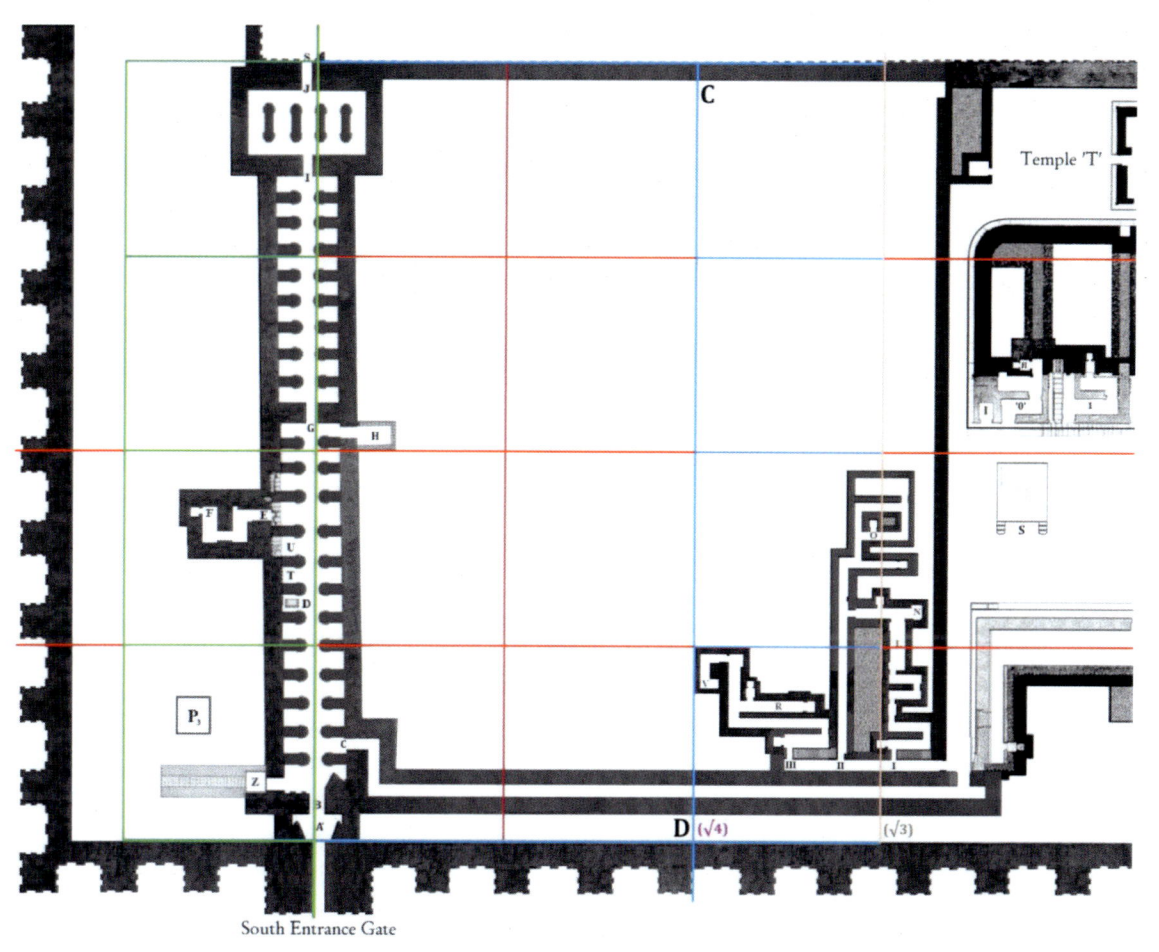

Fig. 7-32 – The underlying grid used in the design of the South Entrance Hall and Ḥeb-Sed Court quadrant

Once the general shape of the South Entrance Hall and Ḥeb-Sed Court was determined, Imhotep proceeded to "fill-in-the-blanks". There are several grid systems based on this underlying 19-by-10 grid of 33⅓ cubit squares that were used to design the South Entrance Hall and Ḥeb-Sed Court quadrant as shown by the layout of many features such as walls, columns, doorways, rooms, and so on.

Sacred Geometry and the South Entrance Hall / Ḥeb-Sed Court Quadrant

After completion of the First Enclosure, how did Imhotep plan the expansion to its present size along with the Ḥeb-Sed Court and the South Entrance Hall?

When the decision was made to upgrade the $M_1/M_2/M_3$ mastaba tombs into the new four-tier Step Pyramid complex including a new Enclosure Wall, Imhotep's first task was to extend the new east wall towards the south to join up with a new south wall. This would also encompass the already built South Tomb (see *Fig. 7-26*). Although the north and west walls of the Second Enclosure Wall were not constructed at this time (see *Figs. 6-81* and *7-27*), nonetheless, Imhotep retained the design for the South Entrance Hall and Ḥeb-Sed Court quadrant and modified his plans as he went along.

Starting with the Sacred Geometry Key as represented in the design of False Gates 1, 2 and 3 (see *Fig. 7-13*), Imhotep proceeded to build this third and final version of the Enclosure by first designing the southern half that incorporated the existing South Tomb. The Great South Court, the South Entrance Gate and Entrance Hall, the Ḥeb-Sed Court and the "House of Beauty" embalming center were probably part of this new design, but their construction had not yet commenced. The following are several plans showing the Sacred Geometry used for these elements.

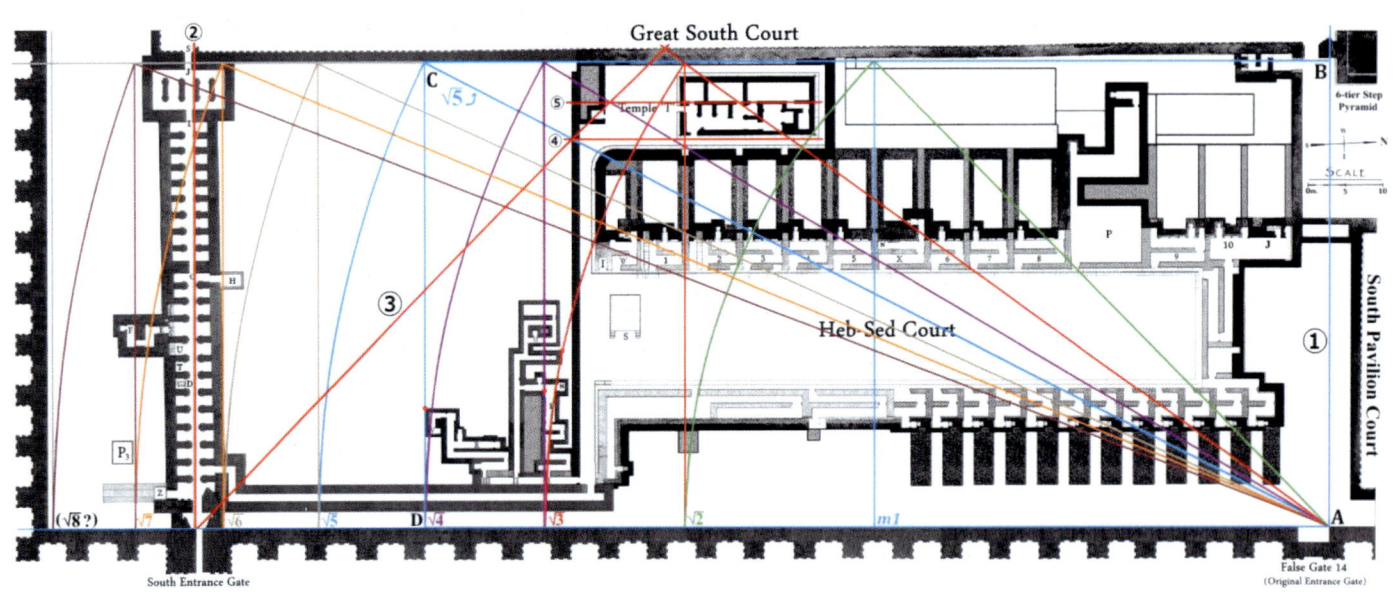

Fig. 7-33 – Proportions of the South Entrance Gate, Ḥeb-Sed Court and "House of Beauty" embalming center using Sacred Geometry

1) Using the center line of the Root 5 ($\sqrt{5}$) Double Square from the unbuilt Second Enclosure Wall project (*Fig. 7-27*), Imhotep drew a new line (**AB**, ①) running east-west (bottom to top, at the right side of *Fig. 7-33*) to a point where the green line ends in *Fig. 7-27*. From the same starting point at False Gate 14, another line (**AD**), twice the length of the east-west line **AB**, was laid out 90° going south along what would become the interior face of the east wall of the new Enclosure. From these two lines, was the creation of a Root 5 ($\sqrt{5}$) Double Square (**ABCD**) ending at Room '**V**', which defined the space where the Ḥeb-Sed Court and "House of Beauty" embalming center would be constructed. Curiously, the length of this initial line, **AB**, is one-quarter the distance between the east and west walls of the finished new Step Pyramid Enclosure. This implies that Imhotep had already planned the final dimensions of this third iteration of the Enclosure Wall before designing and constructing the South Entrance Hall and Ḥeb-Sed Court in the southeast quadrant. This first line is akin to the (red) east-west centerline ② drawn down the middle of the South Entrance Hall (left side of *Fig. 7-35*) that passes through the tip of the outer edge of another wedge-shaped *always-open* door at the end of the Exit Vestibule.

2) The layout of the east wall of the Great South Court (in the middle of *Fig. 7-33*) was along this west line of the Double Square, at least initially. If you notice, this wall isn't perfectly straight: it is offset to the west (up) just a little. It so happens this is the same 1.5° offset as is the South Entrance Hall.[104] Where the south vertical line of

the Double Square denoting the southernmost extent of the "House of Beauty" embalming center touches the interior surface of the east wall of the Great South Court is the point where this wall's 1.5° deflection to the west begins. It is as if the Entrance Hall and the Great South Court's east wall was a single set piece, and Imhotep offset both of them together.

3) Starting from the north (the right side of *Fig. 7-33*) where the south wall of the First Enclosure was once located, Imhotep laid out the basic location of several features for the new South Entrance Hall and Ḥeb-Sed Court quadrant using a 7-Part Root Rectangle Template. The midline (***m1***) of the Double Square lines up with the half-wall and the space between West Chapels 5 and 6. The vertical Root 2 ($\sqrt{2}$) line passes through the middle of the wall between West Chapels 1 and 2, and subsequently runs along the interior face of the south wall of Temple 'T'.

4) A (red) 45° diagonal line, ③, drawn from the eastern point of the center red line in the *Sacrum Room* Entrance Vestibule intersects the (blue) Root 5 ($\sqrt{5}$) line, at which point a line, ④, drawn horizontally north-south aligns with the edge of the base surrounding Temple 'T'.

5) This same diagonal line also intersects the (magenta) Root 4 ($\sqrt{4}$) line, from which another horizontal line, ⑤, drawn from this intersection aligns with the central wall support structures of Temple 'T'.

6) The vertical line created from the Root 2 ($\sqrt{2}$) arc intersects the diagonal Root 3 ($\sqrt{3}$) line, at which point it aligns with the rear walls of the West Chapels. The vertical line stemming from the end of the Root 3 ($\sqrt{3}$) arc also runs along a major wall structure within the "House of Beauty" embalming center near the entrance marked with the Roman numeral 'I'.

7) The vertical Root 4 ($\sqrt{4}$) line runs along the outside wall of Room 'V', and is the southernmost (left) line of the Root 5 ($\sqrt{5}$) Double Square that outlines the Ḥeb-Sed Court and "House of Beauty" medical center. The Root 5 ($\sqrt{5}$) arc does not align with any known feature (unless Imhotep planned something for the area that was never built), but it does aligns with line **GH** as shown in *Fig. 7-37* and line ⑲ of the 19-by-10 grid in *Fig. 7-31*. This Root 5 arc was used to create the Root 6 ($\sqrt{6}$) line, and the arc from this line stakes out the point of the location for the construction of the north wall of the South Entrance Hall where it intersected with the interior face of the east Enclosure Wall. It may be a coincidence, but the vertical Root 7 ($\sqrt{7}$) line derived from an arc generated from the Root 6 ($\sqrt{6}$) line runs along the interior wall of the "T7 Lung Chambers". However, I have long dismissed any notion that most of this mortuary temple's design features are simply the product of *coincidence*.

While Imhotep may have had a 7-Part Root Rectangle Template as part of his architect's *toolkit*, an arc generated from the vertical Root 7 ($\sqrt{7}$) line would create a Root 8 ($\sqrt{8}$) vertical line. This line does not align with any feature in or near the South Entrance Hall, but if it is extended westward (up), it comes fairly close to the exterior of the south wall of the South Tomb. This actually may be one of the few times where this really is a coincidence. *Maybe*.

As part of the process of locating the Ḥeb-Sed Court and South Entrance Hall within the overall plan, Imhotep used two *Phi* (Φ) Rectangles to create the Great South Court (*Fig. 7-34*). In Chapter 6, archeologists have posited the theory that the South Tomb Chapel served to store Djoser's crowns, but when looking at its plan, only a minor part of the South Tomb Chapel's interior volume is taken up by a very small room. We have speculated the "old" Great South Court (now known as the South Pavilion Court) had a small room that served as a robing room and latrine for the king's use during the *Ḥeb-Sed* (see *Fig. 7-21*). Therefore, it is difficult to justify the large size of the South Tomb Chapel based solely on the supposition its design was predicated on its exclusive use for Netjerikhet Djoser prior to running around the two B-shaped boundary markers in the Great South Court as part of the *sed*-festival ceremonies. (See *Figs. 5-5* and *5-6*, and *Fig. 6-19* and "The South Tomb Chapel" section in Chapter 6.) For this reason, it is possible to see that the South Tomb Chapel had an additional different purpose, from not only an architectural design standpoint, but also how it points to Imhotep's symbolic use of hieroglyphs to design various features within the Enclosure. *More on this in Chapter 8.*

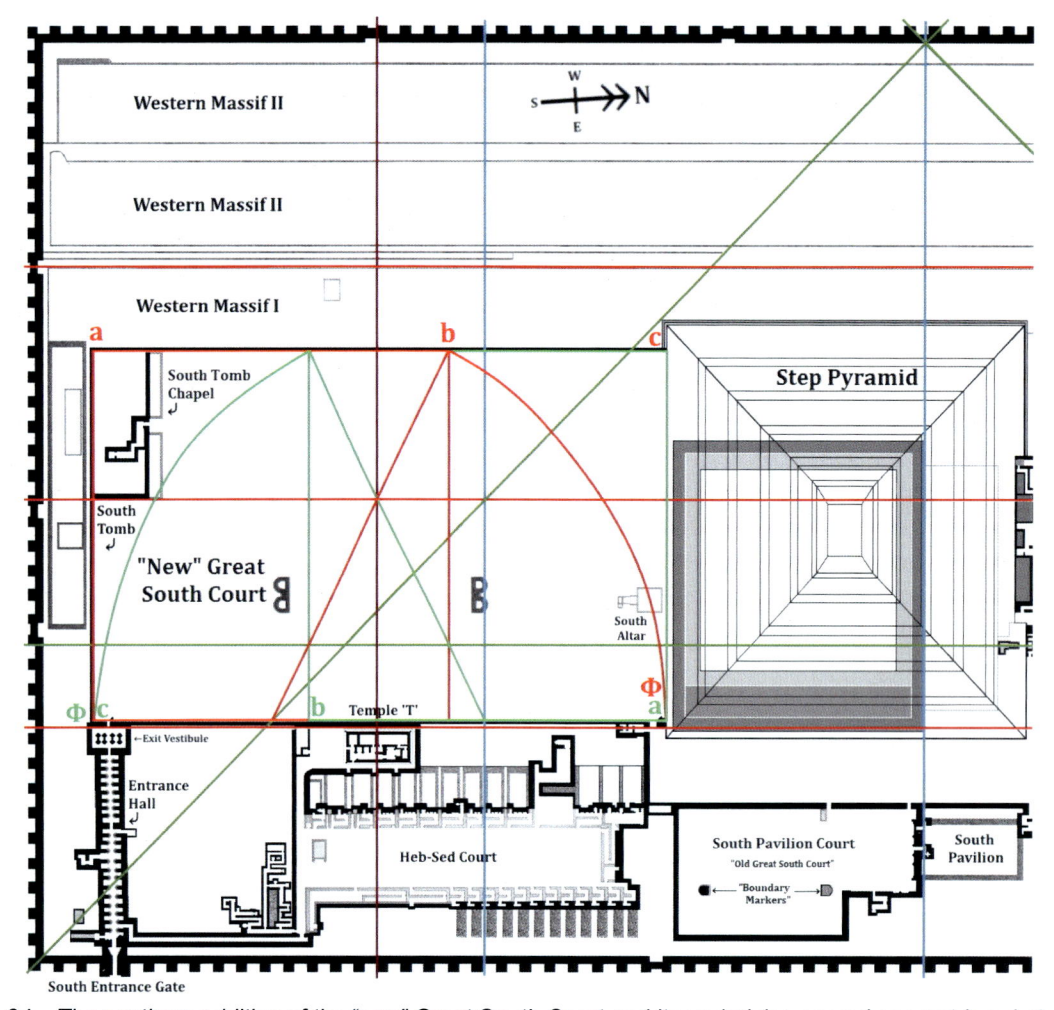

Fig. 7-34 – The southern addition of the "new" Great South Court and its underlying sacred geometric substructure

In the transition from the First Enclosure to the current Third Enclosure, it is possible to see how well balanced this design is when the principles of Sacred Geometry are used to determine where the various architectural elements were positioned within the Enclosure. *Fig. 7-34* shows how the use of two *Phi* (Φ) Rectangles defined the overall space of the new Great South Court. The shape and dimensions of the South Tomb Chapel played a large part in the execution of this design.

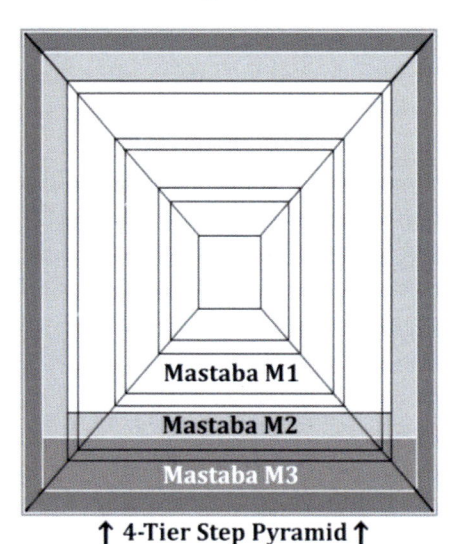

Fig. 7-35 – The Four-Tier Step Pyramid centered over the three nested mastabas

To transform the Mastabas $M_1/M_2/M_3$ into the four-tier Step Pyramid, Imhotep once again used Sacred Geometry to design several structures for the space between the South Tomb and the First Enclosure Wall. When Imhotep wanted to increase this first pyramid to six tiers; it would have been easier to add an equal amount of masonry to each side, centering the six-tier pyramid over it, as he did previously when the he constructed the four-tier pyramid (*Fig. 7-35*). If he did so, centering the added tiers would have shortened the north-south width of the Great South Court, and would have cut into the space designated for the Ḥeb-Sed Court. This can only mean that prior to expanding the four-tier pyramid to six tiers, parts of the First Enclosure Wall still existed, and construction had already begun on the South Entrance Hall, Ḥeb-Sed Court and Great South Court additions along with the construction of the new Third Enclosure Wall. Because of this, Imhotep had to add more masonry only to the four-tier pyramid's north and west sides to enlarge it into the new six-tier pyramid.

When designing the new six-tier Step Pyramid, Imhotep used the lengths of the south and west sides of the four-tier pyramid for the base squares of a pair of Root 2 (√2) Rectangles to define the dimensions of the new pyramid (*Fig. 7-36*). The green Root 2 (√2) Rectangle defines its east-west width. The red Rectangle defines the north-south width of the new pyramid, which coincidentally aligns with line ④ of the 19-by-10 canon of proportion grid used by Imhotep in his initial plans for expanding the First Enclosure (see *Fig. 7-31*). Note, too, because of the four-tier Step Pyramid's rectangular shape, the dimensions of the base squares of the two Root 2 (√2) Rectangles are also different in size, rendering the final shape of the six-tier Step Pyramid to be a rectangle as well, unlike the more common square pyramids found throughout Egypt.

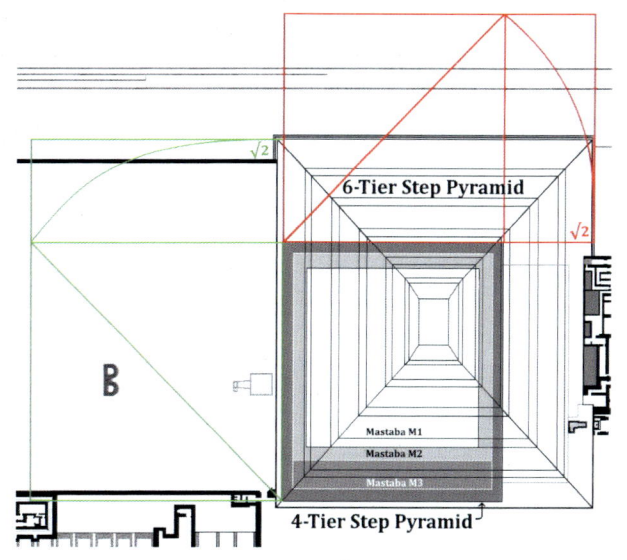

Fig. 7-36 – Two Root 2 (√2) Rectangles were used to design the expanded Step Pyramid

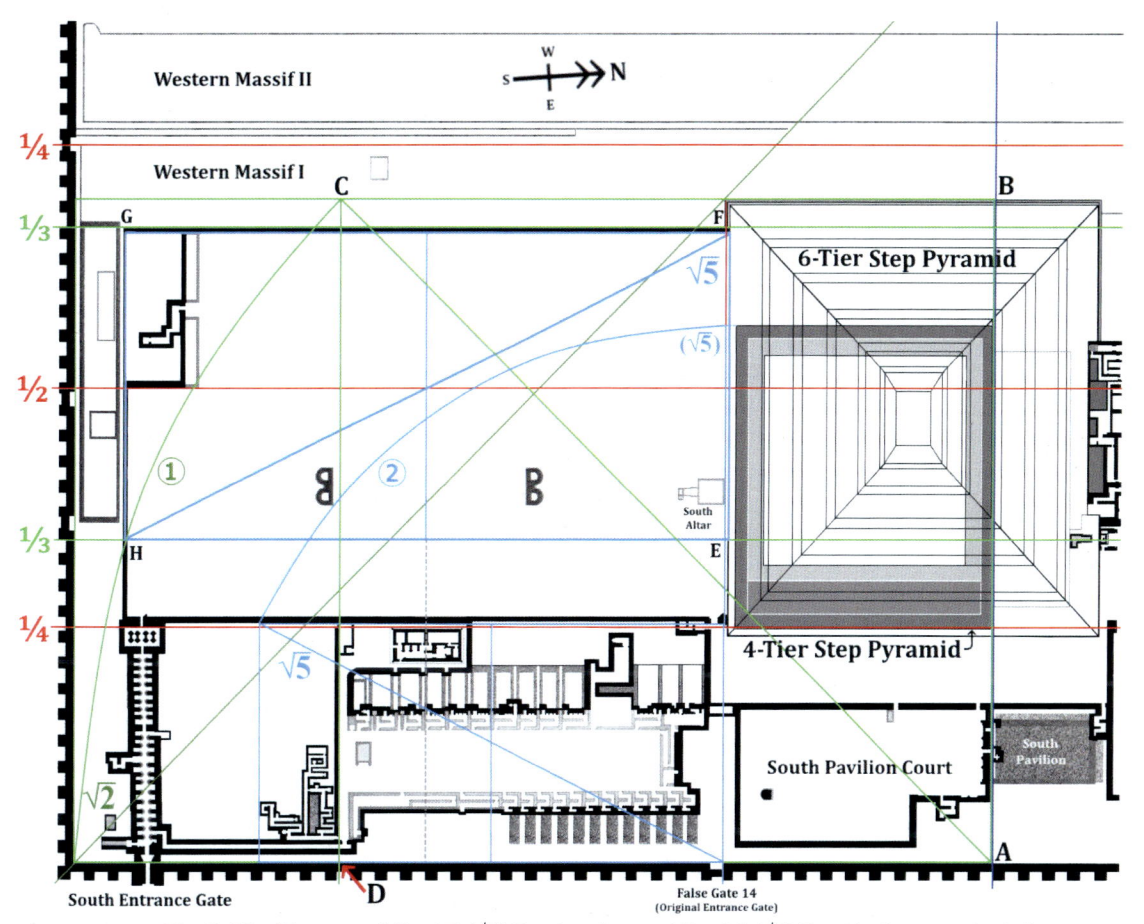

Fig. 7-37 – The use of Root 2 (√2) Rectangles and Root 5 (√5) Double Squares to define the proportions of various features of the south section of the Third Enclosure, Part 1

Figure 7-37 shows a Root 2 (√2) Rectangle and a couple of Root (√5) Double Squares were used to define the proportions of the Great South Court within the horizontal, middle third of the Enclosure, the north-south extent of Ḥeb-Sed Court and embalming center, and the overall size of the Step Pyramid when it was expanded to six tiers.

1) The sides of the base square, **ABCD,** of a Root 2 (√2) Rectangle are derived from the distance between the interior surface of the eastern Enclosure Wall and the southwest corner of the six-tier Step Pyramid (near the letter '**F**').

The north segment of this square, **AB**, runs along the Enclosure's vertical centerline. Its arc, ①, ends at the interior corner of the south wall of the Enclosure, and passes through the northeast corner of the South Tomb Chapel as well as the junction of the lowest ⅓ line and the southeast corner of the Root 5 (√5) Double Square that defines the north-south width of the Great South Court.

2) The east-west width of the South Tomb Chapel is half the width of the Root 5 (√5) Double Square in the Great South Court (lines **EF** and **GH**). The north-south lines (**FG** and **EH**) fit in the space between the south side of the six-tier Step Pyramid and the wall just north of the South Tomb. A line projecting downward from where the two diagonal midpoint lines intersect aligns with the main central east-west wall of Temple 'T' among other features.

3) An east-west line was drawn from False Gate 14 to the southwest corner of the four-tier Step Pyramid. From this point, arc ② was created ending at another point on the interior face of the new east wall of the Great South Court. This second point is the southwestern-most point of a Root 5 (√5) Double Square that encompasses the Ḥeb-Sed Court/"House of Beauty" medical center. Strictly speaking, it is not a Sacred Ratio, but it does show that Imhotep used the length of the initial east-west line to determine the shape of the Ḥeb-Sed Court and the embalming center. This is discussed in greater detail below.

Figure 7-38 is one of the design grids used for the South Entrance Hall/Ḥeb-Sed Court quadrant. This shows a 5-Part Root Rectangle Template was created whose starting point is where the Root 4 (√4) Rectangle shown in *Fig. 7-33* meets the interior face of the Enclosure Wall at point '**D**'. The arcs originating from these Root Squares and Rectangles highlight several key architectural features in the Entrance Hall and Ḥeb-Sed Court designs.

1) The (green) Root 2 (√2) diagonal line ① begins at 'Point **D**' and ends at the Entrance Hall's (red) horizontal midpoint line, which also runs along the exterior of the (lower) east wall of the Heart Chamber (marked as '**H**'). Root 2 arc ② starts at this point and ends at the (blue) horizontal Root 4 (√4) line, touching the **G** corner of the **EFGH** square as it does so.

2) A second (green) diagonal Root 2 (√2) line, ③, extended out from the starting point of the (red) vertical midpoint line in the South Entrance Gate's Entrance Vestibule (marked as '**A**.') From the endpoint of the Root 2 (√2) arc mentioned in #1, line ④ was extended north (right) to this second Root 2 (√2) line (③). The creation of a second Root 2 (√2) arc, ⑤, going south (left), ends at the junction, ⑥, of the (red) vertical Entrance Hall centerline and a horizontal line running along the west face of the east wall of the Great South Court. It is also at this *meeting point* where a (blue) Root 5 (√5) line culminates.

3) The (green) horizontal line ② in #2 was extended to the south (left), meeting up with the endpoint of a (gold) Root 3 (√3) line at the (red) Entrance Hall centerline (⑦). From this line, arc ⑧ meets up with the north-south line (right-left) running through the middle of the Exit Vestibule's interior wall that was created by the primary *Phi* (Φ) Rectangle (see *Fig. 7-31*). Aligned along this line are various architectural features in the "Mystery Building" and in the interior of Temple 'T' such as columns and walls.

4) A (magenta) Root 4 (√4) line, ⑨, was drawn from starting point '**D**' to this same (red) horizontal line ⑩ where it meets the Entrance Hall's (red) vertical centerline (⑪). From this point on the vertical Entrance Hall centerline, arc ⑫ ends at a point where the vertical Root 4 (√4) line and the line running along the west face of the eastern wall of the Great South Court meet (⑬).

5) From a diagonal line in the small base square of the lower *Phi* (Φ) Rectangle (with the crosshairs) in the **EFGH** square, a third diagonal Root 2 (√2) line, ⑭, was created. Where it ends at the vertical Root 4 (√4) line, a (green) horizontal line, ⑮, projects to the north (right) that delineates the front façades of the West Chapels.

6) From the **EF** line of the **EFGH** square, horizontal line ⑯ begins at point '**a**' and extends to the north (right). This aligns with a wall within the "House of Beauty" embalming center, as well as delineates the foundation base of the walls of the East Chapels. The **EF** line, when projected westward until it meets line ⑰, aligns with the upper rear exterior wall of West Chapel '0'. This line then defines where the upper segment for a *Phi* (Φ) Rectangle is located. The vertical line beginning at point '**b**' of the square base of the *Phi* (Φ) Rectangle aligns with an interior wall of West Chapel 2 (⑱). When extended west from point '**c**' of the *Phi* (Φ) Rectangle, vertical line ⑲ of the *Phi* (Φ) Rectangle aligns with several interior walls of West Chapel 5, as well as the exterior face of the wall of the courtyard surrounding Temple 'T'.

7) Another *Phi* (Φ) Rectangle, ⑳, delineates the dimensions of the upper, isolated "intestine" section of the "House of Beauty" embalming center (see Chapter 3).

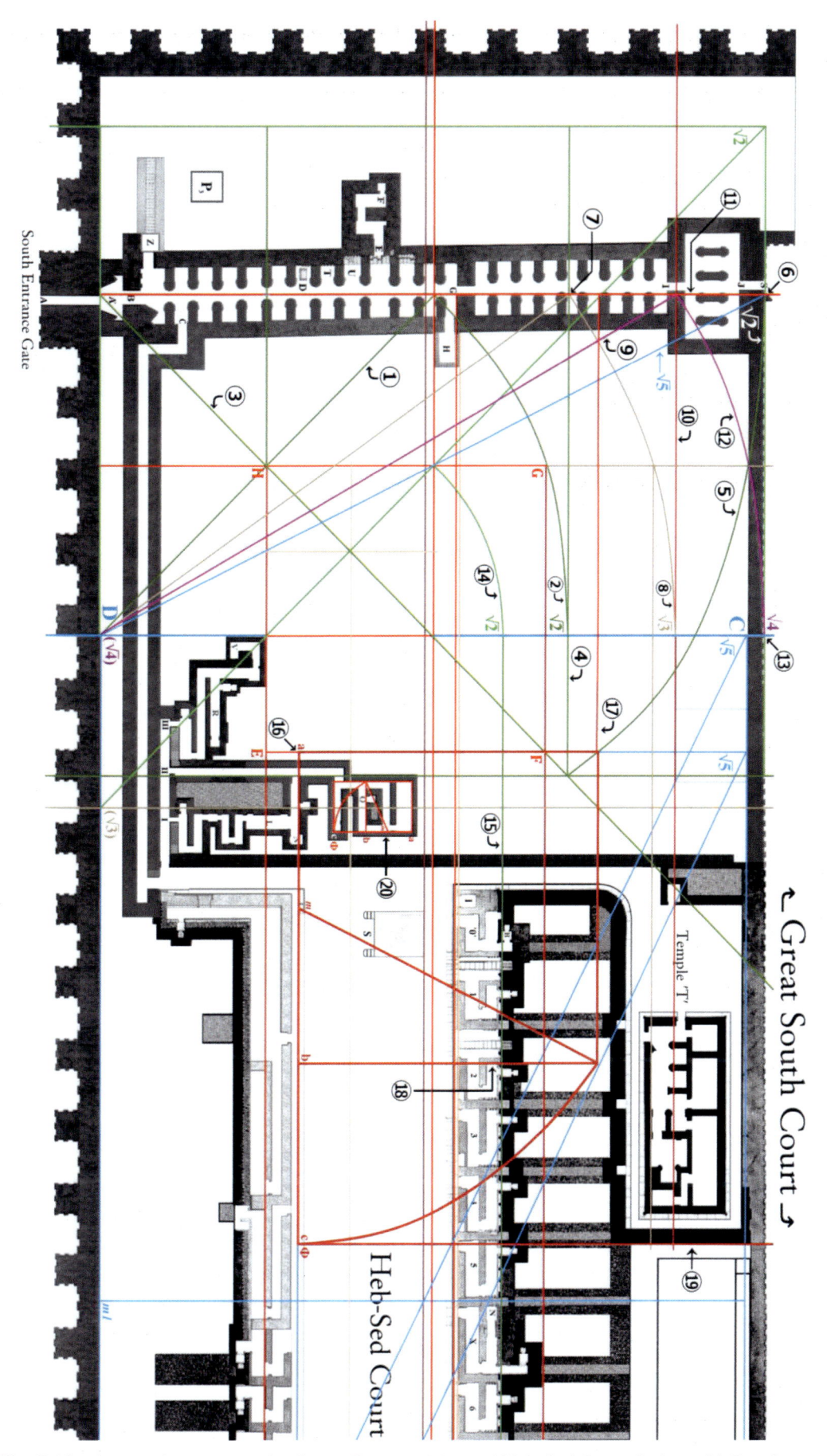

Fig. 7-38 – Sacred Geometry in the South Entrance Hall and Ḥeb-Sed Court design grid, Part 2a

At the other end of the Ḥeb-Sed Court can be found several Root 2 (√2) Squares and Root 5 (√5) Double Squares defining the basic outline of Enclosure 'P' as a whole (*Fig. 7-39*), and the alignment of grid lines with a wall in a room on the far north end of the Ḥeb-Sed Court and East Chapel interior walls. As stated before, architects, like everyone else, are creatures of habit. As such, they tend to use the same dimensions, measurements and ratios repeatedly when creating the architectural features in their plans. An example of this is Imhotep's use of a standard measurement of 33⅓ cubits throughout the Step Pyramid Enclosure. Dimensions *X* and *Y* in *Fig. 7-39* are examples of just such a repetitive use of a dimension. Both of these dimensions are the result of the short part of the rectangle created by the Root 2 (√2) Rectangles. These dimensions define the thickness of the walls in general, as well as the width of the large horizontal double wall in the middle. Dimension *Z* is the width of West Chapel 8's forecourt, and is the same as the base square of a Root 2 (√2) Rectangle that delineates the width of Enclosure 'P'. The combination of the two *Z* segments plus the *X* segment also creates a Silver Rectangle.

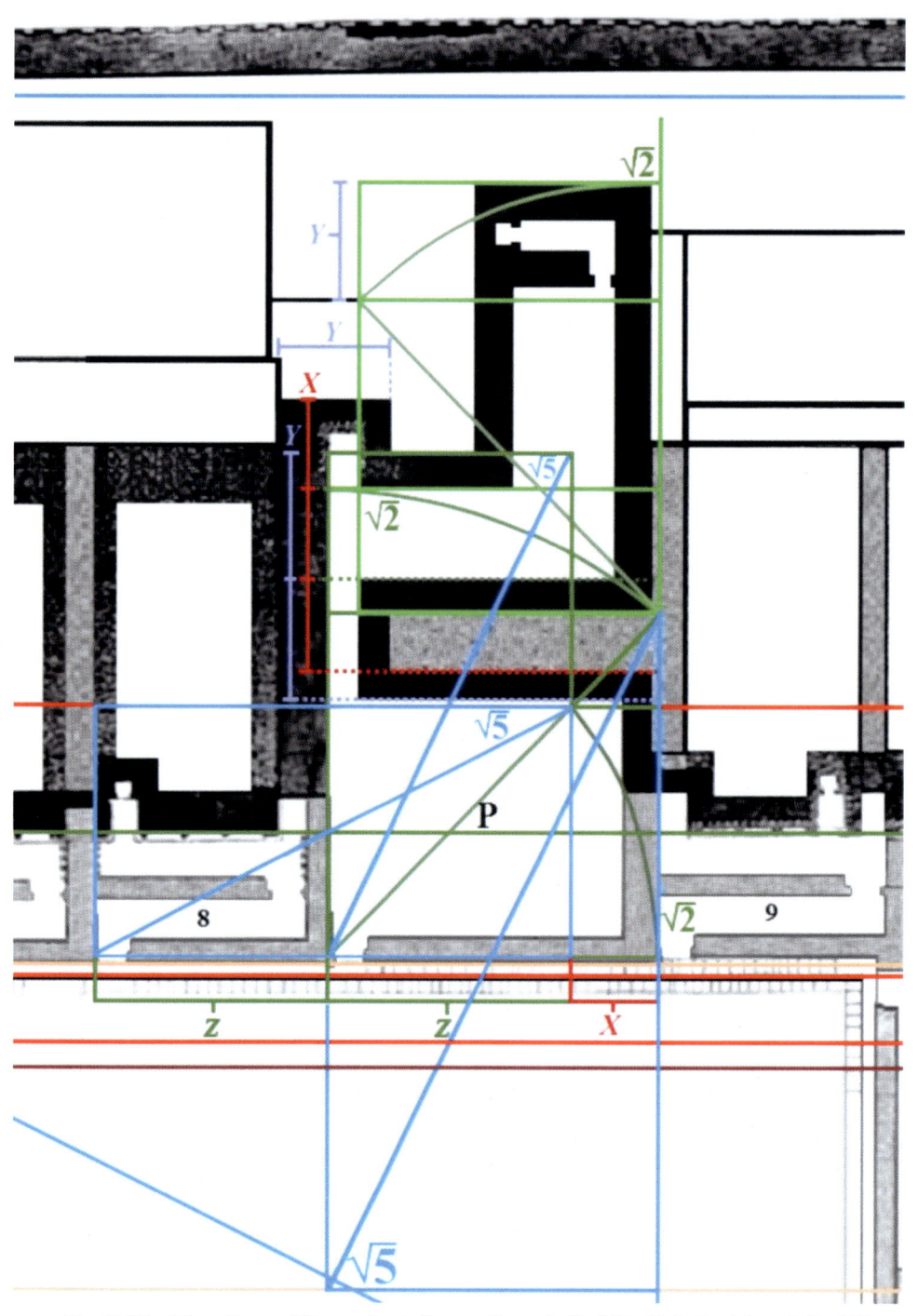

Fig. 7-39 – More Sacred Geometry in the northern half of the Ḥeb-Sed Court, Part 2b

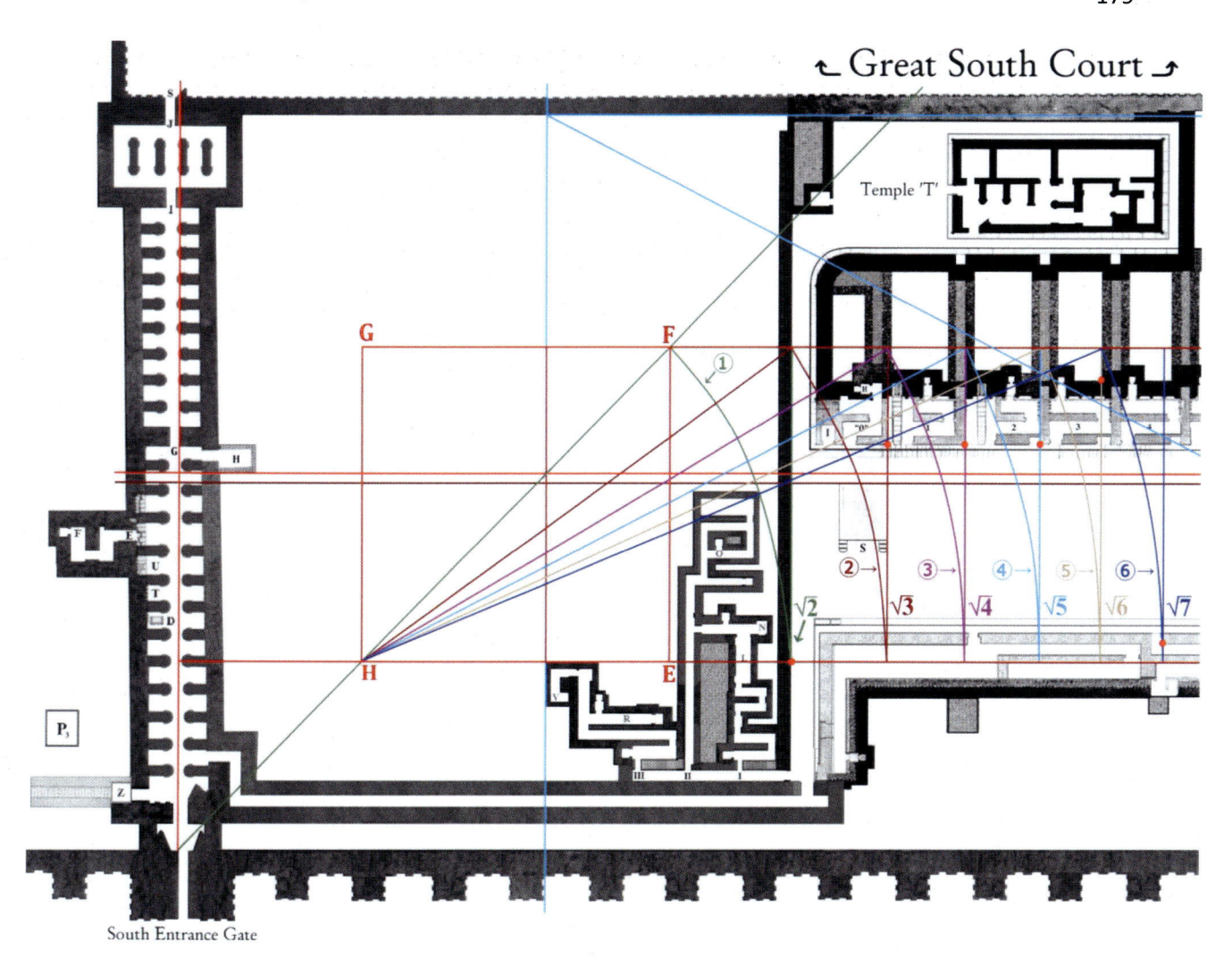

Fig. 7-40 – Sacred Geometry in the South Entrance Hall and Ḥeb-Sed Court design grid, Part 3

Just as hieroglyphs are readable in either direction, Imhotep created another 7-Part Root Rectangle Template grid, this time going left-to-right (*Fig. 7-40*). In this grid projection, the base square of a Root 2 (√2) Rectangle designated as **EFGH**, derived from the two overlapping *Phi* (Φ) Rectangles (see *Fig. 7-41*) is the base square for this 7-Part Root Rectangle Template. Two horizontal lines project north (up) from the lines **HE** and **GF** of this base square into the Ḥeb-Sed Court. What follows are all the correspondences to architectural features of the resultant lines and arcs created by this 7-Part Root Rectangle Template starting at the corner '**H**'.

1) An arc, ①, created from the diagonal Root 2 (√2) line, **HF**, demarcates the interior face of the south wall of the Ḥeb-Sed Court.
2) Arc ②, generated from the Root 3 (√3) line, creates a vertical line that aligns with the north side of the throne dais and the half-wall separating the forecourts of West Chapel '0' and West Chapel 1.
3) The Root 4 (√4) arc ③, created from the vertical line in #2, produces a vertical line, which aligns with a similar half-wall between West Chapels 1 and 2, but also one of the doorways to the southernmost *dormitory* along the East Chapel row.
4) A vertical line derived from the Root 5 (√5) arc ④ created from the Root 4 (√4) line in #3 aligns along the north side of the dividing wall between West Chapels 2 and 3.
5) A Root 6 (√6) line derived from arc ⑤, created from the line in #4 aligns with the interior wall between West Chapels 3 and 4.
6) Arc ⑥ produces the Root 7 (√7) line that aligns with a doorway in another *dormitory* along the East Chapel row.

One of the design grid templates for the South Entrance Hall and "House of Beauty" embalming center consists of six overlapping or interconnected *Phi* (Φ) Rectangles *(Fig. 7-41)* as well as three Root 2 (√2) Squares.

1) The primary *Phi* (Φ) Rectangle, ①, whose base line is the centerline of the Entrance Hall and extends outside the south (leftmost) wall, outlines the general shape of the South Entrance Hall. The '**ab**' line of this *Phi* (Φ) Rectangle ends at a line running along the east faces of the unique "T3" square pillars (marked as '**G**'). (This line extending from the '**b**' point coincides with the '**c**' line of another *Phi* (Φ) Rectangle referred to in *Fig. 7-45*.) The shorter '**bc**' line that derives from the *Phi* (Φ) arc generates a line running through the middle of the wall between the Entrance Hall and the Exit Vestibule (near the doorway to the Exit Vestibule marked as '**I**').

2) The width of the second *Phi* (Φ) Rectangle, ②, comprises two of the four squares of the 4-by-4 grid. It generates a line, which extends north (right) and aligns with the foundation base of Temple '**T**'.

3) Arcs ③ and ④ are generated from two overlapping *Phi* (Φ) Rectangles. Arc ③ demarcates the interior face of the south wall of the Enclosure, while arc ④ delineates the line against which the south wall of Room '**V**' was laid out.

4) *Phi* (Φ) Rectangles ⑤ and ⑥ produce lines **FG** and **EF** respectively of the **EFGH** square used extensively in design work for the other grids below.

5) The Root 2 (√2) arc ⑦, located in the lowest left square of the 4-by-4 grid, demarcates the location of the exterior of the south wall minus the bastions.

6) The Root 2 (√2) arc ⑧ generates an east-west line against which several walls of the "House of Beauty" align.

7) The Root 2 (√2) arc ⑨, generated from the **EFGH** square, aligns with the interior face of the south wall of the Ḥeb-Sed Court.

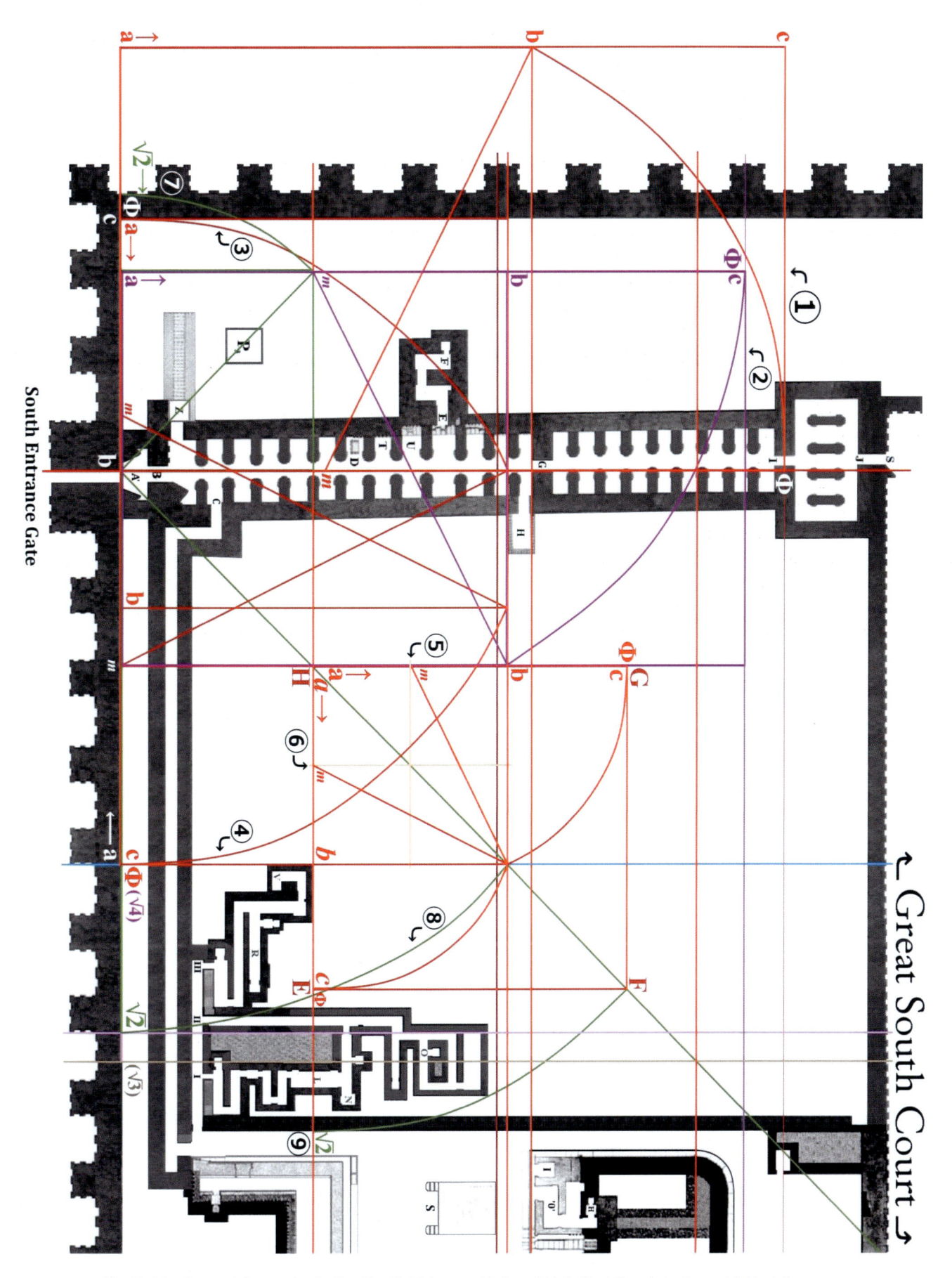

Fig. 7-41 – Sacred Geometry in the South Entrance Hall and Ḥeb-Sed Court design grid, Part 4

Note the double horizontal lines near the "Heart Chamber" (marked as '**H**') in the Entrance Hall that separate the first 22 columns representing Lower Egypt from the 20 columns representing Upper Egypt (see Chapter 5). These double lines *reappear* later on in this chapter. Also note that if the Entrance Hall was not constructed at a 1.5° offset then many – if not all – of the Sacred Ratios would not fit or line up correctly with the various features in the Ḥeb-Sed Court as it presently exists. This is additional proof that Imhotep purposely intended the Entrance Hall to have a 1.5° offset from the beginning to align the various grids used to design the various walls and other elements in the Ḥeb-Sed Court and elsewhere, and wasn't an accidental misalignment during construction as Lauer had asserted.

This rather small sample size of the usage of Root Rectangle Templates may seem somewhat limited, nevertheless it points toward the inescapable conclusion that Imhotep used them with such regularity that it can't be coincidental. Given the prominence of the square **EFGH** in many of the grids used to design the South Entrance Hall and Ḥeb-Sed Court quadrant, it is easy to conclude that Imhotep intended to build something in that spot, but was unable to do so. The most likely reason for this was the death of Djoser, which put a halt to many of the projects within the Step Pyramid Enclosure.

While it may seem several distinctly different grid systems were used to design the South Entrance Hall and Ḥeb-Sed Court quadrant, this by itself may prove that its plan went through several different building phases, each distinctly different from the other in order to accomplish separate design philosophies. This is not out of the question as J.-P. Lauer theorized there is evidence of at least five or six building phases for the Step Pyramid complex as a whole.

When plans for the Entrance Hall and Ḥeb-Sed Court quadrant were complete, Imhotep went on to finish designing the rest of the Step Pyramid Enclosure. After turning the old Entrance and Exit Gates into false gates, Imhotep added 12 more false gates to this third version of the temenos wall. This was to embody the Sacred Number 14 in its design. As it presently exists, the 14 False Gates and 1 Entrance Gate in the Enclosure Wall are mostly evenly spaced around its perimeter, but some are not. For example, on the east wall, False Gates 13 and 14 were likely to have been Exit and Entrance Gates respectively, with the later addition of False Gates 11 and 12 spaced evenly between False Gate 13 and the northeast corner. We have already seen why False Gates 1, 2 and 3 were spaced the way they are now (see *Fig. 7-13*), but it's possible Imhotep used a different arrangement initially at the outset of expanding the Step Pyramid Enclosure to its present size.

A couple of simple renderings of what this original design may have looked like compared to what exists today are depicted below. The squares denote the four corners of the Enclosure Wall. The numbered dots represent the false gates within the wall. The black diamond in the lower left hand (southeast) corner represents the South Entrance Gate. The numbers between the dots represent the number of bastions between the false gates and corners.

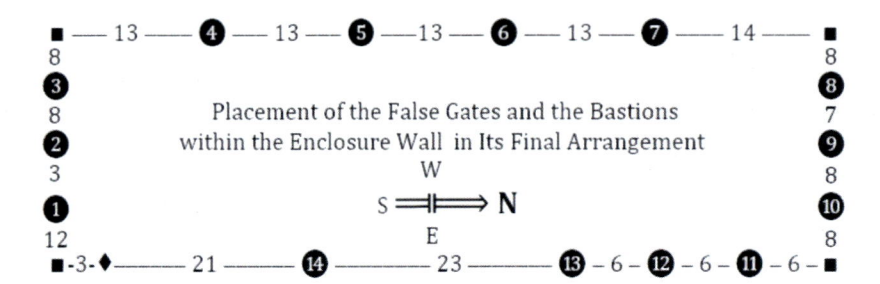

```
■ — 13 —— ❹ — 13 —— ❺ — 13 — ❻ — 13 — ❼ —— 14 —— ■
8                                                      8
❸                                                      ❽
8        Placement of the False Gates and the Bastions 7
❷        within the Enclosure Wall in Its Final Arrangement ❾
3                         W                            8
❶                       S ⇒║⇒ N                        ❿
12                        E                            8
■-3-♦———— 21 ———— ⓮ ———— 23 ———— ⓭ – 6 – ⓬ – 6 – ⓫ – 6 –■
```

Here is what Imhotep may have originally conceived for the Third Enclosure Wall during the initial design phase.

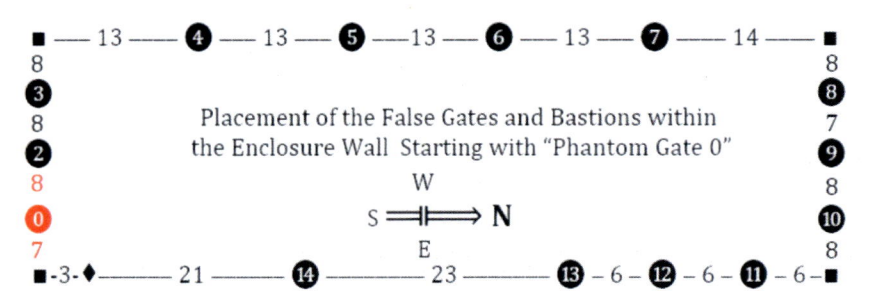

```
■ — 13 —— ❹ — 13 —— ❺ — 13 — ❻ — 13 — ❼ —— 14 —— ■
8                                                      8
❸                                                      ❽
8        Placement of the False Gates and Bastions within 7
❷        the Enclosure Wall Starting with "Phantom Gate 0" ❾
8                         W                            8
⓿                       S ⇒║⇒ N                        ❿
7                         E                            8
■-3-♦———— 21 ———— ⓮ ———— 23 ———— ⓭ – 6 – ⓬ – 6 – ⓫ – 6 –■
```

Figure 7-42 shows a possible design for the south wall where the first False Gate, "Phantom Gate 0", would have been located.

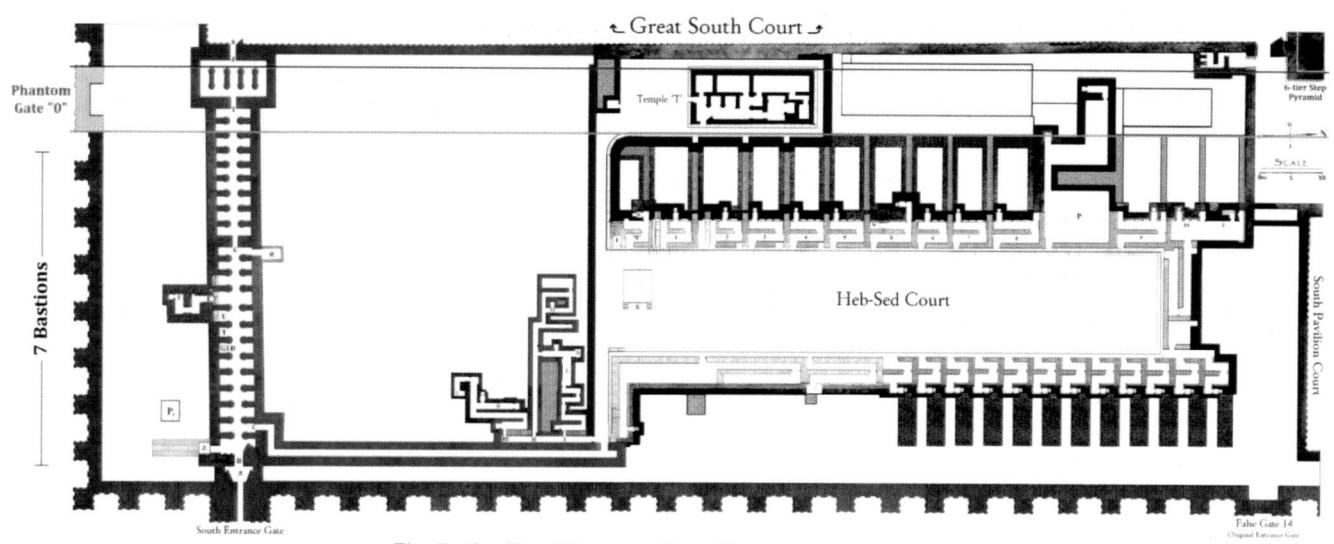

Fig. 7-42 – The "Phantom Gate 0" and the two grid lines derived from it outlining two important features of the Ḥeb-Sed Court

In this unrealized design, seven bastions fill the space between the southeast corner and this *phantom* False Gate instead of the 12 bastions as exist today. Here we have uneven spacing between the first three False Gates on the south wall, but I suspect Imhotep had originally planned mostly even spacing between these gates because two parallel lines bracketing this *phantom* gate are similar to the grid lines employed by Imhotep when he designed the *real* False Gates (see especially False Gate 2, *Fig. 7-13*). These two lines would not have existed otherwise if they had not been derived from this unknown *phantom* gate. Consequently, there are several prominent and important features aligned with the two lines. The most notable features that are aligned with the upper red line are the half-columns of the Exit Vestibule, the west wall of Temple 'T', and the south side of the original four-tier Step Pyramid. The lower green line was aligned with the west foundation platform of the first five West Chapels and the west walls of the other West Chapels.

When it became apparent the construction of the Second Enclosure could not proceed for structural reasons, Imhotep set about expanding the Enclosure to what eventually became its present size. Working from the plans of the First Enclosure and wanting to include Pits P_8 and P_9 as part of an expanded North Court within the new Enclosure, Imhotep began by creating a *Phi* (Φ) Rectangle from the base square **ABCD** in *Fig. 7-43*, also shown in *Figs. 7-22* and *7-23*. Arc ① of this *Phi* (Φ) Rectangle ends at point 'c' that defines the south line, **EF**, of the rectangle, **ABEF**. Imhotep extended this line to the interior of the new east Enclosure Wall (originally designed for the Second Enclosure) to denote the northeast point 'G' of a new square, **GHIJ**, which he used as the base square for a 7-Part Root Rectangle Template. The height of this square is derived from a 45° line, **K**, starting at point 'G' and proceeds diagonally south (left) up to another point, '**I**' on the new south wall. Another 45° line, **L**, extends upward from the interior southeast corner, '**J**' to point '**H**', defining the northwest (upper right) corner of this square. This line continues upward to intersect the midpoint of would become the west wall of the Enclosure. Note a vertical line extending downward from the center point where the two 45° lines intersect in the Great South Court. This line passes through Temple 'T' at the point where walls and columns define the rooms that I have designated as a *surgical suite* (see *Fig. 3-61*). This signifies its importance when repurposing Temple 'T' for use in the Ḥeb-Sed Court medical center after the completion of the *sed*-festival ceremonies.

Several arcs of a 7-Part Root Rectangle Template terminate at important architectural features along the east wall. An arc from the Root 6 ($\sqrt{6}$) line ends at the new northeast corner of the expanded North Court (*Fig. 7-43*).

1) A line extending westward (up) from the midpoint ('*m*') of *Phi* (Φ) Rectangle **ABCD** that creates arc ① marks the doorway that will eventually lead to the new North Mortuary Temple of the six-tier Step Pyramid complex.
2) Arc ② of the Root 2 ($\sqrt{2}$) Rectangle ends at a point which, when extended west (up), aligns with the doorway to the North Pavilion Court.
3) Arc ③, generated from a Root 3 ($\sqrt{3}$) Rectangle, aligns with the north wall of the First Enclosure where it ends at the east Enclosure Wall.
4) Arc ④ doesn't readily align with any architectural feature (if you discount the fact that it ends near the north bastion of False Gate 12), but it does set up the vertical line that defines a Root 5 ($\sqrt{5}$) Double Square. The arc ⑤ coming from this Double

184

Square does align with the interior corner of the north bastion of False Gate 11 along the interior face of the east wall of the Enclosure.

5) The Root 6 (√6) arc ⑥ ends at a point on the east wall where construction of the North Wall would begin in order to avoid building over the subterranean chambers lying beneath Pits **P₈** and **P₉**. The diagonal line that generates arc ⑥ also just happens to touch the southwest (upper left) corner, **F**, of the *Phi* (Φ) Rectangle, **ABFE**, which further adds to the notion that there is a highly cohesive design process at work here.

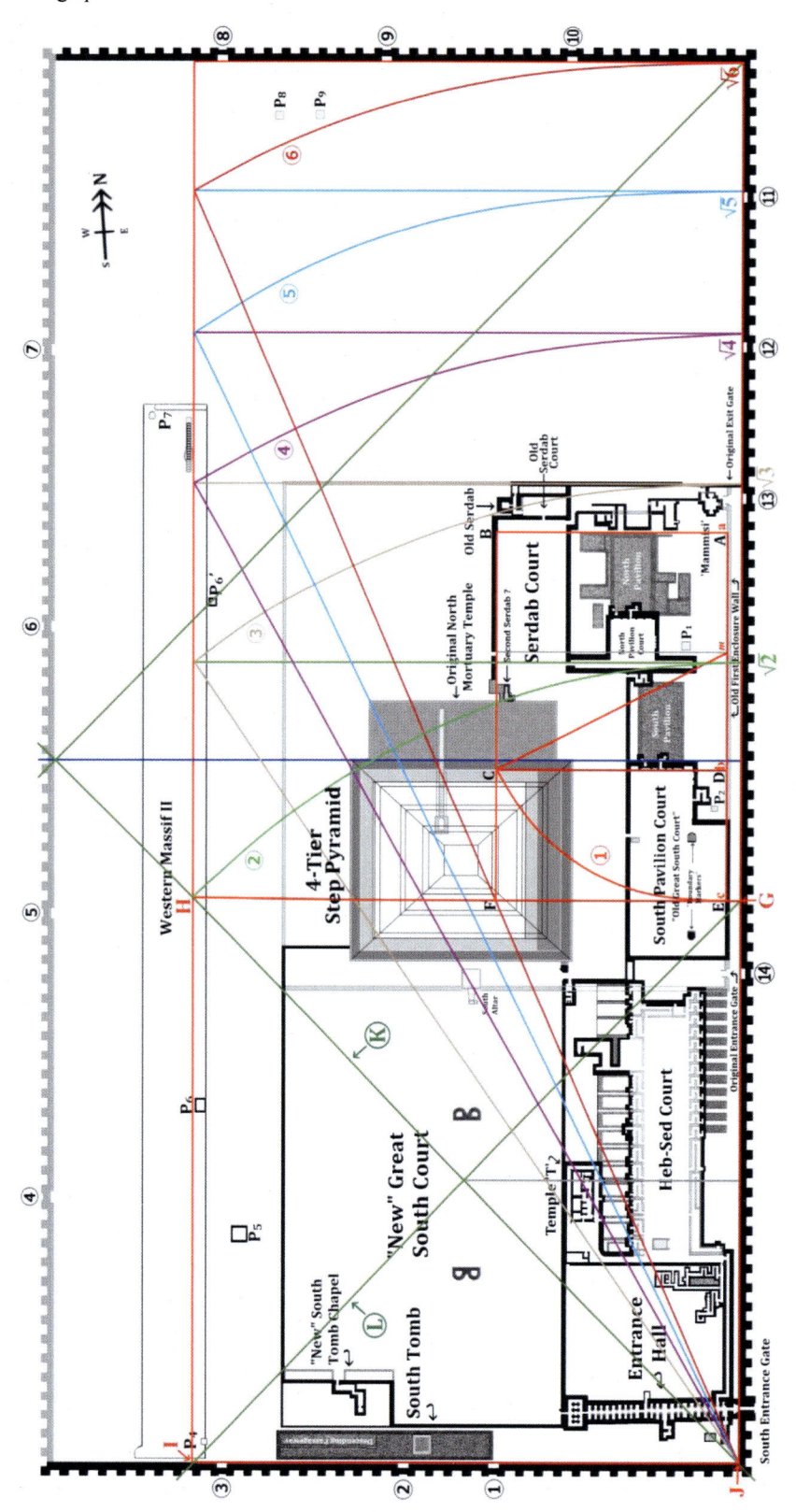

Fig. 7-43 – The layout of the new Third Enclosure derived from a 7-Part Root Rectangle Template

In addition to finalizing the size of the North Court, the location of the new west wall needed to be determined. The obvious necessity of constructing Western Massif III along with Western Massif I was to provide a protective buffer for the much older Western Massif II (see *Fig. 6-68*). For the new west wall (the grayed-out section at the top of the Enclosure Wall in *Fig. 7-43*), Imhotep used a *Phi* (Φ) Rectangle to fix its location (*Fig. 7-44*).

In a nod to the importance of the old North Exit Gate and the soon-to-be constructed *mammisi* birthing rooms, Imhotep placed the '*a*' point of the *Phi* (Φ) Rectangle even with the end of the short exit corridor that leads out of the North Exit Gate. Coincidentally, the location of this point is half the distance between the self-closing door and the interior face of the First Enclosure Wall (see *Fig. 7-25*). Eventually, with the area beyond this point filled in, the self-closing door from the old North Exit Gate was used only to access to the new *mammisi* birthing rooms.

Imhotep also used two *Phi* (Φ) Rectangles to position False Gates 8 and 10 along the north wall. The '*ab*' dimension of the base squares for both of these rectangles are the distance between the (green) ⅓ lines and the center (red) ½ line. The two base squares of the *Phi* Rectangles are different sizes because the distance between the ½ centerline and the ⅓ lines are slightly different due to the off-center position to the west (up) of False Gate 9. As a result, the number of bastions between these two false gates and False Gate 9 reflects this difference.

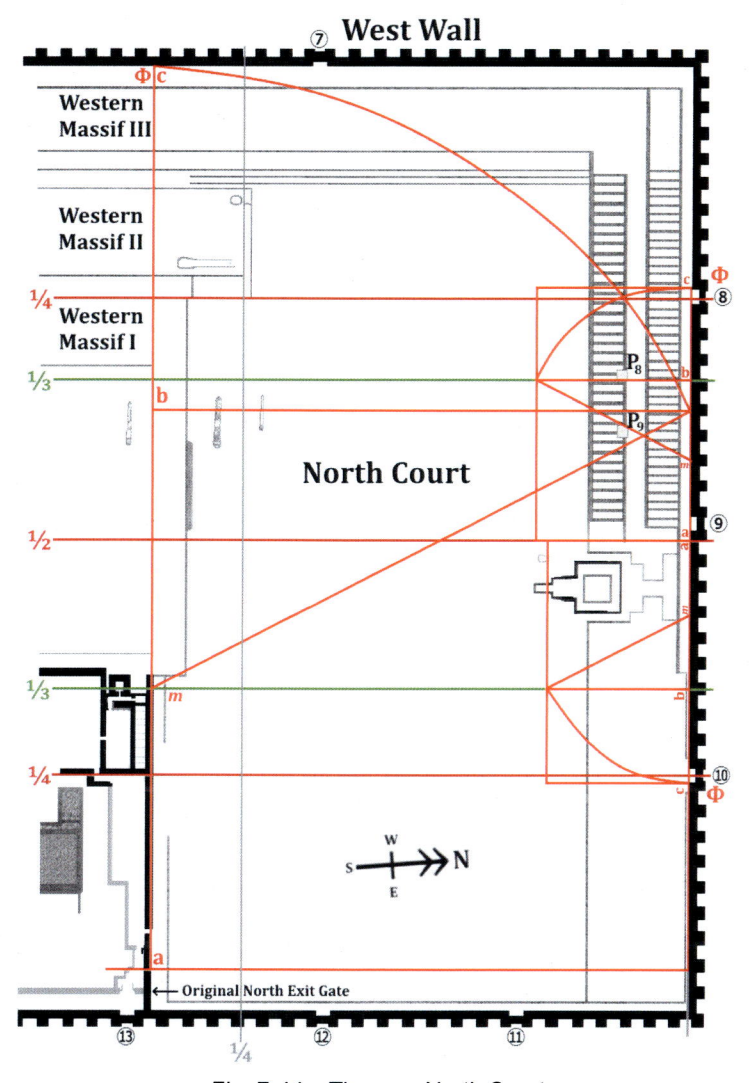

Fig. 7-44 – The new North Court

A new vertical centerline for this third version of the Enclosure needed to be established. Imhotep had used the north side of the Mastabas M₂/M₃ for the vertical centerline of the First Enclosure, which also runs parallel to the new façade installed on the south face of the South Pavilion. This time, he chose to run this new vertical centerline (the blue ½ line in *Fig. 7-45*) the runs along the north side of the four-tier Step Pyramid, which also runs along the south exterior face of the original mastaba that became the South Pavilion.

186

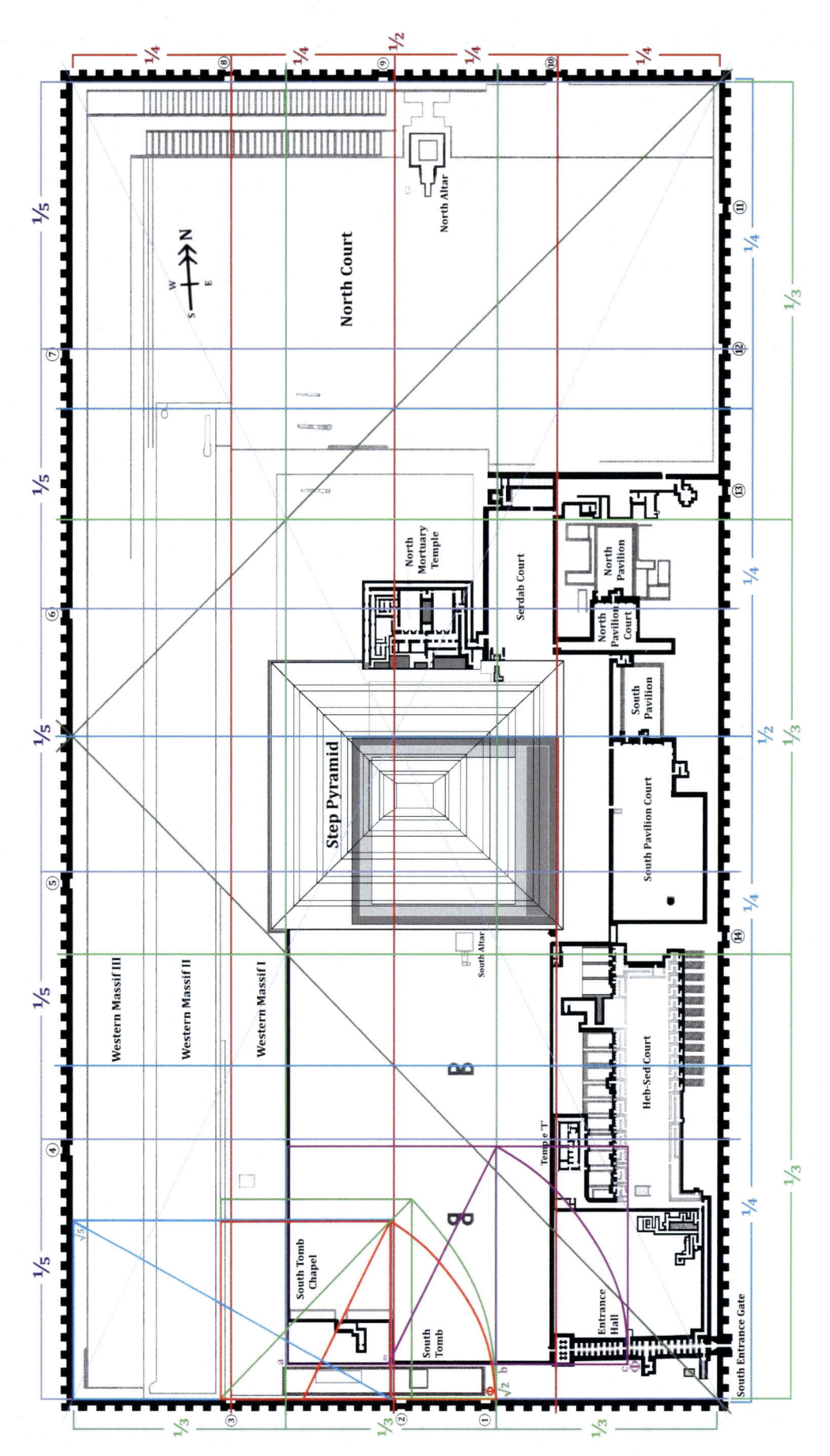

Fig. 7-45 – The new Enclosure subdivided into equal parts with the Key (Fig. 7-13) to the Step Pyramid's design

Once the dimensions of the new Enclosure were stretched to the north creating the new North Court, and also extended to the south encompassing the South Tomb, it is possible to see that the whole of it can be subdivided into equal parts in a number of different ways as part of the design process (*Fig. 7-45*). The overall size of the Enclosure is a Root 5 (√5) Double Square that has a ratio of 2:1, the same as the musical interval of an Octave. Dividing the Enclosure in half and in thirds simultaneously produces a ratio of either 3:2 or 2:3. Dividing 2 by 3 equals 0.67, or roughly a little larger than the short section of a *Phi* (Φ) Rectangle (.61803). In music, the Perfect Fifth has a ratio of 3:2. Dividing the Enclosure again into four vertical and three horizontal parts produces a ratio of 4:3, which is the same as the musical interval of a Perfect Fourth. This 4:3 ratio equals 1.3333, and when multiplied by 100 results in a value of 133.33, one of the more common measurements used in the design of the Step Pyramid Enclosure that was discovered by J.-P. Lauer. [105] When the Enclosure is divided into an additional five vertical and six horizontal parts (implied by dividing the ⅓ horizontal segments in two), it is possible to create ratios of 5:4 and 6:5, the same ratios for the musical intervals of Major and Minor Thirds. All of this implies Imhotep imbued a subtle reference to a 7-note diatonic musical scale within the design of the Step Pyramid Enclosure.

Secretly embedding the musical intervals of the Octave, Perfect Fourth, Perfect Fifth, Major and Minor Thirds into the Step Pyramid Enclosure's architecture lends support to the idea that perhaps the Egyptians believed that all the arts and sciences are fully integrated and complimentary to one another. This is central to the teachings of Pythagoras, the ancient Greek philosopher who studied in the mystery schools of Egypt. He taught that mathematics (the Theory of Proportions), architecture (the Pythagorean Theorem and Sacred Geometry), music (Pythagorean Tuning), astronomy *(musica universalis,* or "music of the spheres", a precursor to modern astronomy), health and medicine (as embraced in vegetarianism) were equal parts of a greater whole.

As you can see, the endpoints of a *Phi* (Φ) and Root 2 (√2) Sacred Ratios contained in the Key (as seen in *Fig. 7-13* and *Fig. 7-45*) to this design aligns with the east ⅓ line, which also passes through the Serdab housing a statue of Djoser. This readily confirms the Imhotep's use of Sacred Geometry and astronomy to design this great monument resulted in the alignment of the entire Enclosure with the circumpolar stars.

The 'c' endpoint of a second *Phi* (Φ) Rectangle, whose base is twice the width of the South Tomb Chapel and runs between the west wall of the Great South Court and the first ⅓ line, which is adjacent to False Gate 1, aligns with the eastern side of the 'T3' square pillars in the Entrance Hall. This is also where the line originating from point '**b**' of primary *Phi* (Φ) Rectangle ① as shown in *Fig. 7-41*.

Carrying the *leitmotif* of overlapping and interconnected Sacred Ratios a little further, Imhotep designed the Exit Vestibule to embody both the Root 2 (√2) Rectangle and the Root 5 (√5) Double Square (*Fig. 7-46*).

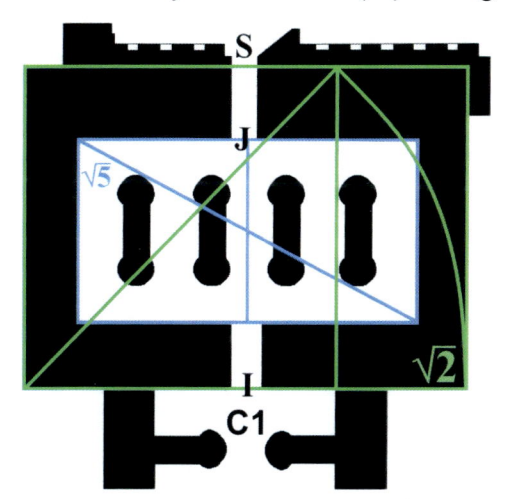

A little confession here: The interior space of the Exit Vestibule isn't exactly a Double Square; it's a little smaller. This may be due to possible inaccuracies inherent in the plans of the Step Pyramid Enclosure that exist today, but does this really make a difference? In the grand scheme of things, no. Why is it so important to notice that some measurements are *slightly off* in Imhotep's use of Sacred Geometry? Did Imhotep subscribe to the notion that "close enough is good enough"?

Fig. 7-46 – Sacred Geometry in the Exit Vestibule

There are many instances of purposeful design errors expressing the concept of *imperfect perfection* scattered throughout the Step Pyramid Enclosure. For example, the Enclosure Wall is 1,040 by 538 cubits. It should be either 1,040-by-528 cubits or 1,056-by- 528 cubits to be an exact 2:1 ratio Double Square. The interior of the Exit Vestibule is 36-by-19 feet. To symbolize the Sacred Ratio of a 2:1 Double Square, it should be either 36-by-18 feet (*my personal choice*) or 38-by-19 feet.

Architects tend to make adjustments as their designs progress to the construction phase. This is why some lines don't match up with architectural elements all the time, but are close enough to consider that Imhotep was using a grid-like system to position the different elements of the Enclosure during the design phase. Someone with a more exacting nature may be rankled by "close enough is good enough", but working architects are not so rigid in their use of Sacred Geometry during the design phase of a building project. Some accommodations always need to take place to realize a completed building project.

Perhaps Imhotep incorporated in his design of the Step Pyramid Enclosure a personal belief that all of physical reality is incomplete without recognizing the element of Divine Spirit (i.e., Ra-Atum) infused within it. Thus, he imbued the Step Pyramid's architecture with the concept that a *perfect* universe is rendered *imperfect* by our own limited vision of it. Inside the Step Pyramid Enclosure walls is a symbolic representation of the Afterlife in the *Sekhet-Aaru*, or *Field of Reeds*. Outside of the Enclosure is the world of the living here on Earth. By not *filling in the blanks*, or overtly incorporating a certain system of Sacred Geometry or spiritual philosophy into the Step Pyramid Enclosure's design, it is as if Imhotep is asking us to acknowledge there is a missing element in our personal belief systems. Because of this, we need to become aware of the presence of Divine Energy within all things, seen and unseen, not unlike *seeing* the human spine and skull within the empty spaces of the Entrance Hall.

This *perfectly imperfect* model of the nature of the universe may have led to Imhotep's *imperfect* application of the inherently *perfect* system of Sacred Geometry, and why the Step Pyramid has only six tiers. Imhotep's later design of the funerary complex of Sekhemkhet, Djoser's successor, was purportedly to have a step pyramid with seven tiers. However, there being one less tier or mastaba on Djoser's pyramid meant that the seventh invisible *step* of Djoser's pyramid was to be that of the pharaoh himself when he became immortal and *one with the gods*.

This *slightly imperfect* utilization of Sacred Geometry is reminiscent of how mathematical fractions were represented in the form of the Eye of Horus (*Fig. 7-47*). Allegedly used in the standard weights and measurement system of the time,[106] the creation of six hieroglyphs from parts of the Eye of Horus to represent fractional values of the number one (1), or *heqat*. When added together, the value of these individual parts is slightly less than one *heqat* (1/2 + 1/4 + 1/8 + 1/16 + 1/32 + 1/64 = 63/64).

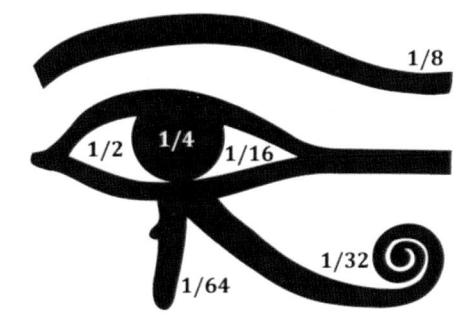

Fig. 7-47 – Fractions embodied within the parts of the Eye of Horus

Though the presumption that the *Eye of Horus method* was commonly used for fractional mathematics has recently been called into question,[107] it nonetheless holds true that this simple method of representing fractions held sway during the Old Kingdom to be replaced by a system that added back the missing 1/64th unit during the Middle Kingdom. More importantly, however, is that the ancient Egyptians did not appear averse to using a system that was outwardly *imperfect*.

Imhotep's deliberately imperfect use of Sacred Geometry can also explain why he may have used the 8:7 and 22:7 ratios mentioned previously to represent *Pi* (π). The 22:7 ratio (3.142857) does not reflect the *true* or *perfect* value of *Pi* ($\pi = 3.14159\infty$). Using a slightly larger value for *Pi* may be an expression of the typically ancient Egyptian belief that if they did not *Live-in-Truth* (*ankes-em-maat*) in their daily lives, they will always *miss the mark* and chaos will ensue. (In Western religions, this often refers to *sin*, the original definition of which was related to archery. When an archer launched their arrow, the spotter observing where the arrow landed would shout out "sin" if the arrow missed hitting its mark.) Although we may not be consciously aware of these slight imperfections when we behold Imhotep's masterpiece, we can rest assured they are *hiding in plain sight*, and it is up to each of us to expand our vision in order to see them, and to recognize what Imhotep is trying to teach us from so long ago.

I freely admit I might be reading more into this than what can be proven by the available archeological discoveries, but not revealing it would be intellectually dishonest, and – who knows – we may yet stumble upon some hidden wisdom along the way. Is this interpretation a product of the author's 21st century mind-set, or could it be the way we think and perceive the modern world around us is an unconscious inheritance from our ancient Egyptian ancestors and we are not even aware of it? How the ancient Egyptians viewed geometry and mathematics as it relates to the expression of Divine Energy within all of nature is unknown. It may well be that Imhotep is talking to us from 4700 years ago by expressing in the design of the Step Pyramid temple complex the idea that everything in nature is interrelated: medicine, architecture, science, music, and so on, and we should live our lives in harmony and balance with it. Ultimately, we must realize the Universe is not imperfect, just our image of it.

The Parthenon

It appears that even the Greeks and Romans, who used Sacred Geometry to design their monuments, were equally prone to *missing the mark* so to speak. For example, the Parthenon of Athens is one of the most aesthetically perfect structures from the ancient world, both in design and execution. Yet, it is hardly *perfect* in any sense of the word. There are no perfect right angles or straight and parallel lines in the entire structure. The columns bulge slightly in the middle, and they are not evenly spaced along the front portico.

The Greek architect's design tricks the eye into seeing harmony and balance in the Parthenon's façade. However, a closer examination reveals the painful truth that strict adherence to the design principles of Sacred Geometry were not executed *perfectly* to create this marvelous building. This is beyond accidental; it is deliberate, and for the same reasons as outlined above. In other words, "close enough is good enough". But there's more going on here than meets the eye. *Literally*.

The Parthenon's architect fine-tuned its final design because the curvature of the human eye would cause the observer to believe something was terribly distorted. For example, a perfectly flat surface would appear concaved because of this anatomical anomaly. Most arguments against the Greeks use of Sacred Geometry in the Parthenon's design usually stem from a few sources who incorrectly measured various features of the Parthenon from sets of poorly drawn illustrations or plans. We can forgive those who used inaccurate plans to formulate their opinions, but for everyone else to quote those same inaccurate sources is nothing more than intellectual laziness of the worst kind. [108] This also appears to be the case with opinions concerning ancient Egyptian architecture. By now, it should become apparent that ancient architects, both Egyptian and their architectural progeny, all used Sacred Geometry as a *guiding principle*, not something adhered to in an unyieldingly dogmatic manner.

While not readily apparent, the West Chapels of the Ḥeb-Sed Court seem to have a hidden organization (*Fig. 7-48*.) When put into groups of similarly sized and embellished structures, the underlying unified design becomes somewhat evident. The reason for this isn't too obvious, but Enclosure 'P' is the same size as Chapels 9 and 10 combined, thus the combination of Enclosure P, West Chapels 9, 10 and J infers a final group of five. A different way of looking at how the West Chapels are organized is that there are two groups of 5 chapels with arched roofs between the 3 flat-roofed chapels, '0', X and J. *Take your pick*. Once again, Imhotep is hiding more things *in plain sight*.

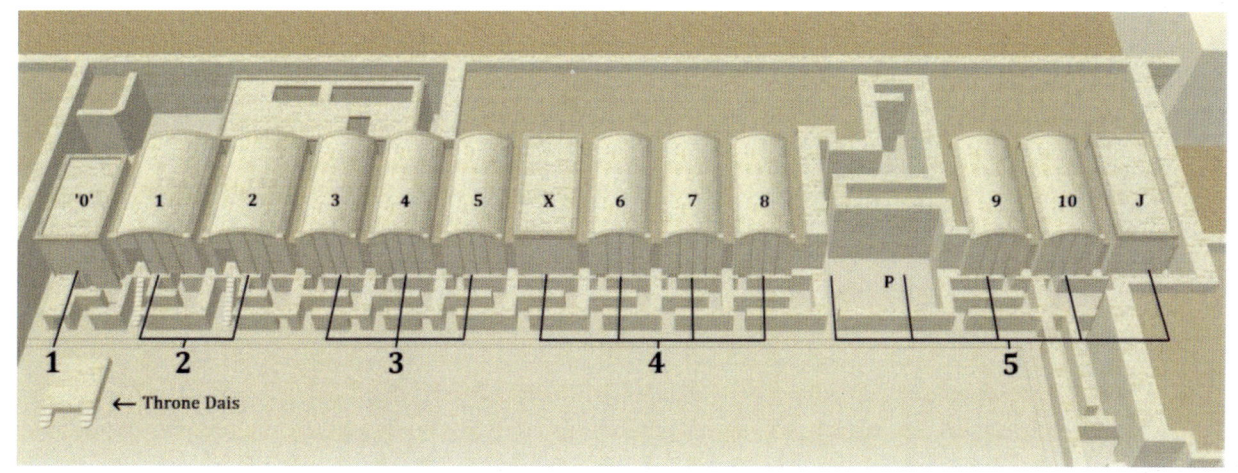

Fig. 7-48 – The hidden organization of the West Chapels of the Ḥeb-Sed Court

The Sacred Geometry of the Entrance Vestibule and the Enclosure Wall

Imhotep's use of Sacred Geometry is apparent even in the smallest and seemingly insignificant of architectural details. Once the design grid using the tools of Sacred Geometry was firmly established, the general plan of the southeast quadrant could be determined. Imhotep then could begin to design the South Entrance Gate and the Entrance Hall. Since the Entrance Vestibule (or, "Sacrum Room") is the first room one encounters when entering the South Entrance Gate, we shall start there with our examination of Imhotep's use of Sacred Geometry in designing this mortuary complex.

The sacrum and the legs attached to it are the foundation of the human skeleton (*Fig. 7-49*). So, too, is the Entrance Hall and the Entrance Vestibule immediately after it is the foundation of the Sacred Geometry used to design the Step Pyramid Enclosure as a whole (*Fig. 7-50*). Many of the Sacred Ratios in the Sacred Geometry *Toolkit* are present in the design of this "Sacrum Room". Imhotep probably had a general concept in mind for the Entrance Vestibule that took the shape of the sacrum from the skeletal system (see *Figs. 3-6* and *3-8*).

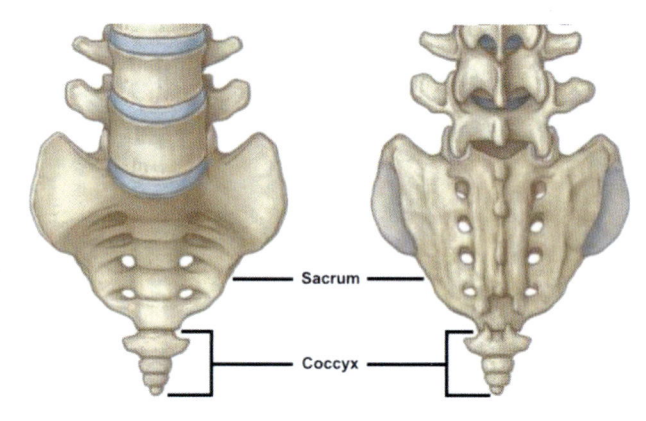

Fig. 7-49 – The Sacrum at the base of the Human Spine

Below is the Entrance Hall and Entrance Vestibule ("Sacrum Room") as it appears on J.-P. Lauer's plan:

The horizontal and vertical patterns in *Fig. 7-50* indicate the remnants of the flooring found *in situ*; and recorded by J.-P. Lauer, in his initial excavation plans in the 1920s. For the sake of clarity, these lines and shaded areas that only depict flooring and infill material no longer appear in subsequent illustrations. Note also that the Vestibule is slightly smaller than indicated in this early drawing. These differences have been corrected in *Fig. 7-51*.

The first thing to notice about this portion of the South Entrance Gate is that the Second Corridor (**B.**) is a bit wider and off center from the Entrance Corridor (**A.**). This is a deliberate design feature, as the 1.5° offset to the south of the entire Entrance Hall begins here (see *Fig. 6-31*). Speculative though it may be, what follows may explain the method used to design the South Entrance Gate, the Entrance Corridor (**A.**), Entrance Vestibule (**A.′**), and subsequent elements of the Entrance Hall from the Second Corridor (**B.**) up to the Exit Vestibule and its exit doorway (marked as '**S**') (see *Fig. 3-6*).

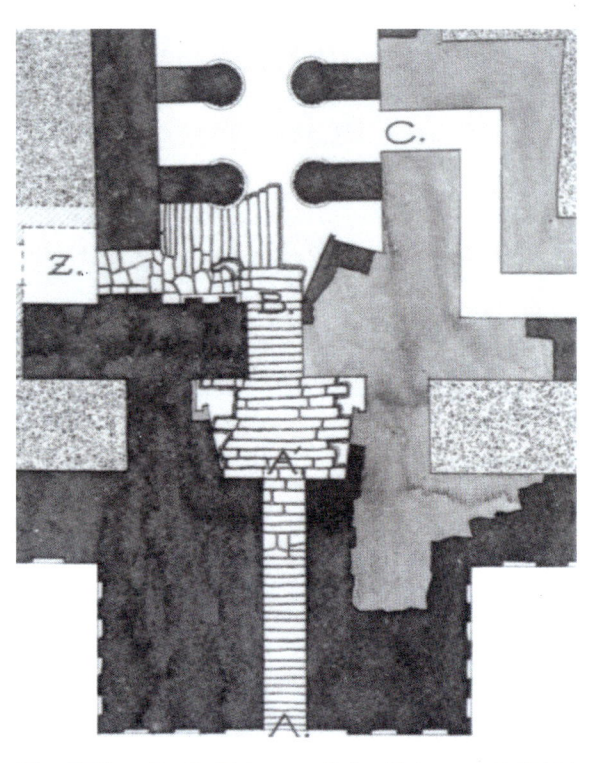

Fig. 7-50 – South Entrance Gate. Entrance Hall (A.), Entrance Vestibule ("Sacrum Room" – A.′) and Second Corridor (B). The 'C.' corridor goes to the Ḥeb-Sed Court

After the location of the South Entrance Gate and its Entrance Corridor (**A.**) was determined, Imhotep created a template using the tools of Sacred Geometry to design the Entrance Vestibule, or "Sacrum Room" (**A.′** in *Fig. 7-51*).

Using a rectangular 8-by-16 grid [itself a Root 5 (√5) Double Square], Imhotep first laid out the shape of the Vestibule within 7 of the 8 vertical units of this grid, a clear expression of the 8:7 ratio discussed above. Starting at the right side of *Fig. 7-51*, the layout of the various features of the South Entrance Vestibule primarily used Root 2 (√2) Rectangles. Red *touch points* highlight these features along the lowest grid line that resulted from using these Sacred Ratios.

1. The base square of a Root 2 (√2) Rectangle created from a 4-by-4 section of the design grid begins at grid line ①. The resultant Root 2 (√2) arc delineates the location of the north walls of corridors (**A.**) and (**B.**).
2. The creation of a Root 2 (√2) Rectangle from a 7-by-7 square starts at grid line ②, and ends at grid line ⑫, which demarcates the south wall of corridor (**B.**).
3. The *hinge* of the north stone door (see *Fig 1-13*) is located at grid line ③. From here, the creation of a Root 2 (√2) Rectangle from a 4-by-4 square indicates the centerline of the Entrance Corridor (**A.**).
4. The creation of yet another 4-by-4 Root 2 (√2) Rectangle starting at grid line ⑤ denotes the south wall of the Entrance Corridor (**A.**).
5. At grid line ⑦, a 7-by-7 Root 2 (√2) Rectangle delineated the southern extent of the Entrance Vestibule ending at grid line ⑰.
6. Finally, Imhotep continued to *think outside the box* by first laying out a 2-by-2 Root 2 (√2) Rectangle starting at grid line ⑪. From this rectangle, he extended out a Root 3 (√3) Rectangle, the *touch point* of which is where the *hinge* of the south stone door is located.

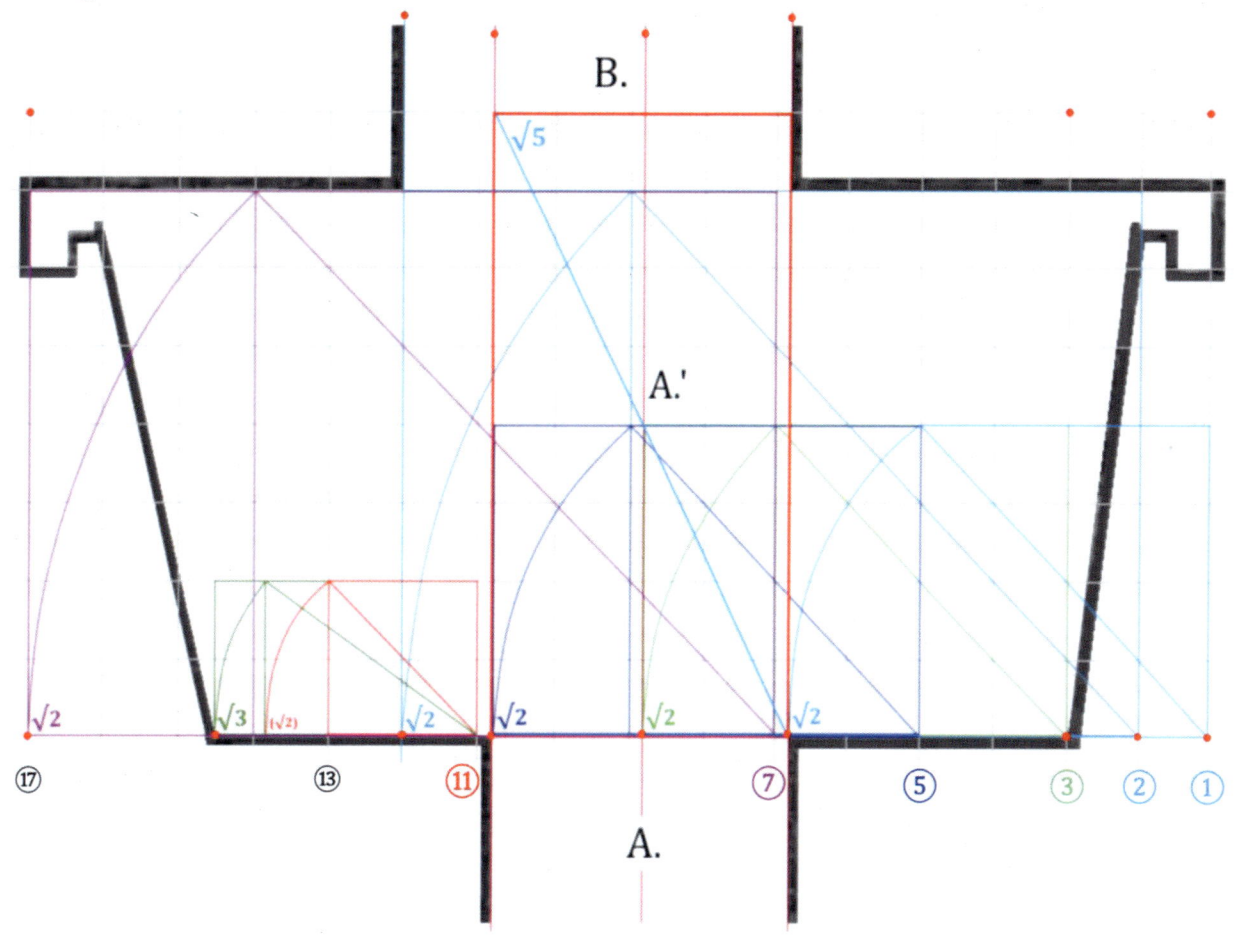

Fig. 7-51 – The Use of a Sacred Geometric Grid System to design the South Entrance Vestibule

On a side note, the reference number of seven of the 8 vertical grid lines used in creating the Sacred Ratios above are the same as the first seven prime numbers (2, 3, 5, 7, 11, 13, and 17). Though previously speculated about in Chapter 6, here may be actual proof of prime numbers used in ancient Egyptian architectural design, and possibly ties into the reason for using a grid with 8 vertical and 16 horizontal squares (2 times 8). In addition, the 16:7 ratio of the South Entrance Vestibule dimension relates directly to the 8:7 ratio. If you divide 16 by 7, the result is 2.285714. When divided by the *Magic Number 2* and adding 2, it equals 3.142857, the Egyptian formula for *Pi* (π), which is more often obtained by dividing 22 by 7 (see *Fig. 7-9*). Also, note that many of the red *touch points* related to various features of the Vestibule do not line up with the grid itself. This is another example of Imhotep employing grids as a starting point for his design, and not being inflexible in his use of Sacred Geometry; thus, making things less obvious and *hiding things in plain sight* once again.

The design of the Enclosure Wall surrounding the Step Pyramid also uses Sacred Geometry (*Fig. 7-52*). The combination of the space between the bastions, a Root 5 ($\sqrt{5}$) Double Square, and the wall immediately behind these spaces becomes a base square (**ab**) for a *Phi* (Φ) Rectangle. The width of the bastions themselves is the smaller portion of the *Phi* (Φ) Rectangle (**bc**).

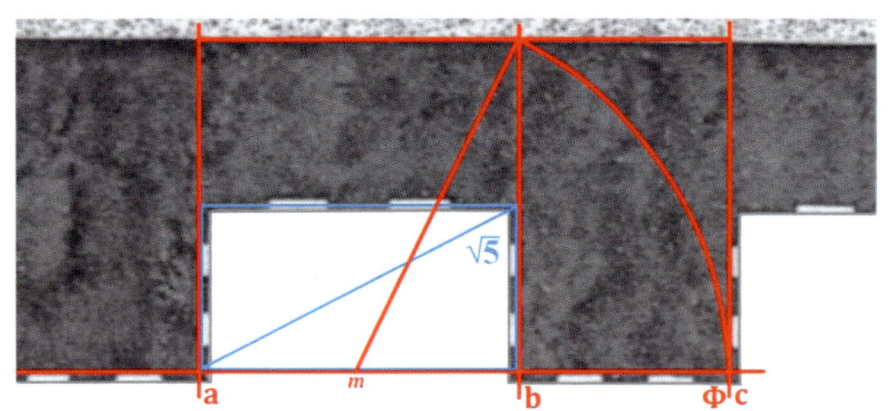

Fig. 7-52 – The Phi (Φ) Rectangle as a template for the design of the Enclosure Wall bastions

The amazing thing about the Step Pyramid complex is that the construction of this monument was from leftover and unfinished structures such as Mastaba M$_1$ and the mastabas that became the North and South Pavilions. Genius that he was, Imhotep was able to create a marvelous temple using Sacred Geometry to the point where the arrangement of all these buildings and their parts appears as if it was designed this way from the beginning.

The Tradition of Using Sacred Geometry by Ancient Egyptian Architects Before and After Imhotep

Studying other funerary monuments in the midst of investigating the secrets contained in the design of the Step Pyramid Enclosure may seem to be an unnecessary diversion. However, in order to understand why Imhotep used Sacred Geometry when designing the Step Pyramid and its ancillary structures, we need to understand how other ancient Egyptian architects used it as well. Indeed, some of these same architects may well have been Imhotep's ancestors who passed down the knowledge of their craft.

Some have argued that there is no proof the ancient Egyptians used Sacred Geometry in the design of their temples and mortuary architecture with the possible exception of temples built by the Greek Ptolemys in later times when they supposedly *imported* Sacred Geometry.[109] (*How ironic!*) This is refuted by the mere fact that such Sacred Geometry *tools* of the square roots of 2, 3, 4, 5, *Pi* (π) and *Phi* (Φ, the Golden Ratio) were used extensively throughout the design of the Step Pyramid Enclosure, and later, in the design of the Great Pyramid. That ancient Egyptian architects were familiar with the language of Sacred Geometry even earlier than Imhotep will now become evident as we go forward. Even if none of what I have discovered proves to be true examples of the use of Sacred Geometry that underlies the plans of these funerary complexes, the fact remains that there appears to be an overall, cohesive architectural design philosophy used by ancient Egyptian architects for much of its history. While it may not appear that Sacred Geometry was used much in architectural design work in later dynasties due to the political and social interruptions caused by the First and Second Intermediate Periods, this does not preclude its extensive use in the Pre-Dynastic and Old Kingdom period.

As we continue to examine the design of the Step Pyramid Enclosure, the obvious must be stated that Imhotep's work as an architect did not exist in a vacuum. Elements of Sacred Geometry as outlined above clearly exist in the plan of the Step Pyramid Enclosure. It is reasonable, therefore, to assume the traditions of using the tools of Sacred Geometry to design temples or funerary architecture must have existed long before Imhotep used them in this, his masterpiece. It also stands to reason these esoteric traditions continued long after Imhotep's death.

The Funerary Enclosure of Khasekhemwui at Abydos

In any scientific inquiry, only repeatable results can determine if a particular theory has any validity. If the presumption that Imhotep used Sacred Geometry to design the Step Pyramid Enclosure without the existence of such a tradition, then logically, any theory that he did so would be no more than wishful thinking. For this reason, I decided to look at the Funerary Enclosure of Khasekhemwui, Pharaoh Djoser's father or stepfather. I half expected only a rudimentary application of some of the Sacred Ratios discussed previously enough to confirm that Sacred Geometry was part of an ancient Egyptian architect's *bag-of-tricks*. Little did I know just how extensive a relative handful of these *sacred tools* were embedded in the design of this earlier monument.

In order to test this theory, I used a plan of the Khasekhemwui Funerary Enclosure I found in a magazine article.[110] Admittedly, the possibility exists that a little bit – or a *lot* – of inaccuracy will creep in when using a plan copied from the pages of a magazine. That being said, however, I was confident the plan was accurate enough to determine if the underlying design of the enclosure was based on Sacred Geometry. If so, then the importance and usage of these design principles inherited by successive generations of architects, including Imhotep, who later used these *sacred tools* to design the Step Pyramid Enclosure would be self-evident.

Before the Third Dynasty, pharaohs traditionally built their tombs and funerary enclosures in southern Egypt at Abydos. Tombs of these First and Second Dynasties monarchs are located in a place called Umm el-Qa'ab, which means 'Mother of Pots' due to the large quantity of broken pottery scattered throughout the site. The last king of the Second Dynasty, Khasekhemwui, like his predecessors, had both a traditional tomb there as well as a separate ceremonial funerary enclosure located a little less than 2 kilometers north of Umm el-Qa'ab in a place called the North Cemetery. No doubt, this massive funerary enclosure inspired the design of the Step Pyramid Enclosure, but Imhotep's design went a step further (*no pun intended*) by combining the Tomb of Djoser and a funerary enclosure into a single unified structure. If what I have discovered about Khasekhemwui's Funerary Enclosure is any indication, its design will no doubt verify that using Sacred Geometry to design temples and other monuments was a well-established tradition in the canon of ancient Egyptian architects long before Imhotep designed the Step Pyramid Enclosure.

As shown in Chapter 6, the similarity between the Step Pyramid Enclosure and Khasekhemwui's Funerary Enclosure, the *"Shunet el-Zebib"* at Abydos, is no coincidence. We do not know the rituals performed within the 'Shuneh', nor do we know what purpose it served. The most likely theory is that it was a *sed*-festival venue or used for other ceremonies. However, as it is devoid of any overt religious or ritual connotation inherent in its design, or what it was supposed to symbolize, it offers us a unique opportunity to assess its architectural design from a purely Sacred Geometry point of view. With a small temple or building of some sort located in the southeast corner, several funerary enclosures in north Abydos including those of Khasekhemwui and Peribsen seem to resemble the hieroglyph for "enclosure" (*Fig. 7-53*).

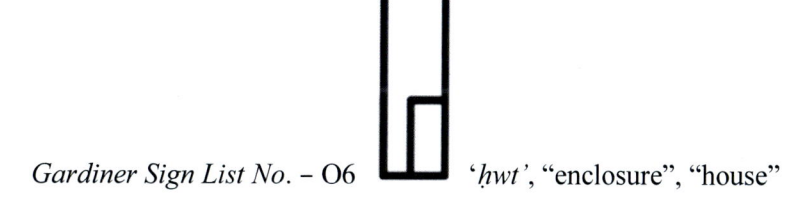

Gardiner Sign List No. - O6   '*ḥwt*', "enclosure", "house"

As seen in Chapter 3, *Fig. 3-57*, Imhotep clearly copied this idea when he designed the Great South Court of the Step Pyramid Enclosure to resemble the hieroglyph for *ḥwt* even more so. (The word, "hut", often defined as a "small house" or "shack" seems to have been derived from this hieroglyph.)

When restoration work on the *Shuneh* commenced in 1986 by David O'Connor and the Penn-Yale Expedition, this old mudbrick structure was in serious danger of collapsing and crumbling into dust. We are most fortunate today because the ongoing restoration work on this ancient enclosure by the North Abydos Expedition and the Institute of Fine Arts at New York City will go a long way in preserving one of Egypt's oldest royal monuments.[111]

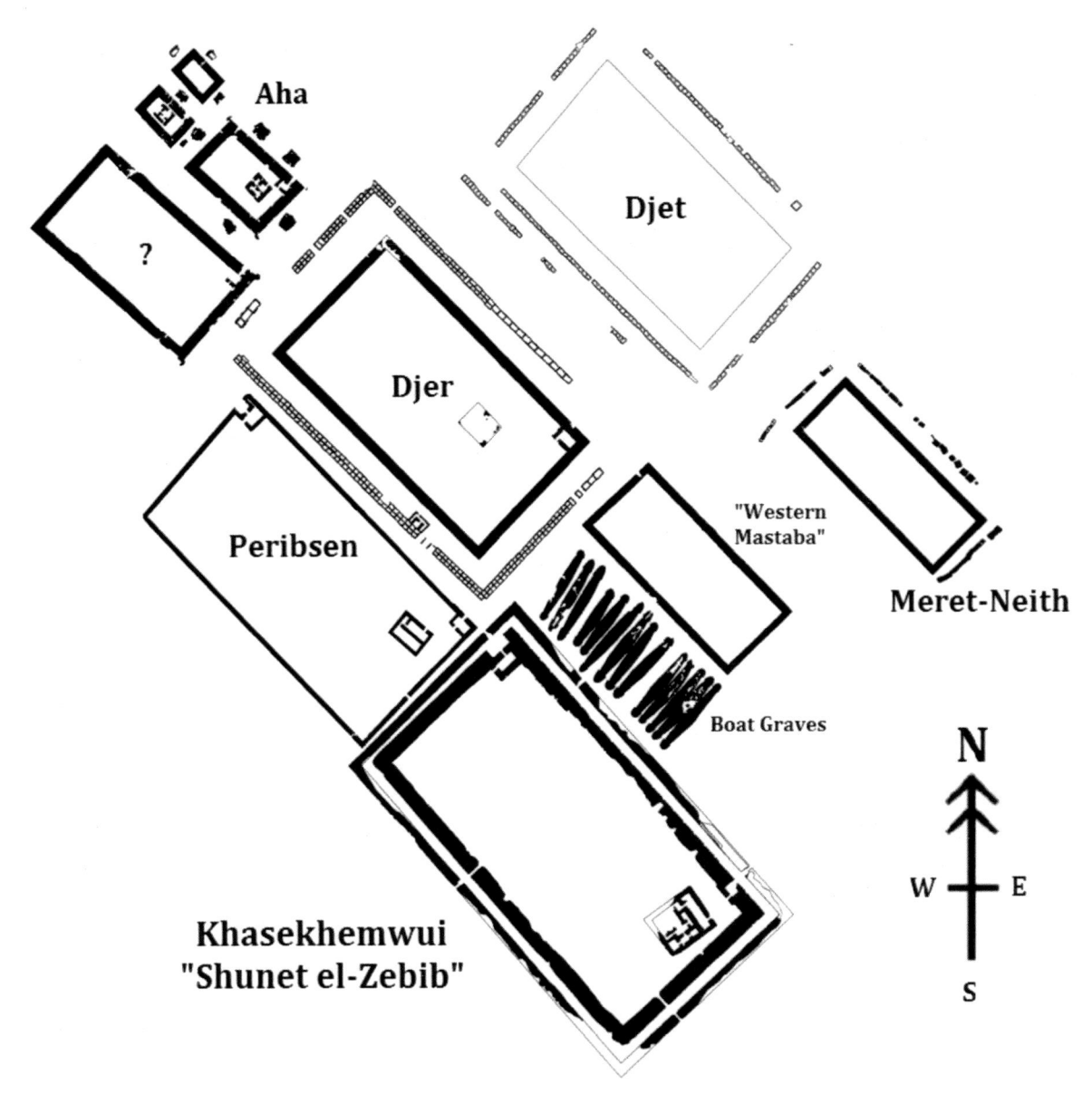

Fig. 7-53 – Funerary Enclosures of First and Second Dynasty Kings at north Abydos

Though larger than every other enclosure in the vicinity, it is easy to see how the architects of Khasekhemwui's Funerary Enclosure constructed it by roughly conforming to the space available. A couple of meters to the north of the *Shuneh* is the older Funerary Enclosure of Peribsen, also known as the 'Middle Fort' because it resembles military architecture. Close by to the east are 14 buried funerary boats (*there's that number 14 again!*), only recently excavated between 1987 and 1991. In *Fig. 7-52*, it is readily apparent how the architectural elements of north, east and south entrances of Peribsen's monument, as well as the position of the small cult chapel in its southeast corner, found their way into the design of Khasekhemwui's monument (*Fig. 7-54*).

The starting point for Khasekhemwui's architects to construct this monument was to first design the perimeter wall. Common belief maintains that the design of the larger interior wall came first and the perimeter wall was a later addition.[112] However, when studying this enclosure, it became obvious the design of the perimeter wall used the tools of Sacred Geometry by which the four gates leading into the enclosure's interior could then be accurately positioned. Subsequently, the larger interior wall's placement within the perimeter wall was determined during the design phase, along with the unique staggered entrances in its north and east walls. This conclusion came about after studying the interior wall by itself and finding only a few instances of Sacred Ratios used in its design. From a planning and construction point of view, building the interior wall must have commenced first, followed by the perimeter wall, which may explain why it seems to have been an afterthought.

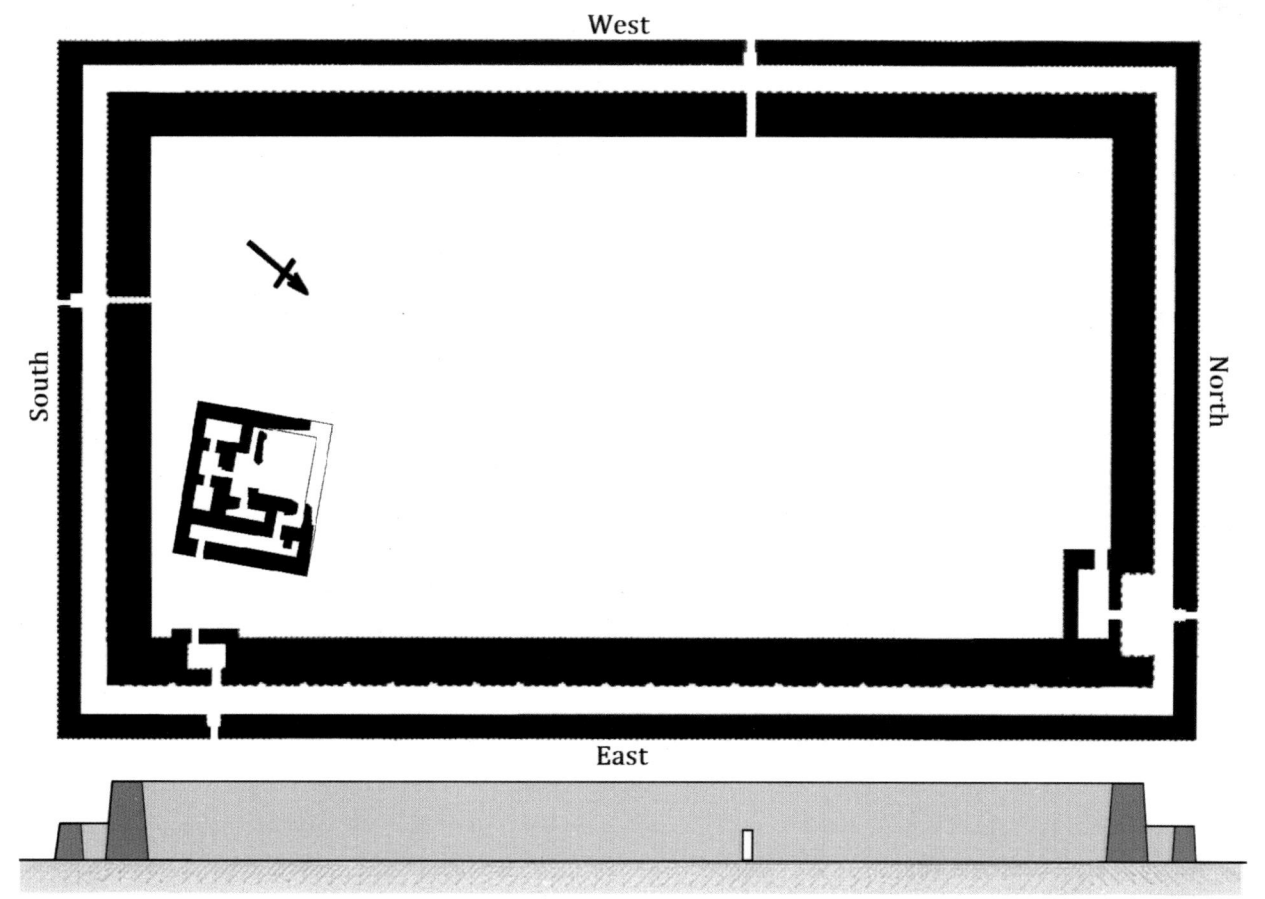

Fig. 7-54 – Khasekhemwui's Funerary Enclosure at Abydos [15]

Despite appearing deceptively simple in its plan, the underlying design of the *Shuneh* is amazingly complex. The first task facing Khasekhemwui's architect was to define the approximate length and width of the perimeter wall. This was to determine where the south entrance was to be located in the south wall, but did not have to be exactly perfect at the outset of constructing the perimeter wall. Only the northeast and southeast corners of the perimeter wall needed to be established at the beginning of construction due to the proximity of the Funerary Enclosure of Peribsen to the north and the 14 boats graves to the east (*Fig. 7-53*).

As stated previously, every *Phi* (Φ) Rectangle has two parts. The first part is a square. The second part comes from drawing a line from the midpoint of the square diagonally to one of the opposite corners, then drawing an arc from that corner to a line even with the base of the square (see *Fig. 7-4*) producing the *Phi* (Φ) Rectangle. Where the south wall entrance is located, it is easy to speculate its off-center position was determined by using the Golden Ratio *Phi* (Φ) in its design.

When designing this enclosure, the architect would have defined a rough length for the south wall. Then, from the southeast corner of the wall at a point roughly ⅗ of the way along its length, the approximate location for the south entrance was located. The temporary length for this segment of the south wall (⅗ is 0.60) is fairly close to the value for *Phi* of 1.61803.) Once this was completed, the finalizing the position of the southwest corner could be done using a *Phi* (Φ) Rectangle. Determination of the location of the north and east entrances used these same Sacred Geometric Ratios. At this point, the layout of the perimeter wall did not have to be exceedingly refined.

Many *Phi* (Φ) Rectangles are detectable in the design of the Khasekhemwui Funerary Enclosure. For all *Phi* (Φ) Rectangles, **ab** is the long segment, **bc** is the short segment and *m* is the midpoint of the **ab** segment from which an arc is drawn to the diagonal corner to create the segment **bc**. Several of the *Phi* (Φ) Rectangles overlap one another. (In the following illustrations, the compass arrow and small building in the southeast corner (*Fig. 7-54*) have been removed and the enclosure's walls have been rendered in grey for purposes of clarity.) Here are some examples of the use of *Phi* (Φ) Rectangles (*Fig. 7-55*).

196

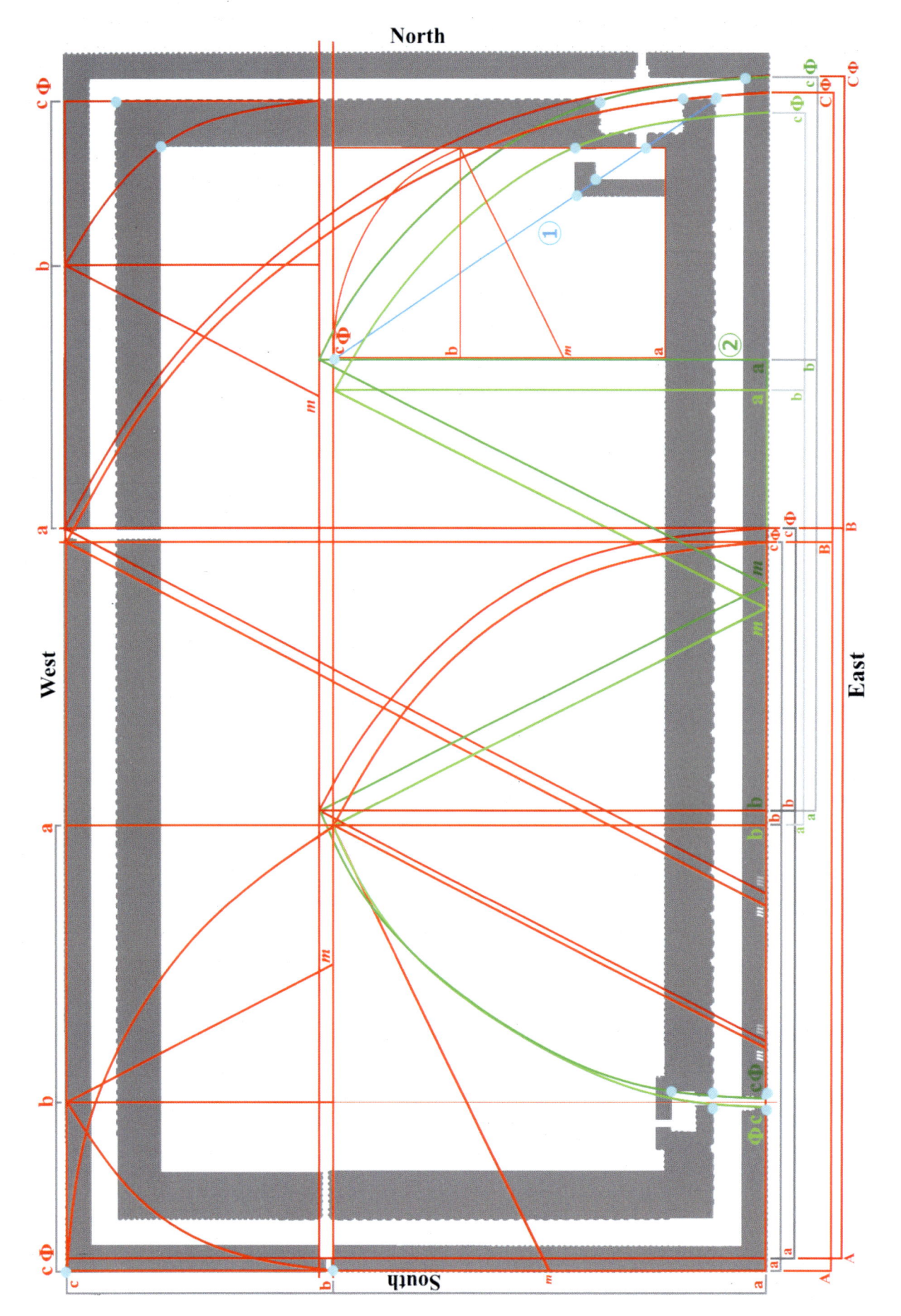

Fig. 7-55 – Several instances of Phi (Φ) Rectangles are used in the design of Khasekhemwui's Funerary Enclosure

The blue dots (*touch points*) indicate where various lines and *Phi* (Φ) Rectangle arcs intersect certain architectural elements in the enclosure's design such as walls, doorways and corners. This suggests that a kind of grid system based on these *touch points* was used to determine their location in the overall plan. (Note the double lines that are similar to ones used by Imhotep in his design of the South Entrance Hall/Ḥeb-Sed Court quadrant [see *Figs. 7-38, 7-40* and *7-41*]. In Imhotep's design, these lines indicate the division between Upper and Lower Egypt as well as other architectural features.) The diagonal line ① in *Fig. 7-55* extends from the '**c**' point of a horizontal *Phi* (Φ) Rectangle (line ②), and intersects several *touch points* denoting several various corners in the north Entrance Vestibule.

As was done with the plans of the Step Pyramid, if the starting point of the Root 2 (√2) Rectangle is reversed, beginning from the north (right) side of the temenos wall, a different set of arcs flesh out more details of the northeast and southeast Entrance Vestibules and the west entrance (*Fig. 7-56*).

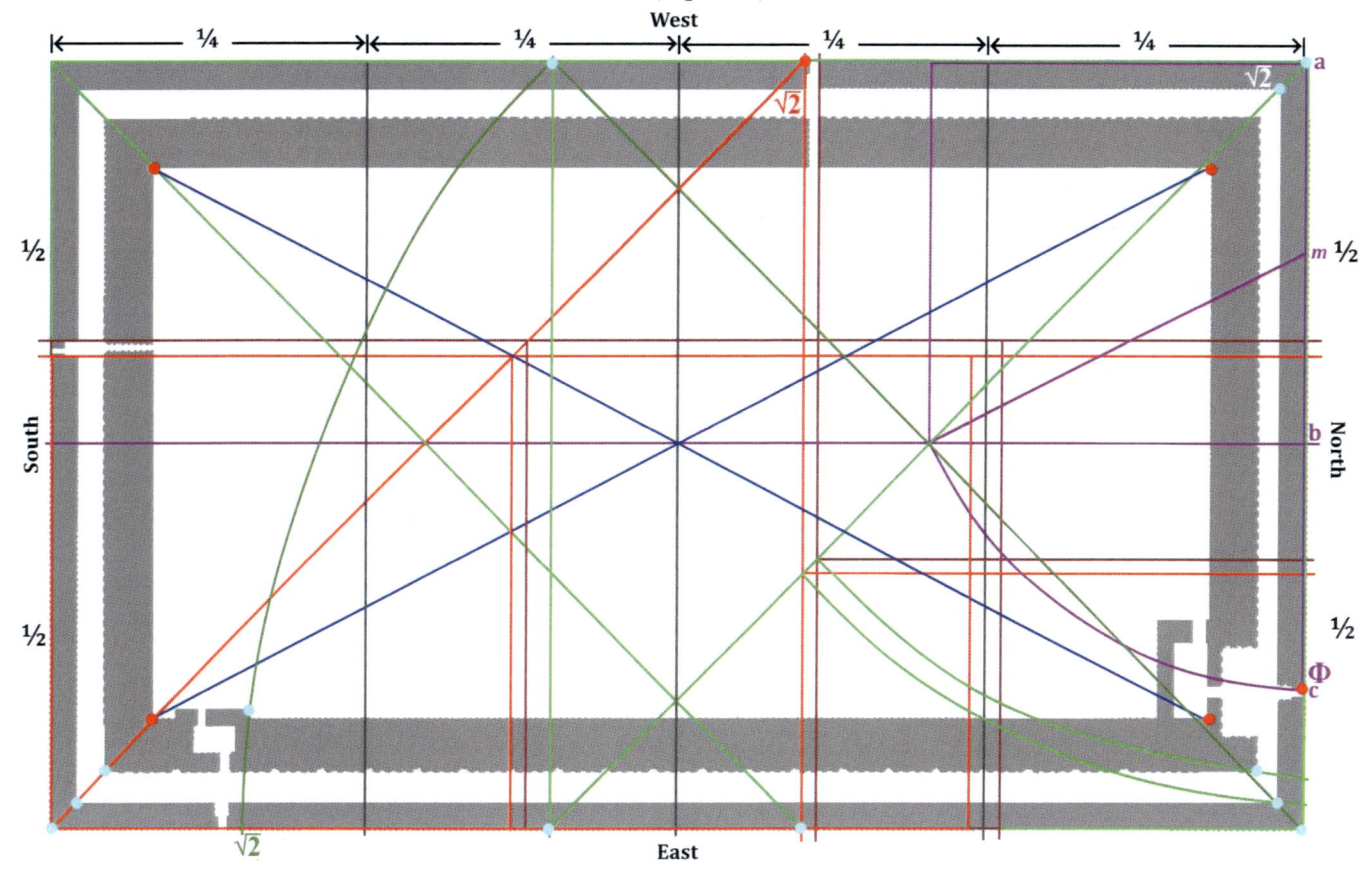

Fig. 7-56 – Superimposing the Root 2 (√2) Rectangle over the funerary enclosure starting from the north temenos wall shows the underlying structure of Khasekhemwui's Funerary Enclosure to be inherently balanced even though it is not readily apparent in the plan of the enclosure

In *Fig. 7-57* are examples of the use of Root 2 (√2) Squares and Root 5 (√5) Double Squares to delineate more features. Vertical lines ① and ② pass through the centers of the eastern entrance in the temenos wall and the interior doorway of the north Entrance Vestibule respectively. These lines were probably used to approximately position the entrances during the design phase. Using mostly the *Phi* (Φ) Golden Ratio and the Root 2 (√2) Rectangle ratio, we can now see how positioning of the four entrances in the temenos and interior walls was accomplished.

198

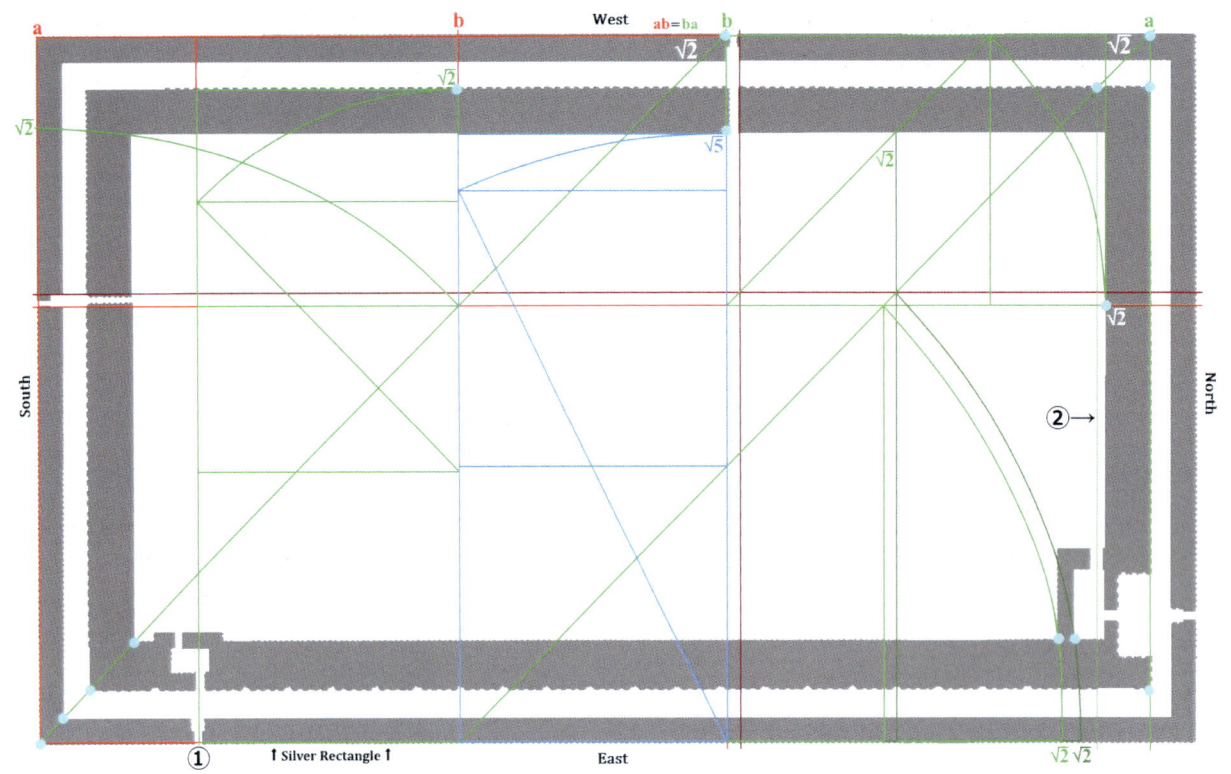

*Fig. 7-56 – The use of Root 2 (√2) Rectangles and a Root 5 (√5)
Double Square in the design of Khasekhemwui's Funerary Enclosure*

When researching the possibility that Khasekhemwui's Funerary Enclosure was designed using principles of Sacred Geometry, I couldn't help but notice a curved set of lines (*Fig. 7-59*) denoting several *touch points* on the Southeast Entrance Gate. These lines bear more than a passing resemblance to a pair of the most widely recognized symbols often associated with Egyptian royalty: the crook and flail. While this may be a perfect example of pareidolia, a phenomenon in which the human mind perceives a recognizable pattern where none exists or is intended, these lines look like a stylized crook and flail (minus the handles, of course, *Fig. 7-58*). The lines terminating at these *touch points* highlight several interior and exterior corners of the southeast Entrance Vestibule, suggesting that this, too, is part of a design grid, though this may be accidental.

Unless, of course, it was completely deliberate.

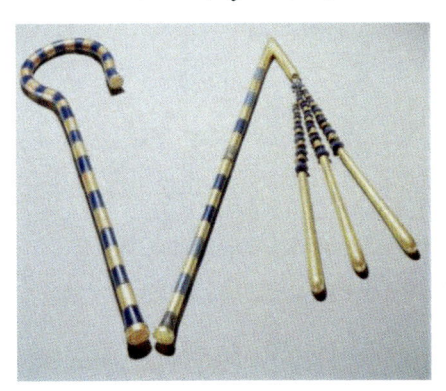

Fig. 7-58 – Tutankhamun's Crook and Flail

The pharaoh's crook (known as a *heka*) is a shepherd's staff that sheepherders used to control and protect their sheep. The royal use of the crook symbolized pharaoh's duty to protect his people. The flail, or *nekhaka*, is a symbolic weapon to defend the flock, but it was also use as tool to separate wheat from the chaff, which also symbolized the king's responsibility to provide for his people.

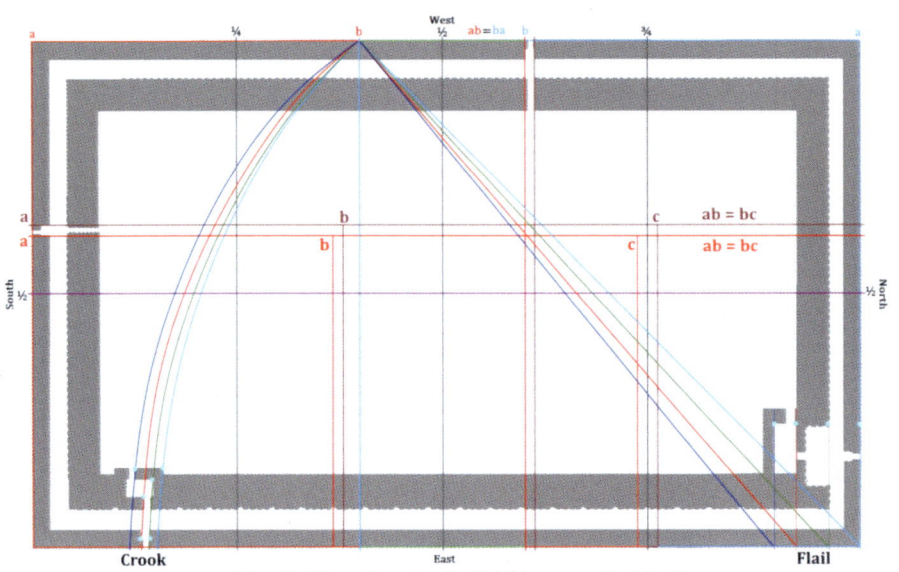

Fig. 7-59 – A potential hidden symbol in the plan of Khasekhemwui's Funerary Enclosure

While most of this funerary enclosure's design as a whole had its beginnings in the exterior temenos wall, the positioning of the interior main wall was also realized using *Phi* (Φ) Rectangles, a Root 2 (√2) Rectangle and a Root 5 (√5) Double Square (*Fig. 7-60*). Note the space between the north temenos wall and the north interior wall. Though barely perceptible, it is slightly smaller than the space between the south temenos and main interior walls. This is a product of using *Phi* (Φ) Rectangle arcs to determine the locations of interior and exterior corners in the northern part of the enclosure.

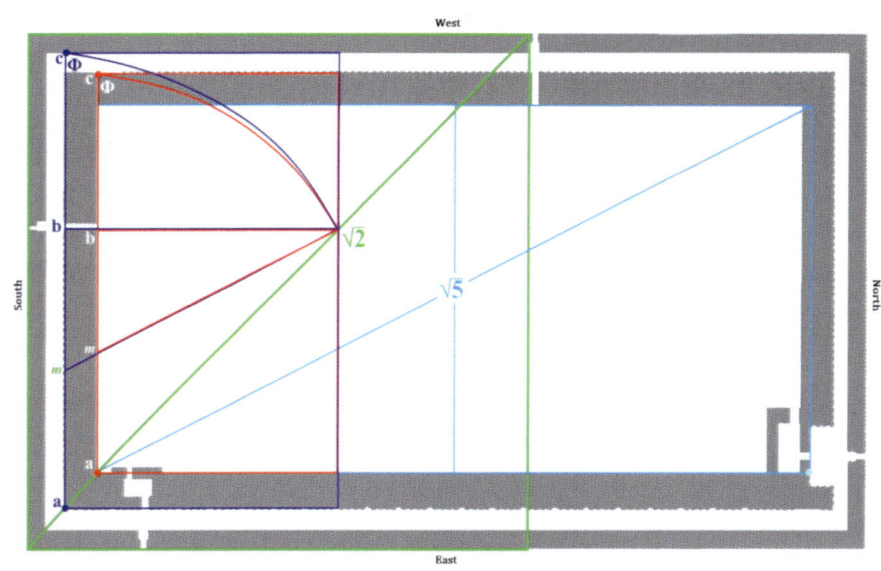

Fig. 7-60 – Sacred Ratios were used to position the Main Interior Wall within the Exterior Temenos Wall

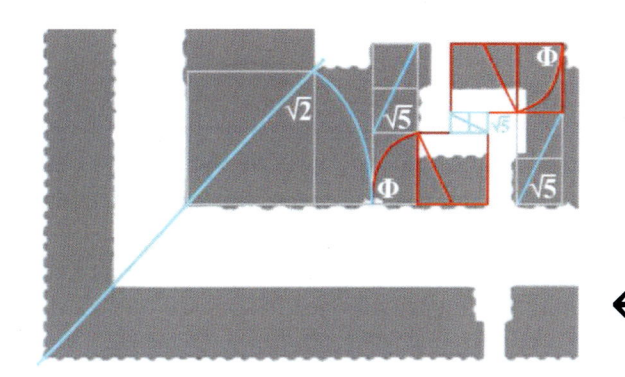

Even the design of something as ordinary looking as the east entrance and its corresponding vestibule located in the inner wall show multiple uses of Sacred Geometry hidden within its design (*Fig. 7-61*).

← *Fig. 7-61 – The Sacred Geometric design of the Southeast Entrance Vestibule*

Finally, if we combine all the above figures into one plan, it would look like *Fig. 7-62*.

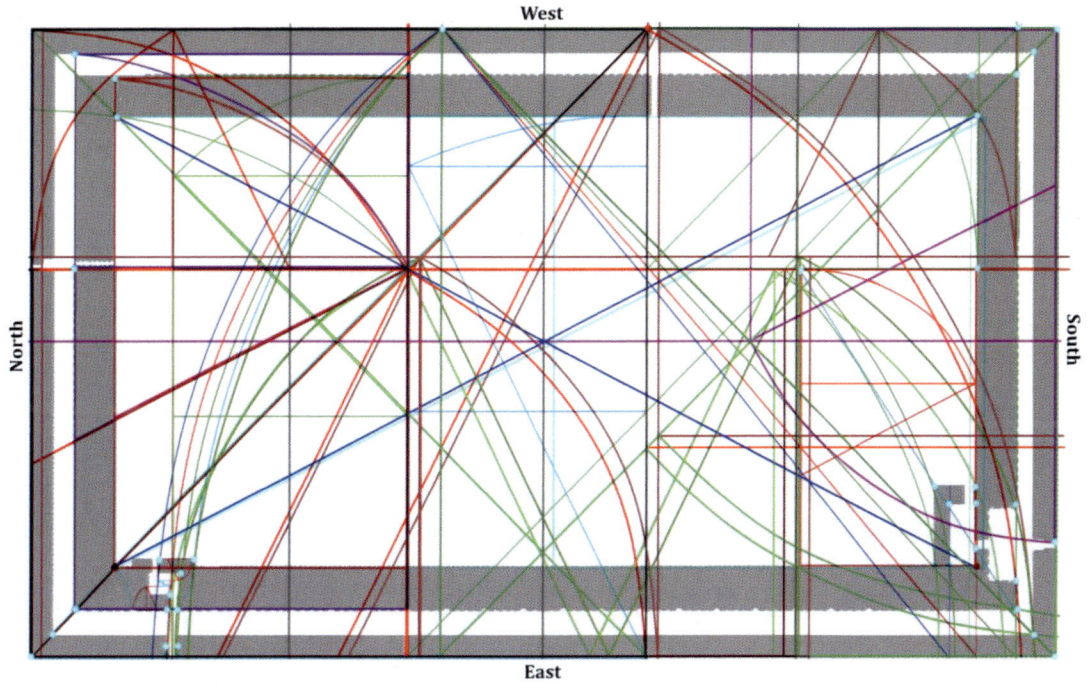

Fig. 7-62 – Every sacred ratio used in the design of Khasekhemwui's Funerary Enclosure merged into one plan

With just a cursory look at *Fig. 7-62*, which contains very easily discernible Sacred Ratios, the practiced eye of one who is conversant with the language of Sacred Geometry will know exactly what it means and understand it immediately. The rest of us will view it as something a tad messy.

The difficulty in determining the exact location of the perimeter wall gateways and the staggered entrances of the interior wall's east and north gateways may be due to their current state of deterioration and the misalignment and absence of many of its mud bricks and any inexact measurements as a result. In other words, if a Sacred Ratio's lines don't quite line up correctly with a wall, a corner of a wall or the intersection of a line that is part of another Sacred Ratio, it's probably due to one of these factors. Except for the ritual cult chapel in the southeast corner, there are indications the interior of the *"Shunet el-Zebib"* was never finished, which include building debris left in place after construction ceased, regretfully so given its complex and sophisticated design. This might explain the attribution of Khasekhemwui as the builder of the Great Enclosure (*Gisr el-Mudir*) at Sakkara if in fact he abandoned the *Shuneh* in favor of a site in the north near Memphis. More recent investigations; however, show the construction of the Great Enclosure may have occurred much later. [113]

We have evidence of several Sacred Ratios inherent in the design of Khasekhemwui's Funerary Enclosure, but can we say with certainty it was designed from the beginning using Sacred Geometry? Just the quantity alone of all these Sacred Ratios should eliminate coincidence as a factor in determining if this were true. This leaves us with the inescapable conclusion that ancient Egyptian architects were working on a whole other level than what we thought previously. There may well be more relationships based on Sacred Ratios in the design of Khasekhemwui's Funerary Enclosure, but these few examples will have to do until a more complete investigation is undertaken.

The Funerary Enclosure of Peribsen at Abydos

It turns out the architects for Khasekhemwui's next-door neighbor, Peribsen, also used Sacred Geometry to design his funerary enclosure (*Fig. 7-63*). Given that the ancient Egyptian royal architects were probably blood relatives, it is no coincidence that these two funerary enclosures are of a similar design. Specifically, double-overlapping *Phi* (Φ) Rectangles analogous to the ones Imhotep used to design Ḥeb-Sed Court chapels (the **EFGH** square in *Fig. 7-41*) can be seen in the layout of the South Gate in the south wall and along the east wall of the Peribsen enclosure. Though the manner of implementation is slightly different, the use of double *Phi* (Φ) Rectangles is similar to the design of Khasekhemwui's Funerary Enclosure, with a Root 5 (√5) Double Square defining the overall shape of the plan.

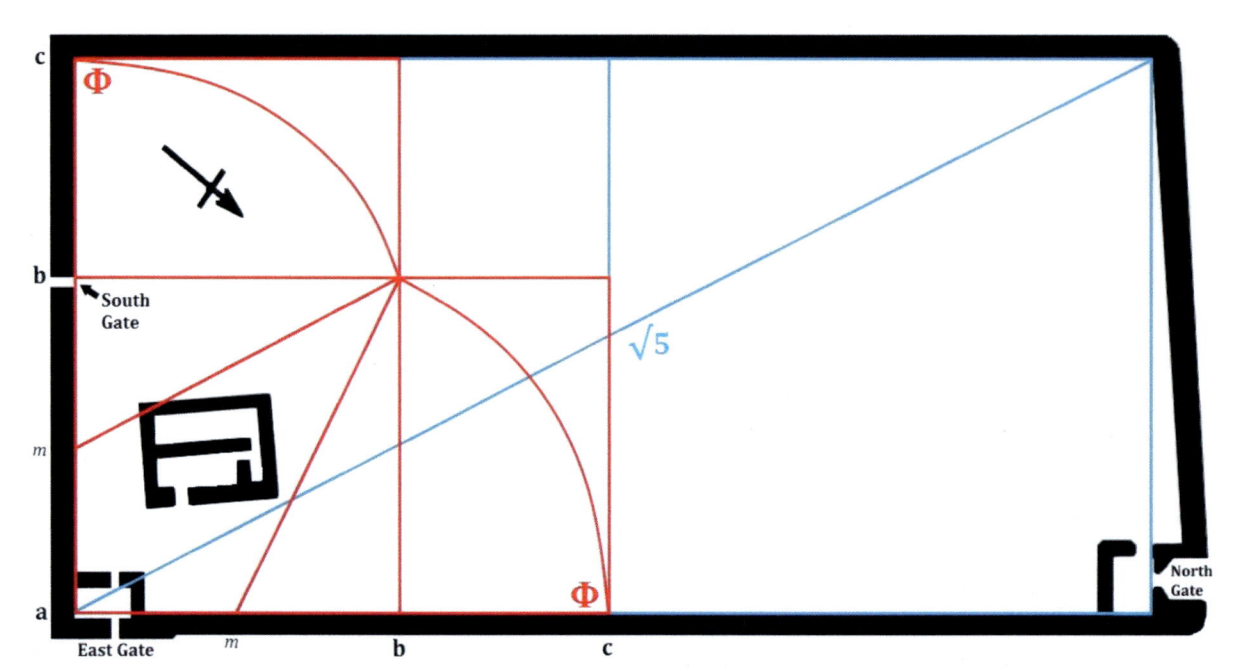

Fig. 7-63 – Peribsen Funerary Enclosure – North Abydos

There are probably more instances of the use of Sacred Ratios inherent in the designs of Khasekhemwui and Peribsen's funerary monuments. Suffice it to say, this small sample, coupled with the use of the 22:7 ratio signifying a uniquely Egyptian value of 3.142857 for *Pi* (π) in the mastaba tomb of the Second Dynasty Pharaoh Djer, indicates that ancient Egyptian architects had knowledge of – and extensively used – Sacred Geometry to design mortuary monuments far earlier than previously thought.

The Step Pyramid of Sekhemkhet

After the death of Pharaoh Netjerikhet Djoser, what did Imhotep do for an encore? Djoser's successor, Sekhemkhet, also built a pyramid and a funerary enclosure at Sakkara (*Fig. 7-64*) just a little to the southwest of Djoser's monument (*Fig. 7-65*). Information about Sekhemkhet is sketchy at best. He may have been either Djoser's son or younger brother, though there is no conclusive evidence to verify their relationship. In addition, there are debates that the name of Sekhemkhet's successor was a pharaoh named Khaba, or another one named Sanakht. Some even think Khaba and Sanakht were the same person, causing even more confusion about the succession of kings during the Third Dynasty.

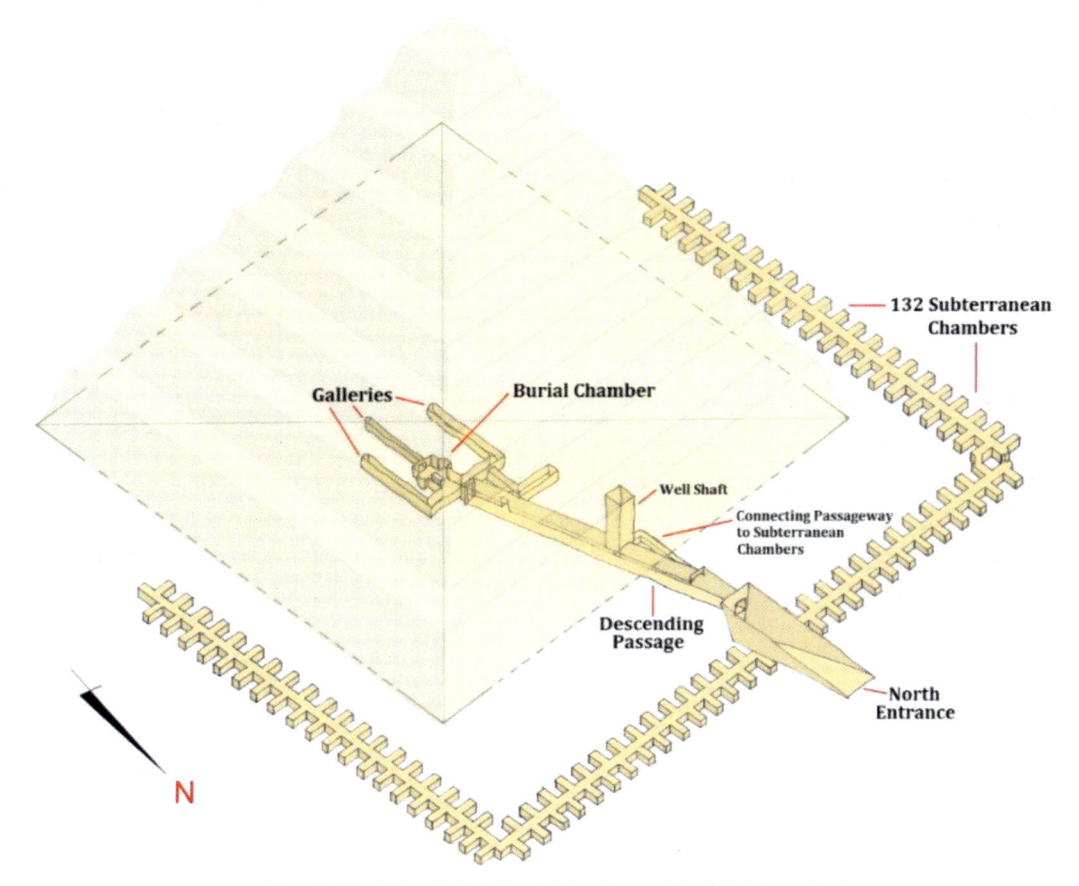

Fig. 7-64 – The Unfinished Step Pyramid of Sekhemkhet

Sekhemkhet's pyramid, often called the "Buried Pyramid" or "Lost Pyramid", was discovered and excavated by Zakaria Goneim in 1952. Left unfinished at the time of Sekhemkhet's death (his reign only lasted six to seven years), the general layout of the pyramid and its funerary enclosure is still recognizable despite all the sand and rubble that once covered it. Though it is difficult to tell if this pyramid was going to have six or seven steps, only the first tier and part of the second was completed giving it the appearance similar to that of a typical mastaba tomb (*Fig. 7-66*).

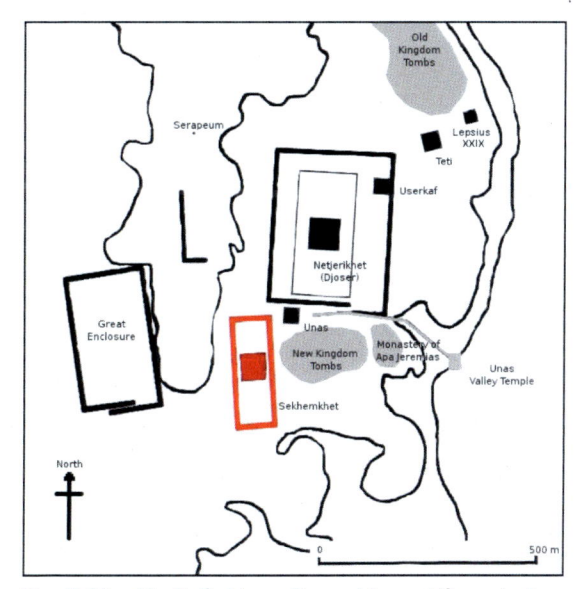

Fig. 7-65 - North Sakkara Pyramids and Cemeteries

M. Zakaria Goneim (1905–1959)

Fig. 7-66 – Sekhemkhet's Pyramid, with the first tier and part of the second tier just after being excavated

When the clearing of the Sekhemkhet's pyramid began, the pharaoh that ordered its construction was unknown. However, the discovery of jar seals with Sekhemkhet's name, along with a graffito on the unfinished enclosure wall bearing the name of Imhotep put this pyramid firmly in the Third Dynasty. As a result, though the evidence is sketchy and incomplete, the belief is that Imhotep may have lived long enough to design Sekhemkhet's pyramid, and maybe even survived into the reigns of later Third Dynasty pharaohs.

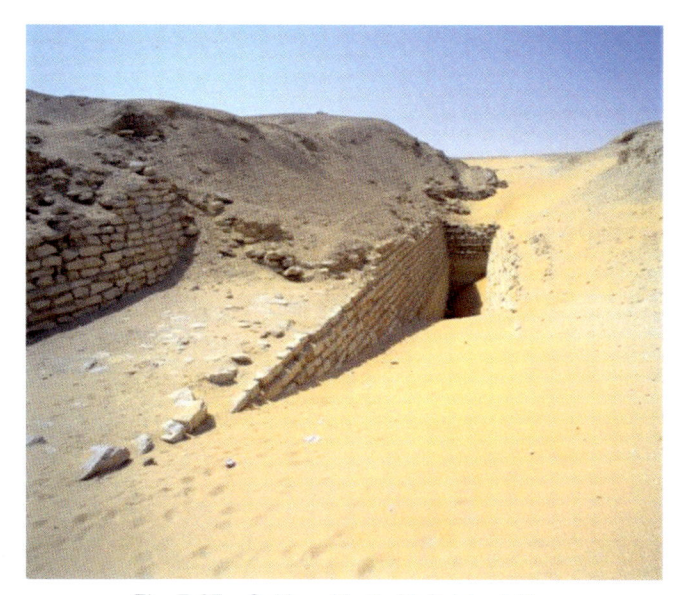

Fig. 7-67 – Sekhemkhet's Unfinished Step Pyramid North Entrance as seen today

Fig. 7-68 – Sekhemkhet's Unfinished Step Pyramid southwest of Djoser's Step Pyramid (in the background)

Fig. 7-69 – The Perimeter Wall of Sekhemkhet's Funerary Enclosure after excavation

This shows the incomplete state of the walls just after the vertical channels had been chiseled out and before the top layers were installed and the square insets carved into them

After the removal of all the sand and rubble from around the pyramid, entry was possible into the unfinished burial chamber, leading to the discovery of a beautifully carved, translucent alabaster sarcophagus along with several dozen other artifacts of gold and pottery retrieved from the pyramid's underground chambers (*Fig. 7-70*). From these finds, the presumption was that Sekhemkhet had quite possibly been buried in the most extraordinary sarcophagus in all of Egypt. It was made of a single piece of hollowed-out alabaster with a T-shaped door fitted at one end. Though completely sealed when first discovered (suggesting a body was still inside), it was completely empty, much to the disappointment of everyone who gathered to witness its opening. One possible reason the sarcophagus was sealed was to prevent the T-shaped door from jarring loose during the move into the burial chamber. To date, there is no trace of Sekhemkhet's mummy.

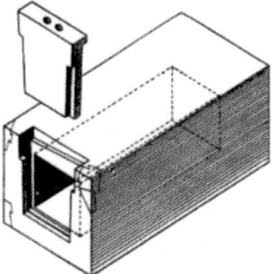

Fig. 7-70 – Sekhemkhet's alabaster sarcophagus in situ (left and middle) and isometric view (right)

As you can see in *Fig. 7-69*, the unfinished perimeter wall uses the same style of bastion as in the Enclosure Wall of the Step Pyramid. From the execution of its stonework, you can tell Imhotep had a hand in its design. Here is a rough plan of what the completed Funerary Enclosure of Sekhemkhet would have looked like had it been finished (*Fig. 7-71*).

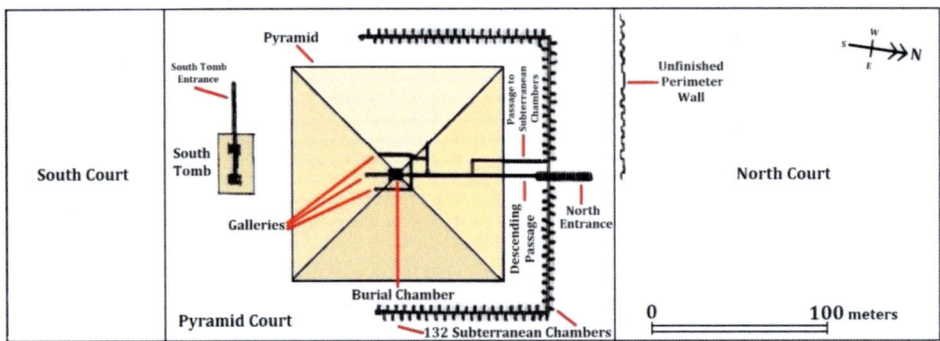

Fig. 7-71 – The unfinished Funerary Enclosure of Sekhemkhet at Sakkara

It is possible to determine that the design of Sekhemkhet's pyramid used the same tools of Sacred Geometry as were used to design Djoser's Step Pyramid Enclosure. What follows is a discussion of the possible design philosophy used to construct Sekhemkhet's Funerary Enclosure, based on the evidence of readily available plans. While these plans may be somewhat crude, limited and possibly prone to some inaccuracy, they serve the purpose to gain an overview of Imhotep's intentions when he designed this pyramid and its enclosure.

At first glance, the Pyramid Court appears to be a standalone single monument with the North and South Courts added later because the unfinished perimeter wall just north of the pyramid bears a strong resemblance to the exterior of the Djoser Step Pyramid's Enclosure Wall. However, as I experimented with various Sacred Geometrical Ratios to determine if Imhotep used them to design Sekhemkhet's funerary monument, it became evident the design of the three courts were constructed as a set piece.

While it isn't readily apparent from a cursory examination of the plan of Sekhemkhet's Pyramid Enclosure, there seems to be an overall guiding principle which renders it into a balanced design. Closer examination of the enclosure's plan shows that it is possible to divide it into equal parts (*Fig. 7-72*). The North Entrance and Descending Passage align with the green north-south dividing line, and the point where the passage to the Subterranean Chambers connects to the Descending Passage aligns with the green east-west dividing line.

The enclosure's plan consists of three different-sized rectangles or squares. From the uneven arrangement of these shapes, the use of Sacred Geometry might not be readily apparent in its design. *Figure 7-71* shows the North Court (far right) is a perfect square with the South Court (far left) being exactly half the half the size of the North Court.

However, during the design phase, the South Court was an *implied* square with both square courts situated on either side of the Root 2 ($\sqrt{2}$) rectangular Pyramid Court (*Fig. 7-72*). This plainly shows the overall plan is a repeat of the A-B-A form used for the three Western Massifs in the Step Pyramid Enclosure. As will be seen below, the presumption that for design purposes, the South Court is twice its actual size directly relates to what Imhotep was attempting to create during the design process.

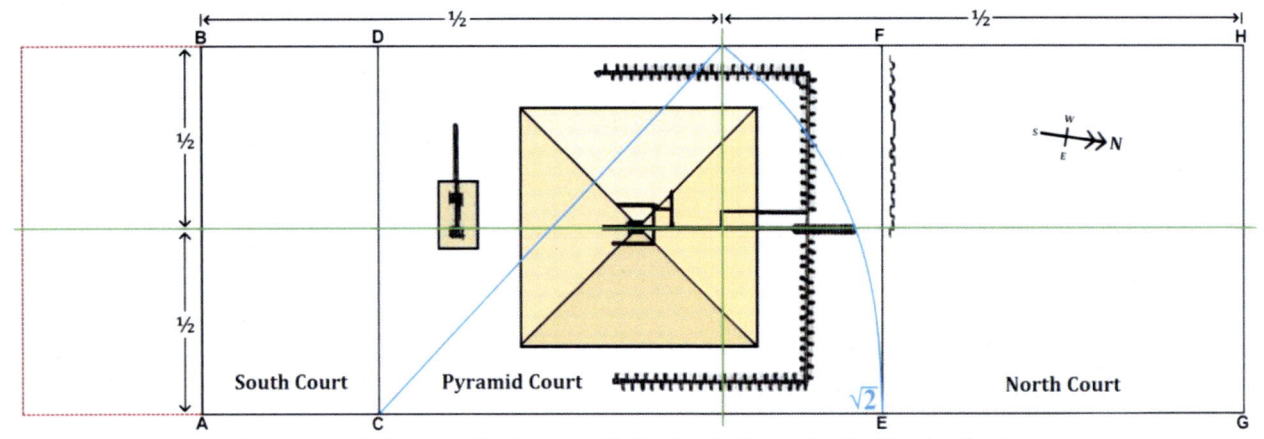

Fig. 7-72 – Sekhemkhet's Pyramid Enclosure with the South Court doubled in size for design purposes

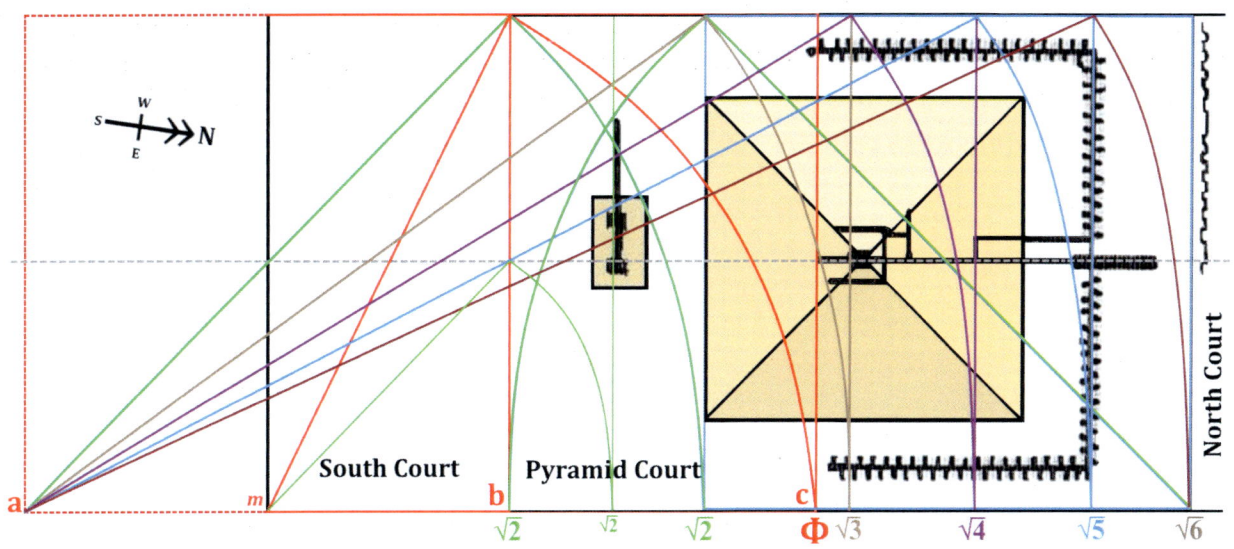

Fig. 7-73 – Sekhemkhet's Unfinished Pyramid – Initial Design Phase

There appears to have been several design and construction phases of Sekhemkhet's mortuary monument. If we start at the south end of the Pyramid Enclosure, the basis of this Pyramid Enclosure's left-to-right design grid using Sacred Ratios starts to become apparent.

1) An implied (blue) square created on the right side of the Pyramid Court is the same size as the North Court (*Fig. 7-73*). The north line of the square aligns with the south wall of the North Court. The south wall of the pyramid is flush against the south line of this square.

2) This square (in #1) is the base square of a Root 2 (√2) Rectangle (blue diagonal line and resultant arc) which determines the location of the north wall of the South Court.

3) Next, the north-south width of the South Court was designed to be exactly one-half the width of the Pyramid Court's initial square (see #1) and the North Court. This suggests the south wall of the South Court is the midpoint (***m***) of the base square of a *Phi* (Φ) Rectangle, only half of which was constructed. The dotted red lines in *Figs. 7-72* and *7-73* imply the *phantom* other half of the South Court's base square. The resultant east-west line at the end of the arc that produces the *Phi* (Φ) Rectangle intersects the south terminus of the central gallery at the end of the Descending Passage, as well as the southernmost point of the western group of Subterranean Chambers.

4) Another Root 2 (√2) Rectangle, whose beginning point is at the southeastern corner of the *phantom* half of the South Court, also intersects the south wall of the pyramid.

5) Additionally, the arc of a smaller Root 2 (√2) Rectangle located in the northeast (lower right) quadrant of the South Court and its *phantom* half aligns with the Descending Corridor of the South Tomb.

6) Another line drawn from this same southeast corner to the east-west line that runs along the south side of the pyramid creates a Root 3 (√3) Rectangle. Its north line is the exact center of the Pyramid Court, and intersects the south wall of the Main Burial Chamber.

7) The east-west line derived from this Root 3 (√3) Rectangle produces a Root 4 (√4) Rectangle that intersects the passage to the Subterranean Chambers. It is also the centerline for the Pyramid Enclosure as a whole.

8) From this midpoint line, a Root 5 (√5) Double Square is created from which an east-west line derived from its arc intersects the northern group of Subterranean Chambers.

9) Lastly, a Root 6 (√6) Rectangle, derived from the arc of the Root 5 (√5) Double Square in #8, meets the south wall of the North Court.

There's a curious thing about the number of Subterranean Chambers beneath Sekhemkhet's pyramid. While there are only 132 carved out of the bedrock, and given the Pyramid Enclosure's unfinished state, it is possible to see that two more chambers could have been added to the eastern section of the chambers totaling 134 before construction on the pyramid stopped. This would have given the shape of these chambers a more cohesive and balanced design. That being said, however, it is equally likely only 132 were planned to be excavated. Here's the reason why: If you divide 22 by 7 [the ancient Egyptian value for *Pi* (π)], and multiply it by the Sacred Number 42, the rounded up answer is 132. *Coincidence? Possibly, but it's still kind of neat anyway!*

Imitating the ability to read hieroglyphics in either direction once again, this time starting from the northeast corner of the North Court and using a right-to-left 7-Part Root Rectangle Template, even more interesting relationships between various elements in Sekhemkhet's Pyramid Enclosure become apparent (*Fig. 7-74*).

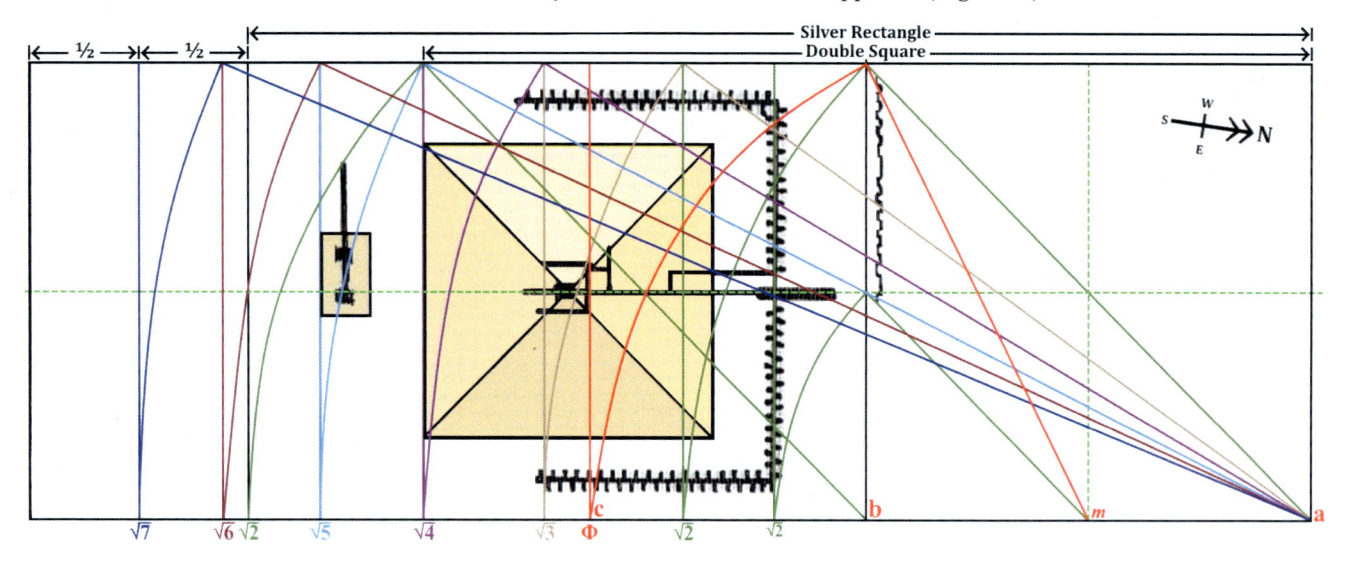

Fig. 7-74 – A 7-Part Root Rectangle Template defining more features within Sekhemkhet's Pyramid Enclosure

Several Sacred Ratios intersect a number of architectural features within the enclosure.

1) Dividing the North Court into four equal squares creates a smaller Root 2 (√2) Rectangle from the square in its southeast (lower left) quadrant. An east-west line extending from the terminus of the Root 2 (√2) arc aligns with the north section of the Subterranean Chambers, and corresponds to the same line drawn from the Root 5 (√5) Double Square arc of #8 in the descriptions for *Fig. 7-73*.

2) A *Phi* (Φ) Rectangle created using the North Court as its base square has its midpoint (*m*) at the northeast corner of the Root 2 (√2) Rectangle in #1 above. The line derived from the *Phi* (Φ) Rectangle arc aligns with the second of two east-west corridors leading from the central axis passageway to two of the north-south galleries.

3) Another Root 2 (√2) Rectangle, as well as other root rectangles, can be derived starting at the northeast (lower right) corner of the North Court. The southern line of this rectangle does not align with any known feature of the Enclosure, but is the basis of a Root 3 (√3) Rectangle that was used to place other features of the Pyramid Enclosure.

4) This Root 3 (√3) Rectangle delineates the end of the west gallery of the Main Burial Chambers. It also passes through the last chamber of the east section of the Subterranean Chambers, which further cements the notion that only 132 chambers were planned to be built.

5) From this Root 3 (√3) Rectangle, a Root 4 (√4) Rectangle can be created. Against the line produced from the arc of the Root 4 (√4) Rectangle is the south side of Sekhemkhet's pyramid, as also confirmed in numbers [1] and [4] of the descriptions for *Fig. 7-73*. The combination of these two squares produces a Root 5 (√5) Double Square. An east-west line created from the Root 2 (√2) arc of the square in the Pyramid Court creates a Silver Rectangle, against which the south wall of the South Tomb was aligned. This reinforces the theory that Sacred Ratios were used extensively in this Pyramid Enclosure's design.

6) From a Root 2 (√2) Rectangle created from this square, the north wall of the South Court is delineated, and along its arc, the beginning of the Entrance Hall of the South Tomb is located.

7) A Root 5 (√5) Double Square is then created from the Root 4 (√4) Rectangle of the Pyramid Court square. This lines up with the south exterior wall of the South Tomb.

8) A Root 6 (√6) Rectangle is created from the Root 5 (√5) Double Square, which doesn't align with anything, but is the basis for a Root 7 (√7) Rectangle, which precisely lands on a point that neatly dissects the north-south width of the South Court in two.

In an odd twist, the space between the south side of the pyramid and the South Court also forms a Root 6 (√6) Rectangle in addition to its delineation by a Root 2 (√2) Rectangle, was used to determine the north side of the pyramid (*Fig. 7-75*). From this dimension, a square pyramid could be designed that was roughly centered within the walls of the Pyramid Court. Once again, Imhotep was thinking *outside the box* as he did with the Step Pyramid Enclosure's Entrance Vestibule.

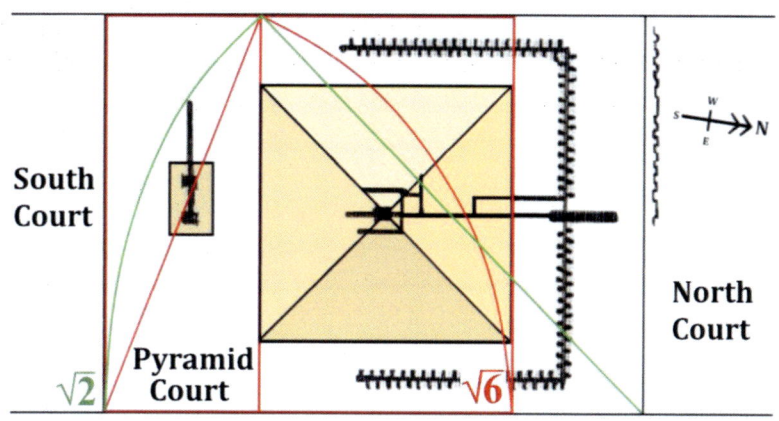

Fig. 7-75 – A Root 6 (√6) Rectangle defines the north side of Sekhemkhet's Pyramid

Continuing with the presumption that Imhotep designed Sekhemkhet's Pyramid Enclosure, and along with the theory that he used the shape of hieroglyphs to create various architectural features in the Step Pyramid Enclosure, the South Tomb in bears a slight resemblance to the hieroglyph for a scribal kit.

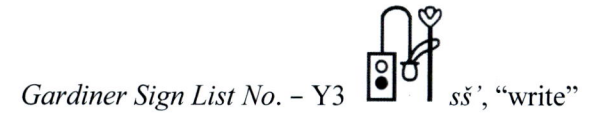

Gardiner Sign List No. – Y3 *sš', "write"*

Being a scribe was a highly respected profession in ancient Egypt. Imhotep, in addition to his other accolades, he was considered the Patron of Scribes. *Coincidence? Possibly, but it is in keeping with Imhotep's primary occupations.*

The hypothesis outlined above is, I believe, how Imhotep probably designed Sekhemkhet's Pyramid Enclosure, but not necessarily how it was eventually constructed, nor how it exists in its current unfinished state. This makes it difficult to ascertain what his real intentions for this monument's design would have been. For example, was he going to include buildings like the North and South Pavilions in this funerary monument?

Because of the similar use of Sacred Ratios in the design of Djoser's Step Pyramid Complex, what I uncovered in this later structure suggests it is more than likely Imhotep's design. Despite Imhotep's name being inscribed on the one remaining section of the north wall, the simplicity of Sekhemkhet's pyramid and funerary enclosure indicates that quite possibly one of his assistants did some of the primary design work on this mortuary monument with guidance from Imhotep. Quite possibly this subordinate was his son whose name we do not know and who would eventually succeed him as Royal Architect. Though it is possible to discern from the limited plans we currently possess that Sacred Geometry was quite probably used as the primary architectural design philosophy for Sekhemkhet's Pyramid Enclosure, it is also wise to wait until further on-site work produces a more detailed and accurate survey that is necessary to determine the veracity of this hypothesis. Still, despite the paucity of precise plans for Sekhemkhet's Step Pyramid, I can't help but think that this simpler design is one that Imhotep may have wished for Netjerikhet Djoser's funerary complex had he not been saddled with the problem of having to use extant, unfinished structures as part of its design.

The difficulty in ascertaining if the design of any of these monuments used the tenets of Sacred Geometry is that any plans currently available only show their state as they presently exist, not the way they were constructed in the past, and certainly not the way in which they were designed. Into this information void is the very real possibility that we have no clear idea what the intentions of the ancient architects were regarding how they designed these monuments. Nor do we have an indication if any variations to the architects' plans took place during the final phases of construction and even decades or centuries later when they might have been altered by later generations of kings and architects, and quite probably, stone harvesters.

Adherence to a strict methodology using Sacred Geometry does not appear to be the case with Imhotep in his design of the Step Pyramid Enclosure. Perhaps, at this early stage of development, the set of *rules* were looser for using Sacred Geometry in art and architecture than that which appeared in later centuries when there was extensive use by *younger* civilizations such as Greece and Rome. This is not to say Imhotep wasn't following architectural practices developed by his predecessors (who were quite possibly his father and grandfathers); it's just that we do not have any point of reference to gauge how strictly he applied those practices, and when he indulged in thinking *out of the box* to affect his designs. Quite clearly, he knew the 'rules', but he also knew when and where to break them. Yet, we have no idea what those *rules* were except to try and divine them from the current archeological site plans made of these old temples.

This reminds me of when I was studying music in college. Music students everywhere often wonder why it is necessary to study the underlying structure of Bach chorales in order to create four-part harmony in a Bach-like manner. Clearly, the music they are composing today does not sound remotely even close to using 18th century harmonic practices. Yet, when it came time to write music firmly rooted in 20th century idioms, many techniques of harmony and voice leading found its way from the 18th century into our music even though we did not consciously choose to do so. There is no confusing Beethoven's Fifth Symphony with Igor Stravinsky's *Rite of Spring*, but good practices in any art form will always be necessary even if it's absolutely required to *break the rules* in order to accomplish a desired end result.

Is it likely that Imhotep used Sacred Geometry to design the Netjerikhet Djoser's Step Pyramid Enclosure and Sekhemkhet's Pyramid Enclosure? *Probably*. Did he occasionally break those rules? *Absolutely*. In the case of Imhotep, his use of Sacred Geometry with his own distinctive *signature and style* is indicative of a facile and expansive mind capable of thinking beyond accepted norms. Proof of this comes by way of his innovative use of stone to realize what would become one of the ancient world's most iconic architectural masterpieces. If only half of what I propose to be the underlying Sacred Geometric design structure of the Step Pyramid Enclosure is true, the word "genius" as it applies to Imhotep is woefully inadequate. The inherent simplicity of design of Sekhemkhet's Funerary Enclosure leads me to conclude that this second attempt at creating a funerary enclosure is the one that Imhotep would have probably preferred. By not having to integrate other structures on the site into the final design allowed for a cleaner, more cohesive realization of his intentions.

Sacred Geometry and the Secret Symbol in the King's Chamber of the Great Pyramid of Giza

Indirect evidence of the use of the 3-4-5 triangle to construct buildings during Imhotep's time can be seen in later generations of architects that used it to construct the pyramids of the Fourth Dynasty, most notably the Great Pyramid of Giza. The Great Pyramid has been measured, analyzed, and virtually dissected for over a hundred years *ad nauseam*. That being said, however, William Flinders Petrie, who made the most extensive – and still accurate – measurements of the Great Pyramid, determined the length of the floor of the King's Chamber to be about 412.25 inches (19.99 cubits /10.47 meters), and the height as 230.05 inches (11.16 cubits /5.84 meters) which creates an exact 30°-60°-90° triangle. Further evidence of the use of Sacred Geometry within the design of the Great Pyramid comes from the width of the King's Chamber being 206.13 inches (9.99 cubits /5.24 meters). This is one-half its length and produces a 2:1 ratio, or a perfect Root 5 ($\sqrt{5}$) Double Square.

A triangle based on a Root 5 ($\sqrt{5}$) Double Square was also incised, albeit very faintly, on the large granite block above the entrance into the King's Chamber (*Fig. 7-76*). Originally discovered in 1880, Flinders Petrie noticed "a remarkable diagonal drafted line across the immense block of granite over the doorway".[114] This inset line turned out to be the long side of a 2:1 triangle, or a Double Square in the vernacular of Sacred Geometry. Mr. Douglas H. Benjamin rediscovered it exactly 100 years later in 1980. *Figure 7-77* shows Mr. Benjamin's rough measurements of what appeared to be a large right triangle.[115]

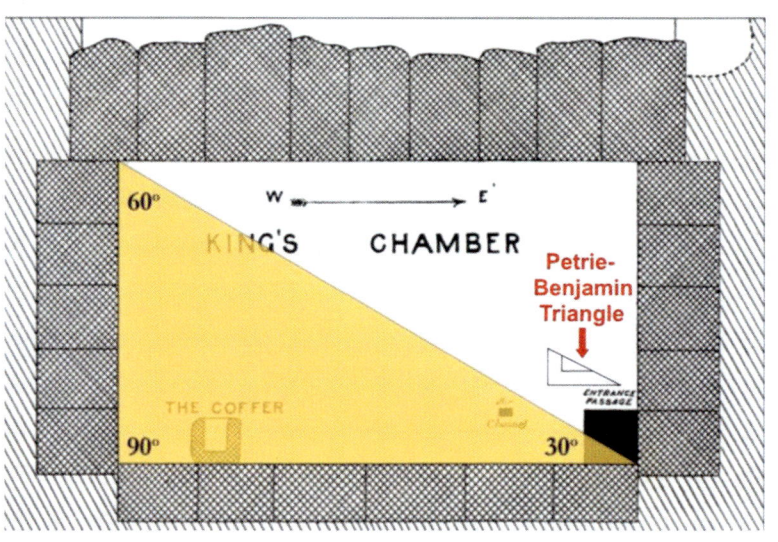

Fig. 7-76 – The Right Triangle as used in the King's Chamber of the Great Pyramid

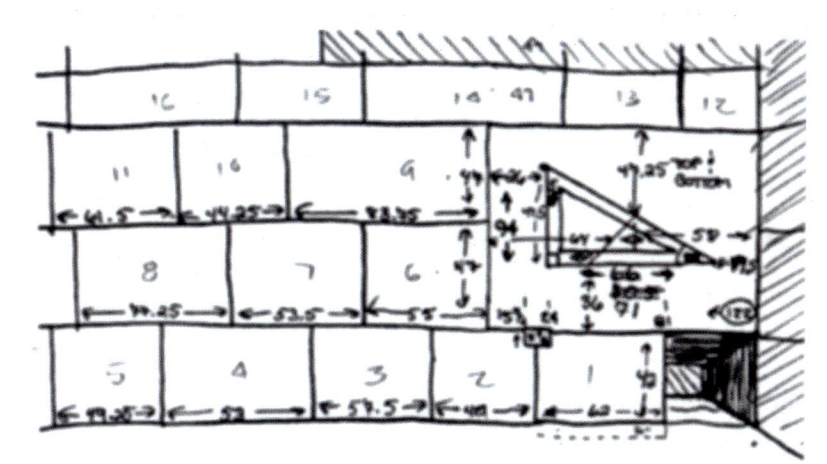

Fig. 7-77 – Mr. Benjamin's rough drawing of the North Wall in the King's Chamber from 1980

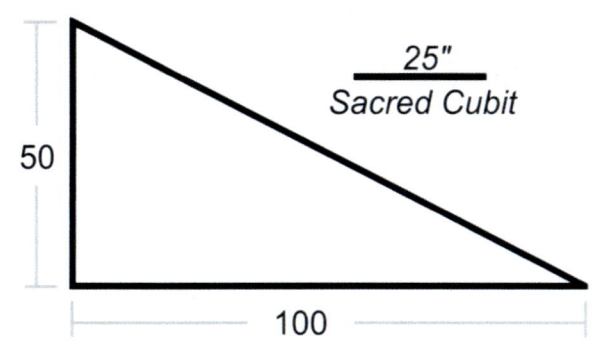

Fig. 7-78 – Dimensions of the Right Triangle in the King's Chamber as first measured in 1980

The Side equals 50" or Two Sacred Cubits. The Base equals 100" or Four Sacred Cubits. Note: A Sacred Cubit of 25" is equal to 1/10,000,000th of the Earth's polar radius

As luck would have it, Mr. Benjamin was able to measure the triangle more accurately due to changes to the lighting system in the King's Chamber when he returned to Egypt in 1989. As a result, he was able to ascertain an intricate relationship between three now visible triangles. One side measured 50 inches while the base measured 100 inches, making a perfect 2:1 ratio triangle (*Fig. 7-78*). This produces a triangle that is approximately 2-by-4 Sacred Cubits.

At that time in 1989, Mr. Benjamin also noticed a *second* right triangle embedded within the first triangle (*Fig. 7-78*).

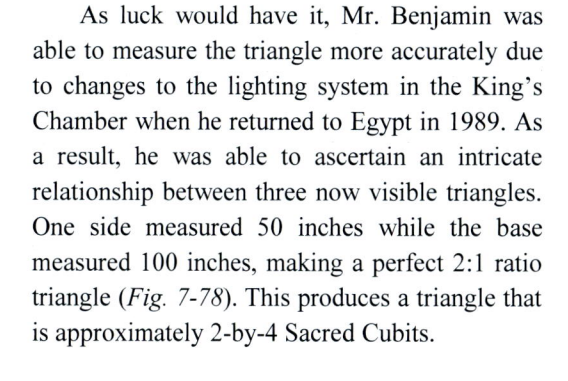

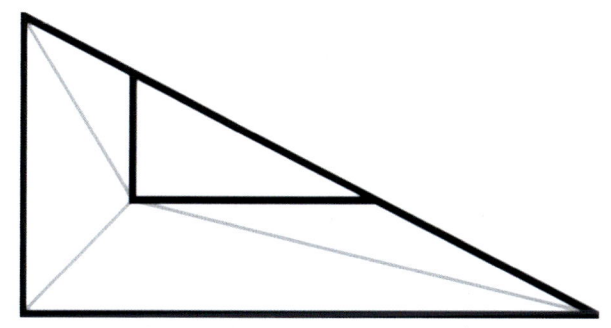

Fig. 7-79 – The Inner Center Triangle of the Hidden 2:1 Right Triangle in the King's Chamber

The inner center triangle of the large right triangle determines the location of the 90° corner angle of the small right triangle. In other words, lines dividing the three corners of the large triangle in half touches the corner of the 90° angle of the smaller triangle. When reviewing his photographs from this trip, Mr. Benjamin discovered several additional details hidden within these two triangles (*Fig. 7-80*).

Fig. 7-80 – The delineation of the four 2:1 Right Triangles within a Double Square

After many millennia of *hiding in plain sight*, a multifaceted connection between the four sides of the two triangles became visible once again. As a result, the four units of measurement used in ancient Egypt can readily be seen in the two right triangles incised in the stone block above entrance to the King's Chamber of the Great Pyramid (*Fig. 7-81*).

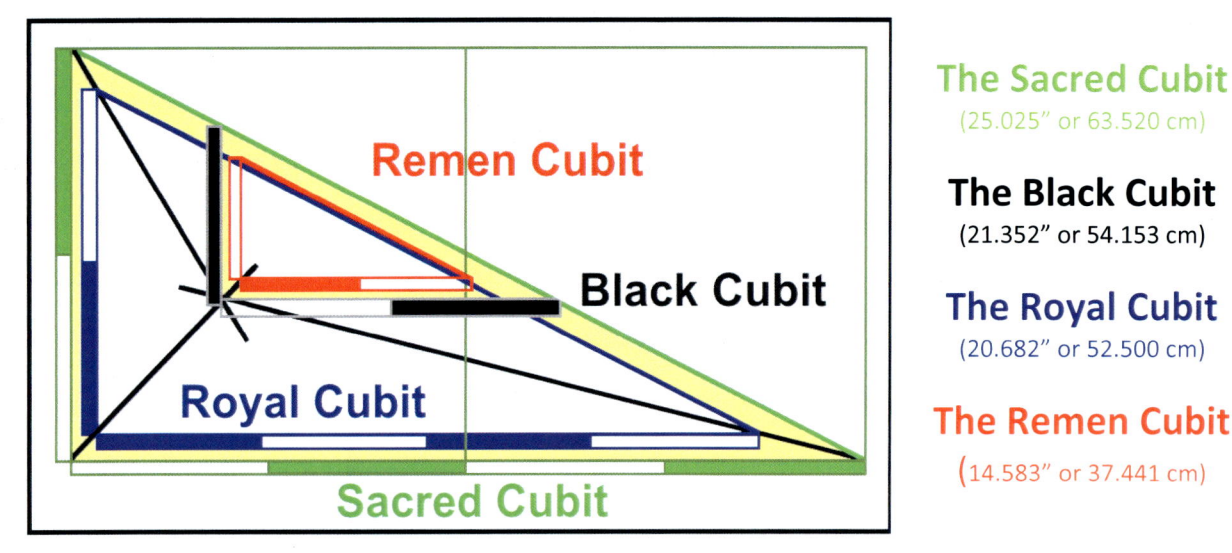

Fig. 7-81 – The Four Primary Cubits of Ancient Egypt

When confronted by the consistent measurements and angles contained within the Great Pyramid, it becomes apparent that a system of Sacred Geometry existed and was in use much earlier than the time of the Fourth Dynasty, that is, during Imhotep's time, and quite likely before. This tradition of Sacred Geometry was passed down to later generations of Egyptian architects, and even to other ancient cultures such as the Greeks, who readily admitted they learned much in the way of esoteric wisdom from the Egyptians. Otherwise, the knowledge and use of Sacred Geometry as embodied in the Step Pyramid as well as the Great Pyramid, and quite probably even earlier structures, could not have been possible.

The Mystery of the Sakkara Ostracon

Is there any definitive, tangible proof that ancient Egyptian architects, in general, and Imhotep specifically, used Sacred Geometry to design their temples, mortuary monuments, and other works of art? In the section, *The Use of Architecture as a Repository of Hidden Esoteric Wisdom* above, it was noted that architectural plans for the Step Pyramid complex – or any ancient Egyptian temple or pyramid for that matter – do not exist, but this is not entirely true. Sometimes, proof for such grand hypotheses sometimes come in small packages. When researching how and when the Mastabas $M_1/M_2/M_3$ were built, as well as the North and South Pavilions, I came upon a relatively obscure artifact that has garnered a disproportionally large amount of attention from Egyptologists given its rather small size.

A curious find was unearthed detailing the construction techniques of these structures during the initial excavations in April 1925 (*Figs. 7-82* and *7-83*). [116] On a small, roughly 6½-inch square flake of limestone called the Sakkara Ostracon is a drawing with an architectural formula depicting the profile of a so-called *saddleback* roof of one of the structures (marked as 'E' on *Fig. 7-99*) next to the North Pavilion (*Figs. 7-85* and *7-86*).

The ubiquitous nature of such ostraca allowed them to be used as writing material for notes, messages, work orders, bills, and so on. It is likely that a staff of architects and construction managers assisted Imhotep in managing the construction of the Step Pyramid and other buildings while he attended to the business of being Vizier of Egypt and other duties. That being said, however, I like to think that maybe Imhotep drew the sketch on the ostraca to guide his work crew on how to build the arched roofs of these two pavilions and their adjacent buildings, even though there could never be any proof for this.

Fig. 7-82 – The Sakkara Ostracon with the formula for creating an arched roof

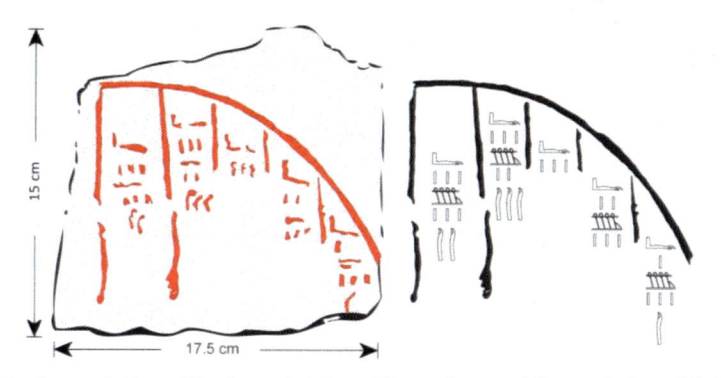

The transcription of the formula into cubits, palms, and fingers (left to right)

3 Cubits, 3 Palms, 2 Fingers = 98 Fingers
3 Cubits, 2 Palms, 3 Fingers = 95 Fingers
3 Cubits, 0 Palms, 0 Fingers = 84 Fingers
2 Cubits, 3 Palms, 0 Fingers = 68 Fingers
1 Cubit, 3 Palms, 1 Finger = 41 Fingers

Fig. 7-83 – The demotic text of the Sakkara Ostracon formula (left) converted into formal hieroglyphs denoting distance and length (right)

That the ancient Egyptians were capable of creating arches or curved roofs is easily verifiable by the blue-green faience-tiled reliefs found in the Subterranean Chambers of the Step Pyramid itself (*Fig. 7-84,* see also *Figs. 6-22* and *6-23.*)

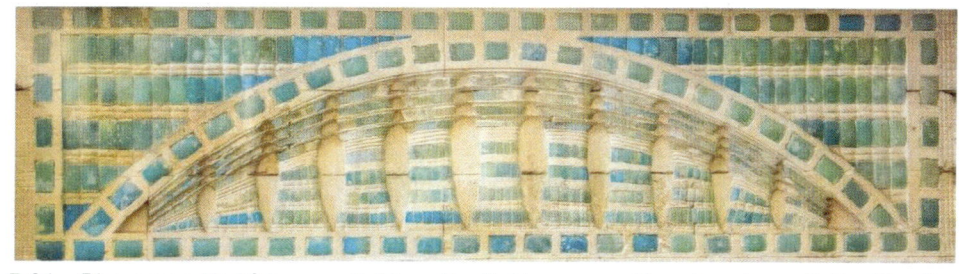

Fig. 7-84 – Blue-green tiled faience relief from the Subterranean Chambers beneath the Step Pyramid

In ancient Egypt, distance and length were measured in *cubits*, said to be the length of the pharaoh's arm from the elbow to the tip of the middle finger. The cubit is further divided into *palms* and *fingers*.

Hieroglyph	Unit	Equals	Modern Equivalent
⌒	Finger or Digit	---	1.87 cm; 0.74 in.
▭	Palm	4 Fingers	7.48 cm; 2.95 in.
⌐	Cubit	7 Palms or 28 Fingers	52.4 cm; 20.63 in.

In modern units of measure, the cubit is about 524 or 525 millimeters, or 20⅝ inches wide depending on which reference you are using. The values depicted on the ostracon are in *fingers*. The English archeologist, Battiscombe Gunn interpreted each of the five segments on the ostracon to be approximately 1 cubit (28 *fingers*) wide.

Fig. 7-85 – The Structure 'E' adjacent to the North Pavilion. The white arrow indicates where the Sakkara Ostracon was found (at "Q" in Fig. 7-99), and the remaining lower portion of the arched roof depicted on it

Fig. 7-86 – The remaining portion of the arched roof of the Structure 'E' adjacent to the North Pavilion (white arrow, Fig. 7-85)

Only half of the roofline is depicted on the ostracon as it gave enough information to the on-site construction manager to recreate its mirror image in order to have his masons build the complete roof (*Fig. 7-87*).

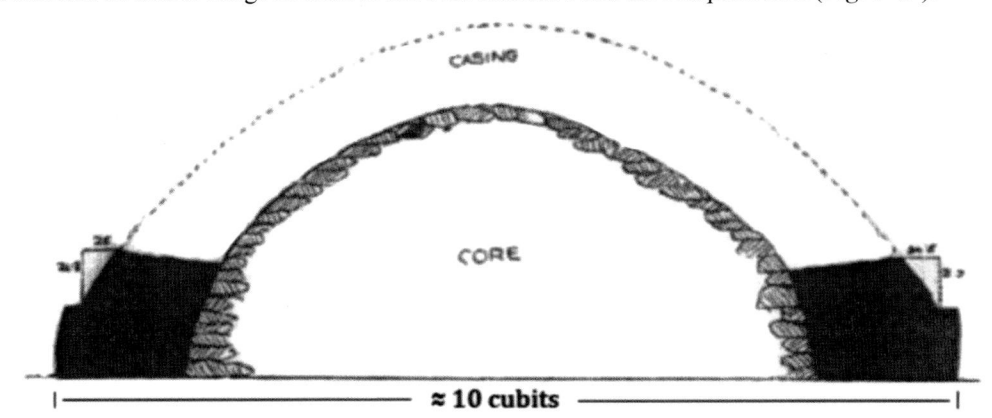

Fig. 7-87 – Cross section of the curved saddleback roof of the building west of the North Pavilion

When first examined by Gunn and Firth, the ostraca did not have a clear indication of the length of its base line. Assuming the distance between the lines of the ostraca were equal, Gunn and Firth extrapolated the width of the base where the zero endpoint would have been on the right side of the ostraca had it not been broken off (*Fig. 7-82*). They estimated it to be 5 cubits, or the equivalent of 140 *fingers* with the total width of the structure being about 10 cubits (280 *fingers*). The ostracon was unearthed next to structure marked as 'E' (*Fig. 7-85* and at 'Q', *Fig. 7-99*), part of the U-shaped structure adjacent to the North Pavilion (see *Fig. 7-85*). For this reason, the belief was that the ostracon was the blueprint used to construct the vaulted roof of Structure 'E' (*Fig. 7-88*). Lauer, however, felt the formula on the ostracon might have been used for Structure 'D' southwest of the North Pavilion, or one of the four structures east of it (marked as 'I', 'J', 'K' and 'L' on *Fig. 7-99*).[117]

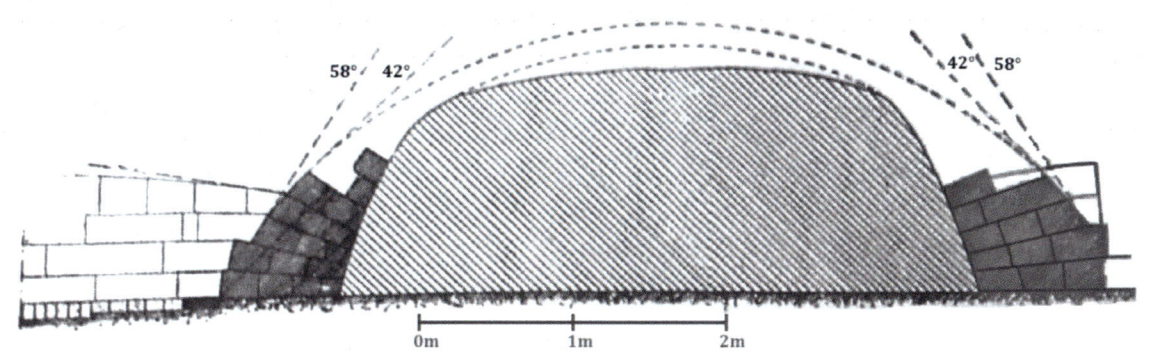

Fig. 7-88 – Cross section of the curved saddleback roof of building 'E' (or 'D') west of the North Pavilion

Other researchers have developed their own interpretations as to what the Sakkara Ostracon formula entails. Andrew Connor, a structural engineer from Great Britain, believes the ancient Egyptians used the 3-4-5 triangle to develop the arched characteristics of the saddleback roof (*Fig. 7-89*). [118] As elegant as Mr. Connor's hypothesis may seem, it falls short of being correct in that the base line in his proposal is about 55 fingers (about 103 centimeters, or 40.56 inches) too wide. Other than that, it shows much promise in solving the Sakkara Ostracon Mystery.

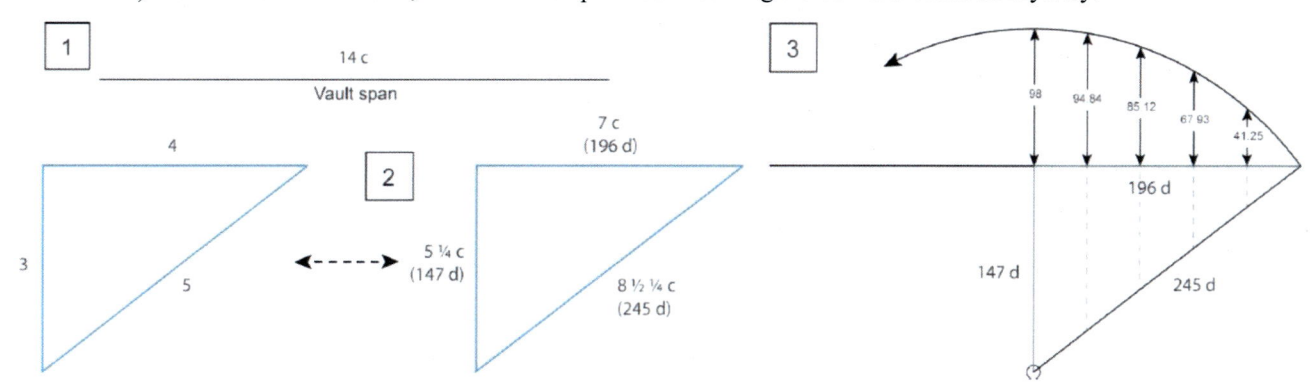

Fig. 7-89 – Andrew Connor's method for calculating the Sakkara Ostracon data

Another interpretation of the Sakkara Ostracon formula appears in the book *Architecture and Mathematics in Ancient Egypt*, by the English Egyptologist, Dr. Corinna Rossi. [119] In her book, Dr. Rossi postulates the formula on the ostracon was determined by using a simple device of a rope and several pegs using a 3-4-5 triangle (a common enough tool in ancient Egypt) to create an ellipse (*Fig. 7-90*). In ancient times, the most likely use of rope and pegs to delineate an elliptical curve would have been to place it horizontally on the ground to map out the foundation for a building with a rounded wall structure. (Maybe Imhotep used this device to determine the foundation for the rear of Chapel '0' in the Ḥeb-Sed Court.)

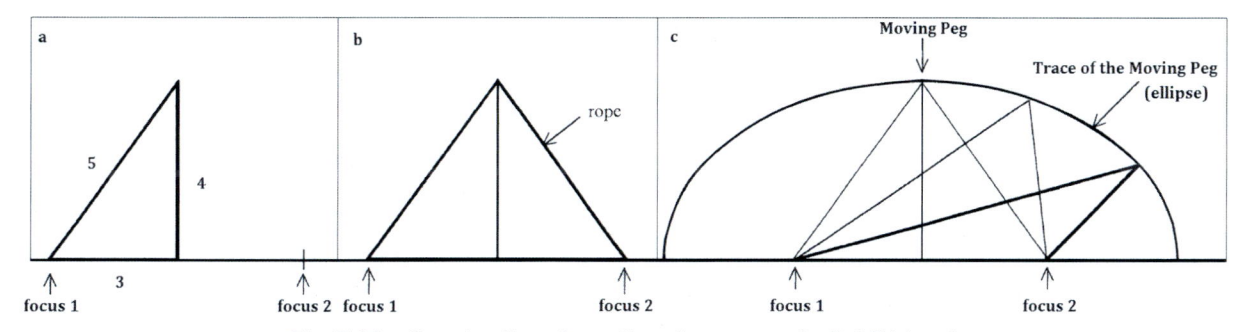

Fig. 7-90 – Construction of an ellipse by means of a 3-4-5 triangle

This theory holds that the architect used a peg and rope on a flat surface (e.g., the ground or a sand table) to lay out the design of the arched roof. He then transferred the final design to the ostracon and gave it to the construction crew to build the roof. This would be plausible if the outer edge of the arched roof curved downward at nearly a 90° angle at its endpoint as in an ellipse. However, since the remains of the roof *in situ* slope at a steep angle to the outside edges of the structure, this theory doesn't match the shape of the roof structure itself (see *Figs. 7-87* and *7-88*).

An amazing solution for the ostracon's formula comes from Arto J. Heino (*Fig. 7-91*).[120] Based on the work of Ben Iverson, Heino uses a rather esoteric form of math called Quantum Arithmetic. Developed in the late 1940's through the 1990s, Iverson's writing sometimes takes on a quality close to mysticism.[121] In one of his articles, he integrates Euclidian geometry, Fibonacci series, prime numbers and musical harmonics using number sets in an array that produce solutions to complex problems in a unique form that defies an easy explanation, so I will not try to do so here (because I would probably mess it up and get it horribly wrong). He stated that the use of Quantum Numbers "were used as early as 2000 BCE in the Rhind Mathematical Papyrus", though he did not divulge the problems in the RMP to which he was referring.

Nevertheless, Heino's solution for the ostracon formula produces an ellipse derived from three nested circles (*Fig. 7-92*) that looks somewhat like the technique of using the rope and peg method advocated by Dr. Rossi, even though Gunn specifically said the curvature of the arched roof was part of a circle, not an ellipse. (Note the Quantum Ellipse also includes the Vesica Pisces Double Circle as part of its design.) A simple visual inspection of the remains of the arched roof (*Figs. 7-85* and *7-86*) shows it could not have derived from an ellipse. In addition, the net outcome of Heino's calculations result in a base line of 294 centimeters, or 588 centimeters for the entire width of the arched roof, far larger than the width of 557 centimeters as measured on site by Gunn and Firth.

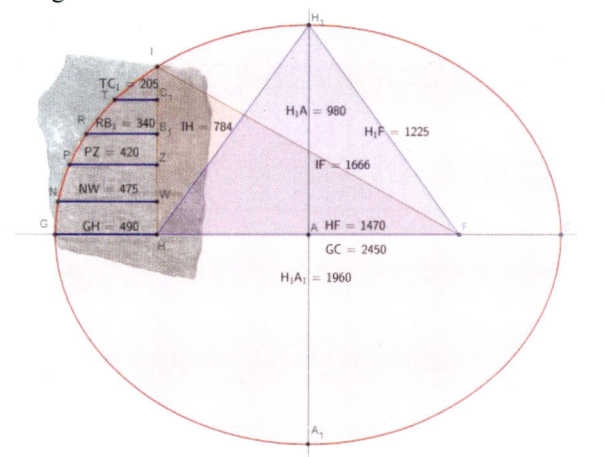

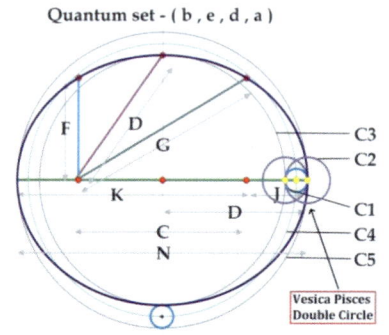

Fig. 7-91 – Arto Heino's solution for the Sakkara Ostracon

Fig. 7-92 – The Quantum Ellipse of Arto Heino

While Quantum Arithmetic looks like it came from an alternate universe, it does bear looking into as a tool for solving complex problems. However, using it to solve the problem of the Sakkara Ostracon formula is not one of them. Not only the reasons given above regarding the solution espoused by Dr. Rossi, but for the obvious reason that the development of Quantum Arithmetic occurred in the 20th century with no evidence it ever existed or was used in any guise circa 2660 BCE.

Finally, a paper by Paolo Di Pasquale also puts forth a similar theory that the curve of the arched roof derived from a circle (*Fig. 7-93*).[122] Though it bears a resemblance to Andrew Connor's work, it is different in that Di Pasquale uses a much larger circle to arrive at a solution. Because of the paucity of data related to the horizontal length of the base line, Di Pasquale assumes the spaces between the vertical lines is 41 fingers (76.875 centimeters, *Fig. 7-94*). However, his conclusion suffers from a base line length of 205 fingers (7.32 cubits, 383.637 centimeters) with a total length of 410 fingers (14.64 cubits, 767.274 centimeters), much larger than the measured width of 557 centimeters of the arched roof of Structure 'E'.

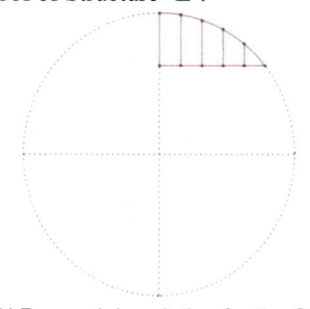

Fig. 7-93 – Di Pasquale's solution for the Sakkara Ostracon formula using part of a circle as the basis for its design

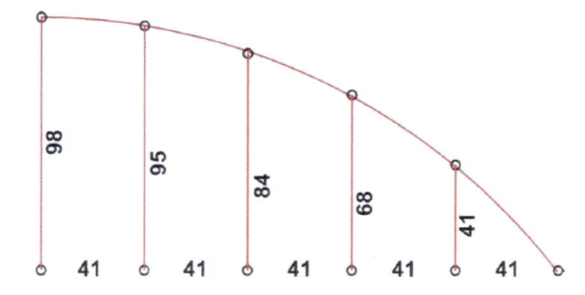

Fig. 7-94 – Di Pasquale's solution for the base line of the Sakkara Ostracon

Within these five analyses are competing theories as to whether the curve of the roofline was determined by the use of a circle or an ellipse. To clarify further, one need only ask if any of these interpretations can be corroborated with known architectural and construction practices that existed during the period before and after the Third Dynasty. With the probable exception of the Arto Heino's solution that uses 20th century Quantum Arithmetic, ancient Egyptian architects may indeed have used one or several of these techniques to create curved roofs or other art during the Old Kingdom as is evident in the Sakkara Ostracon formula. While the above interpretations may eventually be verified with other data from archeological finds, they all share one thing in common: the results of all their computations and suppositions result in a base line, and subsequently, the measured size of the arched roof *that are all much too large.* When placed against the evidence of the true size of Structure 'E' as verified from the measurements recorded by *boots-on-the-ground* archeologists, it becomes readily apparent the space between the five vertical lines is less than 28 fingers, and unequally spaced as well.

Most of the other investigators use a cubit whose length is 525 millimeters, mainly because it seems to be the preferred length used by most Egyptologists, and because it rounds up easily into numbers which have fewer digits after the decimal point. I chose to use the value for the cubit inscribed on a wall near the South Pavilion that was apparently use by Imhotep when designing and building the Step Pyramid Enclosure, that is 524 millimeters. (*After all, what's a silly millimeter among friends?*) While this may seem to be a nonsensically small detail, when scaled up to the size of one of the structures near the North Pavilion, the reasons for using Imhotep's cubit will become obvious.

Given all these disparate and wonderfully elegant, yet complex solutions to the Sakkara Ostracon Mystery, I felt perhaps there was a simpler solution to this problem. When looking at the modern renderings of the drawing on the ostraca, I had another *oh-what-the-heck* moment. I laid out a Root 2 ($\sqrt{2}$) Rectangle using the same 3.5 cubits (98 fingers) of its height along the base line. The resulting curve created from the diagonal of the square landed *precisely* on the zero endpoint (*Fig. 7-95*). The length of the resultant portion of the rectangle was the same length of 41 fingers as the first vertical line on the right, making the base line about 139 fingers long. This difference of a length of one finger from the measurement used by Gunn is no more than 1.87 centimeters ($\approx$ 0.74 inches). The indicated measurements on the ostracon easily proves the total length of the base line ($\approx$139 fingers) can be derived from the maximum height (98 fingers, or 3.5 cubits) of the curved roof by using a Root 2 ($\sqrt{2}$) Rectangle.

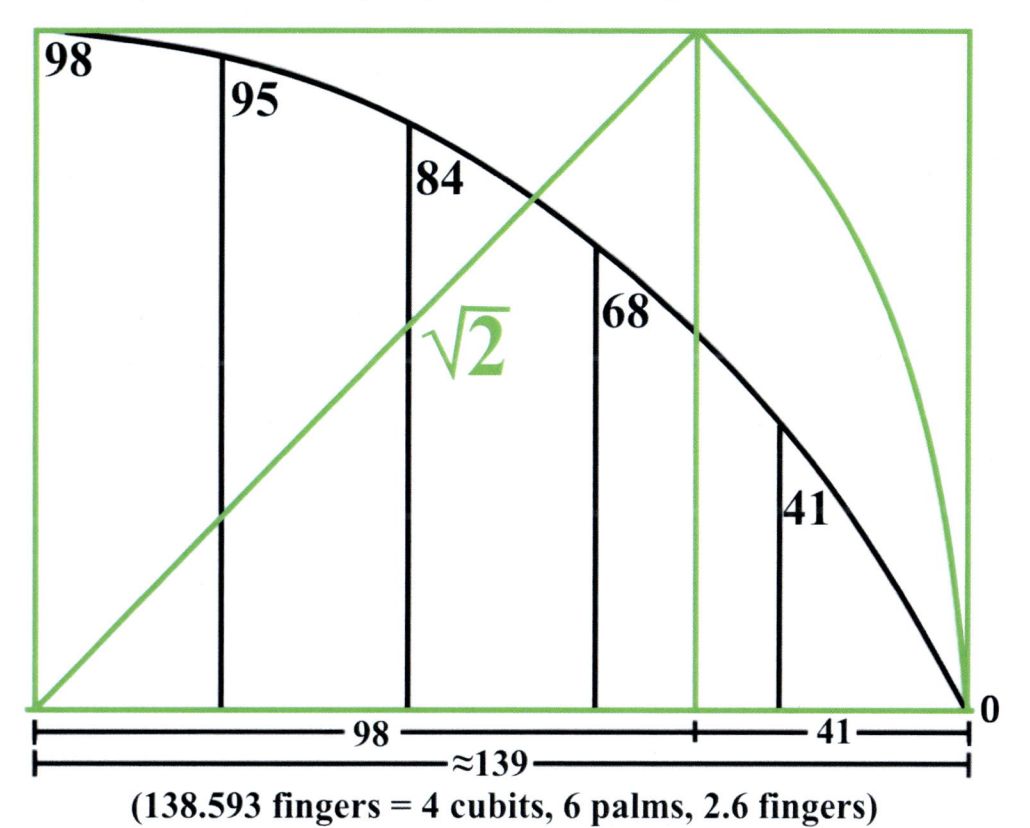

(138.593 fingers = 4 cubits, 6 palms, 2.6 fingers)

Fig. 7-95 – The underlying design principle of sacred geometry used to create the Sakkara Ostracon. All measurements are in 'fingers' (1/28 of a cubit)

Taking a cue from the work of Andrew Collins, I attempted to produce an easier and more accurate method of recreating the curve of the Sakkara Ostracon. On a hunch, I extended the left vertical line downward a length of 49 fingers, half the height of 98 fingers. From this center point, I recreated the curved arch on the ostracon *exactly* (*Fig. 7-96*). (*Boy was I surprised!*) I did not expect it to be very accurate when I began, yet, there it was! Because of its simplicity, this method of reproducing the Sakkara Ostracon formula has the greatest chance of being the correct one than any of the other hypotheses.

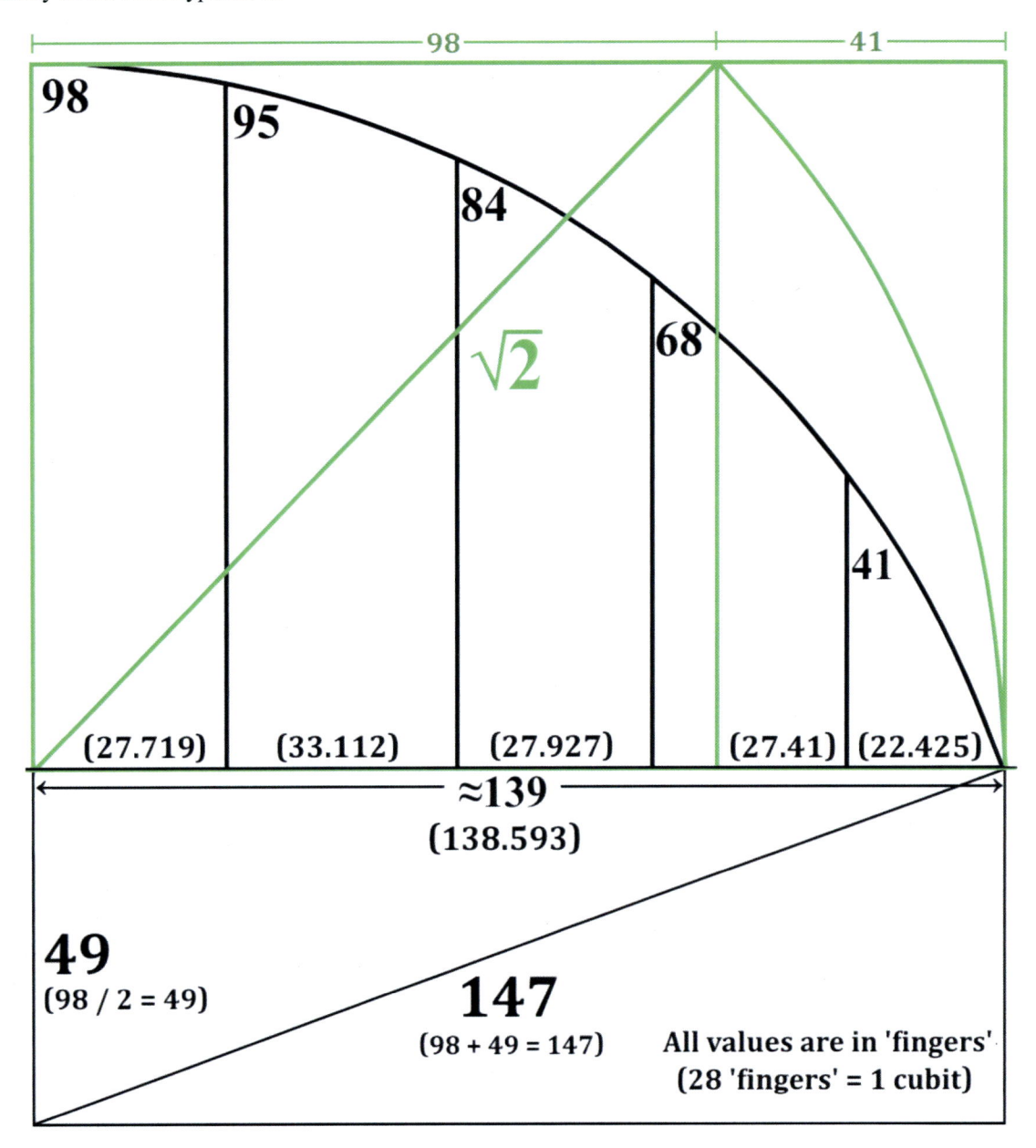

Fig. 7-96 – A simpler method of recreating the formula of the Sakkara Ostracon

Assuming the unfinished group of mastabas existed before work began on the complex, I suspect Imhotep measured the width each of the buildings adjacent to the largest of the mastabas (soon to be the North Pavilion) to create arched roofs for them. The formula on the Sakkara Ostracon was drawn for use in finishing the roof for the nearby structure 'E' or one of the other smaller buildings ('D', 'F', 'I', 'J', 'K' and 'L' in *Fig. 7-99*).

After taking measurements for the unfinished mastabas, Imhotep drew out the base line using a Root 2 ($\sqrt{2}$) Rectangle based on the width of this structure. From this, he determined the height of the arched saddleback roof would be 98 fingers, or 3.5 cubits. During the design process, he took half this height (49 fingers), extended it downwards below the base line, and set the center point for a circle, part of which was the arc that defined the curved roofline. After that, he used the width of the remainder part of the Root 2 ($\sqrt{2}$) Rectangle (41 fingers) for the height of the first vertical line, and created the other three vertical lines (68, 84 and 95 fingers) accordingly.

Not only that, this design template is a rectangle that has 3 vertical and 5 horizontal segments, creating a 3:5 ratio, or 0.6. This ratio of 3:5 appears to have been often used in the initial measurement of temenos walls and other parts of temples when first laid out (*Fig. 7-97*) as we have seen with Khasekhemwui's Funerary Enclosure, as well as the Step Pyramid Enclosure as a whole (see *Fig. 7-45*).

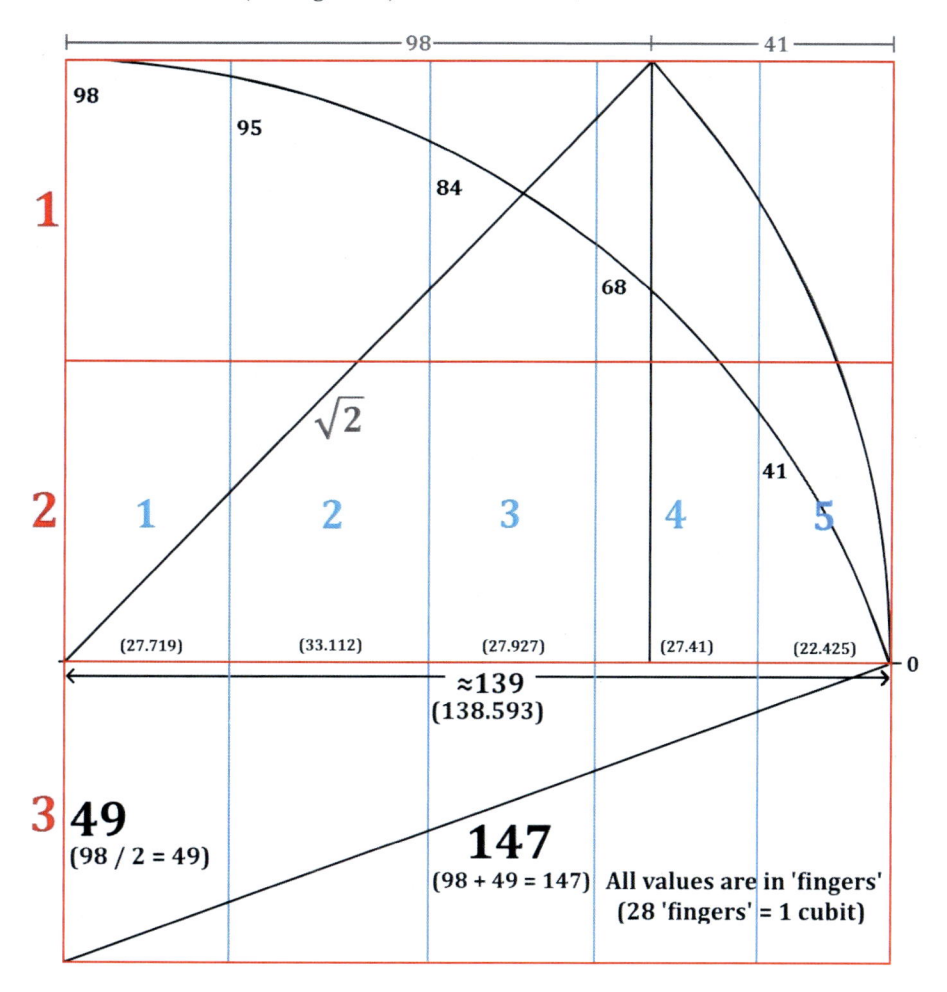

Fig. 7-97 – The 3:5 ratio of the Sakkara Ostracon

Even more amazing is that when fleshing out the formula for the arched roof to its full size, it depicts overlapping Silver Rectangles (*Fig. 7-98*) as found in several other buildings adjacent to the North Pavilion (*Fig. 7-99*), and the First Enclosure (*Fig. 7-22*).

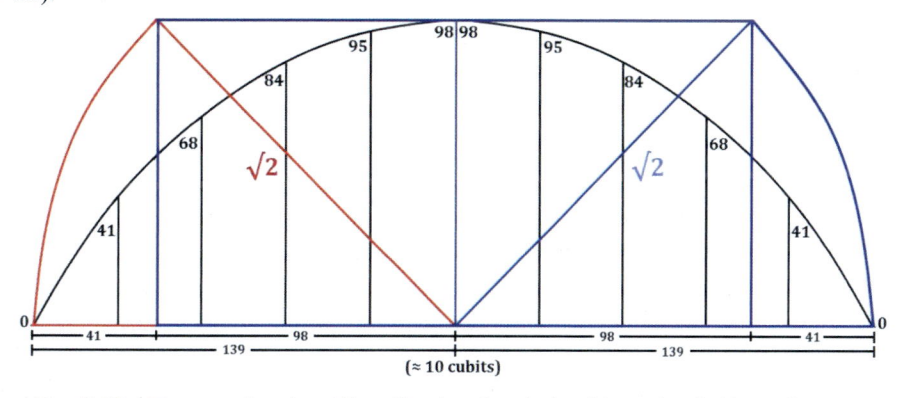

Fig. 7-98 – Two overlapping Silver Rectangles derived from the Sakkara Ostracon

Furthermore, I believe that whoever originally built the North Pavilion cluster of mastabas (perhaps Imhotep's father, Kanofer) certainly used Sacred Geometry to realize their design. In *Fig. 7-99*, you can see the Silver Rectangle is the most used Sacred Ratio in the design of the buildings adjacent to the North Pavilion. [A Silver Rectangle is simply a Root 5 (√5) Double Square Rectangle and the Root 2 (√2) arc from one of the two squares extended along its base.] The Double Square and *Phi* (Φ) Rectangles also make an appearance as well. If indeed, Sacred Geometry was the main tool used to create the formula for the arched roof; this would result in a slightly smaller base line that is a bit less than the 140 fingers proposed by Gunn and Firth, which has been now verified (*Fig. 7-96*). This points to the possibility that the Sakkara Ostracon was meant to guide the construction of an arched roof for the smaller Structure '**D**' (as Lauer had suggested), which is also near the spot where the ostracon was found (marked as '**Q**').

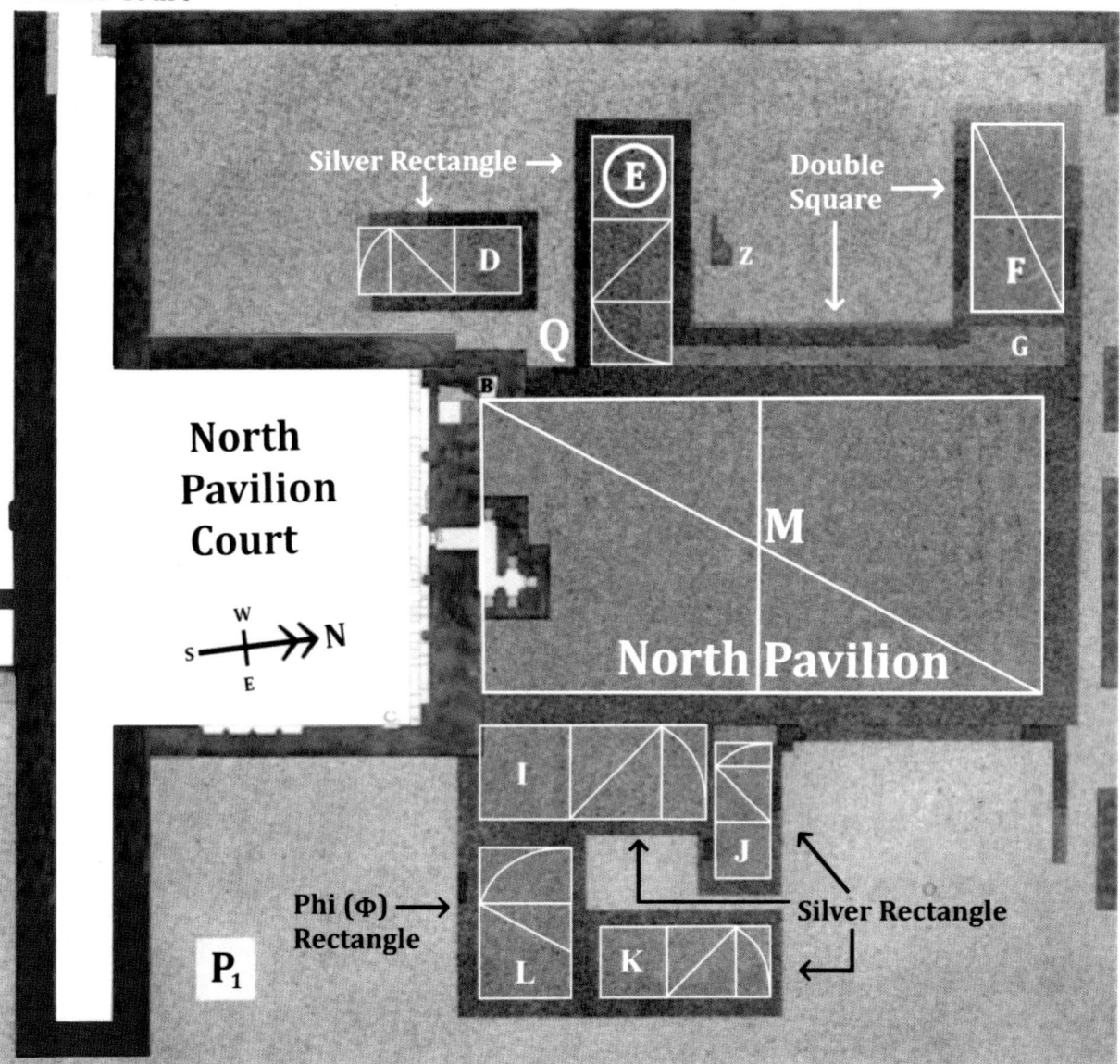

Fig. 7-99 – The Sacred Geometry Ratios used in the design of the North Pavilion and its attached buildings

If nothing else, this little shard of limestone proves that ancient Egyptian architects like Imhotep were using Sacred Geometry to design their temples thousands of years earlier than previously thought.

Given what has been revealed thus far, the only logical conclusion is that the Greeks did not *import* Sacred Geometry during their occupation of Egypt. The ancient Egyptians developed the art first, which the Greeks and other cultures later appropriated when planning their own temples and other structures. Like "sending coals to Newcastle", the Greeks brought Sacred Geometry back to its country of origin when they rebuilt more than a dozen of the older, neglected and rundown temples along the Nile.

Final Thoughts

In our brief examination of the several mortuary monuments built before and after the Step Pyramid Enclosure, it has become apparent that certain mathematical ratios commonly associated with the art of Sacred Geometry were part of the standard 'toolkit' of ancient Egyptian architects. It is safe to say ancient Egyptian architects extensively used Sacred Geometry in their designs from at least the Second Dynasty kings, Peribsen and Khasekhemwui, to the Third Dynasty kings Netjerikhet Djoser and Sekhemkhet, to the later Fourth Dynasty Great Pyramid of Khufu at Giza, and quite possibly beyond. There is an easily discernible set of geometric ratios used in the design of these monuments that can only be explained by their architects using Sacred Geometry to do so. It was pervasive as much as it was *hidden in plain sight*.

By all appearances, it seems ancient Egyptians created a *proto*-Sacred Geometry that is somewhat different from the one used in later periods by the Greeks and Romans. They may have even inherited it from an earlier civilization such as the *Shemsu-Hor*, as previously discussed in Chapter 3. This simpler forerunner of the sacred art was no doubt due in part to the development of, and ensuing experimentation with, this new architectural language by generations of Egyptian architects. It also included several features that are unique to the art these architects practiced to design their monuments and temples. In time, the Greeks and Romans added additional complexities and refinements to the language of Sacred Geometry to become the standard design tool of architects since then.

Trying to perceive unintended Sacred Geometrical relationships in the design of the Step Pyramid Enclosure is fraught with danger, both intellectually and architecturally. Doing so will always divert one's attention away from the true esoteric meaning hidden in the temple's design. We must carefully look at these ancient monuments with fresh eyes so as not to impart something that is not there, as in the phenomenon known as pareidolia. This is akin to seeing an animal or a sailing ship in the shapes of clouds, and is equally ephemeral. Interpreting the spatial relationships between various elements of the Step Pyramid Enclosure as being the result of using Sacred Geometry by ancient architects may appear to be wishful thinking, but the fact remains, these ratios do exist and can be easily detected. In no way am I trying to squeeze a square theory into a round hole of accepted, verifiable facts. Nevertheless, being able to perceive and mentally create geometrical patterns *out of thin air* is not a bad thing. It is a necessary skill that architects and artists of all professions must acquire and use on a daily basis.

Why is it important to understand the design and construction of these monuments? Why would Imhotep go through all the trouble of using Sacred Geometry to design the Step Pyramid Enclosure? It is apparent by all that has been shown thus far that it took a great deal of effort and forethought to build a temple using such complex design principles. Every architect has moments in the design process where "form follows function" gives way to adding elements that break the mold, so to speak. The true answer is that Imhotep was using the practices of his predecessors – probably his father and grandfathers before him – who also used Sacred Geometry to design similar mortuary monuments. Those of us that view the work of these ancient architects are unable to perceive the underlying practices used in their creation because geniuses like Imhotep are able to cleverly disguise the use of Sacred Geometry in the final form of their designs.

While it appears I want to have it both ways, a certain amount of intellectual discipline must be maintained at all times when examining the architecture of ancient Egyptian temples and mortuary shrines so as not miss the obvious – and not-so-obvious – esoteric meanings concealed within the edifices of these monuments. One need only look at the plans of the Step Pyramid Enclosure to realize there is more to its design than any tortured interpretation could possibly conceive. It has often been that said many secrets are still hidden in the sands of Egypt. Yet, it also appears that many secrets are readily visible if we know how and where to look. This is yet another reason why *this book will never be finished*.

Symbolist interpretations of ancient Egyptian architecture may not be a hot topic in Egyptological circles, but it is the "elephant in the room", which cannot be ignored. Symbolism and Sacred Geometry is rampant in ancient Egyptian architecture, and to ignore it or say it does not exist demeans the spirit of the ancient Egyptians who built these marvelous monuments.

Knowing all this, I would venture to say that from now on, whenever you see or walk into any Egyptian temple or pyramid, you will know that deep within its architecture, there lies a hidden meaning to its design, and that meaning will be revealed once you look past the stones that makes up its structure. Then you will truly *see beyond sight*, and become aware of greater ideas and greater worlds than you previously thought possible. In the flash of such moments of insight and intuition, a connection is made with those who built these monuments. The barriers of time and space will seem to disappear, leading to a greater understanding of the world where these ancient architects and priests lived in, and more importantly, what they can teach us about ourselves. The enlightenment they can bring us today will only happen if we shed the constructs and beliefs that anchors us to the present without giving due honor and respect to those who have gone before us, and – oh, by the way – in order to do so, we must also *listen to the intelligence of our hearts*.

Mathematics is the alphabet with which God has written the universe.

Galileo, Italian astronomer

Humanity will only change once our intelligence comes from the heart.

Friedrich Schiller, German Poet and Philosopher

Imhotep the Sage and Scribe – Another Gate and Departure from the World of Spirit

The journey of a thousand miles begins with a single step. – *Lao Tsu, Chinese philosopher*

Let us come full circle and briefly return to the stone artifact that began this "journey of a thousand miles".

Regardless of whether a self-closing door once led out of the Step Pyramid Enclosure or not, we must still look at it in the same symbolic manner as would an ancient Egyptian. They could not have invented a more graphic way of showing the process by which a soul (the ***ka***) leaves the world of the flesh and enters the World of the Spirit by passing through the Entrance Hall out to the Great South Court, the metaphorical *stand-in* for the *Field of Reeds*, the Egyptian heaven. This eternal process continues when the spirit returns to life in the world of flesh in a new body by exiting through the North Exit Gate. One cannot return to the spiritual universe – the Afterlife – except by way of the process of death symbolized in the South Entrance Gate and the Entrance Hall. In this way, Imhotep has brilliantly created in stone an illustration of the cycle of life. If there is a better, more subtle way of teaching this, I cannot think of one.

Our Western-trained minds tend to think in absolutes; something can only be interpreted either one way, or another. All available evidence clearly shows there was no exit corridor in the eastern enclosure wall near the southernmost part of the North Court. Yet, the presence of a doorpost socket designed for a self-closing door implies the architect may have wished us to think beyond our own presumptions regarding the meaning of the Step Pyramid's architectural details. When we see unusual or out-of-place architectural features, are we willing to shed long-held beliefs about them? Do we have the courage to say that, perhaps, there is something more going here than meets the eye?

The stones of these great temples and pyramids are inherently mute. However, there is much they can tell us – if we are willing to listen. After all, temples can tell tales and teach us tremendous truths that transcend the limits of time and the cultural traditions that created them. To that end, let us take a little side trip to another wonderful temple that can give us additional insight into this idea.

Thutmosis III

Many scholars contend that Thutmosis III, the sixth pharaoh of the Eighteenth Dynasty, and his aunt and stepmother, Hatshepsut, the dynasty's fifth pharaoh, had a contentious and bitter relationship because she essentially usurped the throne of Egypt for herself. Though she claimed her father, Thutmosis I, had intended her to be his designated successor, Hatshepsut was only co-regent with Thutmosis III who was the rightful heir to the throne, but Thutmosis III was only two years old when his father, Thutmosis II, died. Because he was the rightful heir to the throne and named co-regent by his father even at such a young age, some believe Thutmosis chafed at the bit, so to speak, but did not dare create a political crisis by overthrowing his aunt/ stepmother.

Hatshepsut was pharaoh for approximately 21 years between 1479 BCE to around 1458 BCE. Towards the end of her reign, Hatshepsut involved Thutmosis more and more in the affairs of state, and eventually put him in charge of Egypt's armies. After she died, it is said Thutmosis rapidly asserted himself and did everything he could to expunge the memory of his co-regent and overshadow her accomplishments. He expanded Egypt's empire by subduing southern and northern enemies, thus earning the sobriquet, "the Napoleon of Ancient Egypt".

There has been speculation that near the end of his reign, Thutmosis III ordered the removal of all traces of Hatshepsut's rule. At her temple at Deir el-Bahari and elsewhere, her statues were torn down, her monuments were defaced or covered up, and her name was removed from the official king list. Some think this was clearly an act of vengeance, though others interpret this as Thutmose III ensuring the succession would run from Thutmose I through Thutmose II to Thutmose III without the incursion of a female ruler in the line.

Hatshepsut

Knowledge of Hatshepsut faded, but in 1822, inscriptions on her magnificent mortuary temple at Deir el-Bahari (*Fig. 8-1*) were finally able to be deciphered. Egyptologists were initially confused because the male image of this unknown pharaoh had a female name, but eventually, the relationship between Hatshepsut and Thutmosis III became clearer.

Or so the story goes. Yet, temples tell a different tale, and their architecture sings a song in stone.

Fig. 8-1 – Mortuary Temples of Hatshepsut (right), Thutmosis III (left rear) and Mentuhotep II (left)

In the recessed bay at Deir el-Bahari across the Nile River from Thebes (modern-day Luxor), between Hatshepsut's glorious three-level mortuary temple and the Eleventh Dynasty temple of Mentuhotep II is the smaller, nearly destroyed temple built by Thutmosis III. Though it is in the process of restoration as of this writing, Thutmosis's temple is somewhat less imposing than Hatshepsut's uniquely graceful and beautiful monument. Had Thutmosis any hard feeling towards Hatshepsut from the outset of his reign, he would have repurposed her temple for his own use and had her name removed and replaced with his own; a not uncommon practice in ancient Egypt. Had he done so, he would not have needed to build his own temple.

Though he was undoubtedly a highly dynamic, testosterone-laden expression of Egyptian manhood, Thutmosis III probably had a great deal of respect for Hatshepsut. He may have resented her authority at times (as most children do), but in his own way, he was, perhaps, grateful to Hatshepsut for teaching him the intricacies of statecraft which he would need when she handed over the reins of power near the end of her reign. More evidence exists of their mutual respect than of any perceived animosity (*Fig. 8-2*).[123]

Instead of erasing Hatshepsut's name altogether from her mortuary temple as other pharaohs would have done, he erected his own comparatively modest temple next to hers, and essentially left her temple alone. Any defacing of her monuments probably occurred no sooner than 20 years into Thutmosis's reign, and may have even happened at the behest of his successor, Amenhotep II. Even then, not all of Hatshepsut's images were erased or defaced. A few of her images tucked away from view in various shrines and tombs were not even touched. Any alleged conflict or acrimony between Thutmosis III and Hatshepsut can be challenged by the presence of their two temples standing side-by-side at Deir el-Bahari. In a sense, these temples mimic depictions of the two pharaohs standing together performing religious and political rituals as seen on Hatshepsut's Red Chapel (*Fig. 8-2*) and elsewhere. Any assumption favoring a rivalry between Hatshepsut and Thutmosis III says more about the late 19th and early 20th century archeologists who fostered these kinds of specious arguments, and are nothing more than a lazy intellectual exercise of those with too much time on their hands or too little evidence to formulate a logical theory. Fortunately, modern Egyptologists rely on more scientific methods to reach their conclusions.

Most likely, the erasures occurred during the reign of Amenhotep II, Thutmosis's heir and co-regent. It is difficult enough ascertain with any accuracy exactly when any of Egypt's ancient monuments were constructed let alone the exact date they were defaced, dismantled or destroyed. Perhaps the succession to the throne of Amenhotep II was not so clear-cut since his mother was a non-royal. By defacing, removing or even covering up Hatshepsut's monuments such as her obelisk in the Temple of Karnak, Amenhotep II sought to legitimize his ascension to the throne by attempting to erase a female pharaoh – albeit a very capable and strong monarch – from the lineage of his family going back to the Pharaoh Ahmose.

Fig. 8-2 – Thutmosis III and Hatshepsut making offerings as equals – The Red Chapel, Karnak (Manna Nader, Gabana Studios, Cairo)

This is consistent with the personality of a misogynistic man that did not even record the names of his queens. Perhaps he felt that royal women who bore the title, God's Wife of Amun – a title used by Hatshepsut – indicated that women at the court had become too powerful. Other reasons may explain why Amenhotep II needed to relegate Hatshepsut to anonymity, but that's subject for a different day.

As we continue in this same vein, if we *listen* to the ancient mortuary temple of Djoser and make similar *out-of-the-box* observations, many things are suddenly revealed in unexpected ways. The existence of a unique element in a temple's architecture can tell us more than the mere assemblage of stones ever could. For example, if evidence exists of a doorpost socket for a self-closing door leading to a North Exit Gate in a location where no proof for such an opening in the Enclosure Wall ever existed, then perhaps we may need to entertain a third possibility: **That both pieces of evidence are correct**.

We have already seen that the South Entrance Hall can be symbolically interpreted in several distinctly different ways. While the North Exit Gate may no longer exist physically since it was, in a sense, decommissioned when the South Entrance Hall/Ḥeb-Sed Court quadrant was constructed, it still existed *etherically*, and thus, *symbolically*. Though our modern way of thinking may prohibit us from entertaining the possibility that two extremely different concepts can exist simultaneously, this does not mean a certain ancient Egyptian physician/architect/priest/vizier was incapable of doing so.

In many carved reliefs, the gods Horus and Seth appear together, symbolically binding the Two Lands together with rope (see *Fig. 3-32*). Thus, it becomes apparent the ancient Egyptians believed that Order could not exist without Chaos, and vice versa. Perhaps, they also held that one could not recognize Order without first experiencing Chaos. In either case, ancient Egyptians saw both Order and Chaos in their daily lives. For example, the chaos of the inundation followed by a subsequent return to order with the planting and harvesting seasons. The *chaotic* life of wild animals such as the lion, crocodile and hippopotamus contrasting with the quiet *order* of domesticated animals like the cat, the cow and sheep. The wild, dust-laden winds, the *khamasīn*, that rush up from the south causing damaging sand and rain storms versus the cool breezes from the north allowing boat traffic on the Nile River to travel against the northbound currents.

Such was the role of duality in Egyptian life where it colored everything and formed every viewpoint. The average Egyptian probably saw their world as being either one way or another, never both at the same time. The rare genius like Imhotep, though, saw life as a multi-dimensional reality that is capable of revealing a deeper meaning and richer truths than the commonly accepted belief of *the way things are*.

Because of this multi-layered perspective as proposed in Chapter 3, Imhotep designed several rooms near the Entrance Hall in the shapes of hieroglyphs relevant to their intended use or symbolic meaning. Apparently, those rooms were not the only instances were Imhotep embedded hieroglyphs within various architectural elements of the Step Pyramid Enclosure. Other *hidden hieroglyphs* can be found throughout the complex. The Great South Court (*Fig. 8-3*) is a giant rendering of the hieroglyph for "temple", "tomb", or "enclosure". In certain contexts, it can also mean "castle", or "mansion"; all of which tie into the functions of this funerary temple.

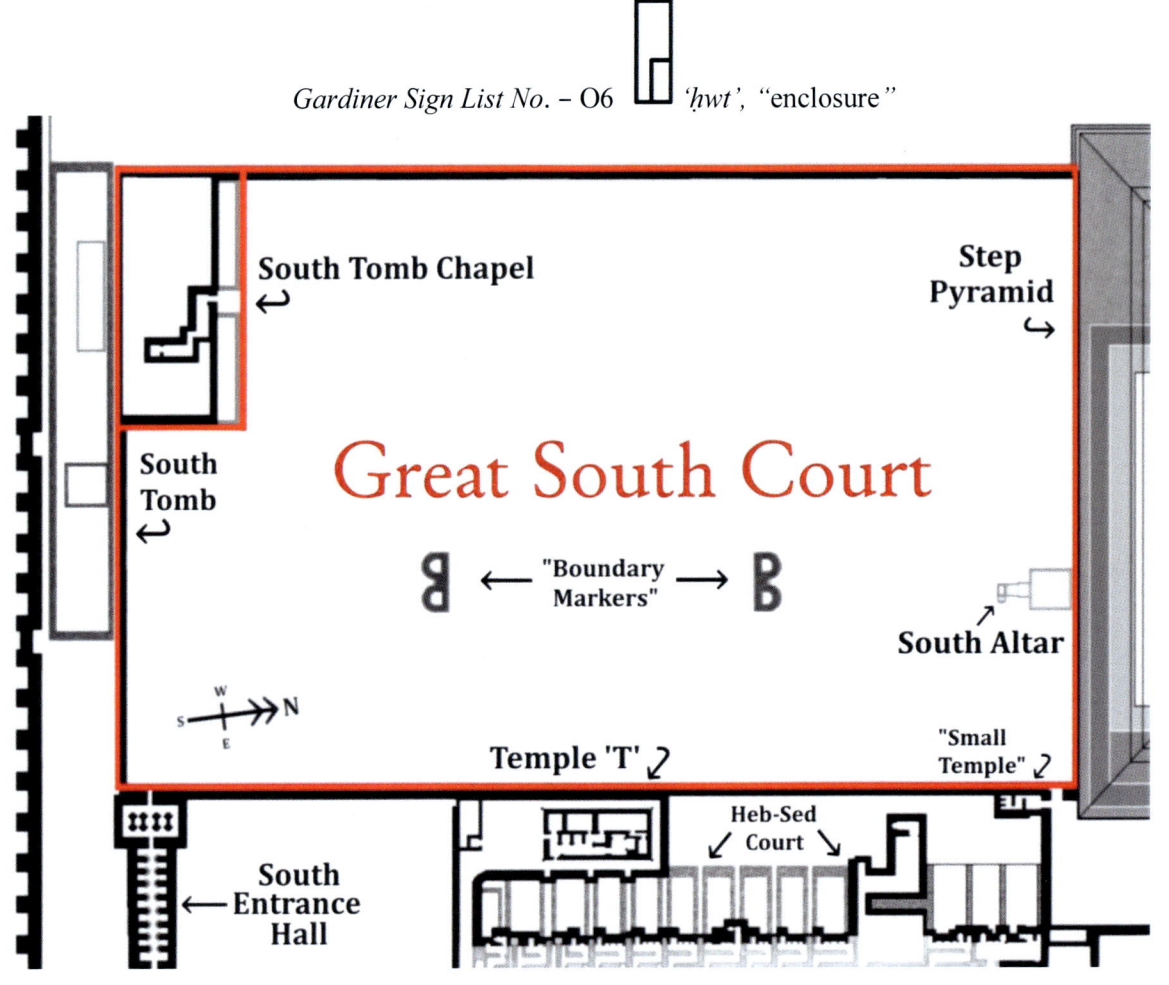

Fig. 8-3 – The Great South Court in its guise as the hieroglyph 'ḥwt'

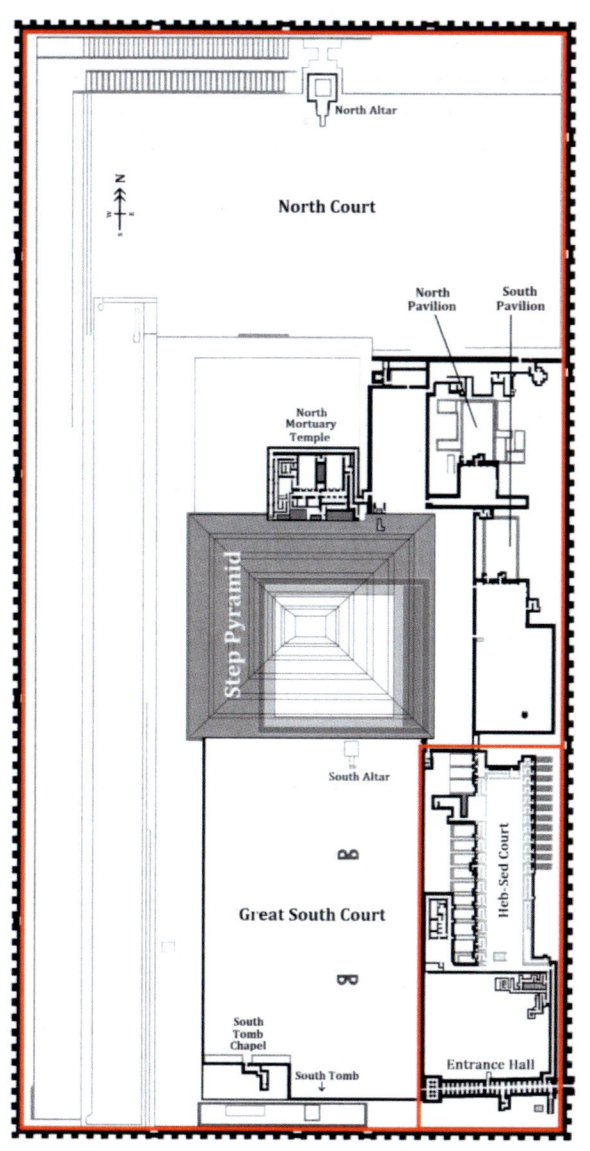

Fig. 8-4 – The Step Pyramid Enclosure in the form of the hieroglyph for "house" or "enclosure"

Even the Step Pyramid Enclosure as a whole resembles the *ḥwt* hieroglyph with the South Entrance Hall/Ḥeb-Sed Court quadrant representing the small rectangle within the larger one (*Fig. 8-4*). The reason emphasis is placed on the South Entrance Hall/Ḥeb-Sed Court quadrant in the southeast corner as opposed to any other part of the Step Pyramid Enclosure is that it saw the most activity on a daily basis than any other part of the temple because it was a medical center for well over a hundred years.

Combined with the hieroglyph of the falcon-headed god, Horus, with whom pharaohs were usually associated, the *ḥwt* hieroglyph becomes the name of the goddess Hathor. This link to Hathor may appear tenuous, but a temple dedicated to this goddess was once located in Memphis. Allegedly as large as the temple precinct of Ptah, its precise location is still unknown. Ramesses II built a smaller temple to Hathor, carrying on the tradition of a temple dedicated to this goddess in the city of Memphis (*Fig. 8-5*). Located near the remains of the Great Temple of Ptah, the Temple of Hathor was excavated in the 1970s.

Gardiner Sign List No. – O10 (O6 + G5)

'Ḥt-ḥr', "Hathor"

Fig. 8-5 – The small Temple of Hathor in Memphis built by Ramesses II, possibly on the site of the original temple

Another feature of the Sakkara plateau that does not receive much attention is the Dry Moat or Great Trench (*Fig. 8-6*). It surrounds the Step Pyramid Enclosure and the pyramid of Userkhaf. It is an enormous feature that, while not easily seen from the ground level, is plainly visible from the air and satellite photos. The Dry Moat is a rock-cut trench covering an area measuring about 750 by 600 meters, and resembles the hieroglyph meaning 'ground plan (for a house)'.

Gardiner Sign List No. – O1 ⌐ ⌐ '*pr*', "house"

The Dry Moat was created as a platform (*Fig. 8-7*) on which the Step Pyramid would eventually be constructed, though it was probably excavated much earlier during the Second Dynasty. Debate about its purpose has been ongoing for some time. The most logical explanation is that the Dry Moat seems to be part of a larger concept concerning the ancient Egyptian creation myth of the god Ra-Atum who formed the universe *out of nothing*. In this myth, darkness and chaos in the form of a primordial *soup* was all that existed. Out of this sea emerged a hill known as the ben-ben stone, on top of which Ra-Atum stood and brought forth the beginnings of life. Curiously, the word *ben-ben* sounds similar to the verb *weben*, which is the Egyptian word meaning 'to rise'. [124]

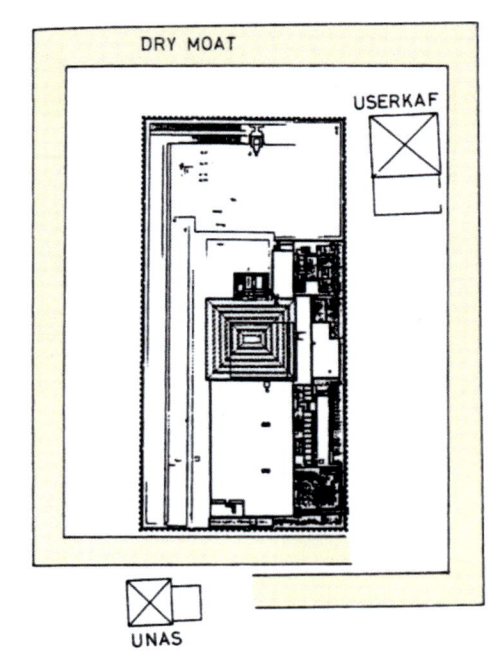

Fig. 8-6 – The Dry Moat and surrounding monuments

This artificially elevated limestone plateau symbolically became the first mountain that rose out of the seas of chaos before recorded history with the Step Pyramid being a solid masonry *stand-in* for the ben-ben stone.

Fig. 8-7 – Artist's concept of the Step Pyramid Enclosure sitting atop a raised mound surrounded by the Dry Moat during the Third Dynasty, minus the pyramids of Unas and Userkaf that were built much later. The two mastaba-like structures on the left are the superstructures of the mortuary monuments thought to have once stood over the entrances to the underground chambers of the first and third Second Dynasty kings, Hotepsekhemwy and Ninetjer (Fr. Monnier)

Fig. 8-8 – Dry Moat south of Step Pyramid Enclosure Wall   *Fig. 8-9 – Part of the Dry Moat near the Pyramid of Unas*

Though it is difficult to imagine given the desert environment of modern Egypt (*Figs. 8-8* and *8-9*), the Sakkara plateau in Egypt during the Third Dynasty was a relatively lush and green environment with many trees and greenery (*Fig. 8-10*), with a resultant higher annual rainfall than there is now. There is even evidence of water intrusion into the Step Pyramid's underground chambers, so the Dry Moat could have also served to keep its substructure dry besides being a symbolic metaphor for one of Egypt's oldest creation myths.

Fig. 8-10 – Artist's impression of the Sakkara plateau during the Old Kingdom (ca. 2686 – 2181 BCE)

Towards the end of the Sixth Dynasty (circa 2345–2181 BCE), a massive, worldwide climactic shift took place, possibly due to a volcanic explosion or other natural disasters taking place elsewhere on the planet. The event, whatever it was, affected all of Africa, especially near the source of the Nile in modern Uganda. This resulted in a 20% drop in annual rainfall due in part to a mini ice age that occurred at that time.[125] Subsequently, Egypt turned into the hot, dry desert we see today with little to no vegetation save that of the fertile Nile valley (*Fig. 8-11*). This enormous disruption in the climate also led to a social and political upheaval culminating in the turmoil of the First Intermediate Period that occurred in about 2180 to 2150 BCE as recounted in Chapter 3.

Given the climatological factors outlined above, the building of the Ḥeb-Sed Court medical center could have only taken place during the relatively peaceful and prosperous time of the Third Dynasty. Such a unique building project needed a stable climate, both politically and environmentally, in which such a forward thinking and expansive concept could be realized. After the disruption of the First Intermediate Period, it is unlikely the combination of a genius like Imhotep and the resources he brought to bear as Vizier and architect could ever produce an edifice such as the Step Pyramid Enclosure ever again. In this respect, the Old Kingdom, that is, the Third Dynasty through the first part of the Sixth Dynasty was truly the *golden age of ancient Egypt*.

Fig. 8-11 – Artist's impression of the Sakkara plateau when it became a desert after the Sixth Dynasty (ca. 2180 BCE)

Even though I initially had misgivings about looking for rooms or other structures in the Step Pyramid Enclosure that resembled hieroglyphs, my *out-of-the-box* thinking eventually proved otherwise. It is highly unlikely that Imhotep secretly embedded symbolic references to relevant hieroglyphs into the design of this temple that is either capricious or accidental. I must admit that searching for hidden hieroglyphs in the architectural details of the Step Pyramid Enclosure began to feel like playing *Where's Waldo*. [126]

As explained in Chapter 7, the phenomenon known as *pareidolia* may account for parts of the Step Pyramid Enclosure resembling hieroglyphs. If so, can this be no more than a mere coincidence? However, there is an old saying: **"a single unique occurrence is an anomaly, two occurrences are a coincidence, but *three or more occurrences are a developing pattern*"**.

As far as the Step Pyramid Enclosure is concerned, this appears to be the case. More than that, designing parts of a structure or a whole building in the shape of a specific hieroglyph that is indicative of its function does not appear to be random or arbitrary, and cannot be attributed to pareidolia or wishful thinking. Because of the number of *hieroglyphic happenstances* scattered throughout the Step Pyramid Enclosure's design, it is safe to say Imhotep was hiding deeply esoteric knowledge *in plain sight*.

After discovering shapes of hieroglyphs embedded in the design of various features within the Step Pyramid Enclosure, I stumbled upon further confirmation from a different source. In the North Court there is a high platform called the North Altar (*Fig. 8-12*). On top of the platform is a raised area about 26-feet square and a couple inches tall.

Debate has surrounded the purpose of this platform/altar since it was uncovered in the 1930s. The Egyptologist Hartwig Altenmüller believed an obelisk may have been erected on the North Altar.[127] However, Rainer Stadelmann later disproved this since large obelisks didn't appear until the Fifth Dynasty sun temple of Niuserre at Abu Ghurob.[128] Others think it was a throne dais used in connection with the *Ḥeb-Sed* ceremonies, but the South Altar is better fit to serve that function (see Chapter 6). Currently, the general consensus is that it was an altar used for giving offerings.[129]

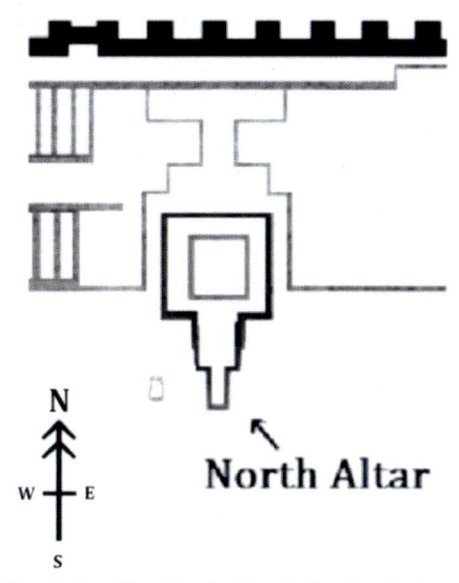

Fig. 8-12 – The North Altar in the North Court

Granted, all of this is highly speculative, but apparently I'm not alone in thinking the shape of hieroglyphs inspired several features in this temple. In his book, *The Treasures of the Pyramids*, Dr. Zahi Hawass noted the North Altar was shaped like the hieroglyph for 'offering'. At first, I could not figure out to which hieroglyph Dr. Hawass was referring. While the North Altar's shape resembled the hieroglyph for "treasury" or "white house", the hieroglyph for "invocation offering" seemed to be the closest one.

Gardiner Sign List No. – O2 'pr-ḥd'
"treasury", "white house"

Gardiner Sign List No. – O3 'prt-ḫrw'
"invocation offering"

Though plausible, something still didn't seem right.

When looking through several photographs of the North Altar, I discovered one that fit the definition of "offering" better than any other image (*Fig. 8-13*). Looking at the North Altar from its north side to the south towards the Step Pyramid, it bears an uncanny resemblance to the hieroglyph for "offering table".

Gardiner Sign List No. – R3

'wḥdw', "offering table"

Fig. 8-13 – The North Altar from the rear looking south

From this viewpoint, it appears the east and west sides of the North Altar are sloping inward, as are the sides of the offering table in the hieroglyph. Abstract though it might be; the resemblance is uncanny. This is all very subjective, but coupled with the evidence of darkened seeds found on top of the North Altar, it appears to be more than plausible (see text at *Fig. 6-65*). Certainly, it can inspire us to stretch our perceptions – and imaginations – beyond what we believe to be true.

As the Ḥeb-Sed Court was also a medical facility, it is highly likely that patients were treated using many of the other rooms located within the complex. Near where I found this doorpost socket are some rooms that today are in a state of near ruin (see *Figs. 1-1* and *1-8*). Few have speculated as to what purpose these rooms may have served, but here I will make a grand intuitive leap: **If this temple was indeed a hospital, then it is equally possible these rooms were for patient examination or even surgical operating rooms**. There is more than enough evidence showing the ancient

Egyptians were skilled in the art of surgery. If these rooms and the halls nearby had roofs and the rooms had doors on them, then it is conceivable a self-closing door in the gate nearby would have helped keep out dust and dirt in a place where such delicate surgical procedures would have been performed.

If not used for surgery, then perhaps the small multi-sided room near the exit (seen in the background in *Fig. 1-8*) was reserved for the most common and universally human experience: childbirth. Such birthing rooms are known as "mammisi". **Located next to the North Exit Gate where one symbolically leaves the world of spirit to be born into the physical world, then naturally, this room could be a labor/delivery room in this temple-hospital complex.** The combination of the shape of the original Old Enclosure Wall with the exit corridor of the North Exit Gate of which I have speculated; and its proximity to this *birthing room* bears a passing resemblance to a womb and the birth canal (*Fig. 8-16*).

In many temples, especially in the temples rebuilt by the Greek Ptolemys such as at Edfu, Dendera, and Kom Ombo, there is a small building called the *mammisi*, or Pharaoh's birth chapel (*Fig. 8-14*). These were small chapel-like structures dedicated to the goddess Isis located within larger temple precincts and are thought to have been for the exclusive use of royal childbirths, making the pharaoh's offspring equal with the gods.

Fig. 8-14 – Mammisi or Birth House at the Temple of Edfu (reconstructed)

The number of niches set into the walls of the Step Pyramid's delivery room show there was accommodations for up to three expectant mothers simultaneously. Unless Djoser and his successors had very large harems (there is no evidence of this), it is probable this mammisi was for use by the general population as well as for royal births, as were the facilities in the Ḥeb-Sed Court medical center.

Looking at the Step Pyramid's birthing rooms, or *Mammisi*, from the west (*Fig. 8-15*), more than one hieroglyph is suggestive in the shape of its design.

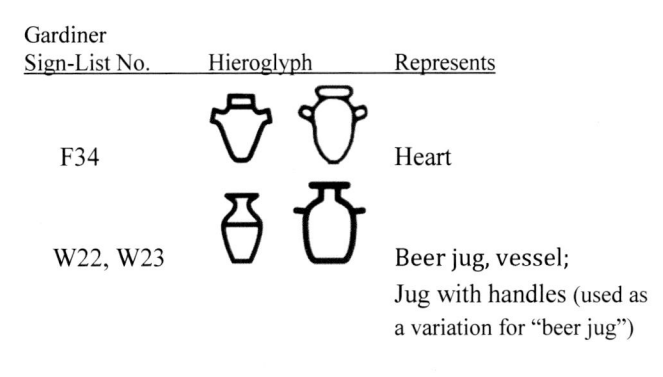

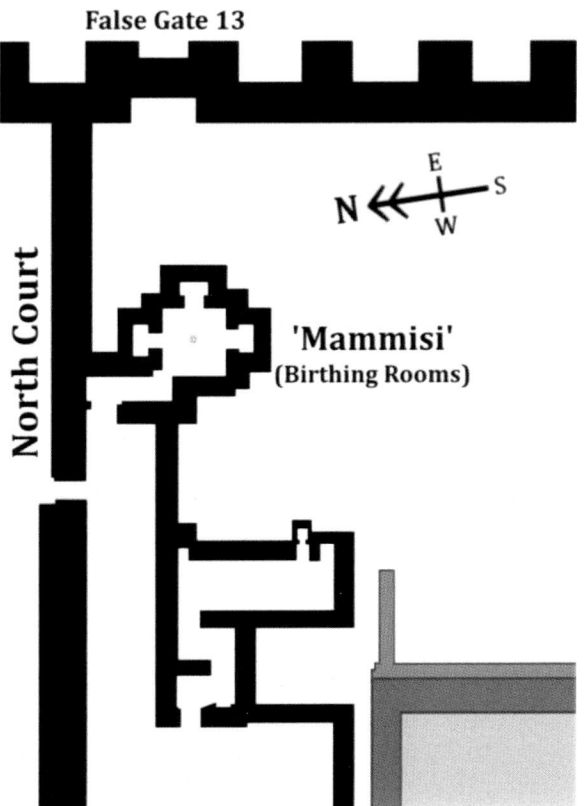

Gardiner Sign-List No.	Hieroglyph	Represents
F34		Heart
W22, W23		Beer jug, vessel; Jug with handles (used as a variation for "beer jug")

Fig. 8-15 – False Gate 13 (the old North Exit Gate) and "Mammisi"

To review: The ancient Egyptians considered the heart to be the most important organ in the human body. It not only performed the most vital function of all the organs within the body, but it was believed to be the seat of wisdom, or the source of higher intuitive faculties, and was the repository of a person's emotions, intellect, will and morality. Within it was recorded the sum total of a person's behavior and actions during their lifetime. When the higher intuitive function of the heart is working at full strength, the heart becomes the gateway to other realms that lie beyond the five senses. To listen to, and be in harmony with the *Wisdom of the Heart*, a person would be *Living-in-Truth*, or *maat* that is, Divine Order, Harmony and Balance. Thus, they would attain the highest level of intelligence and knowledge possible, and live the fullest life for any human.

To be born into the physical world, the spirit or soul must once again live within the confines of a human body. While some may feel living in a human body is a limitation, perhaps ancient Egyptians felt the newborn soul still had a connection to the world of Divine Essence or Spirit from which they came. Being born in a room shaped like the hieroglyph for "heart" tells the soul to remember that link through the heart during their journey here on Earth. They could only do this if they were willing to listen to their heart at all times in order to maintain that connection (*maat*) to the Divine Source that created them and the Universe they lived in.

The three rooms just west of the Mammisi may have also been part of a *maternity wing* of the Step Pyramid Enclosure medical center (*Fig. 8-16*). Related to this in a strange sort of way, the Mammisi also resembles another hieroglyph, this one for a "jug with handles". In certain contexts, it can also mean "beer jug". Beer was an integral part of Egyptian life, and was thought to possess great powers, especially when used as part of religious worship, and often given as a gift to the gods. Along with bread, beer was used as a form of payment for a person's labor. As a staple in the ancient Egyptian diet, men, women and children all drank beer, not as an intoxicant (it did not contain much alcohol), but as a source of nutrition since water was extremely unsanitary. It was also valued for its healing properties, and was often prescribed in medical texts, not as treatment for an illness, but because it was thought to "gladden the heart". [130] (Though it seems odd, this may indicate a closer connection between the similarly shaped 'heart' and 'beer jug' hieroglyphs.)

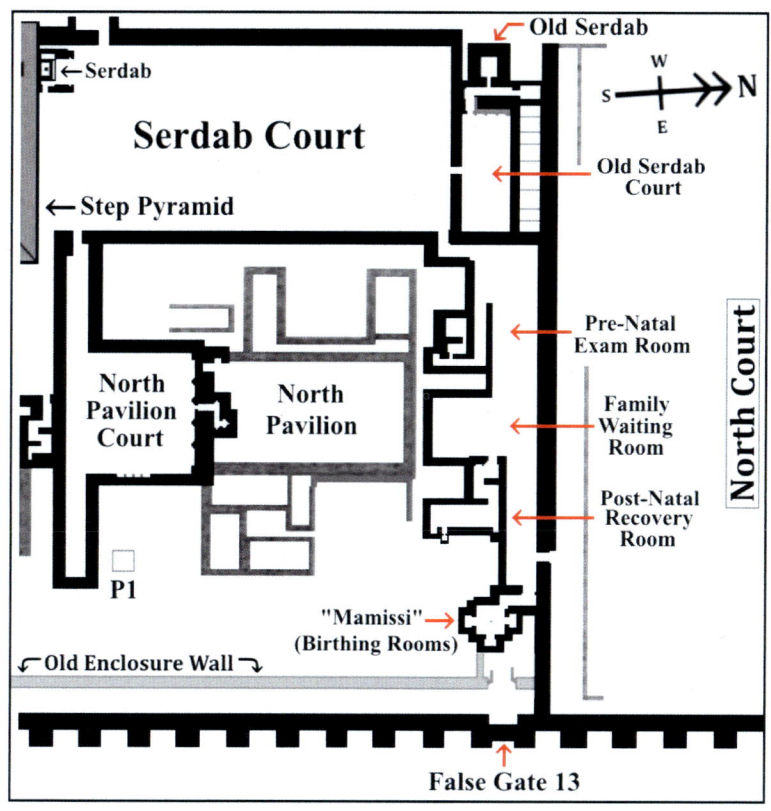

Fig. 8-16 – The rooms just north of the North Pavilion and their possible use as a maternity wing

The association of beer with the shape of the mammisi is not so obtuse. During the time of the Old Kingdom, brewing beer was done primarily by women in the home, and are essentially the first brewers in Egypt. It was only much later in the New Kingdom when beer making became a state-funded industry and run exclusively by men. The deity who presided over the making of beer was also a female, Tenenet, or Tjenenet. She watched over the brewers and made sure they carefully followed the recipe to ensure the quality of the final product. [131] Not coincidentally, Tenenet was also the goddess of pregnancy and childbirth, and protector of the uterus. (In German, *brau* ['to brew beer'] sounds similar to *frau* ['woman' or 'wife']. Is this another linguistic legacy from ancient Egypt?)

The 'beer jug' hieroglyph is often translated as 'vessel' or 'to anoint'. In a highly poetic sense, the expectant mother is a *vessel* for a new life about to be born. In a less poetic (and all too human) sense, the new father would have celebrated with family and friends at the arrival of a new child by consuming copious quantities of beer. (*Sorry! Couldn't help it.*) This may seem silly and frivolous to suggest the shape of the rooms of the mammisi was intended to look like the 'beer jug' hieroglyph, but perhaps ancient Egyptians were not so different from us when it comes to reveling in the joyous, important events of life! As previously stated, there does not need to be only one interpretation for any architectural element in this temple. What is more important to know is that it was deliberate.

Fig. 8-17 – Postnatal Recovery Room

The first room due west of the Mammisi is for new mothers and their babies to rest after childbirth, as the new mother might need to stay one or more days after giving birth. A clue for this is the small notch-like room in the south corner (*Fig. 8-17*, inset) is probably a latrine; similar to the other latrines scattered throughout the complex, and were used by the women during their recovery from childbirth. The second room is for family members awaiting the arrival of the newborn child. The third room to the west may be for the physician/priests and midwives to examine and prepare mothers-to-be before taking them to the birthing rooms for delivery.

The colloquialism for *childbirth* in the ancient Egyptian language literally means "on the bricks".[132] The traditional method for giving birth was to have the woman sit or kneel on a stack of linen-covered bricks (*Figs. 8-18a* and *8-18b*) usually constructed in the shape of a 'U'. The elite may have used a more comfortable *birthing chair* for this purpose.

Fig. 8-18a – A birthing brick from Abydos

Fig. 8-18b – The same birthing brick showing a birthing chair

The interior walls of the Mammisi's three birthing rooms are perfectly designed for the U-shaped birthing seat. Aided by midwives and/or family members, the expectant mother would sit upright on these bricks, or a birthing chair. During childbirth, the mother's groin was positioned over the empty space below her (*Fig. 8-19*, see also *Fig. 3-45*), allowing the midwife to catch the baby as it is being born. This position is purportedly the best for giving birth as it uses gravity to ease the baby out of the womb, and places less stress on both mother and child. The number of rooms in the Mammisi (three) is significant in that it strangely relates to another hieroglyph. It depicts three foxtails tied together. Though translated as "apron of foxes' skins" or in other contexts, "black eye-paint", it also has another meaning more relevant to the design of the Mammisi.

Gardiner Sign List No. – F31   '*msi*', "give birth"

Fig. 8-19 – Isis giving birth ("on the bricks") aided by the goddesses Hathor and Taweret

Further analysis of the birthing rooms of the Mammisi reveals the possibility of a much greater and more esoteric interpretation besides resembling the hieroglyphs for the heart or a two-handled jug. If we view the shape of the birthing room in a more simplified form, it would look something like *Fig. 8-20*.

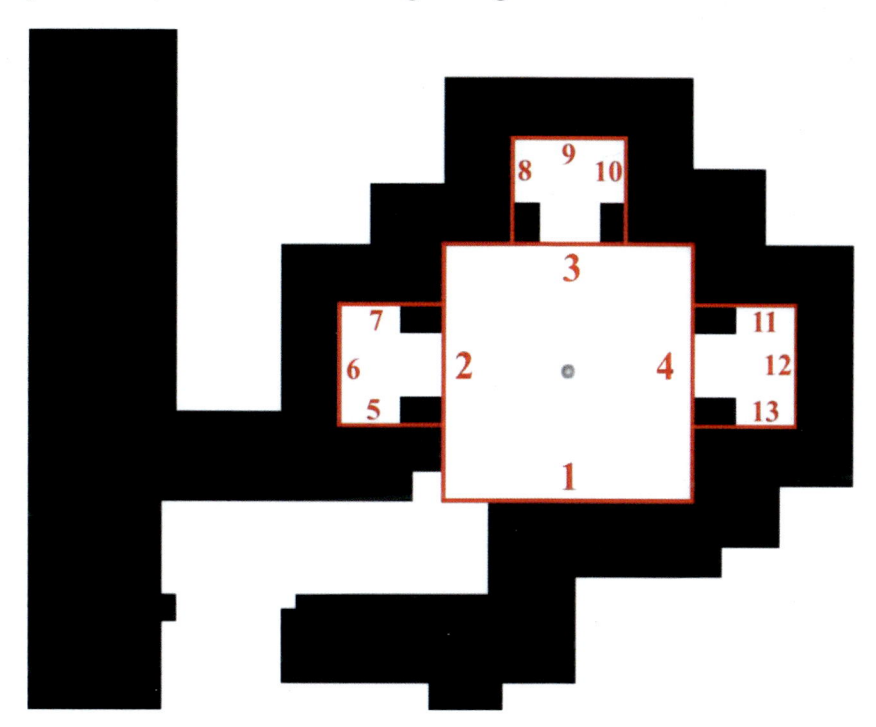

Fig. 8-20 – The Mammisi as a metaphor for "the meaning of life"

The central room and the three birthing chambers outlined in red show the interior of the Mammisi is composed of only 13 walls in its most basic form. Knowing this, why would Imhotep want to hide a 13-sided set of rooms within the design of the Mammisi? Perhaps once again Imhotep is urging us to look beyond the obvious.

The number 13 equals 14 minus 1 (*obviously*). This simple equation (14 – 1 = 13) is symbolic in two ways. Both numbers were associated with the concept of death and resurrection. As noted before, the significance of these two numbers comes from the Osiris myth. The number 13 is the number of pieces of Osiris' body the goddess Isis was able to retrieve in order to resurrect him, symbolizing the creation of a new body. Additionally, Imhotep is reminding us of the age-old maxim that **from the day you are born (13), you are one day closer to your death (14)**.

Though this may seem a bit morbid, herein lies a great truth and Imhotep designed the Mammisi to reflect that truth. This is speculative, of course, but in relation to the Osiris story, maybe ancient Egyptians in general thought the number 13 was a constant reminder of our mortality, and while we are yet alive, we need to live our lives to the fullest, which directly affects how well your life after death will be. From the scenes of the Afterlife painted on the walls of their tombs, it is plain to see the ancient Egyptians wholly embraced this profound belief (*Figs. 8-21* and *8-22*).

Fig. 8-21 – Tomb of Nebamun – Fowling Scene

Fig. 8-22 – Tomb of Nebamun – Banquet Scene

The two scenes in these figures are from the tomb chapel of Nebamun, an official who worked in the temple of Karnak, and are highly evocative of similar scenes found in other tombs throughout Egypt. These scenes are probably reminiscent of Nebamun's life on Earth, but it is equally probable they were an idealized view of what Nebamun wished to enjoy in the Afterlife.

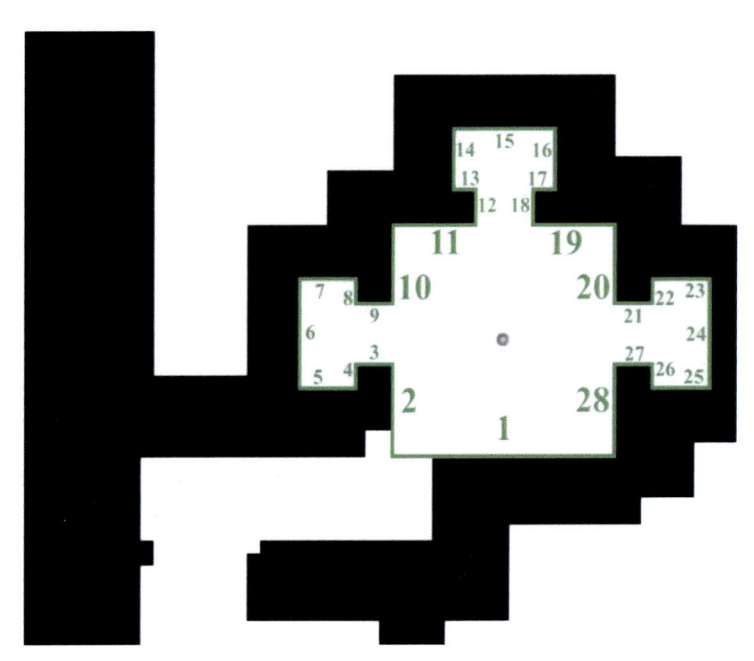

Fig. 8-23 – The Mammisi as a metaphor for the soul returning to life on Earth

Within the design of the walls of the Mammisi is another *hidden* meaning. Its symbolism is revealed when the number of wall surfaces of the three birthing rooms including the smaller wall sections of the door openings are added up, the total comes to 28 (*Fig. 8-23*). Twenty-eight is the number of days in a lunar cycle. The moon is often associated with female deities because 28 is also the average number of days in the female menstrual cycle, further proof that these rooms served the needs of women in childbirth.

I may be reading more into the plan of the Mammisi than Imhotep may have intended, but he could easily have created a simpler design as seen in the red outline of these rooms in *Fig. 8-20* that would have accomplished the same design goals.

In addition, at the risk of being too obvious, 28 is 14 times 2. To put it symbolically, death and resurrection (14) reflects the dual realities (the *Magic Number 2*) of a person's existence on Earth, and their eventual transition to the Afterlife, which the Egyptians believed to be mirror images of one another.

Twenty-eight is also 24 + 4, which represents the 24 vertebrae of the spine plus the 4 unfused bones of the coccyx (*tailbone*) prior to birth. It is only after puberty when the bones of the coccyx become completely fused. The irony here is that the entrance corridor of the South Entrance Gate also represents the coccyx, and along with the Entrance Hall symbolizes the transition of the soul from the world of flesh to the Afterlife. The layout of the rooms in the Mammisi and the reason for their use is a reflection of the idea that a soul is returning to life on Earth from the world of spirit. Of the few medical papyri from ancient Egypt that exist today, quite a few address gynecological issues related to women's health and childbirth, most notably the Kahun, Gardiner, Carlsberg and Berlin papyri. This indicates the level of medical care given to women was vitally important. The Mammisi itself, and the rooms associated with it are also a reflection of this same care given by Imhotep the Physician to the people of Egypt, and gives a feminine counterbalance to the masculine energy of the Step Pyramid.

If there was any doubt that Imhotep designed various architectural elements of the Step Pyramid Enclosure in the shape of hieroglyphs, we need only remember the expansion of the Step Pyramid from a simple mastaba into a four-tier pyramid. The four-tier pyramid-shaped hieroglyph is listed in hieroglyph dictionaries as being a "double stairway" which is often translated as "a high place".

Gardiner Sign List No. - O41   *'q3y'* or *'i'r'*, *"high place"*

However, in certain contexts, this is also translated as **"to ascend"**; a meaning that dovetails nicely into the purpose for which the Step Pyramid was created in the first place: to be a vehicle for the Pharaoh to 'ascend' to the stars.

Am I reading more into this than what is readily apparent? Possibly, but even the most casual observer will find the Mammisi birthing room and the rooms nearby have an unusually unorthodox design the use for which cannot be easily explained otherwise.

We can certainly see that Imhotep was capable of creating architectural features and elements based on the shape of hieroglyphs. That he did so throughout the Step Pyramid Enclosure becomes more apparent the deeper you look. Any reasonable assessment of Imhotep's personality would safely conclude he did not disguise the shapes of certain hieroglyphs in the Step Pyramid Enclosure's design because he had a whimsical sense of humor. Perhaps he wanted to teach future generations the wisdom of ancient Egypt, and did so from a desire to inspire anyone to look beyond the outward appearance of what can be readily seen with their eyes, but instead, to *see* with their hearts. It may also be the reason he chose to use stone when he constructed the Step Pyramid monuments; to give a more lasting expression for all the secret metaphysical knowledge he possessed.

To go through the trouble of creating a *self-closing door* implies that whoever did so possessed an overall guiding principle that necessitated its realization. The ancient Egyptians never designed and constructed their temples in a capricious or arbitrary fashion. There is purpose to every architectural element, every construction detail and every hieroglyph; all incorporated with a great deal of forethought and care. Everything had a specific reason for being included in the design and construction of a temple, even if we do not readily know what those reasons are, and especially if we are unwilling to ascribe higher levels of knowledge and wisdom to a people that many think were only a stone's throw away from *cavemen*.

This misperception is exacerbated by the jumble of tumbled down stones which make up such sites as Karnak, Memphis and Sakkara where it is sometimes difficult to fathom any overarching architectural plan. Even at the pinnacle of these temples' greatest expression, with pharaohs adding their own construction projects to them, it was necessary to have a central design concept inherent in the temple's plan that governed any new project's construction and the part that it would play in adding to the whole. The need to have a coherent design for these large temple complexes were most likely governed by the chief priests rather than by the pharaoh or government officials. Fortunately, the Step Pyramid Enclosure does not suffer from the excesses of other pharaohs adding to Imhotep's most sublime architectural creation, so it is easier to gain an appreciation of his original concept. Sadly, it probably was never completed. [133] Because of this, the world is deprived of the glory of Imhotep's vision and skill as both an architect and a physician when he combined both talents to create one of the world's greatest monuments, but there is enough left of it to give us a tantalizing taste of Imhotep's total vision for this temple.

In order to approach ancient Egyptian sacred art and architecture with any regard for the ideals that lay behind their creation and for the people who created them, we must constantly reminded ourselves that the ancient Egyptians saw their world as a reflection of Divine Truth ('*maat*') or Cosmic Order. The ancient Egyptians made no such distinction between the inner world of the spirit, and its outer manifestation embodied in the physical world we see around us. To ancient Egyptians, religion, art, science and architecture were so interwoven as to be one and the same thing with no distinction between them. It is only in our modern era that we have attempted to *explain away* many of these ancient people's beliefs as mere superstition at best and blasphemous idol worship at worst.

The symbolist method of interpreting ancient Egyptian art and architecture was not widely practiced by those first Egyptologists, perhaps because they were products of their late 19th century European mentality that took a more literal and sometimes condescending view of ancient civilizations. This viewpoint is typical of that era which smugly held such 'uncivilized' cultures with something bordering on contempt. While much of their early work still holds up under close examination, these early Egyptologist's cultural and educational biases prevented them from seeing the potential for interpreting the various monuments and works of art they were excavating on more than one level. We don't have to make that same mistake.

While the popularity of Sakkara as a royal and non-royal cemetery lasted for centuries, when did the hospital in the Step Pyramid Enclosure cease operations as a medical facility?

The best guess would be the Ḥeb-Sed Court hospital closed sometime around the end of the Fifth Dynasty, or early Sixth Dynasty, 2330–2340 BCE; about 330 years after its construction. This is indicated by the addition of a papyrus library to Temple 'T' when it was converted to a construction office during the building of the Pyramid of Teti (see *Fig. 6-53*). The period beginning with the Seventh and Eighth Dynasties, also known as the First Intermediate Period, was a period of civil unrest, social upheaval, political dissolution and general chaos. Military incursions from some of Egypt's enemies, both foreign and domestic, a lack of support from a long list of short-lived pharaohs and even a well-documented severe worldwide drought lasting decades that affected not only the Sahara region, but also as far away as Southeast Asia. This would probably have prevented the healer-priests of Sakkara from continuing to provide for the living as well as to memorialize the dead (Netjerikhet Djoser and other pharaohs). Though the Step Pyramid Enclosure may not have served as a center of healing for many centuries after these periods of political and social turmoil, in ancient times, Imhotep's reputation solely as a physician was secure because of his vision and dedication to create something more lasting than a monumental memorial for his king.

Having come this far, you may well ask, did all these ideas come from stumbling upon an oddly shaped carved stone half-buried beneath the sands of a nearly destroyed temple.

No, not in the least. What the discovery of this artifact has done for me is to bring together and crystallize many disparate chunks of facts and ideas into a cohesive whole. In effect, this doorpost socket has become my own personal Rosetta Stone whereby a much greater architectural language imbued in the overall grand design of this mortuary temple complex has blossomed from the seed of accidently stumbling upon a small, forgotten piece of stonework. It has given me a greater appreciation for the architects who designed these monuments, and for the highly skilled craftsmen who rendered those designs into stone.

The information and speculation given here should not be construed as criticism of those who have written about or worked in the field at Sakkara. Rather, it is my sincerest wish to provide another viewpoint in order to add to the knowledge about the ancient Egyptians in general, and this monument in particular. However, we should not be overly critical of those who have written that there is only one gate in the Enclosure Wall, or missed the enticing idea of a secondary purpose for this temple. As is the common practice in archeology, they base their work on the field reports and publications of those who have worked on the site. It would be impossible for any author writing about ancient civilizations to verify on their own with any degree of certainty the validity of the vast amount of work that others have already done in the field. Therefore, they must depend on the work of other experts whether that work is complete or not – and rightly so. The excavation and restoration work going on at Sakkara is an ever unfolding, ongoing project with no end in sight. We will always be learning new things with every spade full of dirt removed from these ancient sites.

At the same time though, we must try to see the past through the eyes of those who lived in the past, and not perpetuate our own misconceptions and preconceived notions should any subsequent evidence indicate a different and more plausible solution. This is most difficult for us who view these monuments with a different perspective than that possessed by traditional academia. There is inherent danger for all who attempt to learn about ancient cultures. To view them without our ingrained filters and prejudices, and see something different from what is already established fact is our greatest challenge. Thinking *outside the box* can lead us down an empty rabbit hole with nothing to show for our efforts. However, it has produced some of our greatest discoveries, such as when Heinrich Schliemann, a wealthy German businessman and amateur archeologist, whose obsession for the ancient city of Troy led to his pursuing that dream and Troy's eventual discovery.

Science is not a static thing. If it does not grow through change, then it ceases to be true science, and rapidly becomes dogmatic and pedantic. We must be open to new possibilities and new explanations for these monuments, not to challenge those who first worked on them, but to challenge ourselves continually to grow beyond our own limitations. Nothing is more stagnating to the human spirit than clinging to old ideas whose time has long since passed.

As archeological discoveries go (or, as in this case, re-discovery) the unearthing of evidence for a North Exit Gate in the perimeter wall of Djoser's Funerary Temple at Sakkara will never rival that of other discoveries such as finding the tomb of Tutankhamun. Even if this elegantly carved stone proves to be something else entirely, I am certain the other parts of my theories will stand on their own merits. However, if this highly carved stone does indeed turn out to be a socket for a self-closing door, then the genius of Imhotep as an architectural designer – and chief of sculptors – will rightfully be assured.

Excavating further in the area north of the Step Pyramid including the North Court will determine whether this door once led outside the Enclosure Wall. Perhaps we will also learn more of what life was like living and working in this temple, and what its true functions were during the period of the Old Kingdom and beyond. With any luck, this particular re-discovery will stimulate greater interest in the Step Pyramid Enclosure where the acquisition of additional funds can be found to the clean and clear the debris and excavation dirt piles that still clutter the site.

Doing so, I believe, will lead to the continuation of the excellent restoration work begun by Jean-Philippe Lauer, the man most responsible for the reconstruction of the Step Pyramid Enclosure that we see today. Despite many setbacks and interruptions, it is to Mr. Lauer's credit that he diligently worked for more than 70 years at Sakkara until the time of his death in 2001 (*Fig. 8-24*).

Fig. 8-24 – Jean-Philippe Lauer at work

Much of the hypothesis I have developed from what I intuitively uncovered and rediscovered related to various architectural features of the Step Pyramid Enclosure will not be forthcoming any time soon. This is simply because any proof of what I have asserted in this book would have taken the form of a secret, oral tradition. As such, these stories and customs are rarely, if ever, written down because this would have gone against the primary reason for creating an oral-based teaching method in the first place. (*Obviously!*)

In the case of the Step Pyramid complex, Imhotep chose to *write down* this hidden wisdom in stone. Such a rigorous and challenging way of learning required the student-priest to rely on their higher intuitive function – the *intelligence of the heart* – to *see beyond sight* the true intent and purpose beyond the outward expression of a symbolic architectural language, and become aware of the *unwritten language* of the greater wisdom *written* in stone.

Inevitably, at this point, some questions must be asked: *Did Imhotep design the Step Pyramid Enclosure with these hidden meanings, esoteric wisdom and a secret purpose embedded in what is essentially a tomb?* Outside of locating Imhotep's tomb (or better yet, his *library*) which might give us some of these answers, we will never know for certain. It is impossible to discover if these traditions existed in the first place, nor can we know the full extent of the wisdom and knowledge they may have encompassed.

Did subsequent generations of Egyptian architects hide a similar deeply esoteric language within their designs of tombs and temples in the same way as did Imhotep? The only temple we know of that appears to have the human body implicit within its design is the Temple of Amun at Luxor. Other than this one example, it appears there are no other temples in Egypt that we can readily identify that have a representation of the human body in its design. The Step Pyramid Enclosure is indisputably the most unique temple complex in all of Egypt. Though Imhotep was inspired by and relied on the work of previous architects, nothing like the Step Pyramid Enclosure before or after Imhotep's time was constructed in all the history of ancient Egypt. That *hiding in plain sight* such wisdom within the walls of sacred architecture seems to have been unique to Imhotep, and maybe a few architects influenced by his work who came later. Such geniuses as Imhotep are a once in several generations talent who come and go like the brilliant flash of a meteor in the night sky, never to be seen again for millennia.

Maddening and frustrating that attempting to unravel such mysteries may be, perhaps this will give us the incentive to venture into the *land of intuition*; the part of our unconscious mind that connects to a greater universe beyond the five senses – another *terra incognita*, if you will – that allows us to gain so much more than *book knowledge* ever could.

> **We shall not cease from exploration**
> **And the end of all our exploring**
> **Will be to arrive where we started**
> **And know the place for the first time.**
>
> **Through the unknown, remembered gate**
> **When the last of earth left to discover**
> **Is that which was the beginning;**
>
> **At the source of the longest river**
> **The voice of the hidden waterfall**
> **And the children in the apple-tree**
> **Not known, because not looked for**
> **But heard, half-heard, in the stillness**
> **Between two waves of the sea.**
>
> *"Four Quartets"* by *T. S. Eliot*, English Poet

Imhotep the Immortal – The End of One Journey and the Beginning of Another

If you have made it this far in our examination of aspects of ancient Egyptian religion and culture as embodied in the Step Pyramid Enclosure, no doubt you have come away with the distinct impression that the ancient peoples of the Nile saw life as a multifaceted creation of the natural world around them. This led to an equally complex belief system that permeated their religious lives as well. The outward expression of temple rituals and religious festivals were designed to give the average Egyptian a sense of their place in the world around them, and provide a moral code of ethical conduct and behavior that any society requires if it is to flourish and keep the twin evils of chaos and anarchy at bay. Yet, the deeper hidden meaning behind the designs of temple architecture was a natural outgrowth of an equally hidden philosophy, known only to a select few within the priesthood.

As stated in Chapter 1, the revelation of a new idea rarely occurs as a sudden flash of inspiration in the mind. It is an incontrovertible truth that when we seek answers to our deepest and most puzzling questions, we often stumble onto more questions than answers.

Even though the Step Pyramid doesn't garner the same amount of interest as the Great Pyramid of Giza, you may well ask why all the fascination with a semi-famous pyramid and its mortuary temples? What spurred the creative juices so much that writing an in-depth book about it was necessary?

Damned if I know! But there's one thing I do know: I love a mystery!!! Throw in Egyptology and a dash of material related to architecture in general and I'm hooked. The longer I pursued digging into the design of this pyramid complex, the more I kept uncovering even more fascinating details than I could have possibly expected. In so doing, I gained a greater respect and appreciation for the ancient Egyptian's view of their world, and especially Imhotep's sense of order and purpose in his designs, not to mention his genius.

From what has been uncovered in the previous chapters, Imhotep clearly incorporated many, many layers of esoteric and exoteric knowledge in the architectural features of the Step Pyramid Enclosure. For that reason, it is easy to see that Imhotep possessed a keen intellect rarely found in most people, let alone one who lived nearly 5,000 years ago. It is because of his genius that we even know about him today. That he could easily move between the intellectual requirements of widely different professions at the same time is unquestionable.

If there is any doubt as to whether Imhotep, and ancient Egyptians in general, saw life as a multifaceted reality, then one need only look at the Step Pyramid itself. As a metaphor for Imhotep's capacity for working on so many levels at the same time, I can think of no better way of illustrating it.

The Step Pyramid and Ḥeb-Sed Court

Why then hide all this secret knowledge, you may ask? Why should all this matter? Why is it important to know if the ancient Egyptians embedded secret, esoteric wisdom into the design of their temples and funerary monuments? Why should we care if Egypt was the true progenitor of the principles of Sacred Geometry that are often attributed to much younger civilizations like Greece and Rome?

In our journey to discover – and uncover – the hidden secrets of Djoser's Step Pyramid, it becomes readily apparent any hypothetical secret knowledge was *hidden in plain sight*. In reality, there are no *mysteries* and nothing was ever really concealed; it is only our limited thinking that blinds us from seeing the grand scheme of things. Perhaps by designing the Step Pyramid temple in the manner he did, Imhotep wished to inspire those possessed with keen intuitive insight – that is, the *intelligence of the heart* – to discover them once again. Much of our heritage, both spiritual and architectural comes from ancient Egypt, and we don't even know it. We are conditioned to only see the monuments of Egypt in all their faded glory that we so often fail to recognize the esoteric wisdom that went into their design.

It is now plainly obvious to me that there is great wisdom and intelligence inherent in the design of the Step Pyramid Enclosure. Taken as a whole at some point, all of what has been uncovered in this book ceases to be a coincidence. We know with absolute certainty that Imhotep possessed a superior intellect capable of assimilating many different disciplines within his mind, both spiritual and corporal. Therefore, it should not come as a surprise that he was equally capable of integrating these disparate disciplines within the design of this temple.

The final chapter of this book has yet to be written. I believe most of what I have postulated to be the underlying *secrets* buried in the Step Pyramid's design will eventually prove to be true. Some things, upon closer examination, will not. The rest will need to be set aside for now until more data becomes available. At this point, we just do not know which *secret* will eventually prove to be true. This is because the rather fluid nature of archeology will always uncover new evidence adding to our knowledge of the past, and will inevitably call into question earlier accepted interpretations.

While much of what I have written may fall into the class of speculation, I do not believe it falls outside the realm of possibilities. Even though I personally may have some doubts about some of my conclusions, not to report these would be disingenuous and intellectually dishonest. It may seem that I have interpreted my discoveries through the filter of my own experiences and (somewhat scant) knowledge, but isn't that true of anyone engaged in an archeological or historical investigation? It would be a fair criticism that I tend to view ancient Egyptian culture and religion through a philosophical and metaphysical mindset, but isn't that true of the ancient Egyptians as well?

More importantly, any conclusions stemming from my investigations during the last three years before publication are somewhat based on more currently available material than what was available to me in the mid-1990s. Therefore, most of what you find in this book was not part of my personal paradigm before I did even more research and wrote this book. Neither did I glean much of the information in this book from others who have written about the Step Pyramid Enclosure because their focus and conclusions were different from mine. Consequently, I did not have a predisposition towards what developed into my theories from all I uncovered these past few years. Much of what comprised the civilization of ancient Egypt still lies hidden, whether it is beneath the sands of the desert in an unknown tomb, a shattered temple or an undiscovered papyrus. Despite the fact that what I have uncovered and speculated about may generate more questions than provide any answers, it becomes imperative to continue this path of investigation no matter where it may lead. This is why this book *will never be finished*.

I did not write this book strictly for Egyptologists – professional *or* amateur. I wrote it for anyone who wishes to see things from a different perspective and gain whatever knowledge that comes from *thinking-outside-the-box*. If that includes any Egyptologist who stumbles onto this book, that's okay, too. We must always recognize that ancient Egypt – and its *secrets* – are not the property of Egyptology alone. Ancient Egypt belongs to the whole world. True, the exercise of archeological discipline must be the first criteria for unearthing anything concerning the past. After that, looking upon the findings with a *different set of eyes*, be they of professional archeologists or not, can only be an advantage since no one can know everything about anything.

To be even clearer, it is probable that few Egyptologists have ever taken a course in basic human anatomy when working towards their degrees in archeology. Unless they pursue a side discipline in forensic pathology, learning about the nature of human anatomy is something most archeology students are not willing to add to their coursework. This is not an indictment of those who engage in the scholarly pursuit of Egyptology. Most Egyptologists that have studied the Step Pyramid Enclosure do not have a ready knowledge of human anatomy. Because of this, they are not likely to find a relationship of its temple architecture to the human body simply because you cannot find something you were not looking for in the first place! Being able to see the South Entrance Hall and the Ḥeb-Sed Court through the eyes of the various medical professionals it has been my privilege to know has given me greater insight to the real purpose of the Step Pyramid

Enclosure – and especially its architect, Imhotep – than I could have reasonably attained otherwise. To that end, it is my sincerest hope that we all can see beyond the obvious, and embrace new ideas with the eagerness and passion that brought all of us to the study of ancient Egypt in the first place.

My ultimate motive in writing this book was to gather into one place as much as possible the various theories and discoveries scattered over many different sources that wrote about Imhotep and the Step Pyramid. I hope I accomplished that. While it has certainly been an exercise of the mind, some might ask how I came up with the many discoveries I made. I like to think the inspiration for comes from accessing the *intelligence of the heart* as the source of a higher intuitive function, much in the same way as did the ancient Egyptians who created these monuments.

Some of what I have uncovered is undoubtedly coincidental, but if the reader believes I am relying on circuitous and tortured reasoning based on a presumptive predisposition towards fantastical explanations for the various architectural elements and features of the Step Pyramid Enclosure (which some think are the result of mere coincidence), then only one question needs to be asked:

How many coincidences must occur before it becomes mathematically impossible to be simply coincidence?

As Albert Einstein once said, "***Coincidence is God's way of remaining anonymous***". (Or maybe *hiding in plain sight*?)

Finally, nothing in this book would exist without the dedication of the people who have excavated, reconstructed, and renovated the Step Pyramid and its secondary structures, especially the work of Jean-Philippe Lauer, to whom this book is also dedicated. Prior to writing this book, I didn't understand why he spent over seven decades of his life working to unearth, rebuild and document this old pyramid and its temples. It was hard to fathom the attraction, or more precisely, the *obsession* this ancient monument must have had on Mr. Lauer to devote so much time and energy to preserve its history and reconstruct its buildings.

Now I know why.

Thank you, Mr. Lauer. Merci beaucoup.

The only barrier to truth is the certain belief that you already have it.

Voltaire, French Philosopher

Illustration and Photo Credits

All illustrations and photos listed under the author's name are copyrighted © 1990 - 2022 by Stephen R. Kallman. All Rights Reserved. All other illustrations and photos are in the public domain or have their own copyright restrictions. (Abbreviations: A-all, T-top, B-bottom, C-center, L-left, R-right)

Unai Huizi (Shutterstock) – Cover
www.MeretsegerBooks.com – 3, 25T, 36B, 55C, 120T, 121B, 123TR, 203B
Doreen Freedman – 4T
Steve Kallman – 5A, 6, 9, 11, 12CR, 22, 29B, 30L, 31, 47, 53B, 56CR, 57BL, 59BL, 61T, 79B, 91B, 97B, 98, 118, 120BR, 123TL, 125B, 126T, 126BR, 134, 136, 152A, 153T, 153C, 156CR, 158CL, 160TL, 160B, 170T, 182C, 215, 216, 217, 232T
S. Kallman after J.-P. Lauer – 4B, 8B, 10, 12CR, 27, 28B, 29T, 32T, 33, 35C, 35BL, 36TL, 37B, 54T, 55B, 58T, 60T, 61B, 62TL, 66A, 67A, 68TL, 77, 78, 86T, 97T, 102T, 104, 107T, 114B, 115T, 124, 125T, 126BL, 127T, 130T, 131B, 133, 140B, 143T, 144, 146B, 159, 162A, 163, 164, 165, 166A, 167A, 168, 170B, 171, 172, 174, 175, 177, 178, 179, 181, 183, 185, 186, 187, 191, 192, 196, 224, 225T, 229T, 230B, 231, 233C, 234B
R. Willert – 7R, 60B, 129, 130BL
Manna Nader, Gabana Studios, Cairo – 7L, 85BR, 122A, 145TR, 223
Public Domain – 8T, 24BL, 34T, 35B, 36TR, 37TR, 39BL, 40, 41TL, 41TR, 42A, 54B, 59T, 68C, 90, 95CL, 95CR, 112T, 140T, 145TLC, 153B, 156CL, 161C, 188, 189T, 190T, 202TL, 202TR, 203T, 204T, 208, 239
Juan Rodríguez Lázaro – 12CL, 30R, 63R, 117T, 119, 120BL, 121T, 226T, 227TL, 227TR
Bruce Satterfield (Public Domain) – 13
Ernest Board, artist (The Wellcome Collection) – 16T
Louvre Museum – 16B, 37B
Wikimedia Commons (Public Domain) – 17, 19T, 20, 24T, 24BR, 28T, 39BR, 43B, 53T, 79T, 83A, 130BR, 201A, 222C, 229B
C. M. Firth (Public Domain) – 18A, 62TR, 64, 102B, 103, 108, 112B, 127A, 128B, 132, 135, 143BR, 212TL, 212TR, 212B
malemalefica.tumblr.com – 19B
khemitology.com – 23
Jean-Philippe Lauer – 25B, 37TL, 48TL 59BR, 84, 107B, 114C, 146T, 190B, 203B, 213T, 229T
Sandro Vannini, LabritorioRosso – 32B, 234TL, 234TR
Imhotep Museum – 32B, 211T, 237
news.health.doc.com – 34B
Pyreaus.com – 41C
Pinterest – 147BR, 161B
Jonathan Meader/Barbara Demeter – 43T
Turin Museum – 44
Inner Traditions, Bear & Company – 45
Human Genome Project (Public Domain) – 46
Queen Mary University of London – 47TR
Ancient Egypt Foundation – 48B
Wikipedia (Public Domain) – 50, 75B, 85BL, 123CL, 123CR
H. M. Herget, Artist (smithsonianmag.com and Public Domain) – 52, 116
Alexander Badawy – 56B
National Archive – 58B
Cairo Museum – 62B, 65T, 69, 74BL, 131T, 147BL, 154B, 198TL, 233T
Bruce Allardice - 65B
Ludwig Borchardt – 63L
ImpliedLandscapes – 73
British Museum – 74BR, 75T, 91BL, 207BL, 207BR
egyptjordan.blogspot.com – 85C
Jean-Claude Golvin – 86C, 91T
emilyhartsay.com – 89
Ashmolean Museums – 91BR
Jimmy Dunn – 92
B&S Encyclopédie – 94
Egyptian Ministry of Tourism – 101, 105
rpharteyarquitectura.weebly.com – 106
D. Lewis – 113A
R. F. Morgan – 115B
Fr. Monnier – 149B, 211C, 226B

3D Warehouse SketchUp model – 117B, 138, 142A, 143BL, 189B
Royal Air Force, photo courtesy University College London Institute of Archaeology – 137A
Penn-Yale-Institute of Fine Arts, New York University Expedition to Abydos – 139, 194, 200
Latvian Scientific Mission – 148A, 149T
Sherry Towers – 155L
S. Kallman after S. Towers – 155R
J. Belmonte – 158TL
J. Augustus Knapp, artist – 158CR
Paul and Jean Hanna – 160TR
G. Robins, M. Gadallah – 169
Aiden Dodson – KMT Magazine – 195
S. Kallman after Aiden Dodson – 196, 197, 198TR, 199A
S. Kallman after Bahka (Wikimedia Commons) – 204B, 205, 206, 207
F. P. Roy – 202BL, 202BR
Douglas H. Benjamin – 209A, 210
Alain Guilleux – 211T, 211B
Battiscombe Gunn – 211C, 212B
Andrew Connor (David Lightbody, Franck Monnier) – 213C
George Daressy, Corinna Rossi – 213B
Arto Heino – 214CL, 214CR
Paolo Di Pasquale – 214BL, 214BR
Luxor Museum – 221
Metropolitan Museum of Art – 222T
Ancient Egypt Research Associates - 225B
Description De L'EgypTe-1820-1830 (Public Domain) – 230B
Penn Museum – 232CL, 232CR
Cyril Le Tourneur d'Ison – 241

Bibliography

Aldred, Cyril, *Egypt to the End of the Old Kingdom*, New York, 1965
Allen, James Peter, *The Art of Medicine in Ancient Egypt*, Yale University Press, 2005
Altenmüller, H., *Bemerkungen zur frühen und späten Bauphase des Djoserbezirkes in Sakkara* ("Comments on the early and late construction phase of the Djoser district in Saqqara"), MDAIK 28 (1972)
Ancient Egypt Research Associates, *Memphis, Egypt's Ancient Capital: A Plan for Site and Community Development*, Boston and Cairo, 2017
Baker, Rosalie; Baker III, Charles, *Ancient Egyptians: People of the pyramids,* Oxford. 2001
Badawy, Alexander, *A History of Egyptian Architecture: The Empire, or New Kingdom*. University of California Press, 1968
Badawy, Alexander, *A History of Egyptian Architecture: The Empire, or New Kingdom*, Berkeley and Los Angeles, 1968
Bárta, Miroslav, *Serdab and Statue Placement in the Private Tombs Down to the Fourth Dynasty*, Mainz, 1998
Benjamin, Douglas, *A Presentation for Zahi Hawass Secretary General of the Egyptian Supreme Council of Antiquities*, Internet article, 2008
Bestock, Laurel D., *The Early Dynastic Funerary Enclosures of Abydos,* Archeo-Nil, No. 18, March 2008
Beuthe, T., *An animal embalming complex at Saqqara*, JAEA 4, 2020
Breasted, James Henry. *A History of the Ancient Egyptians*, London, 1926
Breasted, James Henry, *Ancient Records of Egypt*, Vol. I, Chicago, paragraph 148, 1906
Di Pasquale, Paolo, *Sakkara's Ostracon and the formula of a circle*, Internet article, 2007
Dodson, Aiden, *The Mysterious 2nd Dynasty*, KMT: A Journal of Ancient Egypt, Summer 1996 (Vol.7, No.2)
Dunn, Jimmy, *The South and North Pavilions, the Sed Festival Complex and the Temple "T" in the Step Pyramid Complex of Djoser At Saqqara in Egypt*, Internet article, 6/13/2011
Dunn, Jimmy, *The Step Pyramid of Djoser at Saqqara in Egypt Part II: The Trench and Perimeter Wall, the South Courtyard, And South Tomb*, Internet article, 6/13/2011
Dunn, Jimmy, *The Step Pyramid of Djoser at Saqqara in Egypt-Part III: The Primary Pyramid Structure*, Internet article, 6/13/2011
Edwards, I. E. S., *The Pyramids of Egypt*, New York, 1972
Egyptology News, internet articles, August 2007
Fairman, Herbert and Blackman, Aylward, *The Myth of Horus at Edfu*, JEA 21 (1935), JEA 30 (1944)
Fitzgerald, F. Scott, *The Crack-Up*, Esquire magazine, essay published February 1936

Flinders Petrie, W. M, *The Pyramids and Temples of Gizeh*, 2nd Ed. Reprint, London, 1990
Foster, John L., *Ancient Egyptian Literature – An Anthology*, Austin, Texas, 2001
Firth, Cecil; Quibell, James; Lauer, Jean-Philippe, *Excavations at Saqqara: the Step Pyramid*, 2 Vols. Cairo, 1935
Gadalla, M., *The Ancient Egyptian Metaphysical Architecture*, Greensboro, NC, 2017
Gahlin, Lucia, *Egypt: Gods, Myths and Religion*, New York, 2002
Gardiner, Alan H., *An Archaic Funerary Stele*. Journal of Egyptian Archæology 4: 256–260, London, 1917
Gardiner, Alan H., *Egyptian Grammar, Being an Introduction to the Study of Hieroglyphs*, 3rd Revised Ed., Oxford, 1957.
Gigal, Antoine, *L'Egypte d'avant les Pharaons* ("Egypt Before the Pharaohs"), Sacrée Planète magazine – April-May 2010
Gunn, Battiscombe, *An Architect's Diagram of the 3rd Dynasty*. Annales du Service des Antiquites de L'Egypte, Vol. 26, Cairo, 1926
Heino, Arto J., *Saqqara Ostrakon a Different and Exact Solution*, Internet article, 2012
Hill, J. *Beer in Ancient Egypt*, internet article, Ancient Egypt Online, 2010
Hirmer, Max; Lange, Kurt and Otto, Eberhard, *Egypt: Architecture, Sculpture and Painting in Three Thousand Years*, Fourth Ed., New York, 1968
Holland, Anthony, *Shattering Cancer With Resonant Frequencies*, TEDx Talk-Skidmore Collage 2017
Hurry, J.B., *IMHOTEP, The Egyptian God of Medicine*, Oxford, 1926
Iverson, Ben, *What is Quantum Arithmetic?*, Internet article
Kemp, Barry J., *Ancient Egypt: Anatomy of a Civilization* (2nd ed.), p. 159, Abingdon-on-Thames, 2005
Lehner, Mark, *The Complete Pyramids*, London, 1997
Lauer, Jean-Philippe, *Étude Sur Quelques Monuments de la IIIE Dynastie (Pyramide á Degrés de Saqqarah)*, Annales du service des antiquites de l'Egypte, Vol. 31, Cairo, 1931
Lauer, Jean-Philippe, *La Pyramide À Degrés, L'Architecture*, Vol. 1, Cairo, 1936
Lauer, Jean-Philippe, *Les Pyramides de Sakkarah* (*The Pyramids of Sakkarah*), Fifth Ed., Cairo, 1977
Lauer, Jean-Philippe, *Sur Certaines Modifications et Extensions Apportées au Complexe Funéraire de Djoser au Cours de Son Règne*, ("On Certain Modifications and Extensions Made To Djoser's Funeral Complex During His Reign"), from *Pyramid studies and other essays presented to I. E. S. Edwards*, London, 1988
Lichtheim, Miriam, *Ancient Egyptian Literature*, Vol. III: The Late Period, Berkeley, Los Angeles and London, 1980
Lightbody, David Ian, Monnier, Franck, *An elegant vault design principle identified in Old and New Kingdom architecture*, JAEA, vol. 2, 2017
Magli, G. and Belmonte, J. A., *IN SEARCH OF COSMIC ORDER*, Cairo 2010
Mark, Joshua, *Beer in Ancient Egypt*, internet article, World History Encyclopedia, 2017
Meader, Jonathan, Demeter, Barbara, *Ancient Egyptian Symbols: 50 New Discoveries (Abridged)*, San Francisco, 2016
Meher, Stephen, *Abd'el Hakim Awyan: The Last of The Dragoman*, Internet article, 2019
Meisner, Gary; *The Parthenon and the Golden Ratio: Myth or Misinformation?*, internet article, 2020
Newberry, Percy, *The Set Rebellion of the IInd Dynasty*, Ancient Egypt, 1922
O'Connor, David, *Boat Graves and Pyramid Origins: New Discoveries at Abydos, Egypt*, Expedition, Vol. 33, No. 3, 1991
Pearsall, Paul, *The Heart's Code: Tapping the Wisdom and Power of Our Heart Energy*, New York City, 1999
Pearsall, Paul, *Transplanting Memories?* U.S. television documentary, 2006
Plato, *Timaeus and Critias*, London, 1971
Quantum Gravity Research, *What is Reality?*, Internet video
Regulski, Ilona, *Investigating a new Dynasty 2 necropolis a South Sakkara*, British Museum Studies in Ancient Egypt and Sudan, 2009
Robins, Gay., *Proportion and style in ancient Egypt Art*, Austin, TX, 1994
Romer, John (2013). *A History of Ancient Egypt from the First Farmers to the Great Pyramid*, London, 2013
Rossi, Corinna, *Architecture and Mathematics in Ancient Egypt*, Cambridge, 2003
Ritter, James, *Closing the Eye of Horus: The Rise and Fall of 'Horus-eye Fractions*, Münster, 2003
Schwaller de Lubicz, R. A., *The Temple of Man*, Rochester, VT, 1998
Segliņš, Valdis, Kukela, Agnese, "*The Structure of the Step Pyramid of Djoser* in Egypt as *a Concept of Primordial Hill*", 17th International Multidisciplinary Scientific GeoConference June 2017
Segliņš, Valdis, Kukela, Agnese, *Damage Assessment and 3D Visualization: An Example of the Step Pyramid*, Egypt, Riga, 2012
Stadelmann, R., *Das vermeintliche Sonnenheiligtum im Norden des Djoserbezirkes* ("The supposed sun sanctuary in the north of the Djoser district [complex]"), ASAE 69 (1983)
Swelim, Nabil, *Cylinder Seals, Cut Stones, and an Update on a King and Monument List of the Third Dynasty*, Budapest, 1992
Täckholm, V. Laurent and Aberg, E., *Plants discovered in the underground passages of the enclosure of king Zoser in Saqqara*, BIE 32, 1951
Taylor, Greg, *The Dying Light: Exploring the strange phenomenon of lights seen at the time of death*, Internet article, 5/20/2020
Towers, Sherry, *Advanced geometrical constructs in a Pueblo ceremonial site*, c 1200 CE, Journal of Archaeological Science: Reports, Jan 2017
Travers, Jason, *Golden Section*, internet article
Warburton, David, *Architecture, Power, and Religion: Hatshepsut, Amun & Karnak in Context. Articles on Archeology*. 7. LIT Verlag Münster, 2012

Notes

Chapter 1

(1) Lauer, Jean-Philippe, *The Pyramids of Saqqara*, Fifth Ed., pp. 5-6, Cairo, 1977.
(2) Hirmer, Max; Lange, Kurt and Otto, Eberhard, *Egypt: Architecture, Sculpture and Painting in Three Thousand Years*, Fourth Ed., p. 399, New York, 1968.
(3) Edwards, I. E. S., *The Pyramids of Egypt*, p. 50, New York, 1972.
(4) Aldred, Cyril, *Egypt to the End of the Old Kingdom*, p. 67, (notes to a photographic plate), New York, 1965. (Actually, there are 15 gates: fourteen false gates plus the South Entrance Gate.)
(5) Breasted, James Henry, *Ancient Records of Egypt*, Vol. I, p. 66, Chicago, paragraph 148, 1906.

Chapter 2

(6) Hurry, J.B., *IMHOTEP, The Egyptian God of Medicine*, pp. 6, 9, 21-24, Oxford, 1926.
(7) en.wikipedia.org/wiki/Polymath
(8) efreedictionary.com/polymath
(9) www.wordnik.com/words/polymath
(10) www.merriam-webster.com/dictionary/polymath
(11) Kemp, Barry J., *Ancient Egypt: Anatomy of a Civilization* (2nd Ed.), p. 159, Oxfordshire, 2005.
(12) Baker, Rosalie; Baker III, Charles, *Ancient Egyptians: People of the pyramids*, pp. 20-24, Oxford. 2001.
(13) Romer, John (2013). *A History of Ancient Egypt from the First Farmers to the Great Pyramid*, pp. 294-295, London, 2013.
(14) Hurry, Jamison B., *IMHOTEP, The Egyptian God of Medicine*, pp. 98-100, Oxford, 1926.
(15) Badawy, Alexander, *A History of Egyptian Architecture: The Empire, or New Kingdom*, pp.362-363, Berkeley and Los Angeles, 1968.
(16) Gahlin, Lucia, *Egypt: Gods, Myths and Religion*, p. 23, New York, 2002.
(17) Lichtheim, Miriam, *Ancient Egyptian Literature*, Vol. III: The Late Period, pp. 104-105, Berkeley, Los Angeles and London, 1980.
(18) Internet Article, *Imhotep | Ancient Egyptian Architecture and Medicine* (www.ancient-egypt-online.com/Imhotep.html)
(19) Allen, James Peter, *The Art of Medicine in Ancient Egypt*, p. 12, Yale University Press, 2005.

Chapter 3

(20) Fitzgerald, F. Scott, *The Crack-Up*, Esquire magazine, essay published February 1936.
(21) Meher, Stephen, *Abd'el Hakim Awyan: The Last of The Dragoman*, Internet article, 2019 (adeptinitiates.com/abdel-hakim-awyan-last-dragoman)
(22) Egyptology News, internet articles, August 2007, (egyptology.blogspot.com/2007/08/special-feature-update-on-most-recent.html, (egyptology.blogspot.com/2007/08/latvian-work-at-saqqara-part-2.html).
(23) Holland, Anthony, *Shattering Cancer With Resonant Frequencies*, TEDx Talk-Skidmore Collage 2017. Holland and his team from Novobiotronics, Inc. tested the procedure called Oscillating Pulsed Electric Field (OPEF) on pancreatic cancer cells and then later with leukemia cells. Pancreatic cancer cells were destroyed at between 100,000 and 300,000 Hz. The procedure was able to destroy the leukemia cells before they had a chance to divide, killing an average of 25 to 40% leukemia cells on average, and up to 60% in some cases. The team also tested the technology on ovarian cancer cells as well as the MRSA "super bug".
(24) Lauer, Jean-Philippe, *Sur Certaines Modifications et Extensions Apportées au Complexe Funéraire de Djoser au Cours de Son Règne*, ("On Certain Modifications and Extensions Made To Djoser's Funeral Complex During His Reign"), *from Pyramid studies and other essays presented to I. E. S. Edwards*, pp. 2-3, London 1988.
(25) Benjamin, Douglas H., unpublished manuscript, 1990.
(26) Meader, Jonathan, Demeter, Barbara, *Ancient Egyptian Symbols: 50 New Discoveries (Abridged)*, San Francisco, 2016.
(27) Breasted, James Henry. *A History of the Ancient Egyptians*, p. 133, London, 1926.
(28) Gigal, Antoine, *L'Egypte d'avant les Pharaons* ("Egypt Before the Pharaohs"), Sacrée Planète magazine – April-May 2010.
(29) Pearsall, Paul, *The Heart's Code: Tapping the Wisdom and Power of Our Heart Energy*, New York City, 1999, and *Transplanting Memories?* U.S. television documentary, 2006.
(30) Wikipedia article, *Cargo cult*, (en.wikipedia.org/wiki/Cargo cult, news.bbc.co.uk/2/hi/asia-pacific/6370991.stm)
(31) History Channel, *Life After People*, U.S. television series, 2008-2010.
(32) Badawy, Alexander, *A History of Egyptian Architecture: The Empire, or New Kingdom*, p. 95, Berkeley and Los Angeles, 1968.
(33) Firth, Cecil; Quibell, James; Lauer, Jean-Philippe, *Excavations at Saqqara: the Step Pyramid*, Vol. 2, plate 54, Cairo, 1935.
(34) Ibid, Vol. 1, p. 66.
(35) Ibid, Vol. 1, pp. 14-15.

(36) Ibid, Introduction, p. III.
(37) Beuthe, T., *An animal embalming complex at Saqqara*, pp. 19-27, JAEA 4, 2020.
(38) Firth, Cecil; Quibell, James; Lauer, Jean-Philippe, *Excavations at Saqqara: the Step Pyramid*, Vol. 1, pp. 112-113, description of Plate 54, Cairo, 1935.
(39) Ibid, pp. 14-15, Cairo, 1935.

Chapter 4

(40) Taylor, Greg, *The Dying Light: Exploring the strange phenomenon of lights seen at the time of death*, Internet article, 5/20/2020 (dailygrail.com/2020/05/the-dying-light-exploring-the-strange-phenomenon-of-lights-seen-at-the-time-of-death/).
(41) Dunn, Jimmy, *The Step Pyramid of Djoser at Saqqara in Egypt Part II: The Trench and Perimeter Wall, the South Courtyard, And South*, Internet article, 6/13/2011 (touregypt.net/featurestories/dsteppyramid5.htm)

Chapter 5

(42) Mr. Lauer could often be seen carrying a rather dog-eared, slightly tattered copy of this book, *Les Pyramides de Sakkarah* (*The Pyramids of Sakkarah*) while working at the Step Pyramid Enclosure.
(43) Lauer, Jean-Philippe, *Les Pyramides de Sakkarah* (*The Pyramids of Sakkarah*), Plate 12, Cairo, 1977.
(44) Firth, Cecil; Quibell, James; Lauer, Jean-Philippe, *Excavations at Saqqara: the Step Pyramid*, Vol. 1, p. 54, Cairo, 1935.
(45) Foster, John L., *Ancient Egyptian Literature – An Anthology*, Austin, Texas, 2001.

Chapter 6

(46) Firth, Cecil; Quibell, James; Lauer, Jean-Philippe, *Excavations at Saqqara: the Step Pyramid*, Vol. 1, p. 78, Cairo, 1935.
(47) Fairman, Herbert and Blackman, Aylward, *The Myth of Horus at Edfu*, JEA 21 (1935), pp. 26-36; JEA 30 (1944), pp. 5-22.
(48) Newberry, Percy, *The Set Rebellion of the IInd Dynasty*, Ancient Egypt magazine, pp. 40-46, 1922.
(49) Fairman, Herbert and Blackman, Aylward, *The Myth of Horus at Edfu*, JEA 21 (1935), p. 28, n. 2.
(50) Dodson, Aiden, *The Mysterious 2nd Dynasty*, KMT: A Journal of Ancient Egypt, Summer 1996 (Vol.7, No.2) p. 26.
(51) Ibid. pp. 26-28.
(52) Lauer, Jean-Philippe, *Sur Certaines Modifications et Extensions Apportées au Complexe Funéraire de Djoser au Cours de Son Règne*, ("On Certain Modifications and Extensions Made To Djoser's Funeral Complex During His Reign"), *from Pyramid studies and other essays presented to I. E. S. Edwards*, pp. 2-3, London 1988.
(53) Firth, Cecil; Quibell, James; Lauer, Jean-Philippe, Excavations at Saqqara: the Step Pyramid, Vol. 1, p. 86, Cairo, 1935.
(54) Ibid. pp. 86, 88, Cairo, 1935.
(55) Dunn, Jimmy, *The Step Pyramid of Djoser at Saqqara in Egypt-Part II: The Trench and Perimeter Wall, the South Courtyard, and South Tomb*, Internet article, 6/13/2011 (touregypt.net).
(56) Ibid. Part I: An Introduction.
(57) Firth, Cecil; Quibell, James; Lauer, Jean-Philippe, *Excavations at Saqqara: the Step Pyramid*, Vol. 1, Introduction, p. ii, Cairo, 1935-1936.
(58) Ibid. p. 32.
(59) Ibid. p. 99.
(60) Ibid. pp. 99-103.
(61) Ibid. p. 32.
(62) Dunn, Jimmy, *The Step Pyramid of Djoser at Saqqara in Egypt-Part III: The Primary Pyramid Structure*, Internet article, 6/13/2011 (touregypt.net).
(63) Swelim, Nabil, *Cylinder Seals, Cut Stones, and an Update on a King and Monument List of the Third Dynasty*, Budapest, 1992
(64) Firth, Cecil; Quibell, James; Lauer, Jean-Philippe, *Excavations at Saqqara: the Step Pyramid*, Vol. 1, p. 15-16, Cairo, 1935.
(65) Lehner, Mark, *The Complete Pyramids*, pp. 84-85, London, 1997.
(66) Dunn, Jimmy, *The South and North Pavilions, the Sed Festival Complex and the Temple "T" in the Step Pyramid Complex of Djoser At Saqqara in Egypt*, Internet article, (touregypt.net).
(67) Firth, Cecil; Quibell, James; Lauer, Jean-Philippe, *Excavations at Saqqara: the Step Pyramid*, Vol. 1, Introduction, p. iii, Cairo, 1936-1936.
(68) The Cobb salad is a main-dish American garden salad typically made with chopped salad greens (iceberg lettuce, watercress, endives and romaine lettuce), tomato, crisp bacon, grilled or roasted (but not fried) chicken breast, hard-boiled eggs, avocado, chives, Roquefort cheese, and red-wine vinaigrette. Various stories recount how the salad was invented. One says that it came about in 1937 at the Hollywood Brown Derby restaurant, where it became a signature dish. It is named after the restaurant's owner, Robert Howard Cobb. Stories vary whether the salad was invented by Cobb or by his chef, Paul J. Posti. The legend is that Cobb had not eaten until near midnight, and so he mixed together leftovers he found in the kitchen, along with some bacon cooked by the line cook, and tossed it with their French dressing. (Yum!) (Wikipedia citation.)
(69) Firth, Cecil; Quibell, James; Lauer, Jean-Philippe, *Excavations at Saqqara*: the Step Pyramid, Vol. 1, pp. 74-76, Cairo, 1935.
(70) *Unearthed*, U.S. television series, *The Hunt for the First Pyramid*, first broadcast 1/5/2020.
(71) Firth, Cecil; Quibell, James Lauer, Jean-Philippe, *Excavations at Saqqara: the Step Pyramid*, Vol. 1, pp. 66, 108, description for Plate 31, Cairo, 1935.

(72) Lauer, Jean-Philippe, *Sur Certaines Modifications et Extensions Apportées au Complexe Funéraire de Djoser au Cours de Son Règne*, ("On Certain Modifications and Extensions Made To Djoser's Funeral Complex During His Reign"), *from Pyramid studies and other essays presented to I .E. S. Edwards*, pp. 2-3, London 1988.
(73) Firth, Cecil; Quibell, James; Lauer, Jean-Philippe, *Excavations at Saqqara: the Step Pyramid*, Vol. 1, p. 54, Cairo, 1935.
(74) Ibid. pp. 49 and 68.
(75) Ibid. p. 88.
(76) Magli, G. and Belmonte, J. A., *IN SEARCH OF COSMIC ORDER*, pp. 318-319, Cairo 2010.
(77) Warburton, David, *Architecture, Power, and Religion: Hatshepsut, Amun & Karnak in Context. Articles on Archeology*. 7. LIT, p. 139, Verlag Münster, 2012.
(78) Gahlin, Lucia, *Egypt: Gods, Myths and Religion*, p. 105, New York, 2002.
(79) Badawy, Alexander, *A History of Egyptian Architecture: The Empire, or New Kingdom*, pp.362-363, Berkeley and Los Angeles, 1968.
(80) Segliņš, Valdis; Kukela, Agnese, "*The Structure of the Step Pyramid of Djoser as a Concept of Primordial Hill*", 17th International Multidisciplinary Scientific GeoConference, June 2017.
(81) Lehner, Mark, *The Complete Pyramids*, London, p. 85, London, 1997.
(82) Ibid. p. 85.
(83) Firth, Cecil; Quibell, James; Lauer, Jean-Philippe, *Excavations at Saqqara: the Step Pyramid*, Vol. 1, p. 86, Cairo, 1935.
(84) Ibid. p. 77.
(85) "Geeked out": an American colloquialism which roughly means a person has become so enthusiastic about a narrow topic, they don't realize that most people listening to the "geek" will fail to understand it or appreciate its nuances.
(86) Bárta, Miroslav, *Serdab and Statue Placement in the Private Tombs Down to the Fourth Dynasty*, Mainz, 1998.
(87) Lauer, Jean-Philippe, *Sur Certaines Modifications et Extensions Apportées au Complexe Funéraire de Djoser au Cours de Son Règne*, ("On Certain Modifications and Extensions Made To Djoser's Funeral Complex During His Reign"), from *Pyramid studies and other essays presented to I. E. S. Edwards*, p. 4, London 1988.
(88) Ibid. p. 3.
(89) Segliņš, Valdis, Kukela, Agnese, *Damage Assessment and 3D Visualization: An Example of the Step*, Egypt, Riga, 2012.

Chapter 7
(90) Meisner, Gary; *The Parthenon and the Golden Ratio: Myth or Misinformation?*, internet article, 2020, (https://www.goldennumber.net/parthenon-golden-ratio-myth-or-misinformation).
(91) Quantum Gravity Research, *What is Reality?*, Internet video, (quantumgravityresearch.org/portfolio/what-is-reality-movie/)
(92) Towers, Sherry, *Advanced geometrical constructs in a Pueblo ceremonial site*, c 1200 CE, Journal of Archaeological Science: Reports, Jan 2017.
(93) Rossi, Corinna, *Architecture and Mathematics in Ancient Egypt*, pp. 93, 173, Cambridge, 2003.
(94) Author unknown, Internet article, (bibliotecapleyades.net/arqueologia/worldwonders/gpd2.htm).
(95) Firth, Cecil; Quibell, James; Lauer, Jean-Philippe, *Excavations at Saqqara, The Step Pyramid*, Vol. I, page 95, Cairo, 1935.
(96) Plato, *Timaeus and Critias*, London, 1971.
(97) Travers, Jason, *Golden Section*, internet article (jtravers.com).
(98) Gahlin, Lucia, *Egypt, Gods, Myths and Religion*, New York, 2002.
(99) Lauer, Jean-Philippe, *Étude Sur Quelques Monuments de la IIIE Dynastie (Pyramide á Degrés de Saqqarah)*, Annales du service des antiquites de l'Egypte, Vol. 31, pp. 49-64, Cairo, 1931.
(100) Lauer, Jean-Philippe, *Sur Certaines Modifications et Extensions Apportées au Complexe Funéraire de Djoser au Cours de Son Règne*, ("On Certain Modifications and Extensions Made To Djoser's Funeral Complex During His Reign"), *from Pyramid studies and other essays presented to I. E. S. Edwards*, pp. 2-3, London 1988.
(101) Schwaller de Lubicz, R. A., *The Temple of Man*, Rochester, VT, 1998.
(102) Robins, G., *Proportion and style in ancient Egypt Art*, p. 46, Austin, TX, 1994.
(103) Gadalla, M., *The Ancient Egyptian Metaphysical Architecture*, Greensboro, NC, 2017.
(104) Lauer thought the offset to the west of the eastern wall of the Great South Court was only 5°.
(105) Lauer, Jean-Philippe, *Étude Sur Quelques Monuments de la IIIE Dynastie (Pyramide á Degrés de Saqqarah)*, Annales du service des antiquites de l'Egypte, Vol. 31, pp. 49-64, Cairo, 1931.
(106) Gardiner, Alan H., *An Archaic Funerary Stele*. Journal of Egyptian Archæology 4, p. 256–260, London, 1917.
(107) Ritter, James, *Closing the Eye of Horus: The Rise and Fall of 'Horus-eye Fractions*, pp. 297-298, Münster, 2003.
(108) Meisner, Gary, *The Parthenon and the Golden Ratio: Myth or Misinformation?*, Internet article, 2020, (goldennumber.net/parthenon-golden-ratio-myth-or-misinformation/).
(109) Rossi, Corinna, *Architecture and Mathematics in Ancient Egypt*, pp. 93, 173, Cambridge, 2003.
(110) Dodson, Aiden, *The Mysterious 2nd Dynasty*, KMT: A Journal of Ancient Egypt, Summer 1996 (Vol.7, No.2), p. 29.
(111) O'Connor, David, *Boat Graves and Pyramid Origins: New Discoveries at Abydos, Egypt*, Expedition, Vol. 33, No. 3, pp. 5–15, 1991.
(112) Bestock, Laurel D., *The Early Dynastic Funerary Enclosures of Abydos*, p. 57, Archeo-Nil, No. 18, March 2008.
(113) Regulski, Ilona, *Investigating a new Dynasty 2 necropolis a South Sakkara*, British Museum Studies in Ancient Egypt and Sudan, pp. 226-227, 2009.

(114) Flinders Petrie, W. M., *The Pyramids and Temples of Gizeh,* 2nd Ed. Reprint, pp.28-29, London, 1990.
(115) Benjamin, Douglas, *A Presentation for Zahi Hawass Secretary General of the Egyptian Supreme Council of Antiquities,* Internet article, 2008, (nileexplorersclub.com/media/pdf/NEC_SecretSymbol_Presentation.pdf).
(116) Gunn, Battiscombe, *An Architect's Diagram of the 3rd Dynasty,* Annales du Service des Antiquites de L'Egypte, Vol. 26, pp. 197-202, Cairo, 1926.
(117) Lauer, Jean-Philippe, *La Pyramide À Degrés, L'Architecture,* Vol. 1, pp. 173 - 175, Cairo, 1936.
(118) Lightbody, David Ian, Monnier, Franck, *An elegant vault design principle identified in Old and New Kingdom architecture,* JAEA, vol. 2, 2017 Internet article, (egyptian-architecture.com).
(119) Rossi, Corinna, *Architecture and Mathematics in Ancient Egypt,* pp. 115-118, Cambridge, 2003.
(120) Heino, Arto J., *Saqqara Ostrakon a Different and Exact Solution,* Internet article, 2012, (artojh.wordpress.com/2012/12/05/saqqara-ostrakon).
(121) Iverson, Ben, *What is Quantum Arithmetic?,* Internet article, (svpvril.com/svpweb17.html).
(122) Di Pasquale, Paolo, *Sakkara's Ostracon and the formula of a circle,* Internet article, 2007, (academia.edu/35169906/Saqqaras_Ostrakon_and_the_formula_of_the_circle).

Chapter 8

(123) Kate Narev-Green, *The relationship Between Hatshepsut and Thutmosis III – Cooperative Co-rulers or Ruthless Rivals?* NSW, Australia, Research Paper, date unknown.
(124) Segliņš, Valdis and Kukela, Agnese, *The Structure of the Step Pyramid of Djoser in Egypt as a Concept of Primordial Hill,* 17th International Multidisciplinary Scientific GeoConference, June 2017.
(125) BBC4 documentary, *Death on the Nile,* 2001.
(126) *Where's Waldo* (known as *Where's Wally* in Britain) is a series of puzzle books for children created by the English illustrator Martin Handford. Readers are challenged to find the character Waldo who is dressed in a red-and-white striped shirt, knit cap and glasses. (Wikipedia).
(127) Altenmüller, H , *Bemerkungen zur frühen und späten Bauphase des Djoserbezirkes in Sakkara* ("Comments on the early and late construction phase of the Djoser district in Saqqara"), MDAIK 28 (1972), part. II, 7-12.
(128) Stadelmann, R., *Das vermeintliche Sonnenheiligtum im Norden des Djoserbezirkes* ("The supposed sun sanctuary in the north of the Djoser district [complex]"), ASAE 69 (1983), 373-8.
(129) Täckholm, V. Laurent and Aberg, E., *Plants discovered in the underground passages of the enclosure of king Zoser in Saqqara,* pp. 121-124 , BIE 32, 1951.
(130) Hill, J. *Beer in Ancient Egypt,* internet article, Ancient Egypt Online, 2010, (ancientegyptonline.co.uk/beer/).
(131) Mark, Joshua, *Beer in Ancient Egypt,* internet article, World History Encyclopedia, 2017. (ancient.eu/article/1033/beer-in-ancient-egypt/).
(132) Romer, John, *Ancient Lives,* Central Television (ITV) documentary; Episode 3 of four, 1984.
(133) Firth, Cecil; Quibell, James; Lauer, Jean-Philippe, *Excavations at Saqqara: the Step Pyramid,* Vol. 1, p. 86, Cairo, 1935.

Index

A

Abd'el Hakim Awyan, "Hakim" 23, 24, 25, 26, 27, 35, 41, 49, 83, 136, 148, 161
Abydos 18, 39, 50, 99, 101, 105, 107, 108, 109, 112, 123, 130, 134, 139, 143, 145, 193, 194, 195, 200, 232
adze..68
Akh 22, 74
Amenhotep III................................. 18, 26, 51, 134, 139, 169
Amenhotep, Son of Hapu................................. 18, 19, 134
Ammit (goddess) 75, 76, 117
Anubis (god) 75, 76
Apis (god) 66, 85, 104
Armour, John Andrew 49
Asclepius 19, 20, 56
Augustus 19

B

Ba 22, 74
Beer 19, 45, 230, 231
Berlin Papyrus 6619 158
Black Cubit 210
Book of the Dead 44, 75, 77, 78
Boundary Markers 51, 69, 85, 97, 129, 143, 163, 165, 173
Brain 20, 35, 49, 54
Breasted, James H.. 11, 12

C

Canon of Proportion 168, 169, 171, 175
Cargo Cults 49, 50
Central Burial Chamber . 93, 96, 100, 101, 102, 103, 104, 105, 106, 108, 109, 116, 132, 136, 141, 142, 149, 157, 165
Circumpolar Stars 118, 130, 131, 132, 187
Coccyx 29, 234
Connor, Andrew 193, 213, 214, 244
Crowns of Egypt 11, 24, 40, 41, 42, 43, 44

D

Di Pasquale, Paolo 214, 244
Djoser (Netjerikhet) . 1, 3, 4, 12, 13, 15, 17, 18, 19, 20, 21, 24, 25, 26, 32, 33, 36, 37, 40, 50, 51, 52, 55, 65, 67, 69, 77, 83, 85, 89, 90, 91, 92, 93, 94, 95, 96, 98, 99, 100, 101, 103, 104, 105, 106, 107, 108, 109, 110, 111, 112, 114, 115, 116, 117, 119, 120, 121, 123, 124, 126, 127, 129, 130, 131, 132, 133, 134, 135, 136, 137, 138, 139, 140, 141, 142, 143, 144, 145, 150, 151, 163, 167, 168, 173, 182, 187, 188, 193, 201, 202, 204, 207, 208, 219, 223, 230, 236, 240
DNA 46, 47, 48, 63, 70
Doorpost Socket..... 6, 7, 8, 9, 10, 11, 12, 13, 27, 84, 146, 221, 223, 229, 236
Dry Moat 26, 148, 226, 227

Duality... 12, 79, 80, 161, 224
Dynasties
Eighteenth Dynasty 19, 26, 44, 65, 120, 155, 221
Eighth Dynasty... 236
Eleventh Dynasty 47, 171, 222
Fifth Dynasty................................48, 63, 96, 115, 229, 236
First Dynasty 18, 48, 51, 65, 90, 92, 93, 95, 96, 99, 107, 111, 112, 140, 141, 144, 145, 146, 193, 194
Fourth Dynasty 12, 92, 147, 208, 210, 219
Nineteenth Dynasty 18
Second Dynasty..18, 65, 89, 90, 91, 92, 93, 95, 96, 99, 100, 104, 107, 111, 119, 124, 138, 140, 141, 145, 147, 155, 156, 193, 194, 200, 219, 226
Seventh Dynasty 30, 47, 236
Sixth Dynasty 30, 127, 227, 228, 236
Third Dynasty....... 17, 18, 24, 30, 63, 79, 87, 90, 100, 108, 110, 132, 136, 138, 156, 193, 201, 202, 215, 219, 226, 227, 228
Twenty-fifth Dynasty 100
Twenty-seventh Dynasty 18
Twenty-sixth Dynasty 97

E

East Chapels..... 50, 53, 54, 55, 56, 57, 58, 61, 126, 176, 178, 179
Edwards, I. E. S.. 1
Edwin Smith Surgical Papyrus 20, 52
Embalming Center......66, 68, 69, 70, 141, 171, 172, 173, 175, 176, 180
Enclosure Wall.........1, 11, 13, 30, 38, 63, 74, 87, 90, 94, 100, 108, 116, 117, 118, 119, 120, 121, 122, 128, 134, 135, 136, 137, 138, 139, 143, 144, 145, 146, 147, 148, 155, 158, 159, 162, 163, 164, 166, 167, 168, 170, 172, 173, 174, 175, 176, 182, 183, 185, 187, 190, 192, 204, 223, 227, 236, 237
Ennead..22, 55
Entrance Vestibule (Khasekhemwui) 197, 198, 199, 207
Entrance Vestibule (Sacrum Room).......12, 29, 35, 173, 176, 190, 191
Exit Vestibule...35, 36, 38, 39, 46, 48, 74, 77, 78, 80, 85, 172, 176, 180, 183, 187, 190

F

False Gates 4, 8, 9, 10, 12, 63, 87, 117, 136, 137, 145, 146, 148, 158, 159, 166, 167, 170, 172, 182, 183, 184, 185, 187
Famine Stele... 17, 18
Field of Reeds (*Sekhet-Aaru*) 44, 51, 67, 75, 76, 78, 188
First Enclosure ...100, 137, 143, 144, 145, 146, 147, 148, 162, 164, 165, 166, 168, 172, 173, 174, 175, 183, 185
First Intermediate Period 47, 49, 168, 227, 228, 236

251

Firth, Cecil M. ... 9, 32, 59, 61, 62, 63, 69, 90, 94, 95, 96, 101, 104, 105, 110, 111, 114, 116, 117, 124, 128, 130, 135, 136, 138, 141, 157, 212, 214, 218

G

Geb (god) 55, 80
Genome 46, 47, 49
Gisr el-Mudir (The Great Enclosure) 105, 119, 145, 200
Giza 1, 4, 23, 89, 90, 147, 208, 219, 239
Goedicke, Hans 77
Granaries 18, 136, 138, 141
Great Pyramid 4, 23, 47, 123, 130, 192, 208, 210, 219, 239
Great South Court 13, 35, 36, 59, 65, 69, 74, 78, 80, 85, 97, 98, 110, 124, 125, 126, 127, 129, 134, 138, 143, 145, 148, 149, 163, 168, 171, 172, 173, 174, 175, 176, 183, 187, 193, 221, 224
Great South Court Small Temple 97, 98
Great Temple of Ptah 18, 135, 225
Gunn, Battiscombe 212, 214, 215, 218, 244

H

Hadrian 19
Hathor (goddess) 225, 233
Heart (anatomy) (***Ib***) 22, 23, 33, 37, 40, 41, 44, 49, 68, 75, 76, 86, 117, 161, 170, 231
Heart Chakra 170
Heart Chamber 33, 37, 86, 176, 182
HeartMath Institute 49
Ḥeb-Sed (sed-festival) 24, 25, 26, 50, 51, 55, 56, 60, 64, 65, 67, 68, 69, 70, 85, 97, 98, 106, 108, 110, 113, 125, 127, 129, 143, 145, 148, 163, 173, 183, 193, 229
Ḥeb-Sed Court 7, 10, 24, 25, 26, 27, 31, 35, 50, 51, 52, 53, 54, 55, 56, 57, 58, 59, 60, 61, 63, 64, 66, 69, 70, 96, 116, 123, 124, 125, 126, 127, 128, 129, 137, 138, 145, 147, 148, 156, 160, 161, 166, 168, 171, 172, 173, 174, 175, 176, 177, 178, 179, 180, 181, 182, 183, 189, 190, 197, 200, 213, 224, 225, 229, 230, 236, 239, 240
Heino, Arto J. 214, 215, 244
Helck, Wolfgang 77
Heliopolis (Onu) 15, 18, 21, 32, 47, 55, 73, 80
Hermes Trismegistus 22
Ḥetepḥernebti 99, 110
Hierakonpolis 47, 92
Horus (god) ... 37, 41, 42, 49, 53, 55, 74, 75, 76, 79, 91, 92, 93, 99, 117, 188, 224, 225
Hotepsekhemwy 89, 91, 99, 226
House of Beauty (*Per Nefer*) 50, 59, 61, 68, 70, 172, 173, 176, 180

I

Imhotep 1, 12, 13, 15, 16, 17, 18, 19, 20, 21, 23, 28, 29, 30, 32, 33, 34, 35, 36, 37, 38, 39, 40, 46, 47, 49, 51, 52, 53, 57, 61, 63, 67, 68, 70, 73, 74, 77, 78, 79, 80, 83, 84, 85, 86, 87, 89, 90, 94, 95, 96, 98, 99, 100, 103, 104, 106, 108, 109, 110, 111, 112,113, 114, 115, 116, 118, 119, 120, 121, 122, 124, 127, 129, 133, 135, 138, 139, 140, 141, 142, 143, 144, 145, 146, 147, 148, 150, 151, 153, 156, 157, 158, 159, 160, 162, 163, 164, 165, 166, 167, 168, 170, 171, 172, 173, 174, 175, 176, 179, 182, 183, 185, 187, 188, 189, 190, 191, 192, 193, 197, 200, 201, 202, 204, 207, 208, 210, 213, 215, 216, 217, 218, 219, 221, 224, 228, 233, 234, 235, 236, 237, 239, 240, 241
Intelligence of the Heart 23, 25, 33, 49, 220, 237, 240
Intkaes 99
Isis (goddess) 53, 55, 63, 75, 76, 80, 117, 230, 233

J

Joseph (son of Jacob) 17

K

Ka 22, 44, 54, 74, 89, 130, 221
Kaleny, Adel 116
Kanofer 18, 100, 104, 113, 139, 217
Karnak 18, 21, 135, 158, 223, 234, 235
Khasekhemwui ... 91, 92, 93, 99, 100, 105, 108, 123, 139, 145, 193, 194, 195, 196, 197, 198, 199, 200, 217, 219
Khat 22, 44, 54
Khnum (god) 17, 18

L

Latrine Chairs 31, 32, 56, 57, 98
Latvian Scientific Mission 26, 101, 148, 149
Lauer, Jean-Philippe ... 1, 4, 8, 9, 24, 25, 30, 32, 33, 35, 55, 59, 60, 61, 84, 85, 87, 90, 95, 96, 105, 109, 110, 114, 116, 118, 123, 124, 126, 129, 130, 131, 136, 139, 141, 145, 146, 151, 155, 157, 166, 167, 182, 187, 190, 212, 218, 237, 241
Lion Base 32, 62, 63, 64, 65, 66, 67, 69, 70
Luxor 18, 45, 99, 169, 238

M

maat ("Living In Truth") .. 21, 22, 39, 42, 49, 76, 79, 155, 159, 188, 231, 235
Maat (goddess) 75, 76
Magic Number 2 .... 79, 80, 156, 157, 161, 169, 191, 234
Manetho 17, 100, 105
Mariette, August 65
Mastaba M₁ 94, 95, 96, 106, 110, 111, 116, 141, 142, 143, 164, 192
Mastaba M₂ 94, 95, 96, 106, 141, 143, 164, 165
Mastaba M₃ 93, 94, 95, 96, 98, 99, 100, 106, 111, 112, 116, 143, 148
Mastabas M₁/M₂ 95, 100, 108
Mastabas M₁/M₂/M₃ 94, 99, 118, 134, 162, 163, 164, 166, 174, 210
Mastabas M₂/M₃ 185
Melanesia 49
Memphis ... 12, 18, 21, 39, 51, 55, 60, 64, 86, 87, 89, 110, 111, 117, 120, 121, 130, 138, 200, 225, 235
Mystery Building 59, 124, 125, 126, 127, 176

N

Natron Table 66, 69
Nebitka (Mastaba) 140
Negative Confessions 76
Nephthys (goddess) 55, 75, 76, 80
New Kingdom 18, 21, 27, 51, 87, 91, 141, 231

Ninetjer..89, 91, 92, 99, 226
Niuserre 63, 229
Nomes...83, 84, 86
North Altar.. 135, 136, 147, 229
North and South Pavilion Courts 166, 171, 173
North and South Pavilions 80, 93, 97, 110, 111, 112, 113, 114, 115, 116, 118, 120, 141, 143, 162, 163, 164, 192, 207, 210
North Court........10, 18, 65, 96, 116, 129, 134, 135, 136, 137, 138, 141, 145, 146, 185, 187, 204, 205, 206, 221, 229, 237
North Descending Passage... 96, 100, 101, 103, 104, 106, 132, 137, 143, 157
North Descending Passage (Sekhemkhet) 204, 205
North Exit Gate.. 8, 9, 10, 12, 13, 78, 134, 135, 136, 137, 146, 165, 166, 185, 221, 223, 230, 236
North Mortuary Temple...... 78, 129, 130, 132, 133, 134, 136, 137, 147, 148, 167, 171, 183
North Pavilion...... 4, 5, 78, 112, 113, 114, 134, 147, 148, 164, 210, 212, 213, 215, 216, 217, 218, 231
North Pavilion Court..115, 162, 164
Nut (Goddess)...55, 80

O

Offering Table 32, 64, 65, 66, 69, 136, 229
Old Kingdom 18, 21, 30, 47, 48, 49, 50, 51, 52, 55, 80, 98, 99, 104, 106, 109, 116, 127, 128, 171, 188, 192, 215, 227, 228, 231, 237
Old Serdab 130, 131, 143, 144, 162, 164, 165, 167, 170
Old Serdab Court 130, 164, 165, 170
Opening of the Mouth Ceremony 68, 75
Osiris (god)............... 41, 55, 63, 74, 75, 76, 80, 117, 233, 234

P

Palermo Stone..48, 49
Patient Suite (East Chapels)........... 55, 56, 57, 58, 61, 124, 126
Pearsall, Paul 49
Pericardium... 33, 40, 41, 43, 44
Pit P$_1$..115, 141
Pit P$_2$..115, 141
Pit P$_3$...30, 31, 141
Pits P$_4$, P$_5$, P$_6$, P$_{6'}$ and P$_7$ 140
Pits P$_8$ and P$_9$.. 140, 141, 147, 183, 184
Plimpton 322 Tablet 158
Prime Numbers 161, 162, 169, 191, 214
Ptah (god) 17, 19, 39, 40, 41, 60, 61, 87, 95, 97, 225
Ptolemy II Philadelphus..19
Ptolemy III Euergetes 19
Ptolemy IV Philopator 19
Pythagoras 156, 158, 187

Q

Quantum Arithmetic 214, 215
Quibell, James E. 9, 61, 63, 69, 90, 96

R

Ra-Atum (god)................ 15, 18, 22, 55, 68, 73, 80, 188, 226
Raneb..91, 99

Reference Dimension 164, 166, 167, 170
Reisner, George 23
Remen Cubit.. 105, 210
Reymond, E. A. E... 49
Rhind Mathematical Papyrus 158, 214
Room 'V' 64, 67, 68, 69, 70, 171, 172, 173, 180
Rossi, Corinna 213, 214, 244
Royal Annals... 48
Royal Canon of Turin 48, 49
Royal Cubit 44, 105, 156, 164, 210

S

Sacred Cubit... 44, 209, 210
Sacred Geometry......80, 151, 152, 153, 155, 158, 159, 160, 162, 163, 164, 165, 167, 168, 170, 172, 174, 177, 178, 179, 181, 187, 188, 189, 190, 192, 193, 194, 198, 199, 200, 204, 207, 208, 210, 215, 217, 218, 219, 240
   5-Part Root Rectangle Template.................... 152, 160, 176
   7-Part Root Rectangle Template.....160, 173, 179, 183, 206
   Golden Ratio (*Phi* Rectangle) 153, 154, 155, 159, 169, 173, 174, 176, 179, 180, 183, 184, 185, 187, 192, 195, 196, 197, 199, 200, 205, 206, 218
   Sacred Geometry Ratios 147, 152, 153, 155, 159, 161, 163, 176, 182, 187, 188, 190, 191, 193, 194, 199, 200, 204, 205, 206, 207, 208, 209, 217, 218, 219
   Silver Rectangle 153, 164, 165, 178, 206, 217
Sacred Number 14 ....63, 117, 118, 148, 161, 170, 182, 194
Sacred Number 42 .... 40, 80, 83, 161, 206
Sacrum 29, 34, 190
Sakkara..... 1, 3, 4, 5, 9, 18, 24, 39, 45, 52, 66, 89, 93, 99, 100, 104, 107, 109, 111, 112, 114, 115, 117, 135, 139, 140, 142, 144, 149, 159, 162, 200, 201, 204, 226, 227, 228, 235, 236, 237
Sakkara Ostracon....... 142, 210, 211, 212, 213, 214, 215, 216, 217, 218
Sanakht (Sa Werskhunum/Nebka).......100, 105, 108, 109, 201
Sarcophagus (Sekhemkhet) 109, 203
Sarcophagus (South Tomb) 108, 109, 141, 142
Sarcophagus (Step Pyramid) 96, 100, 101, 102, 103, 104, 105, 106, 109, 135, 141, 142
Schwaller de Lubicz, R. A... 45, 49
Schwartz, Gary 49
Second Enclosure 146, 147, 167, 168, 170, 172, 183
Second Serdab 131, 132, 167
Sekhemkhet ..19, 108, 109, 115, 119, 188, 201, 202, 203, 204, 205, 206, 207, 208, 219
Serapeum... 65, 104
Serdab...130, 131, 132, 148, 187
Serdab Court.. 130, 167, 171
Seth (god)................ 42, 55, 63, 79, 80, 91, 92, 93, 117, 224
Shemsu-Hor 48, 49, 50, 219
Short Cubit 105
Shu (god) 55, 80
Shunet el-Zebib ('Shuneh') 105, 139, 193, 200
Sneferu 11, 12
Solon 158
South Altar 65, 69, 78, 97, 167, 229

South Entrance Gate 1, 3, 10, 12, 13, 27, 29, 30, 35, 38, 78, 116, 117, 118, 119, 120, 121, 134, 135, 136, 137, 172, 176, 182, 190, 221, 234

South Entrance Hall 1, 3, 7, 10, 11, 21, 24, 27, 28, 29, 30, 31, 32, 33, 35, 36, 37, 38, 39, 40, 46, 48, 51, 52, 61, 62, 63, 65, 66, 68, 69, 70, 73, 74, 75, 77, 78, 80, 83, 84, 85, 86, 87, 97, 113, 116, 118, 120, 125, 126, 129, 134, 137, 147, 166, 167, 168, 171, 172, 173, 174, 176, 177, 179, 180, 181, 182, 187, 188, 190, 191, 197, 206, 221, 223, 224, 225, 234, 240

South Pavilion. 78, 89, 113, 120, 129, 157, 162, 164, 165, 171, 185, 215

South Pavilion Court.. 115, 143, 145, 148, 157, 162, 163, 164, 165, 166

South Tomb 26, 30, 37, 85, 93, 97, 99, 101, 105, 106, 107, 108, 109, 110, 111, 116, 118, 129, 139, 141, 142, 143, 146, 147, 149, 157, 162, 163, 166, 168, 172, 173, 174, 176, 187

South Tomb (Sekhemkhet) 205, 206, 207

South Tomb Chapel 97, 107, 110, 163, 168, 173, 174, 176, 187

South Tomb Main Burial Chamber.................... 103, 109, 141

Spanish Flu Pandemic of 1918 58

Spine (Vertebrae) 27, 28, 29, 30, 31, 32, 33, 34, 35, 37, 40, 62, 234

Step Pyramid (Sekhemkhet) 168, 188, 201, 202, 206, 207

Step Pyramid Enclosure... 1, 3, 4, 5, 7, 8, 9, 10, 11, 12, 13, 15, 17, 23, 25, 26, 27, 30, 33, 35, 37, 38, 39, 40, 45, 50, 51, 52, 55, 61, 63, 65, 66, 68, 69, 70, 74, 75, 78, 80, 85, 89, 95, 96, 98, 99, 100, 104, 110, 111, 112, 114, 115, 116, 117, 118, 119, 121, 127, 128, 129, 130, 133, 134, 135, 136, 137, 139, 141, 145, 146, 147, 148, 149, 150, 151, 153, 155, 156, 157, 158, 159, 160, 161, 162, 163, 164, 168, 169, 170, 171, 172, 182, 186, 187, 188, 190, 192, 193, 204, 207, 208, 215, 219, 224, 225, 226, 227, 228, 229, 231, 235, 236, 237, 238, 239, 240, 241

Step Pyramid P₁ (Four-Tier) 94, 95, 96, 99, 108, 109, 116, 129, 131, 132, 141, 143, 145, 146, 147, 166, 167, 172, 174, 176, 185

Step Pyramid P₂ (Six-Tier).. ..... 1, 3, 4, 7, 9, 13, 17, 18, 19, 20, 23, 26, 38, 47, 51, 52, 55, 56, 64, 65, 68, 78, 80, 84, 85, 89, 90, 92, 93, 94, 95, 96, 97, 98, 99, 100, 101, 102, 106, 108, 109, 110, 111, 114, 115, 116, 118, 119, 126, 127, 128, 129, 130, 131, 132, 135, 136, 137, 138, 139, 141, 147, 148, 149, 150, 151, 157, 158, 160, 161, 163, 166, 168, 171, 175, 176, 182, 183, 188, 189, 192, 197, 202, 204, 207, 210, 211, 221, 226, 227, 229, 230, 235, 237, 239, 240, 241

Sternum..33, 34, 41

Stretching of the Cord (*pedj-shes*) 158

Subterranean Chambers (North Court) 135, 141, 147, 184

Subterranean Chambers (Sekhemkhet Pyramid)........204, 205, 206

Subterranean Chambers (Step Pyramid)... 93, 95, 99, 140, 211

Swelim, Nabil... 108

T

Tefnut (goddess).. 55, 80

Telophase (Mitosis).. 48, 80

Temple 'T' ...50, 59, 60, 61, 64, 124, 125, 127, 128, 173, 176, 180, 183, 236

Temple of Hathor and Maat, Deir el-Medina 19

Temple of Hathor, Dendera.. 53, 230

Temple of Hathor, Memphis 225

Temple of Horus and Sobek, Kom Ombo 53, 79, 230

Temple of Horus, Edfu.. 92, 230

Temple of Isis, Philae... 13, 19

Temple of Khnum, Elephantine Island 17

Tethering Posts... 123, 124

Teti (Pharaoh)... 95, 127, 236

Thebes 19, 47, 56, 89

Third Enclosure 168, 174, 175, 182, 184

Thoth (god)... 15, 22, 75, 76

Throne Base 66

Thymus Gland (anatomy) 41

Tiberius 19

Transverse Processes (Vertebrae)....................................... 28

U

Umm el-Qa'ab...................................105, 107, 112, 145, 193

Unas (Pharaoh).. 95, 115, 226, 227

Units of Measure

Cubit 44, 105, 119, 155, 156, 157, 162, 166, 170, 171, 187, 208, 211, 212, 214, 215, 216

Finger 44, 211, 212, 213, 214, 215, 216, 218

Palm...44, 105, 156, 211, 212

Upper and/or Lower Egypt...15, 18, 24, 32, 40, 42, 43, 51, 83, 85, 86, 110, 114, 134, 182, 197

Userkhaf.. 115, 226

W

Weighing of the Heart Ceremony..........73, 75, 76, 77, 78, 117

West Chapels....... 7, 24, 25, 26, 55, 57, 59, 61, 123, 124, 126, 129, 173, 176, 178, 179, 183, 189

West Descending Passage (South Tomb) 142

Western Massif I 138, 147, 159, 185

Western Massif II ...93, 99, 101, 107, 111, 114, 138, 139, 140, 141, 142, 147, 159, 167, 185

Western Massif III.. 147, 159, 185

White Walls (Memphis) 87, 117, 120

Wilbour, Charles 17